# Coastal Mass Tourism

## ASPECTS OF TOURISM

**Series Editors:** Professor Chris Cooper, *University of Queensland, Australia,*6
Dr Michael Hall, *University of Otago, Dunedin, New Zealand*
and Dr Dallen Timothy, *Arizona State University, Tempe, USA*

**Aspects of Tourism** is an innovative, multifaceted series which will comprise authoritative reference handbooks on global tourism regions, research volumes, texts and monographs. It is designed to provide readers with the latest thinking on tourism world-wide and in so doing will push back the frontiers of tourism knowledge. The series will also introduce a new generation of international tourism authors, writing on leading edge topics. The volumes will be readable and user- friendly, providing accessible sources for further research. The list will be underpinned by an annual authoritative tourism research volume. Books in the series will be commissioned that probe the relationship between tourism and cognate subject areas such as strategy, development, retailing, sport and environmental studies. The publisher and series editors welcome proposals from writers with projects on these topics.

**Other Books in the Series**
Classic Reviews in Tourism
    *Chris Cooper (ed.)*
Dynamic Tourism: Journeying with Change
    *Priscilla Boniface*
Journeys into Otherness: The Representation of Differences and Identity in Tourism
    *Keith Hollinshead and Chuck Burlo (eds)*
Managing Educational Tourism
    *Brent W. Ritchie*
Marine Ecotourism: Issues and Experiences
    *Brian Garrod and Julie C. Wilson (eds)*
Natural Area Tourism: Ecology, Impacts and Management
    *D. Newsome, S.A. Moore and R. Dowling*
Progressing Tourism Research
    *Bill Faulkner, edited by Liz Fredline, Leo Jago and Chris Cooper*
Recreational Tourism: Demand and Impacts
    *Chris Ryan*
Tourism Collaboration and Partnerships
    *Bill Bramwell and Bernard Lane (eds)*
Tourism and Development: Concepts and Issues
    *Richard Sharpley and David Telfer (eds)*
Tourism Employment: Analysis and Planning
    *Michael Riley, Adele Ladkin and Edith Szivas*
Tourism in Peripheral Areas: Case Studies
    *Frances Brown and Derek Hall (eds)*

**Other Books of Interest**
Global Ecotoursim Policies and Case Studies
    *Michael Lück and Torsten Kirstges (eds)*
Irish Tourism: Image, Culture and Identity
    *Michael Cronin and Barbara O'Connor (eds)*

**Please contact us for the latest book information:**
**Channel View Publications, Frankfurt Lodge, Clevedon Hall,**
**Victoria Road, Clevedon, BS21 7HH, England**
**http://www.channelviewpublications.com**

**ASPECTS OF TOURISM 12**
*Series Editors*: Chris Cooper (*University of Queensland, Australia*),
Michael Hall (*University of Otago, New Zealand*)
and Dallen Timothy (*Arizona State University, USA*)

# Coastal Mass Tourism
## Diversification and Sustainable Development in Southern Europe

Edited by
Bill Bramwell

**CHANNEL VIEW PUBLICATIONS**
Clevedon • Buffalo • Toronto • Sydney

**Library of Congress Cataloging in Publication Data**
A catalog record for this book is available from the Library of Congress.

**British Library Cataloguing in Publication Data**
A catalogue entry for this book is available from the British Library.

ISBN 1-873150-69-5 (hbk)
ISBN 1-873150-68-7 (pbk)

**Channel View Publications**
An imprint of Multilingual Matters Ltd

*UK*: Frankfurt Lodge, Clevedon Hall, Victoria Road, Clevedon BS21 7SJ.
*USA*: 2250 Military Road, Tonawanda, NY 14150, USA.
*Canada*: 5201 Dufferin Street, North York, Ontario, Canada M3H 5T8.
*Australia*: Footprint Books, PO Box 418, Church Point, NSW 2103, Australia.

Typeset by Archetype-IT Ltd (http://www.archetype-it.com).
Printed and bound in Great Britain by the Cromwell Press Ltd.

# Contents

# Preface and Acknowledgements

This book arose in part from my surprise that there are relatively few books on the development and planning of coastal tourism, which appeared curious because coastal destinations are so important for global tourism. My research on tourism in the coastal regions of southern Europe also suggested that there was a need for further reflection on the tourism development patterns, impacts and policies in that region, one of the cradles of modern mass tourism.

All the contributions to this volume evaluate coastal tourism in southern Europe in relation to sustainable development. Sustainable development is an important concept, and it is also becoming a key feature of discourses on the future of society, environment and economies in the region. The book was also prompted by a belief there was scope for a book that draws together some of the vast literature on southern Europe that is relevant to an understanding of the tourism industry there. This literature is widely scattered in academic journals and in chapters of books that often have a wider canvas than just tourism itself.

As the book developed it became clear that there was a need for more critical evaluation of two inter linked trends in Europe's Mediterranean coastal regions. These were the upgrading of mass tourism resorts and facilities, and product diversification into small-scale 'alternative' tourism and new types of larger-scale tourism. Not enough is known about these development approaches, about the policy instruments and planning techniques used to support them, or about their advantages and disadvantages. The book, therefore, examines the strengths and weaknesses of these policies and techniques in relation to the objectives of sustainable development. This is one of the book's key themes, and it is one of the features that distinguishes this volume from others that recently have been published on Mediterranean tourism.

The book examines aspects of the complex interactions between market demands and pressures, evolving value systems and policy contexts, and new policies and planning techniques affecting tourism and sustainable development around the shores of Europe's Mediterranean. It provides a commentary on how the implementation of policies affecting tourism and sustainability is a multifaceted and often fraught process. Within the space constraints of this book there are detailed examinations of just some of the major features of tourism and sustainable development in Europe's Mediterranean coastal regions. It must be recognised that there are other important issues not considered in great depth here, such as managing the scale or quantity of tourism development, and efforts to involve local actors in tourism policy-making.

This book was developed alongside a theme issue of the *Journal of Sustainable Tourism*, with nine of the 17 chapters in this book also published in the theme issue (Vol. 11, Nos. 2 & 3, 2003). There are eight completely new contributions in this book, including Chapters 1 and 2 that provide a substantial introduction to the subject and review key themes, and also the Chapters 6, 7, 11, 12, 13 and 14. The link to the journal theme issue helped to attract leading researchers and assisted in the blind referee process: every chapter has been refereed both by the Editor and by up to three experts.

The inspiration for embarking on this book came from two friends who are based in Malta: Karmenu Vella and Gianfranco Selvaggi. Their long experience of the tourism industry in the Mediterranean, and their enthusiasm and generosity, prompted my interest in the issues examined here. I am deeply grateful to Sheela Agarwal, who works at the University of Plymouth, and Andy Smith, a colleague at Sheffield Hallam University, for their insightful comments on drafts of the two introductory chapters. These chapters also benefited greatly from the detailed and perceptive reviews provided by Bernard Lane at the University of Bristol. My regular conversations with Bernard helped me to maintain my own enthusiasm for the book. Joan Butt at Sheffield Hallam University skilfully and quickly produced the figures and tables in Chapter 1. And, of course, I am much indebted to the contributors of the chapters in the book and to the many referees involved. Finally, I would like to express appreciation to Mike and Marjukka Grover at Channel View Publications for their continued support with the project.

Bill Bramwell
*Centre for Tourism and Cultural Change, Sheffield Hallam University, UK*

# The Contributors

**Konstantinos Andriotis** lectures at the Greek Open University and the Technological Education Institute of Crete in Greece. He has an MSc in International Hospitality Management from the University of Strathclyde, and a PhD in Tourism Development and Planning from Bournemouth University. His recent publications include articles on community perceptions of tourism, tourism development and planning, tourism employment, seasonality, the morphology of coastal resorts and public and private sector involvement in tourism, in journals such as *Journal of Travel Research* and *Journal of Sustainable Tourism*.

**Michael Barke** is Reader in Human Geography at the University of Northumbria in Newcastle, UK. He gained a first degree in Geography from the University of Liverpool and a PhD in Geography from the University of Glasgow. He has published widely on social and economic change in Andalucía, including work on tourism impacts. He co-edited the book *Tourism in Spain: Critical Issues*, published in 1996 by CABI. His research interests include recent social and economic change in southern Spain, and the historical geography of Andalucía.

**Bill Bramwell** is Reader in Tourism in the Centre for Tourism and Cultural Change at Sheffield Hallam University, UK. He has an MA and PhD in Geography. He has jointly edited books on tourism and rural areas, tourism partnerships and collaboration, and tourism and sustainability in Europe. In 1993 he co-founded the *Journal of Sustainable Tourism*, which he continues to co-edit. He has written journal articles on various aspects of tourism policy and planning and on sustainability and tourism.

**Helen Briassoulis** is Professor in the Department of Geography at the University of the Aegean, Lesvos, Greece. She holds a PhD in Regional Planning from the University of Illinois at Urbana-Champaign, USA. She has published in refereed journals and books on tourism and the environment, land use change, sustainable development indicators, and integrated economic-environmental analysis.

**Xavier Campillo-Besses** is a Lecturer and Director of the Consultancy Unit in the *Escola Universitària de Turisme i Direcció Hotelera* at the *Universitat Autònoma de Barcelona*, Spain. He holds a PhD in Geography and much of his research and professional activity relates to local development, environment and tourism in mountain areas, countryside access, and ecotourism. He lectures on tourism and the environment and tourism and development, and he has worked on several local rural development programmes.

**Artemios Chatziathanassiou** is an agricultural engineer and project manager for research and demonstration projects in the Centre for Renewable Energy Sources in Greece. He holds an MSc in Energy Management and Environmental Protection from the National Technical University of Athens and the Economics University of Piraeus. His research focuses on tourism eco-labelling schemes, environmental impacts of renewable energy, and the use and promotion of renewable energy. He has published articles on policies for bioenergy technology and its environmental impacts.

**Gonzalo Malvarez Garcia** is a Lecturer in Environmental Science and Assistant Director of the Virtual School at the School of Environmental Studies, University of Ulster, Northern Ireland. His research interests include coastal geomorphology and coastal zone management. Among his recent publications are studies of the measurement and management of environmental stress on the Costa del Sol in the *Journal of Coastal Research* and *Coastal Management*. He has also published on morphodynamic processes and near-shore environments in Britain and Ireland.

**Derek Hall** is Professor of Regional Development and Head of the Tourism Research Group at the Scottish Agricultural College in Auchincruive, Scotland. He has a first degree in Geography and Anthropology and a PhD in Social Geography, both from the University of London. He has numerous publications on tourism and development in central and south-eastern Europe. His research interests include tourism and rural development and EU accession issues in central and eastern Europe and the central and eastern Mediterranean.

**Josep A. Ivars Baidal** is an Associate Lecturer in the Department of Geographical Analysis and a Researcher in the Tourism School at the University of Alicante, Spain. He has a PhD in Geography and he is a member of the Spanish Association of Scientific Experts in Tourism. His research activity focuses on tourism planning, and policy and public management. He combines his teaching activities with professional participation in tourism planning activities.

**Daphne Mavrogiorgos** is a partner in the Environment Section at the Centre for Renewable Energy Sources in Greece. She is a biologist and holds an MSc in Geography – Environmental Change and Management, from the University of London. Her research work examines eco-labelling schemes in tourism, the environmental impacts of renewable energy sources, the rational use and promotion of energy applications, and the Kyoto mechanism for emissions trading.

**Yüksel Öztürk** is Assistant Professor in the Faculty of Trade and Tourism Education at Gazi University, Ankara, Turkey. He is a graduate of the Scottish Hotel School at the University of Strathclyde, Scotland. His research interests include destination marketing, market segmentation and development, the impacts of tourism, and consumer behaviour.

**John Pollard** is a Senior Lecturer in Geography in the School of Environmental Studies at the University of Ulster, Northern Ireland. He has research interests in tourism, recreation management and coastal planning. His recent publications include articles on tourism and coastal management in Spain in the journals *Tourism Management*, *Geography* and *Coastal Management*. His other recent publications concern tourism and the environment in Ireland.

**Gerda K. Priestley** is a Senior Lecturer in the Department of Geography and Director of the International Research Centre at the *Escola Universitària de Turisme i Direcció Hotelera* within the *Universitat Autònoma de Barcelona*. She holds a PhD in Geography, and has research interests in tourism planning, focusing on protected area management and urban and sports tourism. She co-edited the book *Sustainable Tourism? European Experiences*, published in 1996 by CABI. She has directed research projects on tourism and national parks, rural tourism development, and environmental management for golf courses.

**Rafael Dominguez Rodriguez** is Dean of the Faculty of Philosophy and Letters and Titulo Numerario in the Regional Geographical Analysis section of the Department of Geography at the University of Malaga. His research activities relate to tourism, demography and the sustainability of water provision. He has published studies in the fields of coastal tourism and coastal planning.

**Francesc Romagosa** is a Lecturer in the Department of Geography and Lecturer and Consultant in the *Escola Universitària de Turisme i Direcció Hotelera* at the *Universitat Autònoma de Barcelona*. He is preparing a PhD on tourism and the environment in Costa Brava's Empordà wetlands. He holds a first degree and MA in Geography. His research focuses on the relations between geography, tourism and the environment. He has written a book on wetlands and society in Catalonia and several articles on related topics.

**Jon Sadler** is a Lecturer in Outdoor Recreation at the School of Environmental and Information Sciences, Charles Sturt University, Australia. His research examines planning approaches and the use of environmental impact assessments for tourism developments. Other interests are the influences on participation in outdoor activities, and environmental education programmes for the outdoor recreation and ecotourism industries. These interests relate to his work for a degree in adventure ecotourism.

**Julie E. Scott** is an anthropologist in the International Institute for Culture, Tourism and Development at London Metropolitan University, UK. Her research examines gender, ethnic and national identities, community boundaries and tourist space, and the interpretation of heritage and landscape. Her work on the Mediterranean, and notably on Cyprus, includes studies of tour guide itineraries, gender issues in tourism, the use of shrines, and relations between mainstream and casino tourism. Her work has appeared in the *Journal of Travel Research* and *Annals of Tourism Research*.

**Richard Sharpley** is Reader in Travel and Tourism at the University of Northumbria in Newcastle, UK, where he lectures on tourism and international development and tourism in society. The author of several tourism textbooks, he also co-edited the book *Tourism and Development. Concepts and Issues*, published in 2002 by Channel View. His research interests lie in the sociology of tourism, rural tourism and sustainable tourism development. He has published widely on tourism development in Cyprus.

**Konstantinos Sioulas** is a partner in the Environment Section of the Centre for Renewable Energy Sources in Greece, where his role includes promoting environmentally sound energy systems and conducting environmental assessments of projects involving renewable energy. His first degree is in Environmental Science from the University of the Aegean. He is an expert in environmental impact assessments and environmental management strategies, and he has project managed several national and international environmental projects.

**Ioannis Spilanis** is an Assistant Professor in the Department of Environmental Studies at the University of the Aegean, Greece, where his teaching covers the relationships between development and the environment. He is an economist with a PhD on tourism and regional development in Greece, and for three years he worked on regional planning in the Ministry of the Aegean. His research interests are focused on local and regional development, and particularly on sustainable development planning for islands.

**Nadia Theuma** is an anthropologist and holds a BA Honours degree in Mediterranean Studies and a Masters in Anthropology from the University of Malta. Her PhD is in Cultural Tourism Management from the University of Strathclyde. She lectures in tourism and research methods at the University of Malta where she is also Assistant Coordinator of the degree programme in Tourism Studies. She has authored and co-authored papers on tourism's impacts on the social and cultural fabric of the Maltese islands.

**Dallen J. Timothy** is Associate Professor in the Department of Recreation Management and Tourism at Arizona State University, USA. He is Chair of the Recreation, Tourism and Sport Speciality Group of the Association of American Geographers. His research interests include heritage tourism, political boundaries, ethnic communities, heritage and peripheral/rural areas, shopping, and planning in developing countries. He is co-author of books on tourism and political boundaries and on heritage tourism.

**Cevat Tosun** is Associate Professor and Head of the School of Tourism and Hotel Management at Mustafa Kemal University, Iskenderun, Turkey. He was Fulbright Scholar and Visiting Professor at the University of Northern Iowa, USA. His research interests include participatory development, sustainable development, cross-border cooperation, destination marketing, hospitality marketing, the social and economic impacts of tourism, and approaches to development.

**John Towner** is Senior Research Associate in the Department of Child Health at Newcastle University, UK, and he was formerly Senior Lecturer in the Division of Geography and Environmental Management at the University of Northumbria at Newcastle. He has written extensively on aspects of the geography of tourism and on the history of leisure and tourism. His book *An Historical Geography of Recreation and Tourism in the Western World 1540–1940* has won critical acclaim. He is on the editorial board of *Annals of Tourism Research*.

**Paris Tsartas** is Associate Professor of Tourism Development in the Business Administration Department of the University of the Aegean, Greece. His interests lie in tourism development, the sociology of tourism, special interest and alternative tourism, leisure and tourism, and sustainable tourism development. He has published several books in Greek on tourism in Greece, including studies of tourism impacts, female employment in tourism, sociological approaches to tourism, and sustainable tourism development. He has articles in *Annals of Tourism Research* and *Revue de Tourisme*.

**J. Fernando Vera Rebollo** is Professor of Geography, and Director of the Tourism School and of the Tourism Planning Research Group at the University of Alicante, Spain. His research examines tourism and the environment, the geographical analysis of tourism, and tourism planning. He has written many books and articles, including *Análisis Territorial del Turismo,* published in 1997 by Ariel. He is a World Tourism Organisation consultant and a member of the Spanish Association of Scientific Experts in Tourism. He has directed an EU co-funded project on sustainable tourism management.

**Helen Vayanni** works in the Department of Environment of Lesvos Prefecture Authority in Greece. She is an environmentalist who specialises in environmental policy and management. She is studying for a PhD at the University of the Aegean on sustainable tourism development in the Greek insular regions. Her interests include regional information systems as planning tools, and sustainable tourism and environmental planning in insular regions.

# 1 Mass Tourism, Diversification and Sustainability in Southern Europe's Coastal Regions

*Bill Bramwell*
*Sheffield Hallam University, Sheffield S1 1WB, UK*

## Introduction

International mass tourism came of age in the coastal areas and islands of Mediterranean Europe in the decades after the late 1950s. The transformation of Europe's Mediterranean into a tourism belt was the latest in a series of roles that the region has played. Two thousand years ago it had been the cradle of the Greek and Roman empires, gaining supplementary income as a result of military expansion. Subsequently, the Venetian, Turkish and Spanish empires came to exercise their trading and political power. But by the Renaissance period, commercial hegemony had substantially shifted to north-west Europe where wealth was increasingly vested in industrial production and trade. Europe's subsequent industrial revolution was also focused to the north and largely by-passed the Mediterranean, where most of its regions had a largely subordinate role in a wider division of labour, leading to peripherality, dependency, poverty and rural depopulation (Dunford, 1997: 127). From the industrial revolution until the 1960s the economy of Europe's Mediterranean substantially lagged behind that of northern Europe. Paradoxically, it was the population of industrialised northern Europe that fuelled one of the engines for southern Europe's 'renaissance' from the 1960s – through tourist flows from north to south. From that period onwards, tourism activities – alongside commercialised agriculture, industrial development and expanded urban services – have contributed to southern Europe's 'rebirth' (King & Donati, 1999: 134–9).

From the late 1950s onwards many coastal areas of first Spain and Italy, followed by Greece, Malta, Cyprus and former Yugoslavia, began attracting unprecedented numbers of tourists from northern Europe. The holidays offered in this 'pleasure periphery' were largely socially constructed as sun and sea experiences, with better prospects of sun and warmth than in the north (Williams, 1997: 214). It became possible for large numbers of people from diverse social groups to be involved because of the rising incomes of post-war prosperity, longer and paid holidays, and because of innovations in transport technology, notably the commercial jet airliner. Another key element was the tourism industry's large-scale replication of standardised holiday packages combining accommodation and transport, marketed by new types of tour operators. The accommodation and other commercial facilities necessary for these new developments were sometimes financed by capital originating from external, 'core' metropolitan regions, but also often from small-scale investments within the destination areas (Ioannides, 2001a: 117; Sprengel, 1999; Yarcan & Ertuna, 2002: 169, 180). The large volume of package

holidays, aggressively sold, created the scale economies that made these holidays a widely affordable form of mass consumption. In addition, many visitors,
including increasingly significant numbers of domestic tourists, holidayed inde-
pendently, without tour operator involvement (Jenner & Smith, 1993: 51–7;
Williams, 2001: 169).

Overall, therefore, post-war southern Europe has seen major growth in tourism
as an economic activity, which has contributed to wider processes of globalisation.
But tourism's specific character and its impacts vary considerably between
southern Europe's many coastal regions and resorts. Where the industry has
developed it has often been accompanied by economic, sociocultural and environmental changes. These have been more evident because the countries of
southern Europe had been slow to industrialise and modernise, although many
of them – notably Italy, Spain, Greece, Cyprus and Malta – experienced a period
of dynamic economic growth and improved wealth between the 1960s and 1980s
(Dunford, 1997: 127, 134, 150; King & Donati, 1999: 137). Tourism's impacts were
also prominent because large tracts of the Mediterranean littoral had previously
been comparatively undeveloped, were characterised by fairly traditional societies, and they often also had fragile coastal environments (Sapelli, 1995: 13).
However, tourism activity has been only one of many significant influences
working to transform southern Europe in the post-war period, including
economic change from intensified and commercialised agriculture in irrigated
areas, the development of various infrastructural projects, and an expanding
urban economy (Dunford, 1997: 150–52).

While residents in these regions have often responded quite positively to
tourism, their reactions have also varied from place to place (Barke, 1999;
Haralambopoulos & Pizam, 1993; Richez, 1996; Tsartas, 1992). Concerns
about the industry's adverse environmental and sociocultural impacts have
grown in recent years in southern Europe, but these post-materialist sensitivities have developed more slowly here than in more affluent countries. The
views of policy-makers, the industry and NGOs in southern Europe about
tourism's costs and benefits are increasingly framed within discourses on
sustainable development (Kousis & Eder, 2001: 17). While the debates sometimes focus on environmental and sociocultural issues and on inequitable
outcomes, fears about the economic vitality of mass tourism are especially
prominent. Several threats to its economic strength are now identified,
including ageing infrastructure, environmental deterioration, changes in
tourists' expectations of environmental standards, and growing competition
from an ever-expanding choice of holiday destinations both within the region
and across the world.

Over the past 20 years anxiety in southern Europe's coastlands about mass
tourism's future economic health has encouraged policy-makers to advocate
greater product diversification. One policy response has involved developing
new, large-scale products, such as golf courses, marinas, casinos and exhibition
and conference centres, with these often intended to attract high spend visitors.
While these developments may be aimed at 'exclusive', 'up-market' audiences,
they have many mass tourism features as they are large facilities that attract
substantial numbers of users. A second policy response to diversification has
involved developing 'alternative' tourism products that, at least initially, may

be provided on a small scale and may draw on unique features, such as a destination's history, culture or ecology. Typical products of this type include hiking trails in natural areas, agro-tourism facilities, and improved interpretation at small historic sites and museums. 'Alternative' products are often considered better adapted to the changing tastes of consumers, who, it is suggested, are increasingly looking for more specialist and customised holiday experiences. But a rather different set of policies has emerged because of the concern about mass tourism, with these intended to update and improve the environmental performance of the existing infrastructure and products. It is thought that many holiday-makers no longer accept poor environmental standards, and thus environmental quality has to be improved. The environmental upgrading of existing products can be achieved using enhancement schemes in major resorts, tougher land-use planning controls, improvements in water quality and beach cleaning, and initiatives to reduce energy use and recycle waste in the accommodation sector. This upgrading of environmental performance has often been coupled with higher standards of provision generally, with air conditioning, *en suite* facilities and leisure complexes attached to tourist accommodation.

To date, surprisingly few books have been published that focus on the development and planning of coastal mass tourism, and there has been only a limited critical assessment of the strategies of product diversification and environmental enhancement used in coastal regions. This book tackles these topics in the specific context of Europe's Mediterranean. Consideration is given to the policy approaches and planning techniques being used, the intentions and underlying assumptions behind their use, and the types of products that result. Particular attention is paid to the successes and failures of these strategies and techniques in relation to the objectives of achieving sustainable development. Do the policies put forward, and their related products and developments, encourage sustainable outcomes? These themes are considered in case studies from Spain, Greece, Malta, Croatia, Turkey and from both north and south Cyprus. The examples that are examined illustrate how the issues and outcomes depend very much on the contingencies of each case, a point that is not always fully acknowledged in the tourism literature. But, while the book draws on the European Mediterranean experience, there are implications for other coastal areas in the world, such as Bulgaria's Black Sea coast, the beach resorts of West Malaysia, Australia's Gold Coast, and for other parts of the Mediterranean's coasts beyond southern Europe.

This chapter and the next review key themes from the book's subsequent contributions, while also drawing on other relevant studies. The discussion in this chapter focuses on the development of mass, 'alternative' and other tourism forms in southern Europe's coastal regions, as well as their potential disadvantages and advantages for sustainability. Despite its very many potential advantages, it warns against assuming that small-scale 'alternative' tourism is inevitably more appropriate for sustainable development than mass tourism. The second chapter considers the contexts behind the initiation of public policies for coastal mass tourism and sustainable development in southern Europe. This includes policies developed by the European Union and by national and local government.

## Coastal Mass Tourism in Southern Europe

### The geographic context

A regional view of coastal tourism is adopted here. The regions under consideration all border the Mediterranean Sea but they usually also include quite extensive hinterlands within which socioeconomic activities are strongly influenced by their relations with the seaboard and its coastal tourism industry. A regional view is supported by the Blue Plan – the plan for environmental improvement of the Mediterranean Basin that was sponsored by the United Nations Environment Programme. This plan recognises that in the Mediterranean the 'coastal zones might vary in territorial depth from one area to another, depending on the problems to be considered and the nature of the disciplines involved' (Grenon & Batisse, 1989: 16).

Each European Mediterranean region reflects distinctive, multilayered interactions between its climate, environments and landscapes, historical and cultural legacies and contemporary socioeconomic geographies. While each of these regions is unique, there are some characteristics that are quite widely shared (King *et al.*, 2001). For example, while the climate can vary from place to place, in essence it is characterised by the summer heat and drought. This climate has largely been responsible for the distinctive mixes of vegetation and crops, such as the olive, vine, fig and Aleppo pine; and the climate together with the terrain have helped to shape the pastoralism and agriculture in each region. The coastal strips of many Mediterranean regions are backed by hilly or mountainous landscapes. There is intense debate and disagreement among academics about the cultural characteristics of Mediterranean Europe, with some anthropologists suggesting that it has been characterised by the values of honour and shame, together with strong 'traditional' kinship and gender roles, and that these features retain an influence on behaviour (Horden & Purcell, 2000: 485–523; Sapelli, 1995). Other commentators point to 'a rapidly changing reality', with 'trends towards a more individualistic and consumer orientated society' (Hudson & Lewis, 1985: 1, 15). In southern Europe there has also been a long tradition of urban life, with the many port cities around the Mediterranean testifying to this tradition and to the significance of this sea for trade routes. Since the 1960s many of southern Europe's coastal regions have undergone substantial change due to selective development and modernisation. Mass tourism has been just one important economic and sociocultural influence encouraging these changes.

### The growth in international tourism

While there is some discussion of domestic tourism in this chapter, its focus is on international tourism around Europe's Mediterranean shores, starting with a brief history of its development. In the era of élite international tourism before the First World War the French and Italian Rivieras were winter playgrounds for a wealthy upper middle class from northern Europe. From the late 1950s, international tourism gained a mass character based on widening social access and the attractions of warm seas, secure summer sunshine, and often stereotypes or myths about the 'Mediterranean' (Minca, 1998). The industry has spread through a succession of poles of high growth, and its present distribution is highly spatially uneven between and within countries, regions and localities. In the

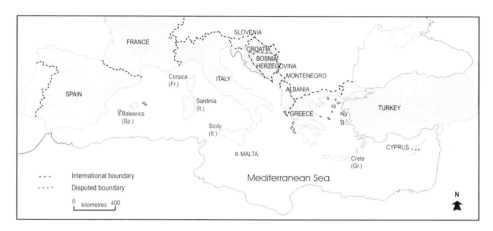

**Figure 1** The Mediterranean countries of southern Europe and Turkey

1950s it grew markedly in Spain, the early market leader, and on the Italian Adriatic. By the early 1970s tourism was expanding in parts of former Yugoslavia, the Greek islands, Malta and Cyprus, and by the late 1970s and 1980s it had reached Turkey (Williams, 1998: 51; 2001: 161). The rapid growth of the 1960s and 1970s meant the southern European littoral was quickly established among the world's premier holiday destinations (Jenner & Smith, 1993; Montanari, 1995: 43). Looking ahead, tourism in many parts of Europe's Mediterranean is likely to continue to grow, but this region's share of the global market is declining because there is increasing competition from newer tourist destinations, and because it is distant from the fastest growing tourist markets, notably Asia with its emerging new economies and rapid population growth.

Figure 1 shows the 12 countries of southern Europe that include a Mediterranean coastline and thus are considered in this book. Within each country the length of this littoral varies from only 20 km in Bosnia-Herzegovina and 32 km in Slovenia to the extensive coasts of Greece (15,000 km), Italy (7953 km) and Croatia (5790 km) (Table 1). The figures for Greece and Croatia are boosted by their many islands. While Portugal is in southern Europe, it is not examined here as it fringes the Atlantic Ocean, but Turkey's regions bordering the Mediterranean are included. Turkey acts as a 'bridge' between East and West and has affinities with Europe as well as Asia; it is striving to join the European Union, and its Mediterranean tourism also depends substantially on visitors from northern Europe (Sapelli, 1995). Table 1 shows that among the 12 countries, those receiving most international tourist arrivals in 2000 were France (75 million), Spain (48 million), Italy (41 million), Greece (12 million) and Turkey (9 million). Unfortunately, these figures include tourists staying elsewhere rather than near the Mediterranean. For example, the proportion in France staying in Mediterranean coastal regions is modest, influenced by these regions comprising less than 10% of the country's land area (Blue Plan, 1999; King *et al.*, 2001). Coastal mass tourism is a particularly prominent influence on the small island states of Cyprus and Malta: in Cyprus there are 3.54 international tourists per head of population and in Malta this ratio is 3.10 (Table 2).

**Table 1** Length of Mediterranean coast and population of coastal areas

|  | Length of Mediterranean coast (km) | Coastal areas as a percentage of area of country (%) | Population of coastal areas, 1995 ('000) | Population density of coastal areas, 1995 (inhabitants /km²) | Average annual population growth rate in coastal areas, 1990-95 (%) |
|---|---|---|---|---|---|
| **West and west central** | | | | | |
| Spain | 2,580 | 19 | 15,307 | 160 | 0.5 |
| France | 1,703 | 9 | 6,066 | 132 | 0.8 |
| Italy | 7,953 | 55 | 32,878 | 198 | −0.2 |
| Malta | 180 | 100 | 372 | 1,178 | 0.9 |
| **Central** | | | | | |
| Slovenia | 32 | 22 | 102 | 98 | 0 |
| Croatia | 5,790 | 46 | 1,590 | 62 | n/a |
| Bosnia-Herzegovina | 20 | 12 | 496 | 44 | n/a |
| Serbia-Montenegro | 274 | 6 | 396 | 61 | n/a |
| Albania | 418 | 31 | 1,326 | 146 | −0.3 |
| **East and east central** | | | | | |
| Greece | 15,000 | 76 | 9,189 | 92 | −0.1 |
| Turkey | 5,191 | 16 | 12,574 | 102 | 2.1 |
| Cyprus | 782 | 100 | 739 | 80 | 1.6 |

*Note*: Coastal areas comprise the administrative regions with Mediterranean coastline equivalent to level 3 of the Nomenclature of Statistical Territorial Units (NUTS 3), such as French departments and Italian provinces.
*Source*: Blue Plan (1999) and www.planbleu.org

The growth in numbers of international tourists visiting southern Europe's coasts has not been continuous. The ups and downs of the economic cycle and military conflicts such as the Gulf War have been important for all destinations. And in some of the 12 countries domestic or regional political problems have halted international tourism growth altogether or for long periods. For instance, military events and political instability mean that Albania largely remains outside of the international tourism system. In the case of the former Yugoslavia, in 1988 it attracted over nine million international tourists, over a million more than neighbouring Greece, but conflict and political disintegration subsequently devastated this industry (Jordan, 2000: 525). However, by 2000 tourist arrivals in Croatia and Slovenia had recovered to six million and one million respectively. Chapters 15 (by Scott) and 7 (by Sadler) describe how the industry's growth in north Cyprus has been limited because this territory lacks international political recognition following the intervention of Turkish troops in 1974. This lack of

**Table 2** International tourist arrivals, 1980 and 2000

| | *International tourist arrivals, 1980 ('000)* | *International tourist arrivals, 2000 ('000)* | *International tourist arrivals per head of population, 2000* |
|---|---|---|---|
| **West and west central** | | | |
| Spain | 22,500 | 48,201 | 1.21 |
| France | 30,100 | 75,500 | 1.27 |
| Italy | 22,087 | 41,182 | 0.71 |
| Malta | 729 | 1,216 | 3.10 |
| **Central** | | | |
| Slovenia | n/a | 1,090 | 0.57 |
| Croatia | n/a | 5,831 | 1.36 |
| Bosnia-Herzegovina | n/a | 110 | 0.03 |
| Serbia-Montenegro | n/a | n/a | n/a |
| Albania | n/a | 39 (1999) | n/a |
| **East and east central** | | | |
| Greece | 4,796 | 12,500 | 1.18 |
| Turkey | 865 | 9,587 | 0.15 |
| Cyprus | 353 | 2,686 | 3.54 |

*Sources*: Grenon and Batisse (1989) and World Tourism Organisation (2001).

recognition means that tourists cannot easily access the north from the more popular south, and tour operators are wary of including this destination, partly due to travel time and costs being greater because charter flights have to land first in Turkey. Prior to 1974 much of the tourism industry on the island had been in the north, but by 1998 tourist arrivals in the north were only 393,000 (including 316,000 from nearby Turkey) compared to 2,222,000 in the south (Altinay, 2000: 301).

## The development of mass tourism

According to Burkart and Medlik (1974: 42), 'Mass tourism is essentially a quantitative notion, based on the proportion of the population participating in tourism or on the volume of tourist activity'. There have been increasing concentrations of tourism development on southern Europe's shores since the 1960s, a process shaped by capital accumulation and expanding market opportunities, and with some aspects embodying Fordist patterns of production and consumption. For example, visitors sometimes seek the experiences of 'collective consumption' to be found on crowded beaches and in bars, nightclubs and shopping malls (Urry, 1995), and parts of the industry are characterised by large-scale, standardised production. The tour operator sector in particular often has Fordist characteristics, and this sector can be a powerful influence on local tourism suppliers. But overall the patterns of tourist consumption and tourism supply are varied, with Fordist features only being tendencies. For example, tourists taking cheap, standardised package holidays may engage in more individual-ised activities and consume products sold by small-scale producers. And, while tourism development is sometimes based on foreign investment and large enter-prises, it also includes a highly significant informal sector, including a strong reliance on family labour, employment of unregistered casual labour and moon-lighting (Dunford & King, 2001: 30–31). The 'black' or 'parallel economy' can be a significant factor in a region's tourism sector. In this book Briassoulis notes that informal labour in the Greek island of Crete is conservatively estimated at 50% of the officially reported tourism employment. In Chapter 4, Tsartas also notes that in Greek coastal regions there is a high incidence of people employed in two or three different jobs, one of which is tourism. His research on this 'multi-employment' in Corfu and Lasithi suggests it is often related to the 'black economy'. Indeed, the economies of southern Europe more generally have been depicted as representing 'a model which, in many respects, is the antithesis of Fordism' (Briassoulis, 2001; King & Donati, 1999: 139).

Fordist systems secure economies of scale through production being large-scale and standardised, as well as inflexible as the products cannot be altered greatly except by paying higher prices. Such features are typified by the low-cost, inclusive package holidays provided by tour operators (Ioannides & Debbage, 1998). Tour operators combine transport to resort areas with destination prod-ucts, such as accommodation and excursions, and through their bulk activities they are well placed to sell holidays to the mass market at relatively affordable prices. They can be dominant in the distribution chain to the consumer, and thus they can depress the prices paid to subcontracting hotels and other local service providers. Some coastal destinations of southern Europe are strongly dependent on a few large tour operators from 'core' metropolitan regions to the north. Buhalis (1999: 353, 2000, & 2001: 461) argues that the considerable power of tour operators in Greece has resulted in hoteliers being forced to accept contracts that minimise their profit margins and also adversely affect the quality of their product. However, the proportion of tourists on inclusive packages varies mark-edly between the countries, regions and resorts of the Mediterranean. For example, domestic tourists are an important market in many resort regions, and they tend to make their own arrangements. Inclusive tours can be especially influential in places that are least accessible by car from northern Europe; when air travel is necessary, the tour operators' control over charter flights can be central to a resort's development. This is reflected in the high proportions of international tourists on inclusive packages visiting Cyprus (over 60% of arrivals by air in 1996) and Malta (estimated at 80% in 2000) (Malta Ministry of Tourism, 2000: 8; Sharpley, 1998: 22). Tour operators are far less important among tourists using their own cars to travel to the Mediterranean. The proportion of interna-tional tourists arriving by car is more than 90% in Croatia (Vukoniæ, 2001: 68), 78% in Italy, 67% in France and 60% in Spain (Williams, 1998: 55). In recent years, the power of tour operators in some southern European resort regions has been challenged by the emergence of 'no frills' airlines, which gain economies of scale through concentrating on air transport, leaving tourists to self-package their own holidays.

In Fordism, production is often concentrated in the hands of a few producers. This quite often applies to the tour operating sector, and in some coastal destinations a few large businesses own or manage much of the tourist accommodation stock, which may include transnational hotel groups. While corporate hegemony can be important, there are also coastal areas where accommodation ownership and management is very fragmented, including many local families renting a single room or running a small hotel, and with numerous locally owned restaurants and shops (Priestley, 1995a: 39). For example, on the Spanish Catalan coast the tourism enterprises are mainly small-scale, and owned and managed by local entrepreneurs. The penetration of foreign capital there is very limited, with outsider involvement largely restricted to the construction sector (Priestley & Mundet, 1998: 92). In a survey of the region in 1982, of 161 hotel firms only eight had foreign owners, and three of these were long-term local residents (Morris & Dickinson, 1987: 19). Similarly, Loukissas and Triantafyllopoulos (1997: 217) describe how much accommodation on the Greek island of Rhodes is family owned, managed and run. The case of Crete, described by Briassoulis in Chapter 3, illustrates how external capital can become increasingly important in a destination over time as globalisation and competition brings in new businesses or local entrepreneurs are bought out. In Crete some local businesses have transferred their management to foreign multinationals, and it is estimated that foreign tour operators now control 70% of tourist beds using various arrangements. At the same time, some local tourism businesses in Crete have been transformed into corporate businesses extending their operations outside the region.

There are many instances on the shores of southern Europe of investment in tourism facilities exceeding the demand for them from tourists and tour operators, this being most evident for accommodation provision. The pursuit of capital accumulation by individual investors in competition with each other can easily lead to a speculative over-supply of products that is counter to all their interests (Harvey, 1978). Over-supply of tourism-related accommodation can be encouraged by there being relatively few other opportunities to secure income from landholdings or from other types of economic activity, and by speculative investment, sometimes fuelled by hopes about rising property prices. In conditions of over-supply, tourist accommodation providers are likely to try to protect their occupancy levels and incomes by offering their facilities to tour operators at very low prices (Sharpley, 2000: 287). Such reductions in prices mean there are insufficient returns to reinvest, and thus the product may deteriorate rather than be upgraded to meet rising tourist expectations. Greece has particularly acute problems of over-supply: between 1983 and 1992 the average annual increase in the supply of official hotel beds was 4.7%, while the average annual increase in international tourist bed nights was 2.7% (Buhalis & Diamantis, 2001: 154). Further, it is claimed that there are many illegal tourist beds in Greece that are not supervised for quality control purposes by the authorities, and their owners often avoid paying local taxes, which reduces the local public sector's ability to provide infrastructure and to restore the environment (Loukissas & Triantafyllopoulos, 1997: 218). Greece's difficulties of over-supply are often encouraged by the failure to enforce planning controls effectively. For example, of the 17,000 tourist beds in Faliraki on the east coast of Rhodes as many as 40%

are 'illegal', and 70% of the buildings are in violation of the law (217). In Rhodes
as a whole, between 1985 and 1995 the average yearly rate of growth of tourist
accommodation was 5%, this being well above the average annual growth in
arrivals of 1.4%. A key influence on this bed surplus in Rhodes is an inability to
implement plans and enforce laws rather than the lack of planning structures
(217).

## Mass tourism's seasonal and spatial concentration

The social construction of Mediterranean, high volume mass tourism as a sun
and sea product means that it is usually highly seasonal. This is largely because
the summer months have most sun and the least chance of cloud or rain, and they
include the longest school holiday period that often determines when families
take their main holiday. In Turkey over 50% of international tourists arrive
between June and September, and over 70% between May and October (Var,
2001: 107–8). Seasonality is marked in Greece, and as a result most hotels are
closed for more than six months each year (Buhalis, 1999: 353). However, the
Spanish Costa del Sol region has a reputation for year-round warm weather and
thus it attracts tourists more evenly over the year. The likely further growth in
properties bought on southern Europe's coasts by north Europeans partly to gain
the benefit of winter sunshine during their retirement years may reduce the
impact of seasonality. The current marked peaking of demand has several potential disadvantages for regional sustainable development. It can lead to periods of
intense congestion, times when the long hours of work disrupt the rhythms and
activities associated with more traditional ways of life, low levels of use of tourist
facilities out of the main season and thus reduced economic returns on investment, the need to invest in such infrastructure as water supplies and sewage
disposal adequate for the days when demand is at its peak, and it can also entail
seasonal unemployment. But the quiet periods resulting from seasonality may
be welcomed by residents and even owners of small tourist businesses as they
offer respite from the tourist pressures, and these periods may also help in the
recovery of local ecosystems.

Coastal mass tourism is also often characterised by its spatial concentration.
Tourism facilities and infrastructure, such as hotels, entertainment venues,
promenades, airports and sewage disposal systems, tend to be clustered within
or near resorts in order to gain agglomeration economies, with these resorts also
usually focused on the sea. In Croatia in 1988, 96% of all tourist accommodation,
93% of all overnight stays, and 97% of all foreign overnight stays were concentrated on the Adriatic littoral. Even within Croatia's coastal fringe, tourism was
often confined to places directly located at the shore (Jordan, 2000: 526). In the
case of Cyprus, intensive development has taken place along fairly narrow strips
of land behind the coast to the east of Limassol and Larnaca (Ioannides, 2001a:
118). Within resorts the most valuable location for tourism real estate is usually
the narrow coastal strip that has sea views and affords tourists easy access to the
beach for sunbathing and the sea (Mullins, 1991, 1993). High-rise building can
help to maximise returns from the land in these prime positions. For example,
near the beaches in the resorts of Santa Ponça, Magaluf and S'Arenal in Mallorca
there are high-rise blocks that are packed on small parcels of land linked by a
grid-iron street pattern (Buswell, 1996: 315). Despite the coastal frontages being

in strong demand, there is, however, much variability in the precise spatial arrangement of tourism urbanisation. Some of these differences are related to whether tourism development took place as accretions to existing settlements or as physically discrete growth on new 'greenfield' sites. Torremolinos, Benidorm and Lloret de Mar in Spain, for example, were based on existing small farming or fishing settlements, while Platja d'Aro on the Costa Brava and Playa de San Juan in Alicante developed in 'greenfield' locations (Valenzuela, 1998: 56). The extent of prior urbanisation can substantially influence the local social structure, tourism's social impacts and the responses of local residents to tourism as well as the morphology of resorts.

## The diversity of coastal tourism development

The diversity of southern Europe's tourism-related coastal development is well illustrated in Italy. Here there are marked differences between the tightly packed, mass tourism landscapes of the Rimini area; the exclusive, carefully managed, and low density development in traditional building styles of the Sardinian Costa Smeralda; and the coast of Calabria that is filled with speculative, second-home developments that often flout local planning regulations (King & Montanari, 1998: 96–97; Manzi, 2001).

There are important variations in the established reputations or status of specific resorts. Based on an analysis of the price of package holidays to larger resorts in the Mediterranean, Papatheodorou (2002: 148) contends that the most successful package tourism resorts are those with a strong brand name. This may be associated with the existence of well-known built attractions, such as theme parks and marinas, or an air of sophistication, which may be related to the presence of old monuments or a reputation for exclusiveness. He also contends that resorts can enhance a luxury image through the presence of high quality accommodation establishments and of leading hotel groups. Resorts also differ in the extent to which they retain or else subsequently gain significant residential or other functions that supplement their immediate tourism functions. For example, in Chapter 11 Campillo-Besses, Priestley and Romagosa describe how the permanent as well as second-home population has grown in Catalan resorts close to Barcelona due to easy accessibility to this city, their comparatively lower property prices, and the obvious attractions of living in these resorts.

The mix of tourism-related accommodation is another source of variation between coastal regions. For example, along some coasts there are notable concentrations of second homes or high-rise apartments owned by 'residential tourists', that are used for short-term or seasonal relocations and many are also rented to other visitors. Second homes often occupy stretches of the Mediterranean coast or are found a little inland outside of the main areas of highest density commercial holiday accommodation (Priestley, 1995a: 52). These second homes and apartment blocks are often increasingly influential in coastal urbanisation, reflecting the changing dynamics of capital-seeking opportunities from real estate development in these regions. Vera Rebollo and Ivars Baidal (Chapter 9) argue that the resulting development of large concentrations of villas and apartment blocks by the construction and real estate industries may be encouraged by local government as a short- and medium-term motor for the local economy and as a source of increasing local tax revenues. Domestic 'residential tourism' is common in Spain, where city inhabitants leave for a period in the summer to stay in a second home, this property often being in the surrounding countryside or near the coast (Barke, 1991; Leontidou & Marmaras, 2001). Aspirations to own a second house or apartment have grown among all social classes in Spain, and this helps to explain the expansion of second homes in recent years. The growth of international 'residential tourism' is highlighted by there being more than 1.5 million foreign-owned dwellings in Spanish coastal areas, with 30% of owners being British nationals and 25% being German (Valenzuela, 1998: 54–5). There are important implications for host communities depending on whether 'residential tourists' buy a property for short holidays and perhaps also to let it out for the rest of the year, or whether they buy it to reside there long-term, possibly as a retirement property. Some of these issues are discussed by Barke and Towner in Chapter 8 in relation to the concentration of foreign residents on the central and eastern Andalucían littoral of Spain (Casado-Diaz, 1999).

## The Impacts of Coastal Mass Tourism in Southern Europe

The increased jobs, spending and wealth that tourism has undoubtedly brought to the Mediterranean coasts have to be balanced against its associated problems. Common socioeconomic disadvantages of this industry include the potential for income leakage from the local economy to tour operators and carriers in origin countries, and its concentration of low-level workers who are badly paid and employed flexibly according to the fluctuations in tourism. Tourism is often associated with problems of seasonal unemployment and periods of long hours of intense work (Urry, 1990: 66–80). The poor pay often contributes to the patterns of inequalities among the residents of tourist areas. There can also be acute disparities in the distribution of tourism income between fractions of capital, such as between external tour operators and local small-scale tourism businesses, and also between different regions. For example, in 1992 as much as 76% of the hotel supply in Spain was found in only five of its 17 regions, four of these being on the Mediterranean (Monfort Mir & Ivars Baidal, 2001: 28–9). In this book Tosun, Timothy and Öztürk show how tourism has contributed to the pronounced economic disparities between Turkey's developed and underdeveloped regions, thereby worsening the country's regional polarisation. They also suggest that in many tourist areas in Turkey the industry's initial growth was established by small local investors, but this was later often replaced by large foreign and non-local domestic capital investors. It is further argued that inequalities between social classes in tourist areas have increased as most local people have remained as low-wage workers.

The industry's rapid growth and its spatial and temporal concentration have often intensified its environmental impacts (Shaw & Williams, 1994). The rapid expansion of some resorts has at times outstripped the capacity of local infrastructure, especially in the busiest summer months, and led to intense environmental problems (Sharpley, 2000: 283). This can sometimes be seen in deficiencies in road provision and surfaces, refuse collection and disposal, and sewage collection systems and treatment plants, especially when local government is unused to the new levels of demand, lacks relevant powers, or is underfunded (Priestley & Mundet, 1998: 92). For example, the burgeoning number of tourists in Malta's resorts has put pressure on an old sewage system with limited capacity that consequently can leak; and the majority of the sewage generated is pumped out into the sea untreated. Since the 1960s tourism has also added to Malta's increasing amounts of solid waste that have been dumped, without being sorted or treated, into poorly managed landfills (Bramwell, 2003; Zanetto & Soriani, 1996).

In Chapter 4 Tsartas notes the problem of weak observation of planning provisions in Greece's coastal tourist areas in the face of pressure for continuing development. In the case of Crete, Briassoulis (Chapter 3) describes how the combination of pro-development laws and the lack of implementation and enforcement of land-use regulations and environmental legislation has resulted in problems such as sea pollution, ecosystem destruction, landscape degradation, loss of productive agricultural land and the mixing of incompatible land uses. While second-home and retirement home developments along southern Europe's coasts are often built at lower densities, this reduced spatial concentration itself can have adverse implications, such as the more extensive loss of farming land and the traffic pollution effects from increased travel distances. Tourism development adds to the varied pressures on environmental resources in coastal regions, including the sand and gravel used for building materials. In Sardinia demand for these materials for new building, including for tourism development, has led to extensive extractive works in the river bed of the Rio Santa Lucia, resulting in landscape degradation and the loss of its unique mixed vegetation (Leontidou *et al.*, 1998: 96–7).

The effects of tourism on the society and culture of these coastal areas are particularly multifaceted, complex and contested. For example, in Chapter 4 Tsartas contends that tourism in Greece has contributed to individuals gaining more financial and social independence from their family and to fathers being less influential in families, but he also argues that the family has retained importance, including as a small 'economic unit' that combines varied income sources from tourism. Similarly, Andriotis (Chapter 6) explains that on some Greek islands tourism has led to depopulation from the villages and a concentration of population in the towns, but he also shows that tourism has reduced emigration from these islands and that returning migrants have become actively involved in the tourism industry. In Chapter 15 Scott emphasises the importance of the specific local sociocultural context for an understanding of tourism's consequences for change in society. She considers the casino industry's rapid expansion from 1997 in north Cyprus, where this industry largely caters for Turkish tourists. It is stressed that gambling problems among north Cypriots did not first arise because of these new casinos, as gambling had long been a fact of life there. Rather, the new gambling opportunities have exacerbated existing problems and have threatened established social and family strategies for managing gambling.

There has been much academic debate about the consequences of the commercialisation of culture for tourism purposes, with some depicting this process as fundamentally destructive of the meanings through which local inhabitants organise their lives (Greenwood, 1989: 179). Certainly, such tourist commercialisation may erode residents' culture, but it must not be assumed that people are necessarily incapable of resisting these pressures or that local cultures should somehow remain fixed. Based on a study of tourism in Malta, Boissevain (1996a:

114) suggests that tourism's influence on Maltese society is 'neither as crude nor as spectacular as the critics of cultural commoditisation have suggested'. While this activity may encourage substantial changes in residents' values, their responses are always mediated by their social relations and beliefs. Thus responses to tourism among the Maltese have depended on their practices and beliefs, including their 'traditional' beliefs in family life and moral standards, and there have also been other key influences on changes in their society, such as the effects of mass media, rising standards of living, and a developing awareness of environmental issues (Bramwell, 2003: 598).

It should also be remembered that tourism is only one influence among others on these regions, although often a highly significant one. In the Spanish Balearic islands, tourism's rapid expansion has encouraged population growth and the islands' emergence as one of the most prosperous regions in southern Europe (Salvà Tomàs, 1991). However, Vidal Bendito (1994) is critical of focusing exclusively on tourism's impact on these islands, as demographic and economic data show that the 'modernisation' of Balearic society was well under way before the advent of mass tourism. And there are also important economic activities other than tourism on the Balearic islands, especially so in the case of Menorca, where its more varied economic structure includes high value agriculture, craft industries and commerce (Mari, 1994). Tourism can be a key factor in littoralisation – that is, the growth of population and economic activity along the coast – but there are usually other processes at work. In the unusual case of south Cyprus, the urbanisation of its coast was substantially encouraged by tourism development; but a second key factor was the island's political division from the north in 1974 and the need to rebuild the economy in the south. Here a stretch of approximately 48 km of once pristine coastal land has been lost to ribbon-like urban and suburban development, including many hotels, tourist villas and apartments, and second homes (Ioannides, 2001a: 120). There are also notable sources of environmental damage in these coastal regions other than from tourism. For example, the Mediterranean is a virtually closed sea that struggles to assimilate the great quantities of pollutants dumped in it from industrialisation, urbanisation, pesticides and oil spillage. Certainly tourism represents a further significant source of sea pollution, although its exact contribution is difficult to measure (King, 1989: 9–15).

## Shifting Modes of Production and Consumption

According to some commentators, more individualised and flexible forms of tourism are gaining in importance, and mass tourism itself is possibly stagnating or even declining. This is said to represent a trend towards post-Fordist forms of consumption and production, with tourism becoming more specialised, customised, flexible and smaller-scale (Britton, 1991; Urry, 1995; Vanhove, 1997; Williams & Shaw, 1998a). Tourist consumption is also more likely to be guided by what it says about the individual consumer and whether the tourism product consumed helps them to accumulate what Bourdieu (1984) refers to as cultural capital, which relies on a person's ability to 'know' or 'appreciate' what holiday to take (Mowforth & Munt 1998: 132). The post-Fordist tourist is considered to be wealthier, better educated, more interested in discovering differing environments and the 'other' in local cultures, and possibly also more 'responsible' (Feifer, 1985). It is thought that holiday choices are more diversified in post-Fordism, often being based on specialist interests, such as golf and sailing, or on 'alternative' products, such as cultural tourism, agro-tourism and ecotourism, that potentially can draw on the distinctive environments, history and culture of each destination (Poon, 1989; Urry, 1995: 151). Increasing use of the Internet by the public has also encouraged more tourists to self-package their holiday components according to their specific needs and interests. 'Alternative' products have potential to be small scale and to involve modest tourist flows to specific places, and thus they may encourage more flexible forms of production (Milne, 1998). Their providers may also deploy links with ecology, conservation and matters sustainable and ethical, perhaps largely for their own ends (Mowforth & Munt, 1998: 327).

However, the arguments about a decline in mass tourism might have been over stated. Williams and Shaw (1998a: 53–4) conclude that,

> The supposed shift away from mass tourism has . . . been exaggerated, not least because of the focus on short-term fluctuations in demand, particularly in Spain in the early 1990s. Despite the much-vaunted decline of mass tourism, there is at best only evidence of relative decline, when contrasted with some other forms of tourism.

There are several potential elements behind this exaggeration. First, it is contended that 'mass tourism coexisted with more individualised forms of tourism even in the 1960s and 1970s; it was often only marginally the dominant form of tourism, and perhaps in many or even most European regions could not even claim to hold this position' (Williams & Shaw, 1998a: 53). Second, southern Europe's resort regions are highly differentiated in terms of their capital structures, natural and built landscapes, extent of geographical concentration, and mix of recreational activities, and thus they already cater for the preferences of a diverse range of consumers. Third, predictions of a decline in southern Europe's resorts are largely based on trends in their northern European markets, and this ignores the potential growth in demand for these resorts from their own domestic markets, such as for holiday homes and apartments, and also from central and eastern Europe (Jenner & Smith, 1993: 51–7, 74–81). Williams and Shaw (1998b: 5), for example, argue that, 'although the growth of mass tourism markets has abated somewhat, and perhaps even stagnated in much of Northern Europe, there is still strong absolute and relative growth in markets in Southern and Eastern Europe'. Fourth, changes in north European markets for mass tourism in the Mediterranean can also easily be exaggerated. For example, in northern Europe there continues to be marked variations in people's lifestyles, and as incomes rise further there is growth in the number of second and third holidays each year. Many of these tourists continue to favour mass resorts, where visitor volumes ensure there are varied recreational activities and relatively low prices, and still tend to use large tour operators that offer convenience, low prices and a degree of quality assurance.

Some researchers also adopt a neo-Fordist view that mass tourism can adapt to the growing demands for more individualised, diversified and flexible forms within what remain as essentially mass products (Agarwal, 2002: 35; Ioannides & Debbage, 1998). This can be achieved by large tour operators offering more choice through the customisation of mass products, increasing choice in the elements of their holiday packages, offering self-provisioning options, developing new products for niche markets, and by promoting destinations outside the main tourist areas (Andriotis, 2002a; Torres, 2002). The rise of 'no frills' airlines has also introduced new, large-scale providers of highly standardised air travel products around which tourists can make their own independent holiday arrangements (Josephides, 2003: 4–5). Mass tourism resorts can also offer a wider choice of activities, both in the resort and in their less exploited hinterland, such as casinos, nightclubs, water sports, craft workshops, scenic rail journeys, historic sites and walking in rural areas. These options are notably increased when tourists use a hire car. Computerised booking procedures have helped make customised holidays easier for large companies to book and control, and sophisticated destination management systems may also assist more in the future in matching destination products to individual tourist preferences.

Developing the case for flexibility even further, Torres (2002) argues that there is a spectrum of modes of tourism production, including pre-Fordist, Fordist, post-Fordist and neo-Fordist, and that these different modes often coexist at particular times and in specific places. The boundaries between these modes are often highly blurred and indistinct, with much permeability and integration between them (Ioannides & Debbage, 1998: 108). This position suggests that there are multiple shades of tourism in many resort areas, creating complex and changing relations, and that there is unlikely to be any simple, linear shift in the modes of production and consumption (Williams & Montanari, 1995: 4).

## Sustainability and Mass and Alternative Tourism

It has been widely assumed that mass tourism is less sustainable than 'alternative' tourism because the former is more likely to entail environmental damage. 'Alternative' tourism would appear much more in tune with the principles of sustainability as it is often characterised by its small scale and involvement of local people, and by an emphasis on appreciating nature, landscapes and cultures. Such potential advantages are clearly important and must be given full recognition. They are likely to favour 'alternative' tourism in perhaps the great majority of cases. But it must also be noted that 'alternative' tourism can be just as problematic as mass tourism, as sometimes it generates intense environmental and social pressures. Hence it is necessary to evaluate the advantages and disadvantages of mass tourism and 'alternative' tourism in different circumstances. Such an evaluation mirrors questions being asked more generally about the environmental consequences of smaller and more geographically dispersed industrial units resulting from post-Fordist restructuring. Here some note that 'a trend towards dispersed small scale businesses is argued to be somehow naturally more environmentally-friendly than large businesses because dispersal is thought to involve local control', while others conclude that the 'issue of whether a small unit or firm automatically leads to greater environmental responsiveness is . . . a highly debatable one' (Gibbs, 1996: 4).

### An adaptive view of sustainability

But conclusions about the relative merits of different types of tourism will depend on the basis by which one judges sustainability. Just how do we evaluate what represents sustainable development? The position taken here is that sustainable development is a 'socially constructed' and contested concept that reflects the interests of those involved. As a consequence, it has taken on diverse meanings, with these alternative interpretations reflecting different economic interests and ethical positions, and also entailing varying conclusions about policy objectives and management strategies. Despite these differences, over the past decade or so sustainability has become a key discourse through which environmentalists, politicians, industry and developers frame environmental issues and advocate differing policies and strategies (Macnaghten & Urry, 1998). Sustainability is also used by a variety of interests in various ways as a means of achieving their desired outcomes, and as such it can support and enhance their basis of power. Viewing sustainable development as a social and political construct and as a terrain of contested discourses makes it possible to move beyond the search for a unitary and precise definition, and to see it instead as reflecting differing beliefs about the world as well as differing interests. It can be seen as similar to concepts such as 'democracy', 'liberty' and 'social justice'. For notions such as these there is a readily understood 'first-level of meaning', but around them there lie a number of fundamental contestations. In liberal democracies the debates around these disputed ideas form an essential component of the political struggle over the direction of social and economic development, this being a struggle embodying unequal power relations. Consequently, the search for a unitary and precise definition of sustainable development may well rest on a mistaken view of the nature and function of political concepts (Barker *et al.*, 1997: 5–7).

Turner (1993) simplifies the contested meanings of sustainable development into four broad positions: very strong, strong, weak and very weak sustainability. A very strong position regards natural resources as having intrinsic value, holds that these resources must be conserved whether or not they provide benefit to society, and rejects the substitution of natural by human-made resources. By contrast, a very weak sustainability position allows resources to be used according to market demand, is strongly oriented to economic growth, and allows the substitution of natural by human-made resources (Bramwell *et al.*, 1996). These four positions should perhaps be conceived as points on a continuum, with very strong and very weak sustainability at its opposite poles. It is suggested by Garrod and Fyall (1998) that different interpretations of tourism and sustainability can be related to Turner's four positions on sustainable development. They distinguish between very strong, strong, weak and very weak positions on how tourism can assist with sustainable development objectives, although this too is best thought of as a continuum. In practice, approaches to tourism and sustainability tend to favour a weaker, economic growth-oriented vision, albeit with growth managed to take account of resource implications through the use of techniques such as environmental impact assessments.

It has been suggested that instead of striving for a single vision of sustainability, this concept should be conceived as a broad framework within which several different development paths may be appropriate according to circumstances. This view of sustainability as an 'adaptive paradigm' according to different contexts has been applied by Hunter (1997) to tourism development. From this perspective, it is considered appropriate for places to adopt different magnitudes, types and locations of tourism development depending on their circumstances. For example, destinations vary according to the fragility of their environments and according to the mix of social groups involved – both hosts and guests – who may have differing views on development. Another source of variation between areas is the extent to which tourism development and related infrastructure already exist (Bramwell & Sharman, 2000: 20; Ioannides, 2001b). Hence, if tourism has hardly developed previously, as is currently the case along many coasts of north Cyprus, it may be decided to discourage the industry so as to protect the destination resources (potentially very strong sustainability) or it may be moderately encouraged because it is considered more sustainable than other economic activities (potentially moderate or weak sustainability). However, if tourism is already a major economic activity then efforts are likely to be directed to at least maintaining it, in order to avoid an unacceptable decline in the local economy and to make the most of prior investment (potentially weak sustainability). But instead, developed areas may promote types of 'alternative' tourism that overtly rely on the maintenance of high-quality environmental and cultural resources (potentially moderate or even quite strong sustainability).

## Sustainability and mass tourism and 'alternative' tourism

The adaptive view of sustainable development suggests that the appropriateness of mass tourism, 'alternative' tourism, or of both in combination for sustainable development depends on the precise context of each destination. Nevertheless, some commentators argue that diversification using 'alternative' tourism is generally necessary in southern Europe's coastal areas, notably because of the emergence of new, competing 'sun and sea' destinations on the Mediterranean's southern littoral and further afield that are often cheaper due to lower wages, land prices and costs of maintaining environmental quality (Formica & Uysal, 1996; Marchena Gómez, 1995: 28; Monfort Mir & Ivars Baidal, 2001). Living standards and demands for environmental improvements have risen over recent years in most of Mediterranean Europe, and this has increased the cost of holidays there. Further, intense competition for low-spending tourists has produced low economic returns, and this jeopardises product upgrading. Consequently, it is argued that southern European countries need to appeal to tourists who will pay higher prices for distinctive 'alternative' products (Jenner & Smith, 1993: 13, 166; WTO/UNEP/Blue Plan, 2000: 6). Such products are also thought to be necessary in order to spread risk in the context of possible shifts in consumer preferences. These products may be encouraged because they promote a sense of place and an awareness of local distinctiveness, and because they provide an economic justification for conserving environments and old buildings and for strengthening 'traditional' ways of life (Sharpley, 2002: 237; Vera Rebollo, 2001: 58–62). Further, these products may help coastal regions to enhance their cultural capital, attracting more tourists because the destinations are better placed to demonstrate tourist taste and style (Bourdieu, 1984; Urry, 1990). These are all important arguments that deserve serious attention.

However, it must be noted that tourists might also pay a premium to stay in mass resorts if their built environment was substantially upgraded and there were more diverse resort-based activities. That is, mass tourism could also move up market. Consequently, it is essential to evaluate the arguments about the potential merits and drawbacks of mass tourism and 'alternative' tourism for sustainable development. In the discussion that follows, slightly more attention is paid to the potential merits of mass tourism and problems of 'alternative' tourism. This is because these arguments feature less often in the literature and not because they are more persuasive. Indeed, it should be remembered that probably only 'alternative' tourism has the potential to meet the strict criteria of strong sustainability, and it is perhaps preferable in the great majority of cases.

One argument is that, by comparison with 'alternative' tourism, mass tourism facilities are more likely to be owned and managed by large businesses based outside of the destination, so that more of the earnings fail to reach local communities and the resort economies are more dependent on external decisions (Weaver, 2000: 218). Andriotis (2002a: 77 and b: 339) compares large with small and medium-sized hospitality firms in Crete, and he finds that larger firms tend to be less economically embedded in the locality, being more likely to import managerial labour, and having far fewer linkages with local suppliers. However, as Williams and Shaw (1998b: 9) suggest, at this point in time 'it is not possible to generalise about the embeddedness of tourism firms; this is a matter of contingent relationships . . . [and] it remains an area long on speculation and short on research'. More studies are needed in southern Europe on the character of tourism businesses according to their size, ownership, management structures and local and external economic linkages (Ioannides, 2001b). It might also be contended that local owners of small hotels are more likely to adopt environmental measures as they are more sensitive to tourism's adverse consequences for destination areas. However, there is evidence that large, multi-facility businesses can quickly diffuse sustainability initiatives through the many parts of their organisations once it is in their business plans, they are well placed to exert pressure on external suppliers to 'go green', and they have the bulk marketing and communication contacts in order to foster wide interest in sustainability issues. And small tourism businesses often lack the resources and expertise to implement sustainability measures (Clarke, 1997: 227; Weaver & Oppermann, 2000: 357–8).

A second set of arguments arise from mass tourism tending to be more spatially concentrated than 'alternative' tourism, with the latter often drawing on spatially scattered environmental, heritage and cultural resources. Concentrated mass tourism resorts are criticised as they can overwhelm local environmental systems, they may exceed the capacity of communities to manage the associated impacts, and they can discourage local economic and employment linkages (Williams & Shaw, 1998a: 53). For example, with spatially concentrated growth it can be easier for a pool of migrant labour to emerge in the area that takes jobs away from long-term inhabitants. In Croatia in the late 1980s there was an extreme concentration of mass tourism on the coast, but the related labour force was often drawn from inland and from Bosnia and Slovenia, because the local residents disliked the low wages and seasonal work. Hence, 'although tourism was concentrated in the coastal zone, it tended not to be organically embedded within the local population and culture. Yet owing to the concentration of "tourist monostructures" in some coastal communities, tourism provided up to 70% of their income' (Jordan, 2000: 527, 534). However, spatially concentrated resorts can benefit by securing economies of scale, and thus they may have additional resources available in order to reduce tourism's harmful impacts. These can include professional planners and skilled urban regeneration practitioners, capable of obtaining funds for and implementing new forms of green urbanism. Such resorts can also reduce the distance that people travel once they are in their holiday region, thus reducing energy consumption and air pollution.

By contrast, there are criticisms that where 'alternative' tourism is spatially dispersed in less developed regions it can unintentionally cause distress to their relatively pristine ecosystems and, in some cases, to specific species. Further, while there may be relatively few tourists in these areas, it is argued that they can produce more sociocultural stress because the local communities they visit are less used to a tourist presence and because visitors often want to experience the 'back' regions of local cultures. Boissevain (1996b) notes that the government of Malta is actively promoting year-round cultural tourism, but he concludes that 'cultural tourism in general and winter tourism in particular are more likely to generate social and cultural tension than seaside tourism in the summer' (236). He offers several reasons why he considers mass tourism is generally more sustainable than cultural tourism in Malta. First, cultural tourism is often less seasonal and he believes that, 'Without some respite from the constant gaze and demands of tourists, hosts become enervated and their behaviour towards tourists [becomes] hostile' (235). Second, cultural activities bring visitors from the coastal resorts into the inland villages and towns where most Maltese reside. The only inland town so far attracting very large numbers of tourists is the historic town of Mdina, and here the residents are described as suffering alienation due to the town's overcommercialisation and loss of tranquillity. This intrusion has led to a loss of privacy: 'As tourists search for the culture they have paid to see, they cross thresholds and boundaries (sometimes, but not always, hidden) to penetrate private domestic space' (234). Excessive attention is depicted as destroying the very culture that the visitors come to experience. In Mdina, 'It does this by transforming natives into entrepreneurs, by destroying the traditional tranquillity and physical environment, and by pricing the local population out of the area, thus transforming the attraction from a living community into a museum or heritage park' (235).

A third set of arguments relate to the level of economic returns from mass tourism and 'alternative' tourism, with small-scale tourism sometimes criticised for providing only modest income benefits (Butler, 1989: 14; Weaver & Oppermann, 2000: 375). For example, in south Cyprus there is public sector encouragement for agro-tourism in inland areas in order to help diversify the tourism industry and also to channel income directly to rural communities (Cyprus Tourism Organisation, 2000). According to Sharpley (2002), agro-tourism on the island has brought new life to old buildings, supplementary income for rural residents, and some new, albeit limited, employment opportunities. But less positively, he suggests that the resulting accommodation generally achieves only low occupancies, in part due to their higher cost relative to resort accommodation, and that their returns have often not covered the initial investment. He concludes that 'long term government subsidy and support is likely to remain an essential element of rural tourism policy and, for destinations such as Cyprus, efforts may be better directed towards sustaining and consolidating the existing coastal resort tourism business' (243). In this book Sharpley contends that mass coastal tourism in south Cyprus has been an effective vehicle for national economic development, and he suggests that a significant policy switch to niche, high quality tourism could hinder the country's further development. But some might question whether further very substantial growth in existing forms of mass tourism in south Cyprus would encourage sufficient 'trickle down' of tourism's benefits to all social groups and geographic regions, and might entail too many environmental costs.

A fourth debate surrounds the potential attitudes of local communities and others in areas engaged in 'alternative' tourism. This is because, while generally there may be good intentions behind seeking this form of development, some individuals or groups within or outside the community may be motivated more by the prospect of quick financial returns, gained from selling land holdings or from tourism-related businesses, even if this has adverse consequences for others. This is one reason why Butler (1989: 16) warns, 'alternative small-scale tourism can change to mass conventional tourism, perhaps will inevitably do so without strict management and control'. Ioannides (1995: 588–90) describes the case of the Akamas peninsula, the last remaining substantial stretch of undeveloped coast in south Cyprus, where there is a long-standing plan to develop small-scale, village-based 'alternative' tourism. However, some villagers as well as some outside interests, including some leaders of the Church of Cyprus that has substantial local landholdings, are pushing for larger-scale tourism development, arguing that it is unfair to stop the inhabitants from getting substantial economic returns similar to those secured by other coastal communities in Cyprus. According to Ioannides, the residents' views on aesthetic controls often differ from those of environmentalists and planners, with many being impressed by the resort developments in Cyprus and relatively unconcerned about their associated environmental problems. And the common problem of a weak application of planning controls has already been noted.

Finally, it could be considered misguided to neglect the vitality of the existing mass tourism resorts in southern Europe: this may be thought to be both an economically inefficient use of prior investment and also socially unacceptable for resort communities. Such considerations relate to the prior development of tourist accommodation and other facilities in resorts which subsequently lose some of their competitiveness, because of their poor quality, their physical deterioration over time, or because of changing tourist expectations. According to Harvey (1978: 123–4), with urban growth

> Spatial structures are created which themselves act as barriers to further [capital] accumulation . . . Capitalist development has therefore to negotiate a knife-edge path between preserving the exchange value of past capital investments in the built environment and destroying the value of these investments in order to open up fresh room for accumulation.

It might also be inappropriate to allow resort decline if it simply diverts tourists into their hinterland areas that have yet to be developed and that have more fragile environments and socio-cultural systems. Butler (1997: 121) has also been critical of adding socially and environmentally sympathetic small-scale additions to the tourism scene, when large-scale and serious negative impacts in mass tourism areas are being ignored. There is a need to consider, therefore, what will lead to the largest gains in impact reduction in the current situation, including in that context the past investments, present resources, and the numbers of tourists involved (Moisey & McCool, 2001: 345).

In some circumstances it may be appropriate for sustainable tourism policies to be focused on existing resorts, through environmental improvements in public spaces, efficiency in waste, water and energy management, and programmes of traffic management (Priestley, 1996: 117–18). In the late 1980s and early 1990s the Balearic islands' government in Spain introduced major public works to improve the physical fabric of some of the oldest tourist resorts, especially in Mallorca, with pedestrianisation, tree planting, the removal of substandard accommodation, and tighter planning regulations on new hotels (Bull, 1997: 148–9). Resort expansion in southern Europe has often been accompanied historically by deficient provision of complementary infrastructure, such as sewage, roads, and waste disposal, and limited consideration of landscape and built environment quality. Such environmental issues in resorts can be tackled directly, and steps can be taken there to improve tourism's local economic and social returns, such as by enhancing training programmes, reducing the over-supply of tourist accommodation, and developing facilities for community use. Unfortunately, too often the political response to the pressures of rapid resort urbanisation is simply to manage development in a more coordinated manner, and to provide some limited additional public expenditure for related infrastructure and a few 'green spaces'. According to Vera Rebollo and Ivars Baidal (Chapter 9), this was the case for the resort of Torrevieja in the Spanish region of Alicante, where opinion leaders appear to accept the need for continued extensive development of tourism and real estate for the municipality's prosperity. The environmental and community pressures resulting from this development are generally considered acceptable locally as local government has protected some areas from development, introduced certain environmental controls, and has also provided waste water treatment. Vera Rebollo and Ivars Baidal depict this approach as comparable to weak sustainability, whereby the loss of natural capital can be substituted by investment in various environmental projects.

The balance of advantages and disadvantages of mass tourism and 'alternative' tourism for sustainable development will vary according to a locality's unique circumstances and character. Each destination differs according to, for example, the range of tourism assets and their potential appeal to tourist markets, its susceptibility to adverse social, cultural or environmental impacts, and its capacity to control tourism's impacts. Whatever form of tourism development is pursued – indeed if tourism is adopted at all – it will require careful planning to ensure that it remains a means to an end – that is, an element of a broader and sustainable socioeconomic development strategy – as opposed to an end in itself. Attention must be directed, for example, to how much tourism development in total to allow. And the affected parties in the host community must participate in the development process, which involves a learning process for all the relevant actors.

### The diversity of mass tourism and 'alternative' tourism

Any comparison of mass tourism and 'alternative' tourism is complicated by the diversity of both of these tourism forms in southern Europe. For example, mass tourism products have become more varied over the past decade, partly due to the greater attention devoted to attracting high spending markets, sometimes including business tourists. For example, in Greece between 1995 and 1998 the state authorities approved investment plans for 13 convention centres, five marinas, three thalassotherapy centres, two golf courses and one thermal spa centre (Moussios, 1999: 47). While such facilities are up-market and geared to 'quality' tourism, they still have many mass tourism features as they are big facilities intended to appeal to large numbers of users. Golf courses and marinas have substantial impacts in their own right, notably environmental problems around water use in the case of golf courses and also problems of social exclusion, and they are often also linked to substantial and luxurious real estate development, such as apartments, timeshares, and hotels, which can have profound landscape impacts. Extensive real estate developments for second homes and residential tourism are also becoming more important in mass tourism resorts on these coasts. But these products can also vary in terms of their implications for sustainability. For example, in Chapter 13 Spilanis and Vayanni make distinctions between large-scale and small-scale conference tourism facilities on the Greek islands. It is suggested that luxury, large-scale conference facilities attached to hotels on the Greek islands of Rhodes and Kos have had negative environmental consequences, make little use of local products and lack connection with the local culture. Conversely, small-scale conference infrastructure on the islands of Chios and Samos are depicted as better suited to the environment and often based on the renovation of old buildings.

There is much variability too within 'alternative' tourism. One example is adventure tourism, where the participants may not be motivated by gaining a greater understanding of the special qualities of the places used for their activities; rather, they may be more interested in being physically active and competitive, and in gaining thrills. Activities such as off-road four-wheel driving, endurance sports, survival games and paragliding that take place in rural areas may reflect the imposition of experiences more readily associated with those found in mass tourism resorts and they may also cause much disturbance (Butler, 1998b: 213–16). The development of cultural tourism in the historic city of Valletta in the Maltese islands, as discussed by Theuma in Chapter 14, may help to diversify the islands' tourism industry away from the mass coastal resorts, but tourism in heritage cities can involve large numbers of visitors and thus may have more mass tourism than 'alternative' tourism characteristics. So-called 'alternative' tourism products may not be associated with small-scale and low-impact activity, as their consumption may demand a high degree of commodification for large numbers of tourists motivated by concerns other than reflection about the products' distinctive characteristics. The potential for the misleading use of labels such as 'ecotourism', 'green' and 'cultural' tourism is illustrated by Spilanis and Vayanni in Chapter 13. They argue that, despite the use of the term 'agro-tourism' for rural accommodation in the Greek island of Lesvos, it actually has little direct connection with agricultural production, local products or landscape conservation, and they conclude that it is largely conventional tourism operated by farmers.

In the future there is likely to be an increased mixture of mass tourism with 'alternative' tourism in southern Europe, so it is important to understand the complexities of combining them so that they promote sustainable development.

One issue is that of matching different products to various potential tourist markets in appropriate ways. For example, cultural tourists and ecotourists may demand high quality, specialised products found outside large resorts, while also requiring the comforts and services of upmarket hotels and other largely resort-based facilities. And some less specialised ecoproducts and cultural activities could be added to a beach vacation or a cruise holiday, in 'sun-plus' rather than just 'sun-lust' vacations. Another issue is the coordinated development of different types of tourism with other economic sectors and activities at a regional scale, with resorts seen in the broader context of their hinterlands (Vera Rebollo & Rippin, 1996: 126). But care needs to be taken to avoid adding to the threats to sustainability due to the new combinations of tourist activities. In the case of Cyprus, companies located in the large resorts now sell 'eco-safaris' in remote rural areas mainly to mass tourists seeking a short break from days on the beach, but these convoys of jeeps have resulted in noise pollution, disturbance to fragile areas, and little economic benefit for rural areas as the food and drink that is provided is brought into these areas by the companies (Ioannides & Holcomb, 2001: 251–2). It is also suggested by Spilanis and Vayanni (Chapter 13) that there may be only limited potential for integrating mass and 'alternative' tourism on the smaller Greek Aegean islands because 'alternative' tourism is handicapped by these islands lacking the diverse resources of a large hinterland and also often being too distant from the mainland for easy access in the winter.

Theuma examines attempts in the Maltese islands to expand cultural tourism based on the islands' capital, the historic city of Valletta (Chapter 14). The development of tourism there can help to diversify the islands' tourism away from a reliance on coastal resorts, as well as to improve the destination's position in the face of fierce competition from other resort areas. Further, an expansion of cultural tourism may assist in Valletta's economic and social revival, with the city having lost some of its vitality due to changing residential patterns, the relocation of the entertainment industry to resort and leisure areas outside the city, and to declining night-time activity. Theuma explains the difficulties of developing cultural tourism in Valletta when currently most visitors from the islands' resorts and from cruise ships only go there for a half day. There may also be problems associated with tourist commercialisation of the city and with bringing visitors into the city's residential areas. There are numerous towns and cities in southern Europe with substantial historic resources that are also coastal resorts or else are near such resorts, and more research is needed on whether and how tourists in these areas use both the resort and the historic resources, and on the implications of this for sustainable development.

## Conclusion and Organisation of the Book

This chapter has considered mass tourism's development in the coastal regions of Mediterranean Europe and its part in the rapid economic growth of many of these regions. While this industry has brought increased wealth, its socio-spatial distribution has been uneven and its dependence on external decision-makers and global markets has grown, and there have also been many adverse impacts on the fragile environments of these coastlands. The effects of tourism on their society and culture have been complex, with some consequences being largely unfavourable. These diverse impacts all raise issues for sustainable development. At the same time, concern has grown over the past two decades about the economic vitality of conventional mass tourism, in part because of deteriorating resort environments. Attempts are being made therefore to diversify from mass tourism by developing 'alternative' products, such as agro-tourism and cultural tourism, and also to improve the environmental quality of mass tourism, through resort upgrading and the 'greening' of tourist facilities. The focus of much of the discussion has been on the potential advantages and disadvantages of these tourism forms for sustainability. It has been shown that it is dangerous to assume that small-scale 'alternative' tourism is necessarily more compatible with sustainable development objectives than is mass tourism. In perhaps the great majority of instances such 'alternative' tourism may be preferable, especially in areas which so far have developed little tourism, but it is important to be wary about policies based on an oversimplified faith in this form of tourism.

It was stressed that the balance of benefits and costs of differing tourism types depends on the specific circumstances found in a destination, and that these circumstances must be understood before deciding on a favoured development path. This adaptive perspective on sustainability focuses on the specificity of each local context and the need for tourism planning and management to be based on careful assessments of the implications of different tourism types for each situation. These types include the avoidance of tourism (a significant development option), small-scale 'alternative' tourism, mixed mass tourism and small-scale 'alternative' tourism, environmentally enhanced mass tourism (such as resorts that invest in sewage treatment), diversified large-scale mass tourism (such as resorts that diversify using marinas or casinos), and more standardised large-scale mass tourism. In many destinations these varied tourism forms may be further combined, and consideration needs to be given to the complexities of their integration in ways that encourage sustainable development.

The discussion has focused on the mix of types of tourism in the coastal regions of southern Europe. But in addition, there must be careful consideration of the quantity of tourism development that is appropriate. Sustainability in a region could require that there is a halt to further tourism growth or else a reduction in the scale of tourism activity, perhaps even a substantial reduction. Such responses could be prompted by specific concerns about an oversupply of tourist facilities, but they may be considered necessary because of the broader issues of tourism's sociocultural, environmental and economic impacts, the views of the various actors in the destination, and the need to secure an appropriate mix between tourism and other economic activities. The focus of this book is on sustainable development within tourism regions, but a full evaluation of sustainability also requires consideration of the environmental impacts of tourists travelling to Mediterranean coastal destinations from their home areas. While this wider aspect of sustainability is not evaluated here, it is of considerable importance.

Many of the case studies that follow assess public sector tourism policies and planning techniques in relation to the goals of sustainable development in specific destinations in southern Europe's littoral. It is helpful to consider these policies and techniques in relation to the various social, economic and political influences on them and to the tiers of public sector involvement, such as the

European Union and local or municipal government. These issues are discussed in the next chapter.

After the two introductory chapters (Section 1), the book is organised in three further sections. Section 2 considers tourism's impacts on southern Europe's coastal regions and the related tourism policies and management tools intended to promote more sustainable forms of development. Section 3 focuses on the problems of mass tourism coastal resorts, techniques to assess sustainability in these resorts, and the successes and failures of 'green' initiatives for mass tourism resorts and facilities in relation to the objectives of sustainability. And the chapters in Section 4 evaluate the development of more diversified forms of tourism – both small-scale 'alternative' tourism and other larger-scale forms – in southern Europe's coastal regions, including their potential advantages and disadvantages for sustainable development.

## Correspondence

Any correspondence should be directed to Bill Bramwell, Centre for Tourism and Cultural Change, Sheffield Hallam University, UK (W.M.Bramwell@ shu.ac.uk).

## References

Agarwal, S. (2002) Restructuring seaside tourism. The resort lifecycle. *Annals of Tourism Research* 29 (1), 25–55.
Altinay, L. (2000) Possible impacts of a federal solution to the Cyprus problem on the tourism industry of North Cyprus. *Hospitality Management* 19, 295–309.
Andriotis, K. (2002a) Options in tourism development: Conscious versus conventional tourism. *Anatolia: An International Journal of Tourism and Hospitality Research* 13 (1), 73–85.
Andriotis, K. (2002b) Scale of hospitality firms and local economic development – evidence from Crete. *Tourism Management* 23 (4), 333–41.
Baker, S., Kousis, M., Richardson, D., and Young, S. (1997) The theory and practice of sustainable development in EU perspective. In S. Baker, M. Kousis, D. Richardson and S. Young (eds) *The Politics of Sustainable Development. Theory, Policy and Practice within the European Union* (pp. 1–40). London: Routledge.
Barke, M. (1991) The growth and changing pattern of second homes in Spain in the 1970s. *Scottish Geographical Magazine* 107 (1), 12–21.
Barke, M. (1999) Tourism and culture in Spain: A case of minimal conflict? In M. Robinson and P. Boniface (eds) *Tourism and Cultural Conflicts* (pp. 247–67). Wallingford: CABI.
Blue Plan (1999) *Indicators for Sustainable Development in the Mediterranean Region. Draft October 1999.* Indicators 2.4 Lands and areas: littoral and 'littoralisation' E. Population density in the coastal areas, and Population growth rate in coastal areas. Sophia-Antipolis: Blue Plan Regional Activity Centre.
Blue Plan (2002) The Mediterranean in brief: The coastline and coastal regions. On WWW at http:www.planbleu.org/vanglaise/4-23a.htm. Accessed 27.2.02.
Boissevain, J. (1996a) Ritual, tourism and cultural commoditization in Malta: Culture by the pound? In T. Selwyn (ed.) *The Tourist Image: Myths and Myth Making in Tourism* (pp. 105–20). Chichester: Wiley.
Boissevain, J. (1996b) 'But we live here!' Perspectives on cultural tourism in Malta. In L. Briguglio, R. Butler, D. Harrison and W. Filho (eds) *Sustainable Tourism in Islands and Small States: Case Studies* (pp. 220–40). London: Pinter.
Bourdieu, P. (1984) *Distinction: A Social Critique of the Judgement of Taste.* London: Routledge.
Bramwell, B. (2003) Maltese responses to tourism. *Annals of Tourism Research* 30 (3), 581–605.

Bramwell, B., Henry, I., Jackson, G., Goytia Prat, A., Richards, G. and van der Straaten, J. (eds) (1996) *Sustainable Tourism Management: Principles and Practice*. Tilburg: Tilburg University Press.

Bramwell, B. and Sharman, A. (2000) Approaches to sustainable tourism planning and community participation. The case of the Hope Valley. In G. Richards and D. Hall (eds) *Tourism and Sustainable Community Development* (pp. 17–35). London: Routledge.

Briassoulis, H. (2001) Sustainable development – the formal or informal way? The case of southern Europe. In K. Eder and M. Kousis (eds) *Environmental Politics in Southern Europe. Actors, Institutions and Discourses in a Europeanizing Society* (pp. 73–99). Dordrecht: Kluwer.

Britton, S. (1991) Tourism, capital and place: Towards a critical geography of tourism. *Environment and Planning D: Society and Space* 9, 451–78.

Buhalis, D. (1999) Tourism on the Greek islands: Issues of peripherality, competitiveness and development. *International Journal of Tourism Research* 1, 341–58.

Buhalis, D. (2000) Relationships in the distribution channel of tourism: Conflicts between hoteliers and tour operators in the Mediterranean region. *International Journal of Hospitality and Tourism Administration* 1 (1), 113–39.

Buhalis, D. (2001) Tourism in Greece: Strategic analysis and challenges. *Current Issues in Tourism* 4 (5), 440–80.

Buhalis, D. and Diamantis, D. (2001) Tourism development and sustainability in the Greek archipelagos. In D. Ioannides, Y. Apostolopoulos and S. Sonmez (eds) *Mediterranean Islands and Sustainable Tourism Development. Practices, Management and Policies* (pp. 143–70). London: Continuum.

Bull, P. (1997) Mass tourism in the Balearic islands: An example of concentrated dependence. In D. Lockhart and D. Dukakis-Smith (eds) *Island Tourism: Trends and Prospects* (pp. 137–51). London: Pinter.

Burkart, J. and Medlik, R. (1974) *Tourism: Past, Present and Future*. London: Heinemann.

Buswell, R.J. (1996) Tourism in the Balearic islands. In M. Barke, J. Towner and M.T. Newton (eds) *Tourism in Spain: Critical Issues* (pp. 309–39). Wallingford: CAB International.

Butler, R.W. (1989) Alternative tourism: Pious hope or Trojan horse? *World Leisure and Recreation* 31 (4), 9–17.

Butler, R.W. (1997) Modelling tourism development: Evolution, growth and decline. In S. Wahab and J.J. Pigram (eds) *Tourism, Development and Growth. The Challenge of Sustainability* (pp. 109–25). London: Routledge.

Butler, R.W. (1998a) Sustainable tourism – looking backwards in order to progress? In C.M. Hall and A.A. Lew (eds) *Sustainable Tourism. A Geographical Perspective* (pp. 25–34). Harlow: Longman.

Butler, R.W. (1998b) Rural recreation and tourism. In B. Ilbery (ed.) *The Geography of Rural Change* (pp. 211–32). Harlow: Longman.

Casado-Diaz, M.A. (1999) Socio-demographic impacts of residential tourism: A case study of Torrevieja, Spain. *International Journal of Tourism Research* 1, 223–37.

Clarke, J. (1997) A framework of approaches to sustainable tourism. *Journal of Sustainable Tourism* 5 (3), 224–33.

Cyprus Tourism Organisation (2000) *Tourism Strategy 2000–2010*.

Dunford, M. (1997) Mediterranean economies: The dynamics of uneven development. In R. King, L. Proudfoot and B. Smith (eds) *The Mediterranean: Environment and Society* (pp. 126–54). London: Arnold.

Dunford, M. and King, R. (2001) Mediterranean economic geography. In R. King, P. de Mas and J.M. Beck (eds) *Geography, Environment and Development in the Mediterranean* (pp. 28–60). Brighton: Sussex Academic Press.

Feifer, M. (1985) *Going Places*. London: Macmillan.

Formica, S. and Uysal, M. (1996) The revitalisation of Italy as a tourist destination. *Tourism Management* 17 (5), 323–31.

Garrod, B. and Fyall, A. (1998) Beyond the rhetoric of sustainable tourism? *Tourism Management* 19 (3), 199–212.

Gibbs, D. (1996) Integrating sustainable development and economic restructuring: A role for regulation theory? *Geoforum* 27 (1), 1–10.

Greenwood, D.J. (1989) Culture by the pound. An anthropological perspective on tourism as cultural commoditization. In V. Smith (ed) *Hosts and Guests. The Anthropology of Tourism* (pp. 171–85). Philadelphia: University of Philadelphia Press.

Grenon, M. and Batisse, M. (1989) *Futures for the Mediterranean Basin: The Blue Plan.* Oxford: Oxford University Press.

Haralambopoulos, N. and Pizam, A. (1993) Perceived impacts of tourism. The case of Samos. *Annals of Tourism Research* 23 (3), 503–26.

Harvey, D. (1978) The urban process under capitalism: A framework for analysis. *International Journal of Urban and Regional Research* 2, 101–31.

Horden, P. and Purcell, N. (2000) *The Corrupting Sea. A Study of Mediterranean History.* Oxford: Blackwell.

Hudson, R. and Lewis, J. (1985) Introduction: Recent economic, social and political changes in southern Europe. In R. Hudson and J. Lewis (eds) *Uneven Development in Southern Europe. Studies of Accumulation, Class, Migration and the State* (pp. 1–53). London: Methuen.

Hunter, C. (1997) Sustainable tourism as an adaptive paradigm. *Annals of Tourism Research* 24 (4), 850–67.

Ioannides, D. (1995) A flawed implementation of sustainable tourism: The experience of Akamas, Cyprus. *Tourism Management* 16 (8), 583–92.

Ioannides, D. (2001a) The dynamics and effects of tourism evolution in Cyprus. In Y. Apostolopoulos, P. Loukissas and L. Leontidou (eds) *Mediterranean Tourism. Facets of Socioeconomic Development and Cultural Change* (pp. 112–28). London: Routledge.

Ioannides, D. (2001b) Sustainable development and the shifting attitudes of tourism stakeholders: Toward a dynamic framework. In S. McCool and R. Moisey (eds) *Tourism, Recreation and Sustainability. Linking Culture and Environment* (pp. 55–76). Wallingford: CAB International.

Ioannides, D. and Debbage, K.G. (1998) Neo-fordism and flexible specialisation in the travel industry: Dissecting the polyglot. In D. Ioannides and K.G. Debbage (eds) *The Economic Geography of the Tourist Industry: A Supply-side Analysis* (pp. 99–122). London: Routledge.

Ioannides, D. and Holcomb, B. (2001) Raising the stakes: Implications of upmarket tourism policies in Cyprus and Malta. In D. Ioannides, Y. Apostolopoulos and S. Sonmez (eds) *Mediterranean Islands and Sustainable Tourism Development. Practices, Management and Policies* (pp. 234–58). London: Continuum.

Jenner, P. and Smith, C. (1993) *Tourism in the Mediterranean.* London: Economist Intelligence Unit.

Jordan, P. (2000) Restructuring Croatia's coastal resorts: Change, sustainable development and the incorporation of rural hinterlands. *Journal of Sustainable Tourism* 8 (6), 525–39.

Josephides, N. (2003) Hold on to your hat. *Tourism in Focus* (Tourism Concern) 46 (Spring), 4–5.

King, R. (1989) The Mediterranean: An environment at risk. *Geographical Viewpoint* 18, 5–31.

King, R., Cori, B. and Vallega, A. (2001) Unity, diversity and the challenge of sustainable development: An introduction to the Mediterranean. In R. King, P. de Mas and J.M. Beck (eds) *Geography, Environment and Development in the Mediterranean* (pp. 1–17). Brighton: Sussex Academic Press.

King, R. and Donati, M. (1999) The 'divided' Mediterranean: Re-defining European relationships. In R. Hudson and A.M. Williams (eds) *Divided Europe. Society and Territory* (pp. 132–62). London: Sage.

King, R. and Montanari, A. (1998) Italy: Diversified tourism. In A.M. Williams and G. Shaw (eds) *Tourism and Economic Development. European Experiences* (pp. 75–100). Chichester: Wiley.

Kousis, M. and Eder, K. (2001) EU policy-making, local action, and the emergence of institutions of collective action. A theoretical perspective on Southern Europe. In K. Eder and M. Kousis (eds) *Environmental Politics in Southern Europe. Actors, Institutions and Discourses in a Europeanizing Society* (pp. 3–21). Dordrecht: Kluwer.

Leontidou, L., Gentileschi, M.L., Aru, A. and Pungetti, G. (1998) Urban expansion and littoralisation. In P. Mairota, J.B. Thornes and N. Geeson (eds) *Atlas of Mediterranean Environments in Europe. The Desertification Context* (pp. 92–7). Chichester: Wiley.

Leontidou, L. and Marmaras, E. (2001) From tourists to migrants. Residential tourism and 'littoralization'. In Y. Apostolopoulos, P. Loukissas and L. Leontidou (eds) *Mediterranean Tourism. Facets of Socioeconomic Development and Cultural Change* (pp. 257–67). London: Routledge.

Loukissas, P. and Triantafyllopoulos, N. (1997) Competitive factors in traditional tourist destinations: The cases of the islands of Rhodes and Myconos (Greece). *Papers de Turisme* 22, 214–18.

Macnaghten, P. and Urry, J. (1998) *Contested Natures*. London: Sage.

Malta Ministry of Tourism (2000) *Carrying Capacity Assessment for Tourism in the Maltese Islands*. Valletta: Ministry of Tourism.

Manzi, E. (2001) Mediterranean concentration and landscape: Six cases. In R. King, P. de Mas and J.M. Beck (eds) *Geography, Environment and Development in the Mediterranean* (pp. 196–215). Brighton: Sussex Academic Press.

Marchena Gómez, M.J. (1995) New tourism trends and the future of Mediterranean Europe. *Tijdschrift voor Economische en Sociale Geografie* 86 (1), 21–31.

Mari, S. (1994) The economic specificity of Menorca in relation to the Balearic islands. In M.R. Carli (ed.) *Economic and Population Trends in the Mediterranean Islands* (pp. 111–28). Collana Alti Seminari 5. Naples: Edizioni Scientifiche Italiane.

Minca, C. (1998) Mediterranean metaphors and tourist space: A theoretical approach. In S. Conti and A. Segre (eds) *Mediterranean Geographies* (pp. 257–73). Rome: Società Geografica Italiana.

Milne, S.S. (1998) Tourism and sustainable development: Exploring the global–local nexus. In C.M. Hall and A.A. Lew (eds) *Sustainable Tourism: A Geographical Perspective* (pp. 35–48). Harlow: Longman.

Moisey, R.N. and McCool, S.F. (2001) Sustainable tourism in the 21st century: Lessons from the past; challenges to address. In S.F. McCool and R.N. Moisey (eds) *Tourism, Recreation and Sustainability. Linking Culture and the Environment* (pp. 343–52). Wallingford: CABI.

Monfort Mir, V.M. and Ivars Baidal, J.A. (2001) Towards a sustained competitiveness of Spanish tourism. In Y. Apostolopoulos, P. Loukissas and L. Leontidou (eds) *Mediterranean Tourism. Facets of Socioeconomic Development and Cultural Change* (pp. 17–38). London: Routledge.

Montanari, A. (1995) The Mediterranean region: Europe's summer leisure space. In A. Montanari and A.M. Williams (eds) *European Tourism. Regions, Spaces and Restructuring* (pp. 41–65). Chichester: Wiley.

Morris, A. and Dickinson, G. (1987) Tourist development in Spain: Growth versus conservation on the Costa Brava. *Geography* 72 (1), 16–25.

Moussios, G. (1999) Greece. *Travel and Tourism Intelligence* 2, 24–49.

Mowforth, M. and Munt. I. (1998) *Tourism and Sustainability. New Tourism in the Third World*. London: Routledge.

Mullins, P. (1991) Tourism urbanization. *International Journal of Urban and Regional Research* 15 (3), 326–42.

Mullins, P. (1993) Cities for pleasure: The emergence of tourism urbanization in Australia. *Built Environment* 18 (3), 187–98.

Papatheodorou, A. (2002) Exploring competitiveness in Mediterranean resorts. *Tourism Economics* 8 (2), 133–50.

Poon, A. (1989) Competitive strategies for a 'new tourism'. In C. Cooper (ed.) *Progress in Tourism, Recreation and Hospitality Management* (vol. 1) (pp. 91–102). London: Belhaven.

Priestley, G K. (1995a) Evolution of tourism on the Spanish coast. In G.J. Ashworth and A.G.J. Dietvorst (eds) *Tourism and Spatial Transformations* (pp. 37–54). Wallingford: CAB International.

Priestley, G.K. (1995b) Problems of tourism development in Spain. In H. Coccossis and P. Nijkamp (eds) *Sustainable Tourism Development* (pp. 187–198). Aldershot: Avebury.

Priestley, G.K. (1996) Structural dynamics of tourism and recreation-related development. In G.K. Priestley, J.A. Edwards and H. Coccossis (eds) *Sustainable Tourism? European Experiences* (pp. 99–119). Wallingford: CAB International.

Priestley, G.K. and Mundet, L. (1998) The post-stagnation phase of the resort cycle. *Annals of Tourism Research* 25 (1), 85–111.

Richez, G. (1996) Sustaining local cultural identity: Social unrest and tourism in Corsica. In G.K. Priestley, J.A. Edwards and H. Coccossis (eds) *Sustainable Tourism? European Experiences* (pp. 176–88). Wallingford: CAB International.

Salvà Tomàs, P.A. (1991) La population des îles Baléares pendent 40 ans de tourisme de masse (1950–1989). *Méditerranée* 1, 7–14.

Sapelli, G. (1995) *Southern Europe Since 1945. Tradition and Modernity in Portugal, Spain, Italy, Greece and Turkey*. London: Longman.

Sharpley, R. (1998) *Island Tourism Development: The Case of Cyprus*. Newcastle: Centre for Travel and Tourism, University of Northumbria at Newcastle.

Sharpley, R. (2000) The influence of the accommodation sector on tourism development: Lessons from Cyprus. *Hospitality Management* 19, 275–93.

Sharpley, R. (2002) Rural tourism and the challenge of tourism diversification: The case of Cyprus. *Tourism Management* 23, 233–44.

Shaw, G. and Williams, A.M. (1994) *Critical Issues in Tourism: A Geographical Perspective*. Oxford: Blackwell.

Sprengel, U. (1999) Luck and bane of tourism. The 'Turkish Riviera' between economic valorization and destruction of landscape. In E. Manzi and M. Schmidt di Friedberg (eds) *Landscape and Sustainability, Global Change, Mediterranean Historic Centres* (pp. 165–78). Milan: Guerini e Associati.

Torres, R. (2002) Cancun's tourism development from a Fordist spectrum of analysis. *Tourist Studies* 2 (1), 87–116.

Tsartas, P. (1992) Socioeconomic impacts of tourism on two Greek Islands. *Annals of Tourism Research* 19, 516–33.

Turner, R.K. (1993) Sustainability: Principles and practice. In R.K. Turner (ed.) *Sustainable Environmental Economics and Management* (pp. 3–36). Chichester: Wiley.

Urry, J. (1990) *The Tourist Gaze. Leisure and Travel in Contemporary Societies*. London: Sage.

Urry, J. (1995) *Consuming Places*. London: Routledge.

Valenzuela, M. (1998) Spain: From the phenomenon of mass tourism to the search for a more diversified model. In A.M. Williams and G. Shaw (eds) *Tourism and Economic Development. European Experiences* (pp. 43–74). Chichester: Wiley.

Vanhove, N. (1997) Mass tourism: Benefits and costs. In S. Wahab and J.J. Pigram (eds) *Tourism, Development and Growth: The Challenge of Sustainability* (pp. 50–77). London: Routledge.

Var, T. (2001) The state, the private sector, and tourism policies in Turkey. In Y. Apostopoulos, P. Loukissas and L. Leontidou (eds) *Mediterranean Tourism. Facets of Socioeconomic Development and Cultural Change* (pp. 91–111). London: Routledge.

Vera Rebollo, J.F. (2001) Increasing the value of natural and cultural resources: Towards sustainable tourism management. In D. Ioannides, Y. Apostolopoulos and S. Sonmez (eds) *Mediterranean Islands and Sustainable Tourism Development. Practices, Management and Policies* (pp. 47–68). London: Continuum.

Vera Rebollo, J.F. and Rippin, R. (1996) Decline of a Mediterranean tourist area and restructuring strategies: The Valencian region. In G.K. Priestley, J.A. Edwards and H. Coccossis (eds) *Sustainable Tourism? European Experiences* (pp. 120–36). Wallingford: CAB International.

Vidal Bendito, T. (1994) The Balearic population in the twentieth century. In M.R. Carli (ed) *Economic and Population Trends in the Mediterranean Islands* (pp. 129–54). Collana Alti Seminari 5. Naples: Edizioni Scientifiche Italiane.

Vukonić, B. (2001) The 'new old' tourist destination: Croatia. In Y. Apostolopoulos, P. Loukissas and L. Leontidou (eds) *Mediterranean Tourism. Facets of Socioeconomic Development and Cultural Change* (pp. 64–71). London: Routledge.

Weaver, D. (2000) A broad context model of destination development scenarios. *Tourism Management* 21, 217–24.

Weaver, D. and Oppermann, M. (2000) *Tourism Management*. Queensland: Wiley Milton.

Williams, A. (1997) Tourism and uneven development in the Mediterranean. In R. King, L. Proudfoot and B. Smith (eds) *The Mediterranean. Environment and Society* (pp. 208–26). London: Arnold.

Williams, A. (2001) Tourism and development in the Mediterranean basin: Evolution and differentiation on the 'fabled shore'. In R. King, P. de Mas and J. M. Beck (eds) *Geography, Environment and Development in the Mediterranean* (pp. 156–75). Brighton: Sussex Academic Press.

Williams, A.M. and Montanari, A. (eds) (1995) *European Tourism. Regions, Spaces and Restructuring*. Chichester: Wiley.

Williams, A. and Shaw, G. (1998a) Tourism and the environment: Sustainability and economic restructuring. In C.M. Hall and A.A. Lew (eds) *Sustainable Tourism: A Geographical Perspective* (pp. 49–59). Harlow: Longman.

Williams, A.M. and Shaw, G. (1998b) Introduction: Tourism and uneven economic development. In A.M. Williams and G. Shaw (eds) *Tourism and Economic Development. European Experiences* (pp. 1–16). Chichester: Wiley.

Williams, S. (1998) *Tourism Geography*. London: Routledge.

World Tourism Organisation (2001) *Yearbook of Tourism Statistics*. Madrid: WTO.

World Tourism Organisation/United Nations Environment Programme and the Blue Plan (2000) *Sustainable Tourism and Competitiveness in the Islands of the Mediterranean. International Seminar*. Capri, Italy, 17–20 May.

Yarcan, S. and Ertuna, B. (2002) What you encourage is what you get: The case of Turkish inbound international tourism. *Anatolia: An International Journal of Tourism and Hospitality Research* 13 (2), 159–83.

Zanetto, G. and Soriani, S. (1996) Tourism and environmental degradation: The Northern Adriatic Sea. In G.K. Priestley, J.A. Edwards and H. Coccossis (eds) *Sustainable Tourism? European Experiences* (pp. 137–52). Wallingford: CAB International.

# 2 The Policy Context for Tourism and Sustainability in Southern Europe's Coastal Regions

*Bill Bramwell*
*Sheffield Hallam University, Sheffield S1 1WB, UK*

## Introduction

Many of the papers in this book look at the policies, and the policy instruments, by which governments try to achieve their goals. These are policies that seek to encourage sustainable development through product diversification and environmental upgrading in the tourism sector in southern Europe's coastal regions. The selection of these policies and policy instruments by policy-makers is, however, only partly a 'technical' question based on identifying which will achieve the desired results most effectively. It is also essentially a moral and political choice that is influenced by diverse economic and societal pressures. Yet much of the tourism literature leaves an impression that the choices are primarily technical ones. Hall (2000: 60–61) recently complained that 'tourism planning is still presented as being primarily a technical issue and not a political problem'. This emphasis in the tourism literature on 'technical' evaluations of policies should not be allowed to mask the moral dilemmas and political choices that lie at the heart of both policy-making and sustainable development. As Hughes (2002: 472) argues: 'In plain terms, the solution of the environmental crisis of tourism does not rest solely with scientific management'.

One aspect of understanding the politics of tourism and sustainability involves considering the influences that shape tourism policies and their application. It is useful to conceive of this political context as a multi-actor field, where different actors have their own specific interests, can espouse certain views, and have varying degrees of influence on the policy process and on the resulting policy direction. At the same time, the tourism policy process takes place within the context of capitalist development and the dynamics of capital accumulation, as well as changing opportunities in the market. There are considerable economic pressures on governments to encourage tourism growth, and policies pursued for tourism development are often those most suited to the interests of the national economy and the tourism industry. Governments frequently talk 'green' but, in practice, usually give priority to economic growth over environmental protection. Of course, such economic imperatives are not determinist. At times, environmental interests will prevail over the short-term interests of the tourism industry, and governments do overrule industry objections. Moreover, it should not be assumed that the tourism industry itself will always oppose measures to protect the environment, if only because these measures may be seen to be in their own best interests.

This chapter reviews the context to policies for tourism and sustainable development in southern Europe's coastal regions. To simplify the discussion, it focuses on the balance between economic growth and environmental protection in policy affecting the tourism sector. The implications of tourism policies for the sociocultural and equity dimensions of sustainable development are clearly very substantial, but they are not the main focus of the analysis here. The chapter assesses evidence for there having been change over recent years in the policies affecting tourism and the environment. As the European Union has been a notable source of environmental and tourism policies affecting member states, attention is directed to whether these policies have promoted sustainability in tourism in southern Europe. Finally, there is discussion of some of the policy instruments in this book that are intended to promote sustainable tourism.

## Influences on Policies Affecting Tourism and Sustainability

This discussion considers the influence of economic interests, public opinion in destinations, environmental groups, different tiers of government, and the European Union on policies affecting tourism and sustainability in southern Europe's coastal regions. It is very difficult to measure the exact impact of these influences, other than through very broad, qualitative assessments. The analysis draws on a range of studies, but in particular on research by Geoffrey Pridham into sustainable tourism policy-making in Greece, Italy and Spain.

It is not possible here to consider all of the potential pressures that are relevant to tourism and the environment in southern Europe. Among other likely sources of influence are the media, such as television and local newspapers, and also political parties, including those not in government. The role of tourists in demanding improved environmental standards is also not considered in any depth. Tourists increasingly seem to demand the environmental qualities of appealing views and scenery and an attractive, relaxing ambience and sense of place. There is also some evidence that certain tourists will boycott areas perceived to have sea pollution or congestion, or that are overdeveloped. The industry has begun to respond to such requirements for environmental quality (Blue Plan and UNEP, 1998: 3; Middleton & Hawkins, 1998: 32–3). Yet many tourists are unlikely to seek out information on specific environmental issues before booking a holiday; they are often very cost conscious, and they may be more likely to forget their consciences when they are on holiday as they seek to relax and enjoy themselves (Bramwell *et al.*, 1996: 60).

### Economic interests

There are various reasons why governments intervene in the operation of the tourism industry and in environmental matters. Some interventions tend to favour economic interests over environmental priorities, while others put more emphasis on environmental concerns. But in the economy the dominant social relations are capitalist and they constrain the form and extent of state involvement. Governments tend to support those policy objectives closely linked to the core relationships of capitalism, and economic growth and the accumulation process often dominate at the expense of the pursuit of sustainability. This is particularly the case in times of crisis.

One reason for state intervention is to provide tourism infrastructure in tourist areas when its provision is likely to be considered commercially unprofitable by potential investors (Williams & Shaw, 1998a: 382). This infrastructure can include airports, sewage systems, and road networks. While this infrastructure is clearly advantageous for the tourism industry, in cases such as sewage systems it can also help to protect the environment. Another reason for government intervention is to ensure that a destination's competitiveness for tourism purposes is not threatened by property owners who damage local resources and generate land-use conflicts, such as by polluting or restricting access to beaches, or by building on sensitive sites (Briassoulis, 2002: 1068). Policies to restrict these activities may be intended to benefit the tourism industry, but they may also lead to environmental improvements. A rather different motive for state intervention seeks to limit the tourism industry's negative environmental impacts primarily so as to protect the environment *per se* rather than to enhance the industry's competitiveness. While in the long-term these restrictions can increase the attraction of tourist areas, the tourism industry may vigorously oppose them if they feel they will damage short-term profitability.

The intense commercial pressures to gain immediate economic returns mean that the tourism sector often opposes government interventions that aim to protect the environment. Based on an assessment of sustainable tourism policy-making in Greece, Italy and Spain, Pridham (1996: 20) argues that the tourism industry remains a major obstacle to sustainability due to its emphasis on profits, with tour operators showing a particularly short-term mentality and having little regard for the long-term environmental quality of destinations.

But Pridham (Pridham, 2001: 379–80) also contends that the recent increase in policy attention related to sustainable tourism in these countries has been influenced by fears that the tourism industry may lose its competitiveness if the environmental quality of tourist areas is not upgraded. There is concern that holiday-makers no longer accept poor environmental standards, especially in the context of growing competition from new tourist destinations that are cheaper and often in the early stages of development and thus suffering less from environmental deterioration (Marchena Gómez, 1995: 28; Monfort Mir & Ivars Baidal, 2001). It is increasingly argued that the low economic returns for tourism businesses from competing for low-spending tourists are damaging the industry and destination areas and, therefore, that there is a need to appeal to more tourists who would pay higher prices for improved environmental standards and distinctive 'alternative' tourism products (Jenner & Smith, 1993: 13, 166; WTO/UNEP/Blue Plan, 2000: 6). Hence, it is suggested that in Greece, Italy and Spain the 'pressure comes from a growing concern that economic interests in the tourist industries there are seriously under threat and that action has to be taken to prevent this worsening in the near and long-term future' (Pridham, 2001: 376). Such concerns are important in these three countries as their tourism industries are economically crucial, and also because business and industry more generally in these nations 'have enjoyed a privileged position and considerable influence in the corridors of power' (Pridham, 1999: 107; Pridham, 2001: 380). It is not just destination policy-makers but also some tourism businesses that nowadays recognise environmental degradation as a threat, and at times they too can support environmental protection policies.

## Public opinion

Public opinion in destinations can be another factor encouraging governments to introduce environmental policies that affect the tourism industry. Although the tourism industry may not be the focus of the public's anxieties about the environment, tourism can still be affected. The views of the public as expressed in opinion polls suggest that, by comparison with northern Europe, awareness of the 'environment' as an issue emerged somewhat later, and is less developed, in Europe's south (Pridham, 2001; Weale *et al.*, 2000). It is argued that environmental concern among the public also 'occurred somewhat earlier in Italy, while in Spain and Greece it did not emerge as an issue . . . until the 1980s, with signs of this growing during the course of the 1990s' (Pridham, 2001: 382). The continuing importance of materialist values in these recently modernised countries presents a powerful obstacle to environmental values (Carter, 2001: 89–91). According to Weale *et al.* (2000: 468), it is northern European countries that 'have a reputation for post-materialist environmental sensitivity, while southern countries, still struggling with developmental problems and motivated by the urge for economic modernisation and higher productivity, place a much lower priority on environmental concerns'. In the case of Malta, environmental concern has emerged only slowly and is still modest. Its growth has been a product of diverse influences, including growing affluence, more widespread education, and advancing urbanisation that has distanced people from an agrarian life and from attitudes to nature fostered through the hardships of working the land (Bramwell, 2003: 594). The strength of localistic cultures in Europe's Mediterranean regions also means that pro-conservation feelings among the public can be sensitised over location-specific environmental issues. It is suggested that this localistic dimension 'seems to have had more effect in Greece and, to some extent, Spain than in Italy' (Pridham, 1994: 81; Pridham 1996: 19).

Government decisions to introduce environmental policies may be influenced by public attitudes in destinations specifically to tourism's adverse environmental and social impacts rather than to environmental problems more generally. Several studies of these attitudes to tourism in local communities in southern Europe suggest that the public is often fairly supportive or at least neutral about tourism's general impact, due to its economic benefits, while also recognising there are various specific negative consequences (Akis *et al.*, 1996; Haralambopoulos & Pizam, 1996; Tosun, 2001). In the case of the Greek island of Ios, Tsartas (1992) argues that the residents tend to accept tourism as it provides many of them with considerable income, although they still recognise specific adverse social consequences, such as deteriorating relationships between residents, and moral problems associated with nudism and the sexual behaviour of young tourists. His conclusion is that 'the money involved proves a stronger argument than the social consequences incurred' (p. 525). Similarly, in a study of the island of Samos, Haralambopoulos and Pizam (1996) found that, while most of the population were positive about tourism's overall effects, they also held mixed views about its specific repercussions. Thus they had positive views on most economic implications, but negative opinions about, for example, the effects on prices of goods and services, and on the frequency of brawls, vandalism, and sexual harassment. Research on Malta suggests that, up to the mid-1980s, many residents made a trade-off, tolerating tourism's unwanted impacts because of their perception of its substantial economic benefits. But more recently some of the population have become concerned about increasing pressure on their society and on the quality of the environment (Boissevain, 1977: 532, 537; Boissevain & Theuma, 1998: 97; Bramwell, 2003: 599).

## Environmental groups

Environmental pressure groups are probably the most visible expression of contemporary environmental concern. Through their protest activity, lobbying and educational work they have become a political actor with a degree of influence on environmental policies in southern Europe. But it seems that environmental pressure groups in Europe's south have for various reasons often been less powerful and effective than in northern Europe. Research in Greece, Italy and Spain suggests that environmental organisations have become 'fairly numerous in these countries, but their political impact on government has with some variation been rather limited' (Pridham, 2001: 385). One constraining influence has been the closed process of environmental policy-making that has left little scope for the lobbying of policy-makers by environmental groups (especially in Spain and Greece), with this having been influenced by their only becoming democracies from the mid-1970s (Pridham & Konstadakopulos, 1997: 141). In the case of Greece's environmental groups, their influence has been constrained by both their lack of political links and also by the fragmentation of ministries in the environmental field (Close, 1999; Fousekis & Lekakis, 1997; Weale *et al.*, 2000; 259). While recognising the considerable constraints on the effectiveness of environmental groups, it is suggested that in the specific context of the tourism sector 'it has been environmental organisations more than the media or political parties that have taken up the cause of environmental quality in tourism especially concerning coastal areas' (Pridham, 2001: 388).

## Government

Government organisations, such as elected bodies and state agencies, shape the policies that influence the tourism industry's repercussions for sustainability. These actors are the main producers and implementers of both environmental and tourism-sector policies. In some southern European countries, the approaches to policy-making adopted by the state reflect their recent transition from authoritarianism. Their relatively large, even 'over-developed' state structures exhibit a reluctance to delegate authority to other economic and social actors (Ruzza, 2001: 117–19; Weale *et al.*, 2000: 339–40). But state institutions work in the context of diverse pressures, including those originating from environmental pressure groups, the media, political parties and producer groups. Hence, the governance regime stems from the particular configuration of relations between the network of multiple actors found in specific places.

Government operates at national, regional and more local geographical scales. Some commentators suggest that differences exist in policy emphases at these different levels of government, and that the broad goals of sustainability may be more prominent at more local scales (Williams & Shaw, 1998a: 376). National governments tend to focus on the economic implications of tourism development for the country's balance of payments and macro-economic objectives, such as creating new jobs, increasing incomes and raising state revenues. Local tiers of government may be relatively more concerned with the wide range of community needs, including environmental, welfare and employment issues. It is also possible that the concept of sustainable development is easier to apply at local or even regional levels: potentially the issues there can be easier to understand and local inputs in policy-making might be achieved more simply. In this context it is notable that in many European Mediterranean countries much power continues to rest with central government, and local government is often quite weak. In the Greek island of Crete local government lacks financial strength and, while the central government in Athens is obliged to consult them about land-use planning and the environment, central government can still circumvent their objections to policies, and it can also determine which tourism-related projects it funds (Andriotis, 2001: 307; Fousekis & Lekakis, 1997: 144). Public administration in Turkey is particularly centralised, and it is claimed in relation to Turkish tourism planning that 'local bodies have been used as an extension of the ruling party to facilitate implementation of the central government's priorities, or they are forced to follow central government decisions via various economic and political pressures' (Tosun & Timothy, 2001: 353; Yuksel *et al.*, 1999: 358). However, there are more decentralised arrangements in some countries, such as the regional authorities established in Italy and Spain (Pridham & Konstadakopulos, 1997: 143). In Greece, while national planning remains very important, there has been a degree of decentralisation to the local authorities, prefectures and regions in the insular and coastal areas (Tsartas, Chapter 4). While such decentralisation may lend some support to the commentators who argue for a 'hollowing-out' of nation states, with national governments losing some power to more localised levels of government and to the European Union, it is clear that national governments in southern Europe generally retain very considerable influence (Anderson, 1995; Jessop, 1994).

Regardless of the institutional arrangements of the state, government efforts to apply sustainability policies to tourism are likely to be hindered by institutional weaknesses affecting the tourism sector's activities (Williams & Shaw, 1998a,b). First, the integration required for sustainability is difficult to achieve as tourism activities are particularly fragmented across diverse economic sectors and policy issues, and among many small businesses (Ruzza, 2001: 107). The degree of 'spillover' between different economic activities and policy sectors is very considerable and multi-dimensional. Second, there are relatively low levels of networking around tourism issues in destinations. Trade union inputs are particularly poorly developed for the tourism industry, and the often crucial tour operator sector can be dominated by businesses based outside the destination which have only a limited interest in its politics and long-term development (Williams & Shaw, 1998a). Third, in Europe's Mediterranean nations there can be administrative weaknesses that hinder the introduction and application of environmental policies. It is suggested that, in some of these countries,

> Until the 1990s, their policy styles were to a large extent reactive to crisis or emergency. Clearly, responding to environmental emergencies is part of any country's policy in this area. But in the south this has been raised to the status of a policy approach. (Weale *et al.*, 2000: 185)

The administrative cultures of government tend to have a reputation for inefficiency, being associated with such characteristics as institutional fragmentation, poor coordination, ponderous bureaucratic procedures and lethargy, lack of bureaucratic openness, and weak controls and enforcement (Pridham, 1994: 81; Pridham, 1996: 22; Pridham & Konstadakopulos, 1997: 127). The consequences of such administrative difficulties can be that 'the only effective way of acting is when the situation is compelling, in the full glare of publicity, whereby crisis management temporarily overcomes bureaucratic sloth' (Weale *et al.*, 2000: 185). Fourth, in some of these countries it can be possible at times for environmental and planning controls to be by-passed because of clientelistic ties between individuals and politicians, based on an obligation to grant favours and support (Güneş-Ayata, 1994: 49; Koker, 1995; Mallia, 1994: 700). However, the characterisation of government in southern European countries as administratively weak may have been overstated by some commentators.

## Trends in Policies Affecting Tourism and Sustainability

During the early development of mass tourism in southern Europe's coastal regions the policy outlook emphasised the opportunities for rapid economic returns, with economic growth taking priority over environmental protection and with few development controls. The rapid overdevelopment that many Spanish coastal municipalities allowed in the 1960s was influenced by the politico-economic environment in the Franco era, in which the drive for economic growth held centre stage and in which relatively free rein was given to private enterprise to secure that growth (Pollard & Dominguez Rodriguez, 1995: 37; Priestley 1995a: 48; Priestley, 1995b: 192–3). At that time there was an absence of national and regional planning in Spain so that each municipality could determine the scale of tourism expansion, and where there were urban development plans it was possible to side-step the adopted land classifications, the requirements to provide for social and economic infrastructure, and to abide by building regulations. Municipal authorities also lacked sufficient funding, and some sought to compensate for this by seeking rapid urban development so as to gain revenue by granting building permits. A high long-term price was paid for this development as valuable natural spaces, forests and agricultural land were lost and sensitive ecological resources were damaged (Priestley, 1995a: 48; Valenzuela, 1998). In this same period in the Maltese islands the lack of planning controls allowed a great deal of haphazard tourism development that disfigured the landscape. This pro-development policy context was encouraged by the need to establish economic activities to compensate for the run down in the islands' military bases and by optimistic views about tourism as a predominantly beneficial vehicle for development (Boissevain, 1977: 532, 537; Italconsult, 1965; King, 1979).

It seems that generally there have been some qualitative changes with respect to policy approach and political behaviour on environmental matters. Based on his study of policies related to tourism and sustainability in Greece, Italy and Spain, Pridham (2001: 379) contends that

> it is possible to say that policy commitment has increased in these Southern countries, but it is a recent development as of the 1990s and especially the past half-decade . . . Cross-national differences are also apparent in the

timing and pace of policy commitment, even though all three countries have in the past subscribed quite distinctly to the economic imperative.

The policy change in relation to tourism and sustainability appears to have occurred 'slightly sooner in Greece, and then Spain, than in Italy. This is surprising, since over environmental policy Italy advanced somewhat sooner than the other two countries over the past decade' (Pridham, 1996: 19). Several influences on this change in policy are noted by Pridham. First, policies promoting sustainability in tourism have often been pushed forward through political pressures and policy actions in the general environmental field (Pridham, 2001: 388). It appears sustainable tourism is often dependent on a general move towards ideas and actions related to environmental issues. Policies coming from the European Union have been a further factor, as have international influences such as Agenda 21 and the work of environmental organisations (Pridham, 2001: 376, 379). A second and more pressing influence has been growing concern about the tourism industry losing its competitiveness due to emerging consumer sensitivities about the deteriorating environment in some resorts. Another economic factor has been the growing interest in increasing tourist expenditure through diversifying the tourism products that are available, although these 'alternative' products can have variable consequences for sustainability.

While there have been some shifts in policy, it is important to note that the changes have often been slow and not radical, have varied between countries and localities, and that they 'do not represent an overturning of different obstacles' to sustainable tourism (Pridham, 2001: 389). In Spain the current policy context for tourism 'may be more attuned to the environmental sensitivities of the market than it was 20 years ago and is also tempered with an increasing mantle of environmental legislation, but the underlying theme is still that of growth' (Robinson, 1996: 408). Garcia *et al.* (Chapter 10) argue that in Spanish coastal regions, while there have been increasing policy controls on the worst excesses of development and some upgrading of the environment of already urbanised areas, there is unlikely to be a significant decline in new construction within the present legal framework. Two notable pressures for further building on these coasts come from residential tourism and from local authorities seeking to expand their local tax base. And in the Maltese islands current planning frameworks mean that new tourism development is only allowed within designated zones, but this development is still a major threat to the environment. This is in part because the pace of construction remains rapid, and also because the zones within which development is permitted encompass an extensive portion of the small land area of these islands. As much new building gains planning approval, the problems of overdevelopment and congestion in existing Maltese resorts have also indirectly been exacerbated by the zoning policy (Bramwell, 2003: 597).

## European Union Policies Affecting Tourism and Sustainability

Over the past 30 years, the European Union (EU) has been a notable source of laws and regulations affecting tourism in member states, although there have been relatively few directed specifically at the tourism sector. The occasional EU policies directly targeted at tourism usually contain a dominant discourse of economic growth (Ruzza, 2001: 110). As a consequence, much encouragement from the EU towards sustainable tourism has come indirectly from environmental and integrated development policies. These include EU directives on environmental impact assessments for development projects and waste water treatment, and the LEADER programmes for integrated rural development, which have funded training, capital grants for agro-tourism, and handicraft production in rural areas. EU programmes such as LEADER and LIFE may impact on sustainable tourism, but their focus is often on other objectives, such as diversifying rural economies, creating demonstration projects in rural development, or bringing increased interaction and understanding between member countries. It should also not be forgotten that EU policies in varied fields indirectly touching on tourism have increasingly disseminated policy styles that some associate with sustainability, such as there being a formal use of partnerships and an emphasis on capacity-building (Bramwell & Lane, 2000; Ruzza, 2001: 117–19). But there have been criticisms that some EU policies, such as the European Regional Development Fund, have at times encouraged developments that contradict sustainability principles (Williams & Shaw, 1998b: 58). An example is found in Crete where EU-funded roads constructed to assist in the development of less developed and unspoilt bays have impeded the beach breeding of loggerhead turtles (Andriotis, 2001: 308). Nevertheless, Ruzza (2001: 117) concludes that in relation to sustainable tourism, 'Southern European resource dependency on EU sources and its late and weak environmental legislation give EU institutions a key policy-shaping role'.

It is argued that environmental thinking called ecological modernisation underpins many EU environmental policies, with this based on the proposition that economic growth can be adapted to meet environmental goals despite increasing constraints from globalisation (Carter, 2001: 211–21; Redclift, 2001: 68–71). In the logic of ecological modernisation it is conceded that environmental problems are a structural outcome of capitalist society, but the political message is that capitalism can be made more 'environmentally friendly' by reform rather than the overthrow of existing economic, social and political institutions. Hence, there is no challenge to global capital; rather it is assumed that business can gain competitive advantage and increased profits from producing high-value, high-quality products that meet high environmental standards. One justification for this is that there will be growing demand for these products from increasingly affluent, sophisticated and environmentally conscious consumers in more global markets (Weale *et al.*, 2000: 78). Attention is also directed to the ways that business can reduce its costs through more efficient ecological practices. It is accepted, however, that industry may need various encouragements from government to engage in this type of production (Harvey, 1996: 377–83). But ecological modernisation seems to offer a weak version of sustainability in which economic growth and environmental protection can be reconciled by further economic development, albeit based on 'greener' products and services. It differs from much sustainable development discourse in its utilitarian emphasis on the idea that business can profit by protecting the environment (Hajer, 1995). It is also distinct from many people's understanding of sustainable development in that it omits the social justice issues that inevitably result from the use of environmental resources.

The ideas of ecological modernisation may have influenced the EU's support for local projects to develop 'alternative' tourism products, such as agro-tourism and cultural tourism, as well as 'green' tourist accommodation and resort areas. The discourses around these projects often have a utilitarian emphasis on the potential to increase profits through the development of high quality products that meet improved environmental standards. The associated thinking also holds out the prospect of further economic growth – although of a more environmentally-friendly kind – in order to reconcile the pressures of economic growth and environmental protection. These projects are also often based on optimistic assumptions that increasing numbers of tourists are prepared to pay for more expensive but higher quality and more environmentally benign products. Ecological modernisation anticipates that business élites and local communities can be encouraged to recognise that instrumental advantages are to be gained from better environmental protection. And in Chapter 4, Tsartas notes that in Greece EU-funded projects involving nature-based and cultural tourism products and other integrated tourism development models have helped to demonstrate to various parties their potential as alternative development paths to that of mass tourism.

There are suggestions that southern European countries can be slow to implement EU environmental norms. Ruzza (2001: 102) claims that 'for cultural and institutional reasons, Southern European environmental policy suffers from delayed and ritualistic incorporation of European policy'. It is contended that in the economically less developed south a 'concern, if not obsession, with economic growth has tended to act as a powerful constraint on environmental initiatives' (Weale *et al.*, 2000: 185). Some commentators highlight problems of administrative inefficiency, poor monitoring, inadequate controls, and clientelistic relations in these countries (Eder, 2001: 29–30). However, recent researchers warn against adopting an over-simplistic stereotype of southern European EU states being 'laggards' in implementing EU environmental norms by comparison with other member countries (Borzel, 2000: 141–2; Eder, 2001: 29–30). It is now thought that there is much variability between member states in both south and north in the timing and pace of their compliance with EU environmental requirements, although some northern countries are generally more advanced (Borzel, 2000: 142; Weale *et al.*, 2000: 302–3). It can also be argued that the discourse of southern European countries as 'laggards' in adopting EU environmental standards actually clouds a situation where the south is paying for the costs of having to adopt standards set by the countries in the north to suit their conditions (Kousis & Eder, 2001: 17–18). It should be remembered that for the southern European countries the financial cost of reaching EU environmental norms are comparatively greater than in the north, because the countries of the south are generally less economically developed and also because they often joined the EU more recently so that they have had less time to adjust (Weale *et al.*, 2000: 469, 478–9).

## Policy Instruments Promoting Sustainable Tourism

A number of policy instruments can be used to promote sustainable tourism; these are the tools by which governments seek to achieve their desired policy goals. The selections of both policies and policy instruments are influenced by economic, moral, and political considerations, and they are usually fought over in the political arena by actors with differing interests. When these selections are being made it is very helpful if policy-makers and other actors are informed about how well or badly different policy tools have performed in practice elsewhere, although their performance is usually greatly influenced by the distinct local circumstances. Several of the chapters in this volume evaluate policy instruments directed at sustainable tourism based on their performance when used in southern Europe's coastal regions.

The discussion that follows relates policy instruments to the broad principles behind their operation. When assessing these instruments, consideration needs to be given to whether they are enforceable, effective and educative in relation to sustainability goals: do they change the behaviour of target groups, do they achieve the stated policy objectives, and do they help spread environmental values throughout society (Bramwell, 1998; Carter, 2001: 285; Jacobs, 1991)? Just three types of policy instrument are discussed here, selected because they are examined in subsequent chapters. These are: encouragement of voluntary action, regulation, and government expenditure.

### Encouragement of voluntary action

The first category is the encouragement of voluntary action. Information, education and general persuasion can be used by the state to encourage voluntary action by various parties in support of sustainable development. This voluntary action involves individuals or organisations, such as tourism operators, tourists or residents in tourist areas, doing things that are neither encouraged by law nor prompted by financial incentives (Carter, 2001: 292–3). Government can encourage this voluntary action through a range of communicative strategies, such as actively encouraging greater take-up of Eco-Management and Audit schemes (EMAS). Organisations enter voluntarily into an EMAS, but they are then involved in an external registration process that requires them to introduce specific changes in their environmental performance.

Government may favour a strategy of voluntary action to achieve its environmental objectives as it offers target groups the freedom to decide for themselves how best to respond. It may also avoid direct political strife. The freedom this approach gives can be advantageous if businesses that voluntarily adopt more extensive pro-environment actions are rewarded with improved sales. A voluntary strategy might be used as it can often be achieved at a low cost to government as it requires little or no 'policing' by the state. But the strategy of encouraging voluntary action also has its weaknesses. In particular, voluntary schemes may have little effect if there is only a limited presence of pro-environment beliefs. They may also be difficult to implement as they lack mechanisms or sanctions for enforcing new behaviour. Consequently, there can be low expectations of voluntary schemes, with some groups going along with them largely as a means of forestalling the threat of tougher approaches. Some related implementation issues are discussed in Chapter 12, which shows that among hotels in tourist areas in Greece there has been relatively little take-up of voluntary environmental improvements schemes, such as EMAS, ISO 14001 standards, and eco-labels. However, many of the hotels have adopted certain 'green' practices that are low-cost and have direct financial benefits, such as the use of energy-saving light bulbs and low energy-consuming appliances. And there are isolated exceptions where more extensive measures have been introduced, notably the Grecotel hotel chain's programme that includes waste management, water and energy saving, pollution control and purchasing policies (Diamantis & Westlake, 1997). The generally limited take-up of the voluntary schemes in Greece is attributed to issues such as the failure of small hotels to appreciate the long-term impacts of their activities, a lack of knowledge of available conservation practices, and the costs of implementation.

## Regulation

Regulation is any direct attempt by government to influence the behaviour of businesses or citizens by setting specific environmental standards that are backed up by the force of the legal system (Jacobs, 1991). Among the potential regulations in tourist areas are land-use zoning requirements, limits to the maximum number of hotel rooms per hectare, and height restrictions on hotels. As well as restrictions on land use, limits can be set for the discharge of pollutants and restrictions can be placed on contracts between tour operators and hoteliers (Nijkamp & Verdonkschot, 1995). Sadler in Chapter 7 considers the regulations in place in north Cyprus for environmental impact assessments (EIAs) that affect proposed tourism projects. He also evaluates the potential to extend these regulations through strategic environmental assessments (SEAs) that would require the potential environmental impacts of individual projects to be evaluated in relation to other projects, programmes and policies.

Regulations have an obvious appeal to policy-makers. They appear to offer precision, predictability and effectiveness: an exact standard is set, the regulator and regulated both know what is expected of them, and enforcement is backed up by the judicial system. Regulations can be administratively efficient, especially when an activity is completely banned, as they do not require complete information about a problem. Assuming there is a high level of compliance, they can also be inexpensive as there is no necessity to examine each case. And they can be perceived as being equitable as in theory all those who do not comply with a regulation are treated equally. It has been argued that, 'In cases where impacts of tourism are considered to be severe or are valued as highly undesirable, the possibilities of introducing more binding instruments (like levies, spatial laws, and compulsory forms of zoning), should be considered' (Van der Duim & Caalders, 2002: 756).

Yet regulations can be subject to criticism. They may be inefficient because they provide no incentive for environmentally harmful activities to be reduced any further than that required by law. They can also be ineffective because the implementation activities of regulatory agencies can be very time consuming and costly. And when pro-environment beliefs are not widespread then even compulsory regulations can lack support and thus may be ignored or by-passed, especially if there is poor enforcement. In Chapter 3 Briassoulis describes attempts to apply land-use planning instruments in Crete that were obstructed by local reactions and resistance. Tourism development plans within Zones of Residential Control were blocked by local resistance, and Special Regional Plans that emphasised environmental protection were blocked by political pressure from both formal and informal groups. And in many Greek islands the state has sometimes failed to set up the mechanisms required to implement certain tourism regulations (Tsartas, Chapter 4).

### Government expenditure

The direct use of government expenditure to achieve sustainability goals may help where the costs of remedial action are too great for individual businesses or citizens to bear. Thus government may fund land purchase and conservation measures in national parks, community development initiatives and waste management projects. Spilanis and Vayanni (Chapter 13) describe how many sewage networks and treatment plants in Greek insular regions have been constructed with finance from the EU and regional and local authorities. They also note attempts by the public sector to secure finance from EU schemes in order to develop small-scale yachting infrastructure on some smaller and less populated Aegean islands, in order to lengthen the stay of sailing tourists and to offer them improved ecotourism opportunities.

Regions that have mass tourism infrastructure but are also developing small-scale 'alternative' tourism products may gain government funding in order to reposition the region in its tourism marketing. Marketing images have a key role in how a region is seen and also in how it wants to be seen in terms of its self-identity. The imagery used in the marketing of tourism in the eastern Adriatic is examined by Hall (Chapter 17). Some of the imagery has reflected the steps taken to diversify tourism products on the coast, such as with nautical tourism, and away from a coastal dominance, including 'alternative' rural, thermal and cultural tourism products, and also the attempts to upgrade and rejuvenate the resorts. But the re-imaging of tourism in Slovenia and Croatia has also reflected attempts to disassociate these countries from any pejorative notions of 'Balkanness', notably to distance them from their Yugoslav political past.

## Conclusion

It has been argued that policy decisions about sustainable tourism in southern Europe's coastal regions have been affected by both technical and political influences. Both past and current decisions about tourism priorities here are informed by moral and political choices. As Moisey and McCool (2001: 349) contend in relation to sustainable tourism:

> Science can provide information about the costs of decisions and the interrelationships between the various players, trade-offs between costs and benefits, and the potential impacts of alternative scenarios. But science cannot decide what is 'right' and what is 'wrong' – these are value-based decisions ideally left up to all affected individuals.

The discussion has focused on some of the varied determinants of policies that have affected tourism and sustainability in these coastal regions, specifically the pressures from economic interests, public opinion in destinations, environmental groups, different government tiers and the European Union. Given the many gaps in our understanding, there needs to be more research on how such influences have impacted on tourism and sustainability around all the northern shores of the Mediterranean.

The general dynamics of policy-making concerning the environment and tourism in the countries of Europe's south were also examined. During the 1990s there have been limited changes in policy approach towards environmental issues and towards tourism and sustainability in at least some of these countries. Where there have been political pressures and policies promoting sustainable tourism they have often been related to the environment and community generally rather than to tourism specifically. The shifts have not been radical and many obstacles to sustainability still remain, notably conservatism, anti-regulation politics, pressures for economic returns and the inequalities endemic in capitalism. While past trends do not encourage great optimism about the future prospects for sustainable tourism, it is contended that, nevertheless, there are likely to be some further changes to the 'business-as-usual' response to sustainability issues.

## References

Akis, S., Peristianis, N., and Warner, J. (1996) Residents' attitudes to tourism development: The case of Cyprus. *Tourism Management* 17 (7), 481–94.

Anderson, J. (1995) The exaggerated death of the nation state. In J. Anderson, C. Brook and A. Cochrane (eds) *A Global World?* (pp. 65–112). Oxford: Oxford University Press.

Andriotis, K. (2001) Tourism planning and development in Crete: Recent tourism policies and their efficacy. *Journal of Sustainable Tourism* 9 (4), 298–316.

Blue Plan and United Nations Environment Programme (1998) *Synthesis Report of the Working Group: Tourism and Sustainable Development in the Mediterranean Region.* Mediterranean Commission for Sustainable Development, Monaco, 20–22 October.

Boissevain, J. (1977) Tourism and development in Malta. *Development and Change* 8, 523–38.

Boissevain J. and Theuma, N. (1998) Contested space. Planners, tourists, developers and environmentalists in Malta. In S. Abram and J. Waldren (eds) *Anthropological Perspectives on Local Development* (pp. 96–119). London: Routledge.

Borzel, T.A. (2000) Why there is no 'southern problem'. On environmental leaders and laggards in the European Union. *Journal of European Public Policy* 7 (1), 141–62.

Bramwell, B. (1998) Selecting policy instruments for sustainable tourism. In W.F. Theobald (ed.) *Global Tourism* (2nd edn) (pp. 361–79). Oxford: Butterworth-Heinemann.

Bramwell, B. (2003) Maltese responses to tourism. *Annals of Tourism Research* 30 (3), 581–605.

Bramwell, B., Henry, I., Jackson, G. and van der Straaten, J. (1996) A framework for understanding sustainable tourism management. In B. Bramwell *et al. Sustainable Tourism Management: Principles and Practice* (pp. 23–71). Tilburg: Tilburg University Press.

Bramwell, B. and Lane, B. (eds) (2000) *Tourism Collaboration and Partnerships. Politics, Practice and Sustainability.* Clevedon: Channel View.

Briassoulis, H. (2002) Sustainable tourism and the question of the commons. *Annals of Tourism Research* 29 (4), 1065–85.

Carter, N. (2001) *The Politics of the Environment. Ideas, Activism, Policy.* Cambridge: Cambridge University Press.

Close, D. (1999) Environmental crisis in Greece and recent challenges to centralised state authority. *Journal of Modern Greek Studies* 17, 325–52.

Diamantis, D. and Westlake, J. (1997) Environmental auditing: An approach towards monitoring the environmental impacts in tourism destinations, with reference to the case of Molyvos. *Progress in Tourism and Hospitality Research* 3, 3–15.

Eder, K. (2001) Sustainability as a discursive device for mobilizing European publics: Beyond the north-south divide. In K. Eder and M. Kousis (eds) *Environmental Politics in Southern Europe* (pp. 25–52). Dordrecht: Kluwer.

Fousekis, P. and Lekakis, J.N. (1997) Greece's institutional response to sustainable development. *Environmental Politics* 6, 131–52.

Güneş-Ayata, A. (1994) Roots and trends of clientelism in Turkey. In L. Roniger and A. Güneş-Ayata (eds) *Democracy, Clientelism, and Civil Society* (pp. 49–66). Boulder, CO: Lynne Rienner.

Hajer, M. (1995) *The Politics of Environmental Discourse: Ecological Modernisation and the Policy Process*. Oxford: Oxford University Press.

Hall, C.M. (2000) *Tourism Planning. Policies, Processes and Relationships*. Harlow: Prentice Hall.

Haralambopoulos, N. and Pizam, A. (1996) Perceived impacts of tourism. The case of Samos. *Annals of Tourism Research* 23 (3), 503–26.

Harvey, D. (1996) *Justice, Nature and the Geography of Difference*. Oxford: Blackwell.

Hughes, G. (2002) Environmental indicators. *Annals of Tourism Research* 29 (2), 457–77.

Koker, L. (1995) Local politics and democracy in Turkey: An appraisal. *Annals of the American Academy of Political and Social Science* 54, 51–63.

Italconsult (1965) *Master Plan for Malta Tourism*. United Nations and Government of Malta.

Jacobs, M. (1991) *The Green Economy. Environment, Sustainable Development and the Politics of the Future*. London: Pluto Press.

Jenner, P. and Smith, C. (1993) *Tourism in the Mediterranean*. London: Economist Intelligence Unit.

Jessop, B. (1994) Post-Fordism and the state. In A. Amin (ed.) *Post-Fordism: A Reader* (pp. 57–84). Oxford: Blackwell.

King, R. (1979) Developments in the political and economic geography of Malta. *Tijdschrift voor Economische En Sociale Geografie* 70, 258–71.

Kousis, M. and Eder, K. (2001) EU policy-making, local action, and the emergence of institutions of collective action. A theoretical perspective on southern Europe. In K. Eder and M. Kousis (eds) *Environmental Politics in Southern Europe* (pp. 3–21). Dordrecht: Kluwer.

Mallia, E. (1994) Land use: An account of environmental stewardship. In R. Sultana and G. Baldacchino (eds) *Maltese Society. A Sociological Inquiry* (pp. 685–705). Msida: Mireva.

Marchena Gómez, M.J. (1995) New tourism trends and the future of Mediterranean Europe. *Tijdschrift voor Economische En Sociale Geografie* 86 (1), 21–31.

Middleton, V.T.C. and Hawkins, R. (1998) *Sustainable Tourism: A Marketing Perspective*. Oxford: Butterworth-Heinemann.

Moisey, R.N. and McCool, S.F. (2001) Sustainable tourism in the 21st century: Lessons from the past; challenges to address. In S.F. McCool and R.N. Moisey (eds) *Tourism, Recreation and Sustainability. Linking Culture and the Environment* (pp. 343–52). Wallingford: CAB International.

Monfort Mir, V.M. and Ivars Baidal, J.A. (2001) Towards a sustained competitiveness of Spanish tourism. In Y. Apostolopoulos, P. Loukissas and L. Leontidou (eds) *Mediterranean Tourism. Facets of Socioeconomic Development and Cultural Change* (pp. 17–38). London: Routledge.

Nijkamp, P. and Verdonkschot, P. (1995) Sustainable tourism development: A case study of Lesbos. In H. Coccossis and P. Nijkamp (eds) *Sustainable Tourism Development* (pp. 127–40). Aldershot: Avebury.

Pollard, J. and Dominguez Rodriguez, R. (1995) Unconstrained growth. The development of a Spanish resort. *Geography* 80 (1), 33–44.

Pridham, G. (1994) National environmental policy-making in the European framework: Spain, Greece and Italy in comparison. *Regional Politics and Policy* 4 (1), 80–101.

Pridham G. (1996) *Tourism Policy in Mediterranean Europe: Towards Sustainable Development?* Centre for Mediterranean Studies, Occasional Paper 15. Bristol: Centre for Mediterranean Studies, University of Bristol.

Pridham, G. (1999) Towards sustainable tourism in the Mediterranean? Policy and practice in Italy, Spain and Greece. *Environmental Politics* 8 (2), 97–116.

Pridham, G. (2001) Tourism policy and sustainability in Italy, Spain and Greece. A comparative politics perspective. In K. Eder and M. Kousis (eds) *Environmental Politics in Southern Europe* (pp. 365–91). Dordrecht: Kluwer.

Pridham, G. and Konstadakopulos, D. (1997) Sustainable development in Mediterranean Europe? Interactions between European, national and sub-national levels. In S. Barker, M. Kousis, D. Richardson and S. Young (eds) *The Politics of Sustainable Development. Theory, Policy and Practice Within the European Union* (pp. 127–51). London: Routledge.

Priestley, G.K. (1995a) Evolution of tourism on the Spanish coast. In G.J. Ashworth and A.G.J. Dietvorst (eds) *Tourism and Spatial Transformations* (pp. 37–54). Wallingford: CAB International.

Priestley, G.K. (1995b) Problems of tourism development in Spain. In H. Coccossis and P. Nijkamp (eds) *Sustainable Tourism Development* (pp. 187–98). Aldershot: Avebury.

Redclift, M. (2001) Sustainability and the North/South divide. Global and European dimensions. In K. Eder and M. Kousis (eds) *Environmental Politics in Southern Europe* (pp. 53–72). Dordrecht: Kluwer.

Robinson, M. (1996) Sustainable tourism for Spain: Principles, prospects and problems. In M. Barke, J. Towner and M.T. Newton (eds) *Tourism in Spain. Critical Issues* (pp. 401–25). Wallingford: CAB International.

Ruzza, C. (2001) Sustainability and tourism. EU environmental policy in Northern and Southern Europe. In K. Eder and M. Kousis (eds) *Environmental Politics in Southern Europe* (pp. 101–26). Dordrecht: Kluwer.

Tosun, C. (2001) Host perceptions of impacts. A comparative tourism study. *Annals of Tourism Research* 29 (1), 231–53.

Tosun, C. and Timothy D.J. (2001) Shortcomings in planning approaches to tourism development in developing countries: The case of Turkey. *International Journal of Contemporary Hospitality Management* 13 (7), 352–9.

Tsartas, P. (1992) Socioeconomic impacts of tourism on two Greek isles. *Annals of Tourism Research* 19, 516–33.

Valenzuela, M. (1998) Spain: From the phenomenon of mass tourism to the search for a more diversified model. In A.M. Williams and G. Shaw (eds) *Tourism and Economic Development. European Experiences* (pp. 43–74). Chichester: Wiley.

Van der Duim, R. and Caalders, J. (2002) Biodiversity and tourism. Impacts and interventions. *Annals of Tourism Research* 29 (3), 743–61.

Weale, A., Pridham, G., Cini, M., Konstadakopulos, D., Porter, M. and Flynn, B. (2000) *Environmental Governance in Europe. An Ever Closer Ecological Union?* Oxford: Oxford University Press.

Williams, A. and Shaw, G. (1998a) Tourism policies in a changing economic environment. In A.M. Williams and G. Shaw (eds) *Tourism and Economic Development. European Experiences* (pp. 375–91). Chichester: Wiley.

Williams, A. and Shaw, G. (1998b) Tourism and the environment: Sustainability and economic restructuring. In C.M. Hall and A.A. Lew (eds) *Sustainable Tourism: A Geographical Perspective* (pp. 49–59). Harlow: Longman.

World Tourism Organisation/United Nations Environment Programme and the Blue Plan (2000) *Sustainable Tourism and Competitiveness in the Islands of the Mediterranean. International Seminar.* Capri, Italy, 17–20 May.

Yuksel, F., Bramwell, B. and Yuksel, A. (1999) Stakeholder interviews and tourism planning at Pamukkale, Turkey. *Tourism Management* 20, 351–60.

# 3   Crete: Endowed by Nature, Privileged by Geography, Threatened by Tourism?

*Helen Briassoulis*
*Department of Geography, University of the Aegean, Lesvos, Greece*

Crete, the fifth largest island in the Mediterranean and the largest Greek island, is a highly heterogeneous region which has experienced rapid tourism development since the mid- to late 1960s when the growth in international tourism and broader socioeconomic changes disturbed past equilibrium patterns. Tourism has become a leading economic sector but has also caused several unwanted economic, environmental and sociocultural impacts and, currently, it appears to threaten the island's sustainability. The principal goal of official development plans is the achievement of sustainable development and the promotion of tourism in the island. To make realistic suggestions for the transition to sustainability it is essential, however, to identify the two-way relationship between tourism and the context within which it develops. The paper offers a broad-brush, integrated analysis of tourism and local development in Crete in three time periods since the late 1960s. It presents its impacts, evaluates them with a consistent set of sustainability criteria and probes into the essential requirements for securing the sustainability of development of the island and of its tourist sector. It concludes with a brief account of theoretical issues related to tourism development in heterogeneous destinations.

## Introduction

Crete, the fifth largest island in the Mediterranean and the largest Greek island, has experienced rapid tourism development since the mid- to late-1960s. Tourism has become a leading economic sector and its promotion features prominently in recent official development plans for the island whose overarching goal is the achievement of sustainable development (Regional Operational Plan (ROP), 2001). At the same time, tourism is blamed as one of the culprits of the recent serious environmental and socioeconomic problems that threaten the island's sustainability. Advocates of tourism development in Crete do not usually question whether this is congruent with the goal of sustainability, perceiving tourism as a development option that is easy to achieve (while this is not always the case) and assuming that development will occur as conceived. Frequently, particular interest groups promote such claims that are rarely (if at all) based on integrated analyses of local/regional and tourism development or employ a comprehensive set of sustainability criteria to evaluate future development options.

Crete represents an interesting case of a large, heterogeneous island tourist destination, located at the periphery of a country that is at an intermediate level of development. It has a historically strong and regionally diverse economic base, a strategic position, abundant natural and cultural resources, a spatio-temporally differentiated pattern of tourism development and a unique value system. The highs of tourism growth between mid-1980s and mid-1990s coincided with broader socioeconomic developments that boosted its economy and tourism –

migration and the influx of European Union (EU) funds to the island being central among them. The challenge in the analysis of tourism development in Crete is to single out, from among a myriad of other factors, the influence of tourism on the island's past, present and future development as well as to assess the influence of these other factors on tourism; in other words, to identify the two-way relationship between tourism and the context within which it develops. Towards this purpose, it is necessary to adopt an integrated methodological framework and to employ a comprehensive set of sustainability criteria. The present paper makes a modest attempt towards this aim as well as suggesting some essential requirements for securing the sustainability of development of the island and its tourist sector.

The next section briefly reviews the literature, while the third outlines the methodological framework adopted. The fourth section presents tourism development in Crete, its impacts and an appraisal of the sustainability of local and tourism development in three time periods. The fifth section suggests critical requirements to secure the sustainable development of the island and its tourist sector. A brief account of the theoretical issues related to tourism development in heterogeneous destinations concludes the paper.

## Brief Review of the Literature

Several theoretical models of tourism development exist, most of which employ the notion of stages in the lifecycle of destinations (Butler, 1980; Forster, 1964; Greenwood, 1972; Miossec, 1977; Noronha, 1979). Butler's (1980) remains the most influential and universal descriptive conceptual device among them, although its applications have revealed several limitations. Reviews of lifecycle models, in general, and Butler's model, in particular, suggest that, although most areas develop in a cyclic and stage-related manner (van den Berg, 1987; van der Borg, 1991), a general lifecycle theory cannot apply to all areas and spatial scales (Loukissas, 1982; Nash, 1977). Tourism development may skip certain stages in some areas (de Kadt, 1979), while elements of several stages may exist at a destination in any given period of time (Hovinen, 2002). More generally, instead of being linear, ordered and deterministic, tourism development is a non-linear, complex and non-deterministic process (McKercher, 1999; Russell & Faulkner, 1999). Because the tourist product is 'an amalgam of different activities' (Lundtorp & Wanhill, 2001: 962), most destinations have multidimensional products each exhibiting their own lifecycle (Agarwal, 1994, cited in Hovinen, 2002); particularly, heterogeneous and special destinations such as heritage cities (Russo, 2002). Moreover, planning regulations, public investment, partnerships and financial incentives are important influences on local and tourism development (Stough & Feldman, 1982, cited in Lundtorp & Wanhill, 2001: 949).

Lifecycle models are supply-oriented, focusing on the tourist product, whereas tourist demand is also critical particularly because it is not uniform and fixed (Lundtorp & Wanhill, 2001). Demand fluctuates with changes in tourist profiles, market evolution, political and business decisions, the interests of international oligopolies and tourism entrepreneurs, competition from other destinations and in the spatial organisation of production (Debbage, 1990;

Haywood, 1991, both cited in Lundtorp & Wanhill, 2001: 949; Russell & Faulkner, 1999; van der Borg, 1991).

The identification of lifecycle stages and their turning points using the number of tourists and available infrastructure only is not unambiguous especially in heterogeneous destinations. The broader geographical context, unit of analysis, tourism policy of the host country, local socioeconomic structure, quantity and quality of environmental and cultural resources, informal activities, migration and long-term structural change also influence the balance between tourist demand and supply and, consequently, the turning points between stages (Agarwal, 1997, 2002; Cooper & Jackson; 1989; McKercher, 1999; Russell & Faulkner, 1999; Tsartas *et al.*, 1995). Because most of these internal and external factors remain unspecified and are revealed *post facto* (Agarwal, 2002; Lundtorp & Wanhill, 2001), the usefulness of lifecycle models for analysis, explanation and forecasting in real world situations is limited (Hovinen, 2002).

Finally, most such models are tourism-centric, focusing on tourism and disregarding the possibility that other development options and functional shifts away from tourism are not necessarily bad; instead, they may be more suitable for the sustainable development of a destination (Agarwal, 2002: 27; Collins, 1999; Hunter, 1995). In fact, the quest for sustainable tourism development, that has become a dominant theme in the tourism literature since the early 1990s necessitates a holistic view of a destination within its broader socioeconomic, political and cultural context.

The discourse on sustainable tourism development has moved gradually from a narrow focus on tourism to a broader view of a destination's state of development, where tourism is one of the sectors making up its economic structure. Despite diverse conceptions and interpretations by different stakeholder groups, a general consensus seems to exist on what constitutes sustainable tourism development and what are the essential requirements to achieve it. These include the economic welfare of host communities, conservative use of natural and human resources, intra- and intergenerational equity, local self-reliance (low dependence on external inputs and assistance), local control and participation in development and tourism decision-making, sectoral coordination and integration, tourist satisfaction and balanced achievement of social, economic and environmental goals (Ahn *et al.*, 2002; Bramwell & Lane, 1993; Butler, 1991; Eber, 1992; Hunter, 1995, 1997; Collins, 1999; Ko, 2001; Mowforth & Munt, 1998; WTO, 1996). These features should characterise all but the stagnation stage of tourism development; however, their achievement and maintenance is most critical for mature destinations.

## The Methodological Framework of the Study

This study adopts a 'stages of development' framework to examine tourism in an integrated and holistic fashion within an area's particular and unique socioeconomic development trajectory (Massey, 1984; cf. Agarwal, 2002). It focuses on strategic issues related to sustainable development; namely, the interaction between demand and supply, internal and external factors impinging on development, the role of foreign and local, tourist and other,

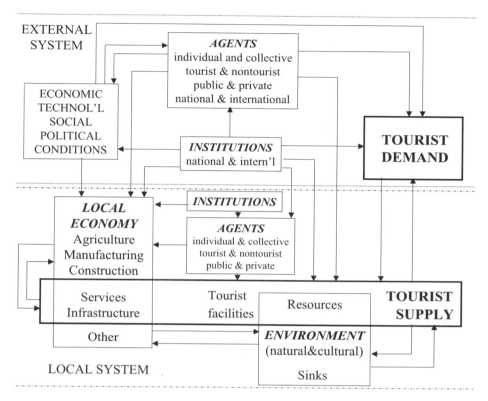

**Figure 1** A scheme for the analysis of tourism development

formal and informal actors, and the state, and the use of local natural and cultural resources.

Crete comprises the local system to be studied, and this is embedded within a broader spatial hierarchy – the external system, which includes Greece, the European Union and other countries. The study period – late 1960s to the present – is divided into time segments. Within each segment, the local and the external system and their interactions are analysed using the scheme shown in Figure 1, with the impacts being identified and the sustainability of the local system being evaluated using selected criteria.

Figure 1 is a simplified representation of the interaction between tourist demand and supply within the broader socio-spatial system, and it depicts only those components on which the present analysis focuses. The *local system* comprises tourist supply, the economy, the environment, institutions, and agents who are vectors of its sociocultural traits. *Tourist supply* intersects with the local economy and the environment because it comprises, in addition to tourist facilities, local facilities, infrastructure and the natural and manmade resources of host areas. The *local economy* comprises all economic sectors and activities. The *environment* comprises the natural, manmade and socio-cultural

**Table 1** Criteria of sustainable local (and tourism) development

| *Criterion* | *Operational measure* |
|---|---|
| Economic welfare | Economic conditions – GDP, employment, unemployment rate (total, by sector, tourism) |
| Sectoral coordination and integration | Integration among sectors<br>Complementarities between sectors |
| Economic diversification | Relative shares of primary, secondary and tertiary sectors<br>Economic monocultures |
| State of natural and human resources (conservative use) | Environmental conditions and impacts (pollution and resource shortages)<br>Social and cultural conditions and impacts<br>Infrastructure – availability and conditions |
| Intra- and intergenerational equity | Regional inequalities<br>Changes in inequalities over time |
| Local self-reliance | Dependence on external inputs and assistance<br>Local and non-local investment<br>Public and private investment |
| Local control and participation in development and tourism decision making | Participation of local and foreign capital<br>Participation of locals in decision making |
| Balance between tourism demand and supply – total and spatial | Degree to which tourism supply (accommodation) meets tourism demand (arrivals)<br>Degree of spatial concentration |
| Tourist satisfaction | Assessment of tourist satisfaction (personal/subjective, survey results, interviews) |
| Balanced achievement of economic, social and environmental objectives | Comparative and combined assessment of relative valuation of economic, social and environmental conditions |

resources of the destination that provide inputs and sink services to tourism and the economy. The *agents* are individuals and public or private collective bodies engaging in tourist and non-tourist activities. Their decisions concerning the use of resources (capital, labour, land, natural resources), are influenced by formal and informal local *institutions* (land tenure and ownership being particularly important), and they determine tourist supply, local economic structure and their relationships.

The *external system* comprises tourist demand, and the prevailing supra-local economic, technological, social and political conditions, institutions and agents. *Tourist demand* is influenced by all the other three components and it interacts with tourist supply. The *prevailing conditions* (nationally and internationally), with competition from other destinations figuring importantly among them, are influenced by national and international, and formal and informal *institutions* and they influence tourist demand, the local system and various types of *agents*. The latter are national and international, public and private, individual or collective entities – national and foreign investors and tour operators, national policy-makers, etc. – that control resources and, thus, influence the functioning of the local and external economic system as well as tourist supply and demand. The strength of the relationships within and between the components of the local and the external systems varies by period and it influences accordingly the sustainability of local (including tourism) development.

Several of the variables use to describe the local and the external system and the impacts of development serve also as operational expressions of the (aggregate) sustainability criteria adopted (Table 1). These draw on the features of sustainable local (and tourism) development presented previously.

The present application of the methodological framework was constrained by data availability, especially for past time periods. Official, published data were used where possible (Katochianou *et al.*, 1997; (National Statistical Service of Greece (NSSG)), 2001; Regional Institute on Tourism, 1998; Regional Operational Plan, 2001; Tourism and Economy, 2001, 2002). However, the most crucial information needed for a thorough, informed analysis was obtained from interviews with key informants, participant observation and the author's personal knowledge and experience.

## Tourism Development in Crete Since the Late 1960s

Crete, the southernmost island of Greece, has an area of 8335 km². It is predominantly mountainous, three-fifths of its area lying 200m above sea level. A mountain range extends from east to west with peaks above 2000m. Crete is divided into four administrative departments (prefectures) (Figure 2). Its population grew by 31.65% between 1971 and 2001. The prefectures of Irakleion and Rethymnon exhibited the highest growth rates, 40.36% and 34.12% respectively. Population change resulted from natural increase and the reversal of outmigration trends that occurred in the 1950s and 1960s. Internal migration contributed to urbanisation of its major towns. Migrants from the Middle East, Balkan and Eastern European countries have also settled in the island.

The urban–rural composition of its population changed from 55.76% rural and 44.24% semi-urban and urban in 1971 to 46.2% rural and 53.8% semi-urban and urban in 1991. The prefecture of Rethymnon remained the most rural of all four prefectures throughout the period (70.23% in 1971, 52.17% in 1991). By the end of the 1990s, inequalities in the urban–rural composition among the four prefectures had diminished.

Crete is renowned for its fabulous natural beauty, diversity of landscape, 1040km-long coastline, mild climate and numerous cultural resources (Minoan palaces and other archaeological and historical monuments and sites) that constitute its principal tourist resources.

The study period is divided into three time segments: (a) mid/late-1960s to mid-1970s, (b) mid-1970s to mid-1980s and (c) mid-1980s to late 1990s/2002 (present) for the following reasons. Tourism development proper started in the mid- to late-1960s in Crete, while the mid-1970s mark a period of accelerating

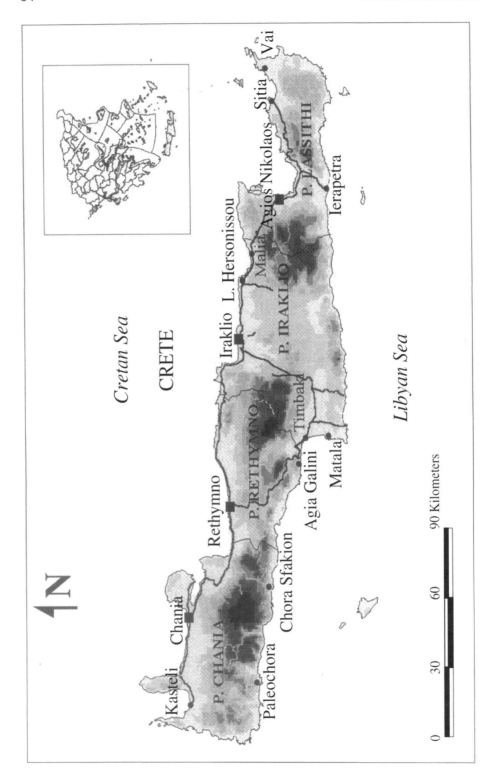

tourism growth and, at the same time, a period of important political changes in Greece. In the mid-1980s, as a result of Greece's accession to the European Union in 1981, significant amounts of funds started flowing to the island that pushed its economy forward. The late 1990s to the present mark a period of mounting problems in tourism (and more generally) and the generation of several initiatives to check the negative repercussions of these trends. The following sections analyse local and tourism development in Crete at an aggregate and selective level of detail due to space and data limitations.

## Mid/late-1960s to mid-1970s period

### Tourist demand and the external system

This first period coincides with a period of dictatorship (1967–74) in Greece and the gradual emergence of the country as a popular tourist destination, mostly for upper-income tourists. Tourists were attracted to Greek destinations renowned for their natural and cultural attractions (Athens, Delphi, Kerkyra, Rodos) that possessed adequate and developed tourist facilities, with Greek tourism policy mostly targeting traditional destinations and providing strong economic incentives for private investment. In 1972, international tourist arrivals by charter to Crete were only 4.1% of the national total. In 1975, overnight stays were 7.95% of the national total, 81.1% of which were in the prefectures of Irakleion and Lassithi that possessed developed tourist accommodation and infrastructure. Upper- to middle-income tourists prevailed.

### Tourism development and the local system

Tourism development in Crete started from the east, as reflected in the 1971 distribution of hotel beds and hotel beds per 1000 inhabitants among the four prefectures. It was based on local capital that took advantage of state-provided economic incentives and was invested in large, luxury hotels in Agios Nikolaos and Irakleion, the capitals of the respective prefectures (Papadaki-Tzedaki, 1999). These localities were basically at the involvement stage and they formed the nuclei of future, mostly mass, tourism development along the northern coast. The rest of the island was entering the involvement stage.

In 1970, Crete's Gross Domestic Product (GDP) was 10.550 million Drs (1970 prices), 4.09% of the national GDP and unemployment was only 1.86% (3.135% in Greece). Most of the 182,644 persons employed in 1971 were concentrated in the primary sector, especially in the prefectures of Rethymnon and Lassithi. The main agricultural products of the island were olive oil, grapes and dairy products. In the 1970s, greenhouse cultivation was introduced in southeast Crete (Ierapetra), and this gradually became very competitive. Trade was well developed and large, locally owned shipping and sea transport companies controlled a large share of the market. The hinterland was relatively undeveloped.

Direct employment in tourism totalled 4206 persons in 1971, 5% of the national total and 10.7% of Crete's tertiary sector employment (national average 8.2%). The island's development was based on local (and national) capital. The most important economic actors of this period were hotel, trade and shipping company owners.

In this first period, Crete did not experience serious environmental problems such as pollution and resource shortages. Culturally, it remained, overall, a traditional society. In sum, economic welfare was high and the economy was relatively well integrated and diverse. Social and environmental conditions were satisfactory and below their critical thresholds. Available infrastructure needed improvement. Regional inequalities did exist, with most development concentrated in the three urban centres of the island. Self-reliance and local control of development were significant and satisfactory. Tourism development was low, highly concentrated spatially and supply was meeting demand satisfactorily. Overall, development was on a sustainable trajectory as economic, social and environmental conditions were in relative balance.

## Mid-1970s to mid-1980s period

*Tourist demand and the external system*

In 1974 democracy was restored and in 1981 Greece acceded to the EU. A period of significant financial flows for development purposes commenced. In the meantime, Greece had become a popular tourist destination in the Mediterranean. Although tourism continued to develop in traditional destinations, new ones emerged including Crete. Foreign tour operators substantially influenced tourist demand. In 1981, 452,375 international tourists arrived by charter in Crete, representing 20.7% of the national total. Their average annual growth rate was 32.5% between 1972 and 1982. Total tourist arrivals reached 953,898. Overnight stays in 1981 increased three-fold over 1975 reaching 6,042,583, 14.72% of the country's total. Their highest concentrations were still in Irakleion and Lassithi but their growth was highest in Rethymnon (517.3% between 1975 and 1981!). Middle- to lower-income tourists prevailed.

*Tourism development and the local system*

Tourist accommodation units attained their highest growth during this period. By 1981 the number of hotel beds and hotel beds per 1000 inhabitants had almost tripled in the island. Tourism development spread to the west. The most dramatic increase occurred in the prefecture of Rethymnon, based significantly on local capital [1] (Papadaki-Tzedaki, 1999), where hotel beds increased more than six-fold and hotel beds per 1000 inhabitants grew ten-fold. In the prefecture of Irakleion hotel beds more than tripled and hotel beds per 1000 inhabitants grew five-fold. The number of unregistered rented rooms also increased considerably. Mass tourism prevailed – mainly along the northern axis and spreading around the major towns of the island – and this was operated primarily by small- and medium-sized family enterprises. Miscellaneous tourist services also developed markedly (car rentals, travel agencies, etc.). Overall, eastern Crete was at the development stage, while western Crete was at the involvement and development stages.

The Cretan economy kept growing. In 1981 the island's GDP was 17,510 million Drs (1970 prices), 4.30% of the national GDP, and unemployment 2.389% (4.382% national average). Employment grew by 3.23% over 1971 to 188,560 persons. Primary sector employment decreased while tertiary sector employment increased. The island retained its rural character, however, especially in the prefectures of Rethymnon and Lassithi, continuing to produce its traditional agricultural products. Greenhouse cultivation spread further, becoming an important export sector. Agriculture benefited from EU subsidies but these were frequently diverted to other uses, such as the construction of tourist facilities and purchase of urban apartments. Trade continued to grow and local shipping and sea transport companies continued to control a large share of the market. The integration of tourism with other economic sectors was very weak and place-dependent.

Direct employment in tourism totalled 9607 persons in 1981 – 7.67% of the national total and 16.1% of Crete's tertiary sector employment (9.2% national average). The tourist product amounted to 8844 million Drs (current prices). The employment opportunities in tourism contributed to the reversal of outmigration trends, especially from the rural hinterland, and to the repatriation of locals. New economic and political migrants augmented the informal labour pool, and they were employed primarily in tourism, agriculture and construction.

In 1980 gross fixed private and public capital investment in the island were 4.47% and 3.61% of the national total respectively. Generous EU funding[2] contributed crucially to the provision of physical and social infrastructure (ports, marinas, highways, health centres, business support, training, etc.).

In the 1980s the University of Crete (in Irakleion and Rethymnon), the Technical University of Chania and research centres of national and international standing were established. Together with tourism, they induced residential development to meet the housing needs of students and new employees. Informally, student housing was rented to tourists in the summer, thereby securing year-round revenues for the owners.

In addition to EU funding, national urban, regional and tourism policy developments – from the early 1980s onwards – greatly influenced the distribution, quantity and quality of local and tourism development. Regional development laws, especially Law 1262/82, provided economic incentives for the establishment of businesses, prioritising peripheral and underdeveloped regions of the country. New tourist units were created very fast. Crete received 21.8% of tourism-related investment and this generated 30,499 beds (23.2% of the national total).

To control haphazard urban and ex-urban development, Law 1337/83, was passed that required master plans for all urban areas. Its special land-use planning instrument – Zones of Residential Control – was used to draft tourism development plans (Kalokardou-Krantonelli, 1995). However, local resistance and reaction postponed and blocked the ratification of most master plans and, in consequence, haphazard urban and tourism growth continued together with their negative side effects.

The combination of development laws, EU-funding, abuse, violation and lack of enforcement and implementation of land-use planning and environmental legislation opened many areas to (frequently illegal) unbridled urban, ex-urban, tourism and tourism-induced development. A host of negative impacts resulted, concentrated on the most developed northern axis. Environmental and physical impacts included sea, coastal and water pollution; water shortages during peak seasons; water conflicts for domestic, agricultural and tourist uses; electricity shortages; uncontrolled solid waste disposal; ecosystem destruction; urban and rural landscape degradation; congestion; noise; land fragmentation; development of the rural–urban fringe; high building densities; congestion and overuse of infrastructure; and proliferation of small tourist units.

Socioeconomic impacts included the development of illegal hotellerie; the loss of high productivity agricultural land, the growth of a tourism monoculture (and, consequently, an increasing dependence on volatile tourist markets) and the ineffectiveness of official, rational development efforts. Tourism intensified regional inequalities, notably those between north and south, coast and hinterland, urban centres and the rest of the island, because tourism was concentrated in places where it developed strong complementarities with agriculture, universities and infrastructure. Serious changes in traditional values and attitudes also made their way into local society, in particular, the unquestioning acceptance of tourism and development as panaceas for economic ills.

In summary, in this second period, there was further growth in economic welfare. Although the island's economy remained relatively well integrated and sectoral complementarities developed, tourism was weakly integrated in the local economy. The environmental condition of coastal areas deteriorated and the sociocultural situation generally changed for the worse. The availability of infrastructure and its conditions improved. Regional inequalities diminished, although not considerably. Tourism and non-tourism development depended significantly on non-local resources and influences, and this weakened self-reliance and local control of development. While tourism development intensified, its degree of spatial concentration diminished but it was still significant. A rising tourist demand was being met satisfactorily by a rapidly growing supply. Tourist satisfaction dropped. Overall, development started to deviate from its sustainable trajectory as there was an emerging relative imbalance between the improved economic conditions, and the deteriorating environmental and sociocultural conditions.

## Mid-1980s to late 1990s/2002 (present) period

*Tourist demand and the external system*

After the mid-1980s, Crete had become an established tourist destination. Foreign tour operators controlled the largest part of tourist demand. Competition from other Mediterranean destinations frequently threatened tourist flows to Greece and to Crete. Tourism in Greece spread over more destinations. Between 1981 and 2001, international tourist arrivals by charter to Crete grew by 9.08 % annually, reaching 2,575,010 in 2001, this being about 30% of the national total. By 1994 total tourist arrivals were 50% above their 1981 levels, reaching 1,423,987. Overnight stays by 1990 had increased almost five-fold over 1975, reaching 9,709,937, which was 19.86% of the country's total. In 2001 they rose by 30% to 12,579,897. In Irakleion they equalled the sum of stays in the other three prefectures. However, the highest growth between 1981 and 2001 occurred in the prefectures of Chania and Rethymnon. The occupancy rate of the registered tourist accommodation units in late 1990s/2002 was 75–80 % (Tourism and Economy 2001, 2002), a high figure as many tourists stayed in unregistered units.

*Tourism development and the local system*

The supply of tourist accommodation units kept growing, although at a slower rate. By the late 1990s, the number of hotel beds and hotel beds per 1000 inhabitants had almost doubled over 1981. Tourism development intensified in the west with the prefectures of Rethymnon and Chania experiencing the most dramatic increase as hotel beds and hotel beds per 1000 inhabitants grew three-fold. In the prefecture of Irakleion the corresponding magnitudes doubled. Mass tourism still prevailed, although alternative and more diverse types and quality classes of accommodation units were being offered to satisfy shifting tourist preferences toward individual and/or family-based holidays.

Greek and foreign entrepreneurs erected luxurious tourist complexes and now control significant proportions of the tourist accommodation and services. The behaviour of local tourism-related capital has become more variegated. In terms of number of firms, family-based businesses dominate but some of them have been transformed into corporate-based businesses that have extended their operations beyond the island. Several others have succumbed to globalisation and competition and have transferred their management to foreign multinationals. It is unofficially estimated that foreign tour operators control 70% of the available tourist beds through various arrangements. Unregistered tourist accommodation has increased considerably. Diverse recreation facilities, such as golf courses, marinas, ports, water parks and miscellaneous tourist services are now available.

The island as a whole is approaching the consolidation stage but individual localities are at different stages of development. The northern axis is in the growth (west) and consolidation (east) stages, with pockets at the stagnation stage in the overdeveloped areas. The northern axis is congested, concentrating four-fifths of total tourist activity and most hotel and transport infrastructure, producing 79% of the island's tourism-related GDP and serving 74% of the population of the region (ROP, 2001). By contrast, the southern axis is in the involvement and development stages, with the acceleration of tourism development there being facilitated by the construction of new infrastructure. The hinterland remains largely undeveloped touristically.

The Cretan economy has kept growing. The 1991 GDP was 3.48% up from 1981 at 23,610 million Drs (1970 prices), 4.77% of the national GDP and unemployment was 5.545% (8.085% national average). In 1997 unemployment dropped to 4.6%, well below the national average (10.3%). In 1996 Crete produced 5.7% of the national GDP, with 31% in the primary sector (15% country), 13% in the secondary sector (25% country) and 56% in the tertiary sector (60% country). Irakleion produced 51.1% of the island's GDP, Chania 23.4%, Lassithi 13.7% and Rethymno 11.8% (ROP, 2001).

Employment grew by 5.79% to 199,475 persons between 1981 and 1991. Primary sector employment decreased. Lassithi and Rethymnon retained the highest shares of agricultural sector employment. Tertiary sector employment increased dramatically due to tourism and public sector growth (local and regional administration, universities, army, etc.) and the sector took the lead in the economy (50% of total employment).

Direct (official) employment in tourism totalled 17,068 persons in 1991 – 9.49% of the national total. Its contribution to the island's tertiary sector employment in 1990 further improved (17.1%) while the national average remained at its 1981 level (9.2%). The 1991 tourist product was 13,863 million Drs, rising to 15,933 million Drs in 1994 (ROP, 2001). Economic and political migrants continued to flow to the island, thus augmenting the informal labour pool. Informal labour is conservatively estimated at 50% of the officially reported employment.

The primary sector continued to receive EU financial support, contributing significantly to the island's GDP despite structural problems hindering its full development. In addition to traditional products, Crete is a leader in the dynamic sector of greenhouse cultivation, possessing around 50% of the country's greenhouses. Strong complementarities between tourism and agriculture have developed in several places. Farmers are involved as owners or workers in tourist enterprises (Tsartas *et al.*, 1995). Informal complementarities have also developed as in the previous period. However, tourism still remains weakly integrated in the local economy.

The physical and social infrastructure improved further through generous EU funding (IMP, Regional Development Programs and other EU initiatives) and national funding. In the 1994–99 period, investment in infrastructure amounted to 56 billion Drs on the northern axis, 13 billion Drs on North–South roads, and 2.8 bill. Drs on the southern axis. Funds for tourism are allocated under EU programmes for 'competitiveness' and 'culture'.

Business activity increased due to considerable private investment and financing provided through development Laws. Cooperation between businesses and local universities and research institutes intensified and helped to boost the economy further. Tourism has benefited from the use of innovative, tourist product-enhancing technologies, such as electronic commerce, advertising, tele-working, medical tourism and sea parks. Local shipping and transport companies maintain their strong position in the economy, producing 7.6% of the island's GDP as well as investing in tourist facilities. Various business associations have been formed together with public–private sector partnerships related to local and tourism development, banking and shipping. However, public sector bodies, and notably the Local Government Organisations, are frequently captive of local interests (Regional Institute on Tourism, 1998), thus blocking the achievement of more equitable, long-term local development.

The mounting problems of environmental degradation caused by unplanned and haphazard tourism and tourism-induced development have led to the reorientation of national tourism policy towards discouraging or even barring further development of 'congested' tourist destinations (Kalokardou-Krantonelli, 1995). Urban and regional development legislation of the 1980s was used for this purpose, in combination with economic instruments. Special Regional Plans – a new instrument emphasising environmental protection – were and are prepared for many municipalities and regions in Crete. However, political pressures by both formal groups (such as local development corporations) and informal groups (such as the 'Union of small landowners and small investors') have blocked the completion of these plans and also their practical implementation (Vogiatzakis, 1995).

The mode of, mostly unplanned, haphazard, and frequently illegal, development of the previous period has intensified in the current period causing similar or more serious negative impacts. Environmental protection and management has progressed but has succeeded in practice in only a few sectors (biological sewage treatment and solid waste disposal). The problems exhibit a strong regional differentiation, with most of them occuring on the northern coast. Spatial and aesthetic conflicts are frequent in the most highly developed areas. Incompatible land uses are mixed together, thus generating economic and environmental externalities (mixtures of greenhouses, hotels, bars, industrial installations, university premises, airport, landfills, biological treatment plants, quarries, fuel storage tanks, monasteries, army fields, etc.). Pockets where there are serious degradations of the tourist resources face problems with their image. In the south, the construction of roads and other infrastructure has led to the invasion, fragmentation and alteration of ecologically sensitive areas by agriculture and tourism. In the hinterland, fires, overgrazing and rural abandonment degrade the natural environment (ROP, 2001). The level of cultural and architectural heritage preservation is generally moderate.

Despite the significant contribution of local capital to vital economic sectors, foreign capital (private and EU) now plays an important role in the island's development. Foreign control of tourist flows, accommodation and services has intensified the unequal distribution of tourism benefits and the loss of self-reliance. This is more serious in areas where tourism is the only viable development alternative. Where tourism develops complementarities with other activities, then the related economic diversification offers brighter prospects, although this still exacerbates regional inequalities. Land value appreciation in tourist areas frequently prohibits the locals from acquiring land for development. Lastly, cultural alteration, such as the loss of traditional values and authenticity, the commercialisation of culture, and attitudes that are pro-development whatever the costs, has become deeper and widespread.

In this most recent period, economic welfare in Crete has remained high, with particular improvements in the rural hinterland, and with a growing economic convergence within the country. Although its economy is still diverse and there are significant sectoral complementarities, economic simplification seems to have set in as the island relies heavily on tourism and it specialises in agricultural products subsidised by the EU. There is growing environmental degradation and simplification, as well as spatial conflicts and cultural alterations. Infrastructure is adequate and keeps improving. Regional inequalities have diminished further. Dependence on external sources of funds is higher than in the past and local participation in decision-making is problematic. Tourist supply may also be exceeding demand. Territorial specialisation in tourism is observed, although the degree of tourism's spatial concentration has dropped. Tourist satisfaction is generally high but fluctuating. The imbalance among the objectives of sustainable development that started in the previous period has grown further and this trend will continue if Crete's limits to development are not respected.

## The Role of Tourism in a Sustainable Future for Crete

Crete is currently in a high growth period, its growth frequently occurring outside of the formal system owing to a tradition of informal sector activity. Its development trajectory exhibits a departure from sustainability as a booming economy coexists with serious environmental and sociocultural problems, dependence on external sources and weakening self-reliance. If the forces underlying this imbalance are left unchecked and those that may counteract it are not encouraged to intervene, then the time may be approaching when Crete's sustainability will be seriously threatened and its irreplaceable natural and cultural resources and valuable tourist resources will be irreversibly damaged.

Regional authorities and business circles are deeply concerned about the sustainability prospects of the island and about the particular role of tourism in this. It is generally agreed that the period of extensive tourism development is over and that little space has been left for development to accommodate the 3.5–4.5 million tourists that are projected for 2010 (ROP, 2001). To secure a sustainable income from tourism and Crete's niche in the tourist market, product transformation and product reorganisation (see Agarwal, 2002) are proposed in order to reduce seasonality and to increase the length of the tourist season, the length of stay and tourist spending by 40%. Proposals include: the development of new facilities; new poles of tourist attraction (e.g. mountainous areas); integrated tourist packages and alternative forms of tourism; alliances among tourist and non-tourist businesses, local government bodies, corporations and associations; the modernisation and improvement of tourist facilities and businesses; improved education and training of personnel; the provision of consulting services for small- and medium-sized tourist enterprises; infrastructure improvement; the protection and enhancement of natural and cultural resources; and a focused promotion of the island for particular types of tourists (ROP, 2001; Tourism and Economy, 2001).

These are supply-side solutions, however, that disregard the critical role of tourist demand and of the broader socioeconomic context. Moreover, they mostly address the supply-side symptoms of unsustainability rather than the essential causes and mechanisms at work (cf. Agarwal, 2002). Drawing on the preceding analysis, two groups of essential requirements to secure sustainability in the development of the island and of its tourist sector are outlined here: (a) decoupling development from the factors causing its current imbalance; and (b) capitalising on factors favouring long-term sustainable development. Both external and internal factors are involved here that, on the one hand, shape demand for the island's products, services and resources and, on the other, provide the necessary financial, human and other resources for development. Internal factors obtain a particular, deeper importance as sustainability is determined crucially by local choices about the preferred development patterns and courses of action.

Development should be decoupled from external factors that are uncertain, volatile or beyond effective local control, although these always remain critical for the viability of any development option. These include EU and national funding, foreign private investment, in-migration, tourist demand, tour operators and other tourism intermediaries. Development should be decoupled also from internal factors that hamper the enforcement and implementation of urban, regional and environmental planning and legislation. These include strong political pressures associated with particular local cultural traits,[3] the unquestioning adoption of short-term, high-revenue (e.g. tourism) development opportunities, weak or non-existent environmental awareness, a diffuse perception of powerlessness (e.g. against tour operators) and risk aversion. Under such conditions, the prescription of the sustainable development literature for formal local participation in decision-making should be viewed with scepticism.

Instead, development should capitalise on such external factors as Crete's mild climate and strategic position and, more selectively, on EU and national funding, foreign private investment, in-migration and favourable future socio-economic developments. It should also capitalise on internal factors that have been instrumental in its past and recent growth. Its inherent potential, due to its physiographic and economic diversity and heterogeneity, for forms of development other than tourism should be protected against current over-exploitation. Development should be managed so as to integrate the economy and the tourist sector and to differentiate the tourist product, thereby providing long-term safety valves against the uncertainty of such external factors as competition from other destinations and unfavourable future socio-economic developments.

Entrepreneurship, local capital and extant collaborations and partnerships – especially between businesses and educational institutes – are crucial, locally controlled assets that should be oriented towards long-run development options in order to increase the island's self-reliance, bargaining power and resilience to future stress. Finally, the tradition of informality, if handled properly, could be turned into a valuable tourist resource and a promising mechanism for flexibility and adaptation to changing socioeconomic circumstances.

The aggregate level of the analysis in this paper permits only broad suggestions how to satisfy these requirements. An absolute priority is the activation – implementation and enforcement – of integrated spatial planning[4] to guide and orchestrate the rational and effective use of Crete's natural and human resources and to provide for foreseeable contingencies; with fluctuations in tourism demand being important among them. Ideally, spatial development plans should be adapted to the island's environmental and sociocultural traits and should involve local actors in the development process. Institutionalising informal tourist and other arrangements and developments is a parallel action to contain the current 'tyranny of small decisions' (Khan, 1966) and to ensure minimum implementation. Lastly, education remains always the longer-term mechanism for the value change needed to support sustainable development choices where tourism develops harmoniously with the other sectors of the Cretan economy.

## Concluding Remarks

The case of Crete demonstrates that the particular model of tourism development of large and heterogeneous destinations results from the historic coincidence of *combinations* of diverse factors rather than from changes in the balance between tourism demand and supply only. Lifecycle models do apply in this case, in general, but description and explanation of a destination's lifecycle cannot be dissociated from its inherent diversity and broader context. Scale (relative size of

the area analysed) and degree of heterogeneity influence the relative contribution of internal and external, tourism-related and other socioeconomic and
cultural factors that determine the particular features of each stage, rate of
tourism development and timing of the lifecycle turning points (Agarwal, 1997,
2002; Cooper & Jackson, 1989).

When a heterogeneous destination enters the involvement stage, the degree of
spatial concentration of tourism is high. Development starts in those localities
where capital (local in the case of Crete) chooses to invest in tourism for place-,
time- and person-dependent reasons. The rest of the destination is essentially
intact. As tourism spreads to other localities, again where capital finds it profit-
able to invest, the destination as a whole moves to the development and
subsequent stages and the degree of spatial concentration diminishes. But,
within any destination-wide stage, different localities are at various stages of
development as the case of Crete illustrates. At more advanced destination-wide
stages (e.g. development, consolidation) the diversity of stages of development
of individual localities seems to increase.

Crete entered the development stage when growth in international tourist
demand coincided with the decline of older, traditional destinations in Greece,
the accession of Greece to the EU, the influx of generous development funds –
that reinforced its economic structure – and place-specific developments. Moreover, this development would not have occurred in the absence of a valuable
stock of active local financial and social capital (entrepreneurship) and this was
mobilised to invest in tourism while developing complementarities with agriculture, trade and local educational institutions. The combination of available local
capital and favourable national tourism and regional policy shaped the island's
tourism supply and stimulated foreign investment and international tourism
demand.

At the consolidation stage, heterogeneous destinations exhibit more complex
patterns of development than less heterogeneous ones (Hovinen, 2002). The
causes and impacts of this development are similarly complex and the role of
tourism becomes less clear unless thorough and informed analyses throw light
on its complex interactions with other sectors as well as the internal and external
factors at work. In Crete, tourism supply keeps on growing – frequently autono-
mously, without consideration of active demand (and its fluctuations),
haphazardly and mostly informally (not officially planned). The behaviour of
local tourism-related capital is more variable. In comparison to earlier periods,
local capital has less power but still remains instrumental for future tourism
development.

The island's self-reliance has weakened overall, pressures from tour operators and competition from other destinations have increased, and national and
EU policy developments may become more stringent in the near future. Its
overall spatial development pattern follows no formal plan. These and many
other socioeconomic developments raise the question as to whether tourism,
from a development motor, will become a source of unsustainability if it
continues developing unchecked in such a broader context. The complexity of
the consolidation stage hinders the specification of solutions that will assist the
area to avoid the stagnation stage and to stay on the sustainable development
path.

The broader theoretical issues that emerge from the present analysis are the path dependent and contingent nature of tourism development in heterogeneous destinations and the importance of external factors in this process (Agarwal, 2002; McKercher, 1999). From the perspective of integrated analysis there is a need to couple destination lifecycle models with more holistic accounts of the destination's complex development history in order to provide a more meaningful and useful basis for tourism planning and decision-making.

## Acknowledgements

The author acknowledges the assistance of George Chamakos, Association of Greek Tourist Enterprises (SETE), and Aris Stratakis, Directorate of Tourism, Region of Crete (Irakleion), who provided relevant information, and of Panagiotis Stratakis, researcher, Department of Geography, University of the Aegean, who prepared the map.

## Correspondence

Any correspondence should be directed to Professor Helen Briassoulis, Department of Geography, University of Aegean, University Hill, Mytilene 81100, Lesvos, Greece (e.briassouli@eagean.gr).

## Notes

1. The case of Rethymnon is particularly interesting because, in a period of local economic crisis, local businessmen invested in large hotel facilities in the area, extended their activities to the rest of the country, and have become supra-local tourism entrepreneurs.
2. The first EU Integrated Mediterranean Programme (IMP) was that of Crete. It commenced officially in 1985.
3. The non-cooperation of locals in formal plan preparation, their non-compliance with regulations and implementation and, consequently, their reliance on informal social networks results from the dominance of individualism, familism and political clientelism and the consequent mistrust in government. This has been termed the 'Mediterranean syndrome' (La Spina and Sciortino, 1993).
4. National legislation exists but remains inactive for the reasons mentioned above.

## References

Agarwal, S. (2002) Restructuring seaside tourism: The resort lifecycle. *Annals of Tourism Research* 29(1), 25–55.

Agarwal, S. (1997) The resort cycle and seaside tourism: An assessment of its applicability and validity. *Tourism Management* 18(2), 65–73.

Ahn, B.Y., Lee, B. and Shafer, C.S. (2002) Operationalising sustainability in regional tourism planning: An application of the limits of acceptable change framework. *Tourism Management* 23, 1–15.

Bramwell, B. and Lane, B. (1993) Interpretation and sustainable tourism: The potentials and the pitfalls. *Journal of Sustainable Tourism* 1(2), 71–80.

Butler, R.W. (1980) The concept of a tourist area cycle of evolution: Implications for management of resources. *Canadian Geographer* 24, 5–12.

Butler, R.W. (1991) Tourism, environment and sustainable development. *Environmental Conservation* 18, 201–9.

Collins, A. (1999) Tourism development and natural capital. *Annals of Tourism Research* 26(1), 98–109.

Cooper, C. and Jackson, S. (1989) Destination lifecycle: The Isle of Man case study. *Annals of Tourism Research* 16, 377–98.

de Kadt, E. (1979) *Tourism: Passport to Development? Perspectives on the Social and Cultural Effects in Developing Countries*. New York: Oxford University Press.

Eber, S. (1992) Beyond the green horizon: Principles for sustainable sevelopment. Discussion paper by Tourism Concern. WWF, UK.

Forster, J. (1964) The sociological consequences of tourism. *International Journal of Comparative Sociology* 5, 217–27.

Greenwood, D.J. (1972) Tourism as an agent of change: A Spanish Basque case. *Ethnology* 11, 80–91.

Hovinen, G. (2002) Revisiting the destination lifecycle model. *Annals of Tourism Research* 29(1), 209–30.

Hunter, C.J. (1995) On the need to reconceptualise sustainable tourism development. *Journal of Sustainable Tourism* 3, 155–65.

Hunter, C.J. (1997) Sustainable tourism as an adaptive paradigm. *Annals of Tourism Research* 24(4), 850–67.

Kalokardou-Krantonelli, R. (1995) Tourism and spatial planning in the Prefectures of Kerkyra and Lassithi. In P. Tsartas, K. Theodoropoulos, R. Kalokardou, K. Maroundas, P. Pappos and N. Fakiolas (eds) *The Social Impacts of Tourism in the Prefectures of Kerkyra and Lassithi* (pp. 201–32) (in Greek). EKKE: Athens.

Katochianou, D., Kavvadias, P. and Tonikidou, P. (1997) *Basic Data of Regional Socio-economic Development in Greece*. Athens: Centre of Planning and Economic Research.

Khan, A.E. (1966) The tyranny of small decisions: Market failures, imperfections and the limits of economics. *Kyklos*, 19(1), 23–47.

Ko, J.T.G. (2001) Assessing progress of tourism sustainability. *Annals of Tourism Research* 28(3), 817–20.

La Spina A. and Sciortino, G. (1993) Common agenda, southern rules: European integration and environmental change in the Mediterranean states. In J.D. Liefferink, P.D. Lowe and A.P.J. Mol (eds) *European Integration and Environmental Policy* (pp. 217–36). London: Belhaven.

Loukissas, P.J. (1982) Tourism's regional development impacts: A comparative analysis of the Greek islands. *Annals of Tourism Research* 9(4), 842–54.

Lundtorp, S. and Wanhill, S. (2001) The resort lifecycle theory: Generating processes and estimation. *Annals of Tourism Research* 28(4), 947–64.

Massey, D. (1984) *Spatial Divisions of Labour*. London: Macmillan.

McKercher, B. (1999) A chaos approach to tourism. *Tourism Management* 20, 425–34.

Miossec, J. (1977) Un modèle de l'espace touristique. *L'Espace Géographique* 6, 41–8.

Mowforth, M. and Munt, I. (1998) *Tourism and Sustainability: New Tourism in the Third World*. London: Routledge.

Nash, D. (1977) Tourism as a form of imperialism. In V. Smith (ed.) *Hosts and Guests: The Anthropology of Tourism*. Pittsburgh: University of Pennsylvania Press.

Noronha, R. (1979) *Social and Cultural Dimensions of Tourism*. Working Paper No. 326. Washington, DC: World Bank.

NSSG (2001) *Population Census 2001*. National Statistical Service of Greece.

Papadaki-Tzedaki, S. (1999) *Endogenous Tourism Development: Structured or Disintegrated Local Development?* (in Greek) Athens: Papazissis.

Research Institute of Tourism (1998) *Regional Development of Greece and of Tourism* (in Greek). Athens: Research Institute on Tourism.

Regional Operational Plan (ROP) (2001) *Regional Operational Plan of Crete, 2000–2006* (in Greek). Irakleion: Region of Crete.

Russell, R. and Faulkner, B. (1999) Movers and shakers: Chaos makers in tourism development. *Tourism Management* 20, 411–23.

Russo, A.P. (2002) The 'vicious circle' of tourism development in heritage cities. *Annals of Tourism Research* 29(1), 165–82.

*Tourism and Economy (T&E)* (2001). Issue 263 (May) (in Greek).

*Tourism and Economy (T&E)* (2002). Issue 275 (May) (in Greek).

Tsartas, P., Theodoropoulos, K., Kalokardou, R., Maroundas, K., Pappas P. and Fakiolas, N. (1995) *The Social Impacts of Tourism in the Prefectures of Kerkyra and Lassithi* (in Greek). Athens: EKKE.

Van den Berg, L. (1991) *Urban Systems in a Dynamic Society*. Aldershot: Gower.

Van der Borg, J. (1991) *Tourism and Urban Development*. Amsterdam: Thesis Publishers.

Vogiatzakis, P.S. (1995) Experience with tourist development in Western Crete. *Proceedings of the Conference Tourism and the Environment in Island Regions* (in Greek). Technical Chamber of Greece, Eastern Crete Section, Irakleion, Crete, 17–19 March.

WTO (1996) *What Tourism Managers Need to Know. A Practical Guide to the Development and Use of Indicators of Sustainable Tourism*. Madrid: World Tourism Organization.

# 4 Tourism Development in Greek Insular and Coastal Areas: Sociocultural Changes and Crucial Policy Issues

*Paris Tsartas*
*University of the Aegean, Michalon 8, 82100 Chios, Greece*

The paper analyses two issues that have characterised tourism development in Greek insular and coastal areas in the period 1970–2000. The first issue concerns the socioeconomic and cultural changes that have taken place in these areas and led to rapid – and usually unplanned – tourism development. The second issue consists of the policies for tourism and tourism development at local, regional and national level. The analysis focuses on the role of the family, social mobility issues, the social role of specific groups, and consequences for the manners, customs and traditions of the local population. It also examines the views and reactions of local communities regarding tourism and tourists. There is consideration of the new productive structures in these areas, including the downgrading of agriculture, the dependence of many economic sectors on tourism, and the large increase in multi-activity and the black economy. Another focus is on the characteristics of mass tourism, and on the related problems and criticisms of current tourism policies. These issues contributed to a model of tourism development that integrates the productive, environmental and cultural characteristics of each region. Finally, the procedures and problems encountered in sustainable development programmes aiming at protecting the environment are considered.

## Social and Cultural Changes Brought About by Tourism Development in the Period 1970–2000

The analysis here focuses on three main areas where these changes are observed: sociocultural life, production and communication. It should be noted that a large proportion of all empirical studies of changes brought about by tourism development in Greece have been of coastal and insular areas.

### Social and cultural changes in the social structure

The most significant of these changes concern the family and its role in the new 'urbanised' social structure, social mobility and the choices of important groups, such as young people and women.

The first changes were registered in areas such as Mykonos (Loukissas, 1982; Stott, 1973), Crete (Kousis, 1989; Tsartas *et al.*, 1995), Corfu (Tsartas, 1991; Tsartas *et al.*, 1995), the Cyclades (Loukissas, 1982; Tsartas, 1992), Samos (Galani-Moutafi, 1993–4, parts I & II; Haralambopoulos & Pizam, 1996), and Rhodes (Kasimati *et al.*, 1995) and concern the special features and functions of a typical family. Gradually, the paternal model, in which the father was the one who decided on the main choices of the family members (such as in relation to profession, education and savings), started to lose its dominant position. The gradual social and financial independence of other members of the family, owing to revenue from tourism, led to a new type of family, in which individualism and collectivism coexist in decision making. In this context, the role of the younger – and usually more educated – members of the family, who have been socialised in the period of rapid tourism development, is being upgraded. The family now operates on the basis of strategies (Kousis, 1989; Stott, 1973; Tsartas 1992) for the expansion of this small 'economic unit', with the aim of taking advantage of opportunities arising from the 'touristification' of the social structure.

A different social structure is being formed, which is directly, but not exclusively, affected by the 'urban-type' social and economic relationships imposed by tourism. In this structure, one may find the social models of the 'closed' agricultural structure typical of the Mediterranean together with urbanised consumption models which, especially in the first phases of tourism development, are restricted to the urban centres, leading to a superficial 'modernisation' (Galani-Moutafi, 1993; Tsartas *et al.* 1995). In this context, the role of customs (e.g. festivities), as elements that reconfirm the tradition and the history of the region, starts to be downgraded. Their place is taken by new 'urban-type' entertainments (e.g. going to restaurants, tavernas and bars). At the same time, the pressing speed of employment and the new production relationships of all people living in these areas (Kousis, 1989) become the key argument for the gradual abandoning – especially by the younger population – of a way of life where the relationship between work and leisure time was more balanced and where social and professional mobility was less intense (Tsartas, 1991).

The social structure of these areas is gaining other new characteristics, the most important of which are an accelerating social mobility and a change in the way in which social positioning is measured. For many generations, social mobility used to be very restricted in these areas, since wealth and political power were usually concentrated within a relatively small social group (Tsartas, 1991, 1992). However, the spread of tourist income to larger groups of the population has led to the creation of an 'expanded' middle class, with high levels of consumption and dynamism in investment. In this context, social positioning has started to be measured more on the basis of income indices (levels of income) and less on social indices (such as education, family tradition and profession). This trend is most probably also related to the downgrading, mainly on the part of men, of education as a means of social mobility. In this new social reality, employment in tourism and the subsequent rise in income are considered to be a more secure way to gain upward social mobility.

Young people and women constitute the two groups in the population that play increasingly important roles in these insular and coastal areas (Stott, 1973; Tsartas *et al.*, 1995). Young people tend to be those initially pressing for rapid tourism development, considering it to be the 'ticket' to modernisation and to change in their way of life. They tend to participate actively in all processes of social and economic change brought about by tourism in their areas, while, more recently, they have also taken the lead in forming groups seeking to change the mass tourism development model, which they now consider to be problematic for local development. Women, too, are benefiting from tourism development, which improves their position not only in the field of production but also in the social structure of these areas. The economic side of this improvement is more important, as in many cases women become employed for the first time, they earn income and they have a significant presence in the creation of businesses. On the social side – although their status is improved – women, and especially the older ones, are often left aside, having at the same time to deal with the quite different and complex reality of their social and family relationships.

## The 'meeting' of tourists and locals: Changes in customs and manners, preferences and stereotypes

Researchers in Greece and elsewhere have argued that tourism is not the only cause of change in a region's customs and manners. Other social changes have moved in the same direction, such as the spread of mass media, expanding urbanisation, better communication, and extended use of information technologies. However, in the case of the Greek coastal, and especially insular, areas where tourism has developed, the historic phase of this development has been a very important influence. In most cases, tourism development took place before the above-mentioned social changes (Galani-Moutafi, 1993; Labiri-Dimaki, 1972; Stott 1973; Tsartas, 1992) so that it functioned as a strong transmitter of messages and it clearly contributed to the change in social relationships. At this point it is useful to consider the views and positions of people living in these insular and coastal areas, as they have been examined in two research studies carried out by the Greek Tourism Organisation for the period 1979–1986 and by *EKKE* for 1980 and 1989. Aspects of these views and positions are presented in Tables 1 and 2.

One may see that the views about tourism among residents of islands at the initial stages of tourism development are often more positive (Naxos, Kalymnos, Leros and Kythira in Table 1, and Serifos and Lasithi in Table 2). On the other hand, people living in islands where tourism had already been developed seem more sceptical and their views are divided between positive and negative assessments of tourism (Mykonos, Paros, Santorini, Ios and Corfu). As regards residents' assessments of the 'bad' or adverse impacts of tourism, it is worth mentioning some of the answers given to the *EKKE* researchers. These related to 'Problems of morals and nudism', the 'Low quality of tourism', 'Vagrancy and bad influences on the young', 'Changes in customs and manners', the 'Destruction of families', increased 'Freedom of the young', 'Disputes', and 'Drunkenness'. Such answers were also registered more frequently in the case of islands where tourism had already been developed.

Thus, a conflicting social situation arises, as the one also identified by Greenwood (1972: 90), whereby at the end of the tourist season the local population is glad to see the tourists go, but at the same time they also worry in case the tourists do not come back next year. This situation is related to the many changes in social customs (derived from the rapid urbanisation brought by tourism), which have affected social relationships, including relationships between the sexes and within families. The result is a new and often conflictual social reality. In this context, there is evidence of a change in social relationships due to the dominance of individualist models and of modernising views in the tourist settlements (as against the rural areas) of Corfu and Lasithi. In these two areas there have also been problems in the relationships between the sexes, usually due to the short-lived relations between men and foreign tourists (the *kamaki* phenomenon) and due to conflicts within the family resulting from the autonomy of the young and the adoption of more modern ways of living.

The locals have also been found to prefer tourists of specific nationalities. This has undoubtedly been affected by the process of stereotyping tourists and also by

**Table 1** Views about tourism among residents of selected Greek insular and coastal areas (in percentages)
Question: 'What does Tourism bring?'

| | Mykonos | | Naxos | | Kalymnos | | Leros | | Paros | | Santorini | | Kythira | |
|---|---|---|---|---|---|---|---|---|---|---|---|---|---|---|
| | 1 | 2 | 1 | 2 | 1 | 2 | 1 | 2 | 1 | 2 | 1 | 2 | 1 | 2 |
| Money and employment | 93.9 | 100.0 | 100.0 | 94.2 | 96.8 | 97.4 | 98.0 | 96.4 | 87.6 | 92.7 | 98.1 | 80.7 | 100.0 | 93.8 |
| Modernisation | 68.2 | 73.7 | 70.0 | 78.3 | 52.3 | 89.6 | 76.0 | 86.1 | 51.4 | 54.9 | 74.5 | 73.7 | 92.3 | 89.1 |
| Corruption of morals | 40.9 | 52.6 | 46.7 | 59.4 | 25.4 | 53.9 | 24.0 | 33.3 | 67.6 | 74.4 | 60.8 | 47.4 | 57.7 | 62.5 |
| High prices | 51.5 | 52.6 | 36.7 | 47.9 | 42.9 | 57.4 | 18.0 | 35.1 | 37.1 | 23.2 | 41.2 | 70.2 | 53.9 | 56.3 |

*Note:* 1. The percentages shown refer to positive answers. The research in Mykonos and Naxos was carried out in 1979, in Kalymnos and Leros in 1980, and in Santorini, Paros and Kythira in 1986. '1' refers to answers given by professionals (in their shops), while '2' refers to answers given by the general public (in their households).

*Sources:* Stavrou (1979), p. 3 (Naxos), p. 2 (Mykonos). Stavrou (1980), Table V (Kalymnos), Table V (Leros); (1986) pp. 13, 33, 65.

**Table 2** Views about tourism among residents of Ios, Serifos, Corfu and Lasithi (in percentages)

| | *First study (1980)* | | *Second study (1989)* | |
|---|---|---|---|---|
| *Questions* | *Ios* | *Serifos* | *Corfu* | *Lasithi* |
| 1. Do you consider that tourism in your area has a good impact? | 15.7 | 60.3 | 22.3 | 42.0 |
| 2. Do you consider that tourism in your area has a bad impact? | 1.4 | 9.5 | 4.5 | 3.8 |
| 3. Do you consider that tourism in your area has both good and bad impacts at the same time? | 82.9 | 30.2 | 72.9 | 53.8 |

*Note*: In the 1989 survey a percentage of the population replied 'I do not know / No reply' (0.3% in Corfu and 0.4% in Lasithi).
*Sources*: Tsartas (1989: 159–68); and Tsartas *et al.* (1995: 166–73).

the economic dynamism of tourism which in most areas is associated with foreign tourists. The views of the locals about differing nationalities of tourists are clearly affected by the related perceived economic benefits (positive attitudes and expectations) and social issues (both positive and negative attitudes and social issues raised). Here it is worth examining the views of the local populations as identified in the two research studies used previously (Tables 3 and 4).

Greek tourists are mainly preferred by the residents of the insular and coastal areas with less tourism development, such as Leros, Kalymnos, Kythira, Serifos and Lasithi (with the exclusion of Naxos). On the other hand, people living in areas with high tourism development are more likely to prefer foreign tourists (Mykonos, Paros, Santorini, Corfu and Ios). These preferences are justified by comments such as, 'Greeks are quieter, you can discuss with them, they have families', while 'foreigners are more easy going, they do not complain, they spend more'. Thus, choices are commercialised and what counts most are the economic characteristics of tourists as a commodity. This trend is increased if we add to it the high percentage who declare that nationality makes no difference, especially when they go on to say that they are only interested in 'how many tourists come, irrespective of their nationality'. The shaping of national stereotypes has been registered quite clearly in research conducted in the Cyclades (Tsartas, 1989: 166), where locals commented that, for example, 'Germans and Scandinavians spend more and are just in their transactions', and the 'French spend enough, but quite often they are demanding and arrogant'. It is very interesting to note that the economic element is very important in these preferences. A good example is the case of Corfu, where the British tourists have been a catalyst for the island's tourism (50–70% of arrivals per annum). However, only a few of the inhabitants seem to prefer them, since the British are often considered to be 'cheap tourists'. Views about tourists among locals seem to be positively affected by factors such as age (younger age groups), work ties with tourism and acquaintance with tourists (a high percentage of interviewees in Corfu and Lasithi noted that they had become friends with foreign tourists and had visited their countries) (Haralambopoulos & Pizam, 1996; Tsartas *et al.*, 1995).

**Table 3** Views about tourists of different nationalities among residents of selected Greek insular and coastal areas (in percentages)
Question: 'What is your order of preference of tourists?'

| | Mykonos | | Naxos | | Kalymnos | | Leros | | Paros | | Santorini | | Kythira | |
|---|---|---|---|---|---|---|---|---|---|---|---|---|---|---|
| | 1 | 2 | 1 | 2 | 1 | 2 | 1 | 2 | 1 | 2 | 1 | 2 | 1 | 2 |
| Greeks | 4.6 | 7.9 | 30.0 | 21.7 | 46.0 | 31.3 | 66.0 | 24.9 | 32.4 | 45.1 | 27.5 | 43.9 | 53.8 | 67.2 |
| Foreigners | 63.6 | 56.6 | 46.7 | 34.8 | 44.4 | 19.1 | 22.0 | 18.2 | 51.4 | 47.6 | 56.9 | 29.8 | 38.6 | 26.6 |
| Makes no difference | 13.6 | 21.0 | – | 29.0 | 4.8 | 2.6 | 8.0 | 29.7 | 14.3 | 7.3 | 15.6 | 26.3 | 7.6 | 6.2 |
| Both Greeks and foreigners | 18.2 | 14.5 | 23.3 | 14.5 | 4.8 | 47.0 | 4.0 | 27.3 | 1.9 | – | – | – | – | – |

*Note:* The research on Mykonos and Naxos was carried out in 1979, in Kalymnos and Leros in 1980, and in Santorini, Paros and Kythira in 1986. '1' refers to answers given by professionals (in their shops), while '2' refers to answers given by the general public (in their households).

*Sources:* Stavrou (1979), p. 5 (Naxos), p. 3 (Mykonos); Stavrou (1980), Table VII (Kalymnos), Table VIII (Leros); Stavrou (1986) pp. 15, 35, 59.

**Table 4** Preferences for tourists of specific nationalities (in percentages)
Question: 'Which tourists do you prefer?'

|  | *Serifos* | *Ios* | *Corfu* | *Lasithi* |
|---|---|---|---|---|
| Greeks | 22.2 | 8.8 | 27.7 | 32.4 |
| Foreigners | 20.6 | 58.8 | 30.8 | 25.9 |
| Makes no difference | 57.1 | 32.4 | 40.4 | 41.6 |
| *Preferred nationalities* | | | | |
|  | (Serifos and Ios combined) Germans 29 French 12 British and Irish 11 Scandinavians 10 Others 17 Makes no difference 21 | | Germans 21 Italians 21 British 14 French, Dutch, Belgians, Americans, Japanese, Swiss, Austrians 10 Scandinavians 9 No difference 24 | Germans 19 Scandinavians 18 British 16 French, Dutch, Belgians, Americans, Japanese, Swiss, Austrians 14 Italians 4 No difference 29 |

*Sources*: Tsartas (1989: 165–6); Tsartas *et al.* (1995: 169–71).

## The new economic structure in coastal and insular areas resulting from tourism development

The holistic presence of tourism in the local production structure constitutes a key feature in most cases under review. Indeed, the tourism sector tends directly or indirectly to become the main source of income for almost all social strata, irrespective of their main occupation. This process starts with the gradual abandonment all other employment sectors, especially agriculture, which traditionally constituted the basic source of income in these areas. This has consolidated tourism as a basic source of income, while occupations in the primary (e.g. agriculture) and secondary sectors (e.g. handicrafts) are on the decline. At this point, it is informative to note Labiri-Dimaki's (1972: 89) description of Mykonos, where 'the number of persons who are exclusively farmers or manual workers is decreasing, and the number of persons who are "partly farmers" and employed in small tourist businesses is increasing'. This transition phase, from an agricultural economy to a 'touristified' productive structure was identified at the beginning of the 1970s, but has gradually been consolidated in subsequent years. In this way, tourism has contributed, directly or indirectly, to the transformation of the local economy and the dominance of the tertiary sector. The research carried out in Corfu and Lasithi (Tsartas *et al.*, 1995: 63–84) showed that the following occupational groups stated that they received income from tourism (at a rate of 25% to 100%). These were traders (82.6% in Corfu and 55.4% in Lasithi), farmers (55.7% in Corfu and 11.7% in Lasithi), builders (69.6% in Corfu and 17.9% in Lasithi), manual workers (48.3% in Corfu and 38% in Lasithi), scientists and self-employed (30.4% in Corfu and 19.4% in Lasithi), and employed persons (40% in Corfu and 19.2% in Lasithi). This situation results from the increasing importance of tourism as a source of income, but also because it is a prestigious employment sector in the local economy.

A consequence of tourism's pervading presence is the high incidence of people employed in two or three different occupations, one of which is related to tourism. This multi-employment concerns both sexes, and it is either of an individual nature or it results from family strategies. An example of the first case is the Sithonia peninsula in Halkidiki, which is mentioned by Bidgianis (1979: 28–9). Here a farmer usually: (1) cultivates his own land, (2) is employed in construction or in the Carras enterprise (involved in agricultural products and hotels), and (3) works in the tertiary sector (rooms to let, or commerce). In the second case, Loukissas (1975: 10) notes that on Mykonos:

> a local, claiming that he is a farmer, may also rent rooms to tourists, or fish, or rent his boat for the recreation of tourists. His wife may work as a cleaning lady, or take care of the rooms-to-let, while at the same time she may sell her handicraft to local shops. Her children may fish with their father, or work in restaurants as waiters.

This multi-employment strategy has also been noted by many other researchers examining Greek insular areas, e.g. in Crete (Kousis, 1998), Samos (Galani-Moutafi, 1994; Haralambopoulos & Pizam, 1996), Corfu and Lasithi (Tsartas *et al.*, 1995), and in Rhodes (Kasimati *et al.*, 1995). It is characteristic that of all people employed in different sectors, 60% in Corfu and 35% in Lasithi declared a certain professional relationship with tourism (shop owners, or employees in rooms to let or hotels) (Tsartas *et al.*, 1995: 77–80). This multi-employment constitutes a characteristic feature of the insular tourist areas of Greece, and the research on Corfu and Lasithi suggests it often related to the black economy. Furthermore, especially in areas with a significant farming tradition, employment in the farming sector is being seriously downgraded, since the dynamism of the sector has been lost. The key source of income in multi-employment is tourism. People residing in Agios Matthaios village in Corfu commented that those having tourism as their main occupation and agriculture as their secondary occupation maintained this second occupation for 'tradition', for 'preserving the family property' and as a 'hobby' (Tsartas, 1991: 128–32).

The social, cultural and economic changes that have been discussed came about very quickly in these insular and coastal regions, and they have had important results. There has been a two-way relationship between these changes and the tourism-related policy exercised in these regions over the past three decades (as explained in the second part of this paper). In this analysis it is assumed that a large share of the problems in the social and cultural field is attributable to the state's decision to promote mass tourism in these regions. The problems are also due to the acceptance of this model by the locals, as they have believed it was the best answer to their regions' low level of development. This situation has changed over recent years, as people started to recognise the associated problems. The influences on this change in people's views include: (1) the shaping of a new institutional framework which allows for participation by locals in the planning process, (2) the upgrading of scientific dialogue on tourism development, and (3) a growing sensitivity to the need to protect the environment. Changes in the basic priorities for tourist policies have also contributed to this direction, as they emphasise development models drawing on local characteristics. In recent years there has been a search for development models designed on the principle of sustainability and that upgrade the tourist product offered in the insular and coastal regions.

## The Search for Locally Integrated Development Models and the Protection of the Environment and Sustainable Development

### The organised mass tourism model as the dominant model of growth: Questions and challenges

The 1980s were crucial for the country's national tourist policy, since new development models began to be sought. The coastal and insular areas of Greece have been developed on the basis of the mass tourism model. Starting with the economic success of the islands, where this model was developed in the 1960s and 1970s (in Rhodes, Corfu, Mykonos etc.), mass tourism has sprung up in most regions of the country. The basic arguments behind this decision were that it produced important economic gains for Greece in terms of foreign exchange, that it increased incomes in the tourist regions, and the tourist resources of the country could keep pace with the demand for this type of tourism (Bouhalis, 1998; Tsartas, 1998a; Varvaressos, 1987). It was also pointed out by the Greek Tourism Organisation (1985: 23–4) that Greece adopted this basic model following the suggestion of international organisations, with a view to increasing its foreign exchange reserves. However, investment was not evenly or rationally distributed among the regions, and the same applied to planning controls. As a result, there are many important problems related to land-use planning and the evolution of this model.

The first problem is the intense seasonality of demand for this type of tourism (Arthur Andersen, 2002; SETE, 2002). In the 1970–2000 period most tourists (35–40%) arrive in Greece in July or August. Hence the infrastructure is not used to its full capacity and it is difficult to achieve full returns on the investment when in most regions the tourist season does not last more than 2–3 months.

A second problem is the progressive reduction of the economic benefits of this model. After a first historical phase when important increases in incomes were observed at the local level (*EKKE*, GNTO), there followed a phase of stagnation or diminishing incomes. This is clearly related to the life cycles of the products in many regions, which were progressively being downgraded (Andersen, 2002; Patsouratis, 2002; Tsartas, 1998a). It is also related to the intense competition among enterprises and among different areas in the same region (e.g. on the same island), among different regions of the country, or between countries.

A third problem is connected with the frequent disregard for land-use planning and urban planning provisions in most regions with a developed and organised infrastructure (Konsolas & Zaharatos, 2001; Spilanis, 2000; Zacharatos, 1989; Zacharatos, 2000a). This fact is connected with the intense pressures that tourism development has created in many areas in terms of the continuing construction of buildings in coastal and island regions. It is also related to the state's failure to set up the mechanisms needed to implement the agreed tourism policies.

Finally, the downgrading of the natural and built environment constitutes a further significant problem for all the regions that have adopted the mass tourism model. The economic dimension of tourist growth is jeopardised by this when the quality of the environment constitutes a key attraction of Greece for Europeans, who constituted the large majority of foreign visitors in the period 1970–2000 (Tsartas, 1998).

From the beginning of the 1980s, these problems contributed to the wider questioning of this type of tourism and led to the search for different development models or to the search for policies to help upgrade this particular model. This questioning came from people living in tourist regions who were directly or indirectly involved in the process of planning tourism development, as well as from many researchers who were involved in the tourist sector. The criticism was initially focused on the inability of the tourist policies to set limits and to manage the growth of organised mass tourism (Buhalis, 1998; Konsolas and Zacharatos, 2001; Tsartas, 1998b).

In the 1980s and 1990s, there were the first studies of the social, economic and political impacts of this type of tourist growth, with these being discussed in the first part of this analysis. These studies demonstrated that many problems exist at the local level and they also identified the intense scepticism of the locals about this development model. Another side of this criticism is that mass tourism was the only type of tourism offered by the country for many decades. This itself has contributed to the downgrading of the Greek tourism product, especially at a time of intense international competition (Arthur Andersen, 2002; Patsouratis, 2002) when many countries have enriched their tourism product with new products and services (mainly related to special interest and alternative forms of tourism). One common denominator in these criticisms, on one side, was the need to find new models of growth in the coastal and insular regions which would be integrated into the local socioeconomic and environmental realities; and, on the other side, the need for this particular model to be upgraded with concrete measures and interventions.

## The progressive shift towards locally integrated tourism development models

Again from the 1980s, tourism development has increasingly tried to promote 'locality' (Tsartas, 1998a; Varvaressos, 1999). Measures, interventions and policies have sought to achieve a softer integration of tourism at the local level, aimed at a more balanced tourism development which combines mass tourism with the development of special interest and alternative forms of tourism. Clearly this was not a concrete and coordinated policy. It was made up more of individual policies (national, regional and local), which together contributed to the promotion of models of balanced local development, particularly in islands and coastal regions. In many cases the policies led to the adoption of new methods and the realisation of development projects, while in other cases the policies were only partly implemented, mainly due to a lack of coordination. Initially, the shift towards 'locality' is located in the planning and management of development, where emphasis is given to programmes of soft tourism development, mainly aimed at the promotion of the local environmental and cultural resources of the region. Thus, the type of holiday is combined with infrastructure and activities originating from the specific special interest, such as cultural tourism, rural tourism, marine tourism, confer-ence tourism, golf tourism, health tourism, agrotourism, adventure tourism, ecotourism, and sports tourism (Anthopoulou *et al.*, 1998; Athanasiou, 2002; Installations for Naval Tourism, 2000; Spathi, 2000; Tsekouras, 1991; WWF, 2000). Considerable amounts of public and private sector funds have been invested in these forms of tourism over the past 20 years. A key aspect of this planning, which is recorded in almost all the studies of tourism development carried out in the last 20 years, is that planners have adopted the special interest and alternative forms of tourism as a basic tool for local tourism development. The argument is related to the specialised demand for these products as well as to the need to promote local tourist resources – an integral part of the local tourism product. In reality, it is a shifting perception of holiday tourism in a country where such resources were previously ignored or downgraded, often considered as a secondary element of a tourism product consisting of only the sea and the sun. A more systematic effort to develop these forms, especially in coastal and insular areas, is best located at the local level (through local devel-opment programmes) or at the regional level (prefectures or tourist areas).

From the 1990s, all insular prefectures and prefectures with coastal regions in Greece have offered a significant amount of infrastructure, services and organ-ised activities related to special interest and alternative tourism. The variety and the large increase of this infrastructure is evidenced in the two tourist fairs (Panorama and Philoxenia) organised in Greece each year, which mainly address the domestic tourist market.

A second element that has enhanced local tourism development has been the progressive decentralisation of competencies to the local level (to the local authorities, prefectures and regions) that has allowed for the direct involvement of representatives of local interests in decision-making processes (Hatzinik-olaou, 1995; Varvaressos, 1999). Institutionally, the upgrading of the role of local authorities has facilitated this process. The municipalities and prefectures now have more competencies in planning, programme development and the management and promotion of local tourism product.

As a result, the number of representatives of professional and institutional bodies involved in local tourism development has increased considerably in the 1990s. Another feature of that decade has been the large increase in the number of institutions dealing with the protection of the environment or the promotion of the cultural heritage in tourist regions all over Greece. These institutions have been established through the activities of locals – mainly young representatives of the local authorities and scientists – who are interested in upgrading the tourism product offered by their region, or they represent the supra-local organi-sations that deal with the protection of flora, fauna and the cultural heritage, such as WWF, MOM and ICOMOS. In both cases, the presence and interventions of these institutions constitute a new feature of the Greek reality, particularly in regions with 'sensitive' environmental resources.

A third axis for interventions and policies that have strengthened local tourism development has come from the European Union (Sotiriadis, 1994; Tsartas, 1998a). Since 1985 there have been a considerable number of initiatives, funding schemes and development programmes financed by the European Union that have focused on local tourism development or on facilitating the completion of infrastructure and activities required for special interest and alternative tourism, such as ecotourism, agrotourism and cultural tourism. Different institutions and organisations have promoted these policies from the European Union, and a large number of different institutions have implemented them at national and regional levels in Greece, and this makes their complete and systematic assessment a very difficult task. It is suggested that their contribution has been very positive for many sectors and activities, and that they have been directly or indirectly related to local tourism development.

A first advantage of these developments has been the transfer of know-how in planning and the realising of local development programmes in the countryside. Much progress has been made through collaborations and the completion of programmes for the upgrading of the countryside, such as through Leader, Life, Envireg and Interreg. Another positive effect was the implementation of training and education activities for employed and unemployed people in occupations related to tourism (and particularly with alternative forms of tourism). In many tourist regions of the country the beneficiaries of these programmes have been primarily young people and women. Such activities were financed by the European Social Fund or by specialised programmes (e.g. Leonardo) and initiatives (NOW, Youthstart, etc.). A third advantage has been the financing of completed local development projects that emphasised the protection of the cultural heritage and the environment, maintaining employment, developing the countryside and promoting balanced tourism development. These projects were undertaken by ministries involved in development and planning issues and by local authorities (municipalities and prefectures). As a result of the above, new infrastructure were created and new services were offered, thus shaping 'new' tourist products, such as ecotourism, health tourism, rural tourism, marine tourism and sports tourism.

All of these policies and actions that have contributed to the emergence of a new type of tourism development in coastal and insular regions of the country have made people realise that new models of viable and integrated tourism development should be sought. These models should play a part in the protection of the natural, the built and the cultural environment of these regions.

## From the protection of the environment to sustainable development

Among all of the different consequences of tourism in insular and coastal areas, the most important for the quality of the tourist product offered is the environment (both natural and man-made). This is primarily explained by the special characteristics of the traditional development model adopted by these areas: tourism both takes up space and downgrades the environment as it consumes resources and it involves large numbers of visitors. As a result, many problems of pollution and aesthetic degradation become apparent in many insular and coastal areas of the country (Briassoulis, 1993; Chiotis and Coccossis, 2000; Kousis, 2000; Loukissas, 1975). This development has caused many problems in Greece because research on the motives of foreign tourists visiting the country suggests that a key parameter for their choice is the environment (see Tsartas, 1998a: 74–5, Table 20, calculations based on EOT data for the 1977–1994 period). Furthermore, the negative effects on the environment have been one of the basic reasons for the forming of organised movements in tourist areas (analysed in the case of Crete by Kousis, 2000). These negative consequences of tourism development, and the policies adopted for the protection of the environment, have pointed to two significant issues for tourism development policy at the local level. The first is the need to protect the environment through specific actions and policies undertaken by both the private and the public sectors. The second is the need to promote soft and environment-friendly tourism infrastructure and activities, such as those of alternative tourism.

As regards the protection of the environment, we should note that there has been substantial investment in the construction of waste treatment networks in Greece's coastal and insular areas, while their use has now been extended to the hotel sector. At the same time, the number of enterprises using quality management standards has increased, and these standards are also related to environmental management and protection. A characteristic example is the Grecotel chain (Middleton & Hawkins, 1998: 155–60) which uses a structured programme of environmental management and protection in its hotels. Apart from the implementation of environmental quality standards, this chain also promotes the training of both its employees and tourists, together with the promotion of local cultural heritage.

Alternative tourism has been considered the opponent of the dominant mass tourism model and, at the same time, a kind of energetic protection of the environment. Its demand, from both foreigners and Greeks (Tsartas *et al.*, 2001), has increased over the years, as stressed previously here, and it is not by chance that it is proposed as a development model in areas with special environmental resources that need to be protected. Skopelos and Naxos offer two characteristic examples. After studies have been completed, it was proposed that different infrastructure and activities of alternative tourism should be developed based on ecotourism, such as trekking trails, birdwatching, ecotourism information centres, environmental training seminars and programmes for the management of specific areas (Vlami & Zogaris, 1997; Zogaris *et al.*, 1996).

From the 1990s, the crucial issue for tourism policy in Greece – directly linked to the need to protect the environment – was the effort to promote policies and actions aiming at sustainable tourism development (Andriotis, 2001; Coccossis & Tsartas, 2001; Pridham, 1999). During this period, the international scientific debate has been centred on sustainability (Bramwell & Lane, 1999; Hunter, 1997), and this issue has become a constant parameter of tourism development policies suggested by such organisations as the WTO and EU (Ruzza, 2001; WTO, 1993). In the same period, the insular and coastal areas in Greece have been a constant reference point in research and analyses carried out on the issue of sustainable development. The most important policy issues that arise concern the selection of appropriate scientific tools and methods in order to control the course of tourism development and to form a framework for its management, so that it could be sustainable. In this context, the carrying capacity of islands and coastal areas with different features and different levels of development has constituted a field for important scientific research in Greece (Coccossis & Parpairis, 1993, 1996, 2000). On the basis of specific examples, the limits of tourism development were assessed and actions and policies necessary to achieve its sustainability were pointed out. A second issue is related to the promotion of appropriate policy measures (for the private sector, the public sector and local authorities) at the local level, so that a tourist area could gradually acquire and maintain sustainable characteristics. Many studies have been carried out in this context, mainly in insular areas (Buhalis, 1999; Butler & Stiakaki, 2000; Spilanis, 2000; Stott 1996) with considerable tourism development. These studies have demonstrated the problems and also suggested solutions, especially in relation to planning, education, the institutional framework, and appropriate policy measures.

The basic parameters in these analyses in the context of sustainable tourism development is the protection of the environment (through a specific institutional framework), the promotion of local culture, the local dimension in planning, and finally, the linkage of tourism development with other production sectors of the economy.

## Conclusions

The considerable cultural, social and environmental impact of tourism in insular and coastal areas has led to changes in two key areas: changes of a social nature (social changes in tourist regions) and changes of an institutional nature (priorities and choices of tourism policies). The 1980s were a crucial decade for Greece because it was then that a stable and dynamic questioning of the dominant tourism development model was registered. Tourism policy now searches for softer and locally integrated models of tourism development. The need to protect the environment, the gradual expansion of alternative tourism and the promotion of 'locality' in planning constitute basic priorities of tourism policy. At a social level, these policies, in combination with the scientific dialogue concerning the repercussions of tourism, have helped the local people to realise that they should promote new models of tourism development. However, the powerful presence of mass organised tourism often functions as an obstacle to these efforts at the local level. The increase in the number of successful local examples of sustainable tourism development in insular and coastal areas constitutes a positive development, and is attributable to the combined effect of institutional changes, scientific debate and social changes at the local level in tourist regions. Two crucial tourism policy issues will arise in the years to come: (1) the ability of a sustainable development model to survive, constituting a basic element of the local tourist product; and (2) the operational linkage between this model and the classic model of mass tourism found in many areas.

## Correspondence

Any correspondence should be directed to Associate Professor Paris Tsartas, Business Administration Department, University of the Aegean, Michalon 8, 82100 Chios, Greece (ptsar@aegean.gr).

## Notes

1. *EKKE*: the National Centre of Social Research.
2. 'A *kamaki* is a harpoon for spearing fish, but the word is also used metaphorically in Greece. It describes the act of a Greek man pursuing a foreign woman with the intention of having sex' (see Zinovieff, 1991: 203).

## References

Andriotis, K. (2001) Tourism planning and development in Crete: Recent tourism policies and their efficacy. *Journal of Sustainable Tourism* 9 (4), 298–316.

Anthopoulou, T., Iakovidou, O., Koutsouris, A. and Spilanis, G. (1998) Spatial and developmental dimensions of agrotourism in Greece [in Greek]. Paper presented at the Fifth Panhellenic Congress of Agricultural Economy, Thessaloniki.

Arthur Andersen (2002) *Consultative Study Relative to the Formation of Strategies for the Development of Greek Tourism* [in Greek]. Athens: SETE.

Athanasiou, L. (2002) *Congress Tourism in Greece: Evolution, Problems, Potentials and Policy* [in Greek]. Athens: ITEP.

Bidgianis, K. (1979) The effects of the Carras company intervention in South Sithonia [in Greek]. *Economy and Society* 7, 25–35.

Bramwell, B. and Lane, B. (1999) Sustainable tourism: Contributing to the debates. *Journal of Sustainable Tourism* 7 (1), 1–5.

Briassoulis, H. (1993) Tourism in Greece. In X. Pompl and P. Lavery (eds) *Tourism in Europe: Structures and Developments* (pp. 285–301). Oxford: CAB International.

Buhalis, D. (1998) Tourism in Greece: Strategic analysis and challenges for the new millennium. *Centre International de Recherches et d'Etudes Touristiques* 18, 1–48.

Buhalis, D. (1999) Tourism on the Greek islands: Issues of peripherality, competitiveness and development. *International Journal of Tourism Research* 1, 341–58.

Butler, R. and Stiakaki, E. (2000) Tourism and sustainability in the Mediterranean: Issues and implications from Hydra. In D. Ioannidis, Y. Apostolopoulos and S. Sommez (eds) *Mediterranean Islands and Sustainable Tourism Development Practices, Management and Policies* (pp. 282–9). London: Continuum.

Chiotis, G. and Coccossis, H. (2000) Tourism development and environmental protection in Greece. In H. Briassoulis and J.V. der Straaten (eds) *Tourism and the Environment: Regional, Economic, Cultural and Policy Issues* (pp. 331–44). Dordrecht: Kluwer Academic.

Coccossis, H.N. and Parpairis, A. (1993) Environment and tourism issues: Preservation of local identity and growth management: Case study of Mykonos. In D. Konsola (ed.) *Culture, Environment and Regional Development* (pp. 79–100). Athens: Regional Development Institute.

Coccossis, H.N. and Parpairis, A. (1996) Tourism and carrying capacity in coastal areas. In G.K. Priestley and H. Coccossis (eds) *Sustainable Tourism* (pp. 153–75). Wallingford: CAB International.

Coccossis, H.N. and Parpairis, A. (2000) Tourism and the environment: Some observations on the concept of carrying capacity. In H. Briassoulis and J.V. der Straaten (eds) *Tourism and the Environment: Regional, Economic, Cultural and Policy Issues* (pp. 91–106). Dordrecht: Kluwer Academic.

Coccossis, H.N. and Tsartas, P. (2001) *Sustainable Tourism Development and the Environment* [in Greek]. Athens: KRITIKI.

Galani-Moutafi, V. (1993) Part One. From agriculture to tourism: Property, labour, gender and kinship in a Greek island village. *Journal of Modern Greek Studies* 11, 241–70.

Galani-Moutafi, V. (1994) Part Two. From agriculture to tourism: Property, labour, gender and kinship in a Greek island village. *Journal of Modern Greek Studies* 12, 113–31.

Greek Tourism Organization (1985) *Tourism '85. Development Participation, Quality of Life.* Athens: GTO.

Greenwood, D.J. (1972) Tourism as an agent of change: A Spanish Basque case, *Ethnology* 11, 80–81.

Haralambopoulos, N. and Pizam, A. (1996) Perceived impacts of tourism: The case of Samos. *Annals of Tourism Research* 23 (3), 503–26.

Hatzinikolaou, E. (1995) *Tourist Promotion at Prefecture Level – The New Institution of Prefectural Committees for Tourist Promotion* [in Greek]. Athens: EETAA.

Hunter, C. (1997) Sustainable tourism as an adaptive paradigm. *Annals of Tourism Research* 24 (4), 850–67.

Installations for Naval Tourism (2000) Athens: ICAP.

Kasimati, K., Thanopoulou, M. and Tsartas, P. (1995) *Female Employment in the Tourist*

*Sector: Investigation of the Labour Market and Prospects* [in Greek]. Athens: Social Morphology and Social Policy Centre, Pantion University, Equal Opportunities Office.

Konsolas, N. and Zacharatos, V. (2001) Regionalisation of tourism activity in Greece: Problems and policies. In H. Briassoulis and J.V. der Straaten (eds) *Tourism and the Environment: Regional, Economic, Cultural and Policy Issues* (pp. 319–30). Dordrecht: Kluwer Academic.

Kousis, M. (1989) Tourism and the family in a rural Cretan community. *Annals of Tourism Research* 16 (3), 318–32.

Koussis, M. (2000) Tourism and the environment: The local social protest in Crete. In P. Tsartas (ed.) *Tourism Development: Multidisciplinary Approaches* [in Greek]. Exantas: Athens.

Labiri-Dimaki, I. (1972) Sociological analysis. In A.S. Kalliga and A.N. Papageorgiou (eds) *Mykonos-Dilos-Rinia, Land-planning Study* [in Greek]. Athens: Governmental Policy Ministry.

Loukissas, P. (1975) Tourism and environmental conflict: The case of the Greek island of Mykonos. Paper presented at the Symposium in Tourism and Culture Change, American Anthropological Association, San Francisco, California, December.

Loukissas, P. (1982) Tourism's regional development impacts: A comparative analysis of the Greek islands. *Annals of Tourism Research*, 9, 523–43.

Middleton, V.T.C. and Hawkins, R. (1998) *Sustainable Tourism: A Marketing Perspective*. London: Butterworth-Heinemann.

Patsouratis, V. (2002) *The Competitiveness of the Greek Tourism Sector* [in Greek]. Athens: ITEP.

Pridham, G. (1999) Towards sustainable tourism in the Mediterranean? Policy and practice in Spain, Italy and Greece. *Environmental Politics* 8, 97–116.

Ruzza, C. (2001) Sustainability and tourism. In K. Eder and M. Koussis (eds) *Environmental Politics in Southern Europe*. Dordrecht: KLUWER.

SETE (2002) *Greek Tourism 2010. Strategy and Aims* [in Greek]. Athens: SETE.

Sotiriadis, M. (1994) *Tourist Policy* [in Greek]. Heraclion: TEI of Heraclion.

Spathi, S. (2000) *Curative Tourism and the Development of Health Tourism in Greece* [in Greek]. Athens: KEPE.

Spilanis, G. (2000) Tourism and regional policy: The case of the Aegean islands. In P. Tsartas(ed.) *Tourism Development: Multidisciplinary Approaches* [in Greek]. Athens: Exantas.

Stavrou, S. (1979) *Social Identification of Tourism in the Islands of Mykonos and Naxos*. Athens: Research and Development Department, Greek Tourism Organisation.

Stavrou, S. (1980) *Social Identification of Tourism in the Islands of Kalymnos and Leros*. Athens: Research and Development Department, Greek Tourism Organisation.

Stavrou, S. (1986) *Social Identification of Tourism in the Islands of Paros, Santorini and Kythira*. Athens: Research and Development Department, Greek Tourism Organisation.

Stott, A.M. (1973) Economic transition and the family in Mykonos. *Greek Review of Social Research* 17, 122–33.

Stott A.M. (1996) Tourism development and the need for community action in Mykonos, Greece. In L. Briguglio, R. Butler, D. Harrison and W.L. Fillio (eds) *Sustainable Tourism in Islands and Small States: Case Studies*. London: Pinter.

Tsartas, P. (1989) *Social and Economic Consequences of Tourism Development in the Prefecture of the Cyclades and Especially the Islands of Ios and Serifos* [in Greek]. Athens: EKKE.

Tsartas, P. (1991) *Research on the Social Characteristics of Employment, Study III, Tourism and Agricultural Multi-activity* [in Greek]. Athens: EKKE.

Tsartas, P. (1992) Socioeconomic impacts of tourism on two Greek isles. *Annals of Tourism Research* 19, 516–33.

Tsartas, P. (1998a) *La Grèce: Du Tourisme de Masse au Tourisme Alternatif*. Série Tourismes et Sociétés. Paris: L'Harmattan.

Tsartas, P. (1998b) Un cadre d'analyse des relations sociales et des caractéristiques de la rencontre touristes–autochtones: le cas de la Grèce. *Revue de Tourisme* 4, 47–55.

Tsartas, P. (ed.) (2000) *Tourism Development: Multidisciplinary Approaches* Athens, Exantas.

Tsartas, P., Theodoropoulos, K., Kalokardou-Krantonelli, R., Manologlou, E., Maroundas,

K., Pappas, P. and Fakiolas, N. (1995) *Social Impact of Tourism in the Prefectures of Corfu and Lasithi* [in Greek]. Athens: EKKE.

Tsekouras, G. and Associates (1991) *Change in the Mass Tourism Model: New Forms of Tourism* [in Greek]. Athens: ETBA.

Varvaressos, S. (1987) Le tourisme en Grèce: Problématique, étude du marche, structure du produit, impact économique, tendances futures. Unpublished PhD thesis, Paris VIII university.

Varvaressos, S. (1999) *Tourism Development and Administrative Decentralisation* [in Greek]. Athens: Propompos.

Vlami, V. and Zogaris, S. (1997) *Ecotourist Development in Skopelos: Trails and Trekking* [in Greek]. Skopelos: Municipality of Skopelos.

WTO (1993) *Sustainable Tourism Development Guide for Local Planners*, Madrid.

WWF (2000) *Planning Actions of Pilot Character to Develop Ecotourism*. Greek Tourism Organisation, Ministry of Development.

Zacharatos, G. (1989) Simple empirism, tourist policy and the time for judgment [in Greek]. *Synchrona Themata* 11 (34), 21–6.

Zacharatos, G. (2000) The required scheme and institutional framework for the conduct of tourist policy in Greece today [in Greek]. In P. Tsartas (ed.) *Tourism Development: Multidisciplinary Approaches* (pp. 39–68). Athens: Exantas.

Zinovieff, S. (1991) Hunters and hunted: Kamaki and the ambiguities of sexual predation in a Greek town. In P. Loizos and E. Papataxiarchis (eds) *Contested Identities, Gender and Kinship in Modern Greece* (pp. 203–20). Princeton, NJ: Princeton University Press.

Zogaris, S., Vlami, V. and Promponas, N. (1996) *The Naxos' Aliki Lagoon: Preparatory Study of Environmental Assessment and Management* [in Greek]. Naxos: Greek Bird Society, Agios Arsenios Community.

# 5 Tourism Growth, National Development and Regional Inequality in Turkey

*Cevat Tosun*
*School of Tourism and Hotel Management, Mustafa Kemal University, 31200 Iskenderun, Turkey*

*Dallen J. Timothy*
*Department of Recreation Management and Tourism, Arizona State University, Tempe, Arizona, USA*

*Yüksel Öztürk*
*Faculty of Trade and Tourism Education, Gazi University, Ankara, Turkey*

The introduction of international tourism as an economic growth strategy in Turkey is relatively recent, and Turkey has experienced rapid tourism growth in terms of volume and value. Despite the significant progress in these respects, tourism has contributed little to development. Instead, it has increased the rate of economic growth at the expense of equality among regions and classes. This paper examines the impacts of intensive coastal tourism growth on the development of rural regions in particular and national development in general. It concludes that spatial concentrations of mass tourism investment induced by tourism incentive policies in relatively developed coastal regions have increased disparities among regions and classes.

## Introduction

Following the Second World War, tourism became a global phenomenon that 'characterises aspects of post industrial society and presents insights into major trends for the future' (Eadington & Redman, 1991: 41). The rapid increase in tourism demand since the 1950s has led many entrepreneurs and governments in various countries to invest in the industry without careful analysis of its costs and benefits (de Kadt 1979a; Timothy, 1999; Tosun & Jenkins, 1998; Tosun & Timothy, 2001). Turkey as a developing country is not exceptional in this regard. It adopted tourism as an alternative economic development strategy to support new export-led growth strategies recommended by international agencies (e.g. the International Monetary Fund and World Bank) to create more jobs and to establish a favourable image on the international platform by exemplifying immediate implementation of an outward-oriented economic development policy, which seemed to have been essential just after the 1980 military coup (Tosun, 1998a). Though the contribution of international tourism to the economic growth of Third World economies appears to be significant, many scholars (e.g. Britton, 1982; Bryden, 1973; de Kadt, 1979b; Tosun, 1999) argue that tourism also perpetuates class and regional inequalities and stimulates economic, environmental and social problems, which have created considerable doubts about tourism being a reliable development strategy in the less-developed world. Evidence from many developing countries in the Mediterranean basin, such as the former Yugoslavia, Turkey, Egypt, Tunisia, Morocco, and Algeria, shows that tourism has been playing an important role in industrialisation and

**Figure 1** Map of regions in Turkey
*Note*: The dotted line shows the coastal strip declared priority for the
concentration of both public and private investment.
*Source*: Derived from data in Duzgunoglu and Karabulut (1999)

economic growth at the cost of regional, class, and inter/intra-generation
equality since the 1970s (Allcock, 1986; Lea, 1988; Poirier, 2001; Tosun, 2001; Var
& Imam, 2001). In this context, Göymen (2000: 1030) contends that 'a pronounced
spatial dichotomy has evolved in Turkish tourism between a privileged space
along the coast and an underprivileged space in the interior of the country'. This
has further increased gaps between the developed and underdeveloped regions
of Turkey. Although tourism development taking place in the more developed
regions has made a considerable contribution to the country's gross national
product (GNP), it has also magnified the developmental problems of Turkey by
inducing regional and class inequities. Seckelmann (2002: 91) recognises that
'currently, the tourism business is focused on the coastal areas of the Mediterranean and the Aegean Sea and so contributes to the further development of those
regions in the western part of the country, which in a national sense already
possess a higher socio-economic status when compared to the east of Turkey'.

It should be noted that the authors do not claim that tourism alone is responsible for increasing inequities between the regions of Turkey. In fact, the way in
which tourism development was encouraged via fiscal and monetary instruments, and the forms of tourism supported by international tour operators, have
widened regional disparities in the country. Clearly, there are many regions in
Turkey that have their own characters, resource endowments, and potential for
tourism development. For example, the industry has not grown in some regions,
including the Black Sea area in the north, and southeast and east Anatolia, which
are relatively less developed and do not have the endowments to satisfy sun, sea,
and sand-driven mass tourism demand (see Figure 1). In these less-developed
areas tourism has not heretofore been a policy for achieving development. The
wealthier coastal regions endowed with amenities required to satisfy the

demands of mass tourism induced by international tour operators have stimulated successive Turkish governments to give preferential treatment to these regions for tourism development without considering its long-term effects on geographical disparities and overall development. Thus, tourism by itself is not the culprit in worsening regional development gaps, with other influences including the tourism policies of successive governments, cultural and natural resource distribution, and political unrest and terrorist activities of the Kurdish Workers Party (*PKK*) in the east and southeast regions.

It is obvious that tourism contributes to the GNPs of nations, and development requires a higher GNP and faster growth rate. The fundamental issue, however, is not solely how to increase GNP but also what stakeholders contribute to it. If a country's GNP grows because of investment by the rich in sectors such as tourism in relatively developed regions, it is most likely to be appropriated by them, and poverty and regional inequality become more of a problem.

> Thus many developing countries that had experienced relatively high rates of economic growth by historical standards began to realise that such growth had brought little in the way of significant benefits to their poor . . . The distribution of incomes seemed to become less equitable with each passing year. Many people felt that rapid economic growth had failed to eliminate or even reduce widespread absolute poverty. (Todaro, 1989: 132)

For years it was thought that improving the GNP would eliminate poverty and unbalanced regional development, but past experience around the world showed that the reverse is often true. Poverty and regional inequality must first be addressed, which in turn will positively affect the GNP (Haq, 1971).

Politicians and media in many developing countries have widely misused the concept of development. Furthermore, they have equated the economic growth induced by tourism and other sectors of the economy with overall national development. This is a faulty assumption because development and economic growth are two related, but distinct, phenomena. In this regard, the main objective of this paper is to examine the degree to which tourism has contributed to a balance in regional development and Turkey's overall development and economic growth in general. Moreover, the contribution of tourism to developing coastal regions, their rural hinterlands and interior regions, is analysed. It is helpful to explain what development and economic growth mean at the outset since there seems to be some degree of confusion regarding these concepts. On the other hand, it should be noted that it might not be possible to find evidence to support entirely every contention about tourism growth and national development owing to formidable difficulties in obtaining information from public and private sources. Likewise, there is a general lack of written material about developmental issues in many developing countries where almost every kind of information is treated confidentially. Therefore, some parts of this paper draw on the authors' observation and first-hand knowledge. Following a review of development concepts and the contribution of tourism to the Turkish economy, the paper considers the spatial concentration of tourism in coastal areas and its impacts on regional inequality. A major conclusion is that while Turkey has been successful in developing resort areas and attracting large numbers of tourists, it has been less successful in using tourism to stimulate development in poorer regions. Consequently, tourism growth has worsened regional inequalities in Turkey,a country whose 'political and bureaucratic elite has the genuine developmental determination and autonomous capacity to define, pursue and implement developmental goals' (Leftwich, 1995: 437). The issue of political stability is also considered as a deterrent to regional equality in development, and the reasons for this are considered.

## The Nature of Development

Most scholars concur that the concepts of growth and development are mistakenly used interchangeably (Nafziger, 1990; Sharpley & Telfer, 2002; Todaro, 1989). Politicians tend to equate economic growth and development. Although economic growth rate is a convenient indicator for politicians to use as a single comprehensive measure (Seers, 1979), and economic growth might seem like development in the early stages, development and growth have two distinct meanings.

'Most economists would accept that economic growth is a rise in real national income, i.e. a rise in money income deflated by index of prices' (Thirlwall, 1978: 23). It also refers to an increase in average per capita income, and more output (Herrick & Kindleberger, 1983; Nafziger, 1990). Economic growth is thus defined as the sustained growth rate in national income and in per capita income. The rate of growth can be censured in that it fails to account for non-marketed production, although it does take into account income distribution and poverty. Besides this, deficiencies in national accounting systems and statistical manipulation in the calculation of GNP are also weak points in the defence that economic growth is a suitable measure of development (Hicks & Streeten, 1995).

As the term development is usually used, it describes the stages of economic and social transformation within countries (Thirlwall, 1989). Todaro (1989: 89) suggests a more complex meaning for development in national contexts:

> Development must be conceived of as a multidimensional process involving major change in social structures, popular attitudes, and national institutions, as well as the acceleration of economic growth, the reduction of inequality, and the eradication of absolute poverty. Development in its essence, must represent the whole gamut of change by which an entire social system, tuned to the diverse basic needs and desires of individuals and social groups within that system, moves away from a condition of life widely perceived as unsatisfactory and toward a situation or condition of life regarded as materially and spiritually better.

Thus, development is demonstrably inter-disciplinary in character. Economics, sociology, anthropology, and political science have all contributed to the framing of a body of related propositions about what happens to a society in the process of development and modernisation (Anderson, 1967). On the other hand, there is also confusion between modernisation and development. It should be noted that modernisation is both a main part, and result, of development. Goulet (1971: 96) points out that 'development is simply one particular form of change, modernisation is a special case of development, and industrialisation is a simple facet of development'. As recognised, modernisation, industrialisation and development are not one and the same. All are interdependent as components of the process of social, economic, cultural and political change in a society, and they do indicate different angles of change from different vantage points. It might be that a country is industrialised, but not necessarily developed and/or modernised.

Despite high growth rates in GNP or GNP per capita in some developing countries, poverty, inequality and unemployment have not been eradicated (Hicks & Streeten, 1995; Ladens, 1995; Seers, 1979; Todaro, 1989). In this context, the contribution of tourism to a nation's GNP may not be interpreted as a contribution to development without examining how the benefits of tourism are distributed among various interest groups and regions. However, according to some economists, inequality is inevitable in the early stage of economic growth (Hunt, 1989). Therefore, development has been argued in the sense of a basic needs approach. Economic growth and the creation of more and better jobs for a few people are not enough; the goals of development should include satisfying the basic needs of everyone in a country. The International Labour Organisation (1976) determined the following as basic human needs: adequate nutrition, shelter, clothing, clean water, sanitation, healthcare, basic education, public transport, household equipment and furniture. Singh (1979) contends that the basic needs approach to development and industrialisation are not obstacles to each other. On the contrary, they have a close interdependent relationship and indeed, they are indispensable to each other. Increasing the rate of growth is a prerequisite to satisfying the basic needs of everyone in the developing world.

Moreover, the Overseas Development Council (ODC) has assessed life expectancy, infant mortality and literacy as indicators of development, which constitute the so-called Physical Quality of Life Index (PQLI) (Wilford, 1979). In addition to the components of a good quality of life and PQLI, other indicators of development can be listed the level of nutrition measured by calorie supply per head, the consumption of energy, quantity of iron and steel produced per head, urbanisation, television and telephone ownership, the share of service sector output in the GNP, school enrolments, numbers of newspapers sold, and so on.

As the above discussion reveals, there are several dimensions of development or underdevelopment, but 'there can be no fixed and final definition of development, only suggestions of what development should imply in particular contexts' (Hettne, 1993: 2). However, it may be useful to offer the following list as basic principles of development to function as guidelines for this study:

- meeting the basic needs of poor people (Seers, 1979; Stewart, 1985);
- making an effort to increase the socio-economic welfare of a society (Bartelmus, 1986);
- reducing spatial inequalities and relative poverty, and eradicating absolute poverty (Todaro, 1989: 89);
- creating all necessary conditions that will lead people to gain self-esteem and to feel free from the three malignancies of want, ignorance, and squalor (Goulet, 1971; Thirwall, 1989), in other words, to help people be 'free or emancipated from alienating material conditions of life and from social servitude to nature, ignorance, other people, misery, institution, and dogmatic beliefs' (Todaro, 1989: 90);

- the acceleration of economic growth is essential (Seers, 1979; Todaro, 1989), but it alone may not be sufficient to achieve development (de Kadt, 1979a).

The contribution of tourism to a country's development should be considered within the scope of the principles of development described above. This is important for making a realistic assessment rather than looking only at tourist receipts, employment in the tourism sector, and the percentage of tourism receipts in total export earnings and in the GDP.

## Contribution of Tourism to the Turkish Economy

Statistical data indicate that there has been a rapid growth in Turkish tourism in volume and value since 1982. As Table 1 shows, tourist arrivals were measured at 200,000 in 1963 and 1,341,500 in 1973, which is a 570% increase in a ten-year period. Between 1974 and 1984, international tourist arrivals increased by 90%. International arrivals accelerated between 1984 and 1994 by 206%, and in 2001 11,619,909 foreigners visited Turkey, an increase of 11% from the previous year. Similar growth trends have also been observed in bed capacity and tourism revenues. Tourism revenues were US$7.7 million in 1963. For 2001, this figure was estimated to be some US$8.1 billion. Bed capacity and number of lodging establishments were 28,354 and 292 respectively in 1970, and these reached 331,023 and 1911 respectively in 2000. In brief, it is clear that Turkey has experienced a rapid growth in international tourist arrivals, revenues, and bed capacity (Ministry of Tourism, 1993, 2001b).

It is not easy to measure the full economic and developmental impacts of tourism because the various components of the industry on both the supply and demand sides are closely linked to other segments of the economy. Furthermore, there is no reliable method to assess the economic contribution to a given economy (Fletcher, 1989; Tosun, 1999). Moreover, while there are some data regarding the benefits of tourism by region, there appear to be no data about how the benefits of tourism are distributed among interest groups. However, related statistical figures have facilitated an examination of the importance of international inbound tourism as a source of foreign currency earnings, as an employment generator, and as a revenue source for GNP. In brief, while it is possible to evaluate the contributions of tourism to a national economy, it is difficult to measure its contribution to overall development, including eradication of poverty, inequalities among classes, and satisfying basic needs of the economically disadvantaged groups. In the following sections, these issues will be examined with special reference to Turkey as a developing country.

### Tourism as an invisible export in the Turkish economy

A negative balance of payments has long been a chronic problem for the Turkish economy (OECD, 2001; SPO, 2002; Tosun, 1999). This suggests that Turkey badly needs foreign currency to reduce the deficits on the current account, to finance the imports that are necessary for economic and social development, as well as to help repay the outstanding national debt. With this knowledge, a cabinet-level body (the Ministry of Culture and Tourism, later changed to the Ministry of Tourism) was established to handle all tourism development issues, but few rights were afforded to local government and local

**Table 1** Tourist arrivals and receipts in Turkey, 1970–2001

| Years | Number of arrivals ('000) | Receipts (million $US) | Years | Number of establishments | Number of beds |
|---|---|---|---|---|---|
| 1963 | 200.0 | 7.7 | 1970 | 292 | 28,354 |
| 1970 | 724.2 | 51.6 | 1973 | 337 | 38,528 |
| 1973 | 1,341.5 | 171.5 | 1974 | 400 | 40,895 |
| 1974 | 1,110.2 | 193.7 | 1975 | 421 | 44,957 |
| 1975 | 1,540.9 | 200.9 | 1982 | 569 | 62,372 |
| 1982 | 1,391.7 | 370.3 | 1983 | 611 | 65,934 |
| 1983 | 1,625.7 | 411.1 | 1984 | 642 | 68,266 |
| 1984 | 2,117.0 | 840.0 | 1985 | 689 | 85,995 |
| 1990 | 5,389.3 | 3,225.0 | 1987 | 834 | 106,214 |
| 1994 | 8,000.0 | 4,700.0 | 1989 | 1102 | 146,086 |
| 1997 | 9,689.0 | 7,000.0 | 1990 | 1260 | 173,227 |
| 1998 | 9,752.0 | 8,300.0 | 1991 | 1404 | 200,678 |
| 1999 | 7,487.0 | 5,203.0 | 1992 | 1498 | 219,940 |
| 2000 | 10,428.0 | 7,636.0 | 2000 | 1911 | 331,023 |
| 2001 | 11,619.9 | 8,090.0 | 2001 | 1673 | 303,211 |

*Sources*: Devlet Planlama Teskilati (2002); Ministry of Tourism (1993, 2001a, 2001b)

communities (see Tosun, 1998a; Tosun & Timothy, 2001). For some time, foreign currency earnings from tourism have been seen as part of a panacea for some of the problems plaguing the Turkish economy. When tourism receipts were compared to export commodities, they ranked second only to manufactured goods, being more than the value of any other export commodity between 1994 and 2000 (Table 2).

Remittances from workers abroad and foreign investments are other contributions to currency flows in the Turkish economy and to the balance of payments. Comparing international tourism receipts to these two items may indicate more clearly the importance of tourism as a source of foreign exchange. Table 3 shows that international tourism receipts are more important to the balance of payments and the economy than workers' remittances and foreign direct investment. In other words, the average ratio of tourism receipts to worker remittances and direct foreign investment were 1.6 and 2.8 respectively between 1990 and 2001. Thus, the importance of tourism is clear (see Table 3).

Tourism's share of export earnings is a viable yardstick to illustrate the place of tourism as a source of foreign currency earnings in an economy. As Table 4 illustrates, the share of tourism receipts in the export economy of Turkey has gradually increased; while it was 5.6% in 1984, it reached 14.7% in 1995 and 27.78% in 2000. As Sezer and Harrison (1994) note, Turkey's international

**Table 2** Exports by commodities and tourism receipts (millions $US), 1994–2000

|  | *1994* | *1996* | *1997* | *2000* |
|---|---|---|---|---|
| Agriculture and forestry | 2,301.4 | 2,454.7 | 2,679.1 | 1,965.4 |
| Fishing | 22.2 | 26.5 | 33.2 | 24.2 |
| Mining and quarrying | 263.0 | 227.6 | 404.8 | 400.0 |
| Manufacturing | 15,517.8 | 20,237.1 | 23,115.9 | 24,058.7 |
| Electricity, gas and water supply | 1.1 | 15.5 | 11.2 | 20.4 |
| Other business activities | 0.0 | 262.2 | 1.0 | 0.4 |
| Social and personal activities | 0.4 | 1.0 | 0.4 | 16.2 |
| Total | 18,105.9 | 23,224.5 | 26,244.7 | 27,485.4 |
| Tourism receipts | 4,616.6 | 5,962.0 | 7,000.0 | 10,428.0 |

*Source*: Compiled from SPO (2001)

tourism receipts increased more rapidly than those of most of the other major destination countries.

Tables 1–4 illustrate that international tourist spending is one of the few alternative sources of foreign exchange earnings in Turkey. In fact, after manufactured goods, tourism is the second most important source of foreign currency earnings, but it is still not at a satisfactory level compared to other competing Mediterranean countries (Tosun, 1999).

## The contribution of international tourist receipts to the GDP

It is difficult to assess the contribution of tourism or the specific segments of tourism to GNP since the scope of the industry is not well defined and there is a serious lack of data. In this sense, therefore, the share of tourism's goods and services in the GNP may be difficult to use to illustrate the importance of tourism in the economy. But the share of international tourism receipts in the gross domestic product (GDP) may be used as an additional measure to illustrate the place of international tourism in an economy. The share of international tourism

**Table 3** Tourism receipts and capital movement in Turkey (millions of $US), 1990–2001

|  | *1990* | *1992* | *1995* | *1996* | *1997* | *1998* | *2000* | *2001* |
|---|---|---|---|---|---|---|---|---|
| (a) Tourism receipts | 3308 | 3640 | 4957 | 5650 | 7000 | 8300 | 7636 | 8090 |
| (b) Workers remittance | 3325 | 3074 | 3327 | 3542 | 4229 | 5240 | 4603 | 2837 |
| (c) Foreign investment | 1784 | 1295 | 2938 | 3837 | 1678 | 1646 | 3060 | 3266 |
| a/b | 0.99 | 1.18 | 1.5 | 1.6 | 1.65 | 1.58 | 1.7 | 2.8 |
| a/c | 1.85 | 2.81 | 1.68 | 1.59 | 4.17 | 5.04 | 2.4 | 2.5 |

*Sources*: Compiled from Istanbul Chamber of Commerce (1997) and SPO (1994a, 1994b, 2002)

**Table 4** Share of tourism receipts in gross domestic product and export earnings, 1963–2000

| Years | GDP (million $US) | Export earnings (million $US) | Tourism receipts (million $US) | % share of tourism receipts in GDP | % share of tourism receipts in export earnings |
|-------|-------------------|-------------------------------|--------------------------------|-------------------------------------|------------------------------------------------|
| 1963 | 7,422.4 | 368.0 | 7.7 | 0.1 | 2.1 |
| 1965 | 8,525.1 | 464.0 | 13.8 | 0.2 | 3.0 |
| 1970 | 9,951.3 | 588.0 | 51.6 | 0.5 | 8.8 |
| 1975 | 37,598.0 | 1,401.1 | 200.9 | 0.5 | 14.3 |
| 1980 | 57,198.3 | 2,910.1 | 326.7 | 0.6 | 11.2 |
| 1985 | 52,597.6 | 7,958.0 | 1,482.0 | 2.8 | 18.6 |
| 1990 | 150,060.7 | 12,960.0 | 3,225.0 | 2.1 | 24.9 |
| 1991 | 147,367.5 | 13,593.0 | 2,654.0 | 1.8 | 19.5 |
| 1992 | 153,627.5 | 14,715.0 | 3,639.0 | 2.4 | 24.7 |
| 1995 | 170,081.0 | 21,636.0 | 4,957.0 | 2.9 | 22.9 |
| 2000 | 201,217.0 | 27,485.0 | 7,636.0 | 3.8 | 27.8 |

*Sources*: Ministry of Tourism (1993, 2001a) and SPO (1994a)

receipts in Turkey's GDP has gradually increased through the years. While it was 0.1% in 1963, it reached 2.9% in 1995 and 3.8% in 2000 (Table 4).

## Employment and tourism development

Tourism is a labour-intensive industry and therefore a major source of employment. In most OECD countries, it is among the largest sources of employment, where the sectors dependent on tourism have recorded above average growth in employment both in absolute terms and in relation to the economy as a whole (OECD, 1988, 1990, 1992). Employment creation is seen as one of tourism's most important effects in Turkey and in many other developing countries in the Mediterranean region, particularly since unemployment is a substantial socio-economic problem. Public and private interests see tourism development as a major source of jobs and have, as a result, been supportive of tourism since the 1980s.

There are varying figures for employment provided by the tourism industry in Turkey. According to a study undertaken jointly by the Turkish Ministry of Tourism (1994) and the International Labour Organisation, 75,069 jobs were directly created by licensed accommodation establishments (58,325), restaurants (5552) and travel agencies (11,192) in 1993. OECD statistical figures indicate that the number of jobs created by tourism was 147,435 in 1990, 160,747 in 1992 and 199,732 in 1995 (Table 5). The Economist Intelligence Unit (1993) suggests a figure of between 200,000 and 250,000 jobs, which would account for some 4% of total employment in the service sector.

**Table 5** Staff employed in tourism in Turkey

|   | *1995* | *1992* | *1990* |
|---|---|---|---|
| HR | 189,755 | 152,709 | 140,363 |
| V | 5,993 | 4,822 | 3,249 |
| A | 2,500 | 1,950 | 2,368 |
| O | 1,484 | 1,264 | 1,456 |

HR: staff employed in hotels and restaurants
V: staff employed in travel agencies
A: staff employed in national tourism administrations
O: staff employed in other sectors of tourist industry
*Sources*: OECD (1992, 1997)

## Tourism Growth and Regional Inequalities

Developing tourism in rural or relatively poor regions of a country may mitigate imbalances between developed and underdeveloped areas. When the tourism sector expands, new revenues flow into the economy of the destination region. As a result, jobs are created and income grows. The level of regional development through tourism generally depends on the degree of integration of the industry into the regional economy and upon the degree to which economic leakage occurs. Tourism growth may decrease the gap between developed and underdeveloped regions in a country, so that tourism may be used as a tool to promote more balanced regional development. However, tourism should not be seen as a panacea for achieving balanced regional development under every condition. Using tourism for this purpose can be difficult, especially in developing countries where the less prosperous regions often experience sociopolitical unrest and a lack of basic infrastructure. Infrastructure development usually requires heavy capital investment since most Western tourists, regardless of the economic position of the destination, require facilities and services to the standards of their own countries.

It is difficult for developing countries to use their scarce capital in their own underdeveloped regions to build infrastructure for tourism, despite the fact that this may create regional external economies for other industries in the long term. It is likely that investing capital in a developed area where infrastructure already exists will be more attractive to administrators since the benefits can be seen more quickly. Likewise, people who live in more affluent areas of developing countries usually wield more political power and can lobby more effectively for development projects.

In the Turkish context, Dinler (1998) argues that inequalities among regions and classes in a single country are rooted in historical and geographical factors and issues of political economy. Thus, to the extent that policies in any sector, such as tourism, reflect the existing socioeconomic situation, including power relations among regions and classes, the development of the sector is likely to reinforce the position of the more powerful classes and regions, confirming existing regional economic and class disparities. For example, the distribution of tourism benefits may generate shifts in the positions of some small coastal towns such as Kusadasi, Marmaris, and Altinkum (on the Aegean coast); Kas, Alanya, and Fethiye (on the Mediterranean coast); and local elites in these towns (see Figure 1). Small local business owners established the initial base of tourism development in many popular destinations and benefited from this for a short period. However, these small local investors were replaced by large foreign and non-local domestic capital owners at a later stage of tourism development, as is commonly the case in destination communities (Butler, 1980). In Urgup, Turkey, at the outset of tourism development local people opened and operated small tourism businesses. However, these locally owned small establishments were closed because of existing patron–client relationships and imperfect market conditions brought on by large-scale, non-local tourism investments that received significant fiscal support from the central Government through the Encouragement of Tourism Law No. 2634, passed by Parliament on 12 March 1982 (Tosun, 1998b).

While there were no legal limitations to prevent local people from benefiting from the Government's generous tourism incentives, there were formidable bureaucratic formalities that could not have been overcome by local people who lack the necessary education and expertise to operate a relatively large tourism establishment. Deliberate help and consultancy services should have been provided to local residents to continue and expand their traditional business operations, which were more compatible with the principles of sustainable tourism development. Unfortunately, these badly needed assistance and consultancy services were not delivered. This may be a result of corrupt party politics, prevailing political culture, and various deep socioeconomic reasons that cannot be explained in depth in this study. Consequently, local human resources have become cheap workers rather than being the main active partners and beneficiaries of a growing industry (Seckelmann, 2002; Tosun, 1998b; Yuksel *et al.*, 1999). The discussion so far may suggest that the way tourism has grown is not only increasing development gaps among regions in Turkey, it is also worsening inequalities among social classes in popular tourist destinations.

It appears that the more developed regions of Turkey have been targeted as growth machines to accelerate the rate of national economic expansion, to maximise the interests of powerful business elites and to achieve the central Government's short-term objectives. Tourism is one of the most important components of this growth machine, which has contributed to widening the gaps between regions and classes (Tosun, 2002). With the 1982 Tourism Incentives Act No. 2634, the Government determined tourism regions, tourism zones, and tourism centres. Tourism regions refer to geographic areas that are defined and declared by the Committee of Ministers with the recommendation of the Ministry of Tourism for the purpose of tourism development. Tourism zones refer to specific physical areas in the tourism regions to which a higher priority is given for tourism investments and whose location and borders are drawn by the Committee of Ministers upon the recommendation of the Ministry of Tourism. Tourism centres refer to geographical areas in the tourist regions or out of the tourism regions whose location and borders are determined by the Committee of Ministers with the recommendation of the Ministry of Tourism, and which have high potential for tourism development (Resmi Gazete, 1982: 3).

Tourism investments outside the predetermined regions, zones and centres were not allowed to benefit from the Encouragement of Tourism Law No. 2634, which provided many generous incentives, including:

- allocation of public land to investors on a long-term basis;
- provision of main infrastructure by the state;
- long-term, medium- and short-term credit lines for construction, furnishings and operations;
- preferential rates for electricity, water, and gas consumption, in priority areas and centres;
- priority for communication installation;
- permitting tourism-related companies to employ up to 20% of their total workforce with foreign personnel;
- some exemptions from customs duties;
- encouragement premiums;
- investment allowances;
- subsidising up to 40% of the total cost of tourism projects;
- exemption of tax, duties and fees for long- and medium-term investment credits;
- exemption from building construction duties;
- postponement of value added taxes (Duzgunoglu & Karabulut, 1999: 12).

According to the Encouragement of Tourism Law No. 2634, 'the criteria for establishing tourism regions, tourism zones and tourism centres are natural, historical, archaeological and socio-cultural attractiveness of geographical locations for tourists, and their potential for winter and water sports and hunting' (Resmi Gazete, 1982: 4). The logic behind the criteria for determining tourism regions, zones and centres was the ability of these locations to attract the maximum numbers of tourists, who would bring in maximum foreign currency earnings – the most critical need for an economy in crisis. The Government gave priority to large-scale tourism investment projects, which targeted mass tourism, in allocating generous monetary and other incentives to meet its short-term policy objectives. Given the economic crisis and socio-political unrest emerging from the leftist–rightist clashes which resulted in the 1980 military coup, the Government had few alternatives but to follow its short-term policy objectives to address the economic crisis and sociopolitical conflicts before it was too late.

However, most of the predetermined tourism regions, centres and zones were in already relatively developed coastal regions (see Figure 1). As the Association of Turkish Travel Agencies (*TURSAB*) noted,

> a coastal strip from Balikesir provincial border, up to the end of Antalya province which included Izmir, Kusadasi, Bodrum, Marmaris and the other popular destinations of today was declared a priority region to concentrate both public and private investments. Then tourism-oriented physical planning works were initiated by the Ministry of Tourism, in co-ordination with the Ministry of Reconstruction and Resettlement, to fill the gap between the development plans which had no spatial dimension and the implementation projects. (Duzgunoglu & Karabulut, 1999: 12)

As can be seen from Table 6, the developed regions (e.g. Marmara and the Aegean and Mediterranean coasts) received the largest share of tourism credits given by the central Government. The less-developed regions (east and south-east Anatolia) received the smallest number of tourism credits, and the smallest number of tourism investment projects (*Turkiye Kalkinma Bankasi*, 1990). In other words, while the Aegean, Marmara and Mediterranean regions, as relatively developed areas, received on average 77.8% of the tourism credits and 78.7% of the bed capacity supported by tourism incentives between 1985 and 2001, the Black Sea and Central, Southeast and East Anatolia, as less-developed areas, obtained only 22.1% of the tourism credits and attracted only 21.3% of the bed capacity developed in the same period. However, this appears to have changed since 2001. For example, while East and Southeast Anatolia received 33% and 30% respectively of the tourism credits given as tourism incentives, the Aegean and Marmara regions obtained only 3% and 1% of this credit. This may suggest that tourism has finally been recognised as an important instrument for balanced regional development.

Content analysis of the tourism development plans included in eight different Five Year Development Plans between 1963 and 1989 suggests that these plans have two main common concerns. The first was to increase the number of international tourist arrivals and the second was to increase international tourism receipts (*Devlet Planlama Teskilati*, 1963–2004; Ekinci & Dogdu, 1992: 115). Additionally, improving the superstructure of tourism (e.g. hotels, shops, and restaurants) was also one of the most important objectives of the tourism development plans between 1963 and 1989. In the early 1990s, enlarging the physical capacities of these tourism facilities has lost its priority status owing to the subsequent oversupply in the predetermined tourism regions, zones and centres of the more developed regions. Consequently, although the central Government has been successful in reaching the desired level of bed capacity, it failed to attract tourism investment to the less-developed regions, particularly in east and south-east Turkey (Table 6).

The relevant figures about Turkish tourism further support the above contention and show that tourism has developed in the more developed regions and functioned as a valuable instrument in achieving the objectives of industrialisation set by the Government and its clients. Table 7 indicates that 91% of Turkey's international tourists visited the most developed regions, and 96% of the nights spent by foreign visitors in 1997 and 2000 were in these regions. The average length of stay was also relatively larger in these developed regions when compared to the average length of stay in relatively less developed regions (i.e. central Anatolia, Eastern Anatolia and Southeast Anatolia) (see Table 7). As can also be seen from Table 8, 84% of licensed beds in tourism operations and 86% of investment in providing licensed beds in tourism establishments are in the Marmara, Aegean and Mediterranean regions – the most developed parts of Turkey.

In 1996 the more prosperous regions' share of licensed beds in tourism operations increased to 87% (Table 8). The regional distribution of tourism employment shows that most tourism employment opportunities are also located in the most developed regions (Table 9). The spatial concentration of tourism in the relatively developed western regions has stimulated labour migration from the

**Table 6** Credit given as incentives to tourism investment by region, 1985–2001 (by percentage)

| Regions | 1985 | | 1986 | | 1987 | | 1988 | | 1989 | | 1990 | | 2000 | | 2001 | | Average | |
|---|---|---|---|---|---|---|---|---|---|---|---|---|---|---|---|---|---|---|
| | a | b | a | b | a | b | a | b | a | b | a | b | a | b | a | b | a | b |
| Aegean | 13.45 | 20.15 | 14.17 | 25.18 | 41.25 | 40.41 | 27.90 | 39.74 | 43.00 | 51.34 | 25.80 | – | 93 | 82 | 3 | 4 | 32.99 | 37.50 |
| Black Sea | 0.86 | 2.29 | 4.31 | 4.72 | 2.09 | 2.16 | 0.71 | 1.04 | 2.28 | 1.72 | 4.30 | – | 3 | 6 | 12 | 7 | 3.99 | 3.56 |
| Central Anatolia | 11.88 | 9.19 | 32.05 | 12.66 | 2.93 | 5.68 | 3.39 | 7.01 | 6.53 | 7.86 | 5.70 | – | 0 | 0 | 1 | 1 | 7.94 | 6.20 |
| East Anatolia | 0.08 | – | 0.10 | 0.71 | 0.46 | 1.25 | 0.30 | 0.78 | 2.58 | 1.93 | 0.31 | – | 4 | 12 | 33 | 29 | 5.10 | 6.52 |
| Mediterranean | 64.70 | 52.49 | 35.26 | 40.47 | 42.22 | 37.50 | 35.85 | 36.91 | 35.20 | 30.05 | 43.36 | – | 0 | 0 | 20 | 30 | 33.40 | 32.48 |
| Marmara | 7.41 | 14.21 | 13.71 | 14.66 | 10.48 | 11.56 | 31.35 | 13.52 | 9.70 | 6.14 | 20.46 | – | 0 | 0 | 1 | 1 | 11.76 | 8.77 |
| Southeast Anatolia | 1.62 | 1.67 | 0.40 | 1.60 | 0.57 | 1.44 | 0.50 | 1.00 | 0.71 | 0.96 | 0.07 | – | 0 | 0 | 30 | 28 | 4.20 | 4.95 |
| Total | 100 | 100 | 100 | 100 | 100 | 100 | 100 | 100 | 100 | 100 | 100 | – | 100 | 100 | 100 | 100 | 100 | 100 |

*Note:* a = amount of credit given; b = number of beds
*Sources:* compiled from *Turkiye Kalkinma Bankasi (TKB)* (1990, 2002)

**Table 7** Number of international tourist arrivals and nights spent by region, 1997 and 2000

| Regions | 1997 | | | 2000 | | |
|---|---|---|---|---|---|---|
| | Arrivals (and %) | Nights spent (and %) | Average length of stay (nights) | Arrivals (and %) | Nights spent (and %) | Average length of stay (nights) |
| Aegean | 2,530,900 27% | 11,077,200 31% | 4.38 | 2,256,103 21.6% | 6,788,307 25% | 4.3 |
| Black Sea | 114,206 1% | 160,708 0.4% | 1.41 | 221,466 2.1% | 161,336 3% | 1.2 |
| Central Anatolia | 735,440 8% | 1,404,036 4% | 1.91 | 195,844 1.8% | 937,620 7% | 1.9 |
| Eastern Anatolia | 63,360 0.7% | 88,379 0.2% | 1.39 | 312,049 2.9% | 55,072 1% | 1.6 |
| Marmara | 3,332,782 36% | 7,175,868 20% | 2.15 | 3,670,904 35.2% | 4,419,277 18% | 2.2 |
| Mediterranean | 2,649,613 28% | 16,233,604 45% | 6.13 | 3,524,355 33.7% | 16,119,574 45% | 6.4 |
| Southeast Anatolia | 16,898 0.2% | 27,401 0.08% | 1.62 | 247,522 2.3% | 401,120 1% | 1.4 |
| Total | 9,443,199 100% | 36,167,196 100% | 2.71 | 10,428,243 100% | 28,510,906 100% | |

*Sources*: Ministry of Tourism (2001a, 2001b)

**Table 8** Regional distribution of licensed beds in tourism operations and of investment in licensed beds in tourism operations, 1991 and 1996

| Regions | Licensed beds in tourism operations (%) | | Investment in licensed beds in tourism operations (%) |
|---|---|---|---|
| | 1996 | 1991 | 1991 |
| Aegean | 31 | 28.42 | 39.88 |
| Black Sea | 1 | 2.74 | 2.74 |
| Central Anatolia | 7 | 9.83 | 5.74 |
| Eastern Anatolia | 4 | 1.50 | 2.60 |
| Marmara | 21 | 24.43 | 12.83 |
| Mediterranean | 35 | 31.76 | 33.29 |
| Southeast Anatolia | 1 | 1.30 | 2.92 |

*Sources*: Ministry of Tourism (1993, 2001b).

**Table 9** Regional distribution of tourism labour, 1993

|  | *Accommodation* | *Restaurants* | *Travel services* | *Total* | *%* |
|---|---|---|---|---|---|
| Aegean | 17,010 | 930 | 2,500 | 20,440 | 27.3 |
| Black Sea | 1,557 | 366 | 151 | 2,074 | 2.7 |
| Central Anatolia | 4,805 | 821 | 1,394 | 7,020 | 9.3 |
| East Anatolia | 510 | 56 | 32 | 598 | 0.8 |
| Marmara | 13,575 | 2,943 | 4,862 | 21,380 | 28.5 |
| Mediterranean | 20,341 | 329 | 2,213 | 22,883 | 30.5 |
| Southeast Anatolia | 525 | 108 | 41 | 674 | 0.9 |
| Total | 58,323 | 5,553 | 11,193 | 75,069 | 100 |

*Source*: Ministry of Tourism (1994)

less-developed, non-coastal areas to work during the summer in the tourism sector and return home after the tourism season. As Seckelmann (2002: 88) notes, 'employment in tourism causes a special form of labour migration with job-seeking people moving to the coast during the summer months and returning to their homes in other parts of the country or to the bigger towns in search for a job during the rest of the year'. Consequently, the underdeveloped, interior regions have become a source of cheap labour for mass tourism development in the more developed regions. The receipts of tourism are in line with the distribution of the tourist bed capacity and employment in tourism. Furthermore, to add an additional dimension, tourism development has taken place in the most developed parts of the affluent regions.

The data in Table 10 also support the arguments about the role of tourism in regional balanced development. There appears to be a positive correlation between the regions contributing most to GNP and regions with higher percentages for landing and departing charter flights, foreign arrivals, employment in tourism, bed capacity, amount of credit given to tourism investment, and number of tourism establishments. On the other hand, it should be recognised that the regional development gap is not only noticeable in relation to GNP and the noted tourism growth indicators, but also with regard to the human development index (HDI) calculated by the United Nations Development Programme (UNDP) for each province in Turkey. This index includes 'life expectancy at birth, adult literacy rate, combined first, second and third level gross enrolment ratio, and the real GDP per capita' (United Nations Development Programme, 1998: 30). A careful analysis of each province's HDI shows that the HDI decreases dramatically from the west to the east and southeast in general (see Figure 2). Based upon these figures, it may be said that the higher the level of GNP and the higher the HDI of the region, the higher the relevant tourism figures for the region will be. This may mean that the way tourism has developed has made a greater contribution to the economies of the developed regions than to the economies of the underdeveloped regions, which further highlights the problem of regional inequities.

**Table 10** Regional development factors

| Regions | GNP 1992–98 (average) (%) | GDP per capita in 1997 | HDI in 1996 | Landing and departing charter flights in 2000 (%) | Foreigners arriving in 2000 (%) | Employment in tourism in 1993 (%) |
|---|---|---|---|---|---|---|
| Aegean | 16 | 2,246,740 | 0.796 | 10 | 9 | 27 |
| Black Sea | 10 | 1,294,737 | 0.687 | 0.9 | 0.5 | 3 |
| Central Anatolia | 16 | 1,639,513 | 0.731 | 4 | 2 | 9 |
| East Anatolia | 4 | 660,216 | 0.557 | 0.04 | 5 | 0.8 |
| Marmara | 36 | 2,684,291 | 0.833 | 23 | 35 | 28 |
| Mediterranean | 12 | 1,706,976 | 0.765 | 62 | 47 | 31 |
| Southeast Anatolia | 5 | 986,350 | 0.554 | 0.2 | 2 | 0.9 |
| Total | 100 | 1,802,763 | 0.696 | 100 | 100 | 100 |

*Sources*: Compiled from Ministry of Tourism, 1994, 2001a, 2001c; State Institute of Statistics, 2000

In other words, the economic data illustrate that development and investment in the Turkish tourism sector have intensified, rather than diversified, economic disparities. Tourism has grown in the most developed regions, which supports the adage that tourism does not bring development but development may bring tourism! However, as tourism development is market driven this is not a particularly surprising outcome, especially in a country where tourism is heavily dependent on package tours and foreign tour operators (Timothy & Ioannides, 2002; Tosun, 1998b, 1999).

The Turkish experience suggests that the development of tourism can be biased towards the uneven distribution of natural and cultural resources/attractions. Given the profile of tourism demand for Turkey, it may be concluded that sun, sea, sand and human-created attractions have become dominant factors in the regional distribution of tourism development. For example, some underdeveloped areas where tourism is also relatively less developed have very high potential for cultural, winter, and rural tourism. However, the main problem is that some of these regions lack basic infrastructure and facilities to meet the European standards of comfort that Western tourists require – the protective ecological bubble of their accustomed environment (Cohen, 1972). Moreover, as Turkish tourism traditionally has been driven by one particular type of tourism associated with the proverbial sun, sea and sand (3S) characteristics, non-coastal parts of the country have been ignored in tourism development. On the other hand, one of the important factors in the concentration of tourist activity in relatively developed regions seems to be the use of air transport for travelling to Turkey. Airports of international standard were built only in large cities, most of which are along the coast. As Table 10 notes, 62% of landing and departing charter flights used airports in the Mediterranean region, 10% in the Aegean region and 23% in the Marmara region. In sum, 95% of landing and departing

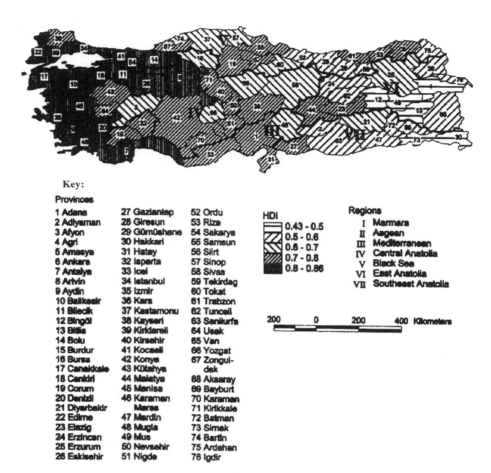

**Figure 2** The Human Development Index (HDI) in the provinces of Turkey
*Sources*: Seckelmann (2002); UNDP (1998)

charter flights used airports in the better-off coastal cities. Lack of proper air transportation infrastructure in the underdeveloped areas restricts the mobility of tourists in Turkey. This is also the case in other developing countries such as the Bahamas, Malaysia, Morocco, and Tunisia (Oppermann, 1993). Ultimately, low mobility levels of tourists within destination countries has limited the diffusion of economic benefits and increased their concentration in primary tourist destinations where the economic and political centres of the destination countries are usually located. As a result, tourism has failed to contribute to the economies of the least affluent regions of developing countries.

## Political unrest and regional tourism growth

It is not entirely known why certain localities in a country or in the world benefit more than others from tourism. As Britton (1979: 78) stated, 'the locations of markets and destinations, and the flow of people, capital, goods, and ideas are at the core of tourism' but the role of these core factors in the spatial distribution of tourism development has not been well considered. In this context, and under the assumption of the Ricardian theory of comparative advantage and the Hecksher-Ohlin factor endowments theorem, it may be argued that the western regions of Turkey have seen more growth because they are better endowed with resources needed to satisfy mass tourism demand driven by sea, sun, and sand.

While the relationship between tourism and unbalanced regional development may be partly explained by the factor endowment theorem and comparative advantage theory, it cannot be separated from the political economy of the industry and broader historical, economic, and political relationships among regions, countries, and classes. In this context, the political dimension of regional tourism development should also be considered. It is obvious that the political and social unrest ushered in by the Kurdish Workers Party's (*PKK*) violence and terror activities have discouraged local, national and international investors from investing in the east and southeast regions of Turkey. As Table 11 demonstrates, between 1987 and 2001 the *PKK* destroyed partly or completely 1884 social welfare facilities including 241 schools, 14 hospitals, 305 post offices and mosques, 500 public vehicles and construction machines, 89 law enforcement stations, 26 bridges, 624 private vehicles, and 85 train wagons. In addition to the destruction of public and private properties, the *PKK* also killed or wounded hundreds of civil servants, including teachers, physicians, governors, and mayors.

After analysing world-wide terrorist incidents, Johnson (2000: 27) stated that

> International and domestic terrorist incidents have declined since 1987 and are approaching historic lows. Since reaching a peak of 665 international terrorist attacks in 1987, incidents fell to 440 in 1995. Even this number overstates the true level of activity because almost forty percent of the attacks were carried out by one group – the Kurdish Workers Party (PKK) inflicting

**Table 11** Terror activities of the Kurdish Worker Party (PKK*), 1987–2001

| Destroyed or attacked | Number | Killed or wounded | Number |
|---|---|---|---|
| Post offices and mosques | 305 | Civilians | 9,940 |
| State vehicles and machinery | 500 | Army officers | 1,554 |
| Police and gendarme stations | 89 | Soldiers | 10,023 |
| Bridges | 26 | Mayors | 6 |
| Schools | 241 | Police and security officers | 10,584 |
| Private sector vehicles and machinery | 624 | Teachers | 141 |
| Hospitals | 14 | Neighbourhood-headmen | 81 |
| Train wagons | 85 | Other public servants | 283† |
| Total | 1,884 | Total | 32,612 |

†This includes judges, physicians, nurses, governors, etc.
*PKK has changed its name to Kurdish Freedom and Democracy Congress.
*Source*: Compiled from Eski Gundem (2002)

terror on Turkey and Turkish interests . . . Exclude the PKK and international terrorism in 1995 was at its lowest level in twenty-five years.

Almost all of *PKK*'s terror activities have occurred in East and Southeast
Anatolia. As the above quotation implies, these terrorist incidents have created
serious security problems for tourists, investors, government officials and local
residents. Therefore, it was not possible for governments in power to encourage
tourism investments by giving only financial and monetary incentives. Moreover, the *PKK*'s terror activities have not only created a disincentive for potential
investors, who could have been attracted to the region, but they have also
prevented optimum utilisation of existing resources. This is particularly true in
tourism, since tourism demand is very sensitive to sociocultural and political
unrest when tourist security is in question (Pizam & Mansfeld, 1996; Richter,
1992; Sönmez, 1998).

If there were no sociopolitical unrest in the east and southeast regions, the level
of development probably would have been higher and the contribution of
tourism to the economies of these regions would have been greater. State authorities in Turkey have recognised the importance of reducing regional disparities
and have prepared an integrated regional development project called the
South-eastern Anatolia Project (*GAP*). 'This project is an ambitious project in
terms of the geographical area it covers, its physical magnitudes and objectives
when compared with the similar other projects throughout the world' (*Turk
Tanitma Fonu*, 2002: 1). It aims to reduce disparities between the country's west
and east, which appear to be a sociocultural and political problem. Investments
by *GAP* in the region constitute 17.5% of the total investments made in Turkey,
despite the fact that the population in the southeast composes only 9% of the
country's total. Annual investment far outpaces tax revenues generated in the
region. Spending on the project, which will ultimately consist of 22 dams, 10
hydroelectric power plants and 37 irrigation systems, proceeds at US$1.7 million
daily. The agricultural and industrial potential to be created by *GAP* will increase
the level of income in the region five-fold and some 3.5 million people will find
employment opportunities, thus creating better education potential and an
overall improvement in standards of living. Moreover, the housing part of the
project includes the construction of 6795 houses in cities and the building of new
homes for villagers left homeless by *PKK* attacks. Nearly 5800 of these houses
have been completed and handed over to owners, and 2321 houses and offices
have been repaired (*Turk Tanitma Fonu*, 2002).

While regional development in the east and southeast has been negatively
affected by the terrorist attacks of the *PKK*, the Government has tried to counteract this by initiating *GAP*. In this context, it is suggested that the effect of *PKK*'s
terrorist activities on regional development and regional tourism development
should be studied on its own in detail based not only on secondary data but also
on primary data, in an effort to understand regional development gaps in
Turkey.

The Ministry of Tourism prepared a regional tourism development plan called
the *GAP* Tourism Development Plan in 1998. Its two main objectives were to
handle tourism investment effectively in the region and to develop forms of
tourism that will be compatible with local values and create jobs for local people.

The plan states that participation of local people will be supported to achieve sustainable tourism development. To achieve these objectives, the following strategies were determined:

- The forms and sources of tourism will be differentiated.
- Factors that allow long-stay holidays in the region will be improved and developed.
- Concentrated tourism development will be shifted from the western regions to the east and southeast regions.
- Foreign arrivals to the south-east region will be increased (GAP Southeast Anatolia Project, 2002).

The plan also states that alternative forms of tourism, including ecotourism, religious tourism, business travel, health-related activities, and trekking, will be particularly encouraged. It is also noted that bed capacity will be increased from 7040 to 12,820 by 2020 (*GAP* South-eastern Anatolia Project, 2002). Obviously, both *GAP* and the *GAP* Tourism Development Plan have great potential to reduce or eradicate regional disparities in Turkey. It is believed that the development level stimulated by *GAP* will attract more tourism investment and tourists to the region. However, it should be kept in mind that these developmental efforts may reduce regional disparities, but they may not be able to decrease the gaps among social classes within the region if deliberate policies and measures are not taken. Widespread patron–client relationships may continue to operate and the disadvantaged groups may not benefit from *GAP* and may get poorer in relative terms.

## Domestic tourism and regional development

Given the large population of Turkey (65 million), one may argue that domestic tourism could be a significant instrument to achieve sustainable regional development. The Ministry of Tourism (1999) conducted a study to determine the potential for, and to profile, domestic tourism demand. Based on an analysis of this survey, *TURSAB* (1999) reported that over US$ five billion was spent by domestic tourists in 1997. However, a careful evaluation of the domestic tourism demand structure suggests that 'domestic tourism is almost as concentrated in the coastal areas as foreign tourism in Turkey and further reinforces the regionally unbalanced structure' (Seckelmann, 2002: 89). As can be seen from Table 12, the vast majority of domestic tourists (66%) visited the coastal regions such as Aegean (24%), Marmara (25%) and Mediterranean (17%), and only a small percentage of them (25%) visited non-coastal regions, including Central (16%), Eastern (4%) and Southeast (5%) Anatolia. However, Table 12 suggests that most nights spent in Central (69%), Eastern (90%) and Southeastern (94.45%) Anatolia were generated by domestic, rather than foreign, tourists. Similarly, foreign visitors contributed only a small proportion to actual daily occupancy rates (e.g. 10.72 of 34.55% in the Central region; 2.94 of 29.54% in the Eastern region; and 1.67 of 30.37% in the Southeast region). These trends may suggest that Turkish authorities should consider domestic tourism demand in these regions as an important basis for tourism development.

Although domestic tourism in the less-developed regions may hold more promise than international tourism demand, domestic tourism is still too small in absolute terms. Thus, in its current state domestic tourism may not be a credible option to be used to achieve balanced regional development. However, it may be used as a supplementary boost for sustainable development in the east and southeast if necessary measures are taken to encourage domestic demand. In this context, a few policies may be recommended. First, income distribution in Turkey should be reconsidered and inequalities among classes must be reduced. The vast majority of employees work for a minimum wage of some US$115 (185 million Turkish lire) per month. This small salary must be stretched to cover a family's housing, water, power, and telephone bills and all other living expenses. While the minimum salary is as low as US$115, even a teacher earns less than US$300, which is hardly enough to satisfy basic family needs. Although there are almost no data about income distribution in Turkey, personal knowledge, participant observations and experience of the authors suggest that most households cannot afford a normal holiday using even simple accommodation facilities. Only a small percentage of Turkish families can afford to have holidays by Western standards. While the wealthy elites desire to vacation abroad or in coastal regions visited by foreigners, travel is not a realistic priority for the masses, because their primary concern is to satisfy their basic needs (i.e. education, food, and housing). In brief, unless new wealth distribution, social welfare and social security policies are implemented (see OECD, 2001), the potential for domestic tourism may never be realised in Turkey.

Second, credit with low interest rates should be given for the purpose of travelling to induce Turkish people to go on holiday in the east and southeast regions. *TURSAB* (2000) has already persuaded the Government and banks to open access to loans for holiday purposes. However, the efficiency of this holiday credit policy appears to depend upon sociocultural, political and economic factors. For example, the current economic crisis and political uncertainty have increased rates of inflation, interest and foreign exchange, which have been detrimental to the banking industry and made this notion difficult to explore. As Dymond (2002) reports

> Turkey's political and economic elite is so fearful of what the future might hold that it is praying that the dying 77-year-old Prime Minister, Bulent Ecevit, can somehow hold on . . . The financial markets shuddered . . . Turkey is now the International Monetary Fund's biggest single debtor . . . the Turkish lira has lost more than 20 per cent of its value since the Prime Minister's illness began (there are almost 2.5 million lire to the pound); interest rates have climbed by 15 per cent.

In brief, it is a fact that the potential domestic demand for tourism is a great opportunity for Turkey to achieve a more balanced regional development and increase bargaining power against international tour operators. Tosun (1999: 244) notes that 'domestic tourism may be utilised as a marketing tactic to overcome a possible crisis due to a possible loss of mass tourism demand for Turkey from Western tourist generating countries'. However, the success of this policy depends largely upon increasing purchasing power of the middle class, which includes the educated poor (e.g. teachers, nurses, physicians, university lecturers, etc.), which is not an objective of oligopolistic Turkish politicians. As reported, 'The contempt for the politicians of all colours spills out . . . Something has to

**Table 12** Number of arrivals, number of nights, average length of stay, and bed occupancy rates by region, 2000

| Regions | Number of arrivals (and % of national total) | | | Number of nights (and % of national total) | | | Average length of stay (nights) | | | Bed occupancy rates (%) | | |
|---|---|---|---|---|---|---|---|---|---|---|---|---|
| | Foreigner | Turkish national | Total | Foreigner | Turkish national | Total | Foreigner | Turkish national | Total | Foreigner | Turkish national | Total |
| Aegean | 2,256,103 21.6% | 2,191,647 24% | 3,761,023 23% | 6,788,307 24% | 4,361,648 26% | 11,149,955 25% | 4.3 | 2.0 | 3.0 | 18.55 | 11.92 | 30.47 |
| Black Sea | 221,466 2.1% | 771,608 9% | 902,646 6% | 161,336 0.6% | 1,060,836 7% | 1,222,172 3% | 1.2 | 1.4 | 1.4 | 4.40 | 28.92 | 33.32 |
| Central Anatolia | 195,844 1.8% | 1,409,820 16% | 1,902,585 12% | 937,620 3% | 2,084,550 13% | 3,022,170 7% | 1.9 | 1.5 | 1.6 | 10.72 | 23.83 | 34.55 |
| East Anatolia | 312,049 2.9% | 346,079 4% | 380,947 2% | 55,072 0.2% | 497,682 3% | 552,754 1% | 1.6 | 1.4 | 1.5 | 2.94 | 26.60 | 29.54 |
| Marmara | 3,670,904 35.2% | 2,218,813 25% | 4,236,432 27% | 4,419,277 16% | 3,802,003 23% | 8,221,280 18% | 2.2 | 1.7 | 1.9 | 18.10 | 15.57 | 33.68 |
| Mediterranean | 3,524,355 33.7% | 1,516,815 17% | 4,054,613 26% | 16,119,574 57% | 4,159,065 25% | 20,278,639 45% | 6.4 | 2.7 | 5.0 | 35.74 | 9.22 | 44.96 |
| Southeast Anatolia | 247,522 2.3% | 401,120 5% | 421,732 3% | 29,720 0.1% | 509,915 3% | 539,635 1% | 1.4 | 1.3 | 1.3 | 1.67 | 28.70 | 30.37 |
| Total | 10,428,243 100% | 8,855,902 100% | 15,659,978 100% | 28,510,906 100% | 15,981,699 100% | 44,986,605 100% | 19.0 | 12.0 | 15.7 | 92.12 | 144.76 | 236.89 |

*Source:* Authors' calculation based upon Ministry of Tourism (2001a; 2001b)

change in the way that politicians affect the economy . . . The politicians do not want to deal with the problems of Turkey. They just want to earn money' (Dymond, 2002). Clearly, Turkey needs a developmental state whose political and bureaucratic elites have a deliberate intention to implement the principles of development stated at the outset of this paper to achieve the goals of development. Without this kind of administration it may not be possible for the masses of the poor to become domestic tourists.

## Conclusions

This study has investigated and discussed the impact of tourism on development balance with special reference to Turkey. Several broad conclusions can be drawn from the discussion that may strengthen some of the points made, function as policy implications for tourism development in Turkey, and provide a summary of this study. First, it is obvious that tourism holds an important place in the Turkish economy. The central Government has accepted and designed tourism to be an important tool for generating badly needed foreign currency earnings and employment. Moreover, it appears to be an economic and political choice for Turkey to use tourism as an instrument for economic growth with the goal of industrialisation and creating a means for international relations without necessarily achieving overall development, including regional balance, equality among classes, and eradication of poverty in the medium term.

Turkey adopted tourism not only as an alternative economic growth strategy, but also as a tool for social change to encourage Europeanization and as an international political strategy to create a favourable image in the eyes of European people. This is supposed to help acceptance of the country for full membership in the European Union. (Tosun & Jenkins, 1996: 519)

This may suggest that the current level, forms, and spatial distribution of tourism development are not a result of pure economic development policies. In this context, it may be argued that the determination of tourism regions, zones, and centres, and the allocation of tourism incentives to predetermined tourism areas reflect, in some senses, the political concerns of central Government. These appear to be myopic and ignorant of many fundamental developmental issues, particularly from the perspective of balanced regional development.

Second, it should be clear that it is not easy to use tourism to achieve balanced regional development in a developing country such as Turkey for a variety of reasons. First, tourism development in Turkey and other developing countries is driven by the needs of tourists from the West. Satisfying the needs of these tourists, who visit the least developed regions of developing countries, requires a larger amount of capital investment in infrastructure and tourism superstructure to Western standards that may be beyond the financial capacity of developing countries or that may not be politically feasible. Second, tourism development in Turkey has been shaped and directed by transnational corporations, including international tour operators, which have marketed the country as a cheap tourist destination to mass tourists seeking sea, sun, and sand – amenities readily available in relatively well-developed coastal areas. It may be difficult for Turkish tourism authorities to attract foreign tourists to underdeveloped regions in non-coastal areas. Öztürk (1996: 278) argues, 'it is rather difficult to claim that the popularity of Turkey as a tourist destination is not the result of conscious and well planned marketing and promotional efforts of the Ministry of Tourism and other related organisations'. Under the given high level of market dependency of tourism development, and the badly needed foreign currency earnings, particularly in the short term, it would be difficult for Turkey to make a radical move to change its current pattern of tourism development. Hence, 'the government's role is to develop ad hoc strategies for tourism to cope with the high bargaining power of international tour operators and adjust policies to the changes caused by external factors' (Tosun, 2001: 299). That is to say, the structure of international tourism and resources to meet the needs of Western tourists are not readily available as a whole in the less developed regions. This appears to be an obstacle for Turkey using tourism as an instrument to achieve balanced regional development. Finally, by using their clientelistic relationship with decision makers, powerful business elites in developed regions may not let the Government devote large amounts of capital to improve infrastructure in the underdeveloped regions. They may not see the profitability of business operations in underdeveloped regions compared to those in the developed regions where several conditions for profitable business investments and operations exist. As a result, they do not want the authorities to use scarce capital in what appears to be non-profitable investments, at least in the short-term. Instead, they lobby to take advantage of generous fiscal and monetary incentives for their own investments in the wealthier regions to accelerate the country's industrialisation process.

Third, although political concerns of the Turkish Governments and the structure of demand for Turkey may partly explain the spatial distribution of tourism development in Turkey, concentration of tourism development on the western and southwestern coasts appears to have been influenced by the supply side of tourism as well. This could be explained within the scope of the Ricardian theory of comparative advantage and the Hecksher-Ohlin factor endowments theorem. Obviously, these coastal regions are better furnished with multitudinous resources needed for tourism, including cultural sites and natural resources. As a result, the Government and tourism operators have been quicker to develop the industry in the western part of the country than in Central, Southeast and East Anatolia and the Black Sea region.

In this context, while the country has been successful in attracting large numbers of tourists and in expanding resort areas, it has been less successful in using tourism to stimulate development in poorer regions. The western, coastal areas, where most tourism development is presently situated, were the most developed parts of Turkey even before tourism grew in the early 1980s. Thus, there are notable developmental gaps between western and eastern Turkey, which has long been a chronic socioeconomic problem. Mass tourism growth in the western provinces has reinforced the hegemony of these more prosperous regions while leaving East and Southeast Anatolia considerably further behind.

Fourth, as noted earlier, Turkey has recognised the importance of reducing regional disparities. Based on this awareness, the nation has prepared an integrated regional programme called the South-eastern Development Project (*GAP*) to address this developmental problem. In connection with the *GAP* project, tourism has been emphasised as an important instrument for improving balanced regional development. For the policy to be effective, several policy recommendations may be made. First, terror activities of the *PKK* must be stopped and long-term stability and security assured. Without establishing long-term stability it may not be possible to attract non-local capital to the region or to keep the local capital and qualified human resources there. Although the terror activities of the *PKK* seem to have reached their lowest level in 2002, there is still a lack of confidence in long-term stability and security. Second, without developing domestic tourism it may not be possible to develop international tourism in the region because of sociocultural reasons and difficulties in meeting the needs of Western tourists. Thus, domestic tourist activities in the eastern provinces should be encouraged. The authors believe that domestic tourism will allow the less affluent areas to prepare themselves for larger and more intensive tourism development in an incremental manner, which is a requisite for sustainable tourism development (Timothy, 1998; Tosun, 2001; Tosun & Jenkins, 1996). In addition, the following deliberate measures should be taken: (1) local people should be educated and trained about how to operate small and medium-sized tourism establishments; (2) continuous consultancy services should be provided for tourism operators; and (3) sudden and rapid tourism development should be avoided.

As a way of achieving balanced regional development, deliberate government policies may promote alternative forms of tourism development in the less-developed regions where sun-, sea-, and sand-driven mass tourism could not be established. This is not only important for balanced regional development, it will also be useful for decreasing some of the negative impacts that occur in the spatially concentrated mass tourist destinations on the coast.

Finally, the concentration of tourism in the more prosperous coastal regions may reflect not only the structure of international demand for the Turkish tourism product, but it may also mirror a constant interaction of the tourism development process with political, social, and economic components of the state. However, for a better understanding of the contribution of tourism to economic growth and overall development in the developing world, comparative cross-national studies and analyses are recommended. The results of these studies may provide a better set of policy recommendations for using tourism as a tool to achieve more balanced regional development, eradicate absolute poverty, reduce relative poverty, meet the basic needs of the poor, and help hitherto excluded people gain self-esteem, self-reliance and freedom from want, ignorance and squalor.

## Correspondence

Any correspondence should be directed to Dr Cevat Tosun, Associate Professor & Director of School of Tourism & Hotel Management, Mustafa Kemal University, Numune Mah. Dr. Sadik Ahmet Cad., 31200 Iskenderum, Hatay, Turkey (cevattosun@hotmail.com).

## References

Allcock, J.B. (1986) Yugoslavia's tourism trade: Pot of gold or pig in a poke. *Annals of Tourism Research* 14, 565–88.
Anderson, C. (1967) *Issues of Political Development*. Englewood Cliffs, NJ: Prentice-Hall.
Bartelmus, P. (1986) *Environment and Development*. Boston: Allen and Unwin.

Britton, S.G. (1982) The political economy of tourism in the Third World. *Annals of Tourism Research* 9, 331–58.

Britton, R.A. (1979) Some notes on the geography of tourism. *Canadian Geographer* 25, 276–82.

Bryden, J. (1973) *Tourism and Development: A Case Study of the Commonwealth Caribbean*. Cambridge: Cambridge University Press.

Butler, R.W. (1980) The concept of a tourism cycle of evolution. *Canadian Geographer* 24, 5–12.

Cohen, E. (1972) Towards a sociology of international tourism. *Social Research* 39, 164–82.

de Kadt, E. (1979a) Politics, planning, and control. In de Kadt, E. (ed.) *Tourism: Passport To Development?* (pp. 18–33). Oxford: Oxford University Press.

de Kadt, E. (1979b) Social planning for tourism in the developing countries. *Annals of Tourism Research* 6, 36–48.

Devlet Planlama Teskilati (1963–2004) *Bes Yillik Kalkinma Planlari*. Ankara: DPT.

Dinler, Z. (1998) *Bolgesel Iktisat*. Regional economics: Decreasing developmental gaps among regions in Turkey. Bursa, Turkey: Ekin Kitapevi Yayinlari.

Duzgunoglu, E. and Karabulut, E. (1999) *Development of Turkish Tourism: Past and Present*. Istanbul: TURSAB, Association of Turkish Travel Agencies.

Dymond, J. (2002) Sickly Turkey gives way to despair. *Observer* (30 June).

Eadington, W.R. and Redman, M. (1991) Economics and tourism. *Annals of Tourism Research* 18, 41–56.

Economist Intelligence Unit (1993) Turkey. *International Tourism Report* 3, 77–97.

Ekinci, Y. and Dogdu, A. (1992) Planli donemde Turk turizmine bakis [Turkish tourism in planned periods] (1963–1990). In *Turizm Yilligi* (pp. 115–23). Ankara: Turkiye Kalkinma Bankasi A.S.

Eski Gundem (2002) PKK Gercegi. Gunluk Siyasi Internet. On WWW at http://www.pkkgercegi.net/ sehitlerimiz.htm.

Fletcher, J.E. (1989) Input–output analysis and tourism impact studies. *Annals of Tourism Research* 16, 514–29.

GAP South-eastern Anatolia Project (2002) Bolgesel Kalkinma Idaresi Baskanligi, Ankara On WWW at http://www.gap.gov.tr or http://www.dpt.gov.tr.

Goulet, D. (1971) *The Cruel Choice: A New Concept in the Theory of Development*. New York: Atheneum.

Göymen, K. (2000) Tourism and governance in Turkey. *Annals of Tourism Research* 22, 1025–48.

Haq, M. (1971) Employment and income distribution in the 1970s: A new perspective. *Development Digest* (7 October).

Herrick, B. and Kindleberger, C.P. (1983) *Economic Development* (4th edn). London: McGraw-Hill.

Hettne, B. (1993) *Development Theory*. Harlow: Longman.

Hicks, N. and Streeten, P. (1995) Indicator of development: The search for a basic needs yardstick. In K.V. Pillai and L.W. Shannon (eds) *Developing Areas: A Book of Readings and Research* (pp. 31–44). Oxford: Berg.

Hunt, D. (1989) *Economic Theories of Development*. London: Harvester Wheatsheaf.

International Labour Organisation (1976) *Employment, Growth and Basic Needs: A One-World Problem*. New York: Praeger.

Istanbul Chamber of Commerce (1997) *Monthly Economic Figures: June, 1997*. Istanbul: Istanbul Chamber of Commerce.

Johnson, L.C. (2000) The threat of terrorism is overstated. In L.K. Egendorf (ed.) *Terrorism: Opposing Viewpoints* (pp. 26–34). San Diego: Greenhaven.

Ladens, D.S. (1995) Why are we so rich and they so poor? In K.V. Pillai and L.W. Shannon (eds) *Developing Areas: A Book of Readings and Research* (pp. 74–85). Oxford: Berg.

Lea, J. (1988) *Tourism and Development in the Third World*. London: Routledge.

Leftwich, A. (1995) Governance, democracy and development in the Third World. In S. Corbridge (ed.) *Development Studies* (pp. 427–37) London: Edward Arnold.

Ministry of Tourism (1993) *Bulletin of Tourism Statistics*. Ankara: Ministry of Tourism.

Ministry of Tourism (1994) *Manpower Survey of the Turkish Hotel and Tourism Industry with Technical Conjunction of International Labour organisation*. Ankara: Ministry of Tourism.

Ministry of Tourism (1999) *Hane Halki Turizm Arastirmasi [Household Tourism Survey] 1997*. Ankara.

Ministry of Tourism (2001a) *Bulletin of Tourism Statistics 2000*. Ankara: Ministry of Tourism.

Ministry of Tourism (2001b) *Bulletin of Accommodation Statistics 2000*. Ankara: Ministry of Tourism.

Ministry of Tourism (2001c) *Bulletin of Charter Flights Statistics 2000*. Ankara: Ministry of Tourism.

Nafziger, E.W. (1990) *The Economics Of Developing Countries* (2nd edn). Englewood Cliffs, NJ: Prentice-Hall.

OECD (1988) *Tourism Policy and International Tourism in OECD Member Countries*. Paris: OECD.

OECD (1990) *Tourism Policy and International Tourism in OECD Member Countries*. Paris: OECD.

OECD (1992) *Tourism Policy and International Tourism in OECD Member Countries*. Paris: OECD.

OECD (1997) *Tourism Policy and International Tourism in OECD Member Countries*. Paris: OECD.

OECD (2001) *OECD Economic Surveys for Turkey, No. 4*. Paris: OECD.

Oppermann, M. (1993) Tourism space in developing countries. *Annals of Tourism Research* 20, 535–56.

Üztürk, Y. (1996) *Marketing Turkey as a Tourist Destination*. PhD Thesis, Scottish Hotel School, University of Strathclyde.

Pizam, A. and Mansfeld, Y. (eds) (1996) *Tourism, Crime and International Security Issues*. Chichester: Wiley.

Poirier, R.A. (2001) The political economy of tourism in Algeria. In Y. Apostolopoulos, P. Loukissas and L. Leontidou (eds) *Mediterranean Tourism: Facets of Socioeconomic Development and Cultural Change* (pp. 211–25). London: Routledge.

Resmi Gazete (1982) *Turizm Tesvik Kanunu, Sayi: 2634; Kabul Tarihi: 12/3/1982 [Tourism Encouragement Law no. 2634; Date of Acceptance: 12/3/1982]*. Ankara: Resmi Gazete.

Richter, L.K. (1992) Political instability and tourism in the Third World. In D. Harrison (ed.) *Tourism and the Less Developed Countries* (pp. 35–46). London: Belhaven.

Seckelmann, A. (2002) Domestic tourism: A chance for regional development in Turkey? *Tourism Management* 23, 85–92.

Seers, D. (1979) The meaning of development with a postscript. In D. Lehmann (ed.) *Development Theory* (pp. 9–32). London: Frank Cass.

Sezer, H. and Harrison, A. (1994) Tourism in Greece and Turkey: An economic view for planners. In A.V. Seaton (ed.) *Tourism: The State of The Art* (pp. 74–83). Chichester: Wiley.

Sharpley, R. and Telfer, D.J. (eds) (2002) *Tourism and Development: Concepts and Issues*. Clevedon: Channel View.

Singh, A. (1979) The basic needs approach to development *vs* the new international economic order: The significance of Third World industrialisation. *World Development* 7, 585–606.

Sönmez, S.S. (1998) Tourism, terrorism, and political instability. *Annals of Tourism Research*, 25, 416–56.

SPO (State Planning Organisation) (1994a) *Main Economic Indicators*. Ankara: State Planning Organisation.

SPO (State Planning Organisation) (1994b) *The Programme of Sixth Year Five Development Planning for 1994*. Ankara: State Planning Organisation.

SPO (State Planning Organisation) (2001) *Main Economic Indicators*. Ankara: State Planning Organisation.

SPO (State Planning Organisation) (2002) *Main Economic Indicators*. Ankara: State Planning Organisation.

State Institute of Statistics (2000) *Statistical Yearbook of Turkey*. Ankara: Prime Minister, Republic of Turkey.

Stewart, F. (1985) *Planning To Meet Basic Needs*. London: MacMillan.

Thirlwall (1978) *Growth and Development* (1st edn). London: MacMillan.

Thirlwall (1989) *Growth and Development* (4th edn). London: MacMillan.

Timothy, D.J. (1998) Incremental tourism planning in Yogyakarta, Indonesia. *Tourism Recreation Research* 23, 72–4.

Timothy, D.J. (1999) Participatory planning: A view of tourism in Indonesia. *Annals of Tourism Research* 26, 371–91.

Timothy, D.J. and Ioannides, D. (2002) Tour operator hegemony: Dependency and oligopoly in insular destinations. In Y. Apostolopoulos and D.J. Gayle (eds) *Island Tourism and Sustainable Development: Caribbean, Pacific and Mediterranean Experience* (pp. 181–98). Westport, CT: Praeger.

Todaro, M.P. (1989) *Economic Development in the Third World*. New York: Longman.

Tosun, C. (1998a) Community participation in the tourism development process at the local level: The case of Urgup in Turkey. PhD Thesis, Strathclyde University.

Tosun, C. (1998b) Roots of unsustainable tourism development at the local level: The case of Urgup in Turkey. *Tourism Management* 19(6), 595–610.

Tosun, C. (1999) An analysis of contributions of international inbound tourism to the Turkish economy. *Tourism Economics* 5(3), 217–50.

Tosun, C. (2001) Challenges of sustainable tourism development in the developing world: The case of Turkey. *Tourism Management* 22, 289–303.

Tosun, C. (2002) Host perceptions of impacts of tourism: A comparative tourism study. *Annals of Tourism Research* 29, 231–53.

Tosun, C. and Jenkins, C.L. (1996) Regional planning approaches to tourism development: The case of Turkey. *Tourism Management* 17, 519–31.

Tosun, C. and Jenkins, C.L. (1998) The evolution of tourism planning in Third World countries: A critique. *Progress in Tourism and Hospitality Research* 4, 101–14.

Tosun, C. and Timothy, D.J. (2001) Shortcomings in planning approaches to tourism development in developing countries: The case of Turkey. *International Journal of Contemporary Hospitality Management* 13(7), 352–9.

Turk Tanitma Fonu (2002) What is being done in the Turkish south east? On WWW at http://www.turkishforum.com/pkk/whats_happening.html.

Türkiye Kalkinma Bankasi (1990) *Turizm El Kitabi [Tourism Handbook]*. Ankara: Turkiye Kalikinma Bankasi.

Türkiye Kalkinma Bankasi (TKB) (2002) *Bölgelere Göre Turizm Yatırımlarına Verilen Krediler (Tourism Investment Incentives by Regions)*. Ankara: Türkiye Kalkınma Bankası.

TURSAB (Turkiye Seyahat Acentalari Birligi/Association of Turkish Travel Agencies) (1999) Arastirma: Yurtici seyahat pazari raporu 1999. *TURSAB Aylik Dergi* 185, 33–56.

TURSAB (Turkiye Seyahat Acentalari Birligi/Association of Turkish Travel Agencies) (2000) *Profile*. Istanbul: TURSAB.

United Nations Development Programme (1998) *Human Development Report Turkey 1998*, Ankara: UNDP.

Var, T. and Imam, K.Z. (2001) Tourism in Egypt: History, policies, and the state. In Y. Apostolopoulos, P. Loukissas and L. Leontidou (eds) *Mediterranean Tourism: Facets of Socioeconomic Development and Cultural Change* (pp. 181–96). London: Routledge.

Wilford, W.T. (1979) The physical quality of life index: A useful social indicator. *World Development* 7, 581–4.

Yuksel, F., Bramwell, B., and Yuksel, A. (1999) Stakeholder interviews and tourism planning at Pamukkale, Turkey. *Tourism Management* 20, 351–60.

# 6 Problems of Island Tourism Development: The Greek Insular Regions

*Konstantinos Andriotis*

*Greek Open University & Technological Educational Institute of Crete, Ionias Street 14, 713 05 Heraklio Crete, Greece*

Growing tourism demand opens new opportunities for island development. Due to the increase in the real income of island populations and the generation of employment, island governments have seen tourism as a promising opportunity for reducing the prosperity gap between themselves and developed mainland regions and as a means of modernising their economic base and retaining their population. Although the positive effects make traditional tourism development inevitable in islands, there are some inherent disadvantages resulting from their insular character and uncontrolled tourism expansion. These include: accessibility difficulties, high transportation costs, external dependency and control of the tourism industry, high leakage rates of foreign exchange earnings, landscape transformations and sociocultural and environmental problems. It is the aim of this paper to review these difficulties and to provide recommendations on the ways in which developers and decision-makers of insular destinations may reduce some of tourism's problems and increase benefits for islands and their inhabitants, taking as a case the Greek insular regions.

## Introduction

In recent years, tourism research into island destinations has grown rapidly. This is attributable mainly to two factors. First, the significance of tourism for the economy of many island destinations. For example, the International Scientific Council for Island Development (INSULA, 2000) estimates that for 70% of European islands, tourism is the mainstay of their economies, in a third accounting for more than 50% of their Gross Domestic Product (GDP). Second, for many researchers, islands hold a particular attraction, because they provide excellent 'laboratory' conditions for the study of international tourism growth where theories can be tested and processes can be observed in the setting of a semi-closed system (Ioannides, 1995a; King, 1993).

Despite the long history of island tourism and the increasing academic research, emphasis on the literature tends to be focused on tourism in island microstates, such as: Caribbean islands (Bryden, 1973; Chen-Young, 1982; Hills & Lundgren, 1977; McElroy & de Albuquerque, 1998; Seward & Spinard, 1982; Weaver, 1993; Wilkinson, 1987), or the Pacific islands (Choy, 1992; Crocombe & Rajotte, 1980; Farrel, 1985; Milne, 1992, 1997; Milne & Nowosielski, 1997); and tourism research on Mediterranean islands has been mainly focused on Malta (Boissevain, 1977, 1979, 1996; Briguglio & Briguglio, 1996; Lockhart, 1997a; Lockhart & Ashton, 1990; Oglethorpe, 1984, 1985; Young, 1983) and Cyprus (e.g. Akis *et al.*, 1996; Andronikos, 1979, 1986; Ioannides, 1992, 1994, 1995b; Kammas, 1993; Lockhart, 1997a). For many islands which are constituent parts of metropolitan countries (e.g. many Mediterranean islands, such as the Greek islands, Corsica,

Balearics, Sicily and Sardinia), few researchers have investigated the impacts of tourism development despite the importance of tourism to their economic base. The reason for this is that data for islands that are parts of a country are often aggregated within the country and cannot be separated out. In contrast, data on island nation states, which are separate political units, are quite easy to find.

To provide a critical analysis of island tourism as an economic blessing and / or a socio-cultural and environmental blight, this paper adopts a case study approach. This study will attempt to contribute to tourism research in relation to islands that are parts of metropolitan countries, taking as a case study the Greek insular regions. Specifically, it is the aim of this paper to provide recommendations on the ways in which developers and decision-makers of insular destinations may reduce some of tourism's problems and increase its benefits for islands and their inhabitants. The paper has three main sections as follows. The first section provides a review of the general characteristics of island tourism, as reported by academic papers. This section illustrates the key elements of the discussion on the nature of island tourism as an economic activity, focusing on the inherent disadvantages of islands in developing their tourism industry; the inevitability of tourism development for islands; and the problems associated with tourism expansion. The second section reviews tourism development in the Greek insular regions and discusses issues referring to the evolution of the tourism industry, the economy, size / development indicators, impacts of tourism, accessibility difficulties and transportation costs and external dependency and control of the industry. The final section provides conclusions and policy implications based on these findings.

## Literature Background

### Inherent disadvantages of islands

By their very nature islands face a number of inherent disadvantages. They are small in size with declining populations; they suffer from isolation, peripherality, external dependency and diseconomies of scale; they are rural in character; and they have a scarcity of resources, meaning mainly that their alternatives for industrialisation and self-sustaining growth are limited (Butler, 1993; Cross & Nutley, 1999; Pearce, 1995; Royle & Scott, 1996).

Despite some commonalities, islands can vary considerably because of their size, range and scale of their separation or isolation (Royle, 1989; Schofield & George, 1997). 'Some are so large as to not have the feeling of islands at all' and others 'cease to exist as true islands, perhaps following the construction of bridges' (Schofield & George, 1997: 5). In a literal sense, 'smaller islands often face severe problems of how to provide their inhabitants with a living from an absolutely restricted resource base and / or find restrictions placed on their development because of the lack of, or shortage of, a necessary resource such as water' (Royle, 1989: 111). Milne (1992: 195) conducted a survey to compare the impacts of tourism in five South Pacific island microstates and found that 'each of the five microstates face a series of binding constraints to traditional forms of economic development'. He stated:

> While each nation differs in terms of population, land area, and relative isolation, they share many characteristics. All suffer from the economic handicaps

associated with small size including small internal markets that limit the ability to adopt import substitution development strategies, remoteness and high shipping costs that raise the price of imports and concomitantly place exports at a comparative disadvantage, a reliance on a limited range of primary commodity exports, problems of underdevelopment, and a labour market characterised by a limited skills base. (Milne, 1992: 195)

While many rural areas of the mainland share these problems, offshore islands have the impediment of a marine barrier. As Baum (1997a: 2) declares, the physical remove from the mainland necessitating a conscious decision to cross the water is an important dimension. The final crossing between the mainland and the island adds on inconvenience cost for both inhabitants and incoming tourists (Royle & Scott, 1996: 111). An island location cannot compete on equal terms with mainland locations, because incoming tourists have to add a transportation cost, often requiring a transfer from one mode of transport to another (Royle, 1989; Royle & Scott, 1996). Therefore, air and sea transport are crucial to the linking of islands with the outside world and with each other, and advances in air and sea transport have positively helped previously inaccessible tourism markets establish themselves (Abeyratne, 1997). For tourism producers the increased transportation costs to visit an island must be reflected in the price of their output, thus reducing islands' competitiveness (Royle & Scott, 1996). An island can therefore never compete on quite equal terms with a neighbouring mainland location – its goods coming in must be more expensive and its goods going out have to be sold at a premium that will cover the extra cost (Royle, 1989: 112).

## The inevitability of tourism for island destinations

However, if islands have so many deficiencies in developing their tourism industry two questions emerge:

*Why do their governments seek to promote the industry through both public and private development?* It is evident that growing tourism demand opens new opportunities for island development. Due to the increase in the real incomes of the island populations and the generation of employment (although mostly seasonal), governments have seen tourism as a promising opportunity for reducing the prosperity gap between themselves and developed countries, and as a means of modernising their economic base and retaining their population and community welfare. Additional positive impacts of island tourism development include heritage and environmental preservation, creation of infrastructure, cultural communication and political stability (Andriotis, 2000; Ioannides, 1995a; Squire, 1996).

*Why do so many people visit island destinations to experience beaches, sea and sun, when the same may be experienced close to home or mainland coastal resorts, often at much less expense?* Island destinations are considered by visitors to offer an appealing environment different to the pace and pressures of 'normal' urban living. 'The feeling of separateness, of being cut off from the mainland, is an important physical and psychological attribute of the successful vacation' (Baum, 1997b: 21). According to King (1993: 14), 'an island is the most enticing form of land. A symbol of the eternal contest between land and water, islands are detached, self-contained entities whose boundaries are obvious; all other land divisions are more or less arbitrary'. As Baum (1997a: 2) states:

> There is something particularly appealing about islands and island living to visitors which cannot be replicated on the mainland. It may be small islands' confined space where, sometimes all corners can be reached by walking, and their relatively large coastline in relation to their land mass makes them different from adjoining mainlands and increases their appeal to the minds of visitors.

## The problems of island tourism development

Island tourism is more vulnerable to the vagaries of the market than mainland destinations. Being completely dependent upon providers of transportation, for example, islands find themselves in the unhappy position of having to rely on the services of airlines and shipping companies which make decisions in the best interests of shareholders and which do not consider the very real concerns of islands (Conlin & Baum, 1995: 6). As a result, many islands have little economic choice but to accept conventional tourism expansion (characterised by mass tourist arrivals, control by external actors and large-scale facilities) as being inevitable (Wilkinson, 1989).

In many islands, multinational companies (e.g. tour operators and international hotels) frequently control the development process and decide whether to encourage tourism. Because government is located off-island and frequently has different priorities and policies to those of the island population, local involvement in tourism development is often at a low level, and the leakage of foreign exchange earnings is very high (Wilkinson, 1989; Butler, 1996: 15; Lockhart, 1997b). Simultaneously, Butler (1993) and Ioannides (1995a) report that because of a lack of diversity in their resources, most island destinations depend overwhelmingly on the three Ss (sun, sand and sea) and only a number of larger island destinations (e.g. Cyprus and Jamaica) are enriched with the resources (e.g. interior mountains) that allow them to sell a diversified tourist product. As a result, tourism in islands (with few exceptions) creates seasonal income and employment (Andriotis, 2000; Baum, 1997a; Vaughan et al., 2000).

Warren (1978) has identified that when tourism evolves in any community many changes occur. The problem is more evident in island communities where stakeholders compete with one another for space. In practice, the tourism industry competes with islanders for a share in the community resources. Limited visitor capacity, fragility and self-containment means that tourism activity puts profound pressure on human life and islands' sensitive and unique environmental resources.

> Tourism is more pervasive in its impacts on the small island community than it is on larger mainland resort destinations. The influx of large numbers of tourists to an island destination is likely to have a profound effect on the community in cultural, social and environmental terms because of size considerations (Baum, 1997a: 3).

As a result, Loukissas (1982) and Wilkinson (1989) believe that the smaller the ratio of local inhabitants to the number of tourists, 'the more risk there is of

negative impact because of the local system's inability to absorb the consequences or to control the nature of tourism development' (Wilkinson, 1989: 159).
Although tourism has effects on all communities, island communities may be
subject to more intense pressures because of their 'contained' nature. Small
islands are likely to be places where everybody knows everyone. Locals know
each other's jobs, politics, families and friends and when contact with the outside
world results, many negative influences emerge.

## The Greek Islands

The Greek islands form the most extensive and significant insular complex in
the European Union, with the most important and fragile resources (Macheridis,
2001). Greece has a coastline of 15,000 km and more than 2000 islands and islets of
varying sizes and shapes (Waters, 1993). (A map of Greece is shown in Figure 1.)
Of these islands, 166 are inhabited, with a population of approximately 1.3
million people, accommodating 12% of the Greek population.

**Figure 1** Map of Greece

## The tourism industry and the economy

The first attempts at developing the tourism industry in the Greek islands were made during the 1950s. Attention was paid to the larger islands (Crete and Rhodes) with historical value and the existence of a basic infrastructure. Later with the construction of some infrastructure and the improvement of transportation systems more Greek islands started to expand their tourism industry. As a result, the local economy of many Greek islands is today characterised by intensive and increasing tourism activity, although the agricultural sector presents declining figures or remains at a low level. This trend has been influenced by public and private investments that are oriented towards promotional activities and the increase of relevant tourism infrastructure all over the insular regions. Giannias (1999) estimates that the Aegean islands have received from the Hellenic National Tourism Organisation (HNTO) the highest amount of money (120 million GRD[1]) for the advertising and promotion of their tourism industry compared to the rest of the Greek regions. In addition, the insular regions have received higher subsidies through development laws, compared to mainland Greek regions, and as result a higher number of hotel establishments was constructed, creating more than half of the jobs and beds in the hotel sector nationwide, attributed to development laws during the period 1982–95 (Table 1).

**Table 1** Subsidies through development laws to the hotel industry from 1 January 1982 to  13 October 1995

|  | No. of invest- ments | Level of invest- ments[a] | Level of subsidy[a] | Special subsidies | Private capital[a] | No. of jobs created | No. of beds |
|---|---|---|---|---|---|---|---|
| Central Greece | 128 | 9.13 | 3.11 | 0.32 | 4.91 | 1088 | 5553 |
| Peloponne sus | 149 | 9.34 | 3.30 | 0.41 | 4.80 | 1517 | 6646 |
| Thessalia | 142 | 12.30 | 3.83 | 0.45 | 6.18 | 1116 | 6520 |
| Epirus | 53 | 4.12 | 1.78 | 0.14 | 1.88 | 435 | 2118 |
| Macedonia | 260 | 33.65 | 10.98 | 1.30 | 16.26 | 3043 | 18131 |
| Thrace | 38 | 1.58 | 0.68 | 0.08 | 0.57 | 246 | 2000 |
| **Ionian Islands** | **231** | **23.33** | **6.88** | **0.86** | **12.91** | **2508** | **13036** |
| **Northern Aegean** | **195** | **21.85** | **10.56** | **1.15** | **8.23** | **2016** | **9505** |
| **Southern Aegean** | **549** | **84.8** | **31.00** | **3.00** | **39.24** | **6791** | **37353** |
| **Crete** | **435** | **55.94** | **14.80** | **1.97** | **33.72** | **5801** | **30449** |
| Greece | 2180 | 256.08 | 86.96 | 9.67 | 128.70 | 24561 | 131361 |

[a] Million Greek Drachma
*Note*: Cases in bold refer to insular regions
*Source*: Pavlopoulos and Kouzelis (1998).

**Table 2** Land area, population, GDP per capita, unemployment, occupancy rate and overnight stays in Greece by region

| | Land area (m²) 2001a | | Population 2001a | | GDP per capita 2001a (Million Drs) | Unemployment 2000b (%) | Hotel beds 1999c | | Average occupancy rate 1999c | Overnights 1999c | | | | | |
| | | | | | | | | | | Greeks | | Foreigners | | Total | |
| | Total | % | Total | % | | | Total | % | | Total | % | Total | % | Total | % |
|---|---|---|---|---|---|---|---|---|---|---|---|---|---|---|---|
| Eastern Macedonia & Thrace | 14,157 | 10.73 | 604,254 | 5.52 | 3.62 | 8.6 | 15,711 | 2.56 | 44.22 | 1,013,089 | 7.01 | 450,026 | 0.98 | 1,463,115 | 2.43 |
| Central Macedonia | 19,147 | 14.51 | 1,862,833 | 17.03 | 3.96 | 10.7 | 61,964 | 10.10 | 58.61 | 1,813,591 | 12.55 | 2,827,047 | 6.17 | 4,640,638 | 7.70 |
| Western Macedonia | 9,451 | 7.16 | 302,750 | 2.77 | 3.88 | 14.7 | 3,745 | 0.61 | 36.63 | 345,704 | 2.39 | 47,859 | 0.10 | 393,563 | 0.65 |
| Thessalia | 14,037 | 10.64 | 754,893 | 6.90 | 3.56 | 12.4 | 23,550 | 3.84 | 42.06 | 1,117,061 | 7.72 | 598,455 | 1.31 | 1,715,516 | 2.85 |
| Epirus | 9,203 | 6.97 | 352,420 | 3.22 | 3.4 | 10.6 | 9,805 | 1.60 | 43.8 | 630,699 | 4.36 | 259,646 | 0.57 | 890,345 | 1.48 |
| Western Greece | 11,350 | 8.60 | 742,419 | 6.79 | 3.39 | 10.2 | 15,068 | 2.46 | 44.45 | 741,844 | 5.13 | 527,245 | 1.15 | 1,269,089 | 2.11 |
| Central Greece | 15,549 | 11.78 | 608,655 | 5.56 | 4.05 | 13.6 | 30,260 | 4.93 | 34.53 | 871,435 | 6.03 | 541,440 | 1.18 | 1,412,875 | 2.34 |
| Attica | 3,808 | 2.89 | 3,764,348 | 34.41 | 4.52 | 12.2 | 67,336 | 10.97 | 47.89 | 2,867,814 | 19.84 | 4,401,598 | 9.61 | 7,269,412 | 12.06 |
| Peloponnesus | 15,490 | 11.74 | 632,955 | 5.79 | 3.41 | 9.3 | 32,513 | 5.30 | 37.58 | 1,158,273 | 8.01 | 874,609 | 1.91 | 2,032,882 | 3.37 |
| Ionian Islands | 2,307 | 1.75 | 214,274 | 1.96 | 3.97 | 5.1 | 65,232 | 10.63 | 76.43 | 951,355 | 6.58 | 5,409,134 | 11.81 | 6,360,489 | 10.56 |
| **Northern Aegean** | 3,836 | 2.91 | 200,066 | 1.83 | 3.53 | 7.4 | 22,326 | 3.64 | 61.40 | 560,812 | 3.88 | 1,426,546 | 3.11 | 1,987,358 | 3.30 |
| **Southern Aegean** | 5,286 | 4.01 | 298,745 | 2.73 | 4.74 | 10.5 | 145,810 | 23.76 | 82.32 | 1,515,816 | 10.49 | 16,189,278 | 35.35 | 17,705,094 | 29.38 |
| **Crete** | 8,336 | 6.32 | 601,159 | 5.50 | 4.07 | 6.7 | 120,316 | 19.61 | 82.27 | 866,049 | 5.99 | 12,250,477 | 26.75 | 13,116,526 | 21.77 |
| **Greece** | 131,957 | 100 | 10,939,771 | 100 | 4.04 | 11.1 | 613,636 | 100 | 63.46 | 14,453,542 | 100 | 45,803,360 | 100 | 60,256,902 | 100 |

*Note:* Cases in bold refer to insular regions

*Sources:* [a]Epilogi (2001); [b]National Statistical Service of Greece (2001); [c]Hellenic National Tourism Organisation (2002)

In 1999 international tourist arrivals in Greece reached 12.6 million and foreign tourists generated 76% of total overnight stays (with two islands, Rhodes and Crete, accounting for 49% of all overnight stays of foreign tourists in Greece). The tourist receipts reached US$3.9, accounting for 6% of the Greek GDP (Moussios, 1999). Moussios (1999) estimates that in Greece approximately 500,000 people are employed in tourism-related activities, reaching 800,000 during the summer season.

In 1999 almost 57.6% of the hotel beds in Greece were located in insular regions, although the insular regions occupy only 15% of the national land area (Table 2). Insular regions recorded more than 65% of total overnights nation-wide, among which 21.8% and 29.4% were recorded in the regions of Crete and Southern Aegean respectively. The insular regions accommodate mainly foreign tourists, since 90.1% of the total overnights in insular regions were recorded by foreign tourists. However, any reference made to statistics by Greek tourists should be taken with caution, since as Leontidou (1998: 113) remarks domestic tourism in Greece is difficult to measure, because they usually prefer rooms to let, the houses of relatives and second homes that are not included in the figures provided. The occupancy rates of the hotel establishments of insular regions are higher compared to mainland regions, ranging from 61.4% for the Northern Aegean region to 82.32% for the Southern Aegean. In addition, the number of hotel beds is not proportionate to the number of inhabitants of each region. As a result, the ratio of inhabitants to hotel beds for the insular regions of Greece is 1:0.269, compared to 1:0.027[2] for the mainland.

The unemployment rates in the Greek insular regions are below the national average, with the lowest in Ionian Islands, 5.1%, followed by Crete, 6.7% (Table 2). In the case of Crete this is due to high agricultural production and the expansion of the tourism industry, although for the Ionian Islands the low unemployment rates are attributed mostly to the increased tourism activity.

The per capita GNP in Greece is below the European Union average (Eurostat, 1999). The inhabitants of the Southern Aegean have the highest GNP per capita in Greece and the GNP per capita in the region of Crete is higher than the national average. However, tourism in the Southern Aegean region has increased regional imbalances since more than half of tourists' overnight stays are recorded in Rhodes. Regional imbalances are also evident in all the other insular Greek regions. As a result, Totsiou *et al.* (1999) state that there are islands (e.g. Kassos, Nissyros, Lipsi, Agathonissi, Sikinos, Folegandros, Kimolos) where the living standard tends to reach poverty conditions.

## Size/development indicators of islands

As Liu and Jenkins (1996) assert, there is no universally accepted definition of what should be considered large and what small. However, it is certain that tourism resources are closely linked to the land area, population and economic diversification, with larger islands tending to have more and richer tourism resource endowments. Likewise, although large islands normally receive more tourism revenues, in small islands tourism is usually developed with more enthusiasm and tourist arrivals are usually more significant both in per capita terms and in share of the national income.

It is certainly very difficult to consider the Greek Islands as a whole, given the huge divergences in the level of tourism development and the size of the islands. On the one hand, there are the well-developed tourist islands (Crete, Corfu, Rhodes, Kos, Myconos, Paros and Santorini) which appear to have deep discrepancies in the main socioeconomic indices when compared to the vast number of small and remote islands that lag behind economically (Totsiou *et al.*, 1999: 1). As Loukissas (1982: 536) reports, 'larger Greek islands are more diversified in accommodations and more able to decrease their vulnerability to external fluctuations'. Smaller islands face higher problems of remoteness, lack of resources and lower levels of development.

Tsartas (1992) classified the Greek islands into three groups. This classification can be useful for explaining the type of tourism development found in each group:

- *Group A*: The islands (mostly large) where the population responded positively to the challenge of tourism evolution and created the necessary infrastructure to attract mass tourism.
- *Group B*: The smaller and poorest islands where the absence of tour operators and the lack of infrastructure have delayed expansion of tourism activity.
- *Group C*: The islands where the economic structure is mixed (tourism and agriculture or tourism and mining) and with some communities having massive organised tourism and others having moderate development.

## Impacts of tourism

The ability of islands to earn foreign exchange through tourism development and generate employment opportunities is often severely restricted by the inherent economic disadvantages associated with their smallness and isolation (Wilkinson, 1989: 157). In the Greek islands, mainly the smaller ones, a fair amount of inputs to the tourism industry are imported. As Dana (1999: 63) writes for the island of Ios:

> The Sweet Irish Dream Bar opened in 1986, serving imported drinks to visitors. Beer, pizza, and hot dogs are being sold where local wine and kadaifi were once the norm. Not long ago, lamb was the staple meat, but packaged, processed ham is now imported instead. Likewise, jams and juices are now imported to an island where figs, oranges, and pears grew in abundance. Perhaps the most remarkable import was a curd labelled feta cheese. Developed in Greece, feta is a cheese made from goat's milk, but the tourist trade was supplied with a cow's milk product that was labeled feta and imported from Denmark.

There is no doubt that patterns of consumption and the behaviour of the local population have changed dramatically (Dana, 1999; Stott, 1996; Tsartas, 1992; Zarkia, 1996). Local teenagers now follow the example set by the incoming tourists; and culture, tradition and even language languishes (Dana, 1999). Young men change their traditional customs and imitate the lifestyle of foreign tourists (Tsartas, 1992; Zarkia, 1996). Tourism converts the host–guest relationship into a commercial one (Andriotis, 2002a; Zarkia, 1996). However, tourism development has halted emigration and returning migrants have been actively involved in the development of the tourism industry (Andriotis, 2002b; Apostolopoulos &

Sönmez, 1999; Galani-Moutafi, 1993; Kenna, 1993; Tsartas, 1992). As a result, Coccosis and Parpairis (1995) report that in Mykonos there has been an increase in the island's population, although there are cases where crime rates have also increased. Concerning the Ionian islands, Eurostat (1994) reports that tourist development has resulted in the depopulation of the villages and the concentration of the population in the urban centres, as well as the gradual abandonment of farming. Nevertheless, the region presents a steady increase of population, mainly due to the expansion of the tourism industry.

During the summer season the islands are submitted to strong pressure due to the arrival of huge numbers of tourists (Apostolopoulos & Sönmez, 1999). There is no doubt that the expansion of the tourism industry in an island destination has direct effects on their sensitive and unique natural and manmade resources (Coccossis, 1987; Coccossis & Parpairis, 1995). Coccossis and Parpairis (1995) for Mykonos and Nijkamp and Verdonkschot (1995) for Lesbos report that because of uncontrolled tourism development the islands face undesirable environmental effects on their resources, such as traffic congestion and the pollution of water and soil, especially during the summer season. In Zakynthos, the construction of holiday accommodation along the coast has posed a serious threat to the breeding of the endangered turtle *caretta caretta* (Marinos, 1983; Prunier *et al.*, 1993). Nijkamp and Verdonkschot (1995) found that in Lesbos the scenery has been greatly affected by the construction of new tourist enterprises. Kousis (1984: 55–6) reports for Drethia (a pseudonym for a coastal community in Crete) various transformations attributable to tourism expansion:

> During the 1950s and early 1960s the village was famous for its fertile gardens, its picturesque windmills, and its beautiful view. In the 1980s the intensive agricultural activities have been replaced by activities promoting tourism. Consequently, the scenery has now changed greatly. The coastal rim, as well as the two kilometres road that connects it with the village centre, have been taken over by various forms of tourist accommodation. Motels, rent-room facilities, camping grounds, hotels of varying sizes, tavernas, restaurants, coffee shops, discotheques, and bouzoukia establishments are encircling and concentrating in and around the north part – closest to the shore – of the village.

Along the same lines, Peterson and McCarthy (1990: 7) vividly illustrate this situation:

> Communities of the north shore of Crete are now facing problems as a result of uncontrolled development. As but one example, much of Stalida, a tourism-oriented beach community, is characterised by small, irregularly shaped parcels; there are few streets and most parcels are land-locked, with only informal, if any, access to either the streets or the beach; building-to-lot coverage ratios are high; and buildings are sometimes so close that one can touch the adjacent structure by leaning out a window or over a balcony. The overall appearance of Stalida is of cluttered and chaotic overbuilding.

The lack of physical planning and the high concentration of buildings have transformed many island resorts into urban space. Undoubtedly, fishing villages such as Malia and Agios Nikolaos in Crete, and Faliraki in Rhodes, have lost their authenticity and architecture due to the easy and quick profit from mass tourism development.

The concentration of visitors and popular attractions in a very limited area is a common feature on many Greek islands (Butler & Stiakaki, 2001: 294). Due to the rapid growth of tourism land values have increased, exacerbating the concentration of hotels, shopping and leisure condominiums. Thus, Papadaki-Tzedaki (1997) reports that in 1993, the value of 1 stremma[3] in Rethymno was equal to the value of 120 stremma during the early 1970s. The problem is accentuated in smaller Greek islands due to the limited availability of land and the intense pressure on their resources.

## Accessibility difficulties and transportation costs

The Greek islands can be reached by air and sea. Since airports exist only on the largest and more developed islands, most of which are capable of receiving charter flights directly from Europe (Buhalis, 1999: 346), sea transport plays a vital role for their connectivity with other insular and mainland regions.

Each island has at least one port. Passenger ships serve the needs of islanders and support any productive activities. In addition, they contribute to the development of each island's tourism industry and function as an infrastructure of the industry (Alexopoulos & Theotokas, 2001).

However, the demand for sea transport by the islands' inhabitants is very low and cannot guarantee an adequate level of use. For example, Alexopoulos and Theotokas (2001) report that during the winter the average number of ferry passengers to the island of Psara is less than 11. As a result, only during the summer do shipping companies achieve an adequate level of use.

The geographical distribution of the Greek islands, the low demand during some periods of the year, and the need to cut down the extra transportation cost and offer better services to islanders and visitors have led the state to design a number of intervention measures. There are obligatory routes to some of the islands as well as a 30% reduction on the VAT paid on air and sea transport (freight and passenger) between most of the islands (Hache, 1996). However, Hache (1996) asserts that the subsidies offered to service providers probably only increase the profit margin of the intermediaries. Likewise, Totsiou *et al.* (1999) criticise the aid provided by the European Union as not corresponding to the actual transportation costs. As they state, 'the distance of the Aegean islands from the main port of central Greece (Piraeous) ranges from 4.5 hours to 17 hours although the aid is not proportional to the distance involved' (Totsiou *et al.*, 1999: 2).

In addition, the sea transportation systems lack regularity and reliability, especially due to bad weather conditions. For example, a study by Darzentas (cited in Hache, 1996) showed that during the winter of 1989, 13.7% of boat arrivals and 18.8% of boat departures were cancelled at the port of Mytilini. Regarding air transport, cancellations due to unstable weather conditions or technical problems comprised an insignificant percentage of approximately 2% during the winter.

Up to now cabotage rules in Greece allow only Greek-owned passenger shipping companies to operate within the Greek islands (Anastasiadou, 2001). However, passenger shipping will enter the era of free competition, due to the regulations of the European Union, and this will increase competition (Alexopoulos & Theotokas, 2001) and may allow better transportation systems for the islands.

Finally, market behaviour in the Greek islands differs substantially to that of mainland areas, mainly due to transportation costs. For example, Totsiou *et al.* (1999) found that the price of flour on the island of Lesvos is 9% higher than in the mainland cities of Athens and Kalamata. The higher prices charged for many products sold on islands are reflected in the price of the output of tourist enterprises and the final price of the tourist package.

## External dependency and control

The Greek tourism industry faces a high dependency on foreign tour operators, with 59% of foreign tourists arriving by charter flights (Moussios, 1999). The problem is also experienced on many Greek islands, because the vast majority rely on a limited range of products since they lack the diversity of resources to attract a broad range of tourists, and depend overwhelmingly on the sun–sand–sea types of tourists. Exceptions include islands rich in alternative resources, such as Tinos, a religious destination, Delos, of archaeological interest, the volcanic island of Santorini and a few others.

However, the vast majority of Greek islands are cheap and mass tourism destinations directed towards the sun, sea and sand mass market, with their increased foreign intrusion contributing to a lack of endogenous development. Tsartas (1992) found that in Ios foreign tour operators played an essential role in the development of the industry, mainly because they linked the island by charters with Western European countries. Likewise, Apostolopoulos (1994) remarks that in Rhodes transnational tourist corporations predominate and the island relies on foreign investments, overseas airlines and metropolitan tour wholesalers.

There are islands, as reported by Apostolopoulos and Sönmez (1999) for Zakynthos, and Zarkia (1996) for Skiathos, where ownership is based on local capital and loans through Greek banks and the European Union. However, Apostolopoulos and Sönmez (1999) believe that the increased demands of foreign tour operators have started to invade the island of Zakynthos, and this will result in the transformation of the island to a mass tourism destination.

Loukissas (1982) found that in the Greek islands outsiders rather than locals took the initiative in developing their tourism industry. Tsartas (1992) notes that in the Greek islands, mainly the large ones, specific catalyst groups such as returned migrants and Athenians have responded positively to tourism development. A recent study by Damer (2001) in Symi found that the majority of tourism enterprises are in the hands of the locals, rather than foreigners, Athenians, or permanent or seasonal return migrants. Perhaps this is due to the smallness of the island, since in larger islands the situation is different. In Crete, Pettifer (1993: 76–7) reports that 'Athenians move in for the summer, open a bar, make a great deal of money and then disappear back to Athens at the end of the season . . . And the next year the Atheneans return, bars open . . . and the whole cycle starts again'. As a result, foreigners control some facets of the Greek islands' tourism industry.

There is hardly any local autonomy on the Greek islands. Although the islands have regional and local government, the planning process for tourism development is controlled by external actors, mainly the central government (Andriotis, 2001). For instance, Hache (1996) conducted a survey to investigate the implications of European Union legislation on the provision of transport services to island regions. According to this study, the Greek islands appear to be the most acute case of centralisation among European islands, as far as transportation is concerned. Specifically, the Ministry of Mercantile Marine, with headquarters in Piraeus, is responsible for the transport of goods or passengers by ferry-boats and passenger-car ferries between the ports of Attica and the islands, and the Civil Aviation Service, with headquarters in Athens, is responsible for regulating air traffic (Hache, 1996).

Despite the existence of regional and local governments the tourism development and planning process of islands is controlled by external actors rather than the locally elected governments (Andriotis, 2001; Lekakis, 1995). The lack of autonomy in the decision-making of the islands' future impedes the accomplishment of an integrated regional policy (Anagnostopoulou *et al.*, 1996: 32). As Lekakis (1995: 22) states, 'the lack of financial strength influences to a large extent the locally elected governments' political will, administrative capacity, and networking with outside organisations'.

In Greece, because the central administration is based in the capital city of Athens, the formulation of development plans does not always reflect the needs of communities (EU, 2000). One major component of the tourist product, the local community, has been neglected in decision-making. The bottom-up approach, through the involvement of the local population in the development process, has not been adopted in tourism planning, and the top-down process has overlooked the local community's desires (Andriotis, 2001, 2002a). Among the limited attempts at considering local community needs and public participation in tourism development and planning are those made by elected members in the public sector, and also improvements to the urban environment and living conditions, e.g. projects associated with transportation, infrastructure and health.

## Implications – Conclusions

Clearly, the introduction of tourism to island communities, either as a planned endogenous activity or as a result of exogenous forces, results in rapid changes in the sociocultural, environmental and economic structures. Despite the substantial economic returns, the limited visitor capacity, fragility and self-containment of islands means that tourism activity has profound pressures on their human life and their sensitive and unique environmental resources. These issues raised in the development of island tourism worldwide are also evident on the Greek islands. However, the plethora of Greek islands makes it difficult to proceed to a detailed analysis at island level in Greece. Thus, the inferences in this paper had to be taken at a regional level. As Macheridis (2001) asserts, the geographical discontinuity of islands means that the use of statistical indices is not feasible and economic assessments should be treated with caution because each island is a microcosm with its own difficulties and peculiarities.

From the review undertaken in this paper various considerations emerge for the development of tourism in the insular Greek regions, which developers and decision-makers should take into account in order to reduce some of tourism's problems and increase its benefits for islands and their inhabitants.

First, accessibility is essential in order to ensure each island's connectivity with tourist-generating countries and other insular and mainland regions. Development support policies should take account of the important differentiations within Greek islands and special attention should be given to the very small islands where they face a 'double insularity' problem. However, increased accessibility may not always be the appropriate response, since the increased tourist arrivals and the subsequent cultural and social costs of greater improved accessibility may have detrimental effects. Therefore, accessibility should increase in a reasonable way and it should not only be directed towards the further expansion of the tourism industry but also towards the improvement of health, education, agriculture and the handicraft industry.

Second, financial and investment considerations are substantial. Although there are many islands rich in the necessary pre-conditions for development (e.g. attractive landscapes and interesting cultural and archaeological sights), not all these islands will move from the potential for development to actual development, because they lack 'sufficient' preconditions, i.e. somebody's will to develop the tourism industry and to invest in infrastructure and accommodation. From one point of view, in cases where the maintenance of an island's local resources is desirable, lack of development or limited development may be better than extensive tourism development. Thus, concentrating tourism activity in a limited number of islands may be used as a government strategy to concentrate the negative impacts to these islands, rather than distributing tourism activity and, hence, the associated adverse effects to more islands.

Third, to avoid social disruption and to ensure economic viability, many island economies are boosted with substantial inflows of public expenditure; and this can give the impression that tourism-related development is a 'villain' for 'hopeless' islanders. However, current inflows of public expenditure do not take into consideration the real needs and concerns of each island. It is common sense that many of the Greek islands need financial support. However, the question arises: is there any limit to how much money should be spent on each island? The response may be a realistic and prioritised list of planning initiatives. It may be better to exploit, in sustainable terms, each island's available resources and its ability to meet genuine demand in the attempt to ensure future economic prosperity. As Royle and Scott (1996: 111–12) propose for the Irish islands, 'public authorities have to consider equity – how to provide the greatest good for the greatest number from their limited resources'.

Fourth, uncontrolled tourism development leads to serious environmental and sociocultural problems. To eliminate these problems future development plans need to be thoroughly assessed on the grounds of future feasibility and economic, environmental and sociocultural sustainability. If tourism does not develop within the framework of sustainability, it will lose its appeal in the future. However, sustainability will not be possible without careful attention to the host society's needs. In areas where foreign developers (either central government or foreign tour operators) control the tourist activity, conflicts between the host population and tourism development may occur. Therefore, autonomy in decision-making for islands, domination of local resources and control of the tourism movement by the host communities are important for the formation of a self-induced tourism industry, supported and encouraged by the locals. Tourism benefits and costs should be distributed more equally within the local population, allowing a larger proportion of the islanders to benefit from tourism expansion, rather than them merely bearing the burden of its costs (Brohman, 1996: 59). For residents to receive benefits from tourism development 'they must be given opportunities to participate in, and gain financially from, tourism' (Timothy, 1999: 375). Therefore, employment opportunities and entrepreneurial activities should be generated for the locals. Careful management and planning initiatives, regarding what sustainable tourism entails and how it can be implemented, should be pursued to ensure that the resources necessary for the tourism industry's survival are not misused and depleted. In addition, any future suggestions and regulations for conservation should be implemented by the local community and should consider local needs and desires.

To conclude, to achieve more sustainable development of the tourism industry in the Greek insular regions, there is a need to draw up a comprehensive tourism plan with listed priorities and strategies. This plan should carefully assess the possible adverse effects of tourism development on environmentally sensitive areas. If island decision-makers want to increase economic returns and improve islanders' standard of living, their main task should be to eliminate negative tourism impacts and to increase the benefits. Through planning and investments in preservation policies the protection of the islands' sensitive cultural and environmental resources can be reinforced. As Dasmann *et al.* (1973: 5) assert, for most other forms of development, some environmental and sociocultural values have to be sacrificed in return for expected benefits but for tourism these values have to be maintained at a high level in order to justify and safeguard the quality of a tourist-receiving destination. Therefore, planning is a determining factor in islands looking for a reasonable expansion in their tourism industry.

### Endnotes

1. 340.75 Dr = 1 Euro
2. It should be noted that a limited number of islands belong administratively to mainland regions and, as a result, statistics for these islands are included within mainland Greek regions. Further, the official statistics of hotel beds do not include a considerable number of undeclared unlicensed units and rooms, known as 'parahoteleria'.
3. 1 stremma = 1000 $m^2$ = 0.24 acres = 0.1 hectare.

### Correspondence

Any correspondence should be directed to Dr Konstantinos Andriotis, Ionias Street 14, 713 05 Heraklio, Crete, Greece (andriotis@angelfire.com).

### References

Abeyratne, R.I.R. (1997) The impact of tourism and air transport on the small island developing states. *Environmental Policy and Law* 27(3), 198–202.
Akis, S., Peristianis, N. and Warner, J. (1996) Residents' attitudes to tourism development: The case of Cyprus. *Tourism Management* 17(7), 481–504.
Alexopoulos, A.B. and Theotokas, I.N. (2001) Quality services in the coastal passenger

shipping sector and its contribution to the development of tourism in small islands. The case of Psara island. Paper presented in the Tourism on Islands and Specific Destinations conference, Chios Island, Greece, 14–16 December.

Anagnostopoulou, K., Arapis, T., Bouchy, I. and Micha, I. (1996) *Tourism and the Structural Funds – The Case for Environmental Integration*. Athens: RSPB.

Anastasiadou, C. (2001) Tourism's social impacts on peripheral islands with diversified economies. Paper presented in the Tourism on Islands and Specific Destinations conference, Chios Island, Greece, 14–16 December.

Andriotis, K. (2000) Local community perceptions of tourism as a development tool: The island of Crete. Unpublished PhD thesis, Bournemouth University.

Andriotis, K. (2001) Tourism planning and development in Crete. Recent tourism policies and their efficacy. *Journal of Sustainable Tourism* 9(4), 298–316.

Andriotis, K. (2002a) Residents' satisfaction or dissatisfaction with public sector governance. The Cretan case. *Tourism and Hospitality Research: The Surrey Quarterly Review* 4(1), 53–68.

Andriotis, K. (2002b) Scale of hospitality firms and local economic development. Evidence from Crete. *Tourism Management* 23(4), 333–41.

Andronikos, A. (1979) Tourism in Cyprus. In E. de Kadt (ed.) *Tourism: Passport to Development?* Oxford: Oxford University Press.

Andronikos, A. (1986). Cyprus: Management of the tourist sector. *Tourism Management* 7(2), 127–9.

Apostolopoulos, Y. (1994) The perceived effects of tourism industry development: A comparison of two Hellenic islands. Unpubished PhD thesis, University of Connecticut, Ann Arbor, MI.

Apostolopoulos, Y. and Sönmz, S.F. (1999) From farmers and shepherds to shopkeepers and hoteliers: Constituency-differentiated experiences of endogenous tourism in the Greek island of Zakynthos. *Tourism Research* 1(6), 413–27.

Baum, T. (1997a) Island tourism as an emerging field of study. *Islander Magazine* 3 (Jan), 1–4.

Baum, T. (1997b) The fascination of islands: A tourism perspective. In D.G. Lockhart, and D. Drakakis-Smith (eds) *Island Tourism: Trends and Prospects* (pp. 21–35). London and New York: Pinter.

Boissevain, J. (1977) Tourism and development in Malta. *Development and Change* 8, 523–38.

Boissevain, J. (1979) The impact of tourism on a dependent island: Gozo, Malta. *Annals of Tourism Research* 6(1), 76–90.

Boissevain, J. (1996) 'But we live here!' Perspectives on cultural tourism in Malta. In L. Briguglio, R. Butler, D. Harison and W.L. Filho (eds) *Sustainable Tourism in Islands and Small States: Case studies* (pp. 220–40). London: Pinter.

Briguglio, L. and Briguglio, M. (1996) Sustainable tourism in Maltese islands. In L. Briguglio, R. Butler, D. Harison and W.L. Filho (eds) *Sustainable Tourism in Islands and Small States: Case Studies* (pp. 162–79). Pinter: London.

Brohman, J. (1996) New directions in tourism for third world development. *Annals of Tourism Research* 23(1), 48–70.

Bryden, J.M. (1973) *Tourism and Development: A Case Study of the Commonwealth Caribbean*. Cambridge: Cambridge University Press.

Buhalis, D. (1999) Tourism on the Greek islands: Issues of peripherality, competitiveness and development. *Tourism Research* 1(3), 341–58.

Butler, R. (1996) Problems and possibilities of sustainable tourism: The case of the Shetland Islands. In L. Briguglio, R. Butler, D. Harrison and W.L. Filho (eds) *Sustainable Tourism in Islands and Small States: Case Studies* (pp. 11–31). London: Pinter.

Butler, R.W. (1993) Tourism development in small islands: Past influences and future directions. In D. Lockhart, D. Drakakis-Smith and J. Schembri (eds) *The Development Process in Small Islands States* (pp. 71–91). London: Routledge.

Butler, R.W. and Stiakaki, E. (2001) Tourism and sustainability in the Mediterranean: Issues and implications from Hydra. In D. Ioannides, Y. Apostolopoulos, and S.

Sommez (eds) *Mediterranean Islands and Sustainable Tourism Development. Practices, Management and Policies* (pp. 282–99). London: Pinter.

Chen-Young, P. (1982) Tourism in the economic development of small states: Jamaica's experience. In B. Jalan (ed) *Problems and Policies in Small Economies* (pp. 221–9), London: St. Martin's.

Choy, D.J.L. (1992) Life cycle models for Pacific Island destinations. *Journal of Travel Research* 30(3), 26–31.

Coccossis, H. and Parpairis, A. (1995) Assessing the interaction between heritage, environment and tourism: Myconos. In H. Coccossis and P. Nijkamp (eds) *Sustainable Tourism Development* (pp. 107–25). London: Avebury.

Coccossis, H.N. (1987) Planning for islands. *Ekistics* 323–4, 84–7.

Conlin, M.V. and Baum, T. (1995) Island tourism: An introduction In M.V. Conlin and T. Baum (eds) *Island Tourism: Management Principles and Practice* (pp. 3–13). Chichester: Wiley.

Crocombe, R. and Rajotte, F. (eds) (1980) *Pacific Tourism as Islanders See it.* Suva: Institute of Pacific Studies.

Cross, M. and Nutley, S. (1999) Insularity and accessibility: The small island communities of Western Ireland. *Journal of Rural Studies* 15(3), 317–30.

Damer, S. (2001) Between God and mammon: The origins of tourism on Symi. Paper presented in the Tourism on Islands and Specific Destinations conference, Chios Island, Greece, 14–16 December.

Dana, L.P. (1999) The social cost of tourism. *Cornell Hotel and Restaurant Administration Quarterly.* 40(4), 60–63.

Dasmann, R.F., Milton, J.R. and Freeman, P.H. (1973) *Ecological Principles for Economic Development.* New York: Wiley.

Epilogi (2001) *Prefectures: The Financial and Social Face of the 52 Prefectures and the 13 Regions.* Athens.

EU (2000) Synthesis of contributions from LEADER groups throughout the European Union. On WWW at http://www.rural-europe.aeidl.be/.

Eurostat (1994) *Portrait of the Islands.* Luxembourg: European Commission.

Eurostat (1999) *Statistics in Focus.* Luxembourg: European Commission.

Farrel, B. (1985) South Pacific tourism in the mid-1980s. *Tourism Management* 6(1), 55–60.

Fousekis. P. and Lekakis, J.N. (1996) Greece's institutional response to sustainable development. *Environmental Politics* 6(1), 131–52.

Galani-Moutafi, V. (1993) From agriculture to tourism: Property, labor, gender, and kinship in a Greek island village. *Journal of Modern Greek Studies* 2(2), 241–70.

Giannias, D. (1999) Regional tourism industry indices and the allocation of European union and state funding: The case of Greece. *Tourism Research* 1(6), 410–12.

Hache, J-D. (1996) The implications of EU legislation upon the provision of transport services with regard to island regions. On WWW at http://www.eurisles.com.

Hills, T.L. and Lundgren, J. (1977) The impact of tourism in the Caribbean: A methodological study. *Annals of Tourism Research* 4(5), 248–67.

Hellenic National Tourism Organisation (HNTO) (2000) *Statistics.* Athens: Hellenic National Tourism Organisation.

Hellenic National Tourism Organisation (HNTO) (2002) *Tourists Movements Bulletin – 2002/1* [in Greek]. Athens: Hellenic National Tourism Organisation.

International Scientific Council for Island Developmeent (INSULA) (2000) European island agenda. Operational Fields. On WWW at http://www.insula.org/.

Ioannides, D. (1992) Tourism development agents: The Cypriot resort cycle. *Annals of Tourism Research* 19(4), 711–31.

Ioannides, D. (1994) The state, transnationals and the dynamics of tourism evolution in small islands nations. Unpublished PhD thesis, Rutgers University, New Jersey.

Ioannides, D. (1995a) Planning for international tourism in less developed countries: Towards sustainability? *Journal of Planning Literature* 9(3), 235–59.

Ioannides, D. (1995b) A flawed implementation of sustainable tourism: The experience of Akamas, Cyprus. *Tourism Management* 16(8), 583–92.

Kammas, M. (1993) The positive and negative effects of tourism development in Cyprus. *Cyprus Review* 5(1), 70–89.

Kenna, M. (1993) Return migrants and tourism development: An example from the Cyclades. *Journal of Modern Greek Studies* 2 (1), 75–96.

King, R. (1993) The geographical fascination of islands. In D. Lockhart, D. Drakakis-Smith and J. Schembri (eds) *The Development Process in Small Islands States* (pp. 13–37). London: Routledge.

Kousis, M. (1984) Tourism as an agent of social change in a rural Cretan community. Unpublished PhD thesis, University of Michigan, Michigan.

Lekakis, J.N. (1995) Environmental management in Greece and the challenge of sustainable development. *Environmentalist* 15, 16–26.

Leontidou, L. (1998) Greece: Hesitant policy and uneven tourism development in the 1990s. In A.M. Williams and G. Shaw (eds) *Tourism and Economic Development: European Experiences* (3rd edn) (pp.101–24). Chichester: Wiley.

Liu, Z-H. and Jenkins, C. (1996) Country size and tourism development: A cross-nation analysis. In L. Briguglio, B. Archer, J. Jafari and G. Wall (eds) *Sustainable Tourism in Islands and Small States: Issues and Policies* (pp. 90–117). London: Pinter.

Lockhart, D.G. (1997a) Tourism to Malta and Cyprus. In D.G. Lockhart and D. Drakakis-Smith (eds) *Island Tourism: Trends and Prospects* (pp.152–80). London and New York: Pinter.

Lockhart, D.G. (1997b) Islands and tourism: An overview. In D.G. Lockhart and D. Drakakis-Smith (eds) *Island Tourism: Trends and Prospects* (pp. 3–20). London and New York: Pinter.

Lockhart, D.G. and Ashton, S. (1990) Tourism in Malta. *Scottish Geographical Magazine* 10(1), 22–32.

Loukissas, P.J. (1978) Tourism and environment in conflict: The case of the Greek island of Mykonos. In *Tourism and Economic: Studies in Third World Societies* (vol. 6) (pp. 105–32). Williamsburg, VA: College of William and Mary.

Loukissas, P.J. (1982) Tourism's regional development impacts: A comparative analysis of the Greek islands. *Annals of Tourism Research* 9(4), 523–41.

Macheridis, I. (2001) Island development: Choices and perspective. On WWW at http://www.eurisles.com.

Marinos, P. (1983) Small islands tourism: The case of Zakynthos, Greece. *Tourism Management* 4(3), 212–15.

McElroy, J.L. and de Albuquerque, K. (1998) Tourism penetration index in small Caribbean islands. *Annals of Tourism Research* 25(1), 145–68.

Milne, S. (1992) Tourism and development in South Pacific microstates. *Annals of Tourism Research* 19(2), 191–22.

Milne, S. (1997) Tourism, dependency and South Pacific micro-states: Beyond the vicious cycle? In D.G. Lockhart and D. Drakakis-Smith (eds) *Island Tourism: Trends and Prospects* (pp. 281–301). London: Pinter.

Milne, S. and Nowosielski, L. (1997). Travel distribution technologies and sustainable tourism development: The case of South Pacific. *Journal of Sustainable Tourism* 5(2), 131–50.

Moussios, G. (1999) *Greece – Travel and Tourism Intelligence Country Reports* 2, 25–49.

National Statistical Service of Greece (NSSG) (2000) *Statistical Yearbook of Greece 1999*. Athens: National Statistical Service of Greece.

National Statistical Service of Greece (NSSG) (2001) *Employment-Unemployment Year 2000* [in Greek]. Athens: National Statistical Services of Greece.

Nijkamp, P. and Verdonkschot, S. (1995) Sustainable tourism development. A case study of Lesbos. In H. Coccossis and P. Nijkamp (eds) *Sustainable Tourism Development* (pp. 127–40). London: Avebury.

Oglethorpe, M. (1984) Tourism in Malta: A crisis of dependence. *Leisure Studies* 3, 147–62.

Oglethorpe, M. (1985) Tourism in a small island economy: The case of Malta. *Tourism Management*. 6(1), 23–31.

Papadaki-Tzedaki, S. (1997) Endogenous tourist development in Rethymno:

Development or underdevelopment [in Greek]. Unpublished PhD thesis, University of Rethymno, Rethymno.

Pavlopoulos, P.G. and Kouzelis, A.K. (1998) *Regional Development of Greece and Tourism* [in Greek]. Athens: Research Institute for Tourism.

Pearce, D.G. (1995) *Tourism Today: A Geographical Analysis* (2nd edn). New York: Longman.

Petersen, C.A. and McCarthy, C. (1990) Greece charts the course: Controlling second home development in coastal areas. Environment Tourism and Development: An Agenda for Action? A workshop to consider strategies for sustainable tourism development, Valetta, Malta, 10 March.

Pettifer, J. (1993) *The Greeks: The Land and People Since the War*. London: Penguin.

Prunier, E., Sweeney, A. and Geen, A. (1993) Tourism and the environment: The case of Zakynthos. *Tourism Management* 14(2), 137–41.

Royle, S. and Scott, D. (1996) Accessibility and the Irish islands. *Geography* 8(12), 111–19.

Royle, S.A. (1989) A human geography of islands. *Geography* 74(2), 106–16.

Schofield, J. and George, J.J. (1997) Why study islands? In R.A. Irving, A.J. Schofield and C.J. Webster (eds) *Island Studies. Fifty Years of the Lundy Field Society* (pp. 5–14). Bideford: Lundy Field Society.

Seward, A.B. and Spinard, B.K. (eds) (1982) *Tourism in the Caribbean: The Economic Impact*. Ottawa: International Development Research Centre.

Squire, S.J. (1996) Literary tourism and sustainable tourism: Promoting 'Anne of Green Gables' in Prince Edward island. *Journal of Sustainable Tourism* 4(3), 119–34.

Stott, A.M. (1996) Tourism development and the need for community action in Mykonos, Greece. In L. Briguglio, R. Butler, D. Harison and W.L. Filho (eds) *Sustainable Tourism in Islands and Small States: Case Studies* (pp. 281–306). London: Pinter.

Timothy, D.J. (1999) Participatory planning. A view of tourism in Indonesia. *Annals of Tourism Research* 26(2), 371–91.

Totsiou, Y., Hatzantonis, D., Karamitropoulou and Lolos, S. (1999) *Evaluation of the Impact of Actions Implementing Regulation (EEC) No 2019/93 on the Economic Situation of the Small Islands in the Aegean Sea*. Athens: European Community.

Tsartas, P. (1992) Socio-economic impacts of tourism on two Greek islands. *Annals of Tourism Research* 19(3), 516–33.

Vaughan, R., Andriotis, K. and Wilkes, K. (2000) Characteristics of tourism employment: The case of Crete. Paper presented in the 7th ATLAS International Conference. North-South: Contrasts and Connections in Global Tourism, Savonlinna, Finland, 18–21 June.

Warren, R.L. (1978) *The community in America* (3rd edn). Chicago: Rand McNally.

Waters, S.R. (1993) *Annual Travel Industry World Yearbook: The Big Picture – 1992*. New York: Child and Waters.

Weaver, D.B. (1993). Model of urban tourism for small Caribbean islands. *Geographical Review* 83(2), 134–40.

Wilkinson, P.F. (1987) Tourism in small island nations: A fragile dependency. *Leisure Studies* 6(2), 127–46.

Wilkinson, P.F. (1989) Development strategies for tourism in island microstates. *Annals of Tourism Research* 16(2), 153–77.

Young, B. (1983) Touristisation of traditional Maltese fishing-farming villages. *Tourism Management* 4(1), 35–41.

Zarkia, C. (1996) Philoxenia: Receiving tourists – but not guests – on a Greek island. In J. Boissevain (eds) *Coping with Tourists: European Reactions to Mass Tourism* (pp. 143–73). Oxford: Berghahm.

# 7 Sustainable Tourism Planning in Northern Cyprus

*Jon Sadler*
*Charles Sturt University, School of Environmental and Information Sciences, PO Box 789, Albury, Australia 2640*

This paper seeks to identify the problems of planning and environmental assessment for tourism in the developing country of Northern Cyprus, known as the Turkish Republic of Northern Cyprus (TRNC). The research provides an overview of tourism in a politically unrecognised and largely unknown state. It investigates the proposition that a politically and geographically isolated *de facto* island state can be an advantage when applying alternative natural resource-based tourism objectives, provided that political and economic influences can favour sustainable planning. Practical frameworks for tourism planning for sustainable development are investigated in the context of this island state. The basic process of strategic environmental assessment (SEA), and the potential organisation and implementation of the SEA process on the island are examined. It is concluded that an integrated SEA and strong tourism planning are urgently required to safeguard the future for tourism and the environment in the TRNC.

## Introduction

This paper examines a hitherto under developed tourism destination, Northern Cyprus or the Turkish Republic of Northern Cyprus (TRNC). It assesses how the economic, social and environmental opportunities afforded by largely undeveloped natural resources can be maximised through alternative approaches. These could involve an integrated tourism development process and the use of strategic environmental assessment (SEA).

Cyprus is the third largest island in the Mediterranean. The TRNC constitutes 38% or 3355 km$^2$ of Cyprus, and it possesses many of the island's best natural and cultural resources. It has the inherent Mediterranean attributes of climate and location. In addition, it contains 55% of the island's coastline; the spectacular Kyrenian Mountains with their associated rich natural history (Viney, 1994); historical and cultural attractions, such as Kyrenia, the Old Town at Famagusta, and the ancient city of Salamis; 'dark tourism' attractions of the recent conflict and war between the Greek National Guard and Greek Cypriots with the Turkish military and Turkish Cypriots (Lennon & Foley, 2000); and the generous Turkish Cypriot hospitality.

Unlike other Mediterranean islands with such tourism resources, the north of the island remains relatively undeveloped for tourism (see Figure 1). Politically, the TRNC is an occupied territory, and it is only recognised and economically supported by Turkey. Any trade is undertaken through Turkey, and international flights have to land there before continuing to Northern Cyprus. While the 28-year deadlocked negotiations for a settlement continue, the *de facto* boundary with the Republic of Cyprus (the part of the island under Greek Cypriot administration) puts the TRNC economy in a precarious position.

In a study of the relative tourism competitiveness of the TRNC with the

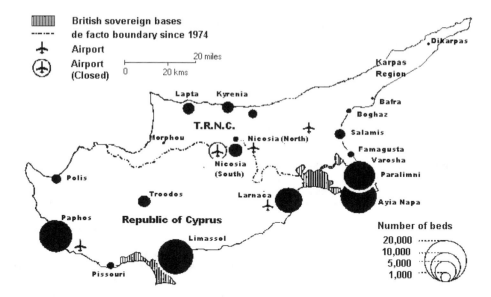

**Figure 1** Distribution of tourist accommodation in Cyprus, 1997
*Source*: Adapted from Lockhart, 1997

Republic of Cyprus (Altinay, 1998), the following factors were assessed: hotel prices, historical places, the administration and organisation, the quality of the product, transport and infrastructure, and promotion. Except for the first two variables, the TRNC was found to be less competitive than the Republic of Cyprus. However, there are a number of long-term competitive indicators that are not measured in conventional economic approaches to competitiveness, such as landscape aesthetics and ecological, wilderness and cultural indicators, and that represent valuable tourism assets for the TRNC (see Table 1). These factors contribute to the 'unspoilt' product label given to the TRNC by tour companies in the UK and Germany. Conversely, the Republic of Cyprus is a highly developed tourist destination. The high-density building and ribbon development in areas such as Larnaca and Ayia Napa have contributed to an over-supply of tourism

**Table 1** Short- and long-term variables of tourism competitiveness

| Short-term variables | Long-term variables |
| --- | --- |
| Accommodation prices | Landscape value |
| Administration | Ecological heritage |
| Transport and infrastructure | Cultural heritage |
| Promotion | Historical heritage |
| Visitor attractions | Wilderness value |

*Source*: Adapted from World Tourism Organisation, 1994

facilities. Associated environmental problems have compelled planners to look to more sustainable approaches to tourism development.

The uncertainties and complexities of the political situation and the need for a strategic approach to tourism development give rise to many critical questions. The aims of the paper are to provide an overview of tourism development in the TRNC, and to present ideas for further research. In particular, it focuses on the following:

- some theoretical procedures for sustainable tourism planning pertinent to Cyprus;
- the existing framework for tourism development in the TRNC;
- possible ways forward and recommendations for further research to secure more effective and sustainable tourism planning in the TRNC and in a federal Cyprus.

## Theoretical Approaches to Sustainable Tourism Planning

### The island paradigm

The value of the present resources in the TRNC for tourism is significantly related to it being part of a small island:

> Islands are detached self-contained entities whose boundaries are obvious . . . on an island, material values lose their despotic influence: one comes more in touch with the elemental – water, land, fire, vegetation, and wildlife. The unity of islands undoubtedly wields an interest over the people who live upon them; life there promotes self-reliance, contentment, a sense of human scale. (Wilstach, 1926: 24).

The idealised qualities of islands sought by tourists include a physical separateness, political independence, cultural distinctiveness, and an attractive climate and environment (Butler, 1993). These qualities contribute to the timeless, changeless and illusory 'Robinson Crusoe Factor' (Lockhart, 1993). For the majority of northern European visitors, the Mediterranean islands to some extent embody these qualities. Destinational differences are perhaps less important than the 'placeless' pleasures of a sun and sea resort with sandy beaches and hospitable locals (Butler, 1993; Dann, 2000). But it can be argued that the uniqueness, sense of intimacy and human scale of islands can be essential ingredients for both 'alternative' and 'mass tourists'.

Small islands often have few economic alternatives to tourism (Wilkinson, 1989). This is because commonly they suffer from the disadvantages of a specialised small economy, a limited range of human and physical resources, a limited ability to react to international market changes, and exogenous decision making by overseas investors and key service providers.

### The competitive sustainability paradigm

The growing interest of tourists in alternative forms of tourism has been well documented (Carey *et al.*, 1997; Orams, 1995). According to Gilbert, the growth of alternative tourism, based on independent, cultural and nature-based activities, is likely to lead to a decrease in mass package holidays. However, this trend would negate the term 'alternative'. If this trend is accepted, then there is a need to identify what is needed to gain a competitive advantage in attracting more discerning tourists. The lack of a sustainable approach to alternative tourism is likely to lead to more environmental damage than mass tourism. Concentrated tourism activity in a resort may have less associated impacts than dispersed alternative tourists seeking new sites and experiences (Warner, 1999). Therefore, long-term competitiveness requires a sustainable approach to tourism. This requires planners to look beyond economic indicators and carrying capacity indicators and to adopt a more holistic approach. In assessing competitiveness, both structural (long-term) and operational (short-term) planning are essential (see Table 1).

It is within the context of long-term competitiveness that this paper investigates tourism planning approaches in the TRNC. It takes into account existing systems as well as the potential application of theoretical environmental assessment (EA) techniques to tourism. First, it is necessary to consider the concept of sustainable development. Sustainability requires that the benefits brought about by tourism development are maintained in an area for an indefinite period of time (Butler, 1993). The benefits can include an equitable increase in per capita consumption, environmental protection, and the involvement of all members of the community in decision making. Realistically, this means there has to be a trade-off between environmental considerations and social and economic goals. In other words, tourism can be sustainable as long as certain irreplaceable natural and cultural elements are protected. These elements are known as 'critical natural and cultural capital' (Bond, 1995) and these need to be defined and protected by policies and legislation.

At the roots of the concept of sustainable development is the notion of carrying capacity. This can be depicted as the maximum number of people who can use a site without an unacceptable alteration in the physical environment and without an unacceptable decline in the quality of experience (Mathieson & Wall, 1982: 88). Thus, carrying capacity is a problematic concept. It can use physical, psychological, biological and social variables and needs to be interpreted and quantified early on in the planning process. Each of these variables also address complex issues. For example, biological carrying capacity indicators may include, *inter alia*, the unacceptable alteration of either individual species, habitat, genetic diversity or ecological diversity, or a combination of these variables. The basis of EA is to guage where the environmental carrying capacity is exceeded by tourism projects.

Projects, such as tourism developments, are not planned, built, operated and decommissioned in isolation, but within a context of regional, national and international change, which includes other projects, programmes, plans and policies (Morris & Therivel, 1995). This requires a strategic approach to planning. Strategic Environmental Assessment (SEA) allows government the opportunity to study environmental impacts at policy, plan, programme and also project levels. The SEA process can be defined as:

> a systematic process for evaluating the environmental consequences of a policy, plan or programme initiatives in order to ensure that they are fully included and appropriately addressed at the earliest stage of the decision-

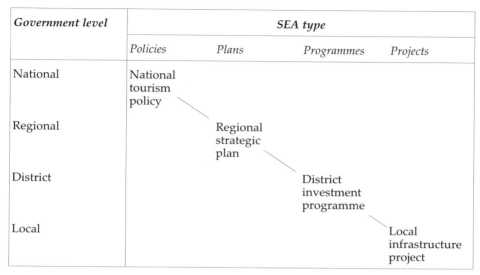

| Government level | SEA type | | | |
| --- | --- | --- | --- | --- |
| | *Policies* | *Plans* | *Programmes* | *Projects* |
| National | National tourism policy | | | |
| Regional | | Regional strategic plan | | |
| District | | | District investment programme | |
| Local | | | | Local infrastructure project |

**Figure 2** Sequence of actions within a comprehensive EIA system
*Source*: Adapted from Wood, 1995.

making process on a par with economic and social considerations. (European Commission, 1998: 1)

According to Glasson *et al.* (1994):

- a policy is an inspiration and guidance for action;
- a plan is a set of coordinated and timed objectives for the implementation of the policy; and
- a programme is a set of projects in a particular area.

The SEA process helps to ensure an acceptable level of sustainable development. This is because SEA provides a higher tier of assessment, so that decision making can be influenced at a time when the framework is established, and this can aid the later formulation of specific projects (see Figure 2).

## The environmental assessment problem

Miller and Szekely (1995) suggest that stakeholders interested in development projects in developed countries are unsure of the systems that need to be developed to assess these projects. These stakeholders include the international community, financial agents, environmental pressure groups and industry. This can be due to:

- insufficient scientific knowledge: in the TRNC information about projects is difficult to obtain due to a lack of trained human resources and of financial resources – this has led to the preparation of inadequate and irrelevant Environmental Statements (Camgoz, 1999; Eren, 1999);
- lack of insight as to what is meant by the reduction of environmental impacts across a project's entire lifecycle: for example, environmental conditions in the TRNC may render inappropriate certain biophysical assumptions

derived in cool temperate zones in the US and Europe, such as in relation to water demand and supply;

- the difficulty of adopting an environmental policy with measurable targets and goals;
- the emphasis of mitigation policies on the visible 'green' principles of environmental conservation, such as on reduction, reuse, recovery, and recycling, rather than more fundamental changes;
- the lack of systems to check whether assessment criteria are applied fairly and consistently;
- the methods used to measure and compare environmental performance being at an early stage of development;
- the methods of monitoring performance being based on comparing it with standards within the industry rather than with best environmental practice;
- EA systems generally relying on what is easily observable or on information that is publicly available, which may not be connected to the full environmental impact.

### The tourism planning problem

Sustainable tourism planning is complex and difficult because practically all natural resources in a given area, such as beaches and mountains, are part of the product. Tourism planning is also multi-tiered and spatially and organisationally fragmented, and there are multiple economic, biophysical, sociocultural and political interrelationships. Hence, it requires a complex and multidisciplinary approach for EA screening (measuring the significance of impacts) and scoping (what impacts should be addressed). Essentially, tourism planning is dynamic and the related processes and impacts are susceptible to change. Conversely, sustainable development implies a degree of stability and permanence. The SEA process entails moulding these disparate concerns into an operational plan.

## Methodology

Due to the shortage of literature and specific data on the topic for the TRNC, some primary research was essential, together with comparison with other island case studies. A total of eight in-depth interviews were conducted with key informants with a good knowledge of the issues in the country.

Interviewee respondents were chosen in terms of their relevance to tourism and environmental planning and management at government, district and community levels, and in the public and private sectors. Interviews were conducted with the Secretary of State responsible for Tourism, the Vice Chairman of the Environmental Protection Agency, the Environment Director of the Famagusta Planning Department, a village *Muhtar* (headman), a local entrepreneur and hotel investor, a hotel manager, and academics in the School of Tourism, Eastern Mediterranean University, Famagusta.

The qualitative framework involved an interpretative approach, although the specificity of the questions aimed to give a focused response to problems and issues. The limitations of the research are influenced by the lack of available data from the TRNC administration, such as environmental statements, and by a perceived lack of communication between the decision makers, other stakeholders and the general public. Some of the interviewees' answers also inevitably lost something of their true meaning and reliability due to the translation process.

## Tourism in the TRNC: The Legacy of a Turbulent History

Cyprus, located on the axis of the Muslim world and Christian civilisations, has always had a significant strategic value, and two dozen contemporary powers through the ages have jockeyed for control (TRNC, 2000). It has been colonised peacefully and forcibly by, amongst others, the Hellenic Minoans and Mycenaeans, the Assyrians, Egyptians, Persians, Phoenicians, Alexander the Great, Byzantines, Lusignans (Frankish), Venetians, Ottomans and finally the British, before achieving independence as the Republic of Cyprus in 1960.

The constitution proved unworkable, as majority rule was explicitly denied by the founding charter. Intercommunal strife occurred, principally from 1963 to 1974, between the Turkish Cypriots and the Greek Cypriots, with the latter wanting greater control with their 80% majority (Dubin, 1996). Extremists exacerbated tensions, with the Greek Cypriot *EOKA* (National Organisation of Cypriot Fighters) wanting union or *enosis* with Greece, and the Turkish Cypriot *TMT* (Turkish Defence Organisation) wanting partition with an ideology similar to today's TRNC administration. Despite the internal conflicts, post-independence economic progress was considerable, particularly with reference to tourism developments now in the TRNC controlled areas.

In July 1974, a *coup d'état* by Greeks and Greek Cypriots, inspired by the Greek junta in Athens, precipitated an invasion and occupation by Turkey of 38% of the island. Subsequently, the TRNC was formed by the Turkish Cypriot administration in 1983. This led to a number of features that placed tourism development in the TRNC in a unique position.

First, and perhaps most significantly, the majority of the generally well-educated, skilled and now perhaps minority Turkish Cypriot community have emigrated to England, Turkey, Australia and elsewhere. Conversely, the immigrants, who are largely uneducated and unskilled Anatolian Turkish settlers, have provided a limited input into tourism initiatives, largely through staffing large hotel developments. It has been suggested that these settlers consisted of families of 1974 campaign veterans, a surplus urban underclass, landless peasants, and low-grade criminals and psychiatric cases (Avci, 1999; Dubin, 1996). However, changes to this pattern are apparent as increasing numbers of educated and qualified Turks assume interests on the island. The establishment of five universities catering for around 20,000 students (TRNC, 2000) to satisfy the largely Turkish and middle-east market, and returning expatriates, has assisted this trend.

Secondly, most of the pre-1974 tourism superstructure and infrastructure in Cyprus were in the possession of the Turkish military and 82% of all accommodation and 96% of hotels under construction were lost to the Turkish (Andronicou, 1979). With the exclusion of Varosha which was left derelict in the demilitarised zone, tourism facilities at Kyrenia and Famagusta proved mostly sufficient to satisfy the small number of tourist arrivals in the decade or so following the war (Mansfield & Kliot, 1996). However, there were only 1369 beds in Kyrenia in

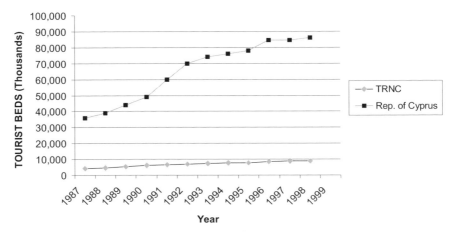

**Figure 3** Number of tourist beds in the TRNC and the Republic of Cyprus, 1987–1997
*Sources*: International Tourism Report, 2000 and TRNC Statistics and Research Department, 1998

1973, so some development was inevitable (TRNC, 1997). It was only in the late 1980s that the increase in tourists from Turkey and Europe necessitated an expansion of tourism infrastructure (Lockhart & Ashton, 1990). The areas that were chosen for development east and west of Kyrenia and north of Famagusta to Boghaz are relatively small and piecemeal.

Thirdly, the TRNC's unstable coalition democracy is continually changing within a climate of party 'tribalism' strongly influenced by Turkey. The TDP (Tourism Development Process) is similar to Turkey in that at a national strategic level the little available expertise and decision making is centralised, following the trait of many developing countries (Tosun, 1998, 2001). Where planning has occurred at a local level, the Department of Town Planning has focused merely on zoning residential development (Lockhart & Drakakis-Smith, 1996).

Fourthly, unlike most island communities, tourism development is not in strong competition with other land uses. Although not all suitable for tourism development, over 8% (26,942 hectares) of land is unused, and a far greater proportion is marginal agricultural land used for rough grazing (TRNC, 1995). Population density in the TRNC is only 58% of that of the Republic of Cyprus (Lockhart & Drakakis-Smith, 1996) and 21% of that of Malta (Godfrey, 1995).

Lastly, the surplus housing stock, which had previously been occupied by Greek Cypriots, has until recently allowed (Haktamir, 1999) for the settlement of displaced Turkish Cypriots, Turkish immigrants and expatriate retirees, and some business and holiday tourists, without large-scale development of new housing.

Therefore, tourism development remained stagnant up until 1987. Since then, the development of new tourism accommodation has been around a tenth of that of the Republic of Cyprus (see Figure 3), and modest in comparison to other competitors in the region. The development that has occurred tends to follow the island characteristics noted by Pearce (1995), whereby larger hotels cluster along a small number of coastal localities which are fairly close to the urban centres: in this case, Famagusta and Kyrenia. About 95% of accommodation in the TRNC is almost exclusively in the form of hotels or hotel apartments, and two-thirds of this accommodation is in the form of large hotels with over 100 beds (TRNC, 1997).

Despite tourism's relatively small contribution to employment compared to agriculture, government services and construction, the TRNC administration views it as the cornerstone of the economy. It is considered as a 'quick fix' solution as it occurs relatively quickly and it has a pervasive effect in assisting the other sectors of the economy (Altinay, 1998), these being essential for a country whose per capita income is a quarter of that of the Republic of Cyprus (Mansfield & Kliot, 1996). This political viewpoint, the lack of competition for land, the *ad hoc* use of existing dwellings, and the deficient financial resources and expertise in the Turkish Cypriot administration, have led to a deficiency in both strategic and local planning for tourism.

## The Reality of Tourism Planning in the TRNC

It has been argued that growing public awareness of environmental problems, reflected in legislation and increased consumer pressure, has led to a competitive advantage for green products, including tourism, throughout Western cultures. In the TRNC, for example, each year some 60 voluntary students from Britain's Glasgow University Turtle Conservation Expedition (GUTCE), together with Cypriot and Turkish students, assist in turtle conservation work. Surveys by the GUTCE team have demonstrated that up to 50% of the largely 2000 foreign visitors per year who view the turtles have come to the TRNC primarily for this purpose (Bell, 1999).

However, there are several reasons for the reluctance to adopt a more sustainable approach to tourism development. First, both Greek and Turkish Cypriots generally only believe in the benefits of mass tourism (Akis *et al.*, 1996). For example, people from the undeveloped areas of Laona and Paphos in the South and Dikarpas in the North favour large-scale tourism developments, despite the above suggested trends and the existing problems of over-capacity at mass tourism destinations. For instance, the TRNC's occupancy rate was 31.8% in 1997 (Altinay, 1998), and although occupancy is greater in the Republic of Cyprus, some areas, such as Ayia Napa and Limassol, have recently suffered occupancy levels of around 30% (Seekings, 1997). Furthermore, even when these areas are totally transformed by tourism developments, which may have around 500,000 tourists visiting in a year (Cope, 2000), the host community appears tolerant, and there is no evidence to suggest that the social carrying capacity is exceeded (Severiades, 2000). Culturally, the protection of natural resources may not be viewed as important as macroeconomic imperatives (Tosun, 2001), particularly as specific tourism impacts on natural resources in the TRNC are perceived to be low.

Secondly, the lack of planning integration in Cyprus, as noted by Ioannides (1995), is partly due to a misconception that comprehensive planning control and environmental conservation strategies contradict political and economic expediency and growth objectives. The Vice-Chairman of the Environmental Protection Agency claims that this explains why local communities are purposefully ignored by technocrats in decision-making processes in the TRNC (Camgoz, 1999).

Thirdly, EA procedures have focused on the condition of the end product and have failed to integrate environmental considerations earlier on in the decision-making process. In the TRNC, the Environmental Protection Act (1998) modelled on the American Federal National Environmental Policy Act (1969) considers impacts at project level (Camgoz, 1999). This project focus is also apparent in developed EU countries, where the SEA policy directive 2001/42/EC has only recently been adopted (European Commission, 2001). The result is that key environmental issues, such as tourism project alternatives, are not adequately considered, and *ad hoc* developments and associated cumulative impacts are not assessed. Such cumulative impacts (Morris & Therivel, 1995) include the development of private housing in tourism development areas, particularly second homes for Turkish Cypriots living overseas. In the Republic of Cyprus, the necessity to build housing for displaced Greek Cypriots meant that between 1977 and 1984 new hotel units at Larnaca and Limassol were outnumbered by new housing by more than six to one (Lockhart & Drakakis-Smith, 1997). Plog (1977) has demonstrated that these developments are a victim of their own success and that if they allow themselves to become over-commercialised they will lose the unique qualities that attracted investment and tourism in the first place.

Lastly, evidence in both Turkey (Alipour, 1995) and the TRNC (Kanol, 1999) suggests that political and economic necessity affects the views taken by both policy makers and developers in their understanding of the problems encountered in tourism development. Policy makers are clearly affected by the lack of policy decisions and tools to indicate the spatial distribution of resources and the priorities, as well as by a shortfall in legislative structures and technical capacity to assess impacts (Hunter & Green, 1995).

The legislative framework for tourism policy in the TRNC is provided by the Tourism Incentive Law (1987). This essentially focuses on investment and encouragement of tourism through the provision of a number of incentives outlined in Table 2. In reality, this has done little for the TRNC economy, with the expatriate Turkish-Cypriot investors repatriating their earnings to their chosen domiciles (Mansfield & Kliot, 1996). In other cases, according to Balgioglu (1999), 'Government aid was promised, but nothing was delivered. Therefore the project could not be completed.'

The Tourism Incentive Law (1987) is planning by 'boosterism' (Getz, 1987), and may be important in the initial stages of tourism development when the focus is on tourism promotion and maximising economic output. However, Getz states that it is led by

> politicians who believe that economic growth is always to be promoted, and by others who will gain financially by tourism. They will go on promoting it until evidence mounts that they have run out of resources to exploit, that the real or opportunity costs are too high, or that political

**Table 2** Investment Incentives for Tourism in the TRNC

1. Import duty exemptions for investment goods concerning a project.

2. Government contribution to charter risk.

3. Contribution to brochure and advertisement expenditure.

4. Exemption from income tax and corporate tax for a period of ten years in the case of investment in tourist accommodation units, and/or operating charter flights. For public companies where the number of shareholders is not less than 50, this exemption is increased by three years.

5. Annual interest and principal instalments of foreign loans enjoy a transfer guarantee.

6. A deduction of 20% of annual foreign exchange gross earnings from taxable income for hotels and travel agencies.

7. Repatriation of profit without any restriction or limitation.

8. Free transfer of proceeds in the case of the liquidation of an investment.

9. Employment of foreign qualified personnel who are not available locally.

10. Transfer of net income earned by foreign personnel is free.

11. Exemption from construction licence fee.

12. Travel and advertisement expenses for promotion and marketing are deducted from taxable profit.

*Source*: Ministry of Economy and Finance, 1994

opposition to growth can no longer be countered. By then the real damage has usually been done.

Evidence from the draft TRNC Tourism Master Plan (Kanol, 1999), the *modus operandi* for tourism policy, indicates that boosterism and economic policies are also prevalent there. Such objectives may prove totally unworkable in practice. An example is the proposal for an increase in bed capacity from 8940 in 1997 (TRNC, 1997) and tourist numbers from 184,434 in 1998, to over 50,000 and 606,775 respectively in 2010, using spatial planning models. Such land-use-based planning models applied at Bafra in the Karpas require 8000 new beds, representing 15% of the physical carrying capacity of the Karpas beaches. However, other sociocultural and environmental parameters are totally ignored, such as the 5000 personnel required that would be imposed on a local population of around 120 (Asikoglu, 1999)!

The European Union could act as a catalyst for more responsible decision making by the TRNC Government (Sertoglu & Bicak, 1998) in relation to tourism planning. There has been some European Union investment in the TRNC, and the leaders of the two communities have finally met. However, the lack of participation in the accession negotiations to the EU by the TRNC administration (European Commission, 2002) does not suggest that supra-national legislative directives supporting sustainable tourism development will be forthcoming.

The status quo is maintained in tourism development because of the sociopolitical structure of the small island community of the TRNC, where the emphasis is on centralised political decision makers and elite business interests

(Dubin, 1996; Kanol, 1999). Furthermore, the lack of political decisiveness is fuelled by concerns among officials as to how the implementation of particular decisions might either improve or degrade a politician's standing in public life. 'Politicians and policy makers have not listened to the technocrats because they consider it not politically viable to do so' (Kanol, 1999). Politically, large, internationally funded hotels produce immediate jobs, and political votes, whereas small-scale local projects do not (Kanol, 1999).

Pressing issues flow from the TRNC's characteristics as a developing country (European Commission, 1998), such as the difficult access to the country, inadequate transport and service infrastructure, substandard facilities, an absence of investment funds, rudimentary technology, a lack of management skills, and a dearth of skilled staff. Local government has all the pressures of providing adequate basic services, and tourism has to be subordinate to these more fundamental responsibilities. For example, a recent priority of the Famagusta Environment Department, with support from the United Nations, was to secure a safe water supply free from sewage contamination (Eren, 1999). The planners clearly require more involvement with relevant stakeholders when considering the location, type and size of tourism developments, as well as a clearer understanding of who and what their market is. The recent building of a large hotel at Boghaz without the local *Muhtar*'s knowledge illustrates this lack of stakeholder participation (Gulu, 1999).

Local authorities have a tradition of not working together when implementing local plans. In Famagusta, for example, the Municipality, Historic Monuments Office, City Planners and The Association for the Revitalisation and Recreation of Old Magusa (Famagusta) had plans for the improvement of the recreation and tourism facilities of the Old Town, but they did not communicate and integrate their ideas. This has led to an over-bureaucratic and inefficient use of resources, delay, and a fragmented approach to the implementation of plans (Biyikoglu & Kursat, 1999).

While the trend of tourist arrivals in the TRNC has been upwards in recent years, there is an over-reliance on low-spending, short-stay Turkish tourists, who comprise 60–70% of overseas arrivals (Lockhart & Drakakis-Smith, 1997). These tourists use lower-quality accommodation and generate little incentive for environmental planning and the improvement of existing and new facilities and services.

Europeans and many Turkish visitors to the TRNC expect a certain quality, reliability and safety standard with respect to both the products and the environment of their holiday destination. Turkey has an absolute advantage over the TRNC in terms of mass tourism for both domestic and international tourists as, although they have a shared currency, Turkey has lower labour and other costs (Warner, 1999).

## Towards Sustainable Tourism Planning in the TRNC

### Island processes

Approaches to sustainable planning must be comprehensive, iterative and dynamic, systematic, integrative, renewable and goal-orientated (Godfrey, 1995). Consequently, attention in the TRNC should be focused on a national

**Table 3** Selected policies in the 1997 Economic Development Plan

| |
|---|
| 1. To develop physical plans and a Tourism Master Plan. |
| 2. To protect historical and natural environments, and protect against environmental pollution by the provision of legally protected areas and National Parks, and to establish statutory agencies. These areas are to be away from tourism developments. |
| 3. To establish an integrated tourism and environmental policy which has legal powers of enforcement. |
| 4. To expand the length of the tourist season, support winter tourism, and increase the length of stay and spend of tourists. |
| 5. To improve tourism facilities and encourage health, golf, village, sailing, third age, youth, cultural and conference tourism. |
| 6. To further encourage the privatisation of industries. |
| 7. To encourage liaison between government employees and tourism industry professionals. |
| 8. To improve quality by the introduction of standards for travel agencies and accommodation units. |
| 9. To introduce environmental studies into the education curriculum so as to improve environmental and tourism awareness. |
| 10. To continue negotiations for direct flights into the TRNC from origin countries. |
| 11. To increase marketing overseas for tourism and improve the image of the TRNC. |
| 12. To participate in international fairs, conferences and festivals, and to research the possibility of the TRNC hosting such activities. |
| 13. To improve the competitive advantage of tourism over regional competitors. |
| 14. To recognise the importance of tourism and to cooperate with local administration, tourism industries, investors and the general public in order to coordinate development. |

*Source*: Devlet Planlama Orgutu (DPO) KKTC, 1996

Master Plan that allows for consultation and decision making at all stages of tourism development. There is a need to achieve a 'top-down' shift in environmental policy and planning from the TRNC Ministry in order to stimulate 'bottom-up' community-based responsibility. This could subsequently raise government and corporate consciousness towards sustainable planning. The 1997 Economic Development Plan (Table 3) outlines a general policy for both sustainable planning and diversification into alternative tourism. These policies should be drafted into a detailed strategic plan. Unfortunately, the use of annual *ad hoc* programmes since 1997 has hindered continuity and the opportunity to translate policy into planning and programming.

In order to decentralise decision making, tourism development planning requires integration into the local structural framework. In turn, local government must bridge the gap between the needs of the local community and those of the tourism industry. Effective local authorities are essential in planning because they construct, operate and maintain economic, social and environmental infrastructure, and they also oversee planning processes (e.g. giving permission for developments, and regulating them). In addition, they establish local policies and regulations (e.g. investment zones, grading hotels), and assist in implementing policy. At the level of governance closest to the people they can play a vital role in education, and in mobilising and responding to the public to promote sustainable development (Quarrie, 1992). Inadequate planning at this level can enable the private sector elite to pursue short-term economic benefits at the expense of the sustainability of local resources (Buhalis, 1999). On the other hand, too much influence from the technocrats involving attempts to re-educate the host community so that they change their preferences, questions the whole community-based decision-making process (Weaver, 1998). Furthermore, budgets for financing tourism superstructure and infrastructure come largely from Turkey (Kanol, 1999). This has political implications for planning and complicates the involvement of the local community in decision making.

Locally planning issues are regularly discussed between the relevant ministry, municipality and the local community. *Muhtars* and members of the community meet with the *belidiye* (town council) and sometimes Members of Parliament five to six times a year, where 'issues affecting street lighting, roads, power and water supply are discussed' (Gulu, 1999). Hence, the structural framework for community participation in decision making is in place. It is the negotiation process in decision making between the host community and other stakeholders that requires attention.

Due to the pervasive nature of tourism, most of the larger tourism developments in Cyprus have regional significance in terms of environmental impacts. In the Republic of Cyprus, the National Tourism Strategy (1990) sought to improve and diversify the tourism product by focusing on regional cultural and natural assets. This was based on habitat conservation and landscape preservation and revitalising rural communities. The expansion of tourism for economic benefit (WTO, 1994) continued, but largely as a result of quality provision at Paphos, and an increase in primarily domestic agritourism in the hill stations, so that tourism increased by nearly 10% from 1997 to 1999 (Cope, 2000).

Other islands place great significance on regional planning. On the largest Mediterranean island, Sardinia, regional law allows specific agreements between a developer, the regional government and a municipal council for new tourist developments at a regional scale (Master Plan Costa Smeralda, 1999). Malta has substantial tourism development and has been divided into 12 zones. These zones range from total preservation of the land area to the upgrading of existing facilities. This is in order to provide for the systematic analysis of relatively homogeneous areas for tourism policy recommendations (Ioannides, 2001).

Social impacts are part of this process and other developing tourism economies recognise that social development and tourism development should not be separated. Pearlman (1990) states that tourism policy in Bulgaria reflects the view that the main task of tourism is not a commercial one, but to satisfy the recreational needs of the Bulgarian people. Ramsara (1989) contends that too many island states, in this case Caribbean states, are preoccupied with increasing tourist numbers rather than increasing benefits to island communities.

What is apparent is that developing and developed countries adopt and adapt

**Table 4** The SEA process in the TRNC

| *Present Practice in Northern Cyprus* | *Recommended Practice* |
|---|---|
| • Environmental Input Assessment (EIA) procedures are at project level | • EIA should be applied to plans andprogrammes, then policy |
| • Screening uses guidelines, including categorical exclusions, thresholds and Findings of No Significant Impact (FONSI) | • Screening should have a more system/process approach with screening guidelines appropriate to Northern Cyprus |
| • Scoping is limited by baseline data but emphasis is on socioeconomic priorities | • Scoping on transboundary impacts, health impacts and carrying capacity should be improved. Scenario planning should be used for assessing alternatives |
| • Predictions undertaken by experts in the Environmental Protection Agency (EPA) and university academics | • Supplementary international prediction and evaluation techniques and models should be used |
| • Environmental Input Statements (EISs) are not made public | • EISs should be accessible to the public and contain comprehensive executive summaries |
| • Public consultation is not practised | • Public participation should be conducted at the screening, scoping, objective and target setting stages, and at the review of the results stages |
| • Decision making on projects requiring an EIA are undertaken unilaterally by the EPA | • Linkages with other tiers of decision making should be ensured, and an increasing number of arguments added to the discussion |
| • Monitoring and evaluation undertaken for completed projects under the Environmental Protection Law, 1998 | • Monitoring should be linked to carrying capacity guidelines and measurable indicators |

the ethos of environmental protection in different ways. The TRNC should shape its own contemporary tourism development approach to suit its unique position. This requires a comprehensive tourism plan which encompasses the methodologies used for SEA in land-use planning, energy, waste management and transport. Some of the methodologies in the SEA process, together with current and recommended practices, are shown in Table 4.

Table 4 highlights that SEA must be a participatory process with decisions made explicitly and transparently; not purely by experts behind 'closed doors'. SEA in tourism is more likely to be effective in cases where the Government has an environmental policy (European Commission, 1999), as it provides a framework for the Tourism Master Plan. In the TRNC, such policies and plans are compiled separately by the Government and they require integration.

The TRNC and the Republic of Cyprus do not have single representation of tourism at ministerial level. At the highest level in the TRNC, the Under-

Secretary of State, Mr Bulent Kanol, has a portfolio that includes tourism marketing and promotion, but he has other related responsibilities, including national and city planning, with subordinate directors for each of these areas (Kanol, 1999).

Research indicates that there is a need to rationalise and depoliticise government operations so that government can fulfil its role as a regulator, coordinator, infrastructure provider and promoter of the destination (Buhalis, 1999). The Tourism Advisory Committee (TAC) could fulfil this role, this having recently been established under the Tourism Incentive Law, 1987. It is essentially the national tourism organisation (NTO), and a think-tank of managers and advisers working in transport, hospitality, travel agencies, airlines and university academics, although at the time of writing, the final composition of its membership is yet to be established. In addition, 'action-orientated' sub-committees have been proposed to look at themes such as casinos, transport, environment etc. Bylaws have been recently prepared by the TAC for approval by the ten Council of Ministers in Parliament (Kanol, 1999).

A quasi-autonomous organisation such as the TAC, with strong ministerial support, could provide good directive leadership from government. In St Lucia in the Carribean, an island in the transition phase of tourism development, the new Ministry of Tourism, together with a statutory tourist board and a community consultative group, proposed the development of the indigenous, small-scale private sector (Wilkinson, 1997). This initiative was financed through government and a gross profit percentage tax revenue from operators, and it proposed product development through marketing, finance and education. This is intended to provide a sense of community ownership in the tourism product, which can help in educating and training the community towards more sustainable tourism development.

### Proposals for managing the process

The present organisational structure in TRNC can provide a good foundation for an integrated planning system. Figure 4 illustrates how this multi-tiered system could incorporate SEA. Such a system requires expertise at all levels and an open-web system of communication (Torkildsen, 1999). All these processes require a strong political will, progressive financial resourcing, and public involvement in order to be effective. Local Agenda 21 Action Plans, compiled at a county (regional) level in the UK, may be an effective tool to consider in order to build bridges between national, district and local policies, as well as tourism and environmental planning. Working groups could be established for key issues, such as transport and pollution, waste and renewables, natural resources and energy, heritage and biodiversity, and education and awareness, along with more business-orientated groups, such as for casino tourism and special interest tourism (see Figure 5).

The TAC could act as the forum, providing a vehicle for wider debate about the process, and an opportunity for the action groups and the working groups to gain a wider audience. The steering group would review the process of the Tourism and Environment Action Plan. In addition, it would identify areas needing further development, and guide and focus future work. Working groups would be charged with overseeing action groups, reviewing and

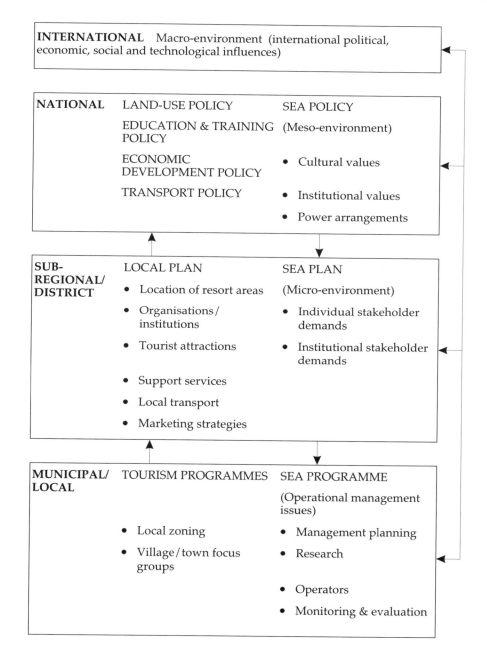

**Figure 4** The Integrated Environmental and Tourism Planning System

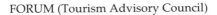

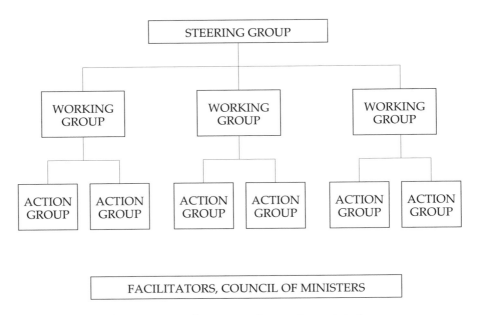

**Figure 5** Suggested organisational structure for tourism-related
sub-committees/working groups in the TRNC

monitoring the role and range of actions within its purview, and nominating representatives to the steering group and other working groups. Action groups would be involved in the implementation of individual or a limited range of actions. An example of how tourism policies could be implemented in a working group is given in Table 5. To work effectively, such a system requires the development of strong leadership and partnerships, the raising of public awareness and empowerment, and the networking of interested agencies and individuals. The potential expertise to contribute to these groups is available from a young, increasingly university-educated Turkish Cypriot workforce.

The TRNC also requires defined land-use zoning with clear policy objectives in order to implement programmes and plans effectively. One option is the division of the TRNC into five sub-regions or zones for the purpose of tourism planning: Karpas (northeast); Lefke (northwest); Kyrenia (northern); Famagusta (eastern); and Nicosia (central) (Yorucu & Jackson, 1996). Each of these regions is administratively viable in terms of their physical size and population, and each has homogeneous characteristics that make them distinct. The working groups would require a sub-regional focus in order to influence programmes and plans. However, a philosophy of integrated multi-use planning needs to be in place before community-based and sustainable models of planning, through SEA, can be developed.

**Table 5** Example working group and project plan for an aspect of alternative tourism in the TRNC

| Working Group X: Alternative tourism through education and awareness | | | | | |
| Project No. Y: Building links with the printed media | | | | | |
| *Issue/problem being addressed* | *Brief resumé of the project* | *Respons-ibility for implement-ation* | *Cost/ source* | *Timescale* | *Indicators/ targets* |
|---|---|---|---|---|---|
| Insufficient and unclear coverage of alternative tourism in newspapers | Training workshops for tourism operators on the effective presentation of their product | Steering group in consultation with TAC | Low. Small charge to tour operators. Seed grant from Ministry | Immediate | Well-presented articles on alternative tourism on a regular basis. Increased inter-national exposure |

*Source*: Adapted from Hereford & Worcester County Council, 1996

## Conclusions

Despite its political, geographical and economic disadvantages, the TRNC has some competitive advantage for alternative tourism because it has a unique and relatively underdeveloped tourism product. The population of only 65% of its pre-occupation level, suggests that there is scope for sustainable development of the tourism industry. A sensitive strategic planning and marketing approach to the resource base for all forms of tourism will give more control to the TRNC, rather than to Turkish and international economic stakeholders.

Tourist destinations that have a relatively long history of resort tourism and have not planned to sustain and enhance their long-term competitive advantage, have had to realign their development policies towards product quality improvement and sustainability. Areas of the Spanish coast and more recently the Republic of Cyprus are examples of this (Seekings, 1997). In these destin-ations the absence of a coherent and integrated planning framework for both alternative tourism and an element of sustainable mass tourism has affected the industry's future. This is due to a decline in the quality of the natural resource base in the former case, and a decline in both the built and natural environment in the latter.

The Tourism Incentive Law (1987) encourages economic 'boosterism' with little attention to social and environmental impacts, this being characteristic of government policies in many incipient tourism destinations. The TRNC has a policy of environmental assessment through the recent Environmental Pro-tection Law (1998) although there is no evidence of any form of EA above project level. Environmental issues and tourism development are considered by the public sector and industry to be conflicting issues rather than interrelated variables. Largely because of this, there is a perceived lack of both political willpower and expertise to implement a broader approach to tourism development at all levels.

Tourism policy and its implementation require a strong, active and experienced national tourist organisation (NTO), preferably with ministerial power. This should have financial and management resources, as well as a commitment from political and administrative leaders. Politicians and decision makers involved in tourism development have traditionally been more interested in patron–client relationships rather than representing a transparent and accountable democracy that improves the environment, the welfare of the community, and ensures long-term economic prosperity. Monitoring and evaluation by independent authorities may be required to ensure this.

Many of the problems are recognised, and the Government is in the process of devolving decision making to a national tourism organisation, that is, the TAC and working group subcommittees. With the development of partnerships, networking, and monitoring and evaluation, this could enable more informed decisions to be made. However, the cultural impacts and resistance to the implementation of such a realignment of thinking is a challenge to a state which has little influence from international systems of governance outside of Turkey.

There is a need to develop a clear strategy for both mass tourism and alternative tourism products, particularly with reference to the market and to customer preferences, tastes and expectations. This is acknowledged by the minister, who proposes that the biggest challenge for the future 'is achieving a balance between the combination of mass [casino] tourism interests and specific purpose tourism' (Kanol, 1999).This necessitates increased development of land-use planning and spatial zoning, together with an emphasis on providing protected areas for preservation, conservation and recreation. Increased research is necessary to support community-based alternative tourism, particularly in relation to small-scale rural tourism, cultural tourism, wildlife tourism and adventure tourism.

There is a requirement for increased communication and coordination between local authorities, environment and tourism departments. A clearer delimitation of responsibilities and linkages in projects is required. This would enable a more informed and integrated framework to be introduced in the decision-making process in areas such as district land use, waste management, transport and tourism strategies. At the same time, policies and guidelines of good management practice should be made available at municipal and district level, so that environmental assessment of developments and best operational practice can be undertaken.

Tourism development planning needs to be responsive to the views of a more informed general public. Thus empowerment of the public is a prerequisite. This would necessitate the use of a more coherent consultation process with local authorities and an educated local community involving 'top-down' guidelines from central government. Such grass-roots involvement could engender a greater sense of collective responsibility towards enhancing cultural, environmental and long-term economic stability. Ideally there should be public consultation both before and after the release of national policies, local plans and tourism programmes at both the scoping and review stages.

In order to sustain such an interest, support needs to be given to tourism and environmental non-government organisations (NGOs). The Society for the Protection of Turtles and *Is Yesil Baris* (Greenpeace), for example, have been a valuable force behind the designation of the first Special Protected Area of the TRNC, made possible by the Environmental Law (1997). The National Trust of North Cyprus is lobbying for a natural park and marine conservation area in the Karpas (National Trust of North Cyprus, 2001). In relation to sustainability, this illustrates the importance of NGOs on small islands and of the bottom-up process of forcing issues at government level.

Finally, and most importantly, the ethos of sustainable tourism needs to be taken more seriously by the corporate international tourism suppliers, including the travel agencies, hotels and lodging operators, and the tour operators. More support for protecting and promoting an unspoilt tourism product is required, particularly from Turkey, Germany, and the approximately 50 operators in Britain (Ioannides, 2001). However, such support may well not be forthcoming in practice.

Evidence indicates that the recently released Master Plan, compiled by the Turkish University of Boghazici, reinforces the policy of economic boosterism. This may simply mimic the philosophy of overseas investors. Such an approach has been demonstrated throughout the world to be unsustainable. Unfortunately, by the time political, social and environmental factors force a change in such policies, the damage has usually already been done. However, the nascent nature of tourism development could encourage a cultural and structural shift in thinking, towards a more sensitive and sustainable approach to policy and planning. With five universities in the TRNC offering tourism and hospitality courses, there is the potential to shift education and training towards more sustainable thinking. With recent signs of reconciliation and political stability in Cyprus, it is now even more crucial for decision makers to adopt this approach before the long-term competitive advantage and unique tourism product are lost for ever.

## Correspondence

Any correspondence should be directed to Mr Jon Sadler, Charles Sturt University, School of Environmental and Information Sciences, PO Box 789, Albury, Australia 2640 (jsadler@csu.edu.au).

## References

Akis, S., Peristianis, N. and Warner J. (1996) Residents' attitudes to tourism development: The case of Cyprus. *Tourism Management* 16 (8), 583–92.

Alipour, H. (1995) Questions about tourism development within planning paradigms: The case of Turkey. *Tourism Management* 15 (5), 327–9.

Altinay, M. (1998) *Tourism and the Economy.* Third Annual Congress of Cyprus Studies, 27 November. Famagusta: Eastern Mediterranean University.

Andronicou, A. (1979) Tourism in Malta and Cyprus. In D.G. Lockhart and D. Drakakis-Smith (eds) *Island Tourism: Trends and Prospects* (pp. 162–77). London and New York: Pinter.

Asikoglu, S. (1999) *Tourism in TRNC.* Famagusta: Eastern Mediterranean University.

Avci, T. (1999) Assistant Professor. Interview, 19 April. Eastern Mediterranean University, Famagusta.

Balgioglu, H. (1999) Hotel Investor. Interview, 21 May.

Bell, I. (1999) Secretary of the Society for the Protection of Turtles. *Newsletter* 4. Kyrenia, Northern Cyprus.

Biyikoglu, Z. and Kursat, E. (1999) Examination of the recreational potential of Gazimagusa old city. BA Tourism Management thesis, Eastern Mediterranean University, Famagusta.

Bond, A. (1995) *MSc Environmental Impact Assessment: Module 8*. Aberystwyth: UWA.

Buhalis, D. (1999) Tourism in the Greek Islands: Issues of peripherality, competitiveness and development. *International Journal of Tourism Research* 1, 341–58.

Butler, R.W. (1993) The dynamics and effects of tourism evolution in Cyprus. In Y. Apostolopoulos, P.J. Loukissas and L. Leontidou (eds) (2001). *Mediterranean Tourism* (p. 127). London: Routledge.

Camgoz, O. (1999) Vice-Chairman of the Environmental Protection Agency. Interview, 24 March. Eastern Mediterranean University, Famagusta.

Carey, S., Gountas, Y. and Gilbert D. (1997) Tour operators and destination sustainability. *Tourism Management* 18 (7), 425–31.

Cope, R. (2000) *Country Reports* 4, 3–21. Cyprus: TTI.

Dann, G. (2000) National tourism organisations and the language of differentiation. In W. Gartner and D. Lime *Trends in Outdoor Recreation, Leisure and Tourism* (pp. 335–45). New York: CABI.

Devlet Planlama Orgutu (DPO) KKTC (1996). *Five Year Development Plan (1993–1997), 1997 Programme*. Nicosia: Prime Minister's Office.

Dubin, M. (1996) *Cyprus. The Rough Guide*. London: Rough Guides.

Eren, A. (1999) Director of Environment. Interview, 16 March. Eastern Mediterranean University, Famagusta.

European Commission (1998) Commission communication on tourism development strategies for developing countries. On WWW at http://europa.eu.int/comm/dg23/.

European Commission (1999) European Union case studies on the use of SEA. On WWW at http://europa.eu.int/dg11/SEAcasestudies.

European Commission (2001) The SEA Directive is adopted! On WWW at http://europa.eu.int/comm/environment/eia/home.htm.

European Commission (2002) Cyprus – European Union: A brief history. On WWW at http://www.cyprus-eu.org.cy/eng/brief_history.htm.

Getz, D. (1987) Approaches to tourism planning. In E. Inskeep (1991) *Tourism Planning: An Integrated and Sustainable Development Approach* (pp. 25–45). Chichester: John Wiley & Sons.

Glasson, J., Therival, R. and Chadwick, A. (1994) *Introduction to Environmental Impact Assessment*. London: University College London.

Godfrey, K. (1995) Towards sustainability? In L. Harrison and W. Husbands (ed.) *Practicing Responsible Tourism* (pp. 58–76). New York: John Wiley and Sons.

Gulu, M. (1999) Village headman (Muhtar), Bogaztepe. Interview, 1 April. Eastern Mediterranean University, Famagusta.

Haktamir, M. (1999) Senior Instructor. Interview, 23 April. Eastern Mediterranean University, Famagusta.

Hereford and Worcester County Council (1996) *The Local Agenda 21 Action Plan*. Worcester: Hereford and Worcester County Council.

Hunter, C. and Green, H. (1995) *Tourism and the Environment*. London: Routledge.

Ioannides, D. (1995) A flawed implementation of sustainable tourism: The experience of Akamas, Cyprus. *Tourism Management* 16 (8), 583–92.

Ioannides, D. (2001) The dynamics and effects of tourism evolution in Cyprus. In Y. Apostolopoulos, P.J. Loukissas and L. Leontidou (eds) *Mediterranean Tourism* (pp. 112–28). London: Routledge.

Kanol, B. (1999) Undersecretary for Ministry of State. Interview. Eastern Mediterranean University, Famagusta.

Lennon, J. and Foley, M. (2000) *Dark Tourism*. London: Continuum.

Lockhart D.G. (1993) *The Development Process in Small Island States*. London: Routledge.

Lockhart, D.G. and Ashton (1990) In D.G. Lockhart (1993) *The Development Process in Small Island States*. London: Routledge.

Lockhart, D.G. and Drakakis-Smith, D. (eds) (1996) *Island Tourism: Trends and Prospects.* London and New York: Pinter.

Mansfield, Y. and Kliot (1996) In Y. Mansfield and A. Pizam (eds) *Tourism, Crime and International Security Issues.* New York: Wiley.

Master Plan Costa Smeralda (1999) On WWW at http://www.vol.it/porto_cervo/cs-mp.htm.

Mathieson, A. and Wall, G. (1982) Patterns and characteristics of the supply of tourism. In C. Cooper and J. Fletcher (1993) *Tourism Principles and Practice* (p. 88). London: Pitman.

Miller, J. and Szekely, F. (1995) What is Green? *Environmental Impact Assessment Review* 15 (5), 418.

Ministry of Economy and Finance (1994) *A Guide for Foreign Investors and Businessmen and Macro Economic Indicators.* Nicosia: Ministry of Economy and Finance.

Morris, P. and Therivel, R. (eds) (1995) *Methods of Environmental Impact Assessment.* London: University College London.

National Trust of North Cyprus (2001) On WWW at http://www.charm.net/~trnc/e019.html.

Orams M. (1995) Towards a more desirable form of ecotourism. *Tourism Management* 16 (1), pp 3–8.

Pearce D. (1995) *Tourism Today – A Geographical Analysis* (2nd edn). London: Longman.

Pearlman, M. (1990) Conflicts and constraints in Bulgaria's tourism sector. *Annals of Tourism Research* 17 (1), 103–22. In J. Costa and L. Ferrone (1995) Sociocultural perspectives on tourism planning and development. *International Journal of Contemporary Hospitality Management* 7 (7).

Plog (1977) In M. Orams (1995) Towards a more desirable form of ecotourism. *Tourism Management* 16 (1), 3–8.

Quarrie, J. (1992) *The Earth Summit 1992.* London: Regency Press.

Ramsara (1989) In P. Wilkinson (1997) *Tourism Policy and Planning.* New York: Cognizant Communication.

Seekings, J. (1997) Cyprus. *EIU International Tourism Report* 4, 29–54.

Sertoglu, K. and Bicak, H. (1998) *Journal for Cyprus Studies* 4 (2) (Spring), 143–59.

Severiades, A. (2000) Establishing the social tourism carrying capacity for the tourist resorts of the east coast of the Republic of Cyprus. *Tourism Management* 21, 147–56

Torkildsen, G. (1999) *Leisure and Recreation Management* (4th edn). London: Routledge.

Tosun, C. (1998) Roots of unsustainable tourism development at the local level: The case of Urgup in Turkey. *Tourism Management* 19 (6), 595–610.

Tosun C. (2001) Challenges of sustainable tourism development in the developing world: The case of Turkey. *Tourism Management* 22, 289–303.

TRNC (1995) *Statistical Yearbook.* TRNC Prime Minister's Office: Nicosia.

TRNC (1997) *Statistical Yearbook.* TRNC Prime Minister's Office: Nicosia.

TRNC Prime Ministry (2000) Education in the TRNC. On WWW at http://www.cm.gov.nc.tr/trnc/.

Viney, D. (1994) *An Illustrated Flora of Northern Cyprus.* Nicosia: TRNC.

Warner, J. (1999) North Cyprus: Tourism and the challenge of non-recognition. *Journal of Sustainable Tourism* 7 (2), 128–45.

Weaver, R. (1998) *Ecotourism in the Less-developed World* (p. 15). London: CAB International.

Wilkinson, P. (1989) The dynamics and effects of tourism evolution in Cyprus. In Y. Apostolopoulos, P.J. Loukissas and L. Leontidou (eds) (2001) *Mediterranean Tourism* (pp. 112–28). London: Routledge.

Wilkinson, P. (1997) *Tourism Policy and Planning: Case Studies from the Commonwealth Caribbean.* New York: Cognizant.

Wilstach, P. (1926) In D.G. Lockhart (1993) *The Development Process in Small Island States.* London: Routledge

Wood, C. (1995) *Environmental Impact Assessment: A Comparative Review.* Harlow: Longman.

World Tourism Organisation (1994) *National and Regional Tourism Planning: Methodologies and Case Studies*. London: Routledge.

Yorucu ,V. and Jackson, P. (1996) *Tourism and Environmental Planning in Small Island States*. Occasional Paper 96/2. University of Leicester.

# 8 Learning From Experience? Progress Towards a Sustainable Future for Tourism in the Central and Eastern Andalucían Littoral

**Michael Barke and John Towner**
*Division of Geography & Environmental Management, University of Northumbria at Newcastle, Newcastle upon Tyne*

This paper examines the recent development of tourism on the coast of Andalucía to the east of Málaga city in the light of explicit assertions of the adoption of sustainability principles by the Spanish tourism authorities. Using a simple model of sustainable tourism and comparing the eastern coastal area with the earlier developed Costa del Sol, it is concluded that any progress towards more sustainable forms of tourism activity in the east are, at best, superficial. An examination of two major proposed developments, at Maro and Retamar, demonstrates the continuing growth-oriented strategy of tourism in the region and a clear failure to engage with the environmental, sociocultural and political contexts of sustainable tourism development.

A recent review of Spanish tourism noted:

> From the environmental point of view, the Spanish tourist [*sic*] development has a special significance, both for its undeniable effects on the environment and for being, at present, an essential way of increasing the sector's competitiveness and of guaranteeing its sustainability. (Monfort Mir & Ivars Baidal, 2001: 23)

In its implied criticism of the past and its implicit, more optimistic reference to a change in the nature of Spanish tourism development this quotation neatly encompasses the scope of this paper. Using the Mediterranean coast of Andalucía (Figure 1), we shall briefly examine some of the problems inherent in the nature of past development, outline some more recent initiatives and, against the background of a simple model of sustainable tourism, discuss the extent to which this more recent generation of tourism developments represent a genuine trend towards a more sustainable form of tourism.

## Mass Tourism on the Costa del Sol

In many ways, the nature of tourism development on the Costa del Sol from the 1960s until the 1990s represents the very antithesis of a form of tourism that is, in most usually accepted sense, sustainable. The staggering rapidity of growth, relatively uncontrolled private sector investment (much of it, unlike Catalonia (Priestley & Mundet, 1998) foreign in origin), lack of coordination with infrastructural development and a breathtaking lack of concern for existing natural, socioeconomic and cultural environments characterised the industry for nearly four decades. Tourist numbers on the Costa del Sol increased from just over 50,000 in 1959 (Fradera, 1961) to almost 1 million in 1968 and nearly 2.5

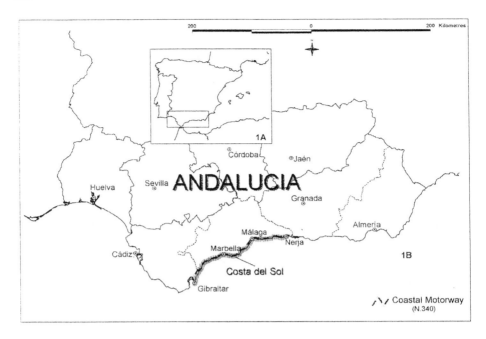

**Figure 1** Location of (a) Andalucía and (b) Andalucía and the Costa del Sol

million in 1975 (Cuadrado Roura & Torres Bernier, 1978). For Spain as a whole by 1987 it was calculated that over 50% of the littoral was developed or classified for urban, port, industrial and, mainly, tourist land use (Secretaría General de Turismo, 1994). On the Málaga coastline of the Costa del Sol it is much higher than this. Furthermore, much of this development is haphazard and uncoordinated in form (Pollard & Domínguez Rodríguez, 1995). The vast majority of the tourist trade was controlled by mainly foreign tour companies whose desire to keep prices down led to lower standards; and the need for economies of scale led to over-development (Gaviria, 1974), often flaunting planning regulations (Parsons, 1973). The nature of mass tourism as experienced in parts of the Costa del Sol also began to attract negative publicity. The area began more openly to celebrate its hedonism (Olano, 1974) but this inevitably led to conflict over aspects of tourist behaviour (Pollard & Domínguez Rodriguez, 1993). Such conflicts were exacerbated by the sheer numbers of foreign visitors and the 'swamping' of traditional villages (Jurdao Arrones, 1990).

There was, therefore, a gradual realisation that the dominant mode of tourism that had emerged so far was increasingly counter-productive and probably not sustainable (Marchena Gómez & Vera Rebollo, 1995), conforming in many ways to Butler's (1980) stagnation stage. Although the sudden oil-crisis-induced downturn in 1974–76 (visitors to Spain fell from 34.5 million in 1973 to 30 million in 1976) did lead to some attempts to diversity, the more recent downturn of 1989–91 (54.2 million in 1988 to 52 million in 1990) was more influential in introducing new thinking on a wider scale. Arrival figures at Málaga airport fell by 20% to 1.56 million in 1990 (Pollard & Domínguez Rodriguez, 1993).

Major conflicts over resources were at first subdued, partly because of the existence of a totalitarian regime until the early 1970s and partly because of the extreme poverty of the majority of the indigenous population. However, conflict over land use, access and, especially, water began to mount in the 1970s (Garcia Manrique, 1985–6; Gomez Moreno, 1983; Tyrakowski, 1986). The general quality of the environment was also increasingly perceived as negative (Vera, 1994), whether in terms of the built environment, represented by the 'concrete *costas*' themselves (Wood & House, 1992), or manifest in issues such as the quality of beaches and bathing water (Jenkins, 1980). Pollard & Domínguez Rodriguez (1993: 258) strongly suggest that in the specific case of Torremolinos 'past neglect of environmental quality now has implications for tourism's viability and profitability'. At the national level the most recent strategic plan for tourism (SECTyPYMEs, 1997) stresses the role of 'environmental sustainability . . . as an essential condition for the survival of products and destinations' (Monfort Mir & Ivars Baidal, 2001: 36).

Mounting concerns over the environmental context of tourism was therefore one of several catalysts for change in Spanish planning law (Fayos Solá, 1992; Keyes *et al.*, 1993). Three major changes took place which are of particular significance for the relationship between sustainable tourism and the environment. First, changes in urban planning law sought to increase the designation of both green open space and conservation areas within urban municipalities. Second, the new law of the coasts (1988) increased protection of the littoral. Third, a series of special plans for the protection of the natural environment were announced.

These developments are frequently cited as evidence that Spain and its tourism authorities have started to take the environment seriously and are engaging with some of the basic requirements of promoting a more sustainable form of tourism. Yet, in coastal Andalucía, the mere designation of a certain percentage of green open space in any new development does not necessarily signal an engagement with sustainability principles. The new purpose-built marina and resort of Almerimar, in one of the driest parts of the region, where major conflicts over water already exist (Provansal & Molina, 1991; Tout, 1990), has vast expanses of planted grass and shrubs whose verdant status is maintained through thousands of sprinklers. It is sometimes difficult to avoid the conclusion that, for some, 'sustainability' in Spanish terms is all too often simplistically equated with ensuring a certain proportion of green space in any new development or with creating more protected 'natural' areas. For example, in the special plans for the protection of the environment:

> Their objective is the protection of all kinds of natural areas, sparing them from deterioration and destruction so as to revalue the territorial resources of Andalucía generally. They regulate the necessary protection and conservation of nature areas and at the same time make the management of natural resources compatible with their optimal utilisation. (Autonomous Government of Andalucía, 1987)

The latter phrase clearly points towards some ambiguity of purpose and a similar ambiguity is evident in *Plan Dia* (Junta de Andalucía, 1993), the most recent major document relating to tourism planning in Andalucía.

*Plan Dia* is described as a 'consensual' plan (p. 25) which, in itself, may be thought enough to set alarm bells ringing. In essence it is a growth-oriented strategy with the necessity of diversifying the Andalucían tourism product at its core. Under the heading of 'the development of sustainable tourism in Andalucía', three 'strategic concepts' are identified (p.75):

- speed of growth – this needs to be at a rate which is in harmony with local areas;
- in new development, concern should be less with the speed at which returns on capital investment take place and more with a recognition that different forms of capital accumulate at different rates; and
- the intention should be to promote ecological balance across the majority of environments and translate this into social and economic development.

At a general level, these three principles seem to be in accord with sustainable tourism, but at the same time *Plan Dia* clearly points to the exploitation of the interior and natural areas as tourism resources and vaguely talks about the 'compatibility between the protection of nature and a conscious tourist development' (p.75).

One of the most worrying features of this desire to diversify the tourism offer and which replicates the ambiguity is the declared intention to direct tourists into the interior (Galiano, 1991). Thus, 'rural tourism' is seen as a universal saviour being, on the one hand, associated with a more sustainable form of tourism and on the other, being about diversifying the rural economy (Barke & Newton, 1997a; Garcia Cuesta, 1996). More worrying is the assertion that increasing the use of 'natural' areas for tourism is not a problem and that any problems that do arise may be resolved by simply applying sustainability principles (Vacas Guerrero, 2001) without any recognition of the real difficulty in putting such principles into practice. This seems to be in accord with Butler's (1998) assertion that, despite widespread adoption of the principles of sustainable tourism, implementation of actual practice is considerably more limited.

In order to assess whether or not the tourism development model in Spain appears to be 'learning from experience', this paper will broadly contrast two areas of the Mediterranean Andalucían coast, the classic Costa del Sol to the west of Málaga city and the area of more recent modern tourism development to the east, extending from Nerja into Almería province. To some extent it is the transport infrastructure, specifically the extension of the N 340 motorway to the east of Málaga city that has provided the stimulus for this eastward expansion of larger scale tourism activity but it is also a product of increasing market diversification within Spanish tourism, not least of which is the growing domestic market (Instituto de Estudios Turisticos, 1995). Given the widespread acknowledgement of the problems associated with the Spanish tourism development model up to the 1980s, the point of contrasting an older tourism area with one of more recent development is to try and assess whether or not there has been a process of 'learning from experience'. A combination of official data sources, media reportage and extensive field observation and data collection will be used to make this assessment. However, in order to provide some structure for this comparison a simple model of sustainable tourism will be used and to this we now turn.

## A Model of Sustainable Tourism

The basic concepts of what may constitute sustainable tourism have been well rehearsed and debated elsewhere, both generally (e.g. Butler, 1991; De Kadt, 1994; Hall & Lew, 1998; Stabler, 1997) and in the context of Spain (Hunter-Jones *et al.*, 1997; Priestley, 1995; Robinson, 1996) and will not be covered here in any detail. However, a broad consensus within the literature would suggest that a process of sustainable tourism development would be based on the substantial re-use of existing manmade and natural resources and would be associated with a low input of energy. It would also be viewed as a process founded in local cultures, producing an equitable distribution of services, managed and administered according to democratic principles, and maintaining and regenerating traditional social values and practices. Yet, whilst these factors may amount to a satisfactory definition of the scope of sustainable tourism, any working model of the concept must recognise the stratification and range of interpretations that surround the notion (House, 1997). Any assessment of whether a particular tourism system exhibits features of sustainable development must therefore recognise the existence of this stratification and the various dimensions of sustainability. The simple model to be used in the present analysis has three such dimensions (Figure 2).

The first dimension consists of the degree of sustainability being assessed; ranging from Turner's (1992) 'weak' or 'shallow' concept to 'strong' or 'deep' sustainability. At the shallow end we have a belief that sustainability is to do with managing tourism impacts in particular destination areas and attempting to minimise those impacts as they arise. The fact that such views remain prevalent is illustrated by Loukissas and Skayannis (2001: 243): 'mass tourism if properly organised might not harm the environment to the extent believed , mainly from the scope of waste, since special infrastructure (technical and organisational) projects can prevent this'. This approach focuses on the reduction or management of social, cultural and physical environmental impacts of tourism without questioning the processes that create them. As we move along the spectrum towards the deep end of sustainability we find a far more radical approach that would challenge existing economic, social and political structures (House, 1997). Under this view, the *whole* tourism system must be incorporated into sustainability; not just the destination area but impacts in the generating area and the modes of transport used to link the two (Robinson & Towner, 1993). Furthermore, tourism has to be integrated into far wider environmental, economic, sociocultural and political contexts. It is these contexts that form the second dimension of our sustainability model. In reality they are, of course, inter-linked but may be considered separately for discussion. The environmental dimension focuses primarily on the physical resources that tourism systems consume both as attractions and for their overall operation and we have noted already how narrowly this can be conceptualised in Spain. Economic sustainability is equally open to a wide range of viewpoints. The tourist industry may well take a considerably shorter-term view of what it would term 'sustainable development' than environmentalists and that view may also be far narrower in terms of integration with other contexts. Similarly, the social and cultural impacts of sustainable tourism can be built upon a

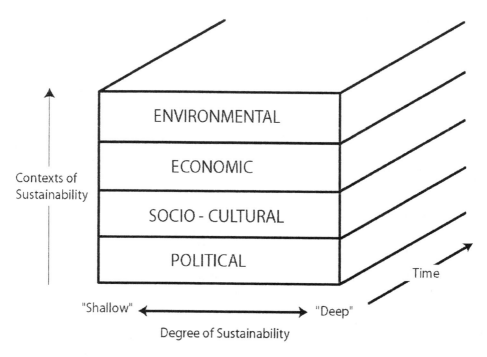

**Figure 2** A simple model of sustainable tourism

'weak' notion of combining consumer satisfaction and tacit rewards for host communities. 'Deeper' sustainability, in contrast, would address whether or not tourism enriched or damaging individuals and cultures over a longer time period. The political dimension is concerned with the issues of power and decision-making that the tourism system creates; the extent to which control of development lies within destination or generating regions and the degree to which that control permeates the social structure.

It is clear that the extent to which these factors can be considered sustainable will depend on the final dimension of the model; time. The success or failure of a tourism system in sustainable terms must incorporate a measure of continuity.

## Sustainability Indicators

The extent to which any particular project may be deemed to be 'sustainable' or where it may fall on the 'sustainability continuum' may be assessed through using a variety of indicators. Many potential lists exist but Table 1 highlights some of the more appropriate indicators in the present context of sustainable tourism.

This is a far from exhaustive list and is obviously capable of being refined into a series of even more specific and measurable criteria. Although it would, theoretically, be possible to apply such measurable criteria to every resort on the Andalucían coast between Gibraltar and Almería, this would be a massive undertaking and not feasible for the present purpose. Although some specific empirical data will be cited, most of the evidence produced in this paper will examine just one or two aspects listed in Table 1. For example, in terms of resource consumption we can characterise coastal tourism as 'narrowly focused' or 'broadly based'. Thus, the earlier developments were focused on a limited range of attractions – the narrow strip of land between the hotel, beach and sea and a limited range of markets – mass package tourism from northern Europe and supporting services including food and drink brought in from elsewhere. A move towards more sustainable tourism at the coast should show evidence of a more broadly based consumption of resources and a direct interest in their continued existence. Attractions would include the hinterland of the coast, especially rural areas and historic and cultural locations, whilst services would also come from this local area. Local and regional food and drink would be significant items of consumption, there would be a recognition of local culture and employment would complement local skills and structures.

**Table 1** Sustainability Indicators Checklist

| Indicator | Sustainability characteristics |
|---|---|
| Energy | Maximise energy efficiency |
| | Generate energy from renewable resources |
| Waste | Reduce waste |
| | Encourage re-use and/or repair |
| | Encourage recycling |
| Transport | Discourage use of cars |
| | Encourage walking or cycling |
| | Encourage use of public transport |
| Pollution | Reduce or minimise local pollution – noise, air, water, land |
| Buildings and Land use | Conserve and/or re-use older buildings |
| | Provide local amenities |
| | Improve access for disabled |
| Wildlife and Open Spaces | Encourage natural plant and animal life |
| | Encourage use of open space for community benefit |
| Economy and Work | Increase local employment |
| | Link local production with local consumption |
| | Improve environmental awareness of local businesses and other key actors |
| Local Community | Involve local community in developments |
| | Encourage local action and decision making |
| | Recognise under-represented groups |

*Source*: Adapted from DETR (2001)

## Recent Growth and Change in Tourism Activity

The growth of mass tourism on the Costa del Sol has been fully described elsewhere (Barke & France, 1996). Initial growth was, of course, to the west of Málaga city and, by 1970, there were over 15,000 hotel bed spaces and a further 70,000 spaces in apartments, chalets, villas and bungalows in this area (Palop, 1970). In the stretch of coastline from Nerja to Almería city at the same time there were less than 4000 bed spaces in hotels, 42% of these in the city of Almería itself.

Growth has continued in the western area with 66, 267 bed spaces in hotels, apartments and pensions in 1988, growing by nearly 20% to 79,500 in 1999 (Junta de Andalucía, 2001). Over the same period, however, the numerically smaller eastern area (Figure 3) grew by 77.5% from 17,200 bed spaces in 1988 to 30,500 in 1999. Formal tourist accommodation is, of course, only one way of measuring increase or decrease in tourism activity and it represents just one segment of the market, albeit the most important in many ways. However, other data point to the same conclusion that the area to the east of Málaga city has, in the last 20 years, seen a significant growth in tourism activity. The number of second homes (admittedly not all necessarily related to tourism, see Barke, 1991) increased by 72% to over 54,000 between 1981 and 1991. The western Costa del Sol area increased by 34.5% from 51,000 to 69,000 over the same period. Employment in *'comercio, restaurantes and hosteleria'* stood at nearly 58,000 in the western area in 1991, 27.2% of the occupied population. In the eastern area the corresponding figures are 23,040 and 21.2%. Given that there is considerably more alternative employment in the east, particularly in agriculture, this again suggests a recent

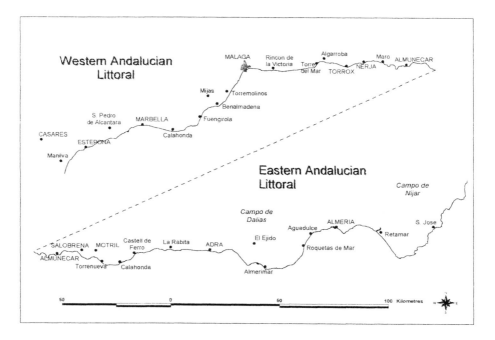

**Figure 3** Location of main resorts: Western and Eastern Andalucían littorals

**Table 2** Eastern Andalucían Coast: Some Dimensions of Tourism Growth, 1970–1999

| Location | Hotel bed spaces, 1970 | Total bed spaces in apartments, hotels and pensions, 1988 | Total bed spaces in apartments, hotels and pensions, 1999 | Percentage change per annum, 1988–99 | Second homes as percentage of total 1991 |
|---|---|---|---|---|---|
| Torrox | – | 127 | 670 | + 42.8 | 45.2 |
| Nerja | 397 | 2225 | 5338 | + 14.0 | 41.8 |
| Almuñécar | 716 | 1713 | 3346 | + 9.5 | 60.2 |
| Salobreña | 177 | 295 | 444 | + 5.1 | 54.4 |
| Motril[a] | 132 | 871 | 1184 | + 3.6 | 29.1 |
| Albuñol[b] | 49 | 40 | 138 | + 24.5 | 8.8 |
| Adra | 60 | 110 | 231 | + 11.0 | 8.7 |
| El Ejido[c] | 52 | 2433 | 5496 | + 12.6 | 7.6 |
| Roquetas de Mar[d] | 322 | 6884 | 11521 | + 6.7 | 42.1 |

[a] includes Calahonda and Torrenueva; [b] La Rabita; [c] mainly Almerimar; [d] includes Aguadulce
*Source*: Junta de Andalucía, (2001)

significant growth in tourism on a large scale. Table 2 shows some of the dimensions of tourism activity in some of the key locations of the eastern area.

## More Recent Growth = A More Sustainable Form of Tourism?

It is clear that the area from Nerja through to Almería city has shown strong growth in tourism activity in the last two decades (Table 2). This has taken place against a background of increasing concern over the sustainability of the tourism development model as experienced in the western area, the classic Costa del Sol. It may be thought, therefore, that there would have been a degree of 'learning from experience', that most of the features that characterised the growth and nature of tourism development in the west would not be repeated in the east. It is to this key issue that we now turn.

Although we have referred to tourism development along the eastern seaboard of Andalucía (eastern Málaga province, the Granada coastline and western Almería) as 'new', in the strictest sense this is not true. Visits to the seaside became increasingly popular for the urban middle classes in the early part of the 20th century, prompting the development of facilities such as the Baños de Octavio at Torre del Mar in the 1920s and *merenderos* in fishing villages and small towns such as Adra (Gathorne-Hardy, 1992). At least one foreign-owned small hotel existed in Almuñécar in the mid-1930s (Lee, 1969) and by the early 1960s sufficient demand existed to justify the building of a new *parador* at Nerja. However, the data noted in the previous section clearly suggest rapid recent growth.

In attempting to assess whether or not the eastern study area demonstrates facets of a more sustainable form of tourism, we can begin with the very issue of speed of growth. A key requirement for any sustainable tourism development must surely be that it allows time for adjustment within local economies, societies and environments (Milne, 1998). However, because tourism is to some extent subject to the dictates of fashion there is a tendency to seek to maximise returns over relatively short periods. Investment may suddenly be abandoned in some sites and new ones rapidly made in other locations. Such features seem unlikely to foster many principles of sustainability. In fact, tourism has grown remarkably rapidly in the eastern zone. In 1968 Nerja could be described as 'in the transitional phase between fishing village and tourist resort'; and, Salobreña had only just been 'discovered', had no hotels and the fact that one English-woman had just bought a plot of land was worthy of mention. The mayor of Motril had just supervised the completion of the first tourist accommodation in the municipality but the rest of the coast, between Motril and Almería was 'African, barren and sparsely inhabited'(Epton, 1968). Between the mid-1970s and the mid-1990s the number of hotel rooms increased fivefold in Nerja, more than doubled in the coastal resorts of Granada province such as La Herradura, Salobreña, Torrenueva and Calahonda but exploded in the Almerían resorts of Aguadulce, El Ejido (several locations) and Roquetas del Mar (Table 2). Many other forms of tourist activity and accommodation have also expanded equally rapidly, for example the very high proportion of second homes in the Costa Tropical of Granada province. Given the significant change in tourist activity away from conventional hotel accommodation to various forms of residential tourism, another indicator of speed of development relates to new construction (Vera & Marchena, 1996), usually taking the form of blocks of apartments or *urbanizaciones* of detached villas which are often segregated from traditional urban settlements at the seaside. This clearly has widespread environmental and sustainability implications relating to land, resources, transport and local communities.

Table 3 provides information on some features of resource consumption in both eastern and western coastal areas of Andalucía. The extraordinarily high levels of real estate development of the western Costa del Sol have not yet been matched in the majority of locations in the eastern area but we should note that, in several of the latter, the proportion of second homes is remarkably high. In other words, new build may be, as yet, less significant but the housing market (mainly externally controlled) is still changing the nature of communities. Whilst still generally lower in the east, electrical energy consumption shows some convergence of the two zones of the Andalucían coast as indicated in the rate of change column. The proportion consumed by the service sector which, of course, includes most tourism activity, is little different between the two zones whilst the effective demand for water, as indicated by current storage capacity, is, if anything, higher in some of the eastern municipalities. Irrigation for advanced agriculture is also, of course, an important part of this demand.

## Representation

Recent brochures produced by several major package tour operators were surveyed to assess whether the central and eastern littoral is being marketed in a way that suggests differences with the region west of Málaga. At the very least,

**Table 3** Some environmental sustainability indicators in Eastern and Western Andalucían coastal areas

| Location | House-building, 1994–2000 per 1000 resident population | Capacity of water supply (m³) per capita, 1995 | Production of residual solids (toneladas) per capita, 1995 | Electrical energy consumption (megavatios per hour) per capita 2000 | Electrical energy consumption: % in service sector | Electrical energy consumption: % change 1987/2000 |
|---|---|---|---|---|---|---|
| **East:** | | | | | | |
| Torrox | 334.0 | 0.655 | 0.393 | 2.327 | 35.1 | +167.6 |
| Nerja | 143.7 | 0.837 | 0.763 | 3.556 | 38.6 | +106.7 |
| Almuñécar | 83.6 | 1.232 | 0.491 | 2.959 | 34.7 | +152.0 |
| Salobreña | 153.1 | 0.427 | 0.265 | 2.615 | 36.7 | + 91.7 |
| Motril[a] | 55.6 | 0.598 | 0.329 | 3.332 | 29.0 | + 66.0 |
| Albuñol[b] | 24.5 | 1.155 | 0.209 | 2.141 | 29.0 | + 92.8 |
| Adra | 27.4 | n.a. | n.a. | 1.523 | 35.8 | +114.0 |
| El Ejido[c] | 44.5 | n.a. | n.a. | 5.242 | 36.4 | +220.6 |
| Roquetas de Mar[d] | 91.8 | n.a. | n.a. | 3.172 | 41.9 | +172.1 |
| **West:** | | | | | | |
| Benalmadena | 498.8 | 1.544 | 1.267 | 5.125 | 29.0 | +143.7 |
| Estepona | 277.6 | 0.178 | 1.248 | 3.664 | 29.0 | +152.2 |
| Fuengirola | 224.5 | 0.099 | 1.032 | 3.517 | 40.3 | + 64.6 |
| Marbella | 550.5 | n.a. | n.a. | 5.206 | 29.0 | +143.6 |
| Mijas | 442.3 | 0.275 | 0.622 | 4.400 | 42.7 | +195.5 |
| Torremolinos | 236.4 | 2.136 | 1.194 | 4.814 | 43.5 | n.a. |

[a] includes Calahonda and Torrenueva; [b] La Rabita; [c] mainly Almerimar; [d] includes Aguadulce
*Source*: Junta de Andalucía (2001)

we would expect to find pictorial images and text more broadly related to the resources of the area. For instance, do pictorial images present a more distinctive setting than the typical beach–hotel–pool scene? Can one resort be distinguished in any way from another, as claimed for the World Travel Market in 1996 (*Sur in English*, November 1996)? Does the text indicate a range of attractions and stress differentiation from other coastal resort regions?

At one level there clearly is an attempt to differentiate the region from that west of Málaga. A number of tour operators (e.g. First Choice, Thomson, Air Tours) refer to the Costa de Almería, although its spatial extent varies between companies and can be confused between a province and a resort. The overall aim appears to be to emphasise a different *pace* of development, with much of the region being represented as unchanged. For example, First Choice claims:

> The province of Almería is a beautiful example of unspoilt Andalucían countryside. The pace of life is much slower than that of many Spanish resorts, with uncrowded beaches, white hill-top villages, narrow winding

streets and surrounding mountains and extensive plains. (First Choice Brochure, Summer 2002: 236)

Thomson (Summer 2002) stresses the 'relaxed atmosphere' and less crowded beaches of 'this little known part of Spain'. Individual resorts are also seen to have particular character. Roquetas de Mar has 'a definite Spanish accent' and Nerja enjoys a 'distinctly traditional ambience' such that visitors 'can feel they are living like locals' (Thomson Brochure, Summer 2002: 295, 305). Meanwhile, Air Tours (2001–02: 50) stresses the care taken in development 'to preserve the unique character of the area'.

However, although the marketing text attempts to distinguish this region from the more lively bustle found to the west of Málaga, the pictorial images hardly convey a sense of uniqueness. The visual impression created is that here is a coastal resort much like any other: non-place images of hotel complexes, pools, beaches, blue sky and yellow sand. Furthermore, not only is a bland non-place visual image presented but that image carries very little recognition that this tourist activity is taking place in the midst of real communities with other forms of economic activity, different traditions and life-styles. The most obvious example of divorcing the tourist enclave from its surroundings is the fact that in the marketing of the resorts, both pictures and text completely ignore a very obvious feature of the area: the massive and adjacent plastic covering for intensive agriculture. In general terms, however, as far as the representation of these relatively new resort areas to the market is concerned, there is little evidence here that sustainability concerns are seen to be a marketing advantage.

## Testing the Four Sustainability Components

In this section we examine some recent evidence from the study area relating to our four key components of sustainability – environmental, socioeconomic, economic and political.

In general terms, although perhaps at a rather superficial level, environmental issues do generate some interest and are reported on within the area. For example, a number of initiatives have been launched in Nerja in recent years, including a scheme to prevent uncontrolled dumping of building rubble and other refuse in the lower reaches of the Rio Chillar and convert the area into a recreational site (*Sur in English*, 27 December 1997 – 2 January 1998: 14). In April 2001 Nerja also announced extra cleaning and refuse collection in the town and on the beaches at a cost of 70 million pesetas and employing 54 people. Almuñécar launched a 'Tourism Excellence Plan' in April 1998 with 454 million pesetas investment. The plan included considerable improvement to the beaches, promenades and gardens, the restoration of the Puente Romano and the creation of a new park in the Cerro Gordo (*Sur in English*, 3–9 April 1998: 22). Also in Almuñécar the first 'environmental rural tourism complex' on the Costa Tropical has been launched as an alternative to the traditional seaside holiday. Located 40 minutes away from the resort the Peña Escrita area covers 350 hectares and provides accommodation in log cabins, traditional small *cortijos* and camp sites. Rural activities are encouraged along with climbing, horse-riding and hang-gliding.

A number of local authorities have also enthusiastically pursued other 'green' policies, especially with various forms of re-cycling. Similarly, there are localised but significant moves to generate energy from renewable sources, especially solar energy. These features may be interpreted as moves towards more sustainable forms of tourism in the environmental sense but it is clear that they mostly lie towards the 'shallow' end of our sustainability continuum.

Further east in our study area, despite the rather bland image presented by the marketing brochures, it is clear that recent development has led to a number of environmental problems, problems that suggest a degree of incompatibility between various sectors of economic development. For example, research at Motril (Marino *et al.*, 1980) demonstrated the toxic effects of a cocktail of effluent from a vegetable oil refinery, a paperworks, herbicides, pesticides, insecticides and fertilisers, together with urban sewage – all this in an area where tourism expansion was being generated. Not all of these problems are necessarily directly attributable to tourism but the growth of that activity has played some part in their generation. One of the most obvious relates to conflict over water as a scarce resource, not just in terms of quantity but also in terms of quality. Intensive agriculture has played a massive role here but tourism also makes its contribution (Smith, 1997: 230; Tout, 1990). In addition to the obvious aspects of water consumption for cleanliness, golf courses and the many green spaces associated with tourism developments and complexes are kept in trim with a high density of sprinklers. But also, for many tourist visitors, local tap water is undrinkable due to the high salt content. Bottled mineral water is, therefore, in high demand which then, of course, generates considerable motor transport and fuel consumption.

Turning to the economic aspects of sustainability, the picture appears to be even less encouraging. Although employment in tourism-related activities has increased, not all of this has necessarily benefited local populations and communities. Similarly, although isolated examples of linking local production with local consumption may be found, in the major new resorts of Almerimar and Roquetas de Mar the patterns of consumption are unquestionably international. One of the main features of economic development relating to tourism is real estate development. Although the rhetoric of development may have changed somewhat and some recognition of a sustainability agenda may be found (for example in the use of solar panels and energy saving etc.), the overall impression remains one of rapacious development. For example, Frigiliana, recommended as a 'white village' in 1968 (Epton, 1968), albeit one where GB car number plates were beginning to appear outside converted cottages, was by 1990 'overrun by foreign settlers' (Jacobs, 1990: 316). In 2000 the municipalities of Nerja and Frigiliana registered over 2000 real estate contracts for the purchase of land for construction, valued at over 30,000 million pesetas, an increase of nearly 20% over 1999 (*Sur in English*, 20– 26 April 2001). In the first three months of 2001 a further 550 contracts were signed. Significantly, 95% of these were non-Spanish with 60% being British or Scandinavians. The president of the local business groups proudly asserted that 'our area is booming' and cited the importance of the extension of the N340 from Torrox to Frigiliana. It is quite clear that Frigiliana and some neighbouring villages of the Axarquia, such as Cómpeta, are going the way of villages such as Mijas and Benahavis further west with 34% and 42%

foreign residents respectively. The local foreign language press positively rejoices in this prospect (*Sur in English*, 8–14 November 1996).

This leads naturally into a third component of the sustainability model – the sociocultural. The, in places, overwhelming presence of foreigners is an important issue in relation to sustainability. This foreign presence is not as obvious in the east as in the west although it is estimated that 40% of Torrox's population of 12,000 is German, with the highest proportion of Germans of any place outside Germany. An intriguing twist is that the local authority is now encouraging local people to learn German (*Sur in English*, 2–8 March, 2001). The major problem arises when a significant proportion of this foreign population is elderly and 'health reasons' are a principal motive for migration (King *et al.*, 2000). Financial, social and psychological problems can start to increase as an already potentially vulnerable population ages still further (Jurdao Arrones & Sánchez, 1990; Rodríguez *et al.*, 1998). Such problems are exacerbated when foreign migrants who regard themselves as permanent residents have considerable problems of integration and consequently of identity (O'Reilly, 2000). Despite considerable natural warmth and hospitality, the attitude of most Spaniards to foreigners remains that they are guests and, conceptually, they are little different (for most Spaniards, no different) from tourists. Questions of control over local resources can also arise when foreign groups start to impose their own development priorities as, for example, in the luxury marina and resort of Almerimar. Clearly, this happened to a massive extent in the western part of the Costa del Sol both in terms of the structure and control of mass tourism (Gaviria, 1974; Valenzuela, 1991) and, later, with real estate development (Jurdao Arrones, 1990). As we have seen, much the same seems to be happening with real estate development in parts of the eastern study area and here also foreigners are taking over some of the local supply of tourist infrastructure. To take just one small example, a British couple have produced a guide to Frigiliana, Maro and Nerja with half-day country trips 'well away from the crowds' (*Sur in English*, 9–15 December 1994).

The fourth component of our sustainability model is concerned with the political dimension. In the present context, this is essentially a question of local democracy and decision-making. We may cite two examples of large-scale contemporary change in the eastern study area that illustrate the extent to which the distribution of power is producing decision-making with regard to tourism that is divorced from many of the key principles of sustainable tourism. The first concerns the proposal for large-scale resort development at the pretty village of Maro, east of Nerja.

Maro is a small enclave resort offering a limited amount of tourist accommodation and services including two locally owned small hotels and six traditional style cottages offering apartment lodgings plus a few restaurants. These facilities are well integrated into a traditional village social and geographical structure where local employment still includes some fishing and, especially, agriculture. The hotels promote local produce and organise trips to local rural areas such as the Alpujarras. The village is also the location of a solar energy firm that installs environmentally friendly heating and cooling systems and advertises these in several languages. Maro, therefore, does have a tourist function and some small-scale local entrepreneurship associated with that but it retains a strong Spanish resident population and a small village atmosphere. However, it is clear that decisions that will fundamentally affect the future of Maro have already been taken elsewhere. A large-scale tourism expansion scheme is planned, covering much of the sea front to east and west of the village and, in effect, forming a tourism conurbation with Nerja, exactly the sort of structural change produced in the western Costa del Sol in the 1970s. The scheme will be predominantly low-rise but will consist of real estate, holiday and retirement homes and associated services. Inevitably, access will be achieved through greater use of the private car. The initial announcement caused massive local resentment and over 200 local agriculturalists who rented land on various leases led a sit-in protest at the famous Caves of Nerja (*Sur in English*, 20–26 December 1996). The caves had to be closed for a period and support was forthcoming from over 4000 local residents in Nerja itself. The principal proponent of the Maro development is the main local landowner, the Larios family, one of Málaga's main aristocratic dynasties. Supremely ironic in the present context, however, is the fact that the land on which the first major *urbanizacion* in Torremolinos in the late 1950s was created, El Pinar, was also owned and promoted by this family (Pollard & Domínguez Rodríguez, 1993). Here we have a significant tourism development about to take place that will destroy an existing harmonious relationship between small-scale tourism and other facets of social and economic life and which, clearly, is totally lacking in local responsiveness.

The second example concerns the on-going development at Retamar, a rather bleak and deserted location in the not very attractive area to the east of Almería city, although actually within that municipality's jurisdiction. At the time of writing, this looks like an over-optimistic and failing real estate development in a poor location. Yet, this is the site of the 2005 Mediterranean Olympics, the first such event having been held in Athens in 1998. As yet there is no sports stadium but an 'Olympic village' is currently under construction adjacent to existing blocks of flats and the area will have Almería's first five star hotel. The intention is that Retamar will become a major resort after the sporting event is over. Interestingly, there is no mention of this in *Plan Dia* where the area was scheduled to become a *Parque Submarino*, with scuba-diving as its principal function. What is evident here is a degree of opportunism of the type that characterised the early stages of mass tourism development on the Costa del Sol. The development is also one that reflects some of the political tensions and rivalries that exist between different locations on the Andalucían coast. Almería has long thought itself to be remote and somewhat neglected by the Autonomous government of the region in Seville (Barke & Newton, 1997b; Hooper, 1995), even to the extent of seeking to ally itself with the non-Andalucían region of Murcia. Over the past decade, most of the other Andalucían provincial capitals have benefited in various ways from regional autonomy (Seville, Málaga, Cadiz) or have had sufficient distinctiveness to remain in the forefront of public consciousness (Cordoba, Granada). Almería has been left somewhat on the fringe and its role in being chosen as the rather unlikely location for these games relates to the perceived political necessity of providing the province and its capital with a high profile event. In other words, political expediency at the broad regional scale overrides any other considerations, including those of sustainability. The development, in its present emerging form, appears no different to those in Fuengirola or Marbella except in the superficial aesthetic sense.

## Conclusion

This paper has attempted to throw some doubt on the extent to which newer tourism developments on the Andalucían littoral have adopted sustainability principles, despite the explicit engagement with such principles by the Spanish tourism authorities (SECTyPYMEs, 1997). Some elements of a more sustainable form of tourism may be identified in a number of localities but these do not amount to any widespread change in the relationship of tourism to local environmental and socioeconomic characteristics in newer compared to older locations. It is our conviction that sustainable tourism, and several other forms of alternative descriptions such as eco-tourism, green tourism, nature tourism etc. – have been adopted more in name than in actual practice in southern Spain. These terms are used to signal an attempted diversification of the tourism product, or as a marketing exercise or simply to improve image and public relations (Butler, 1998). Furthermore, expansion of tourism activity in several locations in the eastern zone reflect an overall policy of promoting the spatial expansion of tourism to 'destinations previously 'untouched' by the main market. It is arguable that such an approach fundamentally conflicts with the aims of sustainable tourism by failing to protect resources for future generations.' (Hunter-Jones *et al.*, 1997).

Applying our simple model of sustainable tourism to the resort developments to the east of Málaga city it is clear that few show any sign of environmental, economic, sociocultural or political sustainability. In the deep sense of sustainability we might question whether many forms of tourism development could ever be attained. Moving numbers of people from one place to another and back again simply for self-gratification will never satisfy the purists. But even if we retreat some way from this position we find little evidence of sustainability. Environmentally, there is perhaps rather more use of 'clean' energy evident, especially solar panels, rather more variation in the nature of the built environment, with lower rise development in various styles being more noticeable, more attempted re-cycling and rather more artificially created 'green' spaces. However, the maintenance of these green spaces requires the use of one of the region's scarcest resources, namely water. Overall energy consumption *per capita* is not massively different from the western Costa del Sol, and transport is even more based on the private car and lorry than in the western area. Economically, the study area is different from the west in that apartments and various other forms of real estate development predominate rather than hotels catering for mass tourism. However, there are many examples from the eastern study area of tourism developments that are essentially short term or opportunistic rather than being based on any deeper consideration of economic sustainability and it has been suggested by Haywood (1986) that tourism areas aimed specifically at new market segments or at exploiting specialised resources have shorter lifecycles than more broadly-based tourist destinations. The eastern area may appeal to a slightly different market niche than the west but that simply means it is competing with other similar developments in the Mediterranean. The area to the east of Málaga also presents a major land-use conflict that stems from two potentially incompatible forms of economic development – advanced agriculture/horticulture and tourism. On the coastline of much of eastern Málaga province, Granada province and Almería province, the tourist gaze falls on plastic. In sociocultural terms, there is little evidence that any of the tourism developments to the east have much local, community input. Indeed, where that does take place it is more likely to be a foreign 'local' or 'community' input and it is certainly the case that, as far as the coastal area is concerned, there is no strong awareness of or attempt to utilise the region's indigenous cultural attributes in marketing. Finally, in political terms there is a similar absence of local decision making and priorities relating to the nature of development. Tourism development in the central and eastern Andalucían littoral shows little sign of learning from experience.

## Correspondence

Any correspondence should be directed to Michael Barke, School of Behavioural and Environmental Sciences, Division of Geography and Environmental Management, University of Northumbria at Newcastle, Lipman Building, Newcastle upon Tyne, NE1 8ST, UK.

## References

Autonomous Government of Andalucía (1987) *Andalucía: A Tourism Investment Handbook.* Seville: Autonomous Government of Andalusia, Economic and Development Council.

Barke, M. (1991) The growth and changing pattern of second homes in Spain in the 1970s. *Scottish Geographical Magazine* 107(1), 12–21.

Barke, M. and France, L.A. (1996) The Costa del Sol. In M. Barke, J. Towner and M.T. Newton (eds) *Tourism in Spain: Critical Issues* (pp. 265–308). Wallingford: CAB International.

Barke, M. and Newton, M.T. (1997a) The EU LEADER Initiative and endogenous rural development: The application of the programme in two rural areas of Andalusia, southern Spain. *Journal of Rural Studies* 13(3), 319–41.

Barke, M. and Newton, M.T. (1997b) Spain, its regions and the EU 'LEADER' initiative: Some critical perspectives on its administration. *Public Policy and Administration* 12(3), 73–90.

Butler, R.W. (1980) The concept of a tourism area cycle of evolution: Implications for the management of resources. *Canadian Geographer* 24, 5–12.

Butler, R.W. (1991) Tourism, environment, and sustainable development. *Environmental Conservation* 18(3), 201–9.

Butler, R.W. (1998) Sustainable tourism – looking backwards in order to progress? In C.M. Hall and A.A. Lew (eds) *Sustainable Tourism: A Geographical Perspective* (pp. 25–34). Harlow: Longman.

Cuadrado Roura, J.R. and Torres Bernier, E. (1978) El sector turístico y su entorno socioeconómico: Una aproximación al caso de la Costa del Sol. *Información Comercial Española* 533, 82–139.

De Kadt, E. (1994) Making the alternative sustainable: Lessons from the development of tourism. In V.L. Smith and W.R. Eadington (eds) *Tourism Alternatives – Potentials and Problems in the Development of Tourism* (pp. 47–76). Chichester: John Wiley.

DETR (2001) *Sustainable Regeneration Good Practice Guide.* London: Department of the Environment, Transport and the Regions.

Epton, N. (1968) *Andalusia.* London: Weidenfeld and Nicolson.

Fayos Solá, E. (1992) A strategic outlook for regional tourism policy. The White Paper on Valencian tourism. *Tourism Management* 13, 45–9.

Fradera, J.V. (1961) *Hoteles, Hoy.* Barcelona: Editur.

Galiano, E. (1991) El turismo rural en España. *Revista de Estudios Turísticos* 110, 39–46.

Garcia Cuesta, J.L. (1996) El turismo rural como factor diversificador de rentas en la tradicional economia agraria. *Estudios Turísticos* 132, 47–61.

Garcia Manrique, E. (1985–86) Turismo y agricultura en la Costa del Sol malagueña. *Revista de Estudios Regionales* 6, 81–96.

Gaviria, M. (1974) *España A Go-Go*. Madrid: Turner.

Gathorne-Hardy, J. (1992) *The Interior Castle: A Life of Gerald Brenan*. London: Sinclair-Stevenson.

Gomez Moreno, M.L. (1983) Competencia entre agricultura y turismo por el dominio del espacio: El caso de Benalmádena. *Baética* 6, 113–58.

Hall, C.M. and Lew, A.A. (eds) (1998) *Sustainable Tourism: A Geographical Perspective*. Harlow: Longman.

Haywood, K.M. (1986) Can the tourist-area life cycle be made operational? *Tourism Management* 7, 154–67.

Hooper, J. (1995) *The New Spaniards*. Harmondsworth: Penguin.

House, J. (1997) Redefining sustainability: A structural approach to sustainable tourism. In M.J. Stabler (ed.) *Tourism and Sustainability: Principles to Practice* (pp. 89–104) Wallingford: CAB International.

Hunter-Jones, P.A., Hughes, H.L., Eastwood, I.W. and Morrison, A.A. (1997) Practical approaches to sustainability: A Spanish perspective. In M.J. Stabler (ed.) *Tourism and Sustainability: Principles to Practice* (pp. 263–74) Wallingford: CAB International.

Instituto de Estudios Turisticos (1995) *Las Vacaciones de los Espanoles, 1995*. Madrid: Secretaria General de Turismo, Ministerio de Comercio y Turismo.

Jacobs. M. (1990) *A Guide to Andalusia*. London: Viking.

Jenkins, S.H. (1980) Coastal pollution of the Mediterranean. *Marine Pollution Bulletin* 11(1), 6–11.

Junta de Anadalucía (1993) *Plan De Desarrollo Integral del Turismo en Andalucía. Plan Dia*. Seville: Dirección General de Turismo. Junta de Andalucía.

Junta de Anadalucía (2001) *Municipios Andaluces. Datos Básicos, 2001*. Seville: Instituto de Estadística de Anadalucía.

Jurdao Arrones, F. (1990) *España en Venta* (2nd edn). Madrid: Endymion.

Jurdao Arrones, F. and Sánchez, M. (1990) *España, Asilo de Europa*. Barcelona: Editorial Planeta.

Keyes, J., Munt, I. and Reira, P. (1993) The control of development in Spain. *Town Planning Review* 64(1), 47–63

King, R., Warnes, T. and Williams, A. (2000) *Sunset Lives: British Retirement Migration to the Mediterranean*. Oxford: Berg.

Lee, L. (1969) *As I Walked out One Midsummer Morning*. London: Atheneum.

Loukissas, P. and Skayannis, P. (2001) Tourism, sustainable development, and the environment. In Y. Apostolopopulos, P. Loukissas and L. Leontidou (eds) *Mediterranean Tourism: Facets of Socioeconomic Development and Cultural Change* (pp. 239–56). London: Routledge.

Marchena Gómez, M.J. and Vera Rebollo, F. (1995) Coastal areas: Processes, typologies and prospects. In A. Montanari and A.M. Williams (eds) *European Tourism: Regions, Spaces and Restructuring* ( pp. 111–26) Chichester: John Wiley & Sons.

Marino, M., Tortajada, R., Ellorietta, J.I., Sánchez, B., Murias, F., Sánchez, Mariscal, T. and Martos, T. (1980) Estudio ecosanitario del litoral de Motril. *Progress in Water Technology* 12(4), 579–96.

Milne, S.S. (1998) Tourism and sustainable development: Exploring the global–local nexus. In C.M. Hall and A.A. Lew (eds) *Sustainable Tourism: A Geographical Perspective* (pp. 35–48) Harlow: Longman.

Monfort Mir, V.M. and Ivars Baidal, J.A. (2001) Towards a sustained competitiveness of Spanish tourism. In Y. Apostolopopulos, P. Loukissas and L. Leontidou (eds) *Mediterranean Tourism: Facets of Socioeconomic Development and Cultural Change* (pp. 17–38) London: Routledge.

Olano, A.D. (1974) *Guia Secreta de la Costa del Sol*. Madrid and Barcelona: Al-Borak.

O'Reilly, K. (2000) *The British on the Costa del Sol: Transnational Identities and Local Communities*. London and New York: Routledge.

Palop, J.J. (1970) *Malaga*. Leon: Editorial Everest.

Parsons, J.J. (1973) Southward to the sun: The impact of mass tourism on the coast of Spain. *Yearbook of the Association of Pacific Coast Geographers* 35, 129–46.

Pollard, J. and Domínguez Rodríguez, R. (1993) Tourism and Torremolinos –recession or reaction to environment? *Tourism Management* 14, 247–258.

Pollard, J. and Domínguez Rodriguez, R. (1995) Unconstrained growth: The development of a Spanish resort. *Geography* 80(1) 33–44.

Priestley, G.K. (1995) Problems of tourism development in Spain. In H. Coccossis and P. Nijkamp (eds) *Sustainable Tourism Development* (pp. 187–98) Aldershot: Avebury.

Priestley, G.K. and Mundet, L. (1998) The post-stagnation phase of the resort cycle. *Annals of Tourism Research* 25(1) 85–111.

Provansal, D. and Molino, P. (1991) El agua en la estepa. In D. Provansal and P. Molina (eds) *Etnología de Andalucía Oriental. Volume 1, Parentesco, Agricultura y Pesca* (pp. 273–83) Barcelona: Editorial Anthropos.

Robinson, M.D. and Towner, J. (1993) *Beyond Beauty – Towards a Sustainable Tourism.* Sunderland: Centre for Travel and Tourism, Business Education Publishers.

Robinson, M.D. (1996) Sustainable tourism for Spain: Principles, prospects and problems. In M. Barke, J. Towner and M.T. Newton (eds) *Tourism in Spain: Critical Issues* (pp. 401–25) Wallingford: CAB International.

Rodríguez, V., Fernández-Mayoralas, G. and Rojo, F. (1998) European retirees on the Costa del Sol: A cross-national comparison. *International Journal of Population Geography* 4(2), 183–200.

Secretaría General de Turismo (1994) *Nota de Coyuntura Turistica.* Enero, Madrid.

SECTyPYMEs (1997) Secretaría de Estado de Comercio, Turismo y de la Pequeña y Mediana Empresa, *Plan de Estrategias y Actuaciones de la Administracion General del Estado en Materia Turística.* Madrid: Ministerio de Economía y Hacienda.

Smith, B. (1997) Water: A critical resource. In R.L. King, L. Proudfoot and B. Smith (eds) *The Mediterranean: Environment and Society* (pp. 227–51) London: Arnold.

Stabler, M.J. (ed.) (1997) *Tourism and Sustainability: Principles to Practice.* Wallingford: CAB International.

Tout, D. (1990) The horticulture industry of Almería Province, Spain. *Geographical Journal* 156(3) 304–12.

Turner, R.K. (1992) *Speculations on Weak and Strong Sustainability.* Working Paper, GEC 92-96, CSERGE. Norwich: University of East Anglia.

Tyrakowski, K. (1986) The role of tourism in land utilisation conflicts on the Spanish Mediterranean coast. *GeoJournal* 13(1) 19–26.

Vacas Guerrero, T. (2001) Las Espacios Naturales Protegidos como recurso turistico. Metodología para el estudio del Parque Nacional de Sierra Nevada. *Estudios Turísticos* 147, 57–84.

Valenzuela, M. (1991) Spain: The phenomenon of mass tourism. In A.M. Williams and G. Shaw (eds) *Tourism and Economic Development: Western European Experience* (2nd edn) (pp. 40–60). London: Belhaven Press.

Vera, J.F. (1994) El modelo turístico del Mediterráneo Español: Agotamiento y estrategias de reestructuracion. *Papers de Turisme* 14–15, 133–147. Valencia: Institut Turístic Valencia.

Vera, J.F and Marchena, M. (1996) El modelo turístico Español: Perspectiva economía y territorial. In A. Pedreno and M. Monfort (eds) *Introduccion a la Economía del Turismo en España.* Madrid: Civitas.

Wood, K. and House, S. (1992) *The Good Tourist.* London: Mandarin.

# 9 Measuring Sustainability in a Mass Tourist Destination: Pressures, Perceptions and Policy Responses in Torrevieja, Spain

*J. Fernando Vera Rebollo and Josep A. Ivars Baidal*
*Escuela de Turismo, Universidad de Alicante, Apartado de Correos 99,*
*03080 Alicante, Spain*

The debate on sustainable tourism development usually focuses on small-scale tourism practices, such as rural tourism or ecotourism, inappropriately referred to as 'alternative' tourism, judging by the problems they start to create. Mature destinations in the Mediterranean are a classic example of inappropriate environmental practices and of disregard for the principles of sustainability, which had been present in scientific discourse long before the 1992 Rio Summit. However, the restructuring processes in traditional destinations led to a more complex reality in which sustainability has become an inescapable reference, both as a competitiveness factor and as a growing social demand. This paper uses an operative definition of sustainable tourism development that makes possible the effective application of its principles. From this basis, a system of sustainability indicators is developed that can be applied to Torrevieja, a Spanish Mediterranean destination that is notable for the size of its tourism industry and for its supply of holiday homes. The territorial and socioeconomic transformations that have resulted from Torrevieja´s tourism development, along with the new local policies in response to these transformations, highlight both the contradictions and the chances of reconciling economic growth with sustainable development.

## Introduction

The development of tourist activities along Spain's coastline, which began during the 1960s, has gradually led to extensive areas of land being devoted entirely to mass tourism, in response to international demand (mostly Northern European) for 'sun-and-sea' holidays. Hotels are used for lodging visitors in a 'package-deal' system, organised mainly by large-scale tour operators who control international demand. Meanwhile, there has been a progressive increase in local demand for holiday lodging, and this is now giving way to the development of enormous 'holiday cities' based on the construction of large housing complexes of villas and blocks of apartments. This relatively recent development has strengthened the real estate side of tourism, which is a lesser-known dimension of the great conglomeration of tourist hotels along the coast, but it is one which must be considered in relation to the desired sustainable development of the sector (Vera Rebollo & Marchena, 1995: 28). This development pattern involves huge extensions of land which has far-reaching ecological and socioeconomic implications and is affecting almost the entire Spanish Mediterranean coast (Montanari & Williams, 1995).

The pattern of tourism development in Torrevieja analysed in the paper has a number of characteristics of wider interest as a topic of research. Its essential features are quite typical of the Mediterranean coast, and it is an excellent example of the contradictions that arise between the principles of sustainability at the global scale and the reality of urban development at the local scale. Some of these areas in Spain have a considerable population. Torrevieja, for instance, went from a stable population of about 9,200 inhabitants in 1960 to more than 70,000 in 2001. With its seasonal population of summer vacationers, however, its population can be as high as 400,000 in August, the most popular month among vacationers. Furthermore, the sheer intensity of urban development (over 90,000 dwellings, 75,000 of which are used exclusively as summer homes), and the related repercussions on employment and on increased demand for goods and services, make it a phenomenon that demands attention.

Local government policies in Torrevieja are quite contradictory. On the one hand, efforts are made in the field of environmental issues, such as in relation to the hydrological cycle and the management of areas of natural interest and in the organising of cultural projects. On the other hand, the rapid growth in housing and infrastructure encouraged by the existing model also permits investment in real estate property of decidedly poor quality. The dynamics of the local system is based almost exclusively on construction, which provides high returns on investment and also additional income that is welcomed by the community. This explains the level of support this kind of policy receives from local communities in general, and especially from those who are directly or indirectly involved in the process.

The new strategies now being employed try to promote more value-added projects like investments in quality hotels or a sound network of urban services. But the reality of the mass-production model, with its continuous construction of holiday homes, seriously limits such initiatives.

## Aims and Methodology

In the current context of the restructuring of tourist destinations in the Mediterranean in a search for new ways of reinforcing competitiveness, the need arises to reconcile mass tourism with sustainable development. It is not unfounded to consider mass tourism destinations as the complete opposite of sustainability within the gradation elaborated by Clarke (1997), but it also represents a simplification of the realities and processes that are much more complex. This paper affirms the need to incorporate the principles of sustainable development within the planning and management of mature tourism destinations. The concept of sustainable development is taken to involve a process of qualitative change that can be assumed by any type of tourist destination, and it is not seen as an ideal state that rules out the possibility of convergence between mass tourism and sustainability.

The recognition of sustainable development as a process of qualitative change that can be adopted by any tourist destination turns sustainability into an operative, measurable paradigm. Within that process, the establishment of a system of indicators is necessary for the analysis, assessment and monitoring of public and private policies. The proposal for indicators we make here implies redesigning pre-existing models. It is adapted to the specificities of tourist activity and focused on a local scale of work, the level at which problems and opportunities are best recognised in relation to the holistic dimension of sustainable development.

The system of indicators has been developed for the municipality of Torrevieja. Three basic vectors have been considered: (1) pressures on the local environment, (2) residents' and tourists' perceptions, and (3) the policy responses (mainly those with a local scope). The design of the system of indicators used various information sources: statistics that were available on different fields (society and economy, the environment, tourism, etc.), in-depth interviews with local agents, and surveys of tourist demand during the summer season. Above all, the application of a Geographical Information System has made possible the georeferencing of primary and secondary data, as well as the analysis of various spatial processes.

## Tourism and Holiday Homes: A Radical Transformation of the Local Scene

Tourist services are nothing new to Torrevieja. Its reputation as a health resort for the surrounding communities dates back to the 19th century. Its income from tourism, however, was nothing more than a supplement to its population's main economic activity as a typical fishing village. Without doubt, the traditional relationships between the locals and their visitors have left their mark on the character of its people, who have learned to quickly assimilate the new and complex social structures resulting from the rapid transformation that the town has undergone in recent years.

Beginning in the 1970s, but particularly during the 1980s, there were massive arrivals of summer vacationers, mainly Spaniards (above all from Madrid, Asturias and the Basque Country), attracted by the supply of economically priced houses and apartments, which were then being promoted by large real estate companies. Over the years, real estate firms and a policy that encourages rapid urban growth, have brought about radical changes to the town's economic, social, cultural and ecological systems.

The urban structure of the Municipality of Torrevieja is divided into two clearly distinct types of areas. One is a large and densely populated town centre, which first began to spread along the shore-line and then, more recently, has begun to move inland. There are more than 100 tourist and leisure settlements in Torrevieja that follow this peculiar urban development model in which thousands of holiday houses and flats are massed together within a relatively small area. In contrast to its densely populated urban zone, however, Torrevieja has a large natural area with two salt-water lagoons that has been declared a Natural Park and included in the Ramsar List of Wetlands of International Importance (Ramsar Convention Bureau, 2002), in recognition of its great ecological value and its natural beauty. In summary, then, the Land Use-Tourism model described here is the result of two apparently opposed realities: (1) the large nature reserve, which is commercially exploited in only one small area, where there is a salt factory, and (2) the other side of the system, the congested urban centre with its growing suburban sprawl (Figure 2).

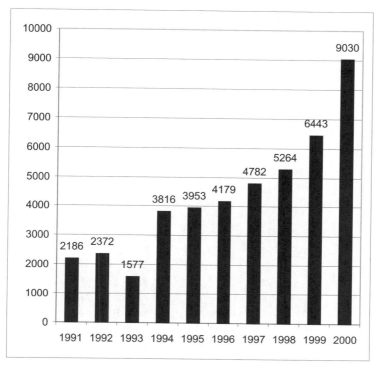

**Figure 1** Number of new dwellings built in Torrevieja, 1991–2000
*Source*: Torrevieja Municipality

## Indicators for Analysis and Management of Sustainable Tourism

Sustainable tourism has become a key issue for tourism policies and management and is becoming increasingly important because of its widespread social acceptance. In spite of the prolific use of the term 'sustainable tourism' and the numerous scientific definitions proposed for it, the ambiguity inherent in the concept and its rhetorical and often inappropriate use have not yet been overcome (Ivars, 2001). After wide acceptance of the initial definition in the Brundtland report and following the tremendous impact of the Earth Summit in Rio de Janeiro (1992), there have been many different points of view expressed in numerous subsequent conferences, documents and international declarations on the topic. These have served to enlarge upon and clarify the theoretical principles of sustainability in tourism. Some outstanding examples of relevant declarations are the Charter for Sustainable Tourism, Lanzarote (1995), Agenda 21 for the Travel and Tourism Industry (World Tourism Organisation *et al.*, 1995), and the Worldwide Code of Ethics in Tourism (Santiago de Chile, 1999).

Such initiatives, together with the growing debates about sustainable tourism, highlight the essence of the sustainability paradigm as the balance between economic growth, environmental preservation and social justice (Bramwell *et al.*, 1996; EEAa; Butler, 1993; Coccossis, 1996; Hall, 2000; OMT, 1993). The key

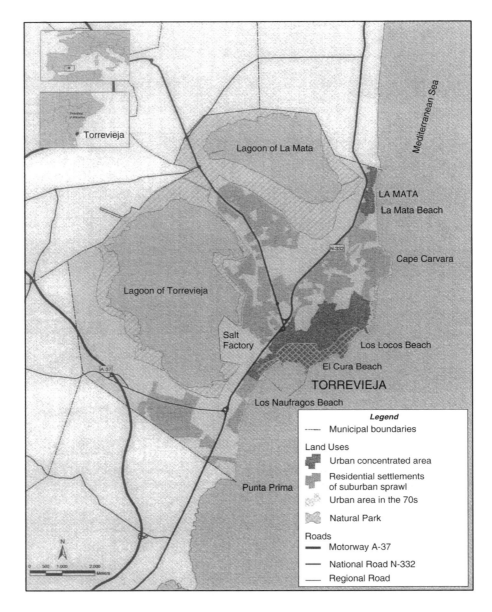

**Figure 2** Land uses in Torrevieja

challenge facing the management of tourism is the attainment of this balance. With such an objective in mind the sustainable development of tourism is identified here as

> a process of quality change resulting from political initiatives that include the indispensable participation of the local population and that adapts the

institutional and legal framework, and the planning and management tools, in order to achieve development based on a balance between the conservation of existing natural and cultural resources, the economic viability of tourism and social equity in tourim development. (Vera Rebollo & Ivars, 2001)

This definition seeks to avoid the identification of sustainable tourism as an ideal or utopian state, which could give rise to logical arguments that exclude the possibility of applying its principles to such major 'sun-and-sea' destinations as Torrevieja. While there are considerable difficulties in such destinations in applying sustainability principles, there is a need for immediate action due to the great pressures on the environment and because the socioeconomic structure is highly dependent on the well-balanced evolution of tourist activities.

The three basic dimensions of sustainable development (preservation of natural and cultural resources, economic viability and social justice) can be measured and analysed using indicators that are adapted to specific realities of each place and that consider environmental, socioeconomic and tourist variables. The identification, monitoring and control of such indicators will assist greatly in working towards more sustainable tourism and in promoting this objective in public- and private-sector decision-making.

## The conceptual framework for a system of indicators

The limitations of traditional development indicators, such as Gross Domestic Product and Gross National Product, have been criticised since the 1970s (OECD, 1978). However, there have been relatively few achievements in terms of defining and applying indicators with a social or environmental content. The huge impact of the Rio Summit and the call in Agenda 21 (chapter 40.6) for the use of sustainability indicators has prompted much theoretical work in the field. There is a long list of international and national organisations as well as non-governmental organisations that have undertaken initiatives related to sustainability indicators: the Organisation for Economic Cooperation and Development (OECD), the United Nations Organisation (Environment and Development Programmes and the Commission for Sustainable Development), the World Bank, the European Union's General Directorate XI, the European Environmental Agency, The International Council for Local Environmental Initiatives, the World Watch Institute, the International Institute of Sustainable Development (Canada), the World Tourism Organisation, the World Wide Fund, etc.

The application of sustainability indicators to tourism arises from the need to introduce environmental considerations in sectorial policies, this being underlined in the European Commission's Programme V on Politics and Action in Environmental Matters (COM (92) 23 final, 1992). The environmental perspective prevails in this approach, and its influence is clearly felt on the genesis of national sustainability indicators in countries such as France, Spain or ·the United Kingdom. Nevertheless, in the planning and management of destinations on a local scale, this perspective is widened to embrace a more comprehensive view that includes the economic and sociocultural dimensions of sustainable development.

Among the earliest studies to deal with tourism planning on the basis of sustainability and the use of indicators is the ECOMOST project, which was promoted by the International Federation of Tour Operators (IFTO) and part-funded by the European Union. This project´s aim was to create a model for sustainable development based on an analysis of tourism development on the islands of Mallorca and Rhodes. The system of indicators was used for analysis, in order to identify the critical problems in the destination, and to develop proposals concerning the actions required to reach higher levels of sustainability (Hughes, 1994).

The World Tourism Organisation´s proposals for the sustainable planning of tourism also led to calls for the use of indicators (WTO, 1995). The definition of such indicators has become an aim shared by a large number of organisations. In France, the *Institut Français de l´Environnement* (IFEN, 2000) and the *Agence Française d´Ingénierie Touristique* (AFIT) have undertaken interesting work. The *IFEN* has identified a series of indicators at a national scale that are classified by types of destination (coastal, mountain, rural or urban) and that seek to facilitate the integration of the environment in tourism policies. And the *AFIT* has outlined a set of criteria for sustainable tourism management in tourist destinations that has been tested in several pilot areas (Céron & Dubois, 2000).

In Spain, the Ministry for the Environment has been working to define a system of environmental indicators for the tourism sector as part of the Spanish System of Environmental Indicators, although Autonomous Communities like the Balearic Islands have already developed their own regional system of indicators (Blázquez *et al.*, 2001). In the local context, the implementation of Agenda 21 in mature coastal resorts such as Calvià (Mallorca) or Sitges (Barcelona) has given a boost to work on tourist sustainability indicators. In the United Kingdom, the design of indicators for sustainable development proposed by the Department of the Environment, Transport and the Regions (DETR) has highlighted the need to develop specific indicators for tourism activity (DETR, 1999). The DETR emphasise the importance of destination indicators which are representative of local conditions and can potentially be aggregated to feed into a national system, with the British Resorts Association collaborating on defining this latter system (Allin *et al.*, 2001).

The system of indicators presented in this paper reflects contributions already made by the OECD's pressure-state-response (PSR) model (1978, 1980, 1993), and by the European Environmental Agency's driving forces-pressure-state- impact-response model (DPSIR) (EEA, 1998b), conceived for urban environments, with these models adapted for responsible management of tourist areas. The system of indicators is shown in Figure 3. It is based on models of causal organisation which measure both the impacts of human activity on local environments and the political and social responses to prevent or mitigate them. It also incorporates the holistic perspective of sustainability by considering the environmental, economic and sociocultural dimensions of tourism development.

The indicators are organised in four interrelated groups: Land Use–Tourism model, pressure indicators, state-quality indicators, and political and social

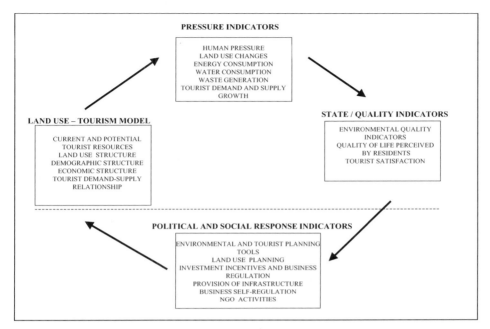

**Figure 3** A system of indicators for the planning and management of tourist areas
*Source:* Adapted from OECD (1993) and EEA (1998b)

response indicators. The Land Use–Tourism model is a prerequisite for identifying the different types of tourist areas (coastal, urban, rural or mountain areas), understanding their different stages of development, and identifying factors that influence the evolution of tourism activities and can also orient it towards a sustainable rate of development. These factors are more easily recognised at the local level, where the principles of sustainability appear directly applicable (Vera Rebollo *et al.*, 1997). The pressure indicators reflect the tensions that tourism activities place on the natural environment and on the socioeconomic structure of the destination, while the state-quality indicators express its current environmental situation, the quality of life as perceived by locals, and the degree of satisfaction experienced by tourists. The political and social response indicators represent the measures taken with regard to the conditions outlined in the Land Use–Tourism model, and the existing pressures as well as the state-quality of the different components of the development process. The placing of management measures at the end of the causal linkage certainly does not imply that the system exclusively promotes a policy of reaction. On the contrary, a periodic revision of these indicators provides useful information for both preventive and proactive measures.

## Application of the system of indicators to Torrevieja

### Indicators in the Land Use-Tourism Model

The group of indicators in the Land Use–Tourism model are adapted to analysing local conditions in order to measure any significant changes in these conditions. Such changes may come about as a result of various causes, such as the advent of a new competitive environment and subsequent impacts on demand, or the adoption of new strategies by the tourist destination. The sustainable planning and management of tourist spaces requires an appropriate definition of local indicators that is sensitive to changes, can easily be included in decision-making processes, and merely supplements the existing local empirical knowledge of the destination and does not substitute for it.

The Land Use–Tourism model used in Torrevieja is based on the ideal characteristics of a place for the development of 'sun-and-sea' tourism: a coastline of attractive sandy beaches and a pleasant climate. These traditional elements provide the basis for the form of tourism that has developed in Torrevieja. In an effort to encourage higher quality forms of tourism and to avoid the homogenisation experienced in other tourist destinations along the Mediterranean (Morgan, 1994), other resources that have a proven potential for tourism have also been included. The types of tourism associated with these resources should not be seen merely as a complement to the traditional tourist supply, as these resources can promote the development of new tourist products and services. This applies to nature or health tourism, which is now offered at the lagoons in Torrevieja's Natural Park. The surface area of the lagoons is almost 40% of the municipal area. The products available at the lagoons are complemented by three golf courses and other new projects sponsored by the City Council, such as the remodelling of the port with a new commercial and entertainment centre, the tourist-oriented use of such cultural and historical traditions as seafaring and salt-making, and the creation of two ecologically oriented paths along the coast.

As a result of these resources, land is now being developed throughout the municipality, with the exception of the lagoons themselves, but with notable pressure being exerted on the coastline where urban development interests seem to prevail. Table 1 shows that the residential area is highly concentrated, and an inevitable consequence of this residential/vacational urban development is the transformation of traditional structures like agriculture. This transformation necessitates the expansion of public services (water supply, sewerage and waste treatment, civilian protection, etc.) and creates demand for larger and more efficient infrastructure (new roads, street lighting, etc.), all of which lead to ever-increasing maintenance costs.

The rapid growth of real estate activities, whose rhythm and intensity are subject to the economic cycles of demand for housing rather than any policy dictated by local politicians, has increased the importance of the construction sector within the local economic structure. The local economy is already highly specialised in the service sector to fulfilling the needs of the growing number of permanent residents and the overwhelming volume of seasonal visitors. The growth in real estate activity and the tertiary sector have been accompanied by a remarkable migration from other provinces in Spain as well as a noticeable presence of foreigners, thus transforming the demographic structure of the municipality. Among the newcomers, a clear distinction should be made between holiday-makers, retired Spanish and foreign couples, and those who have arrived as workers in the construction and service sectors. Most of these workers

**Table 1** Land Use-Tourism model

| Indicator | Parameters |
|---|---|
| *Tourist resources/attractions* | |
| Basic tourist resources | Average temperature of 18°C<br>About 3000 hours of sunshine per year<br>18 km of coastline<br>1500 berths in 2 marinas<br>Natural Park of La Mata and Torrevieja Lagoons<br>3 golf courses within 8 km<br>Events of tourist significance (International Folk Songs Contest, The May Fair, etc.). |
| Potential tourist resources | A better use of the Natural Park for a specific type of tourism.<br>The urban and functional remodelling of the port.<br>Health-oriented tourism in the lagoons (mud-baths, etc.).<br>There is a project to build a hotel-spa resort within the perimeter of the park, although this is not free from controversy. |
| *Land use* | |
| Land for residential use | 16,000,740 m2, which represents 22.3% of the municipality, but reaches 33.5% if the surface area of the lagoons is subtracted. |
| Suburban sprawl versus concentrated areas for residential purposes. | The surface area of open residential land is twice the size of the concentrated area, representing about 15.3% of the municipality's total area. |
| Physical modifications of the coast | The coastal fringe up to 500 m from the sea-shore is classified as either urbanised (74.7%) or urbanisable (9.9%). |
| *Economic activity* | |
| Economic specialisation | 66.7% of the companies belong to one of the following sectors: commerce, restaurants and lodging (51.45%) and construction (15.2%). |
| Employment by sector | The service sector employs the greatest number of workers (65%) according to the latest census (1991). |
| Official unemployment level | Unemployed persons among the resident population: 2.9% (2000) (La Caixa, 2002). |
| *Demographic structure* | |
| Increase in population | The official population has increased tremendously between 1970 and 2001 (622%), totalling 70,262 inhabitants, much higher than the average for the province which was around 53% for the same period. |
| Origins of the resident population | With the recent influx of new residents, the origins of the population have changed considerably: 24.4% born in Torrevieja, 13.8% from the same province as Torrevieja (Alicante), 36.6% from other Spanish provinces and 24.2% foreign born (data from 1996). |

**Table 1** (*cont.*) Land Use-Tourism model

| Indicator | Parameters |
|---|---|
| The ageing of the population | Those of 65 years or over represent 20.8% of the total population (1998), but the ageing trend becomes obvious when we consider that in 1991 this age group was only 15.8% of the total. |
| *Tourist-oriented structure* | |
| Regulated accommodation offer | 5,504 beds in 2000, distributed among apartments (46.5%), hotels (26.8%) and camp sites (25.2%). |
| Potential tourist accommodation available in private homes | An estimated 300,000 beds in both second homes and apartments unofficially rented to visitors. Dwellings allocated exclusively to visitors represent 78.9% of total dwellings. |
| Profile of demand | Majority: vacationing families, middle-income level, Spanish nationals, owners or renters of holiday homes, visits in summer, and highly loyal to the destination. |

*Source*: METASIG Project (Vera Rebollo, 2002)

are of Spanish origin, although recently there has been an influx of foreign workers from developing countries. The arrival of national and foreign pensioners, however, is certainly causing a slow but progressive ageing of the demographic pyramid.

The low bedspace capacity of the regulated supply of tourist accommodation is a basic structural characteristic of Torrevieja's model of tourism. In contrast to this limited supply of hotel accommodation and of registered tourist apartments and camping sites, there is a huge volume of holiday homes and apartments, now estimated to be about 300,000 beds. With such a situation, the prevalence of real estate activities over tourist-oriented ones is evident. In other words, instead of the conventional supply of tourist products (package-tour holidays, etc.), what is on offer are houses and flats for sale or for rent. This explains the main type of demand that Torrevieja has today: visitors of mainly Spanish nationality, of low-middle income level, who organise their vacations without using the services of a travel agency, who are mainly in family groups, who tend to stay in their own homes, who use their own vehicle, whose average stay is of about 21 days, generally in summer, and whose yearly visit is the logical result of the inevitable bond that ownership of a home creates with the destination. The supply–demand interaction described here is quite common for most towns along the Spanish Mediterranean coast. What is truly singular about Torrevieja is the sheer magnitude of its real estate supply for tourism.

## Pressure indicators

The great volume of recently constructed dwellings has led to the rapid extension of the built-up area, which has not only changed the landscape of the municipality but has also encroached considerably on what was agricultural land before the tourist boom. Furthermore, the resident–visitor function of the

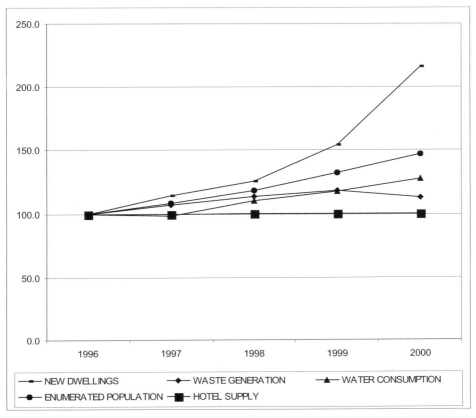

**Figure 4** Evolution of pressure factors, 1996–2000
*Source*: Vera Rebollo, 2002

available land has a great impact on the consumption of water and electricity and the collection of wastes. There are several dimensions to the pressures on the resort, but two aspects should be highlighted: (1) the rapid increase in new dwell-ings, which is the greatest pressure of all, and (2) the extreme seasonality of tourism, which conditions the real impact on the destination. Figure 4 shows the steady increase in the number of homes during the period 1996–2000, which has caused an increase, though not proportional, in the consumption of water and garbage collection. The increase in the enumerated population is a direct effect of the City Council's rapid expansion policy and the efforts it has made to register as many residents as possible. The registered supply of accommodation shows a modest growth, although there are projects underway that could help to increase it by 70%. An increase in hotel accommodation, in contrast to real estate services, is essential for developing new tourist products (health spas, congresses, aquatic sports, golf, nature, etc.), which, in turn, create new job profiles and help consoli-date different types of business that are quite independent of the behaviour of the real estate sector.

The true seasonality of Torrevieja's tourist visits is difficult to measure as there

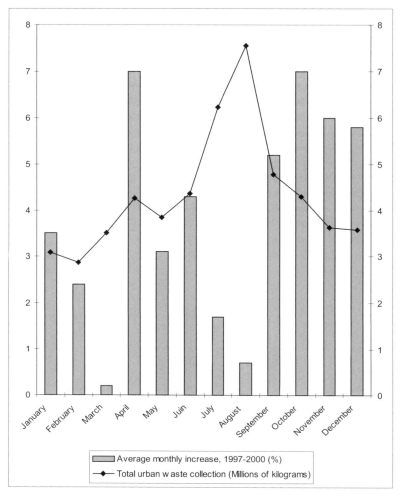

**Figure 5** Urban waste collection. Monthly distribution in 2001 and average
monthly increase, 1997–2001
*Source*: Torrevieja Municipality

are no available data on private accommodation, which, in fact, is greater than
the official hotel supply. This is why indirect indicators should be used, in spite of
their obvious limitations. Both the monthly consumption of water and the
monthly volume of garbage collected have their seasonal peaks in summer. On
the other hand, and parallel to the growth in the registered population, an
increase is also seen in the number of out-of-season visitors, as Figure 5 suggests.
It is also noteworthy that the average monthly increase in garbage collected
during the period 1997–2001 is not highest for the two most popular months for
vacationers (July and August).

*State-quality indicators*
    This set of indicators relates to the state of some easily measured features, like

**Table 2** Pressure indicators

| Indicator | Parameters |
|-----------|------------|
| Human pressure | The population of the municipality during the peak period (August) can be as high as 375,000 people, with a density of about 5252 inhabitants per km². |
| Seasonal human pressure | With the use of an indirect indicator, urban garbage collection, the seasonal summer peak is clearly seen, with the months of July, August and September having the highest rates (36.7%) of annual garbage collection. Water consumption confirms the summer pressure, as the month with the highest consumption rate (August) is triple that of the lowest (January). |
| Increase in land use for residential purposes | Although the surface area of the concentrated residential zone remains stable, the open space dedicated to residential construction grew 10% during the period from April 2001 to January 2002. |
| Increase in number of dwellings | The average annual increase in the number of dwellings for the period 1996–2000 is 16.6%. |
| Increase in official supply of tourist accommodation | The average annual increase in the official supply of accommodation during the period is 13.8% (1996–2000), although it is based on a modest initial volume, and most of the increase took place during the year 2000. |
| Increase in urban garbage collection | The average annual increase in urban garbage collection for the period 1996–2000 is 2.4%. |
| Increase in water consumption | The average annual increase in water consumption during the period 1996–2000 was 4.9%, almost twice the increase in garbage collection. |
| Increase in consumption of electricity | The average increase in domestic consumption of electricity in the service sector was 6.3% for the period 1990–1995, according to the latest available data. |

*Source*: METASIG Project (Vera Rebollo, 2002)

the quality of sea water and the atmosphere, as well as more subjective aspects such as local residents' and tourists' perception of the quality of life. In relation to the most relevant indicators of atmospheric quality, it is suggested that the atmosphere is not negatively affected by the seasonal concentration of tourists although no official measurements are made to confirm this. On the other hand, noise pollution has been observed in the most congested urban areas, due principally to traffic and nightclubs and discos. The quality of the city´s running water meets the official health requirements and, in spite of a total dependence on water supplies from outside, no problems of either quality or supply have arisen so far, in contrast to the situation in many other coastal resorts along the Mediterranean. The sea water is kept at relatively high levels of quality, as attested by the award of six blue flags to the municipality during 2000. This indicator is directly related to policies for the treatment and purification of

**Table 3** State-quality indicators

| *Indicator* | *Parameters* | |
|---|---|---|
| Basic environmental measures | According to conventional standards, there is no atmospheric pollution. Certain areas suffer from noise pollution. Both sea water and tap water are of good quality. | |
| Perceived quality of life | The interviews carried out among the social actors show a positive evaluation of the business sector and the creation of jobs. The areas that need attention are health services, traffic and parking. Other concerns to be addressed are public safety and the loss of local identity. | |
| Tourist satisfaction | Important and satisfactory: Climate Quality of lodging Commercial supply Amusement and entertainment Quality of restaurants and bars Cleaning of public spaces Quality–price ratio Sports facilities Attractiveness of the landscape Public safety Quality of the beaches | Important but unsatisfactory: Quality of urban development and construction Parks and natural areas Historic and cultural attractiveness The pedestrian flow Health services Noise levels Tranquility and non-massification Traffic. Parking |

*Source*: METASIG Project (Vera Rebollo, 2002)

waste water, and a project is now underway to increase the capacity of the water purifying plant.

A survey on the perceived quality of life was carried out through a series of interviews with representatives of the social and political scenes (political parties, business and cultural associations, etc.). The interviewees highlighted the great economic dynamism of Torrevieja and its surrounding areas and the positive effects this has on employment. However, this dynamism which is directly related to real estate and tourist activities and to the increase in population, has negative effects on certain aspects of local life, such as the health services, which is the main concern, and traffic (congestion and parking problems), along with a growing concern for street safety and the loss of local identity. In spite of these concerns, the suggestions made by the interviewees for improving the situation did not include limits being put on either urban growth or tourism. Indeed, both of these are regarded as the key elements in the municipality's development and prosperity which could not have been accomplished by any other sector, and they are therefore accepted as necessary and unavoidable. Consequently, in their opinion the most urgent actions to be taken are all in the realm of public investment (a new hospital, car parks, better roads, etc.).

In order to evaluate the level of satisfaction among tourists, a survey was carried out with 240 interviewees in the Municipality of Torrevieja during the summer of 2001. The sample characteristics sought were basic and simple, considering age, sex and nationality. The questionnaire was divided into two related parts and the responses were based on a five-point Likert-type scoring system. In accordance with the multi-attribute model of attitude measurement presented in Fishbein (Ryan, 1995), the first part of the questionnaire inquired about the factors that a tourist generally considers most important when deciding on a destination for their holiday. The second part evaluated the extent to which Torrevieja fulfilled these attributes. In this way, the information gathered was better than would be obtained from a single indicator of overall satisfaction, which would be extremely difficult to relate to the varied influences on their satisfaction or dissatisfaction. Although the overall evaluation of the destination was quite satisfactory (74%), there are two distinct sets of attributes with different 'importance/adequacy' relationships. There were certain features that the tourists considered as very important that they felt highly satisfied with. This was the case for the municipality's main tourist resources, that is the 'sun-and-sea' elements, as well as for the private sector's service provision (commerce, restaurants, lodging, entertainment, price–quality ratio, etc.). Other services like street cleaning and public safety scored well with visitors, but less well for residents. Paradoxically, the great transformation of the landscape by the built-up area does not seem to have negatively affected the tourists´ perceptions of the destination, perhaps influenced by the attractiveness of the coastline and the large Lagoons Natural Park.

On the negative side, however, there were other aspects that tourists considered important that they were not satisfied with. These seem to have been the direct result of the rapid growth in the population and urban development and its flawed planning. The high concentration of tourists in the summer is the prime cause of traffic jams, difficulty in parking, pedestrian congestion, noise, lack of green areas and insufficient health services. This evaluation of the demand side shows that there are clear weaknesses in the Land Use-Tourism model and that public policies with a new strategic vision are required so as to avoid the problems detected.

### Response indicators

The political response to the factors outlined above does not show any modification to the present policy of rapid urban, tourism and demographic growth; rather it seeks to channel this development in a coordinated way and thus to balance the residential-tourist function with the quality of life through more public spending. Because of tax revenues resulting from its rapid growth, Torrevieja now has the third largest local government budget in the province of Alicante. The environmental and sociocultural losses seem to be accepted politically and socially as inevitable costs, with the opportunities for them to be mitigated through greater investment in certain areas. This undeclared strategy seems to be comparable to the concept of weak sustainability (Hunter, 1997; Pearce & Atkinson, 1998), according to which lost natural capital can be substituted by investment in diverse environmental projects. As such, there is appreciation of the protection of 40.5% of the surface area of the municipality, the progressive increase in the 'green' budget, the treatment of waste water, the selective collection of waste, and the surveillance and control of the environment. Such policies contrast greatly with the common link between coastal mass

**Table 4** Response indicators

| *Indicator* | *Parameters* |
|---|---|
| Actions on tourism resources | Urban remodelling and the creation of new commercial and leisure centres. This project includes the recovery of facilities that were traditionally used for the storage and transport of salt. The 'Integral Plan' for the coast of Torrevieja. |
| Urban planning | The regulation in the 'General Urban Plan' was approved in 1986. The long period that has passed since its introduction, the frequent ad hoc modifications, and the overwhelming real estate activity all indicate the need to revise the municipality's urban plan. |
| Protected non-urbanisable land | 2,906 ha of natural landscape is under protection (40.5% of the municipality's surface area), most of which is included in the Natural Park which is governed by a Management and Use Plan, approved in 1994. |
| Tourism planning | Plan of Excellence in Tourism (2000) and the declaration of Torrevieja as a pilot destination for the 'Green Municipality' programme. |
| Municipal budget | Torrevieja's budget, previously in eighth place in the province of Alicante, has now become the third largest budget in the province with a spectacular increase of 354.7% between 1990 and 2000. |
| Green budget | In spite of the difficulties in separating out the parts of the budget with environmental purposes (changes from year to year, expenses and investments coming from other administrations, etc.), it is estimated that this reaches around 20% of the total. Among the main items in this percentage are the collection, elimination and treatment of garbage, and street cleaning (64% of the green budget), parks and gardens (23%), and beaches and pools (7.6%). |
| Waste water treatment | The purifying station for waste water treated 6,419,231 $m^3$ of water (2001) by means of a system of activated mires. The effluent was used by the City Council for the watering of public gardens, street cleaning and agricultural irrigation. Juárez (2001) estimates that 100% of the recycled water is now used, with a great reduction of loss in the distribution network over the last couple of years. |
| Selective garbage collection | The selective collection of residues has now reached a total volume of 6,780,480 kg per annum (2001), which represents 12% of the total waste generated in the municipality, with a mean increase of 1.4% over 2000. The main residues that are selectively collected are organic remains, most of it from the pruning of trees (37.7%), paper and cardboard (19.2%) and glass (11.8%). |
| Environmental surveillance and control | The municipality has an Environmental Ordinance and an Environmental Surveillance Brigade. |

*Source*: METASIG Project (Vera Rebollo, 2002)

tourism and the progressive and uncontrollable degradation of the environment, and they offer more substance to debates about the mature tourist destinations along the Mediterranean coast.

Contrary to what would be expected of a tourist-oriented municipality of its size, Torrevieja's local policies are not based on sound planning. Its Land Use Plan is obsolete and the opportunities derived from its inclusion in the 'Plans for Excellence in Tourism' and 'The Green Municipality'[1] programmes have not been channelled into any concrete plans for public action, but rather have led to *ad hoc* projects and specific programmes for the renovation and enhancement of the municipality, such as the remodelling of the port, the creation of two ecological paths along the coast, or the recovery of its cultural heritage. This demonstrates a gradual change from tourism based on exotropism (the attractiveness of the environment, like the sea or the beaches) to one of endotropism (the gradual tourism-oriented use of revalued local elements), in accordance with the concepts coined by Dewailly (1990).

## An Assessment of Local Government Policies

Analysis at the local level is important to understand the integration of sustainability in the development and management of tourism. In decentralised Spain, each Autonomous Community develops its own tourist, urban and ecological policies. Furthermore, at local government level there are several different bodies with authority to implement local projects. Indeed, it can be said that the existing national tourism policy is merely a recognition of the diverse strategies that were spontaneously adopted by the different Municipalities from the very start of Spain´s tourism development. There is no other way of explaining the great disparity between neighbouring tourist resorts that share the same natural resources and have developed totally different systems for tourism management, in both their structures and activities. Any attempt to apply the principles of sustainability to tourism, therefore, must consider the diversity of the strategies developed at the local level, a practice that has been widespread in Spain for more than three decades.

In the case of Torrevieja, the Municipality's approach can be classified in several ways, even though the cornerstone of tourism development over the last 20 years has been the promotion of housing construction, devoted almost exclusively to vacationers. It is a low-cost product that is promoted and sold by large real estate companies whose extensive commercial networks are the key to their success in national and international markets. In view of the considerable urban saturation, and in order to avoid the image of a lower-quality mass tourism resort, Torrevieja has for the last five years been implementing an environmental protection policy that involves recovering degraded zones and projecting a new image of itself associated with the Municipality's star product, the Natural Park.

## Development policy

The current Land Use Plan was approved in the mid-1980s and it has become a useful tool for the mass construction of cheap housing. This locally conceived policy has eased the granting of licences for new buildings, as the construction sector has now become an essential factor in the Municipality's economic, social and urban development strategies. Figure 1 showed that, except for brief periods of slight respite that coincided with reductions in real estate investment, there has been an overwhelming growth in the number of private homes and apartments for holiday use.

It was only from the 1990s that the notable lack of green areas, infrastructure and public amenities became manifest, leading to a recognition of the need to promote projects to address this shortage and to create new public areas and better urban services. Nevertheless, the model of rapid growth has not been modified or even questioned, so that the new projects appear to be emergency measures to address specific problems, although they are receiving good responses from the local population. It is not surprising, therefore, that the Plan for urban development, which was originally conceived as an eight-year development plan, has been operating more like an emergency plan for the last 15 years. The most worrying aspect, however, is that the Plan's most important changes have been oriented towards achieving as much urban development as possible, by means of high-rise buildings or invading spaces that had once been declared unsuitable for development.

In short, Torrevieja's urban policy is the result of a desire to continue the model of rapid growth in housing as an essential activity for the town's economy, with profits being made from land that was originally considered unproductive. Indeed, this *modus operandi* is quite common among most other tourist resorts along Spain's Mediterranean coast (López Palomeque & Vera Rebollo, 2001). In the case of Torrevieja, well-known firms are commissioned for large urban projects as a way of creating an image of renewed vitality for their already over-congested areas.

## Tourist promotion policy

After many years of rapid growth and a development plan that favoured real estate activity, certain aspects seem to be changing, although the real estate activity has not slowed down. The new paradigm is a simple change in image, in a desperate attempt to neutralise the impression of congestion. This translates into more limited tourist promotion, with Torrevieja no longer participating in the International Tourism Fair (FITUR) held annually in Madrid, and promotion of more select forms of tourism supply, with a particular emphasis on investment in quality hotels to offset the existing model of private accommodation. The Natural Park is being promoted as the new image of the town, which contrasts sharply with the reality of the existing congestion. In collaboration with both the central and the autonomous governments, a new plan for 'quality tourism' is being implemented (the Excellence Plan). Torrevieja has also been selected as a pilot area for the implementation of the government project, 'the Green Municipality'. The question that remains to be answered, however, is how to achieve a balance between these two different and opposed realities: the conservation of natural spaces and the continued urban development.

## Cultural policy

The benefits obtained from the urban development process and the need to create an image of renewal for this maturing tourist destination have influenced the City Council´s cultural policies. The development of a major cultural programme and the staging of significant events that project the image of the Municipality, like the granting of a literary prize (one of the most important prizes in Spain), have led to Torrevieja appearing in the cultural pages of national newspapers for a few days every year. It is a conscious attempt to overcome the Municipality´s previous image as a destination of cheap real estate promotions that served as prizes for several television shows. Doubts emerge, however, when the cultural policy is dependent on the building sector and on a constant increase in visitor numbers.

## Environmental policy

The environmental policy was created in an effort to offset the image that the process of constant urbanisation has given the Municipality. The considerable progress made in certain areas, like the hydrological cycle and waste management, is relatively unusual among the tourist resorts on Spain's Mediterranean coast. The promotion of the Natural Park and of environmental values is another key element of Torrevieja's new tourism programme, but the granting of licences for buildings at the very borders of the park certainly seems to be in contradiction to the idea of protecting the area. The major challenge, therefore, seems to be in finding a balance between the success in several aspects of environmental management and the maintenance of an undifferentiated 'sun-and-sea' tourist supply.

## Social policy

Whilst Torrevieja's present model of tourism promotion and urban development might be counterproductive for environmental protection, it has certainly been positive with regard to employment and per capita income. The great influx of newcomers (around 10,000 citizens from countries in the European Union and over 50,000 from the different provinces in Spain), has come either seeking the popular 'sun-and-sea' holiday ambience or searching for work and business opportunities. Torrevieja's City Council actively promotes the official registration of all of its residents, since an increase in registered inhabitants results in more tax revenues and larger grants from Spain´s central government and from the European Union. On the other hand, the City Council has also had to increase the volume of social services it provides for the population, e.g. free public transport and subsidies for students and retired citizens with low-level pensions. The important question here, however, is how these social policies will be maintained when the urban development process that now fills the coffers of local government finally stops.

## Conclusions

The definition of a system of indicators helps to show more precisely what sustainable tourist development means and aids in the interpretation of the evolution of tourist destinations according to sustainability principles. Such indicators can also easily be integrated with other approaches and instruments for the planning and management of sustainable tourism, such as Strategic Environmental Assessments, town planning, and environmental management systems for tourist destinations. However, to be more effective the sustainability indicators need a large amount of information as well as improvements in terms of their reliability; for example, a higher degree of scientific-technical elaboration can enhance their scientific consistency, their representativeness, their comparability, and finally, their political and social acceptance.

In this study, the system of indicators was applied to the municipality of Torrevieja. The results are valuable for analysis and diagnosis purposes as they provide a useful point of reference for decision-making in relation to resort management. The causal structure of the proposed indicators allows interactions in the local tourist system to be studied, as well as the degree to which there is integration of sustainable development principles in local policies.

In the municipality under study, a model based on real estate and tourism development continues to prevail. This trend is evident in the increased number of tourist dwellings and the growth of the population registered for the census. Periods of lower growth in building activity are linked with external cycles of recession and do not reflect a will on the part of local authorities to restrain growth. In fact the opposite applies, with local policies fostering demographic growth as well as the further development of real estate activity, which is profit-able for both the building firms and the local administration. The municipal strategy is not exclusively based on the idea of a destination specialised in holiday homes. This strategy has evolved from the massive production of homes for tourist use towards the objective of becoming a centre providing services for the wider urban system in the south of the Valencian Region. However, the persistence of the extensive building model and the predominance of holiday homes necessarily limits its urban function.

Growth takes place under guidelines such as the quality improvement of urban areas, the development of green spaces, encouragement to big projects like the remodelling of the waterfront, and improvements in environmental management (the hydrological cycle and residue treatment). These initia-tives, among others, cannot be separated from the financial benefits that derive from economic dynamism and that materialise in local revenues. In this way, actions are undertaken to overcome negative perceptions of resi-dents (health service shortages, traffic congestion or growing lack of safety) as well as dissatisfaction among tourists, this being particularly associated with summer overcrowding.

Despite the size of the tourism infrastructure and the annual tourist volumes, Torrevieja has not entered the spiral of environmental and tourist degradation that has often been attributed to mature destinations in the Mediterranean. Nevertheless, from the perspective of the interpretations of sustainable develop-ment (Hunter, 1997), the local tourist system reflects a weak sustainability, that is, a type of economic growth is defended that permits the deterioration and consumption of certain natural resources, although there are some specific investments that reduce the negative impacts (such as the reuse of treated sewage water, the treatment of residues and the recovery of degraded areas of landscape). However, the local administration's investing capacity also depends on the maintenance of economic growth, which cannot last for ever. Once the current growth threshold has been reached, more conservationist policies should be applied in order to restore a balance between environmental and socio-cultural dimensions and the economic interests, with the latter so far having prevailed in the model for local development.

## Acknowledgements

This paper arises out of the Research Project 'Planning and Management of Sustainable Tourism. Methodological Proposal and Application of a Tourist Information System' (1FD97–0403), co-funded by the Interministerial Commission of Science and Technology (Spain) and the European Commission (FEDER).

## Correspondence

Any correspondence should be directed to Jose Fernando Vera Rebollo, Escuela de Turismo, Alicante University, Apartado de Correos 99, 03080 Alicante, Spain (JF.Vera@ua.es).

## Notes

1.  The Plans for Excellence in Tourism are applied to mature destinations and are jointly organised by central, regional and local government. Their main objectives are the quest for sustainable development, the mitigating of seasonality, and an increase in the range of tourism products that these coastal destinations offer. The Green Municipality Programme, on the other hand, is sponsored by central government and is devoted to promoting the application of environmental management systems in tourist destinations.

## References

Allin, P. *et al.* (2001) Defining and measuring sustainable tourism: Building the first set of UK indicators. In J. Lennon (ed.) *Tourism Statistics. International Perspectives and Current Issues* (pp. 163–74). London: Continuum.

Blázquez, M., Murray, I. and Garau, J.M. (2001) Indicadores de sostenibilidad del turismo en las Islas Baleares. *Actas del XVII Congreso de Geógrafos Españoles, Oviedo, Noviembre de 2001* (pp. 265–8).

Bramwell, B. *et al.* (eds) (1996) *Sustainable Tourism Management: Principles and Practice*. Tilburg: Tilburg University Press.

Butler, R. (1993) Tourism. An evolutionary perspective. In J. Nelson, R. Butler and G. Wall (eds) *Tourism and Sustainable Development: Monitoring, Planning, Managing* (pp. 27–43). Department of Geography, University of Waterloo.

Céron, J.P. and Dubois, G. (2000) Les indicateurs du tourisme durable. Un outil à manier avec discernement. *Cahiers Espaces* 67, 30–46.

Clarke, J. (1997) A framework of approaches to sustainable tourism. *Journal of Sustainable Tourism* 5 (3), 224–33.

Coccossis, H. (1996) Tourism and sustainability: Perspectives and implications. In G. Priestley, J. Edwards and H. Coccossis (eds): *Sustainable Tourism? European Experiencies* (pp. 1–21). Wallingford: CAB International.

Department of the Environment, Transport and the Regions (DETR) (1999) *Quality of Life Counts: Indicators for a Strategy for Sustainable Development in the United Kingdom*. London: Stationery Office.

Dewailly, J.M. (1990) *Tourisme et Aménagement en Europe du Nord*. Paris: Masson.

European Environment Agency (EEA) (1998a) *Medio Ambiente en Europa. El Informe Dobris.* (First published in 1995, edited by D. Stanners and P. Bourdeau.) Madrid: Oficina de Publicaciones Oficiales de las Comunidades Europeas y Ministerio de Medio Ambiente.

European Environment Agency (1998b) *Europe's Environment: The Second Assessment.* Copenhagen: Elsevier Science.

Hall, C.M. (2000): *Tourism Planning. Policies, Processes and Relationships*, Essex: Prentice Hall.

Hughes, P. (1994) *La Planificación del Turismo Sostenible. El Proyecto Ecomost.* Lewes: International Federation of Tour Operators (IFTO).

Hunter, C. (1997) Sustainable tourism as an adaptive paradigm. *Annals of Tourism Research* 24 (4), 850–67.

Institut Français de l'Environment (IFEN) (2000) *Les Indicateurs. Tourisme, Environnement, Territoires.* Orléans: IFEN.

Ivars Baidal, J.A. (2001) La planificación turística de los espacios regionales en España. Unpublished PhD thesis, Universty of Alicante.

Juárez, C. (2001) Indicadores hídricos de sostenibilidad y desarrollo turístico en la Comarca del Bajo Segura (Alicante). *Actas del XVII Congreso de Geógrafos Españoles, Oviedo, Noviembre de 2001* (pp. 354–8).

La Caixa (2002) *Anuario Económico, 2001.* Barcelona: La Caixa

López Palomeque, F. and Vera Rebollo, J.F. (2001) Espacios y destinos turísticos. In A. Gil Olcina and J. Gómez Mendoza (coord.) *Geografía de España* (pp. 545–71). Barcelona: Ariel.

Montanari, A. & Williams, A. (1995) *European Tourism: Regions, Spaces and Restructuring* (pp. 109–26). London: Wiley.

Morgan, M. (1994) Homogeneous products: The future of established resorts. In W. Theobald (ed.) *Global Tourism. The Next Decade* (pp. 378–95). Oxford: Butteworth-Heinemann.

OECD (1978) *Indicateurs d'Environnement Urbain.* Paris: Organisation de Coopération et de Développement Économiques.

OECD (1980) *L'Impact du Tourisme sur l'Environnement*, Paris: Organisation de Coopération el de Développement Économiques.

OECD (1993) OECD core set of indicators for environmental performance reviews. *Environment Monographs* 83. On WWW at http://www.oecd.org.

Organización Mundial de Turismo (1993) *Guía Para Administraciones Locales: Desarrollo Turístico Sostenible.* Madrid, OMT.

Organización Mundial de Turismo (OMT) (1995) *Lo que todo Gestor Turístico debe Saber. Guía Práctica para el Desarrollo y Uso de Indicadores de Turismo Sostenible.* Madrid: Organización Mundial de Turismo.

Pearce, D. and Atkinson, G. (1998) Concept of sustainable development: An evaluation of its usefulness 10 years after Brundtland. *Environmental Economics and Policy Studies* 1, 95–111.

Ryan, C. (1995) *Researching Tourist Satisfaction. Issues, Concepts, Problems.* London: Routledge.

Ramsar Convention Bureau (2002) The Ramsar Convention on wetlands. On WWW at http://ramsar.org/index_list.htm.

Vera Rebollo, J.F. (2002) *METASIG Project: Planning and Management of Sustainable Tourism.* Alicante University, National Plan of Research and Development.

Vera Rebollo, J.F. and Ivars Baidal, J.A. (2001) Una propuesta de indicadores para la planificación y gestión del turismo sostenible. V Congreso Nacional de Medio Ambiente (2000). CD-ROM edition. Madrid: Colegio Oficial de Físicos, Unión Profesional, Aproma and Instituto de Ingeniería de España.

Vera Rebollo, J.F., López, F., Marchena, M., and Anton, S. (1997) *Análisis Territorial del Turismo.* Barcelona: Ariel.

Vera Rebollo, J.F. and Marchena, M. (1995) Real estate business and tourism development. *Raports 45th Congress AIEST, International Association of Scientific Experts in Tourism* 37, 29–52.

World Tourism Organisation, Earth Council and World Travel and Tourism Council (1995) *Agenda 21 for the Travel and Tourism Industry*. London: WTO, Earth Council and WTTC.

# 10  The Planning and Practice of Coastal Zone Management in Southern Spain

**Gonzalo Malvárez García and John Pollard**
*School of Biological and Environmental Sciences, University of Ulster, Coleraine, N. Ireland*

**Rafael Domínguez Rodríguez**
*Departamento de Geografía, Universidad de Málaga, 29071 Málaga, Spain*

This paper examines coastal management policies in southern Spain in the context of the state's role in the promotion of sustainable development practices. It recognises the critical importance of the coast as a landscape resource for both visitors and residents and, in addition, the latter's rights to enjoy access to it as public property. Attention is directed at both physical protection of the coast through erosion control programmes and urban planning policies, with special emphasis on the 1988 Shores Act that attempts to treat coastal planning in a more integrated manner than has historically been the case. The underlying rationale to introduce a more environmentally sensitive treatment of the coast is discussed together with the attempts to confront illegal occupancy through re-establishment of public ownership and control of land-use in the coastal zone. Positive achievements in beach management, and changing attitudes to the law, are seen as evidence that the message of sustainability is beginning to be heard. However, such success contrasts with failure to control the wider urban development process which continues (even in developments that postdate the Shores Act) to reflect short-term economic rather than environmental prerogatives. Thus severe limitations upon the maintenance of a quality coastal environment are likely to continue without enforcement of buffer zones at the regional level or a more radical designation of more of the coast as 'protected'. Such may well be encouraged eventually by the very same economic interests that are concerned to retain Spain's position in the global tourism market by providing an environment that is attractive to visitors.

## Introduction

The role of the state in the promotion of sustainable development practices is both well established and diverse. Shaw and Williams (2002) have observed that the basis of that role lies in the absence of a market for public goods, including the landscape and ecosystems, thus requiring state intervention to provide overall environmental management. In the context of sustainable tourist development, it is the coast that provides the most extensive landscape resource within the Mediterranean basin, and it is the principal magnet not only for northern European visitors but also significant numbers of the region's own residents. Spain, which occupies the second position in terms of foreign visitor arrivals (Travel and Tourism Intelligence, 2001), welcomes most of these tourists to its coastal margins (Bote Gomez & Sinclair, 1996), so that the well-being of its littoral is of vital concern to the Spanish economy and its workforce.

From the widest perspective that embraces all of Spain's population, there is growing recognition of the rights of citizens as consumers. Within those rights are included entitlement to a quality environment in respect of air, water and scenery (Lash & Urry, 1994; Williams & Shaw, 1998), which has particular resonance for the state's management of the coastal environment. An essential component of sustainable management here relates to the implied concern for social equity and the guarantee of access for both present and future generations to the basic natural resources of water, forests and land (Harrison, 1996). The rapid development of the Spanish coastline has obvious implications for this fundamental right in respect both to aesthetic concerns and to potential adverse impacts upon water quality and access provision.

Enjoyment of access and of an undegraded coastal landscape is an equally paramount demand of visitors to the region. Indeed, environmental factors have been recognised as an important element in the decision-making process (Robinson, 1996), while a reduction in tourism growth rates has often been associated with the serious environmental impacts of mass tourist development (Barke & France, 1996; Vera Rebollo, 2001). Despite the growing promotion of alternative tourism markets and indications of more self-provision and individualisation in holiday-making, it is generally accepted that mass tourism in coastal resorts will continue to play a vital part in the Spanish economy (Williams & Shaw, 1998). Consequently, protection of its economic interests in an increasingly globalised and competitive market demands the sustainable management of such a crucial resource.

The early post-war years of Spanish economic development showed little effective implementation of such sustainable management principles (Morris, 1996). Accordingly, the degradation of coastal resources typified the decades of the 1960s and 1970s when the economic growth paradigm went largely unchallenged and served to confirm the view expressed by Butler (1998) that without 'assigned responsibility for resource protection environmental decline is inevitable'. During that period, coastal management meant little beyond *ad hoc* schemes for the protection of vulnerable stretches of real estate. Although attempts to implement a more effective planning process did follow the advent of democratic government in 1975 and brought some order to development on the coast, it was not until 1988 that the *Ley de Costas* (Shores Act) (Ministerio de Obras Públicas y Urbanisma (MOPU, 1989)) provided a more holistic context in which coastal development could potentially be managed. Dating from that time, greater controls have existed on coastal development, while parallel actions to safeguard the physical integrity of the coastline have also been implemented.

The objective of this paper is to trace the post-war evolution of coastal policies and their impact, emphasising the role of the *Ley de Costas* in providing a theoretically sound framework for a more sympathetic and sustainable treatment of the coastal environment. However, in acknowledgement of the gap that has historically existed between policy formulation and its implementation in Spain, attention is particularly focussed on the effectiveness of the latest legislation in controlling urban development in the south of the country in the autonomous region of Andalucía. Within that region lies the Costa del Sol (Figure 1), which annually receives over 2 million hotel guests alone (Junta de Andalucía, annual). Opportunities to implement the new policies fully are greatly constrained on the Costa del Sol by the intensive urban development that already stretched virtually continuously from Estepona to Nerja by the end of the 1980s. Journey times from Málaga international airport have, until recently, limited pressures for

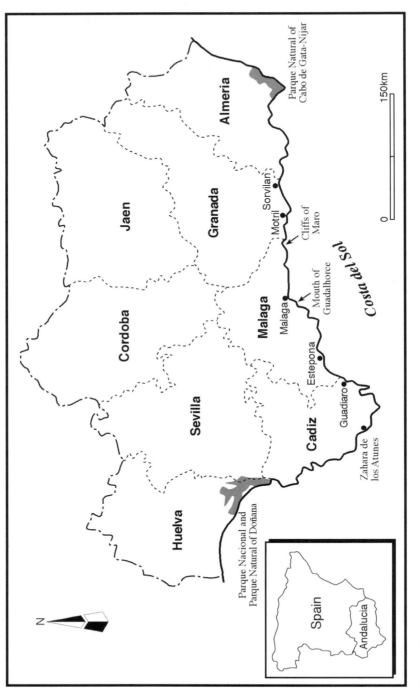

**Figure 1** The Autonomous Region of Andalucía

development to the west of Estepona. However, with the upgrading of the N340 route in the 1990s and the opening of the inland motorway in 2000 (Figure 2), that coastline has been brought well within the compass of the mass holiday market and urbanisation is proceeding apace in Casares and Manilva, the most westerly of Málaga's municipalities (Figure 2). As most of this development post-dates the *Ley de Costas*, this area offers an ideal laboratory in which to test the effectiveness of the legislation and thus the final section of this paper includes an examination of one of these local administrative areas, the municipality of Manilva.

## A Brief History of Coastal Policies and Legislation

Two themes commonly underscore coastal planning: coastal protection and the control of land use on the coastal margins. Until the 1980s these were largely treated as separate issues, although common ground was encountered when the construction of sea-front promenades provided both recreational and protective functions. Both coastal protection and coastal planning offer much scope for debate, the former in terms of the efficacy of alternative protection methods (and consequential effects of protecting one stretch of coast on adjacent sectors); and the latter in respect of the whole panoply of competing interests facing urban planners. On the Costa del Sol, the practice of coastal protection has the longer history, largely because of the failure of the planning process to deal effectively with the early growth of the urban communities that mushroomed with the package holiday industry in the latter part of the 20th century.

### Physical protection and management of the coast

Coastal protection work parallels the urbanisation of the coast and the consequent rise in value of shoreline real estate as fishermen's cottages and vegetable gardens gave way to restaurants, bars, apartments, hotels and residential estates. The first notable engineering works affecting the then villages of the Costa del Sol date to the 1960s with the start of promenade constructions such as those in Marbella and Torremolinos (Figure 2). These were often subject to inundation during storm conditions, leading to demands for further protection or strengthening of the new promenades.

Promenades became important both for their protective and recreational roles, while they also enabled access to the *chiringuitos* or restaurants/bars that were located on the beach itself. Sea-walls fronting the promenades were considered the most feasible and appropriate defensive policy according to the prevailing accepted ideas. However, the western Costa del Sol began to experience an increasing erosion problem in the 1970s after the construction of most of the sea-walled promenades because of erosion induced by their structural characteristics. One of the most serious cases was at Estepona where, following the building in the 1960s of a promenade backing what was at the time an extensive beach, erosion was so serious that the beach suffered a reduction in height and width, so that the promenade itself was threatened with destruction (Fernandez Ranada, 1989).

In an attempt to solve the problem, groynes were set into the beach at right angles to the shore in an attempt to protect the promenade and stabilise the eroding coastline (Fernandez Ranada, 1989). However, the process causing the

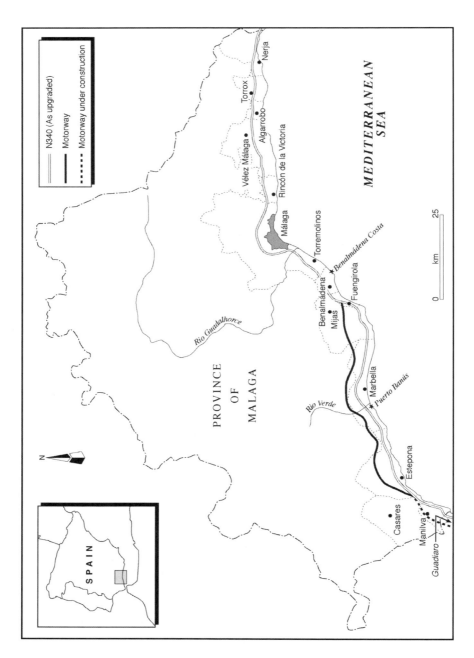

**Figure 2** The Province of Málaga and its municipalities

erosion of the beach was not tackled because, although the groynes did control longshore drift, they failed to stop off-shore directed sediment transport. This led to the subsequent use of hammer-head groynes designed to cope with off-shore as well as long-shore movement. Such groynes became a common feature not only at Estepona but also to the east of Málaga (at Pedregalejo) and later at Benalmádena Costa and Marbella (Figure 2).

Groyne fields have also been deployed in an attempt to minimise erosion and control deposition around the new marinas that now form a regular feature of the coastal infrastructure. Moreover, they helped conserve sand in embayments, so providing expensive condominiums close to the marina in locations like Puerto Banús, Marbella and Benalmádena Costa with permanent beaches (Figure 2).

However, despite the large investment, such fields were removed in the 1990s because of their failure to perform well in practice, and a growing problem of sea-water pollution in the artificial embayments. Benalmádena Costa is a case in point: there, the inadequate design, mainly caused by poor groyne spacing, contributed to further damage to the sea wall and occasional collapsing of the promenade.

A new approach to protection was introduced with the application of beach nourishment. Yet, again, experiences on the Costa del Sol show that the application of beach fill has not been entirely satisfactory partly because of difficulties in solving a fundamental problem of sediment starvation in the coastal system. Inland sources of sediments are restricted by river flows that have been much reduced by dam building, leaving offshore sediment deposits as the only realistic alternative, despite the fact that they are not always sufficient or of ideal composition. Coarseness or shelliness of the sand, and/or a high lime content, have sometimes produced an uncomfortably abrasive surface for recreational use (Malvárez García *et al.,* 2002). In Marbella's case, the beach also failed the durability test as it was subjected to sub-surface erosion. In contrast, sediments utilised for nourishment of Málaga's beach were of ideal characteristics, although it was still prone to sand loss due to the effects of recurrent storms after beach fill, so that replenishment with its attendant costs was demanded. Thus the extent to which coastal protection methods have been successful over the past 50 years is very much an open question despite the complete reversal of techniques from hard to soft structures.

## Urban planning and the coast

The lack of effectiveness of Spanish urban planning in controlling coastal development in both the Franco era and the early years of democratic government has frequently been remarked upon (Naylon, 1986; Wynn, 1984a,b). Economic growth took precedence so that, despite the existence of planning regulations deriving from the 1956 *Ley del Suelo y Ordenación Urbana* (Land and Urban Planning Act), uncontrolled market forces prevailed to the neglect of integrated planning procedures or consideration of environmental parameters (Morris, 1996). The resulting freedom extended to private developers inevitably produced the haphazard development typical of the Spanish Mediterranean coast from Catalonia in the north-east (Morris & Dickinson, 1987) to the Costa del Sol in the south (Pollard & Domínguez Rodríguez, 1993, 1995). While the reflection of such procedures in austere and tightly packed high rise hotel and apartment blocks fronting the shoreline might cause no more than aesthetic offence (García Manrique, 1984), failures in the provision of promenades, means of access to beaches, proper traffic circulation and parking facilities, parks and garden facilities, and sewage systems, offered more practical cause for concern for visitor and resident alike.

New political and administrative structures introduced following Franco's death in 1975 were mirrored in changes in the planning legislation. The principal instrument was the *Reforma de la Ley del Suelo y Ordenación Urbana* (Reform of the Land and Urban Planning Act) with its requirement of each municipality to produce its own urban plan. Although it was the case that the previous 1956 legislation had demanded similar Plans, the response of Town Halls was slow to the point of non-compliance in some instances. On the Costa del Sol, Marbella was quickest off the mark, producing its plan in 1959 followed by a second in 1968: elsewhere Fuengirola delayed until 1969, Málaga until 1970/1, Manilva and Casares until 1973, Benalmádena until 1975 and Estepona and Mijas until the 1980s, i.e. after the original Act had already been superseded by the 1975 *Reforma*.

New Plans produced following the *Reforma* recognised problems inherited from the earlier legislation and made provision for environmental conservation and improvements in the social and economic infrastructure. Moreover, the application of the three broad land-planning categories of 'urban', '*urbanizable*' (programmed for development) and 'non-urban' was more firmly established. Nevertheless, although there was widespread recognition of existing problems, many were beyond remedy, while economic development priorities continued to hold pole position (Morris & Dickinson, 1987). However, growing concerns over the image projected by the old established resorts gradually brought about a shift in emphasis, so that by the end of the century major improvements in the economic and social infrastructure (including promenade completion and sewage provision) had been made (Robinson, 1996).

At the same time a more integrated and holistic approach to coastal planning that took account of both physical coastal protection and coastal amenity could be identified from the 1980s. Neither the 1956 nor 1975 Acts recognised the coast as a zone with any special requirements, although some attempt at coastal legislation had been enacted with the passing of a *Ley de Costas* (Shores Act) in 1969. This empowered the MOPU (*Ministerio de Obras Públicas y Urbanismo* [Ministry of Public Works and Urban Planning]) to undertake defensive and marina construction work, to be carried out by MOPU's *Dirección General de Puertas y Costas* (Ports and Coasts Administration). That Administration's remit comprised three elements, namely the physical protection of the coast, the recovery of public property and legislation for, and management of, that property, but efforts were largely limited to protection work.

A more coordinated programme was introduced in 1982 to bring about a legislative framework empowering the coastal authorities to integrate services and to significantly increase investment. There was little resistance to the increased spending, particularly when it related to coastal protection, but it was a different matter when it came to implementing new regulations that impacted on the operation and siting of businesses located on the shoreline. The *Jefatura de Costas* (Central Office for Coastal Affairs) began lobbying councils and other interested parties from that date, although there was little response, failure to proceed being excused on technical or legal grounds (MOPU, 1988). Some progress with beach management was achieved by the late 1980s, especially in regularising commercial services offered on the foreshore.

It was, however, the passing of the new *Ley de Costas* in 1988, and the formulation of the linked *Plan de Costas 1993–1997*, that seemed to offer the opportunity to open a new era in effective coastal management. The *Ley de Costas* and the *Plan de Costas* provided the legal powers to protect the public coastal zone while underpinning the huge expansion in investment in public works on beach regeneration, promenades and sea-front rehabilitation, and access provision. The *Ley de Costas* established new rights and obligations in respect of use of the public domain and its immediate hinterland. Moreover, it required that any future development of virgin areas (or redevelopment within already urbanised areas) should conform to a more rational and sensitive system of land use. To a significant extent it echoes the language of the Rio declaration in summing up its approach in the following terms:

> It is the responsibility of the legislation of our time to protect the integrity of (the Spanish coast), to preserve (it) as the property of the nation and to bestow (it) as such to future generations. (MOPU, 1989: 18)

Its two principal goals were thus to guarantee that the coast remained public property and to ensure the preservation of natural features, e.g. dune systems, wetlands and important vegetation complexes.

The legislation enunciated the right of the Spanish people to enjoy an acceptable environment and accepted that both planners and the public had an obligation to preserve that environment. In order to provide that acceptable environment, the government clearly spelt out its right to recover possession of coastal public property 'regardless of the time elapsed' (MOPU, 1989: 15). Furthermore, it was recognised that in certain circumstances it might be necessary to act on privately owned land where activities had a serious adverse effect on the coast. In this respect, particular actions were considered necessary:

(a) to avoid interruption of wind transportation of sand;
(b) to avoid closure of visual perspectives by the screening effect of buildings and the shadow projected by buildings;
(c) to control waste disposal; and
(d) to control gravel, sand and stone extraction from the lower courses of rivers where that impedes coastal sedimentation processes (MOPU, 1989: 16).

The geographical limitation of the Act's scope was specified through the setting out of four zones (Figure 3), two of which are designated public property: these are, first, in-shore and territorial waters; and second, shore and beach. Inland from the shoreline are two private property zones, the first being an effective 'buffer zone' of 100 m extendable to 200 m. This is a protected area which may, nevertheless, include a paved pedestrian promenade and public service access covering the first 20 m back from the shoreline. Otherwise the area is designated a *zona verde* ('green zone') in which some leisure uses such as camping and golf can be accepted. Beyond this zone in non-urban areas is a further 500 m strip in which development is restricted.

Further restrictions and prohibitions apply to each of the zones. Of particular relevance is the restriction on residential building, roads (apart from those for access), extractive activity, overhead power-lines, and advertising publicity. Moreover, commercial beach services are restricted up to 20 m from the shore. Of course, along large stretches of the Spanish coast, including much of the Costa del Sol, building already exists to the shoreline. Where building rights are already held, owners can continue subject to the 20 m easement. Beyond the 20 m zone, the Act does not apply to land urbanised prior to 29 July 1988 provided that constructions were legally built, in which case acquired rights were to be respected for the period of any lease, even though no building extensions were to be allowed (Ministerio de Obras Publicas y Transportes (MOPT), 1991). However, where buildings were illegally built, they would be subject to removal unless it were possible to show that they were in the public interest, in which case they could be legalised in retrospect.

The most recent administrative reorganisation has been the 1996 creation of a new Ministry for the Environment to which was transferred the *Dirección General de Costas* (Coasts Administration). This move from its former location within MOPU recognises the shift of emphasis away from infrastructural work and towards the overseeing of the broader coastal environment as encapsulated by the *Ley de Costas* and, theoretically, at least allows for a more sensitive approach to coastal planning. Now that environmental considerations have become the central focus, the emphasis is one of restitution or recuperation of the coast. For the first time, the *dominio público marítimo–terrestre* (public shoreline fringe) is being officially designated both on government maps and plans and physically marked with posts on the ground, while the *Ley de Costas* provides the necessary limitations on concessions within the controlled area. The Act also requires that the coastal municipalities comply with the new provisions when effecting their urban plans. The situation at the beginning of the new millenium is that five distinct activities in respect of the coast now come under the purview of the *Dirección General de Costas*. These are described by M.O.P.T. (1998) as follows.

(1) *Boundary designation.* As noted earlier, this is concerned with defining those parts of the coast that form part of the public domain under the Act. As well as a legal requirement, this provides the first step in the protection or defence of vulnerable areas. Initially planned for completion within a 10-year period from the enactment of the *Ley de Costas*, this was not achieved, although there has been a rapid acceleration in activity since 1997. As far as southern Spain is concerned, boundary designation work is much more conspicuous in parts of the provinces of Huelva and Cádiz (Figure 1), that is those areas that largely escaped the early tourism-based urbanisation of Málaga province immediately to the east.

(2) *Power of Sanction.* This allows the *Dirección* to take action against those abusing the public domain in a wide range of activities that impinge directly on both the physical integrity of the coast and recreational activities. Thus, the unauthorised extraction of materials (sands, gravels, etc.) that might compromise marine processes can be controlled, as can unauthorised construction work, vehicle parking and camping. Almost 6000 prosecutions

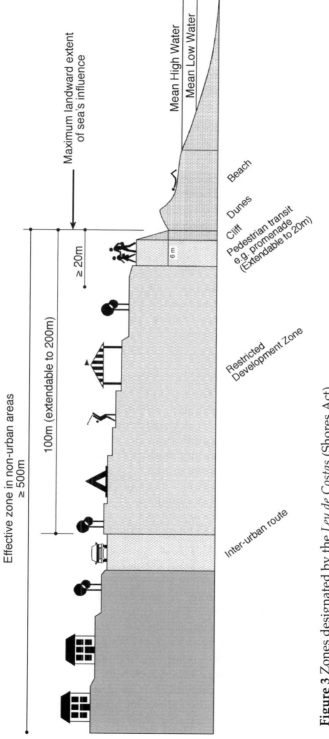

**Figure 3** Zones designated by the *Ley de Costas* (Shores Act)

resulted in the first two years of operation alone and fines have been levied on defaulters.

(3) *Overseeing of urban plans.* The *Dirección* is responsible for ensuring plans comply with the Act and thus municipalities' intentions are examined in respect to whether the sea-front harmonises with the various land-use, access provision and building restrictions.

(4) *Granting of title to use the public domain.* Certain activities, particularly concerning health and public safety, require proximity to the shoreline and the *Dirección* has power to grant title in these cases. Sanitation facilities fall into this category and upgraded units at Sorvilán and Motril in Granada province have been granted title (Figure 1). The growing problem of ensuring sufficient fresh water supplies underpins permission for a desalinisation plant at Marbella, again within the public domain.

(5) *Coastal projects.* Finally, the *Dirección* will assist developments to improve the infrastructure, provided that the law is respected in terms of provision of transit rights and recognition of the public domain and that the work does not promote urban expansion. Improvements to promenades come under this heading, as do the various other works of coastal protection that have traditionally been this authority's responsibility, namely breakwater construction, cliff protection and beach stabilisation, together with the more strictly environmental concerns of dune, marsh and wetland conservation and recuperation of degraded coasts.

## The Legislation in Practice

Evidence of willingness to implement policy rather than sitting on the sidelines while development proceeded actually predates the passing of the *Ley de Costas*. The beaches of the Costa del Sol had, for many years, been characterised by the presence of *chiringuitos* (restaurants and bars) as well as a number of other commercial activities directed mainly to the hiring of recreational equipment for use on both beach and water. Many of these had no legal title and raised important issues about the use of public property, restrictions of access and potential health hazards. In particular, official objections were based upon the restrictions on the beach area available to the public, the reduction in aesthetic or scenic amenity and the vital health consideration of burying of rubbish and sewage effluent in the sand (MOPT, 1993). It was also appreciated that there was an impact upon the seasonal profile of the beach and thus an interference with erosion processes.

MOPU's report upon its activities to re-establish public control over the beaches of the Costa del Sol (MOPU, 1988) referred to the 'anarchic proliferation' of huts and commercial premises along the Spanish beaches. Fishermen's shacks were typical of the two westerly provinces of Cádiz and Huelva, whereas illegally located *chiringuitos* and other commercial enterprises were the principal source of the problem in the more tourism-dominated provinces of Almería, Granada and Málaga (Figure 1). Almost 400 *chiringuitos* had been erected during the era of tourism expansion in Málaga Province alone. Their distribution naturally accorded with business opportunities in that province and thus concentrated on the tourist hot-spots of Torremolinos, Marbella, Fuengirola and

Estepona (Table 1, Figure 2). With an average size of 325 m², they caused a substantial intrusion on beach space in those municipalities. In the absence of legal title in all but 15 cases, almost one-quarter (23%) were removed altogether, whereas a further 42% were forced to relocate outside the beach area (MOPU, 1988). The remainder received authorisation to remain on an annually renewable lease but a prefabricated, sectional construction was required to permit their removal out of season. In practice, removal has not generally occurred with owners arguing on the grounds of difficulty of moving premises, while the extension of the season in recent years provides a stronger business logic to remain *in situ*. Nevertheless, on balance there has been a marked opening up of the area of the sands available for general public use, together with sand levelling and hygiene improvements through sand aeration following cesspit removals. Regular cleaning operations and zoning for commercial and non-commercial uses have, undoubtedly, improved the beach environment in all the major resorts, albeit with some antagonism generated in the business community through its enforced compliance to the new regulations (Malvárez *et al.*, 2002).

**Table 1** The location of *chiringuitos* in Málaga Province, 1988

| Municipality | Number | Municipality | Number |
|---|---|---|---|
| Algarrobo | 2 | Mijas | 17 |
| Benalmádena | 17 | Nerja | 13 |
| Estepona | 26 | Rincón de la Victoria | 22 |
| Fuengirola | 43 | Torremolinos | 85 |
| Málaga | 53 | Torrox | 21 |
| Manilva | 10 | Vélez Málaga | 39 |
| Marbella | 47 | All municipalities | 395 |

*Source*: MOPU (1988)

## Control of Urban Development

Whereas effective management of the beach zone was already being put in place by the time of the passing of the *Ley de Costas*, actions behind the shore-line have met with more limited success. Few localities are more appropriate for studying the impact of the new legislation and coastal management structures upon development than the municipalities situated at the western extremity of Málaga Province (Figure 2). Until recent years the two municipalities of Casares and Manilva had escaped any noteworthy urban development of their coastlines (Marchena Gomez, 1987). In part this may be explained by a complex land-holding structure of small properties discouraging development, and an indifference in earlier years of the governing *Izquierda Unida* (United Left) to tourism development. However, more pertinent is their distance from Málaga's international airport, the principal point of entry for foreign tourists to the Costa del Sol. The main coastal highway, the N340 (Figure 2), provided a dual carriageway as far as Estepona, a distance of approximately 85 km from the airport. Even a journey as far west as this required negotiation of the intervening urban settlements and inevitable congestion until the opening of a series of by-passes between Torremolinos and Estepona brought the latter resort to within an hour of the airport by the end of the 1990s. The construction of an additional motorway paralleling the coast reached Estepona by 2001 (Figure 2), further facilitating access to the west. The last remaining major gap in the road infrastructure will be closed with the provision of a dual carriageway system on the original N340 road between Estepona and Guadiaro. That is due for completion in 2003, and will bind inextricably the municipalities of Casares and Manilva into the tourist nexus of the Costa del Sol.

In anticipation of these developments, urbanisation along the coasts of both Casares and Manilva is already well advanced. Of the two municipalities, it is the latter which is most affected by virtue of its longer coastline, which also significantly includes a long sandy foreshore comprising the beaches of Las Arenas, El Negro, Los Toros, La Duquesa and Sabinillas (Figure 4). These account for over 80% of the coastline of Manilva and represent the last major untapped beach resources in the Province. In many respects their future development has the potential to mirror that of the earlier resorts of the Costa del Sol. As at Carihuela (Torremolinos), El Palo (Málaga) and Marbella, initial occupation of the shoreline was restricted to small fishing communities at San Luis de Sabinillas and Castillo with the main economic focus based upon the agricultural *pueblo* situated inland at Manilva itself. The population of the municipality in 1981 was 3779, a figure that had shown some volatility during the century, but nevertheless was no more than 520 higher than it had been in 1900 (Diputación Provincial de Málaga, 1989).

At the start of the 21st century population has already grown by a further 40% (Instituto de Estadísticas de Andalucía, 2002) but the present infrastructure of hotels and catering establishments remains quite limited showing no more than the incipient development typical of the early stages of resort growth. Two hotels with a capacity for 234 guests are to be found, in addition to four guest-houses capable of boarding a further 43 visitors, while two camp-sites complete the accommodation provision. The focus of much of this development is the marina and golf-course at La Duquesa (Figure 4). Whereas the hotel sector remains quite weak, a number of *urbanizaciones* (private, serviced housing estates) have been constructed as retirement homes, second homes or for rent to visitors. A number of these date back to the 1970s and 1980s (Table 2) and, as such, they can be linked to the 1973 *Plan General de Ordenación* (Development Plan). However, the urban development process was neither massive nor continual at that time, with major breaks occurring especially over the years 1980–85. It is during the period of the current (1990) *Plan General de Ordenación* that the rate of construction has escalated but only from the late 1990s as the projected improved road links moved towards implementation (Table 2). At the start of 2002 less than 10% of the coastal strip has not been sold out of agricultural use, so that the 7 km of Manilva's beaches are virtually continuously backed by actual or projected urban development from Punta Chullera to the boundary with Casares municipality in the east (Figure 4). As a result, the Manilva coastline is well on the way to replicating the remainder of the Costa del Sol in respect of human occupation of the coastline, although the development pattern is more reminiscent of the *urbanizaciones* of Estepona than the high-rise developments further east (Barke & France, 1996).

The precise siting of the new development, which approaches the shoreline to the maximum extent permissible, is particularly relevant in the context of expectations under the *Ley de Costas*. Nowhere was the opportunity taken to establish a buffer zone of 100 m, let alone the 200 m 'green zone' or 500 m set-back area which might have been implemented in a formerly undeveloped area. The protected zone has, in fact, been reduced to its legal minimum of 20 m to provide for a *paseo marítimo* (promenade) and access of public service, including emergency, vehicles. Yet there has been no bending of the law here, for this land had already been designated *urbanizable* as long ago as the 1973 Plan. A prescient Town Hall had, at that time, foreseen the potential for this stretch of coast to follow in the footsteps of municipalities further east, and had accordingly catered to future developers' needs. Even if the land had not been so designated at that earlier date, there is little in town planning legislation to prohibit re-zonation from rural to *urbanizable*, so that an extensive buffer zone at any point along the Mediterranean coast is, in most instances, illusory. Only where environmentally sensitive areas have been officially designated are enforceable restrictions or prohibitions in order. None such exists along the Manilva shoreline. Now that the coast has been effectively urbanised, attention is being directed inland where larger agricultural properties are providing the foundation for golf-course, theme park and villa developments in juxtaposition with the new motorway infrastructure.

Although construction along the Manilva coastline hardly reflects the spirit of the *Ley de Costas*, the latter has been effective in controlling, and indeed reversing, development on the public domain. The case of the *chiringuitos* has been previously mentioned, and Málaga Province has been at the forefront in actions to clear its beaches under the forceful leadership of the head of its *Dirección de Costas* (Coastal Administration). More widely publicised has been the case of El Gran Hotel de Atlanterra, near Zahara de los Atunes in the Tarifa municipality of Cádiz Province (Figure 1), which has been heralded as something of a *cause célèbre* in the efforts of the Ministry of the Environment to reclaim the public domain. The demolition of that hotel at the beginning of 2002 has been described as 'bringing down the major monument to urban aggression' and thus putting a brake on this 'urban invasion of the coast' (*ABC*, 11 January 2002: 38). As a building of nine stories and 45,000 m², its removal (detonated by the Minister of the Environment himself) is not without a certain symbolic value in the application of the *Ley de Costas*. It is especially significant in reflecting a growing willingness to apply the law rather than turning a blind eye, particularly if the promised removal of similarly sited illegal constructions takes place (*El Sur*, 18 January 2002: 68).

However, the demolition of El Gran Hotel is not an indication that urban development of the coast is now under control and that building will be significantly restricted under prevailing legislation. For this hotel, situated as it was on the public domain, had been illegal since its building began in 1970. Litigation over its future had, in fact, proceeded for most of its life: it had consequently never opened to the public, while the owners (who did receive compensation for the demolition) are constructing a new luxury hotel some 200 m from the original building (*El País*, 11 January 2002: 5). The new location will be better integrated with the apartment blocks and *urbanizaciones* that have proliferated in Atlanterra in recent years, but those new estates have themselves been subject to criticism

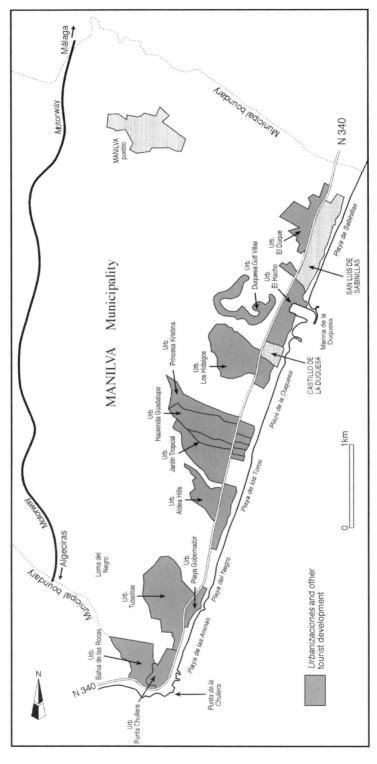

**Figure 4** The urban development of Manilva Municipality

**Table 2** Tourism-based urban development in Manilva Municipality, Málaga Province

| Period | Urbanización | Other Tourist Development |
|---|---|---|
| 1971–75 | Punta Chullera[a]<br>Los Hidalgos[b]<br>El Hacho[b] | |
| 1976–80 | Jardín Tropical<br>Playa Gobernador<br>Tubalitas | |
| 1981–85 | – | |
| 1986–90 | Princesa Kristina<br>Hacienda Guadalupe<br>El Tábano<br>Duquesa Golf Villas[c]<br>El Manantial[c] | Hotel Puerto de la Duquesa |
| 1991–95 | – | |
| 1996– | Loma del negro[d]<br>El Duque<br>Bahía de los Rocas<br>Aldea Hills/Lama Blanca<br>Jardín tropical (ext.)<br>El Tábano (ext.)<br>Magic Hills<br>Los Hidalgos (ext.)<br>La Rondana<br>El Molina | El Tábano Golf Course<br>Magic Hills Golf Courses<br>(2) and Park |

[a] Prior to 1973 Plan.
[b] Post 1973 Plan.
[c] 1990 Plan operational from October of that year.
[d] Not yet implemented.

for their obtrusive location on the shoreline, and allegations that their building resulted from corrupt planning procedures. In those cases licences were awarded for apartment building on *urbanizable* rather than urban land and against rulings of the regional court, the *Tribunal Superior de Justicia de Andalucía* (*El País*, 11 January 2002: 5). However, the *Ley de Costas* is not applicable in this instance as the land is not public domain and there is little indication that the regional government is about to revoke earlier land zonation decisions, however questionable.

## Conclusion

The final two decades of the 20th century witnessed the integration of environmental considerations into planning procedures that apply to all parts of Spain. In particular, the appearance of explicit consideration of the coastal environment represents a focus that many would argue was urgently needed in the aftermath of the rapid and uncontrolled urbanisation of the 'development era' that began in the 1950s and extended well beyond the demise of authoritarian government.

Unfortunately this earlier development has thwarted good intentions by limiting opportunities to implement major environmental improvements in built-up areas. Notwithstanding, there has been substantial investment in specific projects, such as promenade construction and the enhancement of beach conditions and services to more exacting European Union standards, all of which have raised the environmental quality of many sea-fronts. Such is exemplified by the popular Costa de Sol resorts of Torremolinos and Marbella and is replicated elsewhere on Spain's Mediterranean continental coastline (Vera Rebollo, 2001) and the Balearic Islands (Buswell, 1996). Furthermore, noteworthy improvements to sea-water quality have taken place (Kirkby, 1996), and expenditure on coastal protection measures has been heavy, although the means used to control the forces of erosion are still a matter of debate (Malvárez García *et al.,* 2000).

Legislation in the form of the *Ley de Costas* together with the activities of the government department responsible for the administration of coastal affairs clearly reflect a sea-change in both official and public attitudes to the coast. The casual abuse of planning regulations and social infrastructure requirements of earlier times have been held in check, and illegal building within the public domain is no longer ignored. Such progress reflects a change in attitudes towards the law and a growing official intolerance of the worst environmental excesses in the face of development prerogatives, and provides evidence of the 'message of sustainability' having at last been heard (Stabler, 1997).

Despite these undoubted successes in promoting 'a better balance between environmental quality and economic efficiency' (Robinson, 1996), it must be recognised that continued urban development of the coast up to the very limits of the shoreline is, in any practical sense, difficult to tackle effectively. Most construction during the 'development era' took place perfectly legally on land that was designated *urbanizable* (or re-zoned as such by municipalities compliant to developers' wishes). The *Ley de Costas* is impotent to act retrospectively in those circumstances. However, it is of greater concern from a forward-looking perspective, that almost unrestricted development can continue to occur, using the simple expedient of the redrawing of the urban plan. Where economic interests persist in taking precedence, plans submitted to the regional government for final approval are unlikely to be turned down unless territory has been declared *espacio protegido* (protected ground), that is protected by virtue of National/ Natural Park or other environmental designation. At present such land is very restricted on the Mediterranean coast of southern Spain, the major exceptions being the marshlands of the Doñana National Park at the mouth of the Guadalquivir and the Natural Park of Cabo de Gata-Níjar (Figure 1). The core of the Costa del Sol lies in Málaga Province, wherein the only protected areas are the Cliffs of Maro east of Nerja and the mouth of the Río Guadalhorce between Málaga and Torremolinos (Figure 1). There have been no successes in controlling development interests along the lines reported by Morris (1996) with the establishment of a regional park in what remains of the wetlands of Castello in Catalonia.

The overall situation is thus one of some improvements to environmental quality and public access in already urbanised areas but little realistic prospect of significant recovery of coastal land to the public domain. At the same time, any brake on urban development elsewhere is unlikely within the present legal framework, even to the extent of implementing buffer zones between the building line and the coastal margin. Thus, the more wide-ranging expectations for the impact of the *Ley de Costas* seem destined for disappointment, at least in this part of Spain. Consequently, limitations will continue to be imposed on the maintenance of a quality environment for the enjoyment of citizens and visitors alike.

It might be argued that it is in the context of southern Spain's visitors and the region's tourism interests that pressure for further coastal protection may come. The precise part played by an attractive coastline in the potential visitor's decision-making process can be disputed, but it cannot be gainsaid that the role of tourism in the Spanish economy demands the maintenance of a competitive global position. Consequently, the country is in no position to afford any undermining of its image through the degrading of such a prime resource. To date, significant efforts that are made to improve that image tend to be geographically limited to the resorts themselves, and therefore provide evidence of a strong economic underpinning to an environmental rehabilitation that aims to sustain local investment interests. Such would be typical of the efforts made by municipalities on the Costa del Sol supported by the *Patronato Provincial de Turismo* (Barke & France, 1996). The extrapolation of such thinking to safeguard the environment along less developed stretches of the coast is insufficiently supported in the Town Halls where planning responsibility lies. Although the capacity exists to overrule decisions at the regional level, there is little tendency to do so provided that municipal plans are legally sound. Thus the economic directive and development prerogative still dominate. It is true that pressures on the environment of the undeveloped areas are unlikely to come from any expansion of mass tourism, but those pressures are not diminished for that. In their stead, they are replaced by the expansion of the more residential type of tourism that derives from an increasingly affluent European hinterland that promotes a 'gravitational shift of population to the coast' (Buswell, 1996) through demand for second-home ownership, coastal retirement homes, golf courses and support services. All are extensive users of land and will inexorably increase demand for high quality coastal locations, a demand that is satisfied by local authorities eager to maximise their local tax revenues. While development may be less disorderly and aesthetically offensive than in the past, it seems unlikely that it will take sufficient cognizance of the best concepts embodied in the coastal legislation without a significant attitude shift within municipal planning circles, or an extension of protected area status that might otherwise control present economic and social pressures for urban expansion to the very margins of the coastline.

## Correspondence

Any correspondence should be directed to John Pollard, School of Biological and Environmental Sciences, University of Ulster, Coleraine, N. Ireland BT52 1SA.

## References

*ABC* (2002)11 January, p. 38.
Barke, M. and France, L.A. (1996) The Costa del Sol. In M. Barke, J. Towner and M.T. Newton (eds) *Tourism in Spain: Critical Issues.* Wallingford: CAB International.

Bote Gomez, V. and Sinclair M.T. (1996) Tourism demand and supply in Spain. In M. Barke, J. Towner and M.T. Newton (eds) *Tourism in Spain: Critical Issues*. Wallingford: CAB International.

Buswell, R.J. (1996) Tourism in the Balearic Islands. In M. Barke, J. Towner and M.T. Newton (eds) *Tourism in Spain: Critical Issues*. Wallingford: CAB International.

Butler, R. (1998) Sustainable tourism – looking backwards in order to progress? In C.M. Hall and A.A. Lew (eds) *Sustainable Tourism: a Geographical Perspective*. Harlow: Addison Wesley Longman.

Diputación Provincial de Málaga (DPM) (1989) *La Población de la Provincia de Málaga*. Málaga: Servicio de Publicaciones de la Diputación.

*El País* 11 January 2002, 5.

*El Sur* 18 January 2002, 68.

Fernandez Ranada, J.C. (1989) Conditioning of Estepona beach, Málaga, Spain. *Shore and Beach* 57 (2), 10–19.

García Manrique, E. (1984) La costa occidental Malagueña. In M. Alcobendas (ed.) *Málaga*. Colección Nuestra Andalucía (Vol. 1 Geografía) Granada: Editorial Andalucía.

Harrison, D. (1996) Sustainability and tourism: Reflections from a muddy pool. In L. Briguglio, B. Archer, J. Jafari and G. Wall (eds) *Sustainable Tourism in Islands and Small States: Issues and Policies*. London: Cassell.

Instituto de Estadísticas de Andalucía (IEA) (2002) Sistema de información multiterritorial de Andalucía. On WWW at http://www.iea.junta-andalucía.es/sima/htm.

Junta de Andalucía (annual) *Boletín de Indicadores Turísticos de Andalucía*. Sevilla: Dirección General de Planificación Turística, Junta de Andalucía.

Kirby, S.J. (1996) Recreation and the quality of Spanish coastal waters. In M. Barke, J. Towner and M.T. Newton (eds) *Tourism in Spain: Critical Issues*. Wallingford: CAB International.

Lash, S. and Urry, J. (1994) *Economies of Signs and Spaces*. London: Sage.

Malvárez García, G., Pollard, J. and Domínguez Rodríguez, R. (2000) Origins, management and measurement of stress on the coast of Spain. *Coastal Management* 28, 215–34.

Malvárez García, G., Pollard J. and Hughes, R. (2002) Coastal zone management on the Costa del Sol: A small business perspective. *Journal of Coastal Research* 36 (special issue).

Marchena Gomez, M. (1987) *Territorio y Turismo en Andalucía*. Seville: Consejería de Economía y Fomento, Dirección General del Turismo, Junta de Andalucía.

Ministerio de Obras Públicas y Urbanismo (MOPU) (1989) *Ley de Costas/The Shores Act*. Madrid: MOPU.

Ministerio de Obras Públicas y Urbanismo (MOPU) Dirección General de Puertos y Costas (1988) *Actuaciones para la Recuperación de las Playas para el Uso y Dominio Público: Retirada de Instalaciones Ilegales*. Madrid: MOPU.

Ministerio de Obras Públicas y Transportes (MOPT) Dirección de Puertos y Costas (1991) *Principales Contenidos de la Legislación de Costas*. Málaga: M.O.P.T.

Ministerio de Obras Públicas y Transportes (MOPT) Dirección General de Costas (1993) *Recuperando la Costa*. Madrid: MOPT.

Ministerio de Obras Públicas y Transportes (MOPT) (1998) *Hacía una Gestión Sostenible del Litoral Español*. Madrid: MOPT.

Morris A. and Dickinson, G. (1987) Tourist development in Spain: Growth versus conservation on the Costa Brava. *Geography* 72, 16–25.

Morris A.S. (1996) Environmental management in coastal Spain. In M. Barke, J. Towner and M.T. Newton (eds) *Tourism in Spain: Critical Issues*. Wallingford: CAB International.

Naylon, J. (1986) Urban growth under an authoritarian régime: Spain 1939–1975: The case of Madrid. *Iberian Studies* 15, 16–25.

Pollard, J. and Domínguez Rodríguez, R. (1993) Tourism and Torremolinos: Recession or reaction to environment? *Tourism Management*, 14 (4), 247–58.

Pollard, J. and Domínguez Rodríguez, R. (1995) Unconstrained growth: The development of a Spanish resort. *Geography* 80 (1) 33–44.

Robinson, M. (1996) Sustainable tourism for Spain: Principles, prospects and problems. In

M. Barke, J. Towner and M.T. Newton (eds) *Tourism in Spain: Critical Issues.* Wallingford: CAB International.

Shaw, G. and Williams, A.M. (2002) *Critical Issues in Tourism.* Oxford: Blackwell.

Stabler, M.J. (1997) *Tourism Sustainability: Principles to Practice.* Wallingford: CAB International.

Travel and Tourism Intelligence (TTI) (2001) *Country Reports* 1. London: TTI.

Vera Rebollo, J.F. (2001) Increasing the value of natural and cultural resources: Towards sustainable tourism management. In D. Ioannides, Y. Apostolopoulos and S. Sonmez (eds) *Mediterranean Islands and Sustainable Tourism Development: Practices, Management and Policies.* London: Continuum.

Williams, A. and Shaw, G. (1998) Tourism and the environment. In C.M. Hall and A.A. Lew (eds) *Sustainable Tourism: A Geographical Perspective.* Harlow: Addison Wesley Longman.

Wynn, M. (1984a) Spain. In M. Wynn (ed.) *Housing in Europe.* London: Croom Helm.

Wynn, M. (1984b) Spain. In M. Wynn (ed.) *Planning and Urban Growth in Southern Europe.* London: Mansell.

# 11 Using EMAS and Local Agenda 21 as Tools Towards Sustainability: The Case of a Catalan Coastal Resort

*Xavier Campillo-Besses, Gerda K. Priestley and Francesc Romagose*
*Escola Universitària de Turisme i Direcció Hotelera, Universitat Autònoma de Barcelona, Campus de la UAB, 08193 Cerdanyola, Barcelona, Spain*

This paper examines the objectives, underlying principles, methodology and controls involved in the application of two environmental planning tools – Local Agenda 21 and the European Eco-Management and Audit Scheme (EMAS) – to local administrations, in an attempt to identify their strengths and weaknesses. This makes it possible to evaluate their contribution as tools in achieving sustainable development, and to outline the practical difficulties that can be encountered and the political decisions required at community level in their application. The theoretical considerations are illustrated in relation to Sitges, a long-established tourist resort located on the Catalan coast, where, in 2000, the local authorities started a Local Agenda 21 process through the implementation of an EMAS, in an innovative approach to environmental management. Sitges is currently experiencing profound structural changes in its economy, society and urban environment, as the resort is incorporated into the dynamics of Metropolitan Barcelona. These processes are exerting considerable pressure on the urban heritage and valuable natural environment surrounding the town. As a result, the case constitutes an interesting laboratory to analyse the two schemes, as the entire process is being monitored by a series of indicators which constitute an observatory for sustainability.

## Introduction

Since the Earth Summit in 1992, and following the principles of the Aalborg Chart, many European municipalities have adopted Local Agenda 21 (LA21) schemes (Hewitt, 1995) in an attempt to establish management practices which are compatible with sustainable development objectives. Tourism destinations have been particularly active in this respect, which is easily understood, as their survival largely depends on the sustainability of their natural and built environments. The adoption of LA21 schemes has led to some interesting and successful experiences, e.g. the municipality of Calvià in Mallorca (Echenagusia, 1995; Seguí Llinas, 1998). Meanwhile, the European Eco-Management and Audit Scheme (EMAS), originally developed as a tool for improving the environmental performance of industrial companies, has extended its scope to include organisations providing services, following the approval of Regulation (EC) No 761/2001.[1] This has made it possible to apply EMAS to local authorities.

This paper examines the objectives, underlying principles, methodology and controls involved in the application of both LA21 and EMAS schemes by local authorities, in an attempt to identify their strengths and weaknesses. This makes it possible to evaluate their contribution as tools in achieving sustainable development, and to outline the practical difficulties that can be encountered and the political decisions required at community level in their application. The theoretical implications are illustrated in relation to the case of Sitges, a long-established tourist resort located on the Catalan coast, where, in 2000, the local authorities started an LA21 process jointly with the implementation of an EMAS, which will be shown to constitute an innovative approach to environmental management.

## Objectives and Characteristics of Environmental Management Systems

The overall objective of environmental management systems is to promote continual improvement of the environmental performance of economic activities by committing organisations to evaluate and improve their environmental performance and to provide relevant information to the public.

All LA21 and environmental management systems, like EMAS or ISO 14001, can be viewed as planning schemes adopted by organisations. However, in comparison with LA21, environmental management systems rely on a much more comprehensive and well-defined method, which has developed into an international standard. Moreover, these systems are subjected to an external registration process, which obliges the local authority involved in the scheme to introduce real and significant changes in its organisation's environmental performance. This favours working on a more long-term basis, overcoming usually short-dated political commitments. The main difficulties lie in the political nature of local government bodies and in the complexity of registering the environmental performance of a political organisation within its territory.

The link between EMAS and LA21 is based on the methodological coincidences in the two processes (see Figure 1). In reality, both LA21 and eco-management schemes, such as EMAS and ISO 14001, consist of the design and development of an environmental programme. In both cases, the programme is based on an initial environmental review or eco-audit and consensus on a conceptual framework – the so-called Environmental Policy or Philosophy – such as *Agenda 21 for the Travel & Tourism Industry* (WTO, 1997). Moreover, both schemes include a feedback process which seeks to be dynamic, and both require public participation, although LA21 has a more participative approach and EMAS is more systematic.

An important methodological difference between the two schemes is that LA21 is basically a bottom-up process, whereas EMAS is essentially a top-down process, but it also includes bottom-up elements and input at a middle level (from municipal technical staff, for example), as will be demonstrated later. Another difference is related to the content of the two schemes: EMAS, as its name implies, deals only with environmental aspects, while LA21 aims to establish sustainable development not only in the environment but also in economic and social spheres.

The schemes could be interpreted as two parallel processes, which can nourish each other, and therefore perform complementary functions. For example, the Environmental Review which is an initial step in EMAS, also serves as a starting point for LA21 (see Figure 1). Similarly, an Action Plan designed for LA21 can be incorporated into the EMAS Environmental Programme. Hence, the inherent similarities between the two schemes makes integration possible, and this has advantages for both. An important contribution of LA21 is its participative approach, as it requires the involvement of all stakeholders, including the local population, and the inclusion of aspects of a social and economic nature – like

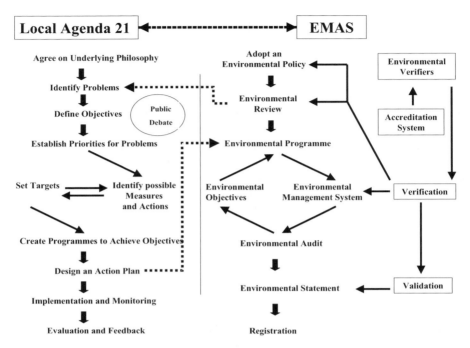

**Figure 1** The relationship between Local Agenda 21 and EMAS
*Source*: The authors

urban planning and tourism policy – within the system. On the other hand, EMAS introduces a more systematic approach than LA21, and exerts more independent and objective controls on the process. As a result, the scheme can more easily maintain its independence on a long-term basis in the face of the winds of political change that can occur as a result of local council elections. Moreover, the widely recognised social prestige of programmes such as EMAS, and the interest which they arouse among the media, bestow on the scheme the appearance of greater solidity and long-term validity.

## Implementation of EMAS and LA21 in Sitges

In the year 2000, the local authorities in Sitges initiated a process of introducing an environmental management programme with an innovative approach: an LA21 process was commenced through the implementation of an EMAS. In this way, the solid and dynamic methodology of EMAS will become linked to the participative process implied in Agenda 21, while the whole process is submitted to an external and objective audit. The project therefore fuses the EMAS and LA21 schemes. The scope of the system is determined by the limits of the responsibilities of the municipal authorities in relation to their administrative activities that exert either a direct or indirect influence on natural systems or environmental vectors within the municipal area.

The project 'Sitges Towards Sustainability' (STS or *Sistema de Gestió per a la Sostenibilitat de Sitges*) is thus a pilot programme for environmental planning and

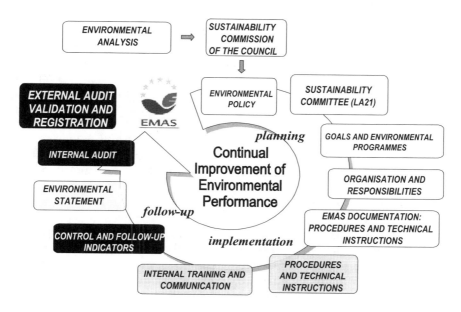

**Figure 2** Phases of the EMAS certification process in the municipality of Sitges
*Source*: ARC research team

management. In order to develop the programme, the local council signed an agreement with the Ministry of the Environment of the regional Government (*Departament de Medi Ambient (DMA) de la Generalitat de Catalunya*) and the School of Tourism and Hotel Management (*Escola Universitària de Turisme i Direcció Hotelera (EUTDH)*) of the Autonomous University of Barcelona (*Universitat Autònoma de Barcelona (UAB)*). A multi-disciplinary technical team from the two organisations led the coordination and direction of the design and implementation of the programme, with collaboration from the council's technical staff. The specific methodology has been developed by the *EUTDH* research team.[2]

Figure 2 shows the proposed phases of the STS programme, which briefly comprise:

- an environmental review;
- the design and implementation of the Environmental Management System;
- municipal staff training and an internal audit;
- certification through an external audit.

The programme requires public participation at certain stages of the process and a public communication and awareness campaign, as will be explained subsequently.

It is proposed that the initial step is an Environmental Review, which assesses the quality of the environment and identifies the existing problems and risks. The municipal council also creates a Sustainability Commission within its Council and a Sustainability Committee, consisting of representatives of the general public, to develop an Environmental Policy. The Policy is based on the Environmental Review and a process of public participation, and it serves as the basis to establish specific Goals and Environmental Programmes. This is followed by the setting up of the organisational structure and its various responsibilities, and preparation of documentation of procedures and technical instructions (which must comply with ISO 14001 standards). The programme requires the definition of specific goals, a series of indicators and benchmarks for each environmental aspect, the drawing up of a work plan, and the introduction of the corresponding control and correction mechanisms, in order to facilitate monitoring of the system. The next step is the implementation of the procedures and instructions laid down, together with in-house training of the municipal technical staff. It is also necessary to carry out a simultaneous communication campaign, both internally and externally.

Subsequently, the effectiveness of the operation of the process is monitored against the pre-established indicators, and an Environmental Statement is elaborated annually to report on resulting environmental improvements. In this way, it is hoped that the indicators will be developed as an 'Observatory of Local Sustainability' (Romagosa & Cúetara, 2001). This phase is followed by an internal audit and, finally, by an external one, undertaken by authorised auditors, which eventually leads to EMAS validation and registration of the municipal council as such.

The ultimate objective is, therefore, to establish a system of continual improvement of environmental performance within the municipal structure, based on an initial statement of a sustainability philosophy. Transparency and public participation, together with an external audit undertaken by authorised auditors, are essential components in order to acquire registration in EMAS.

The Environmental Review is undertaken mainly by the external technical research team,[3] which is expected to be a highly qualified and objective body. Nevertheless, a degree of subjectivity is involved in many decisions. For example, it is the research team that defines which stakeholders are to be consulted when analysing each aspect. In the case of the review of the environmental aspects of beach management in Sitges, the points of view of the tourist sector, the local population and ecologist pressure groups were taken into consideration. On the other hand, the indicators are selected by the research team in conjunction with the municipal technical staff, and are based on objective, quantifiable data. As a result, the annual evolution of each aspect can be measured and an improvement would be interpreted as a trend towards greater sustainability. For example, a reduction in the presence of solid residues in coastal waters would be interpreted as an improvement in quality.

## The Environmental Review

The methodology for the Environmental Review involves tracing back from the environmental impacts[4] in the municipality to the causal environmental aspects,[5] or the elements of council activities that interact with the environment. These in turn can be tracked to the various levels of municipal administration, such as centres, areas, or departments responsible for the aspect in question (see Figure 3). Departments within the municipal administration (such as urbanism,

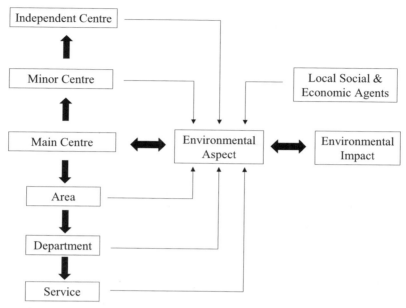

**Figure 3** Methodology of the Environmental Review
*Source*: ARC research team

tourism) are considered main centres, while minor centres are complementary centres dependent on the main ones. Independent centres are those that have an autonomous management structure (such as sports facilities).

The aspects analysed are those identified in Annex VI of the EMAS Regulations as 'direct environmental aspects'. These cover activities over which an organisation has management control, and may include but are not limited to: air-based emissions; releases into water; the avoidance, recycling, reuse, transportation and disposal of solid and other waste, particularly hazardous waste; the use and contamination of land; the use of natural resources and raw materials (including energy); local issues (noise, vibration, odour, dust, visual appearance, etc.); transport issues (both for goods and services and employees); risks of environmental accidents and impacts arising, or likely to arise, as a consequence of incidents, accidents and potential emergency situations; and effects on biodiversity.

Given that the environmental aspect is the core element of the system, the Environmental Review comprises a series of reports, each of which describes the state of a particular aspect, evaluates the council's management and its fulfilment of relevant legislation, describes the resulting impacts, and indicates the stakeholders involved. Thus, through the identification and analysis of environmental aspects, a direct link is established between environmental impact and municipal management. At the same time, the environmental aspects may be directly or indirectly linked to the activities of the various local stakeholders (social, economic and institutional) in the municipality (see Figure 3). Hence, the identification of these stakeholders makes it possible to cross-examine the

Environmental Review from a sectorial viewpoint, for sectors such as tourism, with the aim of incorporating each sector in the participative process through the establishment of sectorial Technical Commissions.

As has already been outlined, this procedure eventually leads to the identification of a number of strategic objectives for each aspect, culminating in the formulation of proposals for specific measures to be introduced. These proposals, together with those arising from the public participation process, which follows LA21 procedures, constitute the Environmental Programme.

## The Participation Process

The EMAS Regulations explicitly stipulate that participation should be made open to all people and elements affected by the environmental performance of those organisations wishing to conform to the Regulations.[6] Hence, in order to take a significant step towards sustainability, a change is required in the behaviour of the multiple stakeholders and, as has been stated, this can only be achieved if the population participate actively throughout. Otherwise, the action plans contemplated in LA21 are limited to measures which local administrative bodies can execute and, although these make a significant and fundamental contribution, they are only a partial solution lacking continuity and, as such, are insufficient. The ultimate objective is for the EMAS to become a vibrant and dynamic instrument in itself, capable of evolving through the formulation of new proposals. Such proposals should be an initiative not only of the Town Council, but also of the population in general, in a constructive climate of consensus. The main questions that must be answered during this process are:

- What do we want the municipality to be like in the future?
- How can we make it more sustainable?
- What can we do to contribute?

The participation process is structured in the form of both internal (governing body) and external (general public) bodies (see Figure 4). Within the town's political structure, a Sustainability Commission of the Council (SCC) is created, with proportional representation of all political parties represented on the council, in order to ensure their support. The council must also create an Environment Commission (EC), composed of one representative of the staff of each department. This facilitates the introduction of changes in the internal structure of municipal management which form part of the EMAS scheme. A Technical Commission (TC) is also created, composed of technical staff of various council departments, together with the temporary incorporation of the assessors and external experts involved in the project. This commission should play a pro-active role in the provision of statistics, the diagnosis of the situation, including the identification of deficits and the collection of opinions during the diagnosis phase, and in formulating proposals for technical measures to be adopted. Personal invitations to participate can be extended to the local stakeholders most seriously affected by the question under debate at a particular stage. This commission must also take on the future technical management of the system.

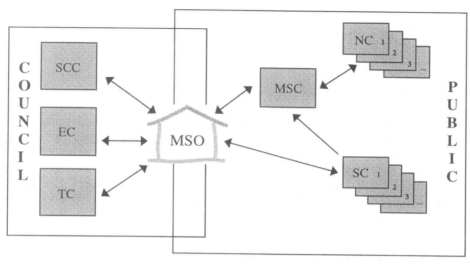

**Figure 4** The participation process
*Source*: The authors

   The general public are encouraged to participate on Sectorial Committees (SC), where representatives of a variety of organisations, associations, unions, etc. from a particular cultural, social or economic sector meet with technical staff to discuss topics which affect or interest them strategically or technically. The number of SCs to be set up can vary according to the needs of each municipality. Urbanism, education, commerce and culture are obviously common denominators in all municipalities, but in Sitges tourism is also an essential sector and, as such, has its corresponding committee. The role of the SCs is to discuss and reach decisions on topics that directly affect their sector, and they must also prepare topics for discussion at the Neighbourhood Committees (see below). They can also assume responsibility for the execution and monitoring of relevant action plans. Themed sessions are held, although the total number, frequency and topics can vary in each case. The meetings should be small in order to make them operative, and the topics to be discussed can be proposed by the Town Council (top down) or by the entities represented (bottom up). The contents discussed are mainly technical, including the completion of the Environmental Review for each aspect, identifying strategic objectives, defining the measures to be applied and the role of each group in their application. For each topic debated, at least two sessions must be held: one to exchange information and hold a preliminary debate, and a second to reach a consensus agreement. In the interim period, the representative of each entity must collect the opinions expressed by the group he or she represents.
   Public participation is also guaranteed through the establishment of Neighbourhood Committees (NC), representing each district. The NCs are provided with a short technical analysis of the state of each topic to be discussed, in order to enrich the debate. Their objective is to identify environmental priorities through consensus. However, one of the most valuable contributions of the NCs is the

synergies that are created between the municipal authorities and the population, rather than specific proposals. As a result, the public are more willing to adopt environmental practices, which often depend on the collaboration of individuals.

A Municipal Sustainability Committee (MSC) is also set up, consisting of a spokesperson from each district committee. This is an essential component of LA21 schemes and it serves as a link with the council commissions and the Municipal Sustainability Office (MSO). This office is the operational centre of the scheme, composed of the external experts and the municipal technical staff responsible for environmental matters. The proposals agreed upon by consensus during the participation process, and eventually ratified by the Town Council, constitute LA21 and are incorporated into the EMAS Action Plan. The corresponding measures must then be scheduled for execution. This process, however, remains open and can be revised.

## The Changing Role of Tourism Resorts on the Mediterranean Coast of Catalonia

The widespread expansion of tourism on the coast of Catalonia dates from the mid-1950s. Prior to that date, only the towns with rail connections to Barcelona were summer holiday resorts[7] (see Figure 5), frequented mainly by the same families year after year, who established their homes there for three months each summer, forming what was known as the 'summer colony' (Barbaza, 1966). International mass tourism, on the other hand, was concentrated in smaller villages or occupied previously deserted coves and beaches, which initially matched the image of 3S (sun, sea and sand) resorts, and where the beach front was still available for development. By 1980, symptoms of stagnation had already been detected on the northern sector of the coast, known as the Costa Brava (Butler, 1980).[8] Certainly, the expansion of international tourism suffered fluctuations after 1973, although the general trend continues to be positive.

Meanwhile, the second-home phenomenon reached boom dimensions during the 1980s. Unlike mass tourism development, which focused on a relatively small number of destinations, second homes sprung up all along the coast,[9] occupying cliff tops and steep slopes as well as beach locations and tagging onto the outskirts of existing towns (Priestley, 1996). However, over the last decade, a new trend has emerged in the resorts close to Barcelona (on the Costas del Maresme, Barcelona and Garraf), as the permanent population has grown. In some cases, second homes have been converted into permanent residences and, in others, new residents have established their permanent homes, although most of them work in the city. This is a result of the high degree of accessibility to the metropolitan capital, by both road and rail, lower property prices outside the city, and the obvious attraction of coastal resorts, where the increase in perceived quality of life, compensates for the additional travel costs and distance.

Many coastal resorts have now become multifunctional towns, which satisfy the needs of various population groups:

- The traditional permanent population who gain their livelihood locally. Most of their families have been attached to the towns for many generations,

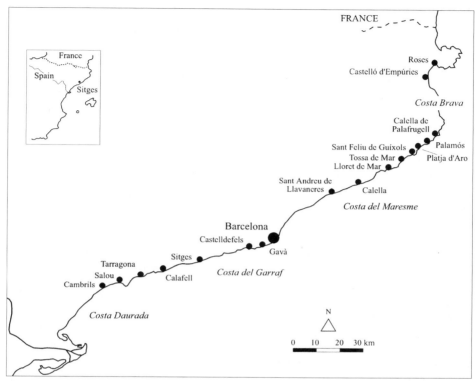

**Figure 5** The coast of Catalonia
*Source*: The authors

although some immigrated from less prosperous regions of Spain during the tourism boom of the 1960s and 1970s.

- The more recent immigrants from Barcelona, with most of them still working in Barcelona and maintaining many links with the city.
- The second home owners, who have expanded in number from a tightly knit and often quite hermetic 'summer colony' into a major component in many towns.
- The short-stay tourist population, which varies greatly in size from one resort to another.
- The day-trippers, not only in summer, but also at weekends throughout the year. In summer, this group tends to be a liability, generating more negative impacts (litter, crowding, noise, etc.) than is compensated for by their direct expenditure. However, in winter, visitors bring economic benefits, especially to the catering and recreation sectors which make a significant contribution to local economies.

It is in this context that coastal towns and villages, such as Sitges, must now be planned and managed, in order to satisfy the quality of urban life expected by the permanent population and also to meet the environmental standards demanded by both residents and visitors.

## The Evolution and Characteristics of Tourism in Sitges

Sitges, situated on the coast 38 km to the southwest of Barcelona, is one of the longest established tourist resorts on the Spanish Mediterranean coast, having welcomed visitors for over a century (see Figure 6). It became a fashionable, high-class holiday resort in the early years of the 20th century, attracting internationally renowned artists and writers, mainly under the auspices of a famous local leader of the arts, Santiago Rusiñol, and a wealthy 'summer colony'. In 1919, the sea-front area not already occupied by the village was laid out for very low density property development and mansions soon began to line the wide, beach-long promenade, an initiative that has had far-reaching repercussions.

The era of international mass tourism dates from 1950, although peak growth rates were experienced between 1956 and 1967. By 1960, Sitges, along with Lloret de Mar and Benidorm, were the three principal international tourism destinations on Spain's east coast (Miguelsanz-Arnalot & Higueras-Miró, 1964). Nevertheless, there is ample evidence that throughout this period and until the present day, large-scale modifications to accommodate mass tourism were rejected, allowing it to maintain its status as a fashionable holiday destination, mainly patronised by Barcelona residents (Priestley & Mundet, 1998). As the number of visitors increased during the peak growth period, they were by and large accommodated in the town centre. Here large mansions were converted into small hotels, while the low density detached housing along most of the sea front survived intact. When the effects of the 1973 oil crisis were felt in 1974 and 1975, the majority of tour operators simply abandoned Sitges, concentrating their business in resorts with large hotel units. Further evidence of the resistance to mass tourism development is provided by the adamant rejection, in the 1960s, of an ambitious, avant garde project for the construction of an offshore marina. It was rejected on the grounds that the project would alter the appearance and character of the village (Priestley, 1984). Hence, after 1974 Sitges reverted to its earlier mission, as an up-market second home resort with a relatively select international tourism component (see Figures 7 and 8).

The build-up to the 1992 Olympic Games marks a minor turning point – the beginning of certain adjustments. On the one hand, the projected demand for hotel accommodation in the metropolitan area at exceptionally high prices during the Olympic Games encouraged the construction of one large hotel and the refurbishing and upgrading of many more. This measure was highly necessary to meet the high quality standards expected and, hence, also the competitiveness of the sector. On the other hand, the general economic thrust associated with the Olympic Games has had repercussions in the surrounding area. These have been particularly strongly felt in Sitges, for the process coincided with the inauguration in 1992 of a toll motorway which reduced the journey from Barcelona to Sitges from 45 to 25 minutes. As a result, Sitges is being incorporated into the dynamics of Metropolitan Barcelona and the resort has experienced profound structural changes in its economy, society and urban environment. The resident population has almost doubled over the last 20 years, urban growth is reaching its physical limits, and the sociocultural structure of the municipality is experiencing dramatic changes (see Figures 9 and 10). These processes are exerting considerable pressure on the urban heritage and valuable natural

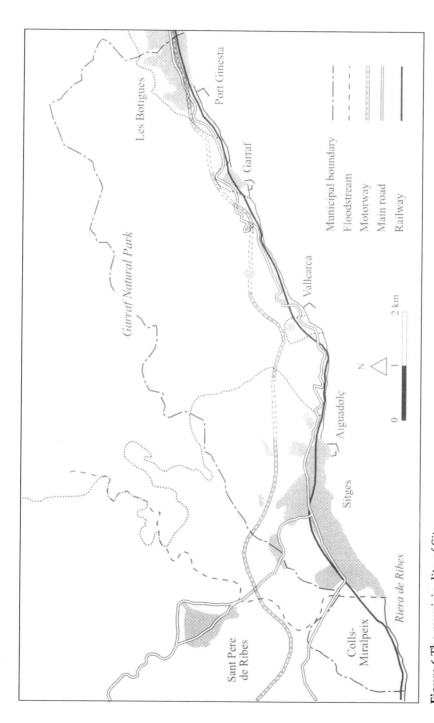

**Figure 6** The municipality of Sitges
*Source:* The authors

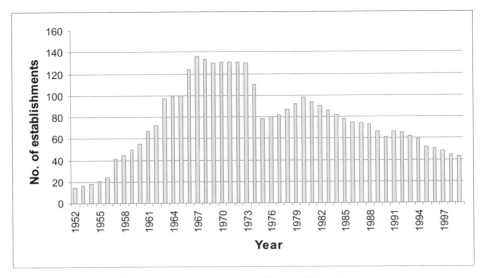

**Figure 7** Number of hotel establishments in Sitges, 1952–1999
*Source*: The authors

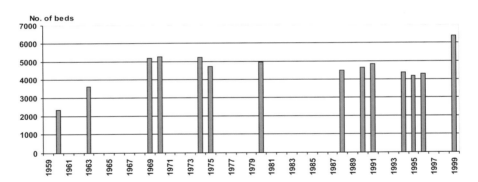

**Figure 8** Hotel accommodation in Sitges, 1960–1999
*Source*: The authors

environment surrounding the town. As a result, the case study presented in this paper constitutes an interesting laboratory to test this new methodological approach to environmental management.

The present Urban Development Plan foresees the construction of 6100 new homes (see Table 1 and Figure 11). This would imply an additional 7000 permanent inhabitants and 11,200 second-home residents, if the 1991 first/second-home ratio is applied. Bearing in mind that, according to the 2000 census, the total number of inhabitants was already 19,707, the completion of the Development Plan (*GC*, 1997) could result in a total permanent population of 27,000 and 42,000 second-home residents. This would culminate in a total of 70,000 inhabitants at peak periods, doubling the figure for 1991. In the light of present trends,

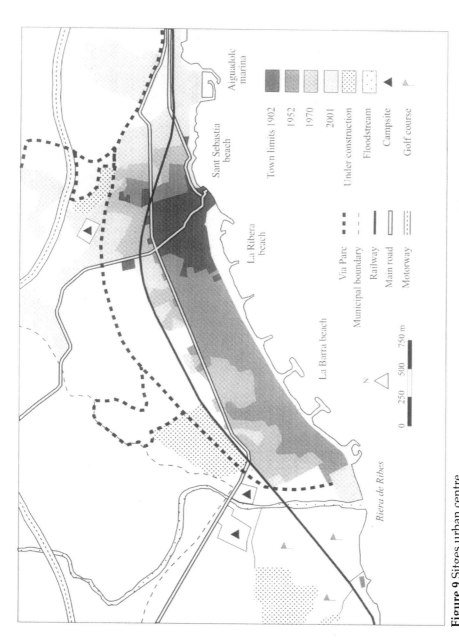

**Figure 9** Sitges urban centre
*Source:* The authors

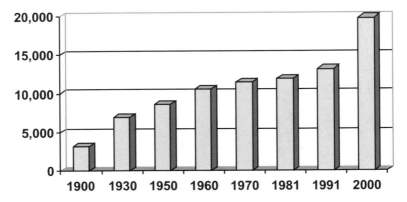

**Figure 10** Population growth in Sitges, 1900–2000
*Source*: The authors

**Table 1** Population and housing in Sitges, 1991 and future projection

|          | *Permanent homes* | *Permanent residents* | *Second homes* | *Seasonal residents* | *Total no. of homes** | *Total population* |
|----------|----------|----------|----------|----------|----------|----------|
| 1991     | 4,408    | 13,109   | 6,934    | *20,802* | 11,342   | *33,911* |
| 2000     | *6,569*** | 19,707   | *10,333* | *31,000* | *16,902* | *50,707* |
| GC       | *2,383*  | *7,149*  | *3,755*  | *11,265* | *6,138*  | *18,414* |
| 2000 + GC | *8,952* | *26,856* | *14,088* | *42,265* | *23,040* | 69,121   |

\* Vacant homes are not included
\*\*Italic numbers are estimates
GC Forecasts under the Urban Development Plan
*Source: GC*, 2002; *IEC*, 2002

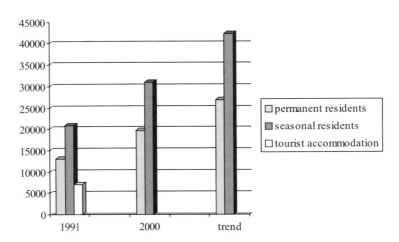

**Figure 11** Population in Sitges, 1991, 2000, and future projection
*Source*: The authors, based on *GC*, 2002; *IEC*, 2002

these estimates might require revision, as municipal records indicate that the permanent population seems to be increasing proportionally more than the second-home population. It must also be remembered that hotels and other tourist accommodation provide additional accommodation. In 2000, they provided 6959 beds, although an increase in capacity is likewise planned. As a result, the total figure could eventually rise to 80,000 inhabitants in the height of the summer season.

## The Environmental Management Programme for Sitges

As has been explained, the Sitges Towards Sustainability (STS) project fuses the EMAS and LA21 schemes. The project is not yet completed, so this analysis is limited to three phases: a consideration of the Environmental Review (including an analysis of the natural heritage of the municipality, followed by the identification of the main environmental problems); the strategic objectives that have been established; and the principal actions that are in progress or are to be undertaken. The entire scheme is intended to consider all environmental aspects of the municipality, but, for this paper, emphasis is placed on aspects that are most relevant to tourism. However, as Sitges is an important tourism resort, a large proportion of all aspects are included.

### The natural heritage

Although Sitges is firmly embedded in the metropolitan area of Barcelona, its natural heritage has considerable value at a regional and even European level.

#### Coastline, sea and beaches

Impressive cliffs spread along half of the 16.5 km coastline, interrupted by a number of coves with small beaches (Garraf, Vallcarca, Cala Morisca). A further quarter of the coast comprises sandy beaches, the longest of which are backed by the main urban centre of Sitges. The coast conserves a number of valuable ecological elements, identified in Directive 92/43/EEC, including flora on the karst Garraf Massif (*Reichardio-Crithmetum maritimi*), which is classified as of European Community interest;[10] one of the last surviving coastal woods in Catalonia in the Colls-Miralpeix sector; dune and marsh land containing salicornia (*Salicornia europaea*) on the Botigues beach; and fauna supporting the nesting of the pallid swift (*Apus pallidus*) and the shag (*Phalacrocorax aristotelis*) on the Garraf coast.

The most noteworthy marine element is the *Posidonia* beds (*Posidonion oceanicae*), an extremely productive ecosystem. They are classified as priority habitat types (code 1120) in the Habitats Directive, and, as such, liable for integration in the European Natura 2000 network. The quality of seawater for bathing is reasonably high, as all the beaches comply with Directive 76/169/CEE standards, and six have been awarded the Foundation for Environmental Education (FEE) Blue Flag (see Table 2). The *Coastwatch* report (Greenpeace, 1999) considers the environmental quality of Sitges beaches and coastline to be, at least, 'satisfactory', awarding a mark of 6 on the INCAS[11] index.

It is therefore fair to conclude that the overall quality of the various components of the littoral area is reasonably high, but there is still considerable

**Table 2** Beach quality in Sitges

| Beach | Star category (2000) | Star average (1999) | Quality diploma (1999) | Blue Flag (2000) |
|---|---|---|---|---|
| Les Botigues | **** good | 3.65 | yes | no |
| Garraf | *** satisfactory | 4.12 | yes | yes |
| Aiguadolç | *** satisfactory | 3.65 | yes | yes |
| Balmins | *** satisfactory | 3.59 | yes | no |
| Sant Sebastià | **** good | 4.06 | yes | yes |
| Ribera | **** good | 4.06 | yes | yes |
| L'Estanyol | **** good | 4.41 | yes | yes |
| La Barra | *** satisfactory | 3.94 | yes | yes |

*Source*: GC, 2002; FEE, 2002

opportunity for improvement, particularly in aspects related to beach and sand quality.

### Vegetation, land use and fauna

The karst Garraf Massif is a nature reserve (*Parc Natural*). Of the entire protected area, 27% (2.865 ha) is located within the boundaries of Sitges, representing 65% of the surface area of the municipality. This situation has certain advantages for Sitges, including the environmental protection which this status ensures through legislation, and access to technical and financial support from the Barcelona Park Authority (*Servei de Parcs de la Diputació de Barcelona*).

No surface watercourses exist on the Massif, as a result of the calcareous surface strata and dry climate, giving rise to a very arid landscape of *garrigue* vegetation, prone to frequent forest fires. Some of the associated vegetation is considered to be of interest to the European Community in the Habitat Directives.[12] In fact, the high ecological value of the flora, fauna and gea on the Massif justify its protected status.

In the municipality, only a few farms are still inhabited and operational. They are involved mainly in sheep, goat and dry farming, although vineyards still dominate the landscape to the southwest of the town. The local wine product, the sweet wine Malvasia, constituted a mainstay of the economy in the past, but is now sold mainly as a souvenir.

## Principal environmental problems and their relation to tourism

The most significant environmental problems for the tourism sector are of two types:

(1) Aspects which have negative consequences for present or potential tourism resources (landscape, fauna, flora and cultural heritage) and/or for the environmental quality of both rural and urban tourism environments (such as mobility and environmental hazards). In this case, the tourist sector can suffer from the negative effects of environmental degradation.

(2) Aspects that provoke environmental impacts directly linked with tourism

activities, such as in tourist enterprises or installations, the over-exploitation of aquifers, and the private appropriation of public maritime areas. In this case, the tourist sector generates, or is responsible for, the damage to the environment, which, in turn, can generate further negative repercussions for tourism activities.

For purposes of analysis, these environmental problems can be grouped more satisfactorily in seven categories, based on the key issues involved: urban planning and management; depletion of the water table; coastal erosion; beach management; natural hazards; access to natural areas and the countryside; and environmental management of economic activities.

### Urban planning and management

During a period of rapid urban expansion, as is occurring at present, it is crucial to conserve the last remaining unspoilt spaces located in the surroundings of the main urban nucleus. Moreover, the widespread infringements by urban development on peripheral steep slopes requires attention in order to mitigate its visual impact. Field observation has also identified a deficit of open spaces within the main urban nucleus, and of pavements and crossings for pedestrians (*Ajuntament de Sitges*, 2001). Private vehicle transport takes precedence, leading to traffic jams on access routes to the town centre and to the beaches.

### Depletion of the water table

In Sitges, as in Mediterranean areas in general, water is a scarce resource. The aquifers are over exploited in summer, mainly due to tourism use,[13] with a consequent increase in salinity. As a result, wastewaters, even after treatment, also register a high degree of salinity, which makes their reuse difficult or impossible, although there would be obvious outlets, such as the watering of the local golf course. The deficit of water and the question of its quality is, therefore, a very complex problem.

### Coastal erosion

The profound transformations to which the Spanish coast has been subjected over the last 50 years have deeply disturbed the coastal dynamics, which, in turn, have caused coastal erosion and beach loss. Sitges is one of many tourist resorts suffering from increasing marine erosion and a reduction in the natural regeneration of its beaches, aggravated by the additional negative effects of occasional storms, which affect not only the beach, but urban infrastructures and even private homes. At the same time, the artificial regeneration of beaches provokes serious environmental impacts, as the removal of sand from the sea-bed disturbs protective vegetation and fishing grounds (Ros & Serra, 1996). Moreover, the economic costs are high: an unpublished report on the Costa del Maresme (Breton *et al.*, 2000b) states that the cost varies according to the amount of work involved. The cost to the coastal authorities of extracting sand close offshore and landing it on the beach is €3 per cubic metre. However, the price rises to €9 when an engineering company is engaged to level the beach and the top layer of sand with heavy machinery, and rises even further to €12 when a prior survey and monitoring of the work is required. The problem is further aggravated by the occupation (both legal and illegal) of the adjoining coastal land fringe by tourist facilities or infrastructures, such as hotels, bars and promenades, which not only disrupt natural environmental processes but also have considerable visual impact.

### Beach management

Reference has already been made to the relatively high quality of the Sitges beaches. However, the *Coastwatch* report (Greenpeace, 1999) is much less favourable in its assessment of solid waste contamination on the beaches (see Figure 12). This report reveals that contamination figures for Sitges are considerably higher than the average for Catalonia, although they are generally similar to the average for the province of Barcelona, and only in a few cases notably higher. The worst conditions were registered in the categories referring to excrement, tins, paper and wood, plastics, sanitary products, polyester and glass, which were found at 60% of the sample points. It should be pointed out that the *Coastwatch* report was carried out in the low tourist season, when beach maintenance rarely occurs, and when solid waste is brought ashore during storms. Regardless of the degree of accuracy of the report, it is obvious from field observation that there is much room for improvement of this area. In addition, the municipal Beach Monitoring Programme (*Programa de Vigilància i Informació de l'Estat de les Platges*) emphasises the problems of rubbish in the parking areas, accesses and other areas bordering the beaches, numerous cigarette butts in the sand, and of solid, floating residues on certain beaches.[14] Obviously, the presence of such objects has a negative impact on the quality of the tourism environment, but they may also constitute a health risk for people and a hazard for marine fauna.

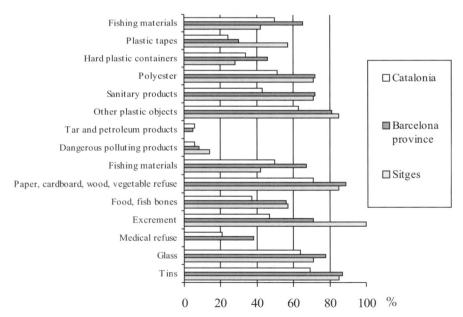

**Figure 12** Probability of the presence of residues in offshore waters in Catalonia, Barcelona province and Sitges
*Source*: Greenpeace, 1999

The use of the beaches only constitutes a problem where valuable natural resources are located. Such is the case for Platja de les Botigues, on the north-eastern limit of the municipality's coast, where dunes exist together with small wetlands which have given rise to the growth of halophile and psammophile vegetation, such as *salicornia*. Access to the beach at present does not follow any environmental criteria, so that trampling is causing damage to the vegetation, while mechanical cleaning prevents further dune development.

### Natural hazards

In Mediterranean environments, flooding and forest fires are recurring catastrophes. Material or human losses in flood conditions are often a result of bad management of river courses. In the case of Sitges, urban expansion has blocked the course of natural flood streams, which formerly released floodwaters without difficulty onto the beaches. The present promenade acts as a retaining dyke, with the consequent flooding of certain sectors of the older part of the town. Moreover, certain tourist installations (a campsite and the local golf club) intrude upon the natural bed of a peripheral flood stream (Riera de Ribes).

With regard to forest fires, the lack of control over access to natural areas is an aggravating factor, and the fires are a serious danger for visitors. Garraf Nature Reserve is particularly vulnerable, as every ten years on average there is an extensive fire destroying up to 700 ha, with serious consequences for flora and fauna on the massif. Statutory fire control measures already exist, but these have proved insufficient to avoid serious fire damage.

### Access to natural areas and the countryside

Uncontrolled access to, and over-frequentation of natural areas, together with a lack of basic fire controls, increase the risk of forest fires and also lead to soil erosion, vegetation destruction, and rubbish accumulation, with the worst effects being felt in the Colls-Miralpeix coastal forest area.

### Environmental management of economic activities

The sphere of economic activities includes the tourist establishments of the town: hotels, restaurants and bars, campsites, golf courses and the three marinas. Such enterprises are responsible for various environmental impacts, such as water and energy consumption, waste water disposal, the production and disposal of solid waste, atmospheric emissions, and noise. The Plan must therefore address these issues.

## The public participation process in Sitges

A total of 14 Neighbourhood Committees have been set up in Sitges, although attendance at their meetings has been variable. The ideal number of participants in each debate, in order to stimulate participation and ensure efficiency, is between eight and ten, so when a large number of residents attend, meetings are subdivided into smaller groups.

Certain conflicts over perceptions have arisen. The population by and large favour urban development based on low density, semi-detached and town houses with gardens. In contrast, the technical experts consider that sustainability parameters are fulfilled much better by constructing higher density blocks of flats of an identical residential capacity, as it is then possible to conserve large areas of 'green' land, provide better infrastructure and services, and to reduce energy and water consumption. Similarly, divergent opinions have been expressed about the beach-front facilities. The long, wide sea-front promenade constitutes a major attraction in Sitges, and it is used by both tourists and the local population. However, the technical experts have drawn attention to the problem of its interference with coastal dynamics.

Within the framework of the participation system described, the main instrument for the participation of the tourism sector in the STS system is the corresponding Sectorial Committee. Representatives of the tourism sector have been involved from the accommodation sector (including hotels and campsites), catering, the marinas and other tourist attractions and installations such as the golf courses. The municipal authorities are represented by four departments – urbanism; government; internal affairs; and environment and beaches – and one service – tourism and economic promotion – which depends on three departments.

## Strategic objectives and proposals for action

The Environmental Review has identified the principal problems and their causes. The following stage of the process is to define the strategic objectives and, subsequently, the actions that are necessary to achieve these goals. A number of strategic objectives which have particular relevance for tourism or for tourist installations in the municipality have already been pinpointed. The various proposals are listed in Table 3 and are grouped according to the three different agents in the municipal administrative structure that are directly or indirectly responsible for implementing the recommendations: Urban Planning and Management; Government, Internal Affairs, Environment and Beaches; and Tourism and Economic Promotion. The table outlines the environmental aspects involved, the objectives identified and the actions that are required. The final column indicates which actions are already being implemented.

### Urban Planning and Management

The main concerns focus on the rapid urban growth that is taking place, with the consequent risk of encroachment on surrounding areas and high density urban construction, which has also led to problems of access and mobility. The two most important priorities in this respect are to ensure the protection of the Colls-Miralpeix coastal forest (in danger of being built upon until recently) and the extension of the limits of Garraf Nature Reserve towards the urban periphery. This will guarantee the quality of the surroundings of the main urban nucleus. Planning measures should also be directed at improving the viability of wine production on the plains area, which will have scenic benefits as well as maintaining production of Malvasia, a product with a high symbolic and cultural value.

Moreover, measures are required to mitigate the visual impact of urban development on peripheral steep slopes. It is also necessary to increase the area designated as green space, and to reduce the scheduled density levels. These problems have already been identified and related measures are being incorporated into the current revision of the Urban Plan (*Pla General d'Ordenació Urbana*).[15] These include the creation of several open spaces and substantial

**Table 3** Strategic objectives and actions proposed for the environmental management of tourism in Sitges

| Area | Environmental aspect | Main strategic objectives | Main actions | Present situation* |
|---|---|---|---|---|
| Urban Planning, Projects, Public Works and Services | Land classification | Guarantee the conservation of those natural areas which contribute to landscape quality in the municipality | Ensure protection of Colls-Miralpeix coastal forest | 1 |
| | | | Extend the limits of Garraf Nature Park | 1 |
| | | | Protect agricultural land for production of Malvasia wine | 1 |
| | Land use categories | Define tourism policy | Revise the Urban Plan to identify future tourism facilities | 1 |
| | | | Draw up a Strategic Plan for tourism | 1 |
| | | Reduce limits or density of construction of property development on surrounding slopes | Revise the Urban Plan | 1 |
| | Systems | Change the pattern of mobility | Improve road connections to the motorway | 2 |
| | | | Facilitate and encourage the use of non-motorised means of transport | 2 |
| | | | Create new peripheral car park network (for access to beaches) | 2 |
| | | | Create a new urban park | 2 |
| | | Extend green spaces | Introduce environmental management systems | 1 |
| | | Introduce environmental improvements in marinas and harbours | Introduce EMAS in marinas | 2 |

**Table 3** Strategic objectives and actions proposed for the environmental management of tourism in Sitges

| Area | Environmental aspect | Main strategic objectives | Main actions | Present situation* |
|---|---|---|---|---|
| | Architecture and construction | Establish environmental practices | Promote model installations as a pilot demonstration | 2 |
| | Mobility | Adjust public transport services to tourist needs | Carry out a study of tourist mobility | 2 |
| Government, Internal Affairs, Environment and Beaches | Extraction of underground water resources | Avoid over-exploitation of the aquifers | Conduct a census of wells and draw up a Control Plan | 2 |
| | Flooding | Minimise risk | Mark the boundaries of the public water course on the Riera de Ribes | 2 |
| | | | Modify sewage system | 1 |
| | Marine erosion and beach management | Ensure strict application of the Coasts Act | Demolish buildings that impinge on public property on the shoreline | 2 |
| | | Improve the quality of coastal waters and beach quality | Carry out a study of coastal dynamics and proposal for an environmentally friendly system of sand regeneration | 1 |
| | | | Revise residue collection measures in coastal waters and on beaches | 1 |
| | Access to the countryside | Restrict motorised access and encourage pedestrian and bicycle access | Draw up an inventory of rights of way | 2 |
| | | | Develop a network of waymarked trails | 2 |
| | | | Regulate motorised access | |

**Table 3** Strategic objectives and actions proposed for the environmental management of tourism in Sitges

| Area | Environmental aspect | Main strategic objectives | Main actions | Present situation* |
|---|---|---|---|---|
| | Use of and access to Les Botigues beach | Establish measures to encourage operation of natural beach dynamics | Restructure access, define the protected vegetation and dune area, install environmental education facilities | 2 |
| Tourism and Economic Promotion | Environmental performance of economic activities | Introduce environmental practices in the tourism sector | Introduce Ecolabels and Environmental Management Systems in hotels, campsites, marinas and harbours, golf courses | 1 |
| | | Introduce additional fire control measures | Adopt self-protection plans on property developments | 2 |

* 1 = Currently being implemented
2 = Planned
*Source:* The authors

modifications to the communication network. Thus, a new transverse artery (*Via Parc*) will provide an alternative route for internal mobility and will connect the urban nucleus with the peripheral natural areas, where the existing network of walking trails will be extended (see Figure 9). In the built-up area, more attention will be paid to the needs of cyclists and pedestrians in general.

Specific planning and sustainability objectives for tourism are also necessary. These objectives should be borne in mind when allocating land for the future provision of hotels and other tourism facilities in the revised Urban Plan. Moreover, the hotel sector is currently developing its own strategic plan, and proposals will be considered for incorporation into the Plan. In this way, the public and private sectors can work together to define the future structure of tourism in Sitges.

### Government, Internal Affairs, Environment and Beaches

The depletion of the water table has been identified as one of the major concerns. It is seen as essential to conduct a census of the numerous wells that exist and to draw up a Control Plan, although its success will largely depend on the cooperation of the tourist and other private sectors. It is something of a paradox that there is also a danger of flooding. Modifications to the sewage system, currently being undertaken, are expected to overcome the problem in the town centre, but it will also be necessary to mark the boundaries more clearly between public and private property along the Riera de Ribas.

The coast and beach areas are essential components of the tourism product, and thus their management is a priority. The drawing up of a conservation strategy for the long-term sustainability of the beaches is certainly necessary. However, the most crucial problems identified are being addressed through certain short-term measures. An immediate improvement would be achieved by demolishing buildings in risk areas, thus complying with the 1988 Coasts Act (*Ley de Costas*),[16] which has not always been strictly enforced in the past. In an attempt to address the problems of beach management, the municipal authorities in Sitges acquired a vessel to collect floating waste, and the report on solid waste collection for 2000, the first year of operation, (Ajuntament de Sitges, 2000) confirms the magnitude of the problem, as two tons of floating residues were collected during the peak tourist season from mid-June to the end of September.

The Platja de les Botigues has been identified as the only beach area where valuable natural resources are located. Given the considerable width of the beach, leisure use can be compatible with the conservation of its natural potential. The design and implementation of a plan for restoration, controlled access and environmental education will help to safeguard the resource while making its use viable.[17]

With regard to access to natural areas and the countryside, the principal recommendation is the restriction of motorised access and encouragement of pedestrian and bicycle access. The implementation of this strategy will require the drawing up of an inventory of the existing public rights of way and private roads. This is intended to lead to the design of a Plan for the development and use of natural areas, which would impose restrictions on vehicle access, and encourage alternative forms of access through the creation of a network of waymarked trails for cyclists and pedestrians. This Plan could have the added advantage of contributing to fire hazard control, although there is also a need for the adoption of self-protection plans for properties located in high-risk areas.

*Tourism and Economic Promotion*

The basic objective for the environmental management of economic activities is to implant and monitor good environmental management practices. The adoption of eco-labels and environmental management systems by the enterprises and installations has been advocated for environmental impacts generated by the tourism sector (UNEP, 1999). Here the Catalan Government has created eco-labels for hotels, campsites and rural accommodation. To date, one of the three campsites (22.5% of total capacity) in Sitges has acquired the relevant certification,[18] one hotel has achieved both ISO 14001 and EMAS certification, another hotel has been awarded EMAS certification, and two additional hotels have initiated the process of implementing it. Further related progress is obviously required, as this represents only a small proportion of the 32 hotels and 13 guest houses in Sitges. Nevertheless, the four hotels constitute 24.5% of total capacity, as the process has focused initially on the larger, higher quality accommodation.

Three marinas within the municipal limits of Sitges have already been awarded a Blue Flag eco-label,[19] although, because of the low environmental standards of this label for marinas, it would be advisable to establish more effective instruments, such as EMAS. In fact, one of the marinas has commenced the necessary steps in order to obtain both EMAS and ISO 14001 certification. The Environmental Management Plan for Golf Courses (*Pla Director Ambiental dels Camps de Golf a Catalunya*[20]), recently introduced in Catalonia, aims to encourage the introduction of EMAS or other eco-management audit schemes, such as Committed to Green,[21] in the region's golf courses. The local golf course and the pitch and putt course will be included in the associated pilot quality plan.

## Conclusions

Sitges is currently approaching the completion of its urban development and its functional integration in the Barcelona metropolitan region, without having lost the most attractive elements which made it a highly regarded tourist resort. Nevertheless, Sitges clearly illustrates the environmental, social and economic problems that face numerous mature tourism destinations, especially in the Mediterranean region. Although Sitges is renowned for its architectural and cultural heritage, combined with its magnificent urban sea-front laid out along the best beaches, the surroundings of the urban nucleus include areas of considerable natural and scenic value. Their intrinsic value is greater because they lie within the Barcelona metropolitan region. Moreover, the natural heritage surrounding Sitges has additional value, as it constitutes a high quality tourism resource which should make a significant contribution to the reorientation of the tourism destination and the renewal of the products offered by the resort.

In this context and by combining EMAS and LA21, the Sitges Towards Sustainability programme represents an innovative approach to the intrinsic complexity of applying environmental criteria to the functioning of urban systems in general, and of tourism destinations in particular. With regard to the tourism sector, the adoption of the system should lead to improvements to some key environmental problems affecting the sector. Perhaps the most significant of the proposed actions are: the revision of urban planning, with the aim of introducing sustainability criteria, especially in mobility patterns; the adoption of environmental criteria in the management of tourism companies and installations, through the introduction of eco-labels and environmental management systems; the control of access to fragile natural areas; and the demolition of tourism-related buildings that impinge on public property on the shoreline.

Certainly the project has aroused the interest of the population, with many participating with considerable enthusiasm. The main difficulty encountered up to the present has been the doubts expressed by the general public about the true effectiveness of the process of participation, as they lack confidence in the willingness or capability of the municipal authorities to convert their proposals into tangible actions. Nevertheless, the STS project is a clear statement of support for sustainability ideals on the part of both local government and society. It is also an opportunity to redefine and reorientate the development model. Moreover, given the direct links that exist between the environment and tourist image, securing a prestigious eco-label – EMAS certification in this case – may be suitably appreciated and valued by the tourist market.

Using an exhaustive environmental review as the starting point, the methodology applied in environmental management systems makes it possible to establish the links between environmental impacts and municipal administration through the analysis of environmental aspects. This, in turn, leads to a more holistic and integrated understanding of the environmental vectors in the destination in question, and it places them in their social and economic context. At the same time, the procedures are capable of identifying existing intersections between environmental impacts and tourism activity. The open and participative nature of the process, a requisite shared by both Local Agenda 21 and environmental management systems, makes it possible to incorporate the tourist sector in the design of the environmental programme and in its application. At this early stage, it is impossible to evaluate the success of the scheme, and a final assessment will only be possible several years after its implementation. Nonetheless, it is argued that the methodological innovation involved justifies the scheme's presentation now.

### Acknowledgement

The authors wish to thank Dr Joan Carles Llurdés for drawing Figures 5, 6 and 9.

### Correspondence

Any correspondence should be directed to Gerda Priestley, EUTDH, Campus de la UAB, 08193 Cerdanyola, Barcelona, Spain (gerda.priestley@campus.uab.es).

### Notes

1. Regulation (EC) No 761/2001 of the European Parliament and of the Council of 19th March 2001 allowing voluntary participation by organisations in a Community eco-management and audit scheme (EMAS).
2. The research team forms part of the staff of *EUTDH* Consulting Department (ARC).

3. *EUTDH* research team in the case of Sitges.
4. According to EMAS Regulations (Article 2): 'Environmental impact shall mean any change to the environment, whether adverse or beneficial, wholly or partially resulting from an organisation's activities, products or services.'
5. According to EMAS Regulations (Article 2): 'Environmental aspect shall mean an element of an organisation's activities, products or services that can interact with the environment; a significant environmental aspect is an environmental aspect that has or can have a significant environmental impact.'
6. According to EMAS Regulations (Annex I, Section B3: External communication and relations): 'Organisations shall be able to demonstrate an open dialogue with the public and other interested parties including local communities and customers with regard to the environmental impact of their activities, products and services in order to identify the public's and other interested parties' concerns.'
7. Towns such as Palamós, Sant Feliu de Guixols, Blanes, Sant Andreu de Llavaneres, and Sitges.
8. In fact, the coast as a whole was still relatively undeveloped, but a few large resorts which dominated the international hotel market (especially Lloret de Mar and Calella and, to a lesser extent, Tossa de Mar and Roses) set the trend in the statistics (Priestley & Mundet, 1998).
9. Key locations include Calella de Palafrugell, Platja d'Aro, Gavà, Castelldefels.
10. Habitats Directive 1240 Vegetated sea cliffs of the Mediterranean coasts with endemic *Limonium* spp.
11. The INCAS index has eight categories: 1. Unsuitable for life; 2. Extremely unsatisfactory; 3. Very unsatisfactory; 4. Unsatisfactory; 5. Satisfactory; 6. Good; 7. Very good; 8. Excellent.
12. Pre-desert scrub dominated by *Ampelodesmos mauritanica* is classified under habitat code 5332 and calcareous rocky slopes with chasmophytic vegetation are classified under habitat code 8211.
13. Tourist usage in hotels and restaurants, but also in second homes.
14. These are frequently found on Aiguadolç beach, due to the proximity of the marina and predominant currents; La Ribera beach, due to the storm flood outlet; and La Barra beach, where the breakwaters retain residues.
15. The Urban Plan, updated at intervals of several years, constitutes the basic planning instrument for each municipality.
16. This would involve the demolition of a discotheque and a hotel, both of which are built within the limits of the beach.
17. Since mechanical cleaning was replaced by manual methods on El Prat beach nearby in the early 1990s, 1.5–2 m high dunes and a complex community of sandy vegetation have formed (Breton *et al.*, 2000a).
18. Denominated *Distintiu de Garantia de Qualitat Ambiental*, awarded by the *Departament de Medi Ambient* of the *Generalitat de Catalunya*.
19. http://www.blueflag.org
20. http://www.gencat.es/mediambient/sosten/pla-golf.htm
21. www.committedtogreen.com

## References

Ajuntament de Sitges (2000) *Informe del Servei de Neteja de Residus Sòlids Flotants de l'Ajuntament, 2000*. Sitges: Ajuntament de Sitges.

Ajuntament de Sitges (2001) *Pla de Mobilitat de Sitges*. Sitges: Ajuntament de Sitges.

Barbaza, Y. (1966) *Le Paysage Humain de la Costa Brava*. Paris: Armand Colin.

Breton, F., Esteban, P. and Miralles, E. (2000a) Rehabilitation of metropolitan beaches by local administrations in Catalonia: New trends in sustainable coastal management. *Journal of Coastal Conservation* 6, 97–106.

Breton, F., Serra, J., López, M.J. and Villeró, D. (2000b) *Anàlisi del Sistema Litoral. Auditoria Ambiental del Baix Maresme*. Bellaterra: Centre d'Estudis Ambientals – UAB

Butler, R.W. (1980) The concept of a tourism area life cycle of evolution: Implications for the management of resources. *Canadian Geographer* 24, 5–12.

Echenagusia, J. (1995) *Calvià, Agenda Local 21*. Calvià: Ajuntament de Calvià.

FEE – Foundation for Environmental Education (2002) On WWW at http://www.blueflag.org.

GC – Generalitat de Catalunya (1997) *Normes Subsidiàries i Complementàries de Planejament de Sitges*. Barcelona: Generalitat de Catalunya, Departament de Política Territorial i Obres Públiques, Direcció General d'Urbanisme.

GC – Generalitat de Catalunya, Departament de Medi Ambient (2002) On WWW at http://www.gencat.es/mediamb/

Greenpeace (1999) *Informe Coastwatch 1998–1999*. Barcelona: Greenpeace.

Hewitt, N. (1995) *European Local Agenda 21 Planning Guide*. Brussels: International Council for Local Environmental Initiatives.

IEC – Institut d'Estadística de Catalunya (2002) On WWW at http://www.idescat.es.

Miguelsanz-Arnalot, A. and Higueras-Miró, G. (1964) *El Turisme a Sitges*. Serra d'Or, 2a època 6 (6), 5–12.

Priestley, G.K. (1984) Sitges, Playa de Oro: La evolución de su industria turística hasta 1976. *Documents d'Anàlisi Geogràfica* 5, 47–69.

Priestley, G.K. (1996) Structural dynamics of tourism and recreation-related development: The Catalan coast. In: G.K. Priestley, J. A. Edwards and H. Coccossis (eds) *Sustainable Tourism? European Experiences* (pp. 99–119). Wallingford: CAB International.

Priestley, G.K. & Mundet, L. (1998) The post-stagnation phase of the resort cycle. *Annals of Tourism Research* 25 (1), 85–111.

Regulation (EC) No 761/2001 of the European Parliament and of the Council of 19 March 2001 allowing voluntary participation by organisations in a Community eco-management and audit scheme (EMAS).

Romagosa, F. and Cuétara, L. (in press) El desarrollo sostenible en destinos turísticos. Propuesta de un sistema de indicadores de sostenibilidad. *Papers de Turisme*.

Ros, J.D. and Serra, J. (1996) Ecosistemes i dinàmica litoral. *Quaderns d'Ecologia Aplicada* 13, 5–43.

Seguí Llinas, M. (1998) Calvià, el futuro de una estación turística madura. In J. Oliveras Samitier and S. Anton Clavé (eds) *Turismo y Planificación del Territorio en la España de Fin de Siglo. Actas de las V Jornadas de Geografía del Turismo* (pp. 233–41). Tarragona: Universitat Rovira i Virgili.

UNEP – United Nations Environment Programme (1999) *Contribution of the United Nations Environment Programme to the Secretary-General's Report on Industry and Sustainable Tourism for the Seventh Session of the Commission for Sustainable Development. Addendum C. Tourism and Environmental Protection*.

WTO – World Tourism Organisation, World Travel and Tourism Council, Earth Council (1997) *Agenda 21 for the Travel & Tourism Industry. Towards Environmentally Sustainable Development*. Madrid: World Tourism Organisation.

## The Authors

Dr Gerda Priestley is Director of the Research Centre (CInERT) at the Escola Universitària de Turisme, and Dr Xavier Campillo-Besses (Director) and Francesc Romagosa (Researcher) are members of the School's Consulting Department (ARC), responsible for carrying out the Sitges Towards Sustainability project.

# 12 Environmental Initiatives in the Hotel Sector in Greece: Case Study of the 'Green Flags' Project

*Artemios Chatziathanassiou, Daphne Mavrogiorgos and Konstantinos Sioulas*

*Centre for Renewable Energy Sources, 19 km Marathonos Av., Pikermi 19 009, Greece*

The hotel sector response to the increasing need for environmental consciousness has been to establish systems and procedures at the core of the decision-making process and to bring sustainable tourism to hotel units through environmental initiatives, such as environmental management systems and eco-labelling schemes. Throughout the last decade in Greece, these types of initiatives were limited due to the hoteliers' reluctance to adopt sustainable practices in their hotel operation. The authors of this paper assessed the environmental performance of 35 hotels in Greece in the context of a LIFE project entitled 'Green Flags', the aim of which was to define a labelling award within the European Union eco-labelling scheme. The results of the environmental reviews of these hotels defined the environmental basis of the criteria to be adopted in the proposed label scheme. The implementation structure and the basic characteristics of this scheme are discussed in relation to the existing conditions that dominate the hospitality industry in Greece.

## Introduction

According to the Mediterranean Commission for Sustainable Development (MCSD), it is estimated that the 135 million tourists visiting the coastal regions of the Mediterranean in 1990 could increase to 235–350 million by 2025. Tourism is a principal economic sector in most Mediterranean countries like Greece, but it is also becoming an important source of negative environmental impacts. In Greece, tourist arrivals amount to 12.6 million, ranking it fifteenth among the world tourism destinations (WTO, 2001) and making the tourism industry one of the most dynamic and productive sectors of the national economy. In particular, it provides 7% of gross domestic product, which amounts to US$9.2 million in tourism receipts (2000), and it employs approximately 10% of the total workforce (Greek National Tourism Organisation, 2001). Although this highly dynamic sector is of primary importance, it has negatively affected the environment in the last two decades, as an unavoidable result of rapid development under competitive conditions (Golphi *et al.*, 1994).

The ultimate goal of tourism is to provide high quality services in a natural and man-made environment, but through its dynamic presence and intensification it has became one of the sectors with the greatest range of environmental pressures. Nowadays, it is well known that the prevailing model of mass tourism, with its mainly seasonal character, its disproportionately large concentration of people and infrastructure in some areas, and its continuously increasing trends of development, has contributed to increased degradation of natural, social and cultural resources in tourism destinations in Greece and elsewhere in the Mediterranean.

The concept of sustainability is being adapted in response to these circumstances. Although tourism was not included in Agenda 21 (Earth Summit, 1992), recognition of the importance of sustainability for the tourism industry resulted in the formulation of 'Agenda 21 for the Travel and Tourism Industry' in 1997 by the World Travel and Tourism Council (WTTC), World Tourism Organisation (WTO) and Earth Council (EC). This is an action plan covering the responsibilities of government, national tourism authorities and representative trade organisations, with the overall aim of establishing systems and procedures to incorporate sustainable development considerations at the core of decision-making processes and of identifying the actions necessary to achieve sustainable tourism (WTTC *et al.*, 1997). According to Middleton and Hawkins (1997), the accommodation sector can have success in the market with sustainable initiatives as long as it makes the most of the opportunities created by incorporating environmental programmes.

## Environmental Initiatives in the Hotel Sector

Tourism, more than any other productive sector, is mainly based on the environment and on maintaining high quality services. To this end, a wide range of instruments can be used to put the tourism industry on a path towards sustainability. These instruments in relation to hotels may include regulations (essential for defining the legal framework), economic instruments, grants to motivate hoteliers, and voluntary approaches such as ISO and the Eco-Management and Audit Schemes – EMAS and eco-label schemes (UNEP, 1998).

Voluntary approaches have been developed by a wide variety of national and international organisations, such as the Hotel Catering & Institutional Management Association, the World Travel and Tourism Council, and UNEP. They emerged at the beginning of the 1990s and are aimed at raising awareness in the hospitality industry about matters concerning environmental policy implementation (Kirk, 1995). The intention was to create awareness of sound environmental policies and management systems among the various stakeholders (Goodall & Stabler, 1997) so that changing business practices and attitudes would reduce the environmental pressures of hotel operations (IHRA & UNEP, 1996; IHEI, 1996). These approaches mainly concerned ways of continually creating more wealth with fewer resources, less raw materials, less energy, less waste and less pollution (Iwanowski & Rushmore, 1994).

Such international schemes as ISO 14001 and EMAS seek to develop an environmental management system (EMS) which certifies the existence of an environmental policy for a hotel as well as its implementation through several practices (managerial or technical). The ultimate aim of an EMS is to continuously improve the environmental performance of these units (Hillary, 1994; Kirk, 1995).

One of the most promising voluntary approaches to attaining high environmental standards is the Eco-label scheme and this favourably supports small and medium firms, such as many hotels (UNEP, 1998). What distinguishes Eco-labels from EMS schemes is that the former adopts the best technical solutions for the prevention and mitigation of environmental impacts. It is worth mentioning that

Eco-labels and EMS are not in competition with each another, as the existence of one does not exclude the application of the other.

The Eco-label schemes operated in the accommodation sector have been developed globally, with approximately 20 of them operating on a regional, national and municipal level throughout Europe (Hamele, 2001). Eco-labels in member states of the EU generally help tourism enterprises on a practical level to determine the crucial points that will accelerate the realisation of improved environmental solutions and lead to the efficient management and monitoring of their environmental performance (CREM & CH21-HILL, 2000). Examples of such schemes include the Emblem of Guarantee of Environmental Quality (Spain), the Environmental Seal of Quality in Tyrol and South Tyrol (Italy and Austria), the Gites Panda (France), and the Blue Flag Campaign (European Union) (Font et al., 2001). In 2000, the European Commission adopted a new Regulation (1980/2000/EC) and revised the previous one for the Eco-labelling award system (880/92/EEC), with these measures taken to satisfy society's increasing demand for market penetration by products that result in minimal environmental degradation. With the current Regulation, the European Commission's purpose is to apply an Eco-labelling system throughout Europe that can be used for any form of economic activity, and particularly for such service sector activity as hotels.

## Environmental Initiatives in Greece

An increasing number of initiatives for the practical promotion of sustainable development have appeared at an international level and within the European Union. In Greece there have been a few cases of the practical application of these environmental programmes, except for a few cases which have received wide recognition both in Europe and internationally. The main reason for this poor environmental performance is the general reluctance of Greece's hoteliers to seriously address the issues by applying ameliorating measures (Stylianopoulou, 1998). In addition, the public sector has been unable to promote and support sustainable practices, especially on the islands, and the small tourism enterprises that dominate the industry often have an inadequate understanding of tourism management and marketing and also fail to appreciate the long-term implications of their actions (Buhalis & Diamantis, 2001).

Grecotel is a leading hotel chain in Greece that has incorporated environmental management, mainly in relation to resort hotels, into its corporate philosophy. It has been referred to as an exemplary tourism company, which has formulated a 'green strategy' (Middleton & Hawkins, 1997; Vellas & Becherel, 1999; WTTC et al., 1997) and has won international awards from the tourism industry in this field, such as the Umwelt Champion Award by the TUI Group in 1997, 1998 and 1999. Its environmental management programme includes actions and measures in the areas of waste management, water and energy saving, pollution control and purchasing policies. In March 2000, a hotel of the Maris Hotels group, Candia Maris, was one of three hotels in the Mediterranean to be certified with the ISO 14001 management by the Hellenic Standards Organisation (ELOT). Nowadays, the Maris chain is one of only three hotel chains in

Europe (Forum and Intercontinental) with all of their hotels having implemented the ISO 14001 management system (Falirea, 2001).

In 1996 a pilot project was carried out to implement the EMAS in hotels in Chalkidiki (Northern Greece) under the auspices of the Union of Chalkidiki Hoteliers. Its primary aim was the adjustment of the EMAS Regulation (1836/93) in order for it to be used for the establishment of EMS's in the tourism industry. Initially environmental reviews were conducted in seven volunteer hotels in Chalkidiki and they were assessed for their environmental performance. The results of the first of these reviews showed that some hotels individually had taken steps to lessen their environmental impact, albeit without proper planning and systemisation (Christophoridis *et al.*, 2000). All of the hotels achieved a medium environmental performance according to the analytical methodology, which had been developed as part of the project (Papazoglou *et al.*, 1999). This project resulted in the publication of guidelines for the implementation of EMAS schemes in hotels. In 1998 one of the participating hotels (Virginia) had its EMS audited by an independent accredited auditor (Gerling CERT Umweltgutachter GmbH) who accepted the hotel's environmental statement. It became the first small-scale hotel (with 30 beds) in the EU to be certified under the EMAS scheme.

While in many EU member states there are Eco-label schemes for accommodation services that are certified at a local and/or national level, these have never been implemented in Greece. And there were only nine members from Greece registered in the Annual Review 1997–1998 of the 'Green Globe' Initiative.

In 2001, the authors established through contact with various Standards Organisations in Greece that only 50 hotels had been certified with ISO standards (ISO 9001 and 9002). Four of these had additionally established EMS's according to the ISO 14001 management system. Among the 50 hotels it is notable that 74% were island hotels and only 14% were city hotels (Athens and Thessalonica).

## The Project 'Green Flags for Greener Hotels'

The project Green Flags for Greener Hotels ENV/F 000338 was carried out within the framework of the LIFE 1998 Programme of the European Commission (Directorate General for the Environment), with a total duration of 26 months (1998 to 2000). Its objective was the determination of environmental measures that a hotel should apply in order for it to be awarded with the 'Green Flag' environmental label.

Six partners took part in the project from various member states of the EU, which are recognised as some of the world's most famous tourist destinations (WTO, 2001). The partners were ADEME (France-the project co-ordinator), ICAEN (Spain), SOFTECH (Italy), ARCS (Austria), IER (Germany) and CRES (Greece). The partners had to take account of national characteristics of the hotel sector in their country, including variations in tourism infrastructure, hoteliers' attitudes and experience, development of Eco-label schemes in relation to hotels, and policy priorities in the tourism sector.

The discussion that follows explains the project methodology, the actions taken to apply it, and the results of the Greek case. The project assessed the applicability of an environmental label in the hotel sector in the six countries.

## Approach

The main purpose of the 'Green Flags' project was for the six partners to agree on a Pan-European Environmental Label Scheme related to the Eco-label philosophy that had already been developed for hotels in Europe. The methodology applied by the partners consisted of the following phases (ADEME, 2001a):

- determining the technical and managerial requirements so as to minimise the environmental pressures from hotel operations;
- formulation of the defined requirements as award criteria, based on the hotel attributes of the six participating countries; and
- review of the applicability of the award criteria for the resulting label system, by the means of a number of environmental reviews of existing hotels.

The approach followed by CRES for the environmental upgrading of a typical hotel operation consisted of the following stages:

- a 'walk through' of a hotel's operations, based on its various areas, such as client contact areas (front), support areas (back) and surrounding areas, and on its layout (Figure 1);
- identification of environmental pressures, such as wastes, heat, noise from various flows, by area and operation as indicated in Figure 2. In addition, the determination of appropriate environmental measures, in the form of technical and managerial requirements in order to minimise the identified pressures; and
- the compilation of a questionnaire, based on the aforementioned environmental requirements and grouped by environmental areas (such as waste,

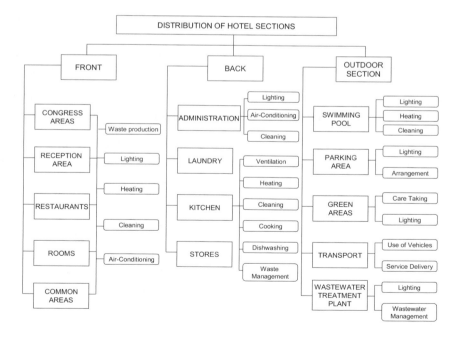

**Figure 1** Layout of sectors, services and environmental areas of a typical hotel unit

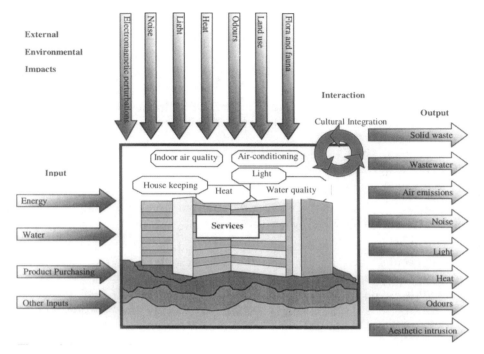

**Figure 2** Structure of environmental aspects (adapted from ADEME, 2001b)

energy, water, air emissions and product purchasing) in order to define the final award criteria for the label scheme.

This approach was supported by the operation of a Greek National Working Group with relevant experience in the hotel sector and in environmental protection issues. It has members from the National Competent Body for Eco-labelling (ASAOS), the Greek National Tourism Organisation (GNTO), eco-tourism experts from hotel groups, and from private enterprises with prior experience in EMS.

Spittler and Haak (2001) stated that 'the quality of the Eco-label and the perception of quality by the potential tourists, depends on how many of the criteria need to be fulfilled and the marks for each one of those necessary to achieve accreditation'. The set of criteria not only has to set high quality standards, but it must also be investigated in order to show how realistic and acceptable they are. This verification of the applicability of the pre-determined set of criteria was checked using environmental reviews of the hotels. The purpose was to reveal potential peculiarities of the tourism product and the ability of hotels to comply with the selected environmental measures.

The preliminary environmental reviews involved questionnaires being completed on site in a limited number of hotels (four). The content of the questionnaires was based on the selected environmental measures and consisted of 11 topics (general issues, waste, hazardous waste, energy, water, wastewater, air-emissions, noise and purchasing policies) and 124 questions. These included

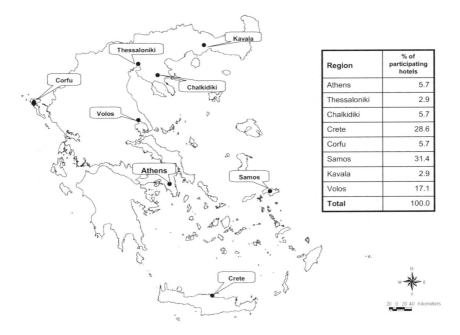

| Region | % of participating hotels |
|---|---|
| Athens | 5.7 |
| Thessaloniki | 2.9 |
| Chalkidiki | 5.7 |
| Crete | 28.6 |
| Corfu | 5.7 |
| Samos | 31.4 |
| Kavala | 2.9 |
| Volos | 17.1 |
| **Total** | **100.0** |

**Figure 3** Geographical distribution of the hotel sample

yes/no answers, request for quantitative data such as the annual energy consumption, and occasionally open-ended questions for clarification or enhancement.

The final environmental review was carried out in 23 island hotels and 12 mainland hotels, these being in various tourist areas throughout Greece, including Samos, Crete, Corfu, Athens, Thessalonica, and Kavala (Figure 3). The

**Table 1** Hotels participated in the environmental reviews and their main characteristics

| *Characteristics* | *Number of hotels* | | *Total* |
|---|---|---|---|
| **Location** | Mainland | 12 | 35 |
| | Island | 23 | |
| **Bed capacity** | < 99 | 9 | 35 |
| | 100–499 | 19 | |
| | > 500 | 7 | |
| **Class** (according to the GNTO) | Luxury | 3 | 35 |
| | A | 14 | |
| | B+C | 18 | |
| **Operational period** | Seasonal | 10 | 35 |
| | Year-round | 25 | |

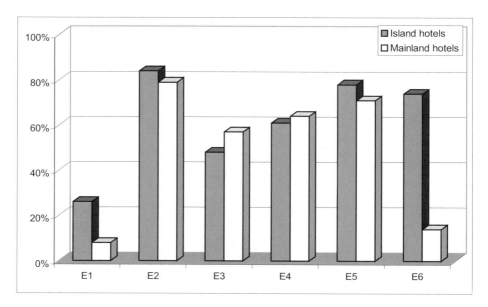

**Figure 4** Application of energy saving techniques and renewable energy in the hotel sample
*Note*: E1=Autonomous measurement of electricity consumption, E2=Energy saving light bulbs, E3=Energy saving systems (e.g. magnetic cards, central energy systems), E4=Double glazed windows, E5=Use of low energy consuming appliances, and E6=Renewable energy sources

hotels were selected to secure a representative sample of the hotel sector, including criteria such as the hotel's class according to the GNTO, its geographical location, its bed capacity and its operational period (seasonal or year-round) (Table 1). The survey was carried out in the summer of 2000, the interviews on average lasted 90 to120 minutes and the correspondent was either the hotel owner (mainly so in small-scale hotels of up to 100 beds) or the hotel director.

## Results of the Environmental Reviews

While the selected hotel sample is small (35), the results of the environmental reviews can still be considered indicative. The reviews reveal a low implementation of environmentally friendly practices. The findings are related to the existing infrastructure in the tourism destination, the geographical area and the environmental awareness of the hoteliers. The results are of intrinsic interest and were also the source of the criteria list used for the labelling award.

The hotels tended to apply low-cost methods and practices when dealing with the environmental impacts arising from hotel operations. This is evident in Figure 4, where the simple energy saving techniques, such as energy saving light bulbs (E2), low energy consuming appliances (E5) and double glazed windows (E4), were more common than the more advanced techniques, such as energy saving systems (e.g. central heating/cooling, magnetic cards, Building Energy Management Systems-BEMs) (E3) and use of renewable energy sources (RES) (E6) in mainland hotels. Because island hotels can face power shortages from

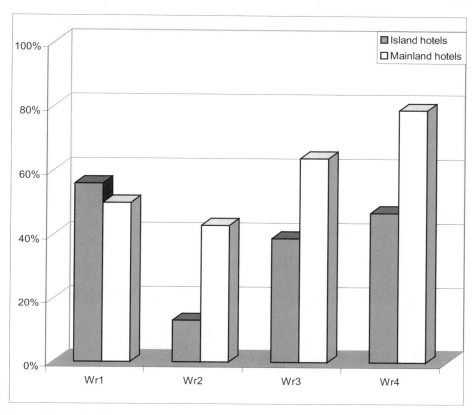

**Figure 5** Application of water management in the hotel sample
*Note*: Wr1=Autonomous measurement of water consumption, Wr2=Water saving techniques (e.g. mixing valves and batteries and regulated cisterns),
Wr3=Recycling systems for swimming pools and rainwater, and Wr4=Automated systems for irrigation

time to time, especially during the summer months which is their main period of operation, one might expect them to apply energy saving techniques and RES technologies on a larger scale than mainland hotels. The survey indicates that they did indeed do this for three (E2, E5 and E6) out of five measures, with a large difference from mainland hotels regarding RES, which relate particularly to solar panels for hot water. The island hoteliers did not apply the highly technologically sophisticated energy saving systems (E3), due to the low financial savings they would achieve since their operation time is during the summer months. As regards double glazed windows (E4), their contribution was probably not what would be expected due to lack of information.

Figure 4 shows that most hotels did not systematically monitor their environmental areas. It indicates that autonomous energy consumption (E1) was measured by very few hotels, and Figure 5 shows that almost half of the hoteliers were unaware of their water consumption levels (Wr1). Water management should be a particular priority for island hotels since there are often problems of freshwater supply. However, the survey shows that it is mostly mainland hotels

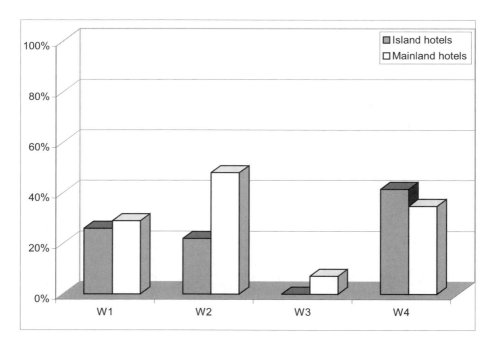

**Figure 6** Application of waste management in the hotel sample
*Note*: W1=Separation of municipal solid waste (MSW), W2=Collection of organic
fraction, W3=Toxic waste, and W4=Chemical wastes

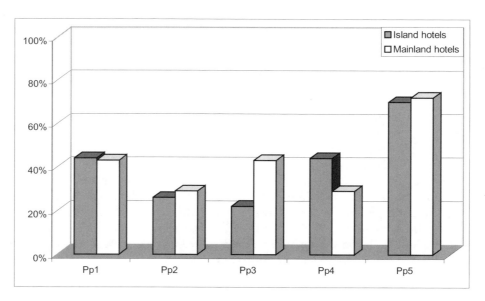

**Figure 7** Product purchasing preferences in the hotel sample
*Note*: Pp1=Ecological food in catering, Pp2=Ecological corridor floor covering,
Pp3=Ecological building material, Pp4=Recyclable packaging material, and
Pp5=Environmentally friendly soaps

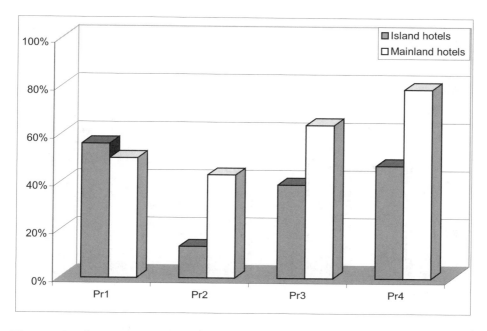

**Figure 8** Purchasing of recyclable materials in the hotel sample
*Note*: Pr1=Toilet paper, Pr2=Office paper, Pr3=Plastic cups, and Pr4=Packaging
material

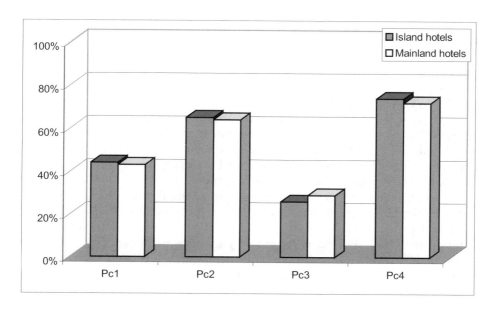

**Figure 9** Purchasing policy on chemicals in the hotel sample
*Note*: Pc1=Environmentally friendly detergents, Pc2=CFC free refrigerators,
Pc3=Low impact agrochemicals, and Pc4=Environmentally friendly cleaning of
pools

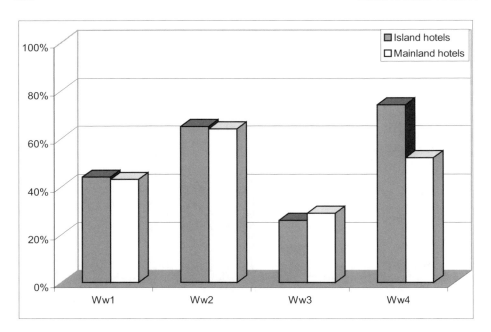

**Figure 10** Application of wastewater management in the hotel sample
*Note*: Ww1=Wastewater treatment plant, Ww2=Water saving washing machines,
Ww3=Separation of kitchen and laundry slops, and Ww4=Grey irrigation

that use water saving techniques, recycling systems and automated irrigation
systems (Wr2-Wr4).

Hotels located far from the large urban centres have a limited infrastructure at
their disposal for dealing with environmental impacts, such as waste management. Figure 6 clearly shows the inefficient separation of municipal solid wastes
(MSW) (W1), with island hotels having lower percentages than the mainland
ones. The collection of the organic fraction (food remains and green ground
litter) (W2) in island hotels was also lower than in mainland hotels, in spite of the
favourable material that would be produced, such as compost. It is also evident
that toxic and chemical waste management was very low, with island hotels
having a zero response rate to toxic management.

There was little use of materials with environmentally friendly specifications.
This is evident in Figures 7, 8 and 9 that concern purchasing policies. In Figure 7,
ecological products such as ecological food (Pp1), corridor floor cover (Pp2),
building materials (Pp3) and recyclable packaging materials (Pp4) were not
really on the hotelier's shopping list. Also, as Figure 8 indicates, there was little
use of recyclable plastic cups (Pr3) and office paper (Pr2), especially in island
hotels. Figure 9 clearly shows the reluctance of hoteliers to purchase environmentally friendly detergents (Pc1) and low impact agrochemicals (Pc3), which
means they mostly used products that may have very severe impacts on the environment and on human health. Furthermore, at least 40% of island hotels made
ecological choices in relation to only five (Pp1, Pp4, Pp5, Pr1 & Pr4) out of the nine
product-purchasing measures, which was maybe influenced by the fact that for

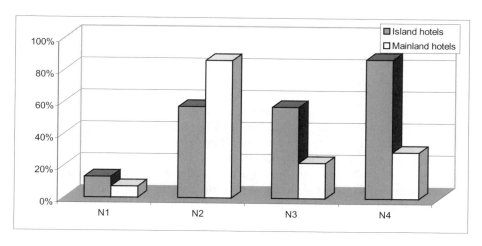

**Figure 11** Application of noise minimization measures in the hotel sample
*Note*: N1=Noise intrusion from air-conditioning, N2=Isolation of laundry/drier areas, N3=Minimisation of noise in restaurant/bar, and N4=Insulation of hotel from external sound sources

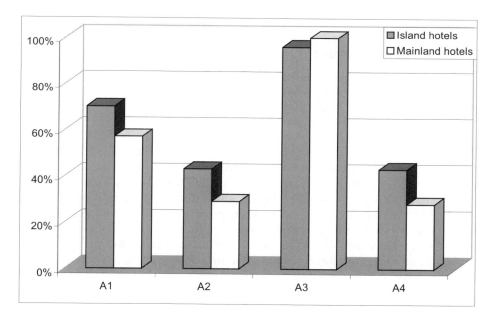

**Figure 12** Application of air emissions minimisation measures in the hotel sample
*Note*: A1=Low emission burners, A2=Ventilation systems in driers, A3=Ventilation system in kitchen, and A4=Designated smoking areas

hoteliers transportation costs are more significant (short term profits) than the conservation of their closed insular ecosystems.

The application of techniques to reduce the negative environmental impacts of hotel operations was not particularly developed, even when they were end-of-pipe solutions. This is clear in the case of wastewater treatment (Figure 10), where only a small number of the hotels had applied biological treatment measures, with the rest using the existing municipal sewage network (Ww1), and even fewer separating the kitchen and laundry slops (Ww3). The former percentage was slightly lower in island hotels compared to mainland ones, which indicates the low importance given to this liquid waste management in these areas. It is also evident in Figure 11, where noise minimisation from air-conditioning (N1) was extremely low, which is very disappointing in the case of Greece since many hotels operate in the summer season and the use of air-conditioning is very high. In the case of mainland hotels the results regarding noise minimisation in restaurants and bars (N3) are rather disappointing, as are the results for the minimisation of external noise (N4). It is observed that more mainland hotels have isolated laundry/drier areas than island hotels (N2), which may be due to the limited available space or restricted capital investment. Also Figure 12 shows that the minimisation of air-emissions from dryers (A2) was quite low, and that the air-quality was quite poor since most hotels did not have designated smoking areas (A4).

## The Proposed Labelling Scheme

The results from the environmental reviews for the Greek hotel sample led to the award criteria that are presented in Table 2. The criteria were set with an emphasis on their easy application and high efficiency, and on the promotion of managerial measures and of low-cost technical solutions.

Based on the results given, it was decided to distinguish between mandatory and optional criteria in the award criteria for the 'Green Flags' label. The mandatory criteria are those considered to be most important for all the hotels under review, and they aim to secure a minimal environmental compliance based on a core set of requirements, such as energy and water saving techniques, environmental awareness procedures, eco-product purchasing, waste management, and so on. The optional criteria are of lesser importance and aim to overcome the obstacles and weaknesses that were identified during the environmental reviews, and to encourage environmental improvements by the hoteliers. They can arise from existing constraints, such as water and electricity shortages, and could be measures such as water flow reducers (in the laundry and kitchen) along with rain and pool water recycling systems. In relation to wastewater, an optional measure could be grey irrigation for hotels that have extensive green grounds or cultivation. Also hoteliers could co-operate with neighbouring enterprises for noise minimisation. As for air-emissions, hotels could provide bicycle rental and maintenance manuals for staff. For the energy field, hoteliers could choose to install energy saving mechanisms, such as central heating/cooling and magnetic cards. They could also install biomass burners for water heating. Another optional measure concerning purchasing policies could be to use returnable packaging and eco-labelling products and to promote local cuisine.

**Table 2** Selected awarding criteria for the proposed label scheme

| Domain | Mandatory | Optional |
|---|---|---|
| **Waste** | 1. Waste management system (purchasing, collection, transportation, storing and disposal under hygiene laws and regulations)<br>2. Separation of different waste categories<br>3. Record and separate collection of hazardous wastes | 1. Large receptacles for food & beverage<br>2. Return of packaging material to the suppliers<br>3. Provision of fat slops to upgrade enterprises |
| **Energy** | 1. Lighting energy saving<br>2. Autonomous energy consumption measurements<br>3. Insulation requirements according to the national code for new buildings | 1. Renewable energy applications<br>2. Energy saving systems, such as central heating/cooling, and magnetic cards |
| **Water** | 1. Regular inspections and maintenance of water pipes and charges<br>2. Autonomous water consumption measurements<br>3. Signs for cautious water use | 1. Water flow reducers and devices (laundry, kitchen)<br>2. Pool and rain water recycling systems |
| **Wastewater** | 1. Compliance with 91/271/EEC (in case of own sewage treatment plant)<br>2. Regular biochemical analysis of effluents | 'Grey' irrigation for hotels that have extensive green grounds or cultivations |
| **Air emissions** | 1. Low emission burners<br>2. Ventilation systems (for the laundry and kitchen)<br>3. Designated smoking area in guest areas | 1. Bicycle rental<br>2. Maintenance manuals for staff |
| **Noise** | 1. Noise emission measurement<br>2. Properly informed staff | Noise minimisation measures |
| **Purchasing policy** | 1. Recyclable packaging material<br>2. Bulk packaging<br>3. Environmentally friendly detergents/agrochemicals | 1. Returnable packaging<br>2. Local cuisine<br>3. Eco-labelling products and/or biologically produced food |

*Note*: The optional criteria list includes only a few from the complete list

The 'Green Flags' label is intended to embrace the following principles:

- it should be voluntary;
- it should seek objectivity and transparency;
- it should seek constantly to update the consumer/client; and
- it should aim at Pan-European application (ADEME, 2001b).

The National Working Group decided on the procedures for awarding the label, including the acceptable total performance score, the method of inspection and the duration period of the validity of the label. These decisions were made under the direction of the National Competent Body (NCB). The former will be both the awarding and funding body, and its operational characteristics are summarised as follows:

- The operation of the NCB will be based on the operational framework of the existing relevant Standards Organisations of the member state (for Greece it is the Hellenic Standards Organisation – ELOT – and the National Competitive body for Eco-labels – ASAOS). It will be a non-profit organisation but its responsiveness will be ensured in some way, such as by the participating hotels making financial contributions.
- The supervision of the NCB will be undertaken by the European Commission and by the Regulatory Committee each member state has for certification issues.
- The executive commission of the NCB will be made up of representatives of tourism agencies, the government, consumers, and experts in the tourism sector and universities.
- The NCB will assign to its sub-commissions such tasks as verifying, training, dissemination and marketing (Figure 13).

The implementation of the 'Green Flags' scheme should take into account the following points concerning market penetration, finance and product development:

- The scheme should not attempt to intrude in areas related to other systems and should avoid any overlaps (Font & Tribe, 2001a).
- Assessing the costs of running the scheme, such as the costs of verification, market penetration and office administration, is vital for economic viability in the long term; the funding body will have to ask for a certain degree of self-financing (Font & Tribe, 2001b).
- The risk of lowering the eco-certification standards should be avoided. This may result from widening the target group when most small-scale hotels find it difficult to meet the costs of investing in innovative technologies needed to comply with standards while still maintaining profit margins (Salzhauer, 1991).

The structure of the proposed 'Green Flags' label scheme is presented in Figure 13.

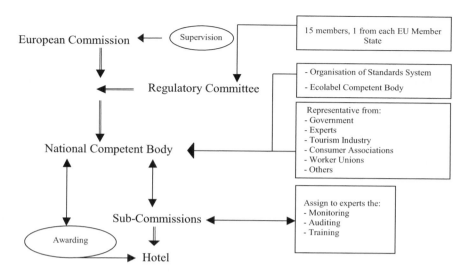

**Figure 13** Structure of the proposed 'Green Flags' labelling scheme

## Discussions and Recommendations

Few voluntary initiatives have taken place in the hotel industry in Greece concerning the environmental improvement of hotel operations. This can be attributed to hoteliers' reluctance to invest in these areas because of the cost of setting up environmentally sound practices and procedures. This has been determined in our survey and is also evident in other studies. In particular, the survey by Damasiotis *et al.* (1999) showed that there was a low penetration of energy saving systems and of renewable energy applications in Greece, apart from solar systems for water heating. This deficiency is attributed to the limited knowledge regarding these practices and the lack of expert personnel. Stylianopoulou (1998) also noted the absence of ameliorating measures to reduce environmental degradation in Cyprus. Furthermore, the inadequate actions to minimise environmental pressures (Christophoridis *et al.*, 2000) are exacerbated by the absence of long-term marketing actions and by the lack of contribution from the state (Buhalis & Diamantis, 2001). The findings of the environmental reviews for the 'Green Flags' scheme show that hoteliers tend to adopt only low-cost methods and practices and that there is weak monitoring of environmental issues, limited use of environmentally friendly materials and a random priority for end-of-pipe solutions. The aforementioned topics defined the final award criteria of the proposed labelling scheme in such a way as to motivate hoteliers toward environmental performance improvements taking into account the constraints and limitations related to their geographical context, existing infrastructure and their own behaviour.

The value of implementing such a label scheme is recognised by many. For example, the last OECD (2000) report on Greece called for more measures to integrate environmental concerns in tourism-related decisions, arguing that '...

further environmental management should be promoted within the tourism industry, using codes of good practice, dissemination of best practices within the profession, staff training programmes, environmental audits and voluntary agreements'. On the other hand, the activities of a few internationally well-known hotels as role models for the implementation of environmental initiatives has resulted in indifference to these issues among the national hotel industry bodies.

According to Miller (2001), the National Government should take a lead role in stimulating involvement in environmental initiatives in tourism by supporting and guiding stakeholders and then mediating their actions through regulation. This is considered to be the only way in which government can produce significant changes. But hoteliers should not be excused of responsibility for developing a voluntary approach. They should take steps despite the weak policy framework, the lack of infrastructure often due to the special problems of islands, and the deficient inspection of environmental matters by relevant local authorities. It is also unreasonable to consider that the existing initiatives (EMAS, ISO 14001 and Eco-labels) are the only approaches towards sustainability in the hotel sector.

Due to the economic context, the hospitality industry has responded to environmental issues mainly in those areas where there are direct financial benefits (energy and waste management) and where they are favoured by the fiscal and/or legislative requirements (Kirk, 1995). Clearly, there is still a vital need to find effective means of turning good intentions into action and of ensuring that hotels help to promote sustainability in Greece's tourism industry.

## Acknowledgements

The authors wish to acknowledge the support on the Greek National Working Group of Maria Valerga (Environment Department of Grecotel), Maria Maraka (GNTO) and Amalia Katsou (ASAOS). Furthermore, they appreciate support for the environmental reviews from Zisimos Evagelou, Vaggelis Piknis and Mania Kirioglou (Planning SA). Finally, the authors express their gratitude to the European Commission DG for the Environment for co-funding the LIFE Project 'Green Flags for Greener Hotels' ENV/F/000338.

## Correspondence

Any correspondence should be directed to Daphne Mavrogiorgos, Centre for Renewable Energy Sources, 19 km Marathonos Av., Pikermi 19 009 Greece (dmavro@cres.gr).

## References

Agence de l'Environnement et de la Maitrice de l'Energie (ADEME) (2001a) *Green Flags for Greener Hotels Project ENV98/338. Final report.* Volbonne, France: ADEME.
ADEME (2001b) *Green Flags for Greener Hotels Project ENV98/338. Summary Report for Dissemination.* Volbonne, France: ADEME.
Buhalis, D. and Diamantis, D. (2001) Tourism development and sustainability in the Greek archipelagos. In Ioannides, Apostolopoulos and S. Sonmez (eds) *Mediterranean Islands and Sustainable Tourism Development – Practices, Management and Policies* (pp. 143–70). London and New York: Continuum.

Centre for Renewable Energy Sources (2001) *Green Flags for Greener Hotels LIFE ENV/F/338 DG XI* [in Greek]. Athens: CRES.

Christoforidis, A., Zacharis, N. and Papazoglou, M. (2000) Implementation of the Eco-Management and Audit Scheme (EMAS) in hotels in Greece. In the *Proceedings of the Workshop EMAS – The Industry is Cleaned in the Whole of Europe, And You?* (pp. 80–91) [in Greek]. Athens: Local Authorities of Piraeus.

Consultancy and Research for Environmental Management (CREM) and CH21-HILL (2000) *Feasibility and Market Study for a European Eco-Label for Tourist Accommodation (FEMATOUR).* Commissioned by the European Commission, DG ENV. Phase I. Amsterdam.

Damasiotis, M., Giannakidis, G., Iatridis, M., Karagiorgas, M., Tzanakaki, E. and Alatopoulou, D.I. (1999) Definition of a strategy for energy efficiency and use of RES in the Mediterranean hotel sector. *Conference on Energy and Environment in the Mediterranean Hotel Sector,* CRES (pp. 15–27).

EEC Council Regulation (2000) No 1980/00, 26 June on a revised Community Ecolabel Award Scheme. *Official Journal of the European Communities* (21 September), 13.

European Commission (DG XI) and Ministry for Environment, Public Works and Siting (1999) *Eco-Management and Audit Scheme for the Greek Hotels – EMAS–H/GR Implementation Guidelines* [in Greek]. Athens.

Falirea, L. (2001) Green Flags from the project of the Centre for Renewable Energy Sources [in Greek]. *Tourism and Economy,* 32–9.

Font, X., Hass, E., Thorpe, K. and Forsyth L. (2001) Directory of tourism ecolabels. In X. Font and R.C. Buckley (eds) *Tourism Ecolabeling – Certification and Promotion of Sustainable Management* (pp. 271–349). Wallingford: CAPI.

Font, X. and Tribe, J. (2001) Promoting green tourism: The future of environmental awards. *International Journal of Tourism Research* 3 (1), 1–13.

Font, X. and Tribe, J. (2001b) The process of developing an ecolabel. In X. Font and R.C. Buckley (eds) *Tourism Ecolabeling – Certification and Promotion of Sustainable Management* (pp. 175–88). Wallingford: CABI.

Golphi, P.A.M., Dagli, K., Kavadias, D., Kradonellis K. and Pashalis P. (1994) Environmental impacts from tourism development. *Tourism and Environment: Opportunities for Sustainable Development* [in Greek] (pp. 8–29). Greek Technical Chamber (11 May).

Goodall, B. and Stabler, M.J. (1997) Principles influencing the determination of environmental standards for sustainable tourism. In M.J. Stabler (ed) *Tourism and Sustainability* (pp. 279–304). Wallingford: CABI.

Greek National Tourism Organisation (GNTO) (2001) Tourism statistics. On WWW at http://www.gnto.gr/2/01/eb10000.html.

Green Globe and World Travel & Tourism Council (1998) *Annual Review 1997/1998.* Cambridge: GG & WTTC.

Hamele, H. (2001) Ecolabels for tourism in Europe: The European Ecolabel for Tourism. In X. Font and R.C. Buckley (eds) *Tourism Ecolabeling – Certification and Promotion of Sustainable Management* (pp. 175–88). Wallingford: CABI.

Hillary, R. (1994) *The Eco-Management and Audit Scheme. A Practical Guide.* London: Stanley Thornes.

International Hotels Environment Initiative (IHEI) (1996) *Environmental Management for Hotels: The Industry Guide to Best Practice* (2nd edn). Butterworth Heinemann.

International Hotel & Restaurant Association (IHRA) and United Nations Environment Programme – Industry and Environment (UNEP) (1996) *Environmental Good Practice in Hotels Case Studies from IHRA Environmental Award.* Paris.

Iwanowski, K. and Rushmore, C. (1994) Introducing the eco-friendly hotel. *Cornell H.R.A. Quarterly* (February), 34–8.

Kirk, D. (1995) Environmental management in hotels. *International Journal of Contemporary Hospitality Management* 7 (6), 3–8.

Mediterranean Commission for Sustainable Development (MCSD), Plan Bleu and United Nations Environment Programme (UNEP) (1998) *Synthesis report of the working group: Tourism and sustainable development in the Mediterranean Region. Mediterranean Action Plan.* Monaco, 20–22 October.

Middleton, V.T.C. and Hawkins, R. (1997) Sustainability in the accommodation sector – with international illustrations. In *Sustainable Tourism: A Marketing Perspective* (pp. 144–58). Butterworth/Heinemann.

Miller, G. (2001) The development of indicators for sustainable tourism: Results of the Delphi survey of tourism researchers. *Tourism Management* 22, 351–62.

Ministry of Development (MD), Special Secretariat of Competitiveness (2001) *Operational Programme 'Competitiveness'* [in Greek]. Athens.

OECD (Organisation for Economic Co-operation and Development) (2000) Environmental performance review: Greece. *Sectoral Integration: Tourism* (pp. 147–64).

Papazoglou, M., Zacharis, N. and Christoforidis, A. (1999) Adaptation of the community Eco-Management and Audit Scheme (EMAS) and implementation in hotel installations. *Proceedings of the Conference Heleco '99* [in Greek] (pp. 238–46). Athens: Greek Technical Chamber.

Salzhauer, A. (1991) Obstacles and opportunities for a consumer ecolabel. *Environment* 33, 10–15, 33–7.

Splitter, R. and Haak, U. (2001) Quality analysis of tourism ecolabels. In X. Font and R.C. Buckley (eds) *Tourism Ecolabeling – Certification and Promotion of Sustainable Management* (pp. 175–88). Wallingford: CABI.

Stylianopoulou, E. (1998) The formulation of an environmental strategy in the Hotel Sector: The introduction of environmental management systems to hotels in Cyprus. In paper presented at the 1st International Scientific Congress 'Tourism and Culture for Sustainable Development', Department of Geography and Regional Planning, National Technical University of Athens, Greece.

Vellas, F. and Becherel, L. (1999) *The International Marketing of Travel and Tourism. A Strategic Approach*.

UNEP (1998) *Ecolabels in the Tourism Industry*. Paris: United Nations.

World Tourism Organisation (WTO) (2001) *Compendium of Tourism Statistics. 2001 Edition*. Madrid.

World Tourism and Travel Council (WTTC), WTO and Earth Council (EC) (1997) *Agenda 21 for the Travel and Tourism Industry – Towards Environmentally Sustainable Development*.

# 13 Sustainable Tourism: Utopia or Necessity? The Role of New Forms of Tourism in the Aegean Islands

*Ioannis Spilanis and Helen Vayanni*
*University of the Aegean, Department of Environmental Studies, Ex 'Xenia' Building, Mytilene, GR-81100, Greece*

Tourism is a major activity in the Greek islands. Its development during recent decades has stopped the economic and demographic decline of the area. The paper develops a framework for the appraisal of tourism's sustainability in the Greek islands, and it is concluded that the conventional tourist model, based on sun, sea and sand (3S) has failed to promote sustainability due to the limited economic benefits for host communities and growing environmental pressures. The latest trend in Greece and elsewhere is a shift from mass tourism to more environmentally friendly and sustainable forms of tourism. Policies to change tourism patterns in the Greek islands will need to take into consideration their unique characteristics, their existing realities, and to be based on the exploitation of the local natural and cultural resources in order to develop new forms of tourism. The purpose of this paper is to identify types of new forms of tourism that are being developed in the Aegean Islands, and to evaluate their impact. Various practical examples are presented, together with the difficulties involved in their implementation. The initiatives are in fact so recent that it is difficult to assess their tangible results.

## Introduction

Tourism is one of the most important, rapidly developing economic activities, especially since the last half of the 20th century (Fayos-Sola, 1996: 405; Koutsouris & Gaki, 1998). In Greece, and particularly in the Aegean archipelago, there are numerous small and medium-sized inhabited islands. For most of them, the basic economic activity for the past three decades has been tourism, which has influenced not only the economic life of the islands, but also their population structure and environmental conditions (Coccossis, 2001: 55–6; Haralambopoulos & Pizam, 1996: 504–6; Loukissas, 1982: 530–4; Mantoglou *et al.*, 1998: 87).

The fast and uncontrolled increase in tourist flows has caused significant negative impacts on the natural and built environment (Mathieson & Wall, 1982). In some cases, the phenomenon is so intense – and thus difficult to reverse – that, in combination with the low quality of services, it contributes to the continuous degradation of the tourist product and the reduction of profits for host communities and for the national economy. If this trend continues, the sustainability of the tourism industry is uncertain. This raises questions about the sustainability of the whole developmental process in the islands (Wall, 1997: 483), bearing in mind the principles of systems theory (Emblemsvang & Bras, 2000: 650; Nir, 1990: 77), since tourism is the most important activity of their economic system.

The emergence of new tourism destinations has increased the competition among existing mass tourism destinations catering for sun, sea and sand (3S). There has also been an increased differentiation of tourist demand and a trend to new forms of active, special interest tourism (Maroudas & Tsartas, 1998: 601). These forms of tourism (such as agrotourism, cultural, conference, maritime, gastronomic, and nature tourism) are based on the unique characteristics and resources of each area (Lagos, 1998: 598; Mantoglou *et al.*, 1998: 87; WWF Hellas, 2000: 8).

In the last two decades the growth of environmental concern and policies has also encouraged the increase in environmentally friendly products and services. The terms 'sustainability' and 'sustainable tourism' are now prevalent in the literature and in most development programmes, even though there is much confusion about their meaning and denotation (Wall, 1997: 483).

The purpose of this paper is to identify initiatives that have involved the development of new forms of tourism in the Aegean Islands and to evaluate their sustainability in comparison with the previous pattern of conventional tourism. In the next section, a framework is developed to evaluate the sustainability of different forms of tourism. There follows a brief consideration of tourism developments that have taken place in the islands. The last section presents some of the initiatives to differentiate the tourism supply in the Aegean Islands.

## Sustainability and New Forms of Tourism

A great problem in the literature is that there is no clear and operational definition of sustainable tourism. That leads to confusion about what sustainable tourism means in practice and about how it can be achieved (Swarbrooke, 1999: 13). Often sustainable tourism is thought to coincide with alternative forms of tourism and especially with ecotourism, which seems to be the most favoured and well known new form of tourism. This section seeks to clarify these terms and to define the way that they are used in the paper.

The World Tourism Organisation (WTO) defines sustainable tourism development as:

> Development that meets the needs of present tourists and host regions while protecting and enhancing opportunities for the future. It is envisaged as leading to management of all resources in such a way that economic, social and aesthetic needs can be fulfilled while maintaining cultural integrity, essential ecological processes, biological diversity and life support systems. (WTO, 2001)

This suggests sustainable tourism is a state of the tourist activity, although this definition needs more explanation and precision in order for it to be operational.

According to Swarbrooke (1999: 14), sustainable tourism differs in meaning from such terms as responsible tourism, alternative tourism, ecotourism, environmentally friendly tourism, minimum impact tourism, soft tourism and green tourism, even though it is related to them. While the majority of these terms are taken to imply tourism that is friendly to the environment, fewer are considered also to refer to tourism's economic and social impacts on host communities.

The inclusion of the term ecotourism in the above list is likely to cause most confusion since it is defined as 'environmentally responsible travel and visitation to relatively undisturbed natural areas, in order to appreciate nature (and any accompanying cultural features) that promotes conservation, has low visitor impacts, and provides for beneficially active socio-economic involvement of local populations' (as proposed by Boo, 1990: xiv, and also accepted by

**Table 1** Different forms and states of tourism activity

| *Approach* | *Conventional tourism* | *New forms of tourism* |
|---|---|---|
| Forms of tourism | • Sun, sea, and sand tourism (3S) | Alternative forms of tourism<br>• Agrotourism<br>• Ecotourism<br>• Cultural<br>• Trekking<br>• Nature |
| | • Mountain (Winter) tourism | Special interest tourism<br>• Conference<br>• Business trips<br>• Maritime<br>• Religious<br>• Health/spa<br>• Educational<br>• Sport<br>• Adventure |
| Mode of organisation | • Mass tourism<br>• Individuals<br>• Social tourism<br>• Second residence | • Small groups of tourists<br>• Individuals<br>• Social tourism |
| Tourist behaviour | • Indifference<br>• High consumption (depletion of resources) | • Responsibility<br>• Use of resources (not consumption) |
| State of tourism activity | Non-sustainable tourism | • Green tourism<br>• Economically sustainable tourism<br>• Sustainable tourism |

Ceballos-Lascurain, 1993; Fennell, 1999; Yunis, 2001). But this definition suggests that we should classify ecotourism as a new form of tourism, alongside agrotourism, cultural tourism, conference tourism, and not as a state of the tourism activity. The confusion is due to ecotourism having been considered to be friendly to the environment and to host communities, and consequently it has been identified with sustainable tourism. While this can be true, it only applies if the activity is also economically and socially viable in a specific region. Table 1 presents a classification of the different forms and states of tourism activity used in the literature.

From this perspective, tourism activity can be divided into two major categories: conventional tourism and new forms of tourism. The term 'conventional tourism' is used in a similar way to that of 'conventional economics' (Turner *et al.*, 1994) in order to highlight the importance of the market, the pricing of resources used as inputs, and a lack of regard for the environment, and of various externalities. It is also preferred to the term 'mass tourism', as mass tourism indicates the way the activity is organised (mass, standardised, low cost, and controlled by tour operators) and not a form of tourism or a conceptual approach. New forms of tourism are divided into alternative forms and special interest forms (Varvaressos, 1998: 76). Special forms of tourism are defined by the special motives that induce travel, while alternative forms of tourism are related to the way the travel is organised (relative autonomy) and to the tourists' willingness to learn about the host area and to consume environmentally friendly products.

New forms of tourism may be either economically viable or environmentally friendly or both. All new forms of tourism do not have the same environmental impacts, even though they are considered more sustainable than conventional tourism. For instance, conference and sport tourism are characterised by the creation of high added value but also by high consumption of resources (available land, water and energy) and by the need for huge installations (big conference centres, hotel resorts, sports fields, swimming pools, marinas etc), that have irreversible impacts on the environment. Moreover, the profits for the local population are not certain as the economic leakages can be very high.

Conventional tourism is not considered to be sustainable, since many problems have been identified in its application up to this time (Butler, 1991; Mathieson & Wall, 1982; Swarbrooke, 1999). Scientists, politicians, planners, the media and the public generate more confusion due to their different uses of the terms 'sustainable development' and 'sustainable tourism'. It is a matter of question whether we could characterise as sustainable tourism, on the one hand, the activities in Calvia (with 120,000 hotel beds and millions of bed nights) where the main objective of the businesses, local authorities and the public is the reduction of water and energy consumption and the management of wastes and ecologically fragile areas; and, on the other hand, the activities in a national park, where the basic objective is the management of a few hundreds of visitors, and the protection of the vulnerable ecosystem. But, despite there being such a difference between these two examples in terms of the scale of the activity and the purpose of the intervention, this can be accepted as long as it is agreed that sustainable development and sustainable tourism may be regarded as a process for the improvement of the economic, social and environmental performance from a given state (different for each area), and not as a well pre-defined situation (the same for all areas). Every attempt which contributes to the reduction of environmental pressures and the maintenance of environmental balance, in combination with the improvement of economic and social conditions in the host area, can be characterised as sustainable because there are different levels of sustainability (Swarbrooke, 1999: 7). The sustainability spectrum varies (Hunter, 1997: 853; Turner *et al.*, 1994: 31) from very weak sustainability (greening – efforts to reduce resource consumption and the production of wastes), to very strong sustainability (change in the model of development and in social behaviour) (Loinger, 1995: 10–15).

According to Inskeep (1991: 166), all types of tourism can be sustainable, under some conditions, such as that they respect the local society and environment of the area in which they are found. This is especially the case for the alternative forms of tourism developed in ecological sensitive areas and in areas with important cultural monuments that should be preserved and protected. Furthermore,

> the position at WTO is that all tourism activities, be they geared to holidays, business, conferences, congresses, or fairs, health, adventure or ecotourism itself, must be sustainable. This means that the planning and the development of tourism infrastructure, its subsequent operation and also its marketing should focus on environmental, social, cultural and economic sustainability criteria, so as to ensure that neither the natural environment, nor the socio-cultural fabric of the host communities will be impaired by the arrival of tourists; on the contrary, local communities should benefit from tourism, both economically and culturally. Sustainability implies that enterprises, as well as the communities in which they operate, have something to gain from tourism. (Yunis, 2001)

Every action plan that seeks to move away from conventional tourism and to apply new forms of tourism is welcome, since it is contributing to the area's sustainability. On the other hand, it is considered as utopian to believe that the development of economically sustainable tourism activities will have absolutely no environmental impact. Figure 1 shows that this change in the pattern of tourism development has at least three dimensions:

- improvement in the environmental performance of enterprises in the tourism industry, and the imposition of limits to tourism growth (green tourism);
- the development of special interest forms of tourism through exploitation of the natural and cultural characteristics of the area, which means that the increase in added value per capita that is created remains within the host area (special interest tourism); and
- the development of forms of tourism that have a low environmental impact and at the same time contribute to the preservation and exploitation of cultural heritage and the maintenance of population and economic activities in remote areas (alternative tourism).

In this proposed scheme in Figure 1 the effects of the socio-demographic system are not considered.

Changing the conventional tourism model is not an easy task because it is based on strong market mechanisms. However, it is not impossible, especially if we consider the recent changes in tourist preferences for vacations, the environmental awareness of consumers, and the development of environmentally friendly technologies.

In this paper, we consider as sustainable any form of tourism that, in a given area, alters the conventional tourist product so that it is a more economically profitable and/ or a more environmentally friendly product. The evaluation of tourism activity can be based on two criteria: first, the tourist performance per capita, which relates to the added value and the employment created per tourist, as well as the consumption of water and energy and the production of wastes per

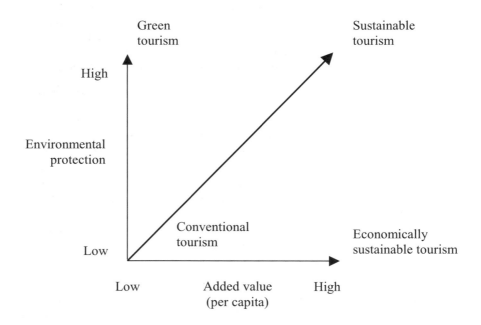

**Figure 1** Model of change in the pattern of tourism development

capita; and, secondly, the scale of the activity compared to the carrying capacity of the host area. Even if the performance per capita is improved, every area has its own environmental, social and economic limits that cannot be surpassed.

## Impacts and Limitations of Conventional Tourism in the Aegean Islands

Chapter 17 of Agenda 21 points out that islands are a special case, both in terms of their environment and development, and that they have specific problems in relation to sustainable development planning (Gortazar & Marin, 1999). Islands demonstrate significant differences and particularities in comparison to continental areas in terms of their natural resources, economic development, society and culture, lifestyles, landscape, and human settlements (Coccossis, 2001: 54). They tend to be ecologically fragile and vulnerable. Their small size, limited resources, geographical dispersion and isolation are characteristics of insularity, and these are considered to be obstacles to the development of islands compared to continental areas (EURISLES, 1997; European Parliament, 1996). These are the reasons why islands are characterised as 'less favoured areas' (LFA) in the European legislation, for which compensatory measures have been established. On the other hand, these specific characteristics make them attractive as tourist destinations (Coccossis, 2001: 54).

In Greece there are 112 inhabited islands, hundreds of uninhabited isles and a coastline of around 15,000 km. The large number of islands, the country's geographical position in the Mediterranean Sea with favourable climatic

**Table 2** Tourist flows in the South Aegean

| Geographical unit | Total number of beds | Annual number of nights spent in hotel establishments (1997) | | | Foreign tourists/ domestic tourists | Average duration of stay in hotel establishments (days), 1997 | | |
|---|---|---|---|---|---|---|---|---|
| | | Total | Domestic | Foreigner | | Total | Domestic | Foreigner |
| *Region of South Aegean* | 214,959 | 14,782,963 | 1,455,741 | 13,327,222 | | 7.78 | 3.69 | 8.84 |
| **Dodecanese** | **120,629** | **13,329,605** | **892,410** | **12,437,195** | **6.3** | **8.77** | **4.37** | **9.39** |
| Agathonissi | 0 | 3,004 | 432 | 2,572 | 2.45 | 7.02 | 3.48 | 8.46 |
| Astipalea | 297 | 2,176 | 1,425 | 751 | 0.56 | 4.01 | 4.11 | 3.85 |
| Kalimnos | 2,243 | 59,372 | 10,636 | 48,736 | 1.31 | 6.09 | 2.51 | 8.83 |
| Karpathos | 4,280 | 210,006 | 8,867 | 201,139 | 14.27 | 8.8 | 5.68 | 9.02 |
| Kassos | 32 | 606 | 536 | 70 | 0.21 | 4.3 | 4.58 | 2.92 |
| Kos | 35,115 | 4,158,247 | 152,324 | 4,005,923 | 10.94 | 9.76 | 4.27 | 10.26 |
| Lipsi | 205 | 1,268 | 393 | 875 | 2.38 | 4.58 | 4.79 | 4.49 |
| Leros | 1,845 | 9,811 | 5,695 | 4,116 | 0.36 | 4.76 | 3.76 | 7.58 |
| Megisti | 32 | 2,568 | 946 | 1,622 | 1.38 | 4.82 | 4.22 | 5.25 |
| Nisiros | 225 | 12,901 | 9,153 | 3,748 | 0.45 | 5.16 | 5.32 | 4.83 |
| Patmos | 2,182 | 45,567 | 23,012 | 22,555 | 0.74 | 3.79 | 3.33 | 4.4 |
| Rhodes | 73,080 | 8,802,027 | 673,558 | 8,128,469 | 5.76 | 8.69 | 4.5 | 9.42 |
| Symi | 678 | 21,459 | 5,244 | 16,215 | 1.64 | 4.16 | 2.68 | 5.06 |
| Tilos | 276 | 593 | 189 | 404 | 1.26 | 2.36 | 1.7 | 2.89 |

**Table 2** (*cont.*) Tourist flows in the South Aegean

| Geographical unit | Total number of beds | Annual number of nights spent in hotel establishments (1997) | | | Foreign tourists/ domestic tourists | Average duration of stay in hotel establishments (days) 1997 | | |
|---|---|---|---|---|---|---|---|---|
| | | Total | Domestic | Foreigner | | Total | Domestic | Foreigner |
| **Cyclades** | **94,330** | **1,453,358** | **563,331** | **890,027** | **1.13** | **3.6** | **3.07** | **4.15** |
| Amorgos | 2,183 | 641 | 513 | 128 | 0.43 | 4.22 | 4.84 | 2.78 |
| Andros | 4,196 | 53,981 | 37,349 | 16,632 | 0.33 | 3.12 | 2.86 | 3.92 |
| Antiparos | 1,689 | 5,585 | 1,315 | 4,270 | 2.45 | 4.97 | 4.03 | 5.35 |
| Ios | 5,228 | 52,343 | 6,238 | 46,105 | 5.34 | 3.67 | 2.78 | 3.84 |
| Kea | 989 | 4,966 | 4,654 | 312 | 0.04 | 2.54 | 2.49 | 3.76 |
| Kythnos | 1,283 | 17,427 | 16,996 | 431 | 0.05 | 7.44 | 7.6 | 3.99 |
| Milos | 3,136 | 32,554 | 22,678 | 9,876 | 0.36 | 3.63 | 3.43 | 4.16 |
| Mykonos | 13,785 | 704,518 | 155,532 | 548,986 | 2.53 | 3.91 | 3.04 | 4.25 |
| Naxos | 8,633 | 58,556 | 23,786 | 34,770 | 1.16 | 3.88 | 3.41 | 4.28 |
| Paros | 18,236 | 191,464 | 84,353 | 107,111 | 1.27 | 3.91 | 3.91 | 3.9 |
| Serifos | 1,455 | 9,176 | 7,196 | 1,980 | 0.21 | 3.31 | 3.15 | 4.06 |
| Sifnos | 3,190 | 13,108 | 9,665 | 3,443 | 0.28 | 2.95 | 2.79 | 3.5 |
| Syros | 3,966 | 104,760 | 87,869 | 16,891 | 0.16 | 2.91 | 2.82 | 3.49 |
| Thira (Santorini) | 20,688 | 105,069 | 21,682 | 83,387 | 2.75 | 3.98 | 3.08 | 4.31 |
| Tinos | 3,607 | 99,210 | 83,505 | 15,705 | 0.11 | 2.26 | 2.1 | 3.65 |

*Source:* National Statistical Service of Greece

conditions, and the area's rich history and ancient Greek civilisation (Buhalis & Diamantis, 2001; Chiotis & Coccossis, 1992) have led to the rapid development of tourism activity.

Tourism development in Greece is for its greatest part based on islands where the 3S model has been applied for many years (Mantoglou *et al.*, 1998: 87). Conventional tourism in the islands is largely based on organised charter flights for foreign tourists (mass tourism). Domestic tourists also form an important part of the market, and they largely travel individually. Finally, there are also many visitors who own secondary residences in the islands, particularly in those close to big urban centres (Egina, Kea, Andros, Spetses, Kythnos, Serifos, Syros) which are gradually becoming integrated into the metropolitan system and zone of influence as areas for recreation and secondary housing (Coccossis, 2001).

Various indicators, such as the size and the amount of tourist accommodation and the number of tourists, demonstrate the importance of islands for Greece's tourism development. As much as 54% of Greece's tourist accommodation is concentrated in six prefectures, four of them being insular. Furthermore, 73.8% of Greece's tourist accommodation is situated in 12 out of the country's 52 prefectures, and nine of the 12 are insular (NSSG, 1999). In the Aegean Islands there is 27.6% of the total hotel beds in Greece (597,855 beds); in Crete there is 19.6% and in the Ionian Islands 10.2%. In total, islands contribute 57.3% of the hotel beds of the whole country. Moreover, 65.0% of the total tourist nights spent are accounted for in insular prefectures (32.7% in the Aegean Islands; 61.4% of which are in Rhodes, 21.8% in Crete and 10.6% in the Ionian Islands).

Even in a rather homogeneous region such as the Region of South Aegean the pattern of tourism development is different for each island. These differences concern the scale and the form of tourism development. For example, big hotels and foreigner tourists are concentrated in a few islands (Rhodes, Kos, Thira, Mykonos, Paros), while domestic tourists visit all of the islands and stay in rooms to let (Table 2).

Conventional tourism has helped to halt previous economic problems and population losses through the creation of new jobs, which to an extent balanced the loss of jobs in agriculture and manufacturing, and through increases in the domestic product and income (Coccossis, 2001: 55; Lagos & Gkrimpa, 2000). The fact that many people are occupied in the tourism sector led to population growth and to a reduction of the out-migration rate that had been very high in the Aegean Islands over previous decades (Sophoulis & Assonitis, 1998: 141) (Table 3).

The percentage of workers in the tourism sector compared to all sectors is very high, especially in the Cyclades and Dodecanese (the Region of South Aegean) where it was 11.97% in 1981 and 26.08% in 1991, compared with 3.69% and 4.95% in Greece as a whole (Coccossis & Tsartas, 2001: 216). Furthermore, according to Buhalis and Diamantis (2001: 146), in most cases the tertiary sector (mainly tourism) generates over 50% of the regional product of the islands, although the multiplier effect increases the impact of tourism and stimulates the entire economy both regionally and nationally. The data indicate that, particularly in the Region of South Aegean, tourism is almost the only economically dynamic activity (and thus could be depicted as a monoculture).

Economic growth is positively related to the intensity and the duration of tourism development, which varies among the insular prefectures of Greece. In

**Table 3** Area, population and tourist growth in the prefectures of the Aegean archipelago

| | Total area (km²) | Total population | | | | | Total number of tourists | | Total nights spent |
|---|---|---|---|---|---|---|---|---|---|
| | | 1951 | 1971 | 1981 | 1991 | 2001* | 1981 | 1991 | 1999 |
| Greece | 131,957 | 7,632,801 | 8,768,641 | 9,740,417 | 10,259,900 | 10,939,605 | 10,332,301 | 9,700,693 | 60,256,902 |
| Lesvos | 2,154 | 154,795 | 114,802 | 104,620 | 105,082 | 108,294 | 35,983 | 62,172 | 685,150 |
| Samos | 778 | 59,709 | 41,709 | 40,519 | 41,965 | 43,574 | 46,424 | 59,877 | 1,088,960 |
| Chios | 904 | 66,823 | 53,948 | 49,865 | 52,184 | 52,290 | 23,089 | 26,792 | 213,248 |
| Dodecanese | 2,714 | 121,480 | 121,017 | 145,071 | 163,476 | 190,564 | 735,314 | 1,051,164 | 16,111,383 |
| Cyclades | 2,572 | 125,959 | 86,337 | 88,458 | 94,005 | 111,181 | 180,179 | 247,751 | 1,593,711 |
| Crete | 8,336 | 462,124 | 456,642 | 502,165 | 540,054 | 601,159 | 953,898 | 1,147,458 | 13,116,526 |

*Source*: National Statistical Service of Greece; Annual socio-economic magazine NOMOI 2001. * Provisional data

**Table 4** Main indicators for the insular prefectures

| | Natural population movement per 1000 inhabitants | GDP per capita (% of the country's average) (million drs) | Deposits per capita (million drs) | Income per capita (% of the country's average) (million drs) |
|---|---|---|---|---|
| | 1998 | 2001 | 1998 | 1999 |
| Greece | -0.16 | 100 | 1.57 | 100 |
| Lesvos | -3.93 | 84 | 1.63 | 80 |
| Samos | -6.52 | 100 | 1.91 | 88 |
| Chios | -4.67 | 83 | 1.91 | 97 |
| Dodecanese | 5.53 | 127 | 1.78 | 88 |
| Cyclades | -0.29 | 102 | 2.22 | 103 |

*Source*: Annual socio-economic magazine NOMOI 2001

the Dodecanese, the prefecture with the greatest number of tourists, almost all indicators (e.g. demographic, economic, and other welfare indicators) are higher than the national average, classifying it among the most developed prefectures in the country (Table 4).

On the other hand, there have been many changes that negatively affect the sustainability of the Aegean Islands. The most important negative impacts are related to: (1) the inability to invest the profits coming from tourism activity in order to increase the physical capital and the local production capacity; (2) the reduction in quality and quantity of natural and cultural capital; and (3) the relatively low educational level of employees (human capital) in the area because conventional tourism offers few opportunities for employees to obtain skills or for the application of innovation (Maroudas & Tsartas, 1998: 606). The main reasons for the emergence of economic problems are the low added value per tourist (mainly due to the oligopolistic tourist market, the low tourist expenditure, the high level of competition among destinations offering the same product (3S), and the instability of demand due to external factors), the leakage of income from the local economy and the transfer of surplus value from the area to origin countries (Aisner & Pluss, 1983: 247; Deprest, 1997: 28–30).

Environmental problems have also appeared because of the construction of large-scale infrastructure, the urbanisation and congestion resulting from increased tourist numbers, the exteriorisation of the operational costs of hotels, and increases in energy and water consumption and in the production of solid wastes. These are the main factors that jeopardise the sustainability of the tourism sector as well as of the whole development process.

In a report of the Greek National Tourism Organisation and the Centre of Planning and Economic Research (GNTO & CPER, 1994: I.3.2 – translation), the economic problems of the tourism sector are clearly identified:

> The Greek tourist product is not reviving, remaining at the status quo. The competitiveness is achieved by continuous reductions in prices. The revenues are also reduced and in many cases the price of the tourist product does not even cover the costs. This is what has happened in many areas in Greece, over the last fifteen-year period.

This conclusion comes out of the analysis of economic data at a national level (expenditure per capita, the GDP generated from tourism and how it compares with other tourist destinations in Europe and elsewhere in the Mediterranean).

Unfortunately, despite the considerable qualitative information indicating the limits to the positive effects of conventional tourism and the sustainability problems, there are no comparable statistical data. This problem also relates to the economic (e.g. the tourist expenditure, the income multiplier etc.) and environmental parameters (e.g. the quantity and consumption of drinking water, the quality of bathing water etc.) at the island level.[1] Such data are essential for the appraisal of the situation and for the evaluation of the policies that are adopted.

Certainly, there are data indicating the increasing tourist pressure on the islands (Figure 2), which do indicate the presence of environmental problems and threats to the sustainability of the system. Analysing these data, it can be seen that there are marked pressures on some islands, such as Mykonos, Kos, Santorini, Paros, Ios and Rhodes, but the data are insufficient to draw firm

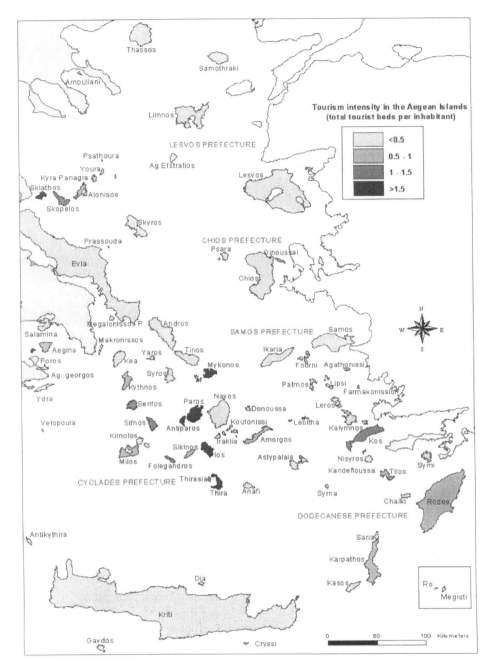

**Figure 2** Tourism intensity in the Aegean Islands

**Table 5** Tourism pressure indicator (beds/surface area and beds/inhabitant)

| Geographical unit | Total number of beds/km² | Total number of beds/inhabitant |
|---|---|---|
| Kassos | 0.48 | 0.03 |
| Astipalea | 2.09 | 0.16 |
| Anafi | 2.58 | 0.36 |
| Kimolos | 2.91 | 0.13 |
| Megisti | 3.50 | 0.08 |
| Tilos | 4.39 | 0.52 |
| Chalki | 5.01 | 0.33 |
| Nisiros | 5.43 | 0.24 |
| Sikinos | 5.48 | 0.93 |
| Schinoussa | 7.46 | 0.28 |
| Kea | 7.68 | 0.33 |
| Andros | 10.53 | 0.40 |
| Amorgos | 11.02 | 0.71 |
| Symi | 11.67 | 0.26 |
| Lipsi | 12.83 | 0.29 |
| Kythnos | 12.93 | 0.80 |
| Karpathos | 14.21 | 0.65 |
| Serifos | 15.77 | 0.83 |
| Tinos | 17.32 | 0.39 |
| Naxos | 17.92 | 0.43 |
| Milos | 19.25 | 0.61 |
| Kalimnos | 20.23 | 0.13 |
| Folegandros | 23.64 | 1.16 |
| **Cyclades** | **32.89** | **0.76** |
| Leros | 33.05 | 0.22 |
| Sifnos | 36.68 | 1.11 |
| *Region of South Aegean* | 38.64 | 0.68 |
| Ios | 38.67 | 2.27 |
| Antiparos | 39.42 | 1.30 |
| Syros | 43.64 | 0.18 |
| **Dodecanese** | **44.10** | **0.63** |
| Rhodes | 52.05 | 0.62 |
| Patmos | 57.39 | 0.65 |

**Table 5** (*cont.*) Tourism pressure indicator (beds/surface area and

| Geographical unit | Total number of beds/km$^2$ | Total number of beds/inhabitant |
|---|---|---|
| Paros | 81.84 | 1.25 |
| Koufonissi | 110.53 | 1.72 |
| Kos | 120.18 | 1.16 |
| Mykonos | 154.25 | 1.36 |
| Thira (Santorini) | 253.37 | 1.60 |

*Source*: National Statistical Service of Greece

conclusions about the overall level of sustainability. There is also useful information showing that some small islands, such as Patmos, Syros, Antiparos, and
Koufonissi, are experiencing relatively high pressures despite tourism activity
not being so important.

## Efforts to Differentiate the Tourism Supply

The problem of the sustainability of tourism in Greece has been recognised
since the early 1990s, and this has led to some dispersed efforts to differentiate
the tourist product, more at the local rather than the national level, but without
any strategic plan. In order to promote sustainable tourism, effort has been
directed to supply high quality, differentiated tourist products instead of mass
and standard tourist services. The latter refers to services – basically accommodation, catering, and entertainment – that are low cost and low added value, and
that involve poorly educated employees and that freely consume natural
resources. By contrast, the former refers to an integrated product, based on the
endogenous characteristics of the area, that has high added value, attracts tourists of a high educational level, incorporates recent research and innovation
techniques, employs skilled employees and has high environmental standards.

The efforts in various islands to move away from the conventional model and
towards new tourist products are discussed next, and are classified in the three
categories presented earlier. The first category is the greening process, where
efforts are made to reduce the environmental impacts of tourism establishments.
The second category involves forms of special interest tourism, where the
economic profits are bigger, but not the environmental benefits. Finally, the third
category of alternative forms of tourism involves activities that are more profit-
able for the local economy than conventional tourism and also more environmentally friendly.

### First category: Green(-ing) tourism

Even though tourism's negative impacts in insular environments have been
identified several times, either in the scientific literature or at a political level, the
actions taken to promote the greening of tourism activity in the Greek islands
have been limited. These actions involved both the private and the public sectors.

As far as the private sector is concerned, there have been few attempts at the
greening of companies by applying one of the environmental management

systems, such as ISO 14000 (International Organisation for Standardisation) or EMAS (Eco-Management and Audit Scheme). In Greece, there is only one hotel (located on the mainland) that possesses the EMAS certification (INEM, 2002). According to the Hellenic Organisation for Standardisation, there are nine hotels in Greece (all of them situated in Crete) that have been certified with ISO 9001, which relates to the quality of service; and four of them also possess ISO 14001 certification (HOS, 2002).

Other actions have been taken that do not relate to the procedures of a specific standard. In 1992, Grecotel, the largest hotel company in Greece, with 22 four- and five-star hotels mostly situated in the islands, became the first hotel group in the Mediterranean to establish an environmental and cultural department (Buhalis & Diamantis, 2001). Furthermore, some hotels have taken steps to reduce their consumption of resources (mainly water and energy) by using the financing opportunities for the upgrading of old hotels contained within the Law for Development. Moreover, steps have been taken to use non-chloride cleaning products in order to reduce toxic wastes, and to use large packages of food so as to reduce solid wastes, etc.

As far as the public sector is concerned, many projects have been introduced since 1987 for the protection of the environment by both regional and local authorities, financed by the European Structural Funds. Specifically, many sewerage networks and plants have been constructed in insular areas to treat wastewater and thus to reduce sea pollution. However, there are few projects involving the management and recycling of solid wastes (Arapis *et al.*, 1996; EC Structural Funds, 1995).

Finally, the application of Local Agenda 21 plans, which can contribute to the reduction of environmental pressures, was not successful in Greece. In the insular regions, it was applied only in Zakynthos, for the management of solid wastes.

It can be concluded that environmental issues are not a high priority for either the public or private sectors, despite the many complaints expressed about mismanagement from tourists and tour operators.

## Second category: Development of special interest tourism

Some distinctive forms of special interest tourism in the Aegean Islands are now examined.

### Conference tourism

This specialist form of tourism is quite developed in such islands as Rhodes, Kos and Crete, where there are hotels with appropriate facilities for this kind of tourism (usually luxury, large-scale units) (Lagos & Gkrimpa, 2000). It is not far removed from conventional tourism as far as its negative environmental impact is concerned, due to the substantial infrastructure, low consumption of local products, and lack of connection to the local culture. The advantage of confer- ence tourism is that it can be applied throughout the year, and especially in the off-season, and thus its importance for hoteliers and local employment is great.

The existence of small-scale conference infrastructure on other islands, such as Santorini, Samos, Chios, Lesvos and Limnos, has helped in the development of this type of tourism, which is smaller in scale and better adapted to the environment. In many cases, the construction of conference centres was based on the renovation of old buildings, which has helped in maintaining the local traditional architectural style, contributing to the conservation and reuse of the cultural heritage and built environment.

## Maritime tourism

A large project for the construction of marinas in the islands, in order to increase the number of yachts in the area year-round, was not successful. In many islands though, smaller projects have taken place to improve existing docks and provide yacht accommodation.

The Minister of the Aegean is trying to invigorate maritime tourism, particularly for the small islands with few or no inhabitants, by securing finance from various European Programmes (e.g. Interreg) to develop small-scale infrastructure for yachts. The objective of the project is to attract more tourists with specific interests in sailing and at the same time to create the conditions to lengthen their stay in the islands. These efforts aim to offer more activities, away from the ports, to watch the unique flora and fauna and to admire the unspoiled landscape. For this purpose, the Minister has established offshore sailing races (Aegean Regatta) among the small islands of the Aegean archipelagos in order to attract more visitors. During the races, many cultural events are organised for the participants and for local people and tourists.

## Sea sport tourism

Even though Greece has an unquestioned comparative advantage in this form of tourism, no major initiatives have been undertaken. In Paros, where the wind and wave conditions are favourable, surfers gather every summer and take part in formal and informal races. Scuba diving is developing, although the National Archaeological Service does not give its permission, in order to restrict the illicit trade of antiquities. Mykonos, Paros, Rhodes, Kos and Kalimnos are the islands in the South Aegean with scuba diving schools.

## Religious tourism

There are a great number of religious monuments (churches and monasteries) on many islands (Tinos, Patmos, Lesvos, Chios, Paros, Amorgos) that are part of the national cultural heritage and attract visitors from all over the country (Lagos & Gkrimpa, 2000). Additional benefits from this form of tourism include its off-season pattern of visitation, the increased demand for the consumption of local products, and the contribution to preserving tradition.

## Therapeutic (health) tourism

This form is based on the great number of hot springs (spas) in many islands (e.g. Ikaria, Kythnos, Lesvos, Rhodes, Kos) (Didaskalou, 2000). The lack of modern facilities and absence of joint promotion with natural and healthy lifestyles has resulted in a comparatively small number of tourists. Moreover, most of these hot spring locations have not diversified their product, and as a result the number of visitors is declining (Didaskalou, 2000).

## Educational tourism

The University of the Aegean and the funding potential from the EU for the development of educational tourism has encouraged summer schools in Lesvos,

Serifos, and Milos, and summer camps in Pserimos and Megisti. Moreover, on their own initiative Norwegian students visit Lesvos every year and study on the island from April to October.

## Third category: Development of alternative tourism activities

This category includes forms of tourism related to natural and cultural resources, and there are a large number of examples.

### Agrotourism

This was one of the first alternative forms of tourism to be applied systematically in Greece, using European funding for rural development. Almost two-thirds of agrotourist accommodation in Greece is located in the islands (NSSG, 1999). In the South Aegean, there are three agrotourist holdings in the Cyclades and 14 in the Dodecanese. However, most agrotourist holdings are in the islands of the North Aegean (56 in Lesvos, 16 in Chios, and 39 in Samos) (Hellenic Ministry of Agriculture, 2002).

The outcomes often sought from agrotourism are: (1) to complement and to raise farmers' income, (2) the improvement of living and working conditions of rural residents, (3) to boast the production of local agricultural and handcraft products, (4) the protection of the environment, (5) the conservation, promotion and the uses of cultural and architectural heritage, and finally (6) the development of a different form of tourism. But in fact the new accommodation facilities have been constructed near to rural areas, and without offering any services, products or activities on the farm, as they were supposed to. The tourists do not stay on farms and do not gain experiences of the farmers' everyday lives. In most cases, there is not even food included in the proposed services, or when it is, the products are not from the farm. Basically, this accommodation was never agrotourist, and it has just operated as a complement to hotels and rooms to let. These assertions have been confirmed by research in Lesvos, where there are the most agrotourist holdings of all insular areas. The results show that, even if the agrotourism programme appears successful in terms of income improvement and farmer willingness to maintain their agricultural activity, most agrotourist holdings in Lesvos operate in the shadow of mass tourism. The customers and the products are the same, and there is no connection with agricultural production, local products, or environmental and cultural landscape conservation. Agrotourism in Lesvos is conventional tourism operated by farmers, but not agrotourism (Gousiou *et al.*, 2001).

### Cultural tourism

Today, efforts to develop cultural tourism aim to expand from inactive archaeological tourism at world-famous sites, to the active exploration of aspects of local contemporary culture: local cuisine, settlements, and traditional activities and customs. In many islands there are thematic museums based on a special natural or cultural characteristic of the area, or a traditional activity. Examples are the olive museums (Andros, Lesvos), soap and ouzo museums (Lesvos), museums of industrial and mine activity (Syros, Milos), and maritime museums (Chios, Crete, Andros, Symi) (Carley & Antonoglou, 2000).

*Ecotourism*

Ecotourism and activities related to nature, especially in protected areas (Ramsar and Natura 2000 sites), were very successful by the early 1990s. The most famous and developed areas in Greece are the forest of Dadia, the Prespes, Kerkini and Plastira lakes, the mountain of Pindos and the deltas of many rivers (e.g. Evros, Nestos, Galikos etc.) (Koutsouris & Gaki, 1998). The main activities in these areas are bird-watching, canoeing, kayak, climbing, mountain bike and trekking (WWF Hellas, 2000).

Until now, the exploitation of natural resources has led to varying results in the islands. A very well-known paradigm is the gorge of Samaria in Crete, which is a protected area, according to the UNESCO's monument list. There are hundreds of visitors every day during the summer, walking and littering for seven hours in the gorge, often having no previous information about the duration of the visit and the hot weather conditions. This activity destroys the natural environment, while at the same time the tourists themselves cannot enjoy their excursion.

The situation is almost the same in the island of Rhodes. In the Valley of Butter-flies (a protected area of the Natura 2000 network), thousands of butterflies gather in a unique ecosystem. This phenomenon, even if it is a matter for protection, has become a tourist resource. Many tourists visit the area every day in order to admire the unique environment, and they impact on the special fauna and its habitat.

However, there are some successful examples of ecotourism, even if they are recent and not very well known. An example is bird watching in Lesvos. In this island there are many wetlands and two salinas, where there are many rare bird species. Numerous tourists with a special interest in birds visit the island just to watch and photograph them during the low tourist season. These tourists travel individually or in small groups during the birds' migration period (March to May and October to November). They are aware and sensitive about environmental protection. This kind of vacation contributes to prolonging the tourist season, and thus it improves the profits from the tourist activity, while at the same time it does not demand specific large-scale infrastructure (Spilanis, 1995).

There are similar patterns in South Crete, where tourism is not developed compared to its northern part, as tourists travel there only for the purpose of watching dolphins and whales. They travel by small boats, studying these species that are rare in the Mediterranean Sea.

Finally, another successful example of ecotourism is practised in Lesvos by the Natural History Museum of the Petrified Forest. The main objective of the museum is to protect and increase awareness of the Petrified Forest. Many activities are organised by the museum for the development of ecotourism and geotourism: there is a network of trails, called 'lava trails', and conferences are organised about the geology. Finally, there are also some educational and research activities, in collaboration with various overseas universities (Zouros, 1996: 179–92).

Trekking activities have been developed in various islands (Lesvos, Chios, Kea, Andros, Syros, Amorgos, Naxos, Folegandros and Serifos). There are paths with the necessary signs and specific guidebooks to help tourists to discover the 'hidden' beauties of the islands.

While there are many success stories, there are also problems in the development of ecotourism. In Greece, most of the successful examples are in rural and mountainous areas of the mainland or in protected areas (WWF Hellas, 2000). This has contributed to the development of 'weekend tourism', with visitors coming from big urban centres. In one study (Tsartas *et al.*, 2001: 39, 41) it was shown that for mountaineering tourism the greatest part of the demand comes from the two large urban centres of the country (about 43.0% of tourists come from Athens and Thessaloniki). For ecotourism the percentage of travellers from the two larger urban centres was 48.0%.

Since the islands are geographically remote and far away from the mainland, travelling to them is rather expensive and difficult, especially in winter due to bad weather conditions, and thus this form of tourism is much less likely to succeed there. Moreover, most of the islands are so small that there is practically no hinterland. There are no ecosystems such as big mountains, forests, wetlands, rivers, and lakes, where many alternative forms of tourism (such as climbing, rafting, and canoeing) take place. Thus, the potential for the development of such forms of tourism in the islands is limited.

One can conclude that the 'coexistence' of mass and alternative tourism is rather difficult in the limited geographical area of an island. For the moment, mass tourism 'allows' the development of some nature activities that enrich its product, but this does not permit a change in the development pattern and the emergence of real alternative tourism products.

## Conclusions

Tourism in Greece and especially in the islands is a major activity. Its development over recent decades has stopped the economic and demographic decline of the area. However, it seems that nowadays the current tourism model based on 3S tourism does not fulfil the tourist demand, and there is a need to change (Lagos, 1998: 593; Mantoglou *et al.*, 1998: 87, 90) in order to continue to generate profits for the local society. On the other hand, pressure from the tourism activity on the environment downgrades the natural and cultural resources of the islands, on which their sustainable development depends.

In order to solve or at least reduce the problems of mass tourism, the policy proposed here is the application of new forms of tourism. However, these forms are not always economically and environmentally sustainable. While most of them have been applied successfully in the mainland, they cannot be applied successfully in the islands as easily due to their unique characteristics (geographical, demographic, economic etc).

There are only limited data for the islands in Greece on which to evaluate their sustainability level, but the efforts that have been undertaken until now for sustainable tourism development can be classified in three categories: the greening of the activity, the development of special interest tourism, and the development of alternative forms of tourism. These forms of tourism have emerged relatively recently in the Aegean Islands, and they are developing without a strategic plan at either national or local levels, so it is difficult to produce tangible results. Furthermore, it is impossible to distinguish between the effects of the different forms of tourism as they are interrelated and no specific survey has been undertaken.

The fact that there is an international trend towards these forms does not necessarily mean that they can be applied in all cases and in every location, without taking into account the local realities and characteristics. The ultimate goal is sustainable development; within this concept the tourism activity should encourage sustainable tourism. Since strong sustainability (both environmental protection and economic development) is a very difficult and long-term task, it seems sensible that it should be accomplished by taking small steps. The first feasible step is the greening of the tourism sector in all areas and in all forms of tourism. This will lead to the improvement of environmental conditions. The second step is the improvement of economic performance.

This means that islands which are already developed as tourist destinations should adopt tourism development strategies with an emphasis on encouraging the control of the tourist activity, while upgrading the quality of services and the environment. In those islands where tourism is not yet a major activity, some forms of alternative tourism can be implemented. This is easier in the bigger islands, such as Lesvos, Chios, and Ikaria, than in the small ones.

It seems that mass tourism can coexist more easily with special interest forms of tourism than with alternative ones, as the hinterland in the islands does not lend itself to the development of markedly different tourism patterns. On islands where the tourism pressure is already high, greening the activity has to be the priority, as well as drawing on the local characteristics in order to develop forms of special interest tourism. The change of the actual tourism pattern to a more sustainable one will be easier if appropriate planning mechanisms are established.

Strategies for tourism need to be based on local particularities and natural and socioeconomic characteristics, taking into account the intensity and the type of tourism development (Mantoglou *et al.*, 1998: 93). These strategies have to reflect the dynamics of tourism development, setting specific objectives for the development of tourism in each island in the context of its general goals of sustainable development (Coccossis, 2001). A new development model is needed that will integrate the islands' particularities in the wider regional planning process and that will facilitate the implementation of tourism strategy and policy based on special interest tourism (Lagos, 1998: 593).

## Correspondence

Any correspondence should be directed to Ioannis Spilanis, University of Aegean, Department of Environmental Studies, Ex "Xenia" Building, Mytilene, GR-81100, Greece (gspi@env.aegean.gr).

## Note

1. The efforts made by the network EURISLES to set up a database for all the European islands (EURISLES, 2002), and by the Laboratory of Local and Island Development of the University of the Aegean for the Greek Islands (GRISLES) cannot overcome the lack of data.

## References

Aisner, P. and Pluss, C. (1983) *La Ruée Vers le Soleil: Le Tourisme à Destination du Tiers Monde*, Paris: L'Harmattan.
Annual socio-economic magazine *NOMOI 2001* [in Greek].

Arapis, T., Anagnostopoulou, K., Bouchy, I. and Micha, I. (1996) *Tourism and the Structural Funds: The Case for Environmental Integration*. Brussels: Birdlife International.

Boo, E. (1990) *Ecotourism: The Potentials and Pitfalls*. Washington: WWF.

Buhalis, D. and Diamantis, D. (2001) Tourism development and sustainability in the Greek archipelagos. In D. Ioannides, Y. Apostolopoulos and S. Sonmez (eds) *Mediterranean Islands and Sustainable Tourism Development: Practices, Management and Policies* (pp. 143–70). New York: Continuum.

Butler, R.W. (1991) Tourism, environment, and sustainable development. *Environmental Conservation* 18 (3), 201–9.

Carley, M. and Antonoglou, D. (2000) Tourist-Dependent Symi: Sustainable future for a small island? *Proceedings of the International Scientific Conference on Tourism on Islands and Specific Destinations*. Chios, Greece: University of the Aegean.

Ceballos-Lascurain, H. (1993) *The IUCN Ecotourism Consultancy Programme*. Mexico: DF.

Chiotis, G. and Coccossis, H. (1992) Tourism development and environmental protection in Greece. In J. Van der Straaten and H. Briassoulis (eds) *Tourism and the Environment: Regional, Economic, and Policy Issues* (pp. 133–43). Dordrecht: Kluwer.

Coccossis, H. (2001) Sustainable development and tourism in small islands: Some lessons from Greece. *Anatolia* 12 (1), 53–8.

Coccossis, H. and Tsartas, P. (2001) *Sustainable Tourism Development and the Environment* [in Greek]. Athens: Kritiki.

Deprest, F. (1997) *Enquête sur le Tourisme de Masse. L'Écologie Face au Territoire*. Paris: Belin.

Didaskalou, E. (2000) Health tourism: A new approach of tourism development on insular areas. *Proceedings of the International Scientific Conference on Tourism on Islands and Specific Destinations*. Chios, Greece: University of the Aegean.

EC (European Commission) Structural Funds (1995) *Greece: Community Support Framework 1994–99*. Brussels: European Commission.

Emblemsvang, J. and Bras, B. (2000) Process thinking – A new paradigm for science and engineering. *Futures* 32, 635–54.

EURISLES (European Islands System of Links and Exchanges) (1997) *Indicateurs Statistiques des Disparités Régionales Engendrées par l'Insularité et l'Ultrapériphéricité*. France: Eurisles.

EURISLES (European Islands System of Links and Exchanges) (2002) Website at http://www.eurisles.com/. Accessed 28.8.02.

European Parliament (1996) *Coastal and Island Regions of the European Union*. Regional Policy Series W-17. Luxembourg: Directorate General for Research.

Fayos-Sola, E. (1996) Tourism policy: A midsummer night's dream? *Tourism Management* 17 (6), 405–12.

Fennell, D.A. (1999) *Ecotourism: An Introduction*. London: Routledge.

Gortazar, L. and Marin, C. (1999) *Tourism and Sustainable Development: From Theory to Practice – The Island Experience*. Canary Islands: Gobierno de Canarias, Consejería de Tourismo y Transportes, Viceconsejería de Tourismo and International Scientific Council for Island Development (INSULA).

Gousiou, A., Spilanis, I. and Kizos, A. (2001) Is agrotourism 'agro' or 'tourism'? Evidence from agrotourist holdings in Lesvos, Greece. *Anatolia* 12 (1) 6–22.

Greek National Tourism Organisation (GNTO) – Centre of Planning and Economic Research (CPER) (1994) *Preliminary National Economic and Spatial Plan for Tourism* 1 (1–3) [in Greek]. Athens.

Haralambopoulos, N. and Pizam, A. (1996) Perceived impacts of tourism – the case of Samos. *Annals of Tourism Research* 23 (3) 503–26.

Hellenic Ministry of Agriculture Website (2002) At http://www.minagric.gr/greek/3.1.4.html. Accessed 12.8.02.

HOS (Hellenic Organization for Standardization) Website (2002) At http://www.elot.gr/home.htm. Accessed 3.1.2002.

Hunter, C. (1997) Sustainable tourism as an adaptive paradigm. *Annals of Tourism Research* 24 (4), 850–67.

INEM (International Network for Environmental Management) Website (2002) At http://www.inem.org/. Accessed 3.1.02.

Inskeep, E. (1991) *Tourism Planning – An Integrated and Sustainable Development Approach*. New York: Van Nostrand Reinhold.

Koutsouris, A. and Gaki, D. (1998) The quest for a sustainable future: Alternative tourism as the level of development. *Proceedings of the First Global Conference on Tourism and Culture in Sustainable Development*. Athens: National Technical University of Athens.

Lagos, D. (1998) Tourism and sustainable development at a regional level: The case of a Greek island region. *Proceedings of the International Congress on Sustainable Development in the Islands and the Role of Research and Higher Education*. Rhodes, Greece.

Lagos, D. and Gkrimpa, E. (2000) The special and alternative forms of tourism: Their contribution to the development of Greek islands and special destinations. *Proceedings of the International Scientific Conference on Tourism on Islands and Specific Destinations*. Chios, Greece: University of the Aegean.

Loinger, G. (1995) *La Problématique du Développement Durable Dans le Contexte de l'Espace Méditerranéen*. Paris.

Loukissas, P. (1982) Tourism's regional development impacts – a comparative analysis of the Greek islands. *Annals of Tourism Research* 9, 523–41.

Mantoglou, A., Hadjibiros, K., Panagopoulos, P. and Varveris, T. (1998) Sustainable development programme for the Greek islands. *Proceedings of the International Congress on Sustainable Development in the Islands and the Role of Research and Higher Education*. Rhodes, Greece.

Maroudas, L. and Tsartas, P. (1998) Parameters of sustainable development and alternative tourism in small and less developed islands of the Aegean. *Proceedings of the International Congress on Sustainable Development in the Islands and the Role of Research and Higher Education*. Rhodes, Greece.

Mathieson, A. and Wall, G. (1982) *Tourism: Economic, Physical and Social Impacts*. Longman.

Nir, D. (1990) *Region as a Socio-environmental System. An Introduction to a Systemic Regional Geography*. Dordrecht: Kluwer Academic.

NSSG (National Statistical Service of Greece) (1999) *Tourism Statistics*.

Sophoulis, C.M. and Assonitis, G. (1998) The 'Aegean-Archipelago Project': Sustainable growth for small islands via high value-added activities. *Proceedings of the International Congress on Sustainable Development in the Islands and the Role of Research and Higher Education*. Rhodes, Greece.

Spilanis, I. (1995) Tourism and environment in the insular regions: The tourism development in Lesvos, with the exploitation of cultural and natural resources [in Greek]. *Proceedings of the Conference in Tourism and Environment in the Insular Regions*. Crete: TEE.

Swarbrooke, J. (1999) *Sustainable Tourism Management*. UK: CAB International.

Tsartas, P., Manologlou, E. and Markou, A. (2001) Domestic tourism in Greece and special interest destinations: The role of alternative forms of tourism. *Anatolia* 12 (1) 35–42.

Turner, R.K., Pearce, D. and Bateman I. (1994) *Environmental Economics: An Elementary Introduction*. Great Britain: Harvester Wheatsheaf.

Varvaressos, St. (1998) *Tourism: Meanings, Size, Structure – the Greek Reality* [in Greek]. Athens: Propompos.

Wall, G. (1997) Is ecotourism sustainable? *Environmental Management* 21 (4) 483–91.

WTO (World Tourism Organisation) Website (2001) At http://www.world-tourism.org. Accessed 13.9.01.

WWF – Hellas (World Wildlife Fund) (2000) *Planning Pilot Activities for the Development of Ecological Tourism* [in Greek]. Athens: European Union, Ministry of Development and Greek National Tourism Organisation.

Yunis, E. (2001) Condition for sustainable ecotourism development and management, Seminar on planning, development and management of ecotourism in Africa, Regional preparatory meeting for the International Year of Ecotourism, Maputo, Mozambique. Available in the WTO internet site.

Zouros, N.K. (1996) The museum and the petrified forest of Lesvos: Exploitation and protection – alternative forms of tourism [in Greek]. *Proceedings of the 1st Conference for the Petrified Forest of Lesvos*. Lesvos: GEOTEE.

# 14 Tourism, Culture and Cultural Tourism in Malta: The Revival of Valletta

*Nadia Theuma*
*University of Malta, Msida, Malta*

The Maltese Islands are a mass tourist destination traditionally renowned for their mild Mediterranean climate and the sea. Recent tourism policy has tried to redress this situation by utilising the extensive historical and cultural heritage of the islands as a market diversification tool and to promote a policy of sustainable tourism development through the development of cultural tourism. Valletta, the islands' capital, is a major tourist attraction. A World Heritage City, this 400-year-old capital offers a rich cultural mix. Its Baroque buildings are a venue for art exhibitions and theatre performances, and its open spaces and gardens offer spectacular views. For the tourist, the day-to-day activities and celebrations of the residents who live there add colour and depth. But Valletta is a bustling city during the day and a dead city by night. In recent years, tourism and local authorities have launched various initiatives to revive Valletta as a bustling centre through the organisation of cultural activities and the creation of new tourist attractions. This paper examines Valletta as a tourist attraction, identifying the current cultural product, and it discusses the recent initiatives to revive the city. Finally, it analyses the extent to which these initiatives have actually led to a revival, including to the city's conservation and to its vitality.

## Introduction

Culture, history, and tourism are intrinsically interrelated. Culture and its manifestations can contribute towards the attractiveness of a tourism region, enhance the tourist experience, and – if well marketed and managed – can distinguish a destination from its competitors. Moreover, cultural tourism is reputed to enhance local identity and can bring about the revival of certain areas.

This chapter focuses on the rejuvenation of Malta's capital city, Valletta, through tourism, and in particular through the development of cultural tourism. The Maltese islands (see Figure 1) are a mass tourist destination, traditionally renowned for their mild Mediterranean climate and the sea. However, the islands are also endowed with an extensive historical and cultural heritage. For more than a decade, the Maltese tourism authorities have seen culture as an attribute that could distinguish Malta as a tourist destination from competitors in the Mediterranean region. Consequently, recent tourism policy has tried to utilise the historical and cultural heritage of the islands as a market diversification tool and to promote a policy of sustainable tourism development through cultural tourism. This chapter will examine Valletta as a tourist attraction, including identifying the current cultural product on offer. It will also discuss the recent initiatives undertaken by certain tourism and local entities to revive Valletta. It will analyse the extent to which these initiatives have successfully led to a revival of this city. Consideration is given to the degree to which any revival has helped its residents, has improved the built environment for the wider cultural heritage and quality of life of the Maltese, and has aided the Maltese

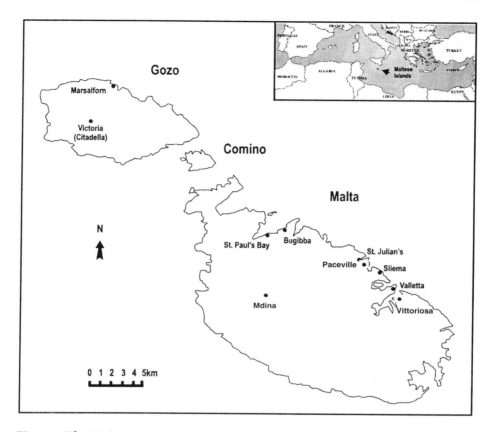

**Figure 1** The Maltese islands

economy by diversifying the tourism industry away from a reliance on resort mass tourism.

## Tourism Development in the Maltese Islands

Tourism is considered the backbone of the Maltese economy, with gross tourism earnings for 2001 reaching Lm271.4 million (Lm1.00 = €2.4) (MTA, 2001). It is responsible for the generation of 40,000 full-time equivalent jobs (Mangion & Vella, 1999). Malta's tourism development is a classic model of tourism development cycles (cf. Butler, 1980). After very modest beginnings in the late 1950s, tourism went through a phase of rapid growth in volume (mid-1960s to the 1970s), followed by decline in the 1980s and rejuvenation during the 1990s.

Early tourism development plans were primarily concerned with increasing the volume of tourists, and due partly to unplanned development and an absence of adequate tourism-planning procedures, enormous pressures were placed on the local infrastructure, leading to water and electricity shortages, and sewage overflow problems. Malta also acquired the image of a low-cost holiday destination and, coupled with the problems of poor infrastructure, it was no longer an attractive tourism destination. Malta's problems were compounded further by it being highly dependent on a single market, the UK, which in 1980 represented 77% of all visitors to the Maltese islands (Lockhart, 1997). These visitors generally came in family groups, stayed in self-catering accommodation, often spent very little, and were highly seasonal (Callus & Bajada, 1992). The over-reliance on a single market had a large impact on the Maltese economy, notably when the economic recession of the early 1980s in Britain led to a 40% decline in visitor numbers between 1981 and 1984 (MTA, 2000).

In 1988 the Maltese Government appointed the UK consultants Horwath and Horwath, who were assisted by a group of Maltese experts to draw up the first Malta Tourism Development Plan. The plan attempted to overcome the problems afflicting Maltese tourism at the end of the 1980s, focusing on seven marketing actions in order to achieve market diversification, an upgrade of its product and tourist markets, and a lengthening of the tourist season. The development of cultural tourism was one of the suggested strategies.

## Culture, tourism and cultural tourism in Malta

The role of culture as a tourist attraction has gone through various phases in the Maltese islands. Through the 1970s, these islands were marketed primarily as a sun, sea and sand destination, and tourist literature published then showed culture and history as an addition to this traditional resort product (Boissevain, 1996a).

This emphasis continued until the beginning of the 1990s when the first phase (1990–1994) of the Malta Tourism Development Plan came into action. In the plan, culture and history were earmarked as attractions that could be used to distinguish the Maltese islands from other Mediterranean destinations. However, it was pointed out that:

> The market for exclusive cultural tourism in Europe is small . . . but the potential of combined cultural and sun holidays is large . . . Malta should not market just its sun . . . but its history, mystique and Mediterranean heritage. (Horwath & Horwath, 1989: 19)

It was suggested that cultural tourism could be developed through an improved management of heritage sites, the marketing of the heritage of the Knights of Malta, the introduction of local festivals and concerts, and the twinning of Maltese historical towns with European towns of similar size (Horwath & Horwath, 1989: 25). The tourism authorities began implementing some of these suggestions to establish a cultural product that would broaden the market base and attract visitors during the low season (December to February) and shoulder months (October to November and March to June). The result was the creation of invented cultural events, mainly in the form of festivals, which supplemented the existing endemic cultural activities of a primarily religious and folk nature. Among the festivals initiated by the Maltese tourism authorities were invented historical pageants depicting events that occurred during the Knights of St John era. The first event was held in the medieval town of Mdina, but protests from local residents (Boissevain, 1996b; Boissevain & Sammut, 1994) led to them being moved to the cities of Valletta and Vittoriosa. Other events were a Choir Festival (first held in 1990), Malta Jazz Festival (organised by the Department of Culture with assistance from the tourism authorities), Fireworks Festival, and a Mediterranean Food Festival (the latter two events were first held in 2002). At the same time, the Malta Tourism Authority (MTA) promoted more indigenous cultural activities, including the patron saint *festas* held during the summer months, and local carnivals and Easter festivities.

Culture and history also featured more strongly in overseas tourism marketing literature (Theuma, 2002), with culture becoming the main thrust of the marketing campaigns by the National Tourism Organisation of Malta (NTOM) and subsequently by the MTA. The MTA's most recent marketing literature emphasised other aspects of culture, in particular 'experiential' aspects of the Maltese atmosphere, and the general feeling of particular towns and villages. An advertisement published in The Netherlands states:

> A visit to Malta will take you back in time.
>
> Experience our Mediterranean heritage and enjoy the friendliness and warmth of our people, join in our 'festas' and celebrations, or get away from it all and savour the tranquility of our villages or secluded beaches.
>
> You will discover that there is so much more to Malta, more than meets the eye. (Verkeersbureau Malta, 2001)

The MTA's strategic plan (MTA, 2000) acknowledges the role of culture as an aspect of Malta's unique selling proposition (MTA, 2000: 22). Moreover, one focus for the MTA's Product Planning Directorate is the 'facilitation of and the support of cultural events, heritage . . . in Malta and Gozo' (MTA, 2000: 50). But it will be shown that the development of cultural tourism in Malta has not been easy, as the tourism industry there, including much of its plant, is geared so strongly to the needs of coastal mass tourism.

## Methodology

Research for this study largely involved qualitative approaches, notably interviews and an analysis of tourist literature. Face-to-face interviews were conducted with Valletta residents (20) and their representative in the Valletta Local Council (1), as well as with people employed in tourism-related activities in Valletta, in particular cultural providers (7), guides (2) and MTA representatives (3). The interviews focused on particular aspects of Valletta, notably on the role of tourism and cultural tourism, the ways in which tourism has helped in its rejuvenation, and on the future of its tourism development. The resulting findings were complemented by a study of guidebooks, tourist brochures and MTA literature. These documents were consulted because they give insights into how Valletta is presented to visitors. Finally, published data and research on Valletta were also consulted. Together, these sources helped to provide a broad picture of the current state of Valletta as a tourism product.

## Valletta: An Overview

The capital city of Malta, Valletta, is located on a promontory flanked by two natural harbours (see Figure 2). For nearly 400 years, Valletta was the centre of

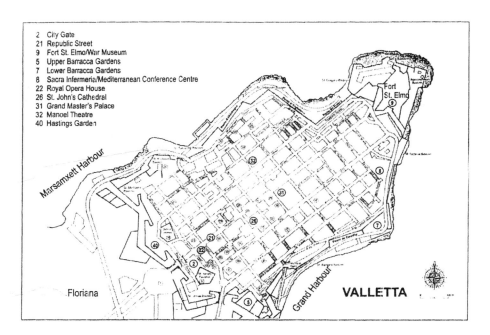

2   City Gate
21  Republic Street
9   Fort St. Elmo/War Museum
5   Upper Barracca Gardens
7   Lower Barracca Gardens
8   Sacra Infermeria/Mediterranean Conference Centre
22  Royal Opera House
26  St. John's Cathedral
31  Grand Master's Palace
32  Manoel Theatre
40  Hastings Garden

**Figure 2** Malta's capital city, Valletta

Maltese life. This importance is evident not only in the many functions that the city has fulfilled (residential, commercial, administrative, leisure and touristic), but also in the local use of its name. Colloquially, Valletta is not referred to by its name but rather by the term *Il-Belt*, which translates as 'the City' – as opposed to the rural areas – and which implies a locus of activity, or a place where things happen.

However, Valletta's importance as the hub of Maltese life has in recent years been the subject of on-going debate. Due to changes in the socioeconomic structure of the Maltese islands, it is no longer considered the main centre of activity, and for a number of years it has been regarded as a city in decline. While over the past ten years (1990s) attempts have been made to revive Valletta, the local authorities and inhabitants talk of it as a locality that needs 'an injection of life'. The main issue is that the city is active by day and 'dead' at night, leading one guidebook to describe it thus:

> Yet, for all its fine architecture and noble birth Valletta lacks character and soul. . . . Valletta is a schizophrenic city. By day it's a thriving and bustling capital . . . By night, however, it wears a sombre mask. Venture into Valletta after sunset, when all shops are shut and the businessmen have returned home and you wonder if it is the same place. (Gaul, 1993: 86–7)

The context to the city is explained next, in particular its many functions as well as some of the problems that it faces which relate most directly to the development of cultural tourism.

Valletta is primarily a residential city, with a population in December 2001 of 7029 (NSO, 2003). Despite its ageing population (in the 1995 census it had an ageing index of 138.01) (NSO, 2003), Valletta has a thriving community. Like most towns and cities of the Maltese islands, Valletta has a life of its own, with the lives of its residents revolving around its own communal and national activities. The residents in Valletta are divided according to its parish communities and by allegiances to the two main political parties, but they share a passion for its football team. The community is endowed with a strong popular culture. The normal day-to-day activities and celebrations of the residents can add colour and depth to the 'cultural' experience of this city.

Valletta is the seat of government, and it is home to the Maltese Parliament, the law courts, and the stock exchange, and major companies and banks have their head offices there. Up to the late 1970s, Valletta was also considered the main commercial, leisure and entertainment centre. Until then it continued to be active by day and vibrant by night, despite the population of Valletta having been on the decline since the beginning of the 20th century (Schembri & Borg, 1997). However, continuing changes in residential population patterns, economic diversification and the relocation of the entertainment industry from Valletta to the newly established resort and leisure areas of St Julian's and Paceville have subsequently led to Valletta's slow decline as a centre of night activity.

Another facet of Valletta is its historic character. It is a planned military city built by the Knights of St John in the 16th century to replace the inland capital city of Mdina so that the islands could be better protected against frequent attacks from Ottoman Turks. It is considered a fine example of baroque architecture and town planning – with both attributes having earned it the title of a World Heritage City. Important buildings are found there that are landmarks of baroque architecture and Maltese history. These include St John's Cathedral, which has a unique floor of tessellated tombstones and which houses Caravaggio's painting of the 'Beheading of St John', as well as auberges and buildings built by the Knights, the oldest baroque theatre in Europe still in use, and the Sacra Infermeria, which has the longest unsupported ceiling in Europe. In addition, there are gardens, numerous churches and palaces, and museums, and the city is surrounded by a fortified wall. At the tip of the peninsula is Fort St Elmo, an important landmark in Malta's chequered history (see Figure 2 for Valletta's main historical attractions). In addition to these sites, Valletta's unique location provides dramatic views across the two main natural harbours. Views of Valletta's cityscape and churches from the harbours are a common image used in tourist literature to introduce the Maltese islands (Theuma, 2002). Valletta's historical elements are important for its position as a cultural city. Besides the popular culture already described, the city has museums (public, private and church), four theatres and a cinema complex. There are also some restaurants that serve local food and thus offer yet another insight into Maltese culture.

Valletta is also a tourist city. It is estimated to attract an average of one million visitors each year. Nearly all tourists visiting the Maltese islands will visit the city at least once, with some returning for a second time during their stay (Mangion & Zammit Trevisan, 2001). Valletta is also on the main itinerary of passengers on cruise liners calling into the Grand Harbour (see Figure 2). Articles on the city also appear regularly in the in-flight magazine published by the national airline, while guidebooks and tourist brochures for Malta dedicate substantial amounts of space to it. In summary, Valletta is central to the general tourist product on offer.

However, the functions of Valletta as a tourist city largely end at its attractions and amenities. More specifically, Valletta provides only 1.5% of the total bed capacity of the Maltese islands, representing a total of only five hotels and five guest houses (see Table 1). The city's current bed-stock contrasts with its role at the beginning of this century when it was also a centre for accommodation (Zarb, in print). Further, Table 1 shows that its accommodation is of a low category, being predominantly three star. There is only one five-star hotel, but this is situated in Floriana – although it is within walking distance of Valletta. In recent years there has been hardly any investment in the city's accommodation sector, and lack of accommodation was identified by interview respondents as a major drawback for the city's sustainable development, since night-time activity in particular can be generated by proximity to tourist accommodation.

Valletta also provides many amenities for visitors in terms of restaurants and eating places (a total of 48) (MTA, 2003), cultural attractions (public, private and church museums, audio-visual centres, and four theatres), and leisure and entertainment (one cinema centre, and shopping facilities). These attractions, together with the historical setting and buildings as well as the local character, make Valletta an important cultural and historical centre with considerable potential tourist appeal.

Whereas the amount of accommodation has declined over the past decade (Mangion & Zammit Trevisan, 2001: 12), the number of businesses offering cultural activities and food has increased. According to Valletta's Mayor, the catering sector has doubled in size. However, a major drawback is that the cultural activities and restaurants are restricted to certain parts of the city, that is, to the upper parts of Valletta, and to certain times of the day, that is, to the mornings. As a result, Valletta is more a tourist attraction rather than a tourist city.

**Table 1** Hotels, guest houses and number of beds in Valletta

| Category of establishment | Quantity | Location | Beds |
|---|---|---|---|
| **Hotels** | | | |
| 5* | 1 | Floriana | 254 |
| 3* | 2 | Valletta | 201 |
| 2* | 1 | Valletta | 80 |
| 1* | 1 | Valletta | 44 |
| **Guest houses** | | | |
| 3 class | 5 | Valletta | 84 |
| **TOTAL** | **10** | | **664** |

*Source*: MTA (2003)

All these features render Valletta something of 'a museum' (Valletta resident), since 'they (the tourists) merely visit rather than stay' (Valletta Local Council representative). Although some tour operators are promoting Valletta as a venue for city breaks, the level of interest in the city as such is still low.

From data provided by the city's museums and from the views of guides, tourist agencies, residents and the Valletta Local Council, it appears that the typical Valletta visitor is one who visits on a half-day guided tour. A guided tour of the city often entails a visit to Upper Barracca Gardens, St John's Co-Cathedral, the Palace State Rooms (the seat of Parliament and office of the President), and an audio-visual show. With the exception of the latter, the tour has hardly changed in 80 years (Theuma, 2002). Occasionally, tour companies include a visit to the museums of fine arts or archaeology, the Sunday market or a drive around the bastions. Only a few companies offer these alternative attractions and only one conducts a full-day tour of Valletta. The city is also visited by individual tourists, who follow the pattern described above but also often venture beyond the prescribed tour, following the guidebooks and their suggestions to venture 'beyond the beaten track'. The average number of hours spent in Valletta by foreign visitors is slightly over five hours for tourists on guided tours, and six hours for individual travellers (Mangion & Zammit Trevisan, 2001). This relatively short stay reduces the tourist impact on the city's economy. Mangion & Zammit Trevisan (2001) calculated that visitors spend an average of Lm13.95 per capita in Valletta, amounting to an estimated Lm15 million each year. Although this is nearly double the amount that tourists in Malta spend per capita per day during their holiday, the political representatives and cultural providers argued that tourists spend 'too little' in view of the city's considerable attractions. They argued that the city has genuine potential to generate more expenditure. The current level of tourist spending goes on food, sites and souvenirs (although the souvenirs and craft items are quite poor and do not provide sufficient incentive to spend more money). The inability of the present craft industry to generate more expenditure is also linked to the cruise industry. Valletta is the main, if not the only, attraction visited by cruise passengers, and the respondents thought that these visitors would spend more money if better quality souvenirs or craft items were available for them to buy, and that therefore the city is losing out on potentially lucrative business.

## Valletta's Revival

The revival of Valletta has been a focus for discussion and debate over the past decade. Both government and tourist entities have tried to reanimate and revive the city and to restore its previous splendour. These attempts have been focused on its monuments and buildings. It has not been targeted at tourism; rather, it has mainly been for the sake of Valletta itself and the restoration of its environs. The city's residents, the Maltese population in general, and the visitors have all been beneficiaries, albeit to different degrees. The discussion that follows outlines the various actions taken to revive Valletta.

Attempts at revival have tried to address different specific aspects of the city's multi-functional uses and character. However, the Valletta Rehabilitation

Committee (VRC), the Valletta Local Council (VLC) and the Malta Tourism Authority (MTA) have sought to promote its regeneration more generally.

The VRC was set up in 1992 as part of the Ministry for Resources and Infrastructure, with the aim of 'giving back to Valletta the mien it deserves' (VRC spokesperson). The brief of the VRC focuses on the restoration of the city's buildings and general environment, with various specific projects being set up to address areas needing immediate attention. These projects have included the restoration of monuments, paving of the main pedestrianised area, replacement of shop fronts so they were more congruent with the character of the city, and the removal of external electricity and telephone cables that had given the streets a shabby appearance. The VRC was also instrumental in making Valletta a more appealing and safer city at night by commissioning a project for the lighting up of Republic Street (the central and main thoroughfare) and parts of the Bastions. However, this project was never completed due to insufficient funds.

The setting up of Local Councils, the smallest scale of local government, was another means of helping to revive the city. Their main aim is to maintain and provide for the upkeep of each locality, with the first being established in 1993. Over time they have assisted in strengthening the local identity of Malta's towns and villages. They have helped by restoring parts of the built heritage, recognising the importance of local artists, poets and philanthropists, and by embellishing the natural environment, and these activities have meant that local inhabitants have become more aware of their surroundings and heritage. In localities such as Valletta which are also major tourist centres, the Local Councils have also ventured into influencing tourism and its impacts on their locality, albeit in a limited way, as tourism does not strictly fall within the remit of Local Council duties.

Valletta Local Council's work has helped in reviving the city and in addressing its major problems. Above all, the council has addressed the problem of street cleaning, this being a major problem as it is a commercial centre, it has a daily open-air market, and it attracts 30,000 commuters each day. A substantial amount of the council budget goes on rubbish collection, and today Valletta is certainly a cleaner city. The residents who were interviewed often commented on the city's improved appearance, with one woman stating that it is now much cleaner and that she is once more proud to live there. Valletta also suffers from visual eyesores and dilapidated buildings. Hence, the Local Council has conducted projects to tidy up and thus revive the lower parts of Valletta, and it has started to work with catering establishments to encourage them to make more use of the public open space in order to encourage activity and business. According to the Local Council's records, catering establishments have doubled in the past ten years, and this has impacted on the general 'feeling' of the city. The Local Council is hampered, however, by lack of funding. Each Local Council's funding is based on the number of its residents, but Valletta receives commuters and visitors each day equivalent to four times its population and these are not taken into consideration. The interviews with locals, owners of retail outlets and political representatives confirm that these visitors leave a substantial impact on the city, which the Council has to cater for.

The Maltese tourism authorities, and in particular the MTA, are a third type of organisation assisting in Valletta's revival. As discussed earlier, following the recommendations of the Malta Tourism Development Plan, the NTOM (the MTA's predecessor) began to organise historical pageantry events in Malta's urban centres. The Valletta Historical and Elegance Festival was first organised in 1996. The criticisms of this festival that had been made by the residents of the inland town of Mdina when it was held there (Boissevain, 1996a) were not evident in Valletta. One possible reason is that, unlike at Mdina, the festival in Valletta is held away from the city's residential areas, being concentrated on the business district and the major buildings, so that its impacts on residents are limited while it still adds to the city's cultural activities. This cultural event includes concerts, recitals, folk music and dancing, art exhibitions and pageantry. The MTA uses the existing architectural heritage, buildings which are normally closed to the public as venues for its concerts and exhibitions. Thus, the MTA enhances the cultural experience of the visitor by providing access to these sites at the same time as it utilises these under-used buildings.

The festival event times are designed to coincide with periods in the day when tourists visit the city, namely between ten in the morning and early afternoon, in order 'to grab the tourist, so that whenever he [*sic*] comes to Valletta during that week he will see something' (MTA official). However, this format elicited criticism from the business community. One shop owner commented that such timings are not conducive for business since they add to the general chaos during the mornings, and there is nothing in the evenings when Valletta needs the activity. Thus, while the Valletta Festival generates interest, it fails to address the city's much-needed revival during the afternoon and evenings.

In addition to the festival, every other Sunday the MTA organises a re-enactment of fort life during the era of the Knights of St John at Fort St Elmo. This event generates interest among foreign visitors and has also led some shops to open on Sunday morning, again helping to revive the central parts of the city, which up to some years ago were devoid of life on Sunday mornings.

In an attempt to enliven Valletta at night the MTA, together with the help of the business community, the Local Council and the museums department, launched a pilot project called 'Valletta Evenings' in April 2001. This involved cultural activities held during the evenings in various localities in Valletta throughout that month. It was envisaged that following the festival the business community would take up the initiative and keep city shops open until later, thus assisting the activities of local restaurants. While the effects of this initiative were not felt immediately, it has aroused enough interest for other pilot projects to be developed. Indeed, towards the end of 2001 the VRC, together with the Manoel Theatre, University of Malta and the MTA, organised a series of evening music programmes. These were held in buildings usually closed to the public, and thus they helped towards ensuring the sustainability of the product.

Various cultural organisations situated in Valletta are a fourth type of agency assisting in the city's rejuvenation. Despite its vast cultural assets, the city currently hosts only two genres of cultural activities during the evenings, namely, food and the visual and performing arts. These evening cultural activities address a need but are still at an embryonic stage. While the number of catering establishments has doubled over the past ten years, very few open during the evenings, with some also opening only on specific days of the week. The majority of owners of catering outlets that were interviewed stated that there was insufficient business to open in the evenings, yet those that did open commented that they had a thriving trade, suggesting that catering activity in Valletta at night is a viable activity. The visual and performing cultural sphere includes an extensive events calendar ranging from cinema shows to art exhibitions, discussions, theatre and music. These activities are gaining momentum, with demand from among specific age brackets of the Maltese population who do not enjoy the current entertainment provision at Paceville and St Julian's. However, this demand is probably not being met fully, in part because the two cultural activities of food and visual and performing arts do not complement one another. Most restaurants are closed by the time performances are over, despite most places having operating licences until 11.00 p.m.

## Discussion of Findings

In assessing the revival of Valletta, one has to look at its various functions and the way in which these have been affected. One aspect that is rarely considered is the residential sphere, with respondents in this research also largely relating the city's revival to its physical environment. Yet the attempts to revive the city have had positive impacts on both businesses and the residential community. This is because Valletta is emerging from the reputation it had acquired for social and cultural deterioration. The residents' comments reinforce this view. They argued that they feel that their city was a better place to live in because the general environment had improved. In addition, the increased commercial activity has had an indirect impact on employment opportunities in Valletta. Although native Valletta shop owners only amount to about 15% of the total (VLC spokesperson), they employ many retail assistants from the city.

While Valletta's residents yearn for a city that is more alive, they are also aware that revival will itself bring problems. One such issue frequently mentioned by residents was parking. Parking problems are already acute, especially during the day when commuters to the city take up very many spaces. The issue of limited parking space is also affecting those areas where there has been an increase in night activity. In addition, residents commented on the state of some buildings, which over the years have been abused or are currently used either for storage or as garages. The VRC and VLC acknowledge that more work is needed in relation to the state of buildings, arguing that, although the registration of buildings has commenced, the completion of this exercise will require time and money, which is in short supply.

Valletta's improvement seems to occur in fits and starts, very often depending on funds and the government of the day (both the Local Council and the VRC are funded by government). Residents and members of the business community who were interviewed, expressed anger at the fact that projects designed to give Valletta a new lease of life as well as to restore its ambience and vitality have been shelved. Projects that had been stopped include the rebuilding of the old opera house, which was severely damaged during the Second World War, the City Gate project, and a number of smaller projects. In addition, there is the need for more coordination and for projects to be linked together. One informant argued that, rather than the Government spending huge amounts of money on major projects, more effort should be focused on finishing the ongoing projects and on

tackling smaller and more feasible projects that can be completed within a particular timeframe. Another respondent argued that Valletta would benefit more
from several small projects being conducted in a specific area rather than one
single major project which would never be finished. One informant even
suggested that penalties should be introduced if projects were not finished on
time.

Another issue that appeared to concern Valletta's political representatives was
that the tourism authorities market the city as part of the overall sun, sea and
sand tourism product – that is, within 'destination Malta' – but they are not keen
on Valletta as a separate and distinct city product, this being similar to the findings for the small historic town of Mdina in Malta, as reported by Boissevain and
Sammut (1994). Although MTA has claimed in its Strategic Plans that it will
encourage further cultural tourism, it does not perceive or treat Valletta as a
cultural destination in its own right. There is very little literature commissioned
by either the MTA or any other organisation that publicises Valletta for tourists.
Moreover, with the exception of a map located at the main city gate, there is no
indication for tourists or locals that Valletta is in fact a World Heritage City. The
respondents argued that Malta has not yet properly exploited Valletta's potential
to attract 'cultural' tourism activity. This city, more than any other Maltese attraction, could attract many tourists interested in culture because it offers a
combination of leisure, entertainment and cultural experiences.

The rejuvenation of Valletta might be hastened if a more holistic approach was
adopted towards the city. At present, its renaissance is too fragmented with
organisations working on their own with very limited collaboration with each
other. One informant, a cultural provider, commented that the 'attractions are
available, but the circumstances are mediocre, and the supporting infrastructure
is not appropriate'.

Valletta's potential as a cultural centre could be much more effectively
exploited by using its World Heritage City status as a brand for the city. In fact,
few Maltese or visitors know it has this status, and more awareness could
generate greater interest in the city and might alter people's expectations and
experiences of it. In this context, a resident mentioned that recently a number of
buskers had occupied the main city entrance selling various items, and she
argued that their licences should be withdrawn as they do not fit in with the city's
character.

Valletta's cultural organisations seem to have identified a particular cultural
product – the performing arts – as the city's attraction, although there were divergent views as to exactly what is meant by the performing arts. A primary concern
was that the current performances do not represent the local culture and do not
promote works by local artists. A theatre director commented:

> What type of performances are we producing? Are we just reproducing
> what the visitor is already familiar with in his [sic] home country? What
> about local productions and local music? We should try to promote these
> more.

This observation raises an important issue that has resonance for the entire cultural
product currently on offer. Valletta's revival has involved exploiting its cultural
assets, but there is the danger that the cultural assets on offer do not reflect the local

culture. This was of major concern to the cultural providers who were interviewed, who cautioned that there is a threat that revival might lead to an overly commercialised version of culture and one which subsequently cannot be sustained because it will not be representative of the population it is supposed to represent. Hence, Valletta's rejuvenation should also involve encouraging the local population to gain its own sense of identity and awareness of the local culture.

Urban revival depends on another key element: the people who live there. Currently, Valletta is seen as an attraction largely devoid of its inhabitants. Yet they are a hugely valuable asset. Their activities can help attract tourists to the city, and tourists are interested in the general atmosphere or ambiance of the city which reflects their activities. In the early 1990s the NTOM published a leaflet on a walking tour of Valletta which highlighted the main attractions of the city but made hardly any reference to Valletta as a 'living city'. More recently, an MTA brochure on Malta included this description of Valletta:

> The impregnable city of the Knights does not allow anyone to take it all in at a glance. You need to caress it with your eyes, stroll along its straight streets, pausing to admire a carved façade, a balcony, a beautiful staircase, a courtyard surrounded by arched passageways, a fountain, or magnificent coat-of-arms. (MTA, 2002: 10)

Although focused on the built structures, this description does begin to give more depth to the city's qualities.

Transport represents a major problem for the city. During the day it is easily accessed by public transport from all localities, but it is less easy at night when services to and from certain localities stop as early as nine o'clock in the evening. This can limit Valletta as an attraction for tourists. Although Malta's other two main entertainment centres, Paceville and St Julian's, suffer from the same problem, they have the advantage of being within walking distance of a large amount of tourist accommodation. In addition, Valletta also has an acute parking space shortage and in order to park in Valletta car owners have to pay a surcharge on their road licence fee.

Effective tourism management often requires that the several affected stakeholders are involved in arriving at a consensus as to how to manage a particular site or activity in a mutually beneficial manner. The links and relationships among stakeholders relevant to tourism in Valletta vary from mere acknowledgement of their existence to active collaboration on various projects, but it is clear that more coordination is needed. For example, in terms of marketing of certain facilities, there is no single publication that details all the restaurants in Valletta. More generally, there is a clear need for a comprehensive information leaflet describing the city and its attractions and facilities. The city's revival could also be promoted through a tourist information office entirely dedicated to Valletta – the current office located at the main city entrance is a general tourist office and it does not provide comprehensive information on Valletta.

## Conclusions

To date, initiatives for Valletta's rejuvenation have largely focused on improving the general environment, restoring monuments, encouraging business in the evenings, and attracting people through 'cultural' entertainment. These community- and tourism organisation-based actions are beginning to have a positive outcome as Maltese people are becoming increasingly aware of the city. However, Valletta's renaissance should go beyond an increase in cultural events or the embellishment of buildings. Valletta has to be seen holistically and in its entirety, which so far has not been the case. Some suggestions are offered here on how this could be encouraged in relation to tourism.

In terms of tourism, the city needs to be recognised as an object of art and culture in its own right. Further, more recognition is needed that it is the combination of buildings, open spaces and also people living in Valletta that give this city its unique characteristics. However, while the buildings and open spaces are mentioned in the tourist literature and have been the focus of recent initiatives, the character and vitality of the inhabitants' local ways of life have been very largely absent from them.

Secondly, Valletta appears to be divided into four parts – geographically into 'the upper part' and 'beyond Palace Square', and culturally into 'high' culture and 'popular' culture. Yet, if Valletta is to be fully revived then all four elements need to be considered. Cultural initiatives to revive Valletta should include the lower parts of Valletta 'beyond Palace Square', partly because they have much to offer tourists. This includes gardens, fortifications, buildings, the recently refurbished War Museum and War Memorial, and views of the Three Cities across the Grand Harbour. Importantly, Valletta's lower parts are replete with opportunities for visitors to sample the 'living experience of the city'. It is here that one can find the traditional vegetable vendor, the tea shop, the age-old parish rivalry and rich religious pageantry, and people gossiping and going about their daily lives. Here there are old and unused bars and tavernas that could benefit from more business. When visitors go to this area on Sunday mornings for the *InGurdia* event at Fort St. Elmo, there is currently nowhere for them to have a snack. These parts could be developed with care to encourage more tourist activity and also to limit pressure on the other parts of the city.

The community-based organisations often lack funds, which helps explain why projects remain incomplete, and this issue needs attention. One way of generating funds would be to channel money from the vast numbers of commuters and tourists who come to the city, perhaps through very small payments by tour-based groups and from car licence fees directed to the VLC and VRC. These would add up to a significant sum to fund several necessary projects. Such a scheme would mean that Valletta is also being sustained by all those who use it – for the benefit of current and future generations.

## References

Boissevain, J. (1996a) 'But we live here!' Problems with cultural tourism. In L. Brigulio *et al.* (eds) *Sustainable Tourism in Islands and Small States. Case Studies* (pp. 220–40). New York: Pinter.

Boissevain, J. (1996b) Ritual, tourism and cultural commoditization in Malta. In T. Selwyn (ed.) *The Tourist Image: Myths and Myth Making in Tourism* (pp. 105–120). Chichester: Wiley.

Boissevain, J. and Sammut, N. (1994) *Mdina: Its Residents and Cultural Tourism. Findings and Recommendations.* Report. Malta: Med-Campus Euromed Sustainable Tourism Project.

Butler, R.J. (1980) The concept of a tourist area resort cycle of evolution: Implications for management of resources. *Canadian Geographer* 24 (11), 5–12.

Callus, M.L. and Bajada, S. (1992) *The British Visitor*. Unpublished report, NTOM, Valletta.

Gaul, S. (1993) *Malta, Gozo and Comino*. Cadogan Island Guides.

Horwath and Horwath (1989) *The Maltese Islands Tourism Development Plan*. London: Horwath and Horwath.

Lockhart, D.G. (1997) 'We promise you a warm welcome': Tourism to Malta since the 1960s. *GeoJournal* 41 (2), 145–52.

Mangion, M.L. and Vella, L. (1999) *Economic Survey*. Valletta: Research and Information Division, MTA.

Mangion, M.L. and Zammit Trevisan, C. (2001) *The Significance of Valletta as a Tourism Product: Findings of a Tourism Survey*. Valletta: Research and Information Division, MTA.

MTA (2000) *Malta Tourism Authority Strategic Plan 2000–2002*. Valletta: MTA.

MTA (2001) *Malta Tourism Authority Annual Report and Financial Statements 2000*. Valletta: Communications and Business Development Division, MTA.

MTA (2002) *Malta: The Island at the Heart of the Mediterranean*. Valletta: MTA.

MTA (2003) *Accommodation Data*. Unpublished report. Valletta: MTA.

NSO (2003) Enumerated population by gender, single years of age and by locality. On WWW at http://www.nso.gov.mt/publications/census'95. Accessed 27.02.03.

Schembri, J. and Borg, M. (1997) Population changes in the walled cities of Malta. In C. Fsadni and T. Selwyn (eds) *Sustainable Tourism in Mediterranean Islands and Small Cities* (pp. 114–23). Malta and London: Med-Campus and Euromed.

Theuma, N. (2002) Identifying the Maltese Cultural Tourism Product: Marketing and Management Issues. Unpublished PhD thesis, University of Strathclyde.

Verkeersbureau Malta (2001) *MTA Adverts*. Amsterdam: MTA.

Zarb, J. (in print) *L-Istorja tat-Turizmu f'Malta*. Malta.

# 15 Coffee Shop Meets Casino: Cultural Responses to Casino Tourism in Northern Cyprus

*Julie E. Scott*
*International Institute for Culture, Tourism and Development, London Metropolitan University, Stapleton House, London*

Taking the case of northern Cyprus, this paper moves beyond a 'social impact' approach to casino tourism to focus on how the rapidly growing global casino industry connects with, mediates and is mediated by, the existing local gambling culture. Gambling has an ambivalent place within the cultural values and traditions of Cyprus. On the one hand, it is seen as a disreputable and somewhat shameful activity with potentially anti-social (and, particularly, anti-family) consequences. On the other hand, when viewed in terms of qualities of risk-taking, daring and recklessness, it is celebrated in some ideals of Cypriot masculinity and the rebellious, independent and individualistic spirit of 'Cypriotness'. This ambivalent attitude produces a tension, which can be perceived, for example, in gender-differentiated attitudes to and participation in gambling and in the manner in which social controls on gambling are exercised (both formal/legal and informal controls). The paper considers the implications for the ways gambling is managed in the traditional and casino contexts and for our understanding of what constitutes 'cultural sustainability'.

## Introduction

In 1997, following mounting reports of widespread problem gambling and stories linking casinos with organised crime and corrupt politicians, the government of Turkey finally bowed to public and political pressure and closed down its commercial casino sector.[1] A large part of the industry immediately shifted operations to the Turkish Republic of Northern Cyprus (TRNC). This small, unrecognised territory (population: ca 250,000) emerged from the 1974 division of Cyprus, when 14 years after the island's independence from British rule, the military junta in Greece engineered a coup against the Cypriot President Makarios. Turkey responded to the perceived threat to the Turkish Cypriot population with a decisive military intervention and Turkish troops have remained on the island ever since. The Greek and Turkish Cypriot populations which, prior to 1974, were distributed throughout the island in contiguous neighbourhoods of towns and villages, or in separate Greek and Turkish villages, were exchanged and resettled south and north respectively of a UN controlled 'Green Line'. The government of the Republic of Cyprus, whose remit since 1974 has been effectively limited to the southern two-thirds of the island, retains international recognition, whilst the TRNC is subject to international boycotts and embargoes which have reinforced its political and economic dependence on Turkey.[2] Despite numerous rounds of negotiations, political agreement has so far eluded the parties to the Cyprus dispute.

Although commercial casino gambling was established in northern Cyprus as early as 1975 as part of an effort to encourage investment and diversify the north's struggling tourism product, over the past ten years the tourist economy of northern Cyprus has become increasingly dependent on its casinos, and this dependence has intensified since the ban on commercial gaming in Turkey (Scott, 2001a). The casino market is overwhelmingly composed of Turkish tourists, although at different times the Israeli market has also been significant. Many are repeat visitors who make the short flight from Istanbul, Izmir or Ankara on all inclusive week-end trips (Scott & Aşıkoğlu, 2001). Since 1997, the number of casinos has more than quadrupled to over 20, with licence applications pending for another 20, and local expressions of concern over the possible social effects have multiplied.

Turkish Cypriot citizens, and students of all nationalities studying in the TRNC, are technically banned from gambling in casinos, and indeed from all forms of gambling on the island, with the social stigma of a court case and its attendant publicity a more effective deterrent than the low levels of fine incurred. However, whilst researching casino tourism in northern Cyprus (see Scott, 2001a; Scott & Aþýkoðlu, 2001) I was surprised by the number of stories I heard, during the course of casual conversations with friends and acquaintances, of cases of heavy gambling in Turkish Cypriot families. Even more surprising to me was the fact that many of the stories I was told stemmed from long before the introduction of commercial casino gambling, yet they had never surfaced previously during five years of living and working on the island with my Turkish Cypriot husband and family. Gambling, it seemed, was an underlying fact of life: persistent, relatively widespread, sometimes problematic, yet socially managed and accommodated. It was also evident that a shift had occurred with the opening of the casinos and the particular gambling opportunities they offered, exacerbating existing tensions and threatening established social and family strategies for managing gambling and its sometimes difficult consequences.

Such experiences are not unique to northern Cyprus. Over the past ten years, commercial gambling has undergone, and continues to undergo, rapid global expansion (Thompson, 1998). Its effects have been charted by a growing body of literature, characterised on the whole by a narrow focus on the economic impacts of casino developments and the social and psychological effects of problem gambling. Studies employing positivistic frameworks and quantitative methodologies predominate, and the widespread application of diagnostic tests such as the South Oaks Gambling Screen (SOGS) and DSM-IV criteria (Diagnostic and Statistical Manual of Mental Disorders) tends towards the medicalisation of gambling behaviour across a variety of cultural settings according to a dominant ethnocentric north American model (e.g. Becoña *et al.*, 1995; Duvarcý *et al.*, 1997). The focus on the a-cultural individual as the unit of research has meant that little attention has been paid to the significance of 'traditional' gambling cultures which pre-date the arrival of commercial casino gambling, except, as McMillan (1996a) notes, to reduce their diversity to a 'legal/illegal' dichotomy. Yet, as McMillan goes on to observe, although gambling is today widely understood as a form of risk-taking behaviour involving financial transactions, it is an activity which has taken and continues to take many different forms throughout the world, fulfilling diverse social functions, of which the economic is often the least important (McMillan, 1996a: 7). In order to understand the dynamics of the global casino industry, she argues, we need to address 'the fusion of global and local influences in contemporary gambling' (McMillan, 1996b: 264).

This paper presents an anthropological perspective on gambling which attempts to move beyond an 'impacts' approach to casino tourism in order to explore how the global casino industry connects with, mediates, and is mediated by, existing local gambling culture. The approach adopted emphasises the significance of the sociocultural context for an understanding of casino tourism. At the same time, it highlights certain conceptual difficulties in applying what Harrison (1996: 69) has termed the 'sustainability quasi-paradigm' to sociocultural dimensions of tourism development. As Harrison (1996) points out, it is not immediately obvious how the Brundtland (WCED, 1987) definition of sustainability (development meeting the needs of both present and future generations) should be interpreted in the context of the social and cultural institutions of tourism destinations. Efforts to apply the concept wholesale to the sociocultural structures of host communities make little sociological sense and are particularly prone to *over-estimating* locally prevailing levels of social cohesion (Harrison, 1996), whilst *under-estimating* the porous nature of cultural boundaries and the interpenetration of 'global' and 'local', 'modern' and 'traditional', i.e. 'internal' and 'external' worlds (Scott, 1995, 2001b). A further problem lies in the positive valuation cultural sustainability approaches place on manifestations of 'the traditional' which, as Harrison (1996: 84) points out, may themselves be spurious or rest on highly inegalitarian structures. It is perhaps significant that public concern about the possible consequences of gambling liberalisation in the UK (see Gambling Review Body, 2001) – concerns which focus, in particular, on associated criminality and a potential rise in problem gambling – have not been framed in terms of the threat to British cultural sustainability. As de Kadt (1990) points out, 'cultural sustainability' tends to be conflated with issues of authenticity, which are generally of more concern to tourists than to hosts.

The initial piece of exploratory research into the sociocultural context of casino tourism development in northern Cyprus was carried out during a month-long period of fieldwork in April 1999, building on previous anthropological fieldwork in 1992–94, and a period of residence and research from 1996–1998. The 1999 research employed multiple methods, including a questionnaire survey of 750 Turkish casino and non-casino tourists (published as Scott & Aþýkoðlu, 2001); participant observation in a variety of gambling settings, including 10 out of the 20 casinos; and extended semi-structured interviews with seven local casino/hotel managers, members of the Turkish Cypriot Restaurateurs' Association (in the course of their monthly meeting), the head of the Turkish Cypriot Hoteliers' Association, and numerous traders and small business owners in the tourist towns of Kyrenia and Famagusta. In addition, I worked with six key informants who had themselves worked as croupiers, were aficionados of cock-fighting and coffee-shop gambling, or who had family members who were. Information gained by these means was supplemented and triangulated through a detailed survey of local newspaper archives and through countless conversations with a wide variety of men and women of all ages, in the course of day-to-day interactions in the two principal tourist towns of Kyrenia and Famagusta and in four outlying villages. Conversations and interviews were conducted in Turkish, and were not taped, in order not to inhibit discussion of what for many informants were sensitive issues. Detailed short-hand notes were made in the course of interviews, or immediately afterwards, and written up on the same day (cf. Ellen, 1984: 278–85; Sanger, 1996: 65–72). Verbatim extracts from these interviews have been translated by the author.

I start by examining the background to the development of gambling and its place in Turkish Cypriot culture. I then consider what the new forms of casino gambling reveal about changes in Turkish Cypriot society and the challenges they present to the way gambling is managed by families and the community.

## The Development of Gambling within Turkish Cypriot Culture

Gambling has been a well-established part of Cypriot life since long before the advent of the casinos,[3] but in asking informants to tell me what they knew about different forms of gambling in Cyprus, it soon became apparent that their narratives were coloured by the current gambling boom. People's accounts of the development of gambling in the Turkish Cypriot community commonly trace a trajectory from a pastime rooted in non-monetary relations of sociability, through increasingly large money wagers, to the highly commercialised gambling of the modern casino sector. Despite the fact that gambling is a sin in Islam and illegal, both during the British rule of Cyprus and subsequently various forms of gambling have always been common and tolerated to different degrees. During the 1960s, family bingo was played during the intermission at the Turkish-language cinemas, and the British football pools were popular (and, indeed, are still played). Tombola and raffles were and remain common at local fairs and fund-raising events. Cockfighting was a common pastime and many informants in their thirties, forties and older had memories of cockfights taking place for wagers in town and village centres. There is no national lottery in northern Cyprus, but agents sell tickets for Turkey's national lottery, offering big cash prizes (see Duvarcý *et al.*, 1997) .

Outside the family context, card playing is traditionally a common focus for single-sex sociability. In the coffee shops, men play *gonga* and *pokerize*, a version of poker. I was told that before the 1950s there was 'no Turkish gambling', meaning that money transactions were not involved. The loser in a village cafe card game would treat the others to coffee or the traditional sweets, *lokum* or *sudam*. Middle-class women of the urban elite – the '*sosyete*' – would meet in each others' houses to pass the time playing *konken*, another card game. Yet other accounts of the time paint a slightly different picture, presenting gambling as a deeply embedded social and cultural activity with a pronounced monetary dimension. One common anecdote recounts the time when the British colonial authorities were enforcing the gambling ban in village cafes and men would lay bets on the colour of the next car to pass by. I was also told that large Turkish estates in the Kyrenia region (on the northern coast) had been lost to Greeks in card games. This contradicts both the present-day insistence that gambling was traditionally non-monetary in character and also the denials, from other informants, that gambling had ever taken place between Greek and Turkish Cypriots.

Village coffee shops and sports clubs – so called because they support a particular local football team – are important loci for the expression of the competitive egalitarianism which is an important cultural ideal of Cypriot masculinity (Herzfeld 1985; Peristiany, 1965[4]). Meeting in the village coffee shop, playing cards and attending the increasingly clandestine village cockfights are activities which permit men from across the social and occupational spectrum to indulge in forms of collective banter and play which are ultimately opportunities for the controlled yet competitive display of manhood. A rather different milieu is provided by the *şehir kulûbleri* – literally, 'town clubs' which are more akin to the idea of a 'gentlemen's club'. The reports of informants in Cyprus about the higher amounts of money gambled in such clubs accord with what Duvarcı *et al.* (1997) write about similar clubs in Turkey and explain the self-selecting, more socially homogenous membership of such clubs which, in contrast to the village coffee shops and sports clubs, is drawn almost exclusively from higher income groups.

Whilst male gambling has traditionally provided an arena for the expression of culturally-sanctioned masculine values in Cyprus, female gambling is a different matter and attitudes to it highlight a number of interesting tensions. Most male informants maintained that women's card playing was a rare and frivolous accompaniment to the main female social activity of 'visiting'. However, a memoir of a 1930s childhood in Cyprus recounts how the wife of the writer's uncle frequently lost money at afternoon card sessions, which took place according to rota in the house of confirmed female card 'addicts'. Later the ladies formed a club and rented a house in the Arab Ahmet district of Nicosia where they could gamble, free of husbands and 'grizzling children' (Baybars, 1970: 49). A poem by the noted feminist and journalist Uliviye Mithat, which appeared in the newspaper *Ses* in December 1936, provides a fascinating insight into such female card circles. Entitled *Rami – Fantazi* (Rummy – Fantasy) she writes about the game of rummy as a passion, a fickle lover and the husbands' rival. She describes the cheating, the arguments, the nicknames given to the players and ends:

> Ne Taundur ne de Veba
> Onlardan da saridir,
> Hep şilinler olur heba
> Ah bu Rami belası.

> [Neither plague nor pestilence
> It's more contagious than either of those,
> Shillings all are wasted on it
> Oh this cursed Rummy.]
> (Mithat, 1936; my translation.)[5]

It seems that, for women, gambling at cards was restricted to the members of the high society elite who had both the social standing to flout conventional norms regarding 'appropriate' female behaviour and access to the material means to do so – thus, paradoxically, reinforcing the existence of the norm for other, 'ordinary' women. Whilst, as a male activity, gambling promoted a sense of a common masculine identity transcending social class, for women it is traditionally tied to notions of respectability which mirror and reinforce the awareness of gendered class differences.

## The Meaning of Stories about 'Traditional Gambling'

Class and gender differences in gambling practices clearly emerge from the foregoing accounts. But differences also exist in the distribution of social knowledge concerning gambling and the ways and purposes for which this social knowledge is deployed. The idealisation of traditional gambling, with its emphasis on masculine sociability and non-monetary relations, can be read as part of a discourse of the loss of traditional Cypriot village ways and their replacement by a modern, urban commercial nexus which originates outside the island and primarily in Turkey. This discourse is clearly exemplified in the story of Şevket Kısmet, as featured in the series 'İçimizden Biri' (which could be translated as 'one of us') in the Turkish Cypriot daily newspaper *Kıbrıs* (17 July 1998 20–21).

The double-page feature tells the story of a 'man of the people' (*Halk Adamı*), whose life embodies 'typical Cypriotness' (*tipik Kıbrıslı 'lık*). In the story this takes the form of humble origins, hard work and cheerful irreverence; a colourful and chequered past in the multi-ethnic harbour town of Limasol; a lust for life lived in all its highs and lows; injustices suffered and hardships overcome; and a philosophy of life reflected in the name chosen for the family business, '*Kısmet*', meaning 'fate' or 'chance'. The gamble and the big gesture are an integral part of this emblematic life, with the subject recounting at one point how

> I got mixed up with a bad crowd! I got into gambling . . . drinking, cigarettes, this, that . . . you understand, I squandered the capital:
> (*Sonra, kötü arkadaşlarla düşdüg, garışdıg! Gumara alışdıg... işgi, sigara, şu, bu ... anadın; batırdık sermayeyi*).[6]

The story demonstrates the ambivalent position of gambling in the cultural values of the island and the mythologies of 'Cypriotness'. On the one hand it is portrayed as a disreputable and somewhat shameful activity with potentially anti-social and, in particular, anti-family consequences. In this particular story the gambling and other vicissitudes of life are overcome with the support of a loyal wife, a woman of strong character who tells the journalist 'Oh! He hasn't even been to the coffee shop for years!' ('*Uuuu! E'ya seneler vardır o gahveye bile gitmez ki!*'). The narrative ends happily with the foundation of a prosperous and secure family business and stable way of life. On the other hand, the story celebrates the qualities of risk-taking, daring and recklessness; the rebellious, independent and individualistic spirit of Cypriot masculinity, with which gambling is also associated. The complementary gender roles demonstrated in the story also represent a cultural ideal, with Şevket Bey's wife restoring order and stability by the exercise of female good sense and restraint.

In addition to the nostalgic discourse of Cypriotness, the stories of traditional gambling contain an implicit critique of modern casinos and the new forms of gambling. It is the casinos to which I now turn.

## Casino Stories

Casinos are becoming the focus for new stories about gambling. These stories are set within a different social space and reflect an apparently different social morality from the stories of traditional gambling, especially with regard to gender roles. One question to be addressed, however, concerns the extent to which these changes are substantive, or only apparent.

The casinos of northern Cyprus are, on the whole, very small by international standards, with an average of 10 tables and 70 slot machines per casino. The smallest has seven gaming tables and 18 slot machines, whilst the largest has 22 tables and 377 slot machines. All are attached to, or located within, hotels, holiday villages or other tourist accommodation. These too tend to be fairly small scale, although the largest, the recently refurbished Salamis Bay Hotel, has 960 beds. Most are situated out of town, either on the coast or, in some cases, in mountain locations. As northern Cyprus has so far seen very little coastal strip development, the casinos are often fairly isolated, apart from the surrounding holiday complex of which they form part.

The shift from village centre to peripheral tourist space represents more than a change in the physical location of gambling activities. Whereas stories of traditional gambling hinge on the local and the familiar, casino stories highlight the exotic, the extreme and the unfamiliar: from the behaviour of the tourists who visit the casinos, to the sexual attraction and danger of the foreign croupiers who work there (Scott, 1995). Stories of huge amounts of money gambled and won – or, more frequently, lost – replay the local story of Şevket Kısmet in a more dramatic key. But the most notorious incident along these lines – the extremely public suicide of a gambler who shot himself in a Turkish casino and whose death, captured on CCTV, was subsequently broadcast on Turkish television – represents the logic of the grand gesture taken to unacceptable limits, and was frequently cited by respondents in northern Cyprus as a warning of the dangerous extremes to which casino gambling can lead.

On a more mundane level, the identification of casino gambling with the tourism sector, with its local associations of modernisation and economic development, has facilitated its acceptance as a new kind of leisure activity amongst some sections of the population. Their location in holiday complexes, which often host annual dinner dances of clubs, trade unions, and professional and trade associations, encourages many Cypriot couples attending such social events to round off their evening by dropping into the casino to try their luck. In this way, casinos have become the focus for a new kind of 'couple-based' sociability, favoured in particular by younger, middle-class couples, in contrast to the more old-fashioned, traditional gender-segregated patterns of socialising. Indeed, in Kyrenia, the north's most fashionable resort for locals and tourists alike, the previously thriving coffee shop and sports club culture of the town was said by many to be dying out.

The casinos themselves have fostered their image as a modern, mainstream leisure product by sponsoring fashion shows, bringing top-flight celebrity entertainers over from Turkey, and providing free meals and drinks for customers. The provision of free entertainment, food and drink, exercises particular appeal given the economic problems of northern Cyprus, the extremely high annual rate of inflation (ca 70%) and low level of most local earnings. An evening spent observing the comings and goings in the Emperyal Casino in Kyrenia – the biggest and most modern casino in northern Cyprus – suggested that for many local couples, the casino had taken over from the town's picturesque Venetian harbour as the place for strolling, meeting friends, chatting and taking a drink and a bite to eat. Whilst the harbour remains popular with tourists and overseas students, the little harbour bars and restaurants have started to price themselves beyond the means of local residents.

Stories abound about the effects of these developments on Turkish Cypriot social life and on the family. A barber in Kyrenia, himself an habitué of the casinos, estimated in conversation that

> at least 80% of the local youth who have a nightlife go to the casinos for eating, drinking and playing. They go first of all for free food and drink. Then they bring their girlfriends. If they want to get drunk, they go the casinos first to drink whiskey and beer ... The young generation don't eat at home any more.

He himself, he maintained, had not eaten at home in two years. Gender role reversal is another popular theme of these stories, with anecdotes of heavy gambling by women and husbands who had to sell land in order to pay their wife's debts. Nevertheless, other accounts underline the persistence of more traditionally conventional gender norms. According to one casino manager, wives act as a brake on their husbands' gambling:

> The true gambler does not know the value of money – they like to play with chips and continue. The presence of a wife in the casino – somebody who *does* know the value of money – after a dinner dance or a reception for example – well, that can stop the man playing – 'Come on, we've won the cost of our night out, let's go.' If everyone just stayed and played for half an hour, the sector would go out of business.

The casino manager's view appears to confirm the opinion, widely expressed in northern Cyprus, about the dangerously addictive nature of gambling. Many informants saw the trappings of casino gambling as a lure to entice the weak and unwary.

> It's an attractive environment. Men like to go and see the croupiers in their short skirts. They gamble more.

> In Istanbul, before they banned the casinos, 2000 families had stopped eating at home – they go out and eat in casinos, say they are gambling their kitchen money, and end up gambling away their house money. The same thing is happening here now.

Despite the new trend for couples to visit casinos together, all-male gambling is still common. In the course of participant observation in small, out-of-town casinos, the only women observed gambling were tourists, whilst all-male groups of gamblers from local villages congregated around other tables. Town-centre casinos located in four- and five-star hotels, however, attracted a more urban, middle- and upper-class Cypriot clientele which included couples –

further evidence of the gender / class differential in relation to gambling, alluded to earlier.

Despite the growing popularity of the casinos as a leisure venue, gambling remains illegal for Turkish Cypriots and, from time to time, police raids are carried out at casinos to remind citizens of that fact – although they are often warned of an impending raid by an alarm bell and given time to escape via a back door. Although a nominal fine may be levied, in the tightly-knit Turkish Cypriot community, where reputation remains important and each individual is widely known through networks of friends, neighbours and extended kin, the real sanction remains the 'naming and shaming' of those charged and taken to court. Informants were emphatic that public humiliation remains a real deterrent to gambling in the casinos. According to the manager of one town-centre casino in the capital Nicosia, it is the reason why women, in particular, are reluctant to visit the casinos, and evidence of the continuing ambivalence towards the casinos in Turkish Cypriot society.

So far I have concentrated on social discourse about traditional and casino gambling. A number of parallels can be discerned in the stories told about both: the ambivalence towards gambling; the strong association with gender ideology; and the contradictory tendencies towards the subversion, reinforcement and transformation of conventional gender norms. It is also worth noting the significance of these gambling stories as points of reference for the construction of Turkish Cypriot ethnic identity; for whereas many of the stories of 'traditional' gambling invoke previous contacts and commonalities with Greek Cypriots, the casinos provide a setting for contrast and comparison with modern metropolitan Turkish culture. In the next section, I want to consider how these discourses are reflected in some of the practices and social relationships surrounding gambling in the traditional and casino contexts.

## Casinos and the Transformation of Gambling Spaces

According to many informants, the only difference between casino gambling and coffee shop gambling is one of scale. As one informant, a village school teacher observed, with the casinos, gambling has been 'industrialised'. Yet 'problem gambling' is a feature of the coffee shop as much as the casino. In the words of a casino manager: '"Big money" is what you can spend. It can be a large or small amount, depending on the individual'.

Gambling was said by many informants to be a major cause of divorce and domestic violence. The following account tells of an attempt to solve the problem in one village:

> I was the head of the sports club in X village, and some of the women started coming to me complaining that their men were gambling and losing and then coming home and beating up them and the kids. The coffee shop owner was getting commission, and there were 6–7 tables gambling. I got together with some of the men from the village who were gamblers, and also with the local police chief who was living in the village. He said he would like to help stop the gambling because he could not go to the café in his own village because of the gambling. Together, we managed to stop it for a while. We put an extra pool table in the cafe, and some table tennis

tables so there would be no room for gambling. But I had to go to London for eight months and when I came back, they had started up again. Every so often the police do a raid – they take away the money and the tables and chairs, then they bring them back again . . .

This account echoes several familiar themes, particularly with regard to the gender roles represented, the ambivalence suggested by the police's informal tolerance of the illegal gambling and their periodic ineffectual raids. But what is also interesting is the women's mobilisation of informal social networks in the village in order to curb the men's gambling, a recourse which was made possible by the location of the gambling in the highly visible village centre café, at the heart of male social relations in the village.

There is a curious symmetry in the construction of the social space of the casino and the village coffee shop. The coffee shop remains the primordial masculine space within what is still the sharply gender-segregated geography of the village. As with the villages studied by Reiter (1975: 257) in the south of France, women and girls will make considerable detours in order to avoid the main street where men sit outside the cafés, playing backgammon and watching the world go by. Casinos, in contrast, offer themselves, as we have seen, as a new kind of leisure space for men, women and couples; but they are located in 'liminal' tourist spaces, away from the social constraints of the village. Gambling in the casinos takes place mainly at night, in enclosed, windowless rooms and lubricated by the free flow of alcohol. Coffee shop gambling, in contrast, takes place in the broad light of day as well as at night time, with the life of the village going on all around. There are further contrasts in the types of games played and the way they are played. Gambling in the casinos consists of a one-to-one relationship between the gambler and the slot machine; or it is mediated by, and directed towards, the croupier who spins the roulette wheel or deals the hand. Coffee shop gambling, in contrast, is embedded in the multi-stranded relationships of the village. This is particularly evident in the matter of the extension of credit for gambling. At present there are no regulations in northern Cyprus governing minimum or maximum stakes or the giving of credit, which is made widely available in casinos. During fieldwork I came across several reports of families having to sell the car or some land in order to cover gambling debts and, in two extreme cases, even of individuals who had fled the island because they were unable to pay their gambling debts. Credit is also extended in coffee shop gambling. Coffee shop owners make a minimal charge per hour for each gambler at their table or take a percentage of the pot after each hand and therefore have an interest in prolonging the game. In certain villages, informants told me that coffee shop games had been known to go on for days. However, the amount of credit extended is limited according to the coffee shop owner's expectation of recouping the loan, his knowledge of the individuals involved and their circum-stances. Social pressure – including threats to inform a gambler's wife of his debts – may be the only means available to enforce collection of the debt. These debts can sometimes be substantial. Although they may not equal the thousands of pounds run up at casinos, they may amount to two or three hundred pounds in a night – the equivalent of an unskilled labourer's monthly wage.

Despite some exceptions to the contrary, gambling in northern Cyprus is largely perceived as an activity for men – and a problem for women. Their ability to deal with this problem is arguably much greater in the village context than in the casino context – despite the fact that the casino is presented as a leisure space for men *and* women, whereas the village coffee shop remains a resolutely masculine space. Informal social pressure, and the manipulation of social knowledge, cannot be effectively brought to bear on casino owners and managers, who are seldom from the locality. Requests to the police to conduct a raid – a frequent expedient in the village context to put a temporary stop to a husband's gambling – are unlikely to be acceded to in the case of a casino, as frequent raids would put off casino tourists. The teacher's comment about the industrialisation of gambling, mentioned earlier, seems apposite, not only in relation to the increased scale of gambling but also in its implicit reference to the alienation of casino gambling space from informal local control.

## Conclusion

The current spread of casino tourism is part of a broader global trend which includes the growth of national lotteries, the deregulation of existing restrictive gambling regimes, and the rising popularity of internet gambling. Accompanying and facilitating the enormous financial flows involved is a cultural shift in which gambling is being reinvented as a modern, global, mainstream leisure and tourism product, not a vice to be controlled, as it has been traditionally viewed in, for example, European jurisdictions (McMillan 1996b; Gambling Review Body, 2001; Lemon, 1998). The 'individualisation' of gambling – with its focus on the rights and freedoms of the a-cultural individual as a leisure consumer – is integral to this shift and goes hand in hand with the promotion of the American 'corporate casino' model worldwide. As Thompson (1998: 16–17) puts it:

> the basic political philosophy that dominates policymaking in Europe has its roots in notions of collective responsibility . . . On the other hand, in America, and especially in the American West, people are expected to control their own behaviors.

But this is only part of the story, for as the anthropologists Kasmir and Wilson (1999: 377) observe, in the globalised economy, 'even the hyper-rapid transnational flows of capital, discourse and power emerge from and "land" *somewhere*' (emphasis added). The 'somewhere' they land is not a *tabula rasa* and my aim in this paper has been to draw attention to the existing social and cultural landscape which mediates the 'localisation' of casino tourism development in northern Cyprus.

Cultural responses to casino tourism development in northern Cyprus clearly demonstrate the interpenetration of global and local, 'the modern' and 'the traditional' in Turkish Cypriot society, and the ambivalence with which gambling is regarded reveals much about the tensions and contradictions in Turkish Cypriot life. The stories people tell about casino, coffee shop and other forms of gambling, which make conscious reference to categories such as 'tradition' and 'modernity', are demonstrations of reflexive discourse which both reinforce and subvert entrenched social values. On the one hand, coffee shop gambling, the *şehir kulûbleri*, and the ladies card circles evoke the 'old' Cyprus with its certainties of established gender and class norms and its informal sociability. On the other hand, the luxury, formality and modernity of the casinos speak to the aspirations of the upwardly mobile and, in particular, younger generation, which increasingly identifies with urban metropolitan popular culture as reflected on satellite and Turkish television. Furthermore, the individualistic model of the gambler promoted by the global casino industry chimes well with certain cultural ideals of Cypriot masculinity as embodied in male gambling. At the same time, these gambling stories also embody a variety of critiques of Cypriot society, whether it is the incidence of domestic violence which is an element of the 'traditional' masculinist culture of Cyprus, or the extension of Turkey's cultural and economic dominance of Turkish Cypriot society via the casino sector.

Elsewhere (Scott, 2001a) I have argued that casino tourism development is, generally speaking, an opportunistic and contingent form of development, largely concentrated in marginal locations with few other development options and tending to reinforce existing relations of dependency. In this sense, the long-term viability of casino tourism is open to doubt – and to the extent that it may also detract from or undermine other aspects of the local tourism product, it may pose wider problems of sustainability for tourist destinations (Scott & Aşýkoğlu, 2001). Cultural sustainability, however, is not, I would suggest, an appropriate means of conceptualising and addressing the issues. Culture does not constitute a limited local resource. Gambling holds an established if problematic place in Cypriot social and cultural practices. Whilst the question of whether the increased availability of gambling necessarily stimulates 'problem gambling' (however that is defined) is still a matter of debate (see Bellringer, 2001; Gambling Review Body, 2001), it seems clear in the case of northern Cyprus that the opportunities for gambling have always been plentiful. What has changed is the constitution of the social and moral space in which gambling occurs. The emergence of gambling activity in 'liminal' locations away from highly visible village-centre settings has, it seems, limited the effectiveness of traditional strategies for managing the new 'industrialised' forms of gambling. It seems likely that the *privatisation* of gambling, and consequent undermining of local coping mechanisms constitutes a significant shift in local gambling practices. It remains to be seen what social and cultural resources will be brought to bear on this change.

## Correspondence

Any correspondence should be directed to Dr Julie Scott, London Metropolitan University, Stapleton House, 277–281 Holloway Road, London, N7 8HN (j.scott@londonmet.ac.uk).

## Notes

1.  Closure of the casinos became inevitable with the electoral success of the Islamic Welfare Party in Turkey in 1997.
2.  For more detail on the division of Cyprus and its effects on tourism see Ioannides (1992) and Scott (2000).
3.  The opening of a casino in the (Greek Cypriot) Republic of Cyprus has long been debated in the south but so far not sanctioned (Miller, 2000).
4.  Peristiany was writing about a Greek Cypriot village and Herzfeld about Crete, but

their observations are equally valid reflections of Turkish Cypriot views on masculinity.
5.  I am indebted to Mr Taçgey Debeş of Eastern Mediterranean University for drawing
    my attention to this poem.
6.  In the newspaper article, speech is rendered in the local Cypriot dialect, thus reinforc-
    ing the sense of the 'local' and 'intimate' in the story.

## References

Baybars, T. (1970) *Plucked in a Far-off Land. Images in Self Biography*. London: Gollancz.
Becoña, E., Labrador, F., Echeburúa, E., Ochoa, E. and Vallejo, M.A. (1995) Slot machine
    gambling in Spain: An important and new social problem. *Journal of Gambling Studies*
    11, 265–86.
Bellringer, P. (2001) Gamcare's response to gambling review recommendations. Unpub-
    lished conference paper, Gamcare Annual Conference, 17 October.
de Kadt, E. (1990) *Making the Alternative Sustainable: Lessons from Development for Tourism*.
    Institute of Development Studies Discussion Paper No. 272. Brighton: University of
    Sussex
Duvarcı, İ., Varan, A., Coşkunol, H. and Ersoy, M.A. (1997) DSM-IV and the South Oaks
    gambling screen: Diagnosing and assessing pathological gambling in Turkey. *Journal of
    Gambling Studies* 13, 193–206.
Ellen, R.F. (1984) *Ethnographic Research: A Guide to General Conduct. (Research Methods in
    Social Anthropology* 1). London: Academic Press.
Gambling Review Body (2001) *Gambling Review Report (The Budd Report)*. London: Depart-
    ment for Culture, Media and Sport.
Harrison, D. (1996) Sustainability and tourism: Reflections from a muddy pool. In L.
    Briguglio (ed.) *Sustainable Tourism in Islands and Small States* (pp. 69–89). London:
    Pinter.
Herzfeld, M. (1985) *The Poetics of Manhood: Contest and Identity in a Cretan Mountain Village*.
    Princeton: Princeton University Press.
Ioannides, D. (1992) Tourism development agents: The Cypriot resort cycle. *Annals of
    Tourism Research* 19, 711–31.
Kasmir, S. and Wilson, A. (1999) Introduction. *Critique of Anthropology* 19 (4), 376–8.
Lemon, B. (1998) Weighing up the odds. *Leisure Management* 18 (9), 62–3.
McMillan, J. (1996a) Understanding gambling. History, concepts, theories. In J. McMillan
    (ed.) *Gambling Cultures: Studies in History and Interpretation* (pp. 6–42). London:
    Routledge.
McMillan, J. (1996b) From glamour to grind. The globalisation of casinos. In J. McMillan
    (ed.) *Gambling Cultures: Studies in History and Interpretation* (pp. 263–87). London:
    Routledge.
Miller, A.O. (2000) The bets are off. *Sunday Mail* (17 September), 14.
Mithat, U. (1936) Rami – Fantazi. In F. Azgın (ed.) (1998) *Ulviye Mithat: Feminist Buluşma* (pp.
    38–9). Nicosia: Meral Tekin Birinci Vakfı/Kıbrıs Tûrk Üniversiteli Kadınlar Derneği.
Peristiany, J.G. (1965) Honour and shame in a Cypriot highland village. In J.G. Peristiany
    (ed.) *Honour and Shame, the Values of Mediterranean Society* (pp. 171–90). London:
    Weidenfeld and Nicholson.
Reiter, R.R. (1975) Men and women in the south of France: Public and private domains. In
    R.R. Reiter (ed.) *Toward an Anthropology of Women* (pp. 252–82). New York: Monthly
    Review Press.
Sanger, J. *The Compleat Observer? A Field Research Guide to Observation*. Qualitative Studies
    Series 2. London: Falmer.
Scott, J. (1995) Sexual and national boundaries in tourism. *Annals of Tourism Research* 22 (2),
    385–403.
Scott, J. (2000) Peripheries, artificial peripheries and centres. In F. Brown and D. Hall (eds)
    *Tourism in Peripheral Regions* (pp. 58–73) Clevedon: Channel View.
Scott, J. (2001a) 'Everything's bubbling, but we don't know what the ingredients are.'
    Casino politics and policy in the periphery. *Electronic Journal of Gambling Issues* 4. On
    WWW at http://www.camh.net/egambling.

Scott, J. (2001b) Gender and sustainability in Mediterranean island tourism. In D. Ioannides, Y. Apostolopoulos and S. Sönmez (eds) *Sustainable Tourism in Mediterranean Islands: Policy and Practice* (pp. 87–107). London: Continuum International.

Scott, J. and A. Aşızkoğlu (2001) Gambling with paradise? Casino tourism development in northern Cyprus. *Journal of Tourism and Travel Research* 26 (3), 47–57.

Thompson, W.N. (1998) Casinos de Juegos del Mundo: A survey of world gambling. *Annals of the American Academy of Political and Social Science* 556, 11–21.

WCED (World Commission on Environment and Development) (1987) *Our Common Future (The Brundtland Report)*. Oxford: Oxford University Press.

# 16 Tourism, Modernisation and Development on the Island of Cyprus: Challenges and Policy Responses

*Richard Sharpley*
*Centre for Travel and Tourism, University of Northumbria, Morpeth,*
*Northumberland NE61 3LL, UK*

The role of tourism as an agent of development in small island states is virtually universal. Indeed, for many islands, tourism is the principal source of employment and foreign exchange earnings and the dominant economic sector. Nevertheless, many commentators suggest that island tourism is characterised by dependency, a condition which, according to development theory, restricts development. As a result, sustainable tourism development is widely seen as a solution to the problem of island tourism. This paper, however, argues that this is not necessarily the case. Based on a case study of Cyprus, it demonstrates that, despite its inherent dependency, tourism has proved to be an effective vehicle of development. Moreover, it is the development of mass tourism as a modernising growth pole that has contributed to the remarkable socioeconomic development of the island since the mid-1970s. Therefore, it suggests that, far from being a solution, the current policy for promoting sustainable or 'quality' tourism is not only inappropriate but may actually hinder the further development of Cyprus.

## Introduction

Tourism has long been considered an effective vehicle of development in general, and in island micro-states in particular. Indeed, it has been observed that, in an island context, reliance upon tourism as a means of development is almost universal (Lockhart, 1997), whilst recent figures indicate that the top 20 nations ranked according to the contribution of tourism to GDP are all island destinations (World Travel and Tourism Council, WTTC, 2001a). Certainly, tourism has played a dominant role in the socioeconomic development and is the principal economic sector of many islands within the Mediterranean region. At the same time, for islands in the developing world 'gross receipts from tourism are larger than all visible exports put together' (King, 1993: 28).

However, the virtually ubiquitous development of tourism in island micro-states has, perhaps inevitably, been accompanied by increasing concern about the consequences of such development (Conlin & Baum, 1995; Harrison, 2001; Lockhart & Drakakis-Smith 1997; Wrangham, 1999). Not only do the specific physical and socioeconomic characteristics of islands, representing their attraction to tourists, serve to increase their potential vulnerability to the pressures of tourism on natural and human resources but also island tourism development is widely considered to be typified by a condition of dependency (Bastin, 1984; MacNaught, 1982; Milne, 1992). That is, island economies may become dependent upon a dominant tourism sector, whilst the tourism sector itself is often subject to the external domination of, for example, overseas tour operators, airlines or hotel chains (Sastre & Benito, 2001). Indeed, some have suggested that island tourism development inevitably follows a 'vicious circle' of dependency (Milne, 1997; also Palmer, 1994; Wilkinson, 1989) and, thus, reflects the 'centre–periphery' dependency model of development. Not surprisingly, therefore, attention has been increasingly focused on sustainable tourism as a means of addressing, if not solving, the inherent challenges of island tourism development (Briguglio *et al.*, 1996; Ioannides *et al.*, 2001b).

This paper adopts the counter-position. It argues that dependency (in the broader, dependency paradigm context) is not the inevitable outcome of island tourism development and that, consequently, the commonly proposed 'antidote' to dependency – sustainable tourism development (in a form most commonly manifested in practice) – may not represent the most appropriate policy response. This is not to suggest that sustainable tourism should not be an objective; however, using the development of tourism in Cyprus[1] as a case study, it will be suggested that, under certain circumstances, the use of more traditional, mass forms of tourism as a modernising economic 'growth pole' may be a more effective means of optimising the contribution of tourism to the development of island micro-states. The purpose of this paper, therefore, is to identify lessons from the developmental experience of Cyprus that may be relevant to other island destinations. The first task, however, is to review briefly the contrasting development paradigms of modernisation, dependency and sustainable development as a theoretical framework for the subsequent analysis of tourism in Cyprus.

## Development Theory: Modernisation, Dependency and Sustainable Development

As noted, tourism is widely justified as a vehicle of development, yet the meaning and objectives of 'development' often remain unclear. Traditionally, it has been equated with economic growth, socioeconomic development being seen as the inevitable consequence of an increase in per capita wealth (Mabogunje, 1980). However, development is more commonly considered a multi-dimensional process embracing not only economic but also social, political, cultural and environmental factors – it is a 'continuous and positively evaluated change in the totality of human experience' (Harrison, 1998: xiii). Through what processes, then, may development be achieved?

### Modernisation theory

The core premise of modernisation theory is that all societies follow an evolutionary path to development and that, according to their stage of development, societies can be located at different positions or stages on a path from traditional to modern (Telfer, 2002: 40). Once a particular society attains the so-called 'take-off' stage (Rostow, 1960), modernisation or development can occur as a result of economic growth and diffusion – economic growth being synonymous, from the modernisation perspective, with development. Such economic growth may be induced in a variety of ways, such as the balanced 'big push' approach, although it is the notion of 'poles of growth', which may be either urban centres or economic sectors, that is of most relevance to tourism-related development. That is, tourism represents an economic growth pole from which economic benefits 'trickle down' or diffuse throughout the economy through the promotion of backward linkages, the income multiplier effect, and so on. As observed by Wall

(1997), the Mexican policy of developing large resorts, such as Cancun, is one example of the application of this approach. Thus, modernisation is, in effect, a process of 'westernisation', with economic growth underpinning western-style sociocultural development.

Not surprisingly, modernisation theory is criticised for its assumption of inevitable modernisation, its western ethnocentrism and its fundamental doctrine of economic growth, the latter frequently reliant on investment from the metropolitan centres as well as the implicit exclusion of local input into the development process. Nevertheless, it most closely reflects the process of tourism-related development, the benefits of which are most commonly measured in economic terms.

## Dependency theory

Dependency theory, sometimes referred to as underdevelopment theory, emerged in the 1960s as a critique of the modernisation paradigm. Based upon Marxist theory, it has been defined as 'a conditioning situation in which the economies of one group of countries are conditioned by the development and expansion of others' (Dos Santos, 1970: 231). In other words, within the single, capitalist world system, wealthy western nations utilise their dominant position to exploit weaker, peripheral nations, often mirroring earlier colonial ties (Frank, 1969). Thus, less developed countries display external political and economic structures that maintain their dependency on the metropolitan centre; they are unable to develop unless 'permitted' to do so by the West.

Given the inherent political economy of international tourism (Bianchi, 2002), it is evident that there exist parallels between tourism development and dependency theory, particularly in an island context. As Lea (1988: 10) observes, tourism 'has evolved in a way that closely matches historical patterns of colonialism and economic dependency'. The focus here, however, is on the potential underdevelopment that results from dependency.

## Sustainable development

In contrast to modernisation theory, sustainable development gives primacy to the satisfaction of basic needs, such as food, shelter, healthcare and education, although economic growth remains a fundamental prerequisite – the 'pollution of poverty' must first be addressed before development in form can occur. Importantly, the principal focus of sustainable development is also upon a local, 'bottom-up' or grassroots approach in order to ensure both development according to local needs and the promotion of local choice and political freedom, whilst development itself must be environmentally sustainable. Thus, sustainable development proposes a long-term, holistic perspective that espouses equity, choice, political freedom (from dependency), cultural integrity and development within environmental parameters.

The extent to which tourism may contribute to sustainable development remains the subject of rigorous debate (Butler, 1998, 1999; Sharpley, 2000a; Sharpley & Telfer, 2002). Indeed, given both the characteristics of the production of tourism with its inherently unbalanced power relationships and the nature of tourism consumption as, essentially, an ego-centric activity, it is not surprising, perhaps, that sustainable tourism development in practice is largely manifested in small-scale, localised projects which, though laudable in themselves, bear little relation to global requirements of sustainable development. Nevertheless, sustainable development has become, according to Hall (2000), the 'imperative' of tourism planning in general whilst, for Mediterranean islands in particular, the rate and impacts of tourism development, the degree of dependency on international tour operators and the loss of competitiveness have meant that sustainability, frequently equated with the search for 'quality tourism', is considered a pressing need (Ioannides *et al.*, 2001).

Certainly, this is the case in Cyprus. By the mid 1980s, the rate and scale of tourism development was considered to be unsustainable (EIU, 1992) and, as a consequence, the Cyprus Tourism Organisation (CTO) attempted to implement, albeit unsuccessfully, a succession of policies aimed at developing higher quality, more sustainable forms of tourism. Nevertheless, tourism has underpinned the rapid and remarkable economic development of the country since 1974 and continues to drive economic growth and development (Ayers, 2000; Sharpley, 2001a). Thus, as this paper now argues, the development of traditional, mass tourism has proved to be an effective economic growth pole in Cyprus, providing the foundation for broader 'modernisation' and development of the island.

## Cyprus: Tourism and Development

Since 1960, when the island gained its independence from Britain, tourism development in Cyprus has occurred in two distinct phases (for more detail, see Andonikou, 1987; Cope, 2000; Ioannides, 1992; Seekings, 1997; Sharpley, 2001a, b).

### Tourism development in Cyprus: phase 1

The first phase, up to 1974, witnessed the beginning of the island's transformation into a major Mediterranean summer sun destination as the focus of tourism development shifted from the traditional hill resorts of the Troodos mountains to the coastal resorts of Kyrenia and Famagusta (Figure 1).

During this period, and particularly from the late 1960s onwards, tourism grew rapidly. Annual arrivals, which totalled just 25,700 in 1960, exceeded 264,000 by 1973, representing an average annual growth rate of over 20%, whilst tourist receipts grew at an annual average of 22% (Table 1). At the same time, the characteristics of tourism development on the island, even at this early stage, were following a pattern typical of many Mediterranean destinations. That is, development was focused primarily on coastal resorts (by 1973, Kyrenia and Famagusta accounted for 58% of accommodation and 73% of arrivals), demand was highly seasonal and the UK had already emerged as the principal market (Andronikou, 1987; Lockhart, 1993).

Not surprisingly, perhaps, this first period of tourism development coincided with a rapid growth of the island's economy. In 1960, Cyprus was relatively undeveloped; for example, agriculture, though providing almost half of all employment, contributed just 16% of GDP, whilst manufacturing (10% of GDP) was restricted to the processing of locally produced agricultural raw materials (Andronikou, 1987). Thus, 'one of the major goals of the island's first development plan called for an import substitution policy as a tool to achieve

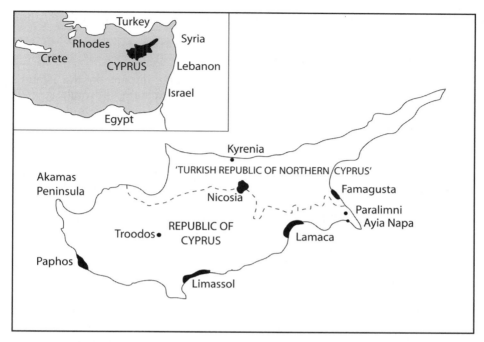

**Figure 1** Map of Cyprus

**Table 1** Tourism growth rates in Cyprus 1960–73

| | Arrivals/earnings | | | | Rates of growth (%) | | |
|---|---|---|---|---|---|---|---|
| | 1960 | 1966 | 1971 | 1973 | 1960–66 | 1966–73 | 1960–73 |
| Tourist arrivals ('000s) | 25.4 | 54.1 | 178.6 | 264.1 | 13 | 25 | 20 |
| Foreign exchange earnings (CY£m) | 1.8 | 3.6 | 13.6 | 23.8 | 12 | 31 | 22 |
| Contribution of earnings to GDP (%) | 2.0 | 2.5 | 5.2 | 7.2 | | | |

*Source*: PIO (1997: 251); Ayers (2000)

industrialisation and greater economic development . . . taking advantage of the island's natural resources' (Kammas, 1993: 71).

This was certainly achieved; as Brey (1995: 92) observes: 'in the 14 years after independence . . . Cyprus, with a free enterprise economy based on trade and agriculture, achieved a higher standing of living than any of its neighbours, with the exception of Israel'. Not only did the economy grow remarkably, but tourism's contribution to GDP grew from around 2.0% in 1960 to 7.2% in 1973 (Table 1). At the same time, some 3.8% of the working population were employed in tourism (Ayers, 2000). Thus, even then, tourism was emerging as an effective economic growth pole, underpinning the economic growth and modernisation of Cyprus.

## Tourism development in Cyprus: phase 2

The Turkish invasion in 1974 had a devastating impact on the island's economy in general and on the tourism sector in particular (Andronikou, 1979; Gillmor, 1989; Lockhart, 1993). The great majority of existing and planned accommodation, as well as the island's international airport at Nicosia and many other tourist facilities, were lost and arrivals in 1975 amounted to just 47,000.

However, despite the enormous problems facing the country, the second phase of tourism development in Cyprus from 1975 onwards again witnessed remarkable growth. Between 1976 and 1989, for example, annual arrivals increased by 700% (Witt, 1991), whilst the receipts from tourism also grew rapidly. Indeed, the 1973 figure of CY£23.8 million was re-attained by 1977 and, during the 1980s as a whole, tourism receipts grew at an average annual rate of 23% (CTO, 1990). Since 1990, arrivals and receipts figures have been somewhat erratic. Over 2.6 million arrivals were recorded in 2000, generating CY£1,194 million in receipts (CTO, 2001), whilst, at the time of writing, over 2.8 million tourists were expected to have visited Cyprus during 2001 (Kattamis, 2001). In 2002, however, a 10–15% fall in arrivals is expected as a result of increased tension in the Middle East, capacity reductions on the part of tour operators following the events of 11 September 2001and the Agia Napa factor (see later).

Such overall dramatic growth has reflected the island's rapid emergence as a major Mediterranean summer sun destination, in particular since the mid-1980s when overseas charter airlines were first permitted to operate to Cyprus. This, in turn, has been driven by the no less rapid growth in accommodation facilities (Sharpley, 2000b), primarily in the coastal resorts of Paphos, Limassol, Agia Napa and Paralimni, the latter two resorts currently accounting for over 40% of the island's accommodation stock and attracting 32% of all arrivals in 2000 (CTO, 2001). Indeed, the popularity of Agia Napa as one of the Mediterranean's premier clubbing/nightlife centres has been a major contributor to the recent growth in arrivals in Cyprus, although by early 2002, bookings for Agia Napa were some 40% down on 2001 (Machalepis, 2002) – the family market has been deterred by the clubbing image, whilst the resort's popularity as a nightlife centre has proved to be short-lived. The key indicators of tourism development on the island since 1975 are provided in Table 2.

## The economic impact of tourism in Cyprus

Inevitably, tourism has assumed an increasingly important role in the Cypriot economy. Tourism receipts which, in 1975, contributed just over 2% of GDP, currently contribute some 20% of GDP. However, as Ayers (2000) points out, this figure does not indicate the true impact of tourism on the economy. That is, the rapid growth in tourism has stimulated growth in other sectors, particularly construction, as well as in related industries such as financial services, communications and transport, whilst 'agriculture and manufacturing also benefited from the increasing number of arrivals who boosted demand for a wide range of locally produced products' (Ayers, 2000). At the same time, the production of other products and handicrafts, such as wines and lace, has been revitalised by

**Table 2** Tourism in Cyprus 1975–2000 – key indicators

| Year | Arrivals (000s) | Receipts (CY£mn) | Average tourist spending (C£) | Tourism receipts as % of GDP | Total licensed bedspaces |
|------|------|------|------|------|------|
| 1975 | 47 | 5 | n.a. | 2.1 | 5,685 |
| 1980 | 349 | 72 | 200 | 9.4 | 12,830 |
| 1985 | 770 | 232 | 299 | 15.7 | 30,375 |
| 1986 | 828 | 256 | 308 | 16.0 | 33,301 |
| 1987 | 949 | 320 | 334 | 18.0 | 45,855 |
| 1988 | 1,112 | 386 | 344 | 19.4 | 48,518 |
| 1989 | 1,379 | 490 | 350 | 21.7 | 54,857 |
| 1990 | 1,561 | 573 | 364 | 23.4 | 59,574 |
| 1991 | 1,385 | 476 | 343 | 18.4 | 63,564 |
| 1992 | 1,991 | 694 | 351 | 23.8 | 69,759 |
| 1993 | 1,841 | 696 | 379 | 21.4 | 73,657 |
| 1994 | 2,069 | 810 | 389 | 22.3 | 76,117 |
| 1995 | 2,100 | 810 | 383 | 20.5 | 78,427 |
| 1996 | 1,950 | 780 | 382 | 19.0 | 78,427 |
| 1997 | 2,088 | 843 | 393 | 20.4 | 84,368 |
| 1998 | 2,222 | 878 | 380 | 20.2 | 86,151 |
| 1999 | 2,434 | 1,025 | 400 | 22.0 | 84,173 |
| 2000 | 2,686 | 1,194 | n.a. | 21.7 | 85,303 |

*Source*: CTO Reports; Department of Statistics and Research; Ayers (2000)

tourism demand. It is surprising, therefore, that in a country so dependent upon tourism, no figures are published that provide a indication of the overall value of tourism. Nevertheless, according to the World Travel & Tourism Council's satellite accounting research, the tourism economy in Cyprus contributed almost 31% of GDP in 2001, a figure forecast to rise to 34.2% by 2011 (WTTC, 2001b).

Tourism is also the dominant source of employment on the island. In 2000, 40,500 people were directly employed in tourism, around 18,000 of whom work in the hotel sector (Department of Statistics and Research, 2002) whilst, overall, some 25% of the working population are directly and indirectly dependent on the tourism sector. Thus, in a social development sense, tourism has made a vital contribution by maintaining virtually full employment on the island – for the last two decades, unemployment has remained at about 3%. This has, in turn, stimulated the entry of women into the labour market – their participation rate has increased from under 29% in 1976 to around 50% at present – but, at the same time, it has been necessary to recruit a significant number of foreign nationals to make up for a shortage in the labour market. Indeed, it is paradoxical that, as the

**Table 3** Contribution of tourism's foreign exchange earnings

|  | Tourism receipts (CY£mn) | Tourism receipts as a percentage of | | | | |
|---|---|---|---|---|---|---|
|  |  | *Export of goods* | *Invisible exports* | *Total exports* | *Imports of goods* | *Total imports* |
| 1980 | 72 | 41.5 | 29.2 | 17.2 | 18.8 | 14.4 |
| 1985 | 232 | 90.8 | 39.8 | 27.7 | 32.7 | 24.0 |
| 1990 | 573 | 147.6 | 52.8 | 38.7 | 49.9 | 36.8 |
| 1995 | 810 | 158.8 | 51.0 | 38.6 | 54.0 | 37.3 |
| 1996 | 780 | 130.6 | 49.4 | 35.8 | 46.8 | 32.6 |
| 1997 | 843 | 139.3 | 49.5 | 36.5 | 49.4 | 33.9 |
| 1998 | 878 | 169.2 | 48.7 | 37.8 | 48.6 | 33.3 |
| 1999 | 1,025 | 203.3 | 49.8 | 40.0 | 57.0 | 38.2 |
| 2000 | 1,194 | 228.3 | 48.4 | 39.9 | 53.9 | 36.5 |

*Source*: Adapted from Department of Statistics and Research (2001)

labour force as a whole has become better educated and trained, there are too few Cypriots willing to take lower-grade jobs in hotels (but too many chasing relatively few management positions). As a result, in Paphos hotels alone there were some 1000 vacancies in early 2002 (Pyrillos, 2002).

Moreover, high employment levels coupled with powerful trade unions representing the majority of employees have also resulted in rapid increases in wages in the tourism sector. For example, the average cost of labour in hotels rose by 94% between 1992 and 1997 (Karis, 1998), leading to a significant fall in productivity, employment levels and, ultimately, the level of service. However, likely membership of the EU will make it easier to recruit (cheaper) overseas staff although, importantly, a greater proportion of foreign workers is likely to dilute the traditional hospitality for which Cyprus is renowned, further diminishing the island's competitiveness.

Tourism has also played a vital role in terms of foreign exchange earnings. As with most small island states, Cyprus is obliged to import many raw materials and manufactured goods and, unless such essential imports can be financed by export earnings, economic growth – and, hence, development – may be constrained. Since 1980, tourism has made an increasingly important contribution to invisible earnings and, by 2000, represented over 48% of invisible earnings, 40% of all exports and covered 54% of the import of goods (see Table 3).

As is evident from Table 3, receipts from tourism have had a significant influence on the island's balance of payments, particularly in the context of relatively static earnings from the export of goods. Inevitably, leakages occur to support the needs of the tourism sector as well as to meet the demands of an increasingly prosperous local population but although specific figures are not available, it can be assumed that the ability of local producers to supply hotels, restaurants, souvenir shops and so on has maintained such leakages at a relatively low level. Tourism receipts have also, therefore, helped to sustain a high rate of overall economic growth, which has averaged around 10% per annum since 1980 (Ayers, 2000) and which reached 5% in real terms in 2000 compared with an EU average of 3.4% (Press and Information Office (PIO), 2001: 165).

## Tourism, economic growth and development

There is little doubt, then, that tourism has long been and continues to be the engine driving economic growth in Cyprus. To what extent, however, can such economic growth be equated with the broader development of the island? In other words, modernisation theory implies that economic growth and development are synonymous – the former inevitably stimulates the latter. Has this been the case in Cyprus?

Certainly, the evidence suggests that tourism has proved to be an effective growth pole, underpinning both dramatic economic growth and also the fundamental structural modernisation of the economy. Moreover, per capita income has risen from around US$3000 in 1980 to an estimated US$13,125 in 2000 (PIO, 2001), the third highest of all Mediterranean countries. The island also, in effect, enjoys full employment and there is virtually no poverty. At the same time, according to other typical development indicators, such as access to health care, life expectancy, infant mortality rates, literacy and educational attainment, Cyprus is classed amongst those countries which enjoy 'high human development'. Indeed, in 1999 the island ranked 25th on the UNDP's Human Development Index, above countries such as Portugal, Singapore and Malta. Therefore, in terms of both economic growth and social development, Cyprus now compares favourably with other developed nations and it is clear that this achievement is directly related to the growth of mass tourism on the island. Importantly, this rapid development has also been achieved despite the fact that the development of tourism on the island is characterised by dependency, a 'condition' that, as observed earlier, is widely seen as preventing or retarding development.

Nevertheless, there has long been concern over the costs of the apparently successful development of tourism in Cyprus. In other words, the nature and impacts of tourism development have given rise to doubts about the longer term contribution of tourism to the island's continued, sustainable development. As a result, successive tourism policies since the early 1980s have sought a more balanced approach to tourism development, whilst the most recent strategy for 2000–10 focuses explicitly on sustainable tourism development, 'the notion of sustainability . . . [being] . . . consistent with the concept of quality. Sustainable tourism development aims at the safeguarding of the quality of tourist experience, of environmental quality and of the quality of life of the inhabitants of all areas' (CTO, 2000b: 6).

However, this latest policy, though addressing some of the problems, is not necessarily the most appropriate response to the challenges of tourism development in Cyprus, in particular with respect to tourism's continuing contribution to the island's development. Indeed, as this paper will now suggest, the principal issue is not tourism *policy* (that is, the promotion of sustainable/quality tourism as opposed to traditional, mass tourism) but the *management* of tourism development in Cyprus. First, however, it is necessary to review briefly the challenges facing tourism on the island that have led to the new policy for sustainable/quality tourism development.

## Tourism in Cyprus: The Challenges

Despite its evident contribution to the island's development, tourism in Cyprus is characterised by a number of challenges that collectively point to dependency both on and within the tourism sector and, hence, a lack of longer term sustainability. The challenges include:

*(1) Arrivals.* Rapid growth in arrivals throughout the 1980s was followed by fluctuating annual figures in the 1990s – from 1994 to 1998, annual arrivals grew over by just 7%, less than half the global rate. Most recently, annual arrivals have again increased (see Table 2), the popularity of Agia Napa being a significant factor, though it remains to be seen whether the CTO's present target of 4 million arrivals by 2010 is achievable.

*(2) Main markets.* Continuing the trend set in the early 1970s, the UK remains the principal market for tourism in Cyprus. British visitors accounted for 47.4% of total arrivals in 1970; by 1999, despite attempts to diversify into new markets, the UK's share of the market was identical and, by 2000, had risen to 50.7%. Cyprus' other traditional markets, Scandinavia and Germany, each continue to account for roughly 10% of arrivals (Table 4). This dependence on the UK is considered a particular problem, particularly as major British tour operators have cut capacity to Cyprus in 2002 by between 10 and 20% (Pyrillos, 2001). However, though justified on the initial downturn in demand following the terrorist attacks of 11 September 2001, many view the cutbacks as a ploy on the part of tour operators to force down hotel prices in an over-supplied market (Evangalides, 2002), thereby challenging the CTO's longer term policy of developing quality tourism.

*(3) Mode of travel.* One of the most significant factors in the rapid growth of tourism to Cyprus, particularly since the mid-1980s, has been the expansion of the inclusive-tour by charter (ITC) sector – prior to this, a no-charter flight policy was enforced to protect the national carrier, Cyprus Airways. Nevertheless, significant restrictions remain on many routes, particularly with respect to

**Table 4** Arrivals from major markets 1990–2000 (% share)

|  | 1990 | 1991 | 1992 | 1993 | 1994 | 1995 | 1996 | 1997 | 1998 | 1999 | 2000 |
|---|---|---|---|---|---|---|---|---|---|---|---|
| United Kingdom | 44.3 | 49 | 54.6 | 51.6 | 46.9 | 40.5 | 36.9 | 38.3 | 45.7 | 47.6 | 50.7 |
| Scandinavia | 17.6 | 14.1 | 12.1 | 8.6 | 9.9 | 10.9 | 12.1 | 10.8 | 10.9 | 10.9 | 9.8 |
| Germany | 6.4 | 4.8 | 5.1 | 6.5 | 8.4 | 11.2 | 12.3 | 11.9 | 9.4 | 9.8 | 8.7 |
| Greece | 4.5 | 4.3 | 3.3 | 3.0 | 2.7 | 3.1 | 4.5 | 3.2 | 3.2 | 3.4 | 3.7 |
| Switzerland | 2.9 | 2.8 | 2.6 | 4.1 | 4.7 | 5.2 | 5.4 | 4.6 | 3.8 | 3.6 | 2.9 |
| Russia/other ex-USSR | – | – | – | – | 2.9 | 4.5 | 6.7 | 10.6 | 8.9 | 5.5 | 5.4 |

*Source*: Adapted from CTO 1990–99; CTO 2001

seat-only sales on charter flights. As a result, almost two-thirds of all arrivals now travel on inclusive arrangements, whilst 80% of UK visitors and 100% of Scandinavian arrivals are on package holidays. Not only has this given enormous power to the major tour operators but also the potentially lucrative independent market has remained limited. However, it is expected that the Cypriot authorities will have implemented an air liberalisation policy in accordance with EU requirements by 2003, allowing companies such as EasyJet, the budget airline, to operate flights to Cyprus. Thus, EU membership will not only serve to diminish the power of tour operators, but will also encourage what is likely to be a flourishing independent market.

(4) *Seasonality*. Tourism in Cyprus remain stubbornly seasonal. Over a quarter of all tourists arrive in the peak months of July and August, with the summer quarter (July to September) accounting for almost 40% of total annual arrivals. Conversely, reflecting a pattern that has remained reasonably consistent since the mid-1980s, around 15% of annual arrivals visit the island between November and February.

(5) *Accommodation trends*. As suggested earlier, the rapid growth in tourism has been fuelled by an equally rapid growth in the supply of accommodation facilities, the vast majority of which are owned by Cypriot companies or individuals. Importantly, the development of accommodation has also directly influenced the nature and scale of tourism on the island (Sharpley, 2000b). In particular, accommodation development has been spatially concentrated in the coastal areas, whilst the latter half of the 1980s was notable for a rapid expansion in the provision of self-catering/apartment accommodation. Thus, although more recent growth has focused on the higher-graded hotel sector, the island's accommodation supply remains predominantly that of mid-range hotels and self-catering accommodation located in coastal resorts, underpinning the position of Cyprus as a summer-sun, mass-market destination. At the same time, the over-supply of accommodation has played into the hands of tour operators who are able to command heavy discounts, thereby reinforcing the mass market appeal of the island.

(6) *Social/environmental impacts*. Inevitably, 'there has been unprecedented pressure on the natural environment of the island due to the uncontrolled expansion of tourism' (Kammas, 1993). These are widely discussed in the literature (Akis *et al.*, 1996; Apostilides, 1995; Mansfeld & Kliot, 1996) and include 'typical' consequences such as: architectural pollution; loss of flora and fauna; the loss of agricultural land; coastal erosion; air, water, ground and noise pollution; and excessive demands on natural resources. The most commonly cited resource problem is the lack of water – the island has long suffered water shortages – and it is widely believed that tourism has significantly exacerbated the problem. As Mansfeld and Kliot (1996: 197) comment, water scarcity 'should have acted as a severe constraint on tourism development'. Interestingly, however, a survey undertaken by the Department of Water Development found that 77% of metered consumption is used by agriculture, 21% for domestic services and just 2% is consumed by the tourism sector (Metaxa, 1998).

With respect to sociocultural impacts, the development of tourism in Cyprus has been less problematic than might be expected, although in the popular resorts, such as Agia Napa, a degree of resentment against tourists has been found to exist (Akis *et al.*, 1996). Nevertheless, most local people feel that the benefits of tourism outweigh the costs (Akis *et al.*, 1996), an unsurprising finding given the high level of tourism-related employment and income.

To summarise, then, since the early 1980s Cyprus has emerged as a relatively expensive (owing to its distance from its main markets) yet mass-market, summer-sun destination, highly dependent on traditional markets. At the same time, the island's economy as a whole has become increasingly dependent upon the tourism sector which, in recent years, has suffered erratic demand, low profit margins and dependence on dominant overseas tour operators. In short, Cyprus, in common with many other island tourism destinations, appears to be following the unsustainable, 'centre–periphery' model of development referred to in the introduction to this paper (although, as already demonstrated, the island has achieved a remarkable rate and level of development).

## Tourism: Policy Responses

These challenges have not, of course, gone unrecognised by the Cypriot tourism authorities. Indeed, both the contribution of tourism to socioeconomic development and the need to control and manage tourism development effectively have long been recognised – since 1975, tourism has been prominent in national development plans, as have proposals with respect to the scope, scale and nature of tourism development.

Initial tourism policies focused on rebuilding the industry in the immediate post-invasion period, underpinned by various forms of financial support and incentives to encourage tourism development (Ioannides, 1992). However, by the early 1980s, it was evident that the re-development of tourism was too successful – the rapid development of accommodation and facilities and the equally rapid growth in arrivals was not being matched by associated infrastructural development or the provision of ancillary tourist facilities. Moreover, planning controls to protect the environment were proving to be inadequate.

Accordingly, a number of measures were introduced which, in effect, sought to limit the development of mass tourism on the coast, with 'the highest attention being paid to the protection and enhancement of the environment' (Andronikou, 1986). These included a variety of financial incentives to encourage hotel and other tourism-related development in the hinterland and the controlled development of luxury hotels in selected coastal areas. At the same time, marketing policy re-focused on attracting higher spending, 'quality' tourists, the purpose being to increase the value, rather than the scale, of tourism in order to reduce the island's increasing dependence upon the mass, summer-sun market. Efforts were also made to attract niche markets, such as conference/incentive tourism, special interest tourism and winter tourism, in order to address the problem of seasonality. In other words, the policy called for a more balanced, sustainable approach to tourism (Andronikou, 1986).

In practice, the opposite occurred. As already noted, the 1980s as a whole witnessed a dramatic increase in annual arrivals which, from 1986 onwards, was exacerbated by the introduction of charter flights. More specifically, between 1985 and 1990 the supply of accommodation on the island almost doubled, with

30% of the increase attributable to new apartment accommodation in the coastal resorts. Nevertheless, in recognition of the fact that 'if the present course of [tourism] development is continued, it will in the long run have serious adverse effects on the competitiveness of our tourist product in the international market' (Central Planning Commission (CPC) 1989: 156), many of the policy objectives were embodied in subsequent economic development plans and tourism policies. These collectively reflected the CTO's long-held objectives of

- reducing the rate of growth in tourism development;
- upgrading and diversifying the tourism product, utilising the island's environmental and cultural attractions;
- spreading the benefits of tourism around the island;
- attracting more diverse, quality markets;
- increasing off-season tourism; and
- increasing the level of spending per tourist.

Attempts were also made to limit the environmental impacts of excessive development. For example, a moratorium on new hotel building was imposed in 1989 (though this proved ineffectual given the large number applications approved prior to its imposition). Furthermore, in 1990, a Town and Country Planning Law was enforced, requiring all municipalities to submit local development plans for approval and, in particular, major hotel developments costing over CY£1 million had to undergo an Environmental Impact Assessment.

Over the last decade, some – though limited – success has been realised in achieving these policies. For example, golf tourism has received a significant boost through the opening of two golf courses in the Paphos district, with three more under construction (though some would argue that, owing to perennial water shortages, golf tourism is an inappropriate development). The construction of six marinas has recently been approved, laying the foundation for developing potentially lucrative yacht-based tourism and significant attempts have been made to develop agrotourism as a means of spreading the benefits of tourism away from the coast. Some 60 traditional rural properties have been redeveloped into tourism accommodation, whilst a number of villages have benefited from regeneration programmes. However, only about 450 bedspaces have been created and occupancy levels remain low.

In contrast, traditional summer-sun tourism to Cyprus remains strong, although the anticipated fall in arrivals in 2002 coupled with downward pressure on prices is evidence of the sector's continuing susceptibility to external influences. In other words, there has been a consistent failure to fully implement the desired tourism policy on the island or, more precisely, the CTO has been unable to manage effectively the development of tourism. A variety of factors have contributed to this:

- The continuing dominance of the UK market has diminished the opportunity for diversifying and repositioning the island as an upmarket destination. Whilst its attraction to British tourists is easy to explain – English is widely spoken, it is seen as a safe destination, cars drive on the left and the local currency, the Cyprus Pound, is the 'same' – historical and cultural ties have resulted in a mutual dependence. It is no coincidence that, following the collapse in tourism following the Gulf War in 1991, the CTO's primary marketing effort and expenditure was directed towards the UK, resulting in a record proportion of British visitors to the island in 1993.

- The combination of a relatively high proportion of visitors travelling on package holidays, increasing concentration of ownership within the European tour operating industry and an oversupply of accommodation on the island have given the major operators a significant degree of power and influence. It is estimated, for example, that the German company Preussag now controls up to 30% of all arrivals in Cyprus. As a result, operators are able to control not only the nature and flow of tourism to the island but also prices. Thus, whilst the CTO is seeking to attract higher spending tourists, the major operators are increasingly selling on price to maintain volumes.

- Local political structures do not facilitate central control on the island (Sharpley, 2001). At the national level, formal structures for the implementation of policy do not exist; rather, there is a reliance on informal contact and agreement between political and industry leaders which, arguably, allows for political deals which circumvent official policy whilst also permitting conflicts of interest. At the same time, a complex, multi-layered democratic system delegates a significant degree of authority to the local level. As a result, decisions regarding planning applications, infrastructural investment and development and other tourism-related activities are made by local politicians who, for electoral or other reasons, may not always make decisions in the wider regional or national interest.

- The CTO itself enjoys little statutory authority. For example, although it has the power to license and grade new accommodation facilities, it is not in the position to decide whether such facilities should be built in the first place. Conversely, various political groups, such as the trade unions and the Cyprus Hotels Association (CHA), are relatively powerful. Thus, attempts to limit the growth of mass tourism in recent years have been thwarted by fierce lobbying on the part of the CHA to maintain occupancy levels (Ioannides & Holcomb, 2001), whilst rapid increases in wages have had a significant impact on profitability, productivity, investment and service levels.

Despite this apparent failure to control tourism, the authorities continue to pursue a quality / sustainable tourism development policy. The current strategy for 2000–2010, focusing on the development of quality tourism, sets out a number of objectives (CTO, 2001). These include:

- maximising the income from tourism (and, hence, its contribution to the national economy) through balancing a growth in arrivals with increasing visitors' length of stay and spending – the strategy proposes a 'value-volume strategy' which, by 2010, seeks to increase receipts to CY£1.8 billion based on arrivals of around 3.5 million;

- reducing seasonality, with the peak season's share falling from 40% to 33% of total annual arrivals;

- increasing competitiveness by re-positioning Cyprus as a tourism destination; in particular, less emphasis to be placed on sun-sea-sand tourism, whilst attention is to be focused on developing products, such as agrotourism, that are based around the island's culture, natural environment and people;

- attracting 'quality' tourists (defined in the strategy as older, better off, more culturally / environmentally aware and demanding flexibility, higher levels of service, better value for money) through more effective targeting and segmentation;
- in general, marketing the island as 'a mosaic of nature and culture, a whole, magical world concentrated in a small, warm and hospitable island in the Mediterranean at the crossroads of three continents, between West and East, that offers a multidimensional qualitative tourist experience' (CTO, 2001: 33).

In essence, the current strategy is little more than a re-working of previous policies although, for the first time, sustainable development is an explicit objective;

> the achievement of the strategy's vision will be accomplished through a strategy that will focus on sustainable development . . . [aiming at] . . . tourism development that will exploit the available resources without destroying or exhausting them, allowing in this way for the destination to successfully respond to the present and future needs of the visitor as well as of the locals. (CTO, 2001: 6) To what extent, however, does this represent an appropriate policy for both the development of tourism and, more importantly, the continued overall development of Cyprus?

## Tourism and Development: The Way Forward?

From the foregoing discussion, it is evident that the development of tourism in Cyprus has created a developmental paradox. On the one hand, the country appears to be facing many of the 'typical' challenges of island tourism development – economic dependence on the tourism sector, a significant degree of dependence on principal markets and overseas tour operators, mass market appeal and diminishing competitiveness, excessive demands on limited natural and human resources, and so on. Collectively, these problems point to a lack of longer term sustainability of tourism and, consequently, economic growth and it is not surprising, therefore, that the sustainable development 'imperative' has been adopted in tourism policy and planning.

On the other hand, the development of mass tourism – in effect, using tourism as a modernising growth pole – has made a spectacular contribution to economic growth and development in Cyprus. It has stimulated and supported other sectors of the economy, it has created virtually full employment and it has directly contributed to the transformation of the island into a relatively wealthy, modern state. Undoubtedly, this has not been achieved without associated environmental consequences, yet tourism to Cyprus has continued to grow despite the over-development of coastal regions, the lack of infrastructural development and the other problems that have beset the island since the 1980s.

It could be argued, therefore, that re-focusing on quality tourism / sustainable tourism development, manifested in policies that emphasise specialist, niche products that promote the island's culture, environment and people is not only an inappropriate course of action, but also one that could restrict, rather than encourage, the future development of Cyprus. Three points, in particular, support this position.

*(1) Local management/control.* There is no doubt that the dominance of major tour operators poses significant problems for the tourism authorities in Cyprus; planned capacity reductions and heavy discounting in 2002 are, for example, likely to result in falling occupancy and profitability levels in hotels and an overall fall in receipts. However, international tourism, whether mass or niche market, is inherently dependent (Britton, 1991) and, thus, the dependency issue in Cyprus has been exacerbated not by the development of mass tourism but by the inability of the authorities to manage it effectively. In other words, it is principally the over-supply of accommodation relative to demand that has increased the power of the tour operators, whilst the lack of cooperation amongst all stakeholders, the lack of authority invested in the CTO and the lack of political mechanisms to translate policy into practice at the national level have collectively resulted in the uncontrolled development of tourism. It may justifiably be queried, for example, how Agia Napa has been 'allowed' to become one of the Mediterranean's clubbing capitals when a principal element of tourism policy is to develop quality, cultural tourism! Thus, rather than tinkering with policy, attention should be focused on implementing structures and mechanisms of control at the national level in order to sustain tourism and its contribution to development.

*(2) The tourism product.* Sustainable tourism, according to the latest CTO policy, is equated with quality tourism. However, quality tourism demands a quality product and, subsequently, a sufficient volume of 'quality tourists' to meet projected arrivals and spending targets. Therefore, as Ioannides and Holcomb (2001: 253) observe, the CTO's 'blind faith in an upmarket tourism product in order to rectify the impacts of mass tourism has a number of flaws'. First, the lack of control, planning and infrastructural investment means that a number of basic problems, such as inadequate airport facilities, poor roads and pavements and a lack of public spaces or green areas in resorts remain to be addressed. Thus, although, for example the motorway running the length of the island between Paphos and Agia Napa is virtually complete, significant improvements are required in basic infrastructure and facilities. Second, the island's cultural and archaeological sites are poorly maintained, interpreted and marketed. Even at major sites, such as the Tombs of the Kings in Paphos, there is a lack of basic amenities, such as shaded seating areas. Third, in reality Cyprus does not possess enough cultural sites to attract sufficient numbers of 'quality' tourists, particularly in comparison with other Mediterranean destinations, whilst, finally, the island has a firmly established image as a mass, summer-sun destination. The development of agrotourism, for example, has not yet proved to be successful, the problem of low occupancy levels amplified by the fact that the majority of guests are domestic, as opposed to overseas, tourists. Generally, therefore, as Ioannides and Holcomb (2002: 253) ask, why would 'quality' tourists wish to 'visit Cyprus as a destination in the first place, especially as there are so many other competing upmarket destinations . . . offering vastly superior products'? Conversely, well over 2.5 million 'mass' tourists are attracted to the island each

year, despite the relatively high cost of holidays given its distance from its principal markets.

*(3) Tourism's developmental role.* Perhaps most importantly, tourism in its present form (i.e. principally coastal, summer-sun tourism) has been and remains, as this paper has demonstrated, the engine that drives the Cypriot economy. Economic growth, high levels of employment, increasing wealth and the expansion of other sectors of the economy have all resulted from the development of tourism as a volume industry, whilst tourism has also proved to be an effective agent of modernisation and development. To an extent this has been facilitated by the inherent desire and ability of the Cypriot people to take advantage of the opportunities offered by tourism, yet it is the scale of tourism development that has been a principal factor in its successful contribution to development. Quality tourism, in contrast, may lead to higher per capita tourist spending and reduced environmental impacts, but restricting the growth in arrivals will, inevitably, impact upon employment levels, growth in other sectors of the economy and, ultimately, continued development.

Collectively, these points imply that tourism in Cyprus, and its contribution to the island's future development, would be best served by policies that focus on consolidating or sustaining the existing mass tourism product. This, in turn, may be achieved through more effective control over development at the national level, higher public investment in infrastructure, facilities and environmental improvements in resort areas in order to improve the quality of the overall tourist experience, and associated policies with respect to, for example, air liberalisation, that will go some way to reducing the dominance of tour operators. In other words, it is the CTO's interpretation of sustainable tourism development in the Cypriot tourism context that is at fault; sustainable development through tourism can be achieved but through improving the standards, quality and management of its existing products.

This is not to say that attempts should not be made to develop niche, quality products in order to spread the benefits of tourism and address the problem of seasonality. Indeed, the post 11 September capacity cutbacks have heightened the need for Cyprus to reduce its dependency on tour operators, something that will undoubtedly be facilitated by EU-required air liberalisation. However, tourism policy should be based on the acceptance that Cyprus is, and is likely to remain, a mass, summer-sun destination. Therefore, planning should focus on sustaining and improving the current mass tourism product (within environmental limits), whilst seeking to develop additional economic activities, such as offshore banking or hi-tech industries. In this way, tourism will continue to underpin economic growth and modernisation, providing a sound platform upon which to build a more diverse and sustainable economy. In short, tourism policy should not be directed towards sustainable tourism development but towards sustained (mass) tourism as the foundation for the longer-term sustainable development of Cyprus.

## Correspondence

Any correspondence should be directed to Dr Richard Sharpley, Centre for Travel and Tourism, University of Northumbria, Longhirst Campus, Longhirst Hall, Morpeth, Northumberland NE61 3LL, UK (richard.sharpley@unn.ac.uk).

## Notes

1.  The paper focuses upon the 'second phase' of tourism development in the (Greek) Republic of Cyprus which, following the occupation by Turkish forces of the northern third of the island in 1974, has experienced the more significant and rapid development of tourism. In contrast, the self-proclaimed Turkish Republic of Northern Cyprus (TRNC) remains relatively undeveloped and accounts for less than 3% of international tourist arrivals on the island as a whole (Warner, 1999).

## References

Akis, S., Peristianis, N. and Warner, J. (1996) Resident attitudes to tourism development: The case of Cyprus. *Tourism Management* 17 (7), 481–94.

Andronikou, A. (1979) Tourism in Cyprus. In E. de Kadt (ed.) *Tourism: Passport to Decvelopment?* (pp. 237–64) New York: OUP.

Andronikou, A. (1986) Cyprus – management of the tourism sector. *Tourism Management* 7 (2), 127–9.

Andronikou, A. (1987) *Development of Tourism in Cyprus: Harmonisation of Tourism with the Environment.* Nicosia: Cosmos.

Apostilides, P. (1995) Tourism development policy and environmental protection in Cyprus. In *Sustainable Tourism Development* (pp. 31–40). Environmental Encounters No. 32. Strasbourg: Council of Europe.

Ayers, R. (2000) Tourism as a passport to development in small states: The case of Cyprus. *International Journal of Social Economics* 27 (2), 114–33.

Bastin, R. (1984) Small island tourism: Development or dependency? *Development Policy Review* 2 (1), 79–90.

Bianchi, R. (2002) Towards a new political economy of global tourism. In R. Sharpley and D. Telfer (eds) *Tourism and Development: Concepts and Issues* (pp. 265–99). Clevedon: Channel View.

Brey, H. (1995) A booming economy. In H. Brey and C. Muller (eds) *Cyprus* (pp. 92–3). London: APA Publications (HK) Ltd.

Briguglio, L., Archer, B., Jafari, J. and Wall, G. (eds) (1996) *Sustainable Tourism in Island and Small States: Issues and Policies.* London: Pinter.

Britton, S. (1991) Tourism, capital and place: Towards a critical geography of tourism. *Environment and Planning D: Society and Space* 9 (4), 451–78.

Butler, R. (1998) Sustainable tourism – looking backwards in order to progress? In C.M. Hall and A. Lew (eds) *Sustainable Tourism: A Geographical Perspective* (pp. 25–34). Harlow: Longman.

Butler, R. (1999) Sustainable tourism: A state-of-the-art review. *Tourism Geographies* 1 (1), 7–25.

Conlin, M. and Baum, T. (1995) *Island Tourism: Management Principles and Practice.* Chichester: John Wiley & Sons.

Cope, R. (2000) Republic of Cyprus. *Travel & Tourism Intelligence, Country Reports* 4, 3–21.

Central Planning Commission (CPC) (1989) *Five Year Development Plan, 1989–1993.* Nicosia: Planning Bureau.

Cyprus Tourism Organisation (1990–2000a) *Annual Reports.* Nicosia: Cyprus Tourism Organisation.

Cyprus Tourism Organisation (2000b) *Tourism Strategy 2000–2010.* Nicosia: Cyprus Tourism Organisation.

Cyprus Tourism Organisation (2001) Tourism in Cyprus 2000. Nicosia: Cyprus Tourism Organisation.

Department of Statistics and Research (2001) Statistical Service. On WWW at http://www.kypros.org/DSR/key_figures.htm.

Department of Statistics and Research (2002) *Census of Establishments 2000.* Republic of Cyprus, Statistical Service.

Dos Santos, T. (1970) The structure of dependency. *American Economic Review* 60 (2), 231–6.

EIU (1992) Cyprus. *International Tourism Reports* 2, 43–64.

Evangalides, M. (2002) (Chairman, Cyprus Hotel Managers' Association), personal communication.

Frank, A. (1969) The development of underdevelopment. *Monthly Review* 18 (4), 17–31.

Gillmor, D. (1989) Recent tourism developments in Cyprus. *Geography* 74 (2), 262–5.

Hall, C.M. (2000) *Tourism Planning: Policies, Processes and Relationships.* Harlow: Pearson Education.

Harrison, D. (1998) *The Sociology of Modernisation and Development.* London: Routledge.

Harrison, D. (2001) Tourism in small islands and microstates. *Tourism Recreation Research* 26 (3), 3–8.

Ioannides, D. (1992) Tourism development agents: The Cypriot resort cycle. *Annals of Tourism Research* 19 (4), 711–31.

Ioannides, D., Apostolopoulos, Y. and Sonmez, S. (2001a) Searching for sustainable tourism development in the insular Mediterranean. In D. Ioannides, Y. Apostolopoulos and S. Sonmez (eds) *Mediterranean Islands and Sustainable Tourism Development: Practices, Management and Policies* (pp. 3–22). London: Continuum.

Ioannides, D., Apostolopoulos, Y. and Sonmez, S. (eds) (2001b) *Mediterranean Islands and Sustainable Tourism Development: Practices, Management and Policies.* London: Continuum.

Ioannides, D. and Holcomb, B. (2001) Raising the stakes: Implications of upmarket tourism policies in Cyprus and Malta. In D. Ioannides, Y. Apostolopoulo and S. Sommez (eds). *Mediterranean Islands and Sustainable Tourism Development: Practice, Management and Policies* (pp. 234–58). London: Continuum.

Kammas, M. (1993) The positive and negative influences of tourism development in Cyprus. *Cyprus Review* 5 (1), 70–89.

Karis, P. (1998) (General Manager, Association of Cyprus Tourist Enterprises), personal communication.

Kattamis, K. (2001) (Tourism officer, CTO), personal communication.

King, R. (1993) The geographical fascination of islands. In D. Lockhart, D. Drakakis-Smith and J. Schembri (eds) *The Development Process in Small Island States* (pp. 13–37). London: Routledge.

Lea, J. (1988) *Tourism and Development in the Third World.* London: Routledge.

Lockhart, D. (1993) Tourism and politics: The example of Cyprus. In D. Lockhart, D. Drakakis-Smith and J. Schembri (eds) *The Development Process in Small Island States* (pp. 228–46). London: Routledge.

Lockhart, D. (1997) Islands and tourism: An overview. In D. Lockhart and D. Drakakis-Smith (eds) *Island Tourism: Trends and Prospects* (pp. 3–20). London: Pinter.

Lockhart, D. and Drakakis-Smith, D. (eds) (1997) *Island Tourism: Trends an Prospects.* London: Routledge.

Mabogunje, A. (1980) *The Development Process: A Spatial Perspective.* London: Hutchinson.

Machalepis, P. (2002) (General Manager, Dome Hotel, Agia Napa), personal communication.

MacNaught, T. (1982) Mass tourism and the dilemmas of modernization in Pacific Island communities. *Annals of Tourism Research* 9 (3), 359–81.

Mansfeld, Y. and Kliot, N. (1996) The tourism industry in the partitioned island of Cyprus. In A. Pizam and Y. Mansfeld (eds) *Tourism, Crime and International Security Issues* (pp. 187–202). Chichester: John Wiley.

Metaxa, A. (1998) (Planning Department, Cyprus Tourism Organisation), personal communication.

Milne, S. (1992) Tourism and development in south Pacific microstates. *Annals of Tourism Research* 19 (2), 191–212.

Milne, S. (1997) Tourism, dependency and south Pacific microstates: Beyond the vicious circle? In D. Lockhart and D. Drakakis-Smith (eds) *Island Tourism: Trends and Prospects* (pp. 281–301). London: Pinter.

Palmer, C. (1994) Tourism and colonialism: the experience of the Bahamas. *Annals of Tourism Research* 21 (4), 792–811.

Press and Information Office (PIO) (1997) *The Almanac of Cyprus 1997.* Nicosia: Press and Information Office.

Press and Information Office (PIO) (2001) *About Cyprus*. Nicosia: Press and Information Office.

Pyrillos, K. (2001, 2002) (General Manager, Imperial Beach Hotel, Paphos), personal communication.

Rostow, W. (1960) *The Stages of Economic Growth: A Non-Communist Manifesto*. Cambridge: Cambridge University Press.

Sastre, F. and Benito, I. (2001) The role of transnational tour operators in the development of Mediterranean island tourism. In D. Ioannides, Y. Apostolopoulos and S. Sonmez (eds) *Mediterranean Islands and Sustainable Tourism Development: Practices, Management and Policies* (pp. 69–86). London: Continuum.

Seekings, J. (1997) Cyprus. *International Tourism Reports* 4, 29–54.

Sharpley, R. (2000a) Tourism and sustainable development: Exploring the theoretical divide. *Journal of Sustainable Tourism* 8 (1), 1–19.

Sharpley, R. (2000b) The influence of the accommodation sector on tourism development: Lessons from Cyprus. *International Journal of Hospitality Management* 19 (3), 275–93.

Sharpley, R. (2001a) Tourism in Cyprus: Challenges and opportunities. *Tourism Geographies* 3 (1), 64–85.

Sharpley, R. (2001b) Sustainability and the political economy of tourism in Cyprus. *Tourism* 49 (3), 241–54.

Sharpley, R. and Telfer, D. (eds) (2002) *Tourism and Development: Concepts and Issues*. Clevedon: Channel View.

Telfer, D. (2002) The evolution of tourism and development theory. In R. Sharpley and D. Telfer (eds) *Tourism and Development: Concepts and Issues* (pp. 35–78). Clevedon: Channel View.

Wall, G. (1997) Sustainable tourism – unsustainable development. In S. Wahab and J. Pigram (eds) *Tourism, Development and Growth: The Challenge of Sustainability* (pp. 33–49). London: Routledge.

Warner, J. (1999) North Cyprus: Tourism and the challenge of non-recognition. *Journal of Sustainable Tourism* 7 (2), 128–45.

Wilkinson, P. (1989) Strategies for tourism in island microstates. *Annals of Tourism Research* 16 (2), 153–77.

Witt, S. (1991) Tourism in Cyprus: Balancing the benefits and costs. *Tourism Management* 12 (1), 37–46.

Wrangham, R. (1999) Management or domination? Planning tourism in the Banda Islands, Eastern Indonesia, *International Journal of Contemporary Hospitality Management* 11 (2/3), 111–15.

WTTC (2001a) Economic research: Country league tables. On WWW at http://www.wttc.org/ecres/league.asp.

WTTC (2001b) Year 2001 TSA research summary and highlights: Cyprus. On WWW at www.wttc.org/ecres/a-cy.asp.

# 17 Rejuvenation, Diversification and Imagery: Sustainability Conflicts for Tourism Policy in the Eastern Adriatic

**Derek Hall**
*Leisure and Tourism Management Department, The Scottish Agricultural College, Auchincruive, Ayr KA6 5HW*

Employing a comparative perspective, this paper offers a critical evaluation of the post-conflict tourism policies of the former Yugoslav republics bordering on the eastern Adriatic. Policies for destination rejuvenation and national re-imaging are evaluated. The role of coastal areas within national policy is examined. Two aspects are emphasised: variations in ability to diversify and upgrade coastal destinations; and the capacity to diversify, at a national level, away from coastal dominance. The extent to which tourism imagery articulates national identity is assessed. This analysis is set within the context of the region's trajectory away from a period of bitter conflict and from the heritage of a state socialist past. The paper concludes that the challenges, tensions and conflicts of sustainability reveal both similarities and contrasts for each of the three 'countries' under review.

## Aims and Objectives

The aim of this paper is to critically evaluate the post-conflict tourism policies of Slovenia, Croatia and Montenegro – the three (former) Yugoslav states abutting the eastern Adriatic (Figure 1). It first sets the context in which tourism developed along the eastern Adriatic after the Second World War. Second, it examines policies adopted by the three former Yugoslav littoral states towards coastal tourism in the wake of half a decade of regional conflict and instability in the 1990s and evaluates these in the light of the need to pursue both structural and spatial diversification at destination and national levels. It then examines the implications of policy for national identity and image, and evaluates the sustainability challenges for, and arising from, such policies. A broad, holistic interpretation of sustainability is adopted, although the empirical context of the paper tends to focus on natural and built environmental and economic dimensions with less emphasis on social and cultural ones. Finally, conclusions are drawn.

In pursuing this aim, the paper raises a number of issues of wider significance relating to

- the nature and role of Mediterranean tourism;
- the rejuvenation and diversification of coastal tourism destinations;
- tourism's role in trajectories away from state socialism and from conflict and its effects;
- challenges for newly independent states of image promotion for tourism and foreign direct investment;
- the requirements of EU accession; and
- similarities and contrasts in sustainability challenges, conflicts and tensions.

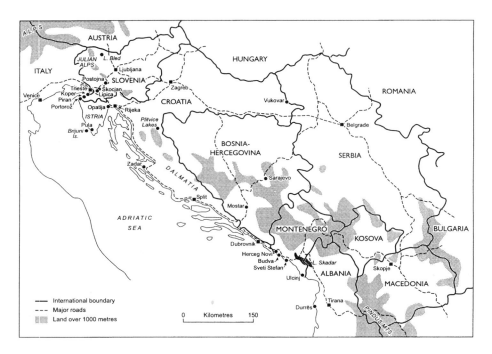

**Figure 1** The eastern Adriatic and the former Yugoslavia

## Context

The coast of former Yugoslavia has been latterly somewhat neglected in English language appraisals of Mediterranean tourism (e.g. Apostolopoulos *et al.*, 2001). Indeed, despite its significant contribution to the region's tourism product in the 1970s and 1980s and its re-emergence from half a decade of regional conflict and instability in the 1990s, apart from Croatian and Slovenian publications (e.g. *Turizam*), only a handful of English language researchers have devoted attention to it: most notably the sociologist John Allcock (e.g. 1983, 1991) and the geographer Peter Jordan (albeit mostly in his native German, e.g. 1982, 1989, 2000). Continuing southwards, Albania too has been neglected, perhaps more understandably given the low level of development and continuing relative instability of the country (e.g. Hall, 2000b; Holland, 2000). As a consequence, there has remained something of a spatial void in our perceptions of contemporary Mediterranean tourism in this important sub-region situated between EU member states Italy and Greece and which straddles a deep cultural fault line within Europe.

At the end of the Second World War the Yugoslav Adriatic coast was an economic backwater. Following expulsion from the soviet-dominated organisation Cominform in 1948, Yugoslavia was required to steer a delicate political and economic path between East and West which was to change that role dramatically. Economic and political reforms during the 1950s saw a new constitution in 1963 allowing Yugoslav citizens to live and work abroad, and allowed for a much greater degree of private investment than hitherto in economic sectors such as tourism. Further constitutional reform culminated in 1974 with the devolution of wide powers to six states and two autonomous regions within the federal republic.

Between 1961 and 1965, the Adriatic Highway was constructed, with western assistance, to extend virtually the whole length of the Yugoslav coast. Although intended to integrate often isolated communities, completion of this key piece of infrastructure encouraged and focused coastal tourism development (Allcock, 1991). By the mid-1970s, emigré workers' remittances and tourism receipts represented by far the two most important sources of foreign currency. The complex series of two-way linkages which this generated with Western Europe, and notably with German-speaking countries, provided the context within which Yugoslavia proceeded to cement a national identity in the West around experiences of inexpensive coastal mass tourism reinforced with the images of such cultural-historic icons as the medieval walled city of Dubrovnik (e.g. Antunac, 1992).

Such an identity was based largely upon the attributes of a geographically narrow 'Mediterranean' (Adriatic) strip of the country steeped (untypically for Yugoslavia as a whole) in heritage derived from two major historic maritime ('western') colonial powers: Rome and Venice. The country's often rugged interior – including most of its major cities and centuries-old ('eastern') Slavic cultures – was largely excluded from the western tourist's mental map. Thus, a somewhat skewed and unrepresentative set of images of 'Yugoslavia' was projected westwards. In 1988, the last full year of stability, 96% of all Croatian accommodation capacity and 97% of all foreign tourist overnight stays were concentrated on the Adriatic coast (mainland and islands) (Republički Zavod za Statistiku, 1989). Attempts to involve hinterlands enjoyed little success. Conversely about 90% of seasonal labour in coastal tourism was drawn from non-coastal regions (Jordan, 1989; Poulsen, 1977).

Rare exceptions to the coastal dominance of tourism included the lakes and mountains of Slovenia, immediately accessible to the Austrian, north-western Italian and southern German markets and hallmark events such as the 1984 winter Olympic Games in Sarajevo (Bosnia-Hercegovina). Although by the late 1980s Yugoslavia was generating more tourism hard currency income than the rest of communist Central and Eastern Europe combined (Hall, 1998a), per tourist spend was generally much lower than in 'western' Mediterranean destination countries such as Spain or Italy. The subsequent political fragmentation of the country and the conflict between some of its former component parts both destroyed a positive unitary image and put in abeyance potential tourism development and modernisation for at least half a decade.

## Policies for Coastal Tourism: Structural Shifts

'Yugoslavia's' negative experience of conflict in the early 1990s was in stark contrast to that of most other Central and East European countries (CEECs), for whom the immediate post-communist period of 1989–92 stimulated new and relatively distinct images of countries, regions and particular destinations. Some, such as Prague, saw visitor numbers increase dramatically as they rapidly acquired a fashionable 'cool' cachet. By contrast, in the formerly relatively open Yugoslavia, bitter conflict acted as a strong repellent to international tourism over much of south-east Europe.

As a consequence, three sets of questions faced tourism policy-makers by the mid-1990s:

- how to compensate for half a decade of neglect and reassure markets of destination security for tourism and investment purposes;
- how to rejuvenate resorts many of which had reached a critical point in their evolutionary cycle by the late 1980s; and
- how to diffuse higher-value tourism development more widely to interior locations.

In response, Slovenia, Croatia and Montenegro have sought to overcome the lost years of conflict through processes of reconstruction, diversification and re-imaging. These have involved:

- refurbishing and upgrading physical structures and infrastructure;
- innovating products and raising quality;
- diversifying attractions at both coastal destination and national levels; and
- recapturing former markets and seeking new ones.

Slovenia's five-fold niche approach to national tourism development and promotion views coastal tourism as one element in the small country's diverse portfolio of tourism resources. The Slovenian coast supports just three main tourist centres – Izola, Pirin and Portorož– the latter with a century-old spa tradition. The port of Koper acts as the country's major maritime trade outlet with associated industrial development, although a new residential spa complex was opened in 2001 on the outskirts of the town (Slovenia Tourist Board, 2001b). But with a coastline of just 40 km and with coastal products little different from those more extensively found further south in Croatia, from necessity Slovenia has diversified its coastal product provision in a number of ways: (a) active pursuits such as cycling and walking trails along and from the coast (e.g. Maher, 2000); (b) non-sand–sea–sun activities such as a rejuvenation of spa tourism; (c) excursions to the Slovenian interior; (d) excursions to neighbouring countries: by hydrofoil to Venice and to Brijuni Island (Croatia) (with consequent economic leakages); and (e) targeting higher income visitors through the attraction of nautical tourism (Logar, 2000).

With 1777 km of mainland coastline and 1185 islands, and with over 80% of the tourist turnover of former Yugoslavia, Croatia has been faced with both the greatest problems and opportunities for rejuvenation. A resurgence of mass demand from the more advanced states of Central Europe and from Russia was significant in assisting the early stages of rehabilitation of the Dalmatian coast when demand was otherwise low but it also reflects both a low value product and the rather ambivalent market position of the eastern Adriatic. However, (mass) tourism marketing has been directed to entice West Europeans: Italians, Austrians and Germans led a 190% increase in both international tourist arrivals and overnight stays between 1995 and 1997 (WTO, 1998) and still play an important role (Table 1).

**Table 1** Croatia: Interntional tourist arrivals and overnights by country of origin, 2001

|  | Arrivals | | Overnights | |
|---|---|---|---|---|
|  | *Nos. (000s)* | *% of total* | *Nos. (000s)* | *% of total* |
| Germany | 1,300 | 19.9 | 9,686 | 25.2 |
| Italy | 1,060 | 16.6 | 4,724 | 12.3 |
| Slovenia | 877 | 13.4 | 5,119 | 13.3 |
| Czech Republic | 742 | 11.3 | 4,921 | 12.8 |
| Austria | 687 | 10.5 | 3,601 | 9.4 |
| Poland | 392 | 6.0 | 2,514 | 6.6 |
| Hungary | 280 | 4.3 | 1,554 | 4.0 |
| Slovakia | 203 | 3.1 | 1,335 | 3.5 |
| Bosnia and Hercegovina | 172 | 2.6 | 802 | 2.1 |
| The Netherlands | 125 | 1.9 | 1,059 | 2.8 |
| Other countries | 706 | 10.8 | 3,069 | 8.0 |
| Total | 6,544 | 100.0 | 38,384 | 100.0 |

*Source*: Republic of Croatia Ministry of Tourism (2002: 4)

Croatia has pursued a twin policy of (a) rejuvenating and upgrading the coastal tourism which had acted as the core of former Yugoslavia's mass tourism product, and (b) promoting niche (cultural, rural) tourism development and diversification. Although attractions may be similar to those of Slovenia, Croatia can offer a greater and more diverse range. Thermal tourism has seen substantial re-investment, as at Opatija, a centre favoured by the Austrian nobility and artist colonies in the 19th century. Former President Tito's former retreat on Brijuni island – including a safari park, casino and race course – has been re-opened and cultural events such as the Croatian film festival at Pula have multiplied.

Most critically, since the late 1990s the Croatian authorities have paid particular attention to the attraction of wealthy clientele involved in nautical tourism. The Croatian National Tourist Board has widely publicised the presence of members of European royalty and international show business personalities visiting the country's 48 marinas aboard luxury yachts (Croatian National Tourist Board, 2001e). Paradoxically, by its very scale marine tourism has become part of the mass product. There are some 20,000 moorings to attract foreign vessels, while 75 registered charter companies provide 14,000 vessels catering annually for more than 150,000 tourists with over one million onboard overnight stays. The 2000 World Cup in dual sailing, held in Split, further helped to draw attention to Croatia's marine tourism capacity (Croatian National Tourist Board, 2001d). But further south into Dalmatia, product diversification has been less successful.

Montenegro's relatively traditional approach and appeal to coastal mass markets generated more than 400,000 foreign tourist arrivals in 1987. Largely as a consequence of the Yugoslav wars, in 1998 only 36,000 arrived, and numbers declined yet again as the Kosova conflict deterred travellers in the region during 1999 (Balmer, 2000). Further, Albanian refugees from Kosova were housed in settlements along the coast. Ulcinj, for example, was the temporary home to some 40,000 displaced Kosovars who filled the town's hotels and campsites. Ironically, the Montenegrin government had declared 1999 the 'Year of Tourism', in an aborted attempt to entice international visitors back to its 293 km coastline and 117 beaches (Republic of Montenegro, 2001). Although hotel capacity of about 30,000 beds and 100,000 spaces in apartments and campsites appealed to international and domestic (Yugoslav) mass markets, the 122-bedroom promontary hotel complex of Sveti Stefan gained a particular international cachet during the 1970s and 1980s hosting royalty and such 'celebrities' as Sophia Loren and Richard Burton. This market was supplemented by small-scale congress and business tourism at Budva and health tourism at Herceg Novi.

## Diversification: Spatial Shifts

Part of an escape strategy from the immediate past and its images is the desire to diversify away from mass coastal tourism and to emphasise the uniqueness of cultural and natural resources such as, somewhat ironically, drawing on the earlier aristocratic connotations of Habsburg patronage (Hall, 1999; Jelincic, 2001; Meler & Ruzic, 1999). This has entailed an implicit spatial shift to promote countries' interiors: notably urban-based cultural, business and thermal tourism, with rural and nature tourism becoming more niche-oriented (e.g. Slovenia Tourist Board, 2000; Stifanic, 2000), and rural areas being re-imaged to portray traditional 'idylls' of timeless sustainability as part of a wider trend across Europe (Roberts & Hall, 2001).

With such a short coastline, Slovenia has long placed an emphasis upon its interior attractions, the development of which in many cases dates from Austro-Hungarian times and reflects ease of access from Austria, southern Germany and north-eastern Italy. These natural and cultural attractions include Lake Bled and the Julian Alps; Škocjan, Postojna and other extensive karstic cave systems; a network of spas (e.g. Rogaška Slatina, Radenci, Dobrna) and the Lipica stud farm, renown as the original source of Lipizzaner horses for the Spanish Riding School in Vienna (Bozic, 1999). Given the small scale of Slovenia, most of these attractions can also be encompassed in day excursions from coastal resorts and thus assist product diversification at both national and coastal destination levels.

This spatial diffusion was implicit in the marketing adopted in 1995 to promote the country's tourism resources in terms of five sector 'clusters': coast and karst, mountains and lakes, health resorts, cities and towns, and the countryside. By this time Slovenia was enjoying the highest level of receipts per international tourist arrival in former communist CEECs. With near neighbours Italy, Austria and Germany providing almost 60% of the country's tourist arrivals, as well as generating high-spending cross-border excursionists, Slovenia's emphasis on accessibility and security has been relatively successful. Health tourism has managed to combine elements of the natural and cultural attributes and to attract relatively wealthy clientele from neighbouring 'western' countries to render Slovenia the most important health tourism destination of post-communist CEECs, representing around 18% of international overnight stays in the country.

But as evident in the case of Croatia, rural infrastructure to support tourism may often be inadequate (Jordan, 2000): road, transport and accommodation quality, provision of paths, trails, signposting, park furniture, retailing and evening entertainment facilities may not be of a level which Western tourists might expect, thereby constraining diversification. The market potential for 'extreme' activities such as mountaineering, caving, paragliding, hunting and diving has yet to be realised, largely because of infrastructure shortcomings, even though the coastal hinterland offers a range of suitable natural resources, with high coastal ranges (up to 2000 m high) and mountains on the islands. A major environmental factor constraining such interior diversification as cultural sightseeing, hiking, cycling and visiting nature attractions, is the enervating high summer temperatures experienced away from the cooling influence of the sea. A number of relatively low value-added natural attractions have been promoted, such as the Plitvice Lakes national park world heritage site (16 lakes and 92 waterfalls extending over 7 km), located 100 km from the coast. Promotion of urban 'cultural' destinations and notably the country's capital Zagreb ('the new European metropolis': Goluza, 1996), has been undertaken in an attempt to embed them within themes of 'European' heritage and progress and to tap into the relatively lucrative conference and business tourism market.

By contrast, although the coast of contemporary Montenegro was successively part of the Venetian and Habsburg empires, its interior lacks 'western' heritage and the cachet of former dynastic patronage. This has encouraged Montenegro to draw on natural environmental qualities and the heritage of its own earlier monarchy, which, throughout the 19th century, ruled a state with fluctuating boundaries which did not reach the sea until 1878 (Pounds, 1985: 28). But it is the natural environment which has tended to dominate diversification strategies. The Montenegrin constitution, as ratified in October 1992, recognises and promotes Montenegro as an 'ecological state' (e.g. Montenet, 1997), and such national identity is being employed to promote natural tourism products. These embrace coastal features, such as the Bay of Kotor, the largest fjord on the Adriatic and a UNESCO world heritage site, and inland attractions such as Lake Skadar, shared with Albania, home to rare fauna including pelicans, storks and herons. The importance of these assets has been embraced by an economic recovery programme supported by the World Bank and other agencies (e.g. CEEBIC, 2001). To complement this, cooperation and partnership, both domestically between newly privatised tourism enterprises and internationally with neighbouring countries, is being emphasised (e.g. Klub & FitzPatrick, 2000).

## Implications for National Identity and Image

(Re-)imaging of newly independent countries on the fringe of South-eastern Europe has been required for the purposes of securing investment, gaining acceptability in the European home and encouraging tourism development. At least for Slovenia and Croatia an important element has been to disassociate themselves from any pejorative notions of 'Balkan-ness' (Hall & Danta, 1996;

Todorova, 1994, 1997). This has been a particularly important task in the paradox of seeking to distance themselves from their Yugoslav political past while attempting to recapture the 1980s markets for Yugoslav tourism and to emphasise for new and evolving markets both a Central European-ness in culture and history and a Mediterranean-ness in coastal tourism products. For example, marketing emphasises 'Western' characteristics of the Istrian peninsula, the most highly developed region of the eastern Adriatic, shared by Slovenia and Croatia: coastal settlements typified by labyrinths of narrow streets of Venetian architecture topped by dominating towered stone churches, such that the 'picturesque landscape is often compared to Provence or Tuscany' (Balkan Holidays, 2002: 46).

As an important element of the (re-)imaging process, on independence, Slovenia adopted the national tourism 'strapline' *'The sunny side of the Alps'*. This was intended to convey the availability of summer and winter attractions through climate and topography as well as contiguity with, and thus accessibility for, Western Europe and its markets. Italian objections saw this superseded in the mid-1990s with *'The green piece of Europe'*, placing an emphasis on smallness of scale and ecological awareness, and indicating a significance not just for tourism. This integral role of tourism in national development was underlined when, in 1996, the newly established Slovenia Tourist Board's mission statement firmly intertwined tourism with national political aspirations:

> to promote Slovenia as a country with a clear and distinctive identity and clearly defined comparative and competitive advantages and thereby assist the Slovene economy by marketing Slovene tourism in a concrete manner. (Slovenia Tourist Board, 1998: 1)

As a consequence, Slovenia's self-imagery and promotion for tourism purposes closely mirrors national efforts to attract foreign investment and to present an acceptable face to the wider European political community. It emphasises four key elements. First, a fashionable/politically correct ecologically friendly ethos is emphasised. Second, a Central European character is expressed through the Habsburg heritage, Alpine associations and contiguity with Austria and Italy. Thus tourism promotion emphasises:

- being firmly part of ('western'/'civilised') Europe – 'delightful villages and warm and hospitable people, whose lives are still steeped in the traditions of centuries of Austrian rule' (Transun, 1998: i);
- being a natural component of Mediterranean tourism – 'the proximity of the Italian border produces a distinctly Mediterranean feel' (Crystal Holidays, 2001: 167); and
- disengagement from any Balkan and former communist connotations – 'Slovenia is actually situated in Central Europe not in Eastern Europe at all!' (Slovenia Tourist Board, 1999: 1).

Third, security is emphasised by claiming to be 'one of the safest countries in Europe' with ' a very high level of political, economic and social stability' (Slovenia Tourist Board, 2001a: 1). Finally, a sense of order and planned development is projected: a tourism development strategy promulgated as part of a national economic plan, with local strategies being developed for tourist centres.

Like Slovenia, Croatia was a former Austro-Hungarian, and thus Roman Catholic, constituent member of Yugoslavia. Over 95% of the former Yugoslavia's coastline (including islands) and thus much of its tourism industry was in Croatia. As such, Croatia's long coastline became the key element of Yugoslavia's tourism product in the 1960s, 1970s and 1980s. Until the disastrous events of the early 1990s, the Croatian coast may have been many Westerners' only experience of 'Yugoslavia' and may have remained closely associated with that construction. Unlike Slovenia, Croatia was enmeshed during the first half of the 1990s in continuing hostilities both on its own soil and in Bosnia, with a consequent collapse of the country's tourism industry. The most notable cultural image of the Yugoslav coast – the medieval walled city of Dubrovnik – was deliberately shelled by Serbs and Montenegrins in attempts to undermine the Croatian economy (Oberreit, 1996).

Following the cessation of conflict, it was therefore vital that Croatia should establish a national tourism marketing policy which, closely allied to national image rebuilding, would achieve three goals. First, to clearly differentiate the country from its neighbours, although, for example, rural, sports and activity tourism in Istria is inevitably similar to that found in neighbouring Slovenia. Second, to reassure former markets that quality and value had been restored (not necessarily reconcilable objectives). Finally, to secure long-term competitive advantage through the country's major tourism attributes.

Until 1999 'niche-oriented' promotion tended to emphasise Croatia's Central European cultural credentials but was clearly aimed more at the world political community than its tourists and, as such, any 'benchmarking' was geared to longer-term aspirations for European acceptance and EU accession rather than necessarily shorter-term requirements of tourism regeneration (Hall, 2000a). Since the death of President Tudjman in 1999, the state has removed itself further from the development process, except for offering incentives for mass tourism promoters (e.g. see Republic of Croatia Ministry of Tourism, 2001b,c). Tourism promotion has been more product-related (e.g. Orlic, 2000) and market-specific, particularly in relation to those former mass markets, such as the UK, which have exhibited slow post-conflict recovery. Thus in its English-language web-pages the tourist board reflects on how Edward VIII encouraged tourism on the island of Rab when he stayed there with Mrs Wallis Simpson and claims it was he who inaugurated the fashion for nude bathing there (Croatian National Tourist Board, 2001a).

For the Montenegrin authorities there is no denying a Balkan location and situation. Yet as the most rugged part of former Yugoslavia, Montenegro never fully succumbed to Turkish domination from the 15th century, and thus did not embrace Islam as did its Bosnian and Albanian neighbours. But while Montenegro avoided this element of Balkan 'Otherness', being located to the east of the Christian schismatic fault line, the dominant religion is, as for Serbs, Christian Orthodox. Montenegro's current national identity is compromised by its position within 'rump' Yugoslavia: attraction of tourists and foreign investors to the country's long delayed privatisation programme has been constrained by the slow and highly sensitive separation from Serbia (Anderson, 2001). For tourism rejuvenation, this is exacerbated in the short term by tourism marketing and promotion employing a 'Montenegro' brand which may be unfamiliar to, and ambiguous for, former markets. However, a recently developed promotional website (National Tourism Organisation of Montenegro, 2002) may help to overcome this in the medium term.

## Policy Challenges for Sustainability

The sustainability of tourism policy and promotion confronts a number of challenges in the eastern Adriatic (Hall, 1998b; Jordan, 2000). These are underscored by a geographical transition from north to south of increasing distance from major west European markets, decreasing (incentive for?) product diversification, increasing ambivalence towards organisational restructuring, an increasing length of season and increasing proximity to potential regional instability. From this generalisation, three models can be projected:

- the consolidation of an existing spatial diffusion of inland attractions, stimulated by strong adjacent markets (Slovenia);
- limited success in such diffusion attempts such that coastal tourism still heavily dominates (Croatia): by 2000 no less than 88.1% of tourist arrivals (international and domestic) and 95.3% of tourist nights in Croatia were still located on the coast, compared to, for example, just 1.1% and 0.8% at health resorts (Table 2); and
- despite an institutionalised ethos of ecological awareness, limited apparent attempt to diffuse tourism from a coastal dominance, partly influenced by slow privatisation processes and an ambivalence towards foreign investment (Montenegro).

Such policy variations both articulate and result in a number of sustainability challenges and tensions, both explicit and implicit.

Continued spatial concentration of activities along much of the eastern Adriatic coast has induced a number of physical planning impacts. First, infrastructural pressures are expressed, notably in Croatia, in public sector under-investment and the lack of land-use and urban spatial planning strategies for tourism destination resorts. This has resulted in the unplanned construction

**Table 2** Croatia: Tourist arrivals and overnights by types of locality, 2000

|  | *Arrivals* | | *Overnights* | |
|---|---|---|---|---|
|  | *Nos. (000s)* | *% of total* | *Nos. (000s)* | *% of total* |
| Sea coast | 5832 | 88.1 | 36,616 | 95.3 |
| Health resorts | 75 | 1.1 | 299 | 0.8 |
| Mountains | 128 | 1.9 | 208 | 0.5 |
| Other tourist localities | 75 | 1.1 | 180 | 0.5 |
| Zagreb | 341 | 5.2 | 599 | 1.6 |
| Non-tourist locations | 169 | 2.6 | 504 | 1.3 |
| Total | 6620 | 100.0 | 38,406 | 100.0 |

*Source*: Republic of Croatia Ministry of Tourism (2001a: 11)

and use of weekend houses and apartments, producing visual pollution and blight and placing major, imbalanced and often disproportionate, demands on infrastructural services such as water supply and sewage treatment. Although an 'I love Croatia' campaign was instituted in the spring of 2001, whose objectives included a 'tidying up' of the visual environment of tourist locations and towns (Croatian National Tourist Board, 2001c), it did not address this critical issue. Montenegro's economic reform and recovery strategy (MFRM/NACPU, 2001) has pointed to substantial problems of fresh water supply shortage and quality at coastal resorts which are seen to jeopardise the potential for coastal tourism regeneration.

Second, use of motor vehicles as the predominant means of tourist mobility exerts substantial pressures on the built environment and atmosphere in terms of exhaust emission pollution, congestion and parking problems inducing aesthetic degradation, despite attempts to enhance images of environmental friendliness (e.g. Schneider-Jacoby, 1996). As several coastal and island settlements enjoy – as an implicit attraction – limited accessibility, policy requirements would seem to point to sensitive congestion rationing and charging schemes such as the permit and cordon system used in Piran, a small compact settlement located on a peninsular. The Croatian authorities are considering ways to reduce motor vehicle numbers on some of the offshore islands.

Third, continued spatial concentration along the coast has also fuelled demand for accessible airport development and has intensified air transport links. Currently, for example, there are plans to expand Portorož airport, located within Slovenia's built-up coastal zone: driving time from the country's main airport at Ljubljana to coastal resorts is currently around two and a half hours. Airfields have been established on three Croatian islands and more may follow. Any intensification of sea ferry links is unlikely to divert this demand significantly, particularly if the short-break market is further developed.

Fourth, a spatial concentration along the coast perpetuates a seasonal concentration for the sun–sea–sand market: in 1988 Croatia saw 61% of coastal overnight stays concentrated in July and August, and 93% from May to October (Republički Zavod za Statistiku, 1989), while for 2000 the concentration had actually increased slightly to 65 and 94% respectively (Republic of Croatia Ministry of Tourism, 2001a: 9). Despite the reinvigoration of health tourism and other 'niche' activities which can act to extend the season, this concentration has resulted in overall low annual occupation rates, with consequent inadequate finance to re-invest in structural and infrastructural refurbishment and upgrading, and to support appropriate environmental safeguards. Further, it has provided only a limited number of permanent jobs in tourism and related branches. Employment in this sector has been largely unattractive for local people, such that migrants from other, particularly interior, regions have needed to be recruited as seasonal workers, arguably reducing the quality of the tourist product because of their temporary presence and lower skill levels. As a consequence of these interrelated factors, tourism has tended not to be organically embedded within the local population and culture of much of the eastern Adriatic coast (Jordan, 2000). There would, therefore, appear to be substantial untapped potential for stimulating local participation and control and for encouraging the development of local networks and partnerships. At a time when cultural tourism has gained popularity globally, a lack of local involvement would appear to present major constraints on generating cultural authenticity and sustainability.

Fifth, while nautical tourism may be viewed as offering a relatively high income product, it can generate marine pollution and congestion offshore and at marinas, is also seasonally concentrated, and can undermine the role of on-shore accommodation. Although Slovenia was awarded eight blue flags in 2001, substantial marine pollution results from shipping activities to and from Koper, Trieste and northern Italy, with current effects concentrating pollution in the northern Adriatic, and industrial and agricultural waste run-off flowing into discharging rivers. Although environmental considerations are claimed to hold a high priority in tourism development, marine pollution problems are evident along the Croatian littoral. Although in 2000 22 blue flags were awarded for environmental quality (Croatian National Tourist Board, 2001b), there is a perception among Croatians, rightly or wrongly, that the 'blue flag' award is a distraction and cover for pollution problems rather than acting as an award for genuinely clean beaches.

An infrastructural element which notably suffered from half a decade of neglect and which has negatively influenced images of service quality is a need for appropriate education and training of tourism and hospitality managers and entrepreneurs. In Montenegro, as part of a reconstruction programme based on a tourism master plan drawn up by German consultants (DEG, 2000), the tourism ministry is establishing a centre for tourism and hotel education on the coast to act as a training and vocational education centre and to also house the University of Montenegro's recently established faculty of tourism. Its impact remains to be seen. But in Croatia, national tourism development strategies and a tourism master plan have been criticised for paying little attention to such crucial constraints as inherited poor management practices (Dragičević *et al.*, 1998). For a range of reasons, therefore, the realism of proposals for improved 'sustainability', however interpreted (e.g. Kunst, 1998; Petrić, 1998), has been widely contested (e.g. Jordan, 2000; Poljanec-Borić, 2000).

## Conclusions

Within the context of Mediterranean tourism development and change, this paper has set out to critically evaluate the post-conflict tourism policies of Slovenia, Croatia and Montenegro – the three (former) Yugoslav states abutting the eastern Adriatic. It has briefly set the context in which tourism developed along the eastern Adriatic after the Second World War. It has examined policies adopted by the three towards coastal tourism, and evaluated these in the light of the need to pursue both structural and spatial diversification at destination and national levels. Two aspects have been emphasised: variations in ability to diversify and upgrade coastal destinations, and the capacity to diversify, at a national level, away from coastal dominance. It has examined the implications of policy for national identity and image. Finally, it has discussed the challenges such policies face in their attempts to be (seen to be) 'sustainable'.

Issues of wider significance raised in this analysis have included the nature and role of Mediterranean tourism; the rejuvenation and diversification of coastal tourism destinations; tourism's role in trajectories away from state socialism and from conflict and its effects; challenges for newly independent states of image promotion for tourism and foreign direct investment; the requirements of EU accession; and similarities and contrasts in sustainability challenges, conflicts and tensions. Variations in spatial, structural and seasonal concentration and a general north-south transition patterning have suggested a three-fold diversification typology into which policies and their sustainability challenges can be placed. Post-conflict eastern Adriatic represents a significant, distinctive and still evolving element of Mediterranean tourism. Yet the reality and sustainability of that element will remain variable both within and between the Yugoslavian successor states, providing considerable interest for policy analysts and substantial challenges for policy makers.

## Correspondence

Any correspondence should be directed to Derek Hall, Leisure and Tourism Management Department, The Scottish Agricultural College, Auchincruive, Ayr KA6 5HW, Scotland (d.hall@au.sac.ac.uk).

## References

Allcock, J.B. (1983) Tourism and social change in Dalmatia. *Journal of Development Studies* 20(1), 35–55.

Allcock, J.B. (1991) Yugoslavia. In D. Hall (ed.) *Tourism and Economic Development in Eastern Europe and the Soviet Union* (pp. 236–58). London: Belhaven.

Anderson, P. (2001) Montenegro's tourism hopes. BBC News, London. On WWW at http://www.bbc.co.uk/hi/english/world/europe/newsid_1287000/1287791.stm.

Antunac, I. (1992) Udio Hrvatske u turizmu bivse Jugoslavije. *Turizam* 40(7/8), 111–24.

Apostolopoulos, Y., Loukissas, P. and Leontidou, L. (eds) (2001) *Mediterranean Tourism. Facets of Socio-Economic Development and Cultural Change*. London: Routledge.

Balkan Holidays (2002) *Bulgaria, Croatia, Slovenia, Romania*. London: Balkan Holidays.

Balmer, C. (2000) Montenegrin tourism evaporates because of war. *Nando Times* (7 June). On WWW at http://archive.nandotimes.com/Kosovo/story/general/0,2773,57174-91290-648875-0-nandotimes,00.htm.

Bozic, M. (1999) *Lipica 1580*. Lipica: Kobilarna Lipica.

CEEBIC (Central and Eastern Europe Business Information Center) (2001) Firm Level Assistance Group (FLAG) Montenegro. CEEBICnet. Om WWW at http://www.mac.doc.gov/eebic/countryr/fyrsm/flagcrnagora.htm.

Croatian National Tourist Board (2001a) Adriatic sea. On WWW at http://www.croatia.hr/about/index.php?mmit = adriatic&mit = islands.

Croatian National Tourist Board (2001b) Blue Flag. On WWW at http://www.croatia.hr/about/index.php?mmit = bluef&cont = bfl.

Croatian National Tourist Board (2001c) I love Croatia. On WWW http://www.htz.hr/misc/index.php?mmit = menu_root&mit = volim.

Croatian National Tourist Board (2001d) Nautics. On WWW at http://www.croatia.hr/activities/index.php?mmit = nautics.

Croatian National Tourist Board (2001e) The jet set is discovering Croatia. On WWW at http://www.htz.hr/news.php?id = 14.

Crystal Holidays (2001) *Lakes and Mountains, Including Fjords, Coastlines, Cities and Tours*. Kingston-upon-Thames: Crystal Holidays.

DEG (2000), *Montenegro: Tourism Master Plan*. Cologne: DEG. On WWW at http://www.donors.cg.yu/project/6.pdf.

Dragičević, M., Čižmar, S. and Poljanec-Borić, S. (1998) Contribution to the development strategy of Croatian tourism. *Turizam* 46 (5–6), 243–53.

Goluza, M. (1996) *Zagreb: The New European Metropolis*. Zagreb: Tourist Association of the City of Zagreb.

Hall, D.R. (1998a) Central and Eastern Europe. In A.M. Williams and G. Shaw (eds) *Tourism and Economic Development in Europe* (pp. 345–73). Chichester and New York: John Wiley & Sons.

Hall, D.R. (1998b) Tourism development and sustainability issues in Central and South-eastern Europe. *Tourism Management* 19, 423–31.

Hall, D.R. (1999) Destination branding, niche marketing and national image projection in Central and Eastern Europe. *Journal of Vacation Marketing* 5, 227–37.

Hall, D. (2000a) Croatia. In D. Hall and D. Danta (eds) *Europe Goes East: EU Enlargement, Diversity and Uncertainty* (pp. 275–88). London: Stationery Office.

Hall, D. (2000b) Tourism as sustainable development? The Albanian experience of 'transition'. *International Journal of Tourism Research* 2(1), 31–46.

Hall, D. and Danta, D. (1996) The Balkans: Perceptions and realities. In D. Hall and D. Danta (eds) *Reconstructing the Balkans* (pp. 3–13). Chichester and New York: John Wiley and Sons.

Holland, J. (2000) Consensus and conflict: The socio-economic challenge facing sustainable tourism development in southern Albania. *Journal of Sustainable Tourism* 8(6), 510–24.

Jelincic, D. (2001) *Theoretical Approaches to Regional Cultural Tourism Planning: Croatian Strategy – Culture = Future*. 41st Congress of the European Regional Science Association. 29 August – 1 September, Zagreb.

Jordan, P. (1982) Fremdenverkehr und Einzelhandel auf den Kvarnerinseln. Eine Untersuchung über Wirkungen des Fremdenverkehrs in peripheren Gebieten. *Münchner Studien zur Sozial- und Wirtschaftsgeographie* 23, 193–209.

Jordan, P. (1989) Gastarbeiter im eigenen Land. Das Problem der saisonalen Arbeitskräfte im Fremdenverkehr der jugoslawischen Küste am Beispiel des Touristikunternehmens 'Jadranka', Mali Lošinj. *Österreichische Osthefte* 31(4), 683–714.

Jordan, P (2000) Restructuring Croatia's coastal resorts: Change, sustainable development and the incorporation of rural hinterlands. *Journal of Sustainable Tourism* 8(6), 525–39.

Klub, M. and FitzPatrick, P. (2000) Tourism: A solution for Prevlaka? *Central Europe Review* 2(30), 2. On WWW at http://www.ce-review.org/00/30/montengronews30.html.

Kunst, I. (1998) Market structure of Croatian tourism sector. *Turizam* 46(3), 123–39.

Logar, M. (2000) *Information for Nautical Guests*. Ljubljana: Slovenia Tourist Board.

Maher, I. (2000) *Slovenia by Bicycle*. Ljubljana: Slovenia Tourist Board.

Meler, M. and Ruzic, D. (1999) Marketing identity of the tourist product of the Republic of Croatia. *Tourism Management* 20, 635–43.

MFRM (Ministry of Finance of the Republic of Montenegro)/NACPU (National Aid Coordinating Policy Unit) (2001) *Economic Reform and Recovery Strategy: Infrastructure Development*. On WWW at http://www.donors.cg.yu/economic_reform/infrastructure.htm. Podgorica: Ministry of Finance of the Republic of Montenegro.

Montenet (1997) Ecological state of Montenegro. On WWW at http://www.montenet.org/econ/ecostate.htm. Podgorica: Montenet.

National Tourism Organisation of Montenegro (2002) Visit Montenegro. On WWW at http://www.visit-montenegro.com/.

Oberreit, J. (1996) Destruction and reconstruction: The case of Dubrovnik. In D. Hall and D. Danta (eds) *Reconstructing the Balkans: A Geography of the New Southeast Europe* (pp. 67–77). Chichester and New York: John Wiley and Sons.

Orlic, D. (2000) *Istra: the Wine Road of the Buje Region*. Porec: The Association of Vintners and Wine-growers of Istria.

Petrić, L. (1998) Tourism policy – goals and instruments. *Turizam* 46(3), 140–68.

Poljanec-Borić, S. (2000) System conditions for the development of tourism in the underdeveloped areas of Croatia. *Tourism/Turizam* 48(4), 353–60.

Poulsen, T.M. (1977) Migration on the Adriatic coast: Some processes associated with the development of tourism. In H.L. Kostanick (ed.) *Population and Migration Trends in Eastern Europe* (pp. 197–215). Boulder, CO: Westview.

Pounds, N.J.G. (1985) *An Historical Geography of Europe 1800–1914*. Cambridge: Cambridge University Press.

Republic of Croatia Ministry of Tourism (2001a) Croatian tourism 2000 in figures. On WWW at http://www.mint.hr/ENGTUR2001. pdf.

Republic of Croatia Ministry of Tourism (2001) Instructions for subsidized foreign organized tourist traffic in 2002. On WWW at http://www.mint.hr/subeng_2002.htm.

Republic of Croatia Ministry of Tourism (2001c) Investment opportunities in the Croatian tourism sector through the privatisation process. On WWW at http://www.mint.hr/privatisation_guidelines.htm.

Republic of Croatia Ministry of Tourism (2002) Tourist traffic 2001.On WWW at http://www.mint.hr/TRAFFIC1201.pdf.

Republic of Montenegro (2001) Tourism. On WWW at http://www.montenegro.yu/english/turizam.htm.

Republički Zavod za Statistiku (ed.) (1989) *Promet Turista u Primorskim Općinama 1988*. Zagreb: Republićki Zavod za Statistiku.

Roberts, L. and Hall, D. (2001) *Rural Tourism and Recreation: Principles to Practice*. Wallingford: CAB International.

Schneider-Jacoby, M. (1996) A view from abroad: Nature preservation in Croatia – an investment in the future of the country. *Turizam* 44(11–12), 276–92.

Slovenia Tourist Board (1998) Marketing of Slovenia's tourism: Corporate image. On WWW at http://www.tourist-board.si/podoba-eng.html.

Slovenia Tourist Board (1999) Slovenia at a glance: Some brief notes for press visitors. On WWW at http://www.slovenia-tourism.si/enews/article-01.html.

Slovenia Tourist Board (2000) *Slovenia By Bicycle*. Ljubljana: Slovenia Tourist Board.

Slovenia Tourist Board (2001a) Slovenia at a glance: Some brief notes for press visitors. On WWW at http://www.slovenia-tourism.si/enews/article-01.html.

Slovenia Tourist Board (2001b) Tourist industry invests in new programme. On WWW at http://www.slovenia-tourism.si/enews/EARTICLE2001-03.HTM.

Stifanic, D. (2000) *Vrsar: Bike Eco Ride*. Vrsar: Tourist Association of Vrsar.

Todorova, M. (1994) The Balkans: From discovery to invention. *Slavic Review* 53, 453–82.

Todorova, M. (1997) *Imagining the Balkans*. Oxford and New York: Oxford University Press.

Transun (1998) *Transun's Croatia*. Oxford: Transun.

WTO (World Tourism Organization) (1998) *Tourism Market Trends: Europe*. Madrid: WTO.

# Index